ADVANCED APPELLATE ADVOCACY

ASPEN COURSEBOOK SERIES

ADVANCED APPELLATE ADVOCACY

Susan E. Provenzano
Professor of Practice
Northwestern University School of Law

Sarah O. Schrup
Director, Appellate Advocacy Center
Northwestern University School of Law

Carter G. Phillips
Partner, Sidley Austin LLP

Jeffrey T. Green
Partner, Sidley Austin LLP

Wolters Kluwer

Published by Wolters Kluwer in New York.

Wolters Kluwer Legal & Regulatory Solutions U.S. serves customers worldwide with CCH, Aspen Publishers, and Kluwer Law International products. (www.WKLegaledu.com)

To contact Customer Service, e-mail customer.service@wolterskluwer.com,
call 1-800-234-1660, fax 1-800-901-9075, or mail correspondence to:

Wolters Kluwer
Attn: Order Department
PO Box 990
Frederick, MD 21705

Printed in the United States of America.

1 2 3 4 5 6 7 8 9 0

ISBN 978-1-4548-4720-5

Library of Congress Cataloging-in-Publication Data

Names: Provenzano, Susan E., author. | Schrup, Sarah O., author. | Phillips,
    Carter G., author.
Title: Advanced appellate advocacy / Susan E. Provenzano, Professor of
    Practice Northwestern University School of Law, Sarah O. Schrup, Director,
    Appellate Advocacy Center Northwestern University School of Law, Carter G.
    Phillips, Partner, Sidley Austin LLP, Jeffrey T. Green, Partner, Sidley
    Austin LLP.
Description: New York : Wolters Kluwer, 2016. | Includes index.
Identifiers: LCCN 2015049827 | ISBN 9781454847205
Subjects: LCSH: Appellate procedure — United States. | Trial practice — United States.
Classification: LCC KF9050 .P77 2016 | DDC 347.73/8 — dc23
LC record available at http://lccn.loc.gov/2015049827

About Wolters Kluwer Legal & Regulatory Solutions U.S.

Wolters Kluwer Legal & Regulatory Solutions U.S. delivers expert content and solutions in the areas of law, corporate compliance, health compliance, reimbursement, and legal education. Its practical solutions help customers successfully navigate the demands of a changing environment to drive their daily activities, enhance decision quality, and inspire confident outcomes.

Serving customers worldwide, its legal and regulatory solutions portfolio includes products under the Aspen Publishers, CCH Incorporated, Kluwer Law International, ftwilliam.com, and MediRegs names. They are regarded as exceptional and trusted resources for general legal and practice-specific knowledge, compliance and risk management, dynamic workflow solutions, and expert commentary.

For Sophia, Henry, Sofia, and Summer

SUMMARY OF CONTENTS

CONTENTS

 OVERVIEW OF THIS BOOK AND THE APPELLATE PROCESS 1

 GETTING TO AND STAYING IN APPELLATE COURT 5

 THE STANDARDS AND SCOPE OF REVIEW 25

4 THE PLANNING AND LEARNING PHASE: DIGESTING THE RECORD AND SPOTTING ISSUES   49

5 THE PLANNING AND LEARNING PHASE: RESEARCHING THE MERITS AND SYNTHESIZING AUTHORITIES   69

6 THE PLANNING AND LEARNING PHASE: SELECTING AND REFINING ISSUES AND DEVELOPING ARGUMENTS   87

7 THE WRITING PHASE: DEVELOPING A PERSONAL WRITING PROCESS   115

8   THE WRITING PHASE: THE BASICS OF JUDICIAL AUDIENCE, RHETORIC, AND PERSUASION   137

9   THE WRITING PHASE: FRAMING YOUR CLIENT'S STORY   161

10 | THE WRITING PHASE: STRUCTURING ARGUMENTS BEYOND IRAC   205

11 | THE WRITING PHASE: FRAMING ARGUMENTS BEYOND IRAC   249

12 THE WRITING PHASE: DRAFTING SPECIALIZED SECTIONS, REVISING TO PERFECTION, AND FILING THE BRIEF   295

13 SPECIAL TYPES OF BRIEFS   327

14   PREPARING FOR AND DELIVERING ORAL ARGUMENT   351

PREFACE

This book is for law students and new lawyers seeking deeper instruction on the craft of appellate advocacy, one of the most rewarding and intellectually challenging practices a lawyer can choose. The book is a first of its kind collaboration among diverse authors: a director of an appellate clinic, a writing and advocacy professor, and two experienced appellate practitioners with many appeals behind them. We designed the book for use in a wide range of law school contexts: appellate simulation courses, appellate and Supreme Court clinics, moot court competitions, and upper-level advocacy courses. Using our text, faculty can teach appellate advocacy in a complementary and consistent manner, with keen attention to the realities of pursuing and defending appeals. The book can also serve as a handbook for new lawyers entering appellate practice.

In our experience, the best way to learn appellate advocacy is to stand in the shoes and enter the mind of an appellate lawyer, facing the same strategic decisions that appellate lawyers make at every step, doing the same intensive work. To that end, the book's organization tracks the appellate process. It begins with the decision to appeal and preliminary appellate strategy considerations and continues through briefing to oral argument. As the reader reaches each step of the real or simulated appeal she is working on, the book provides, precisely at that moment, the guidance needed to execute that step. And that guidance is comprehensive, covering everything from appellate doctrine and procedure, to client counseling and ethics, to visual rhetoric and nonverbal persuasion, to amicus briefs and petitions for certiorari. In this respect, the text aims to provide a three-dimensional educational experience that conveys the creativity, strategy, and sophistication behind real appeals.

In addition to its whole-appeal orientation, the book offers readers a jump-start towards mastery — a vigorous push up the novice-expert learning curve in all facets of an appeal. For example, our planning and learning chapters deconstruct the approaches that experts have internalized for learning their cases, for conducting appellate research, for selecting and framing issues, and for formulating appellate arguments. Our writing chapters raise the bar as well. Going "Beyond IRAC," these chapters facilitate the shedding of formulaic novice legal writing approaches in favor of more flexible, sophisticated approaches used by expert appellate writers. Our coverage of these expert approaches is informed by the latest thinking in composition theory, rhetoric, and cognitive psychology. To bring these expert writing approaches to life, a plentiful crop of expert brief samples populates the chapters. These briefs represent some of the best work that the appellate bar has to offer. In the text, we annotate those briefs to highlight the expert techniques they employ, harnessing the powerful pedagogy of modeling. Our oral argument instruction is equally robust, going well beyond the fundamentals to map out expert preparation and delivery approaches, complete with insider advice on handling questions from the bench and troubleshooting the argument. At every stage, the book aims to bridge the gap between foundational written advocacy instruction and the skill set that a budding appellate lawyer must have.

To engage readers and enhance their learning experience, our book has three distinctive features. First, the text includes the expert annotated briefs that we have already described. Second, the text contains reflection, discussion, and challenge questions at the close of sections. These questions aim to promote critical thinking, to allow readers to self-test their understanding of concepts, and to help readers immediately apply what they have learned to their appellate projects. Third, the text has a password-protected online companion. The online companion enriches the text's instruction with: (1) exercises that can be assigned for classroom or independent use; (2) additional examples of briefs and working documents; (3) video and audiotaped interviews with prominent appellate practitioners; and (4) argument dissection classes taught by coauthors Carter Phillips and Jeff Green. Within the text, each chapter contains several "Practice Alert" boxes that call readers' attention to any exercises, briefs, or working documents that are keyed to the topics discussed in that portion of the text.

This book was borne of our joint passion for teaching and advocacy, and we are delighted to share with you our enthusiasm for both. We hope this book is just your first step towards a long and fulfilling career as an appellate advocate.

ACKNOWLEDGMENTS

This book would not have been possible without the invaluable contributions of our research and faculty assistants. Our profound thanks goes to Melissa Goldman, who supplied the graphics that translated our prose into appealing visuals. We also appreciate the very fine work of faculty assistant Aileen Reid, who worked tirelessly to perfect the final product. And we cannot adequately express our gratitude to the many students who assisted with nearly every aspect of the book, performing research, vetting expert briefs, reviewing chapters, critiquing exercises, helping with the appellate specialist interviews, and providing samples of their work. Those students are Will Carpenter, Jack Chen, Joe Delich, Jeremy Dunnaback, Leigh Gordon-Patti, Michelle Goyke, Matthew Heins, Margaret Heitkamp, Heath Ingram, Alan Iverson, Andrew Jaco, Kathleena Kruck, Trevor Lee, Michael Meneghini, Julia Prochazka, Mike Rizza, Scott Shelton, Brian Smith, Lauren Swadley, Anthony Todd, and Jeff Van Dam.

The children's T-shirt graphic in Chapter 12 appears courtesy of Edward Tufte and Graphics Press.

The graphic timeline and demonstrative visual in Chapter 12 appear courtesy of Bartlit Beck Herman Paldncher & Scott LLP.

ADVANCED
APPELLATE
ADVOCACY

1 Overview of this Book and the Appellate Process

Most lawyers are professional writers,[1] but this statement particularly describes appellate advocates. In fact, the appellate writing process is like no other. It requires the lawyer to digest large quantities of factual and legal information and then to transform that information into a succinct, straightforward written presentation that persuades an exacting and skeptical audience. These days, most state and federal appeals are decided on the briefs; the percentage of cases granted oral argument in federal appellate court stands at an all-time low.[2] It is no over-statement to say that the brief's quality has become dispositive in virtually all cases.

Given the judicial audience, the appellate writing process requires more than meets the eye. Consider all the steps needed to transform a trial court record and raw legal material into an appellate brief:

- Issue spotting and digesting the record, which could be thousands of pages
- Researching authorities on rules, procedures, the court, and the merits
- Synthesizing facts and law into viable arguments with compelling themes
- Brainstorming, outlining, writing, and revising the brief
- Soliciting and incorporating feedback from "cold readers," because your colleagues may be too familiar with the case
- More researching, brainstorming, outlining, and rewriting (a recursive cycle)
- Finalizing the brief for filing.

Typically, you must complete these tasks in a month or less, often with a full trial or appellate caseload (or if you are a student, a full course load). Then, if you represent the appellant, you must repeat the process on a smaller scale — but in a more compressed time frame — when you file the reply brief. Whichever side you represent, you may need to prepare for oral argument as well. Oral argument planning should start as soon as you take the case and should continue while you write, peaking in an intense preparation period as soon as the case is set for argument. The immense project of taking or defending an appeal will not go well

1

unless you come to it with a full grasp of all the tasks you must perform and have a master plan for executing them.

This book is designed to put you in that position. It tracks the progression of an appeal from the standpoint of the lawyer pursuing or defending it. The only exceptions to the book's process-based organization are Chapters 2, 3, and 13. Chapters 2 and 3 introduce foundational appellate doctrines and processes that you must understand *before* you set eyes on an appellate record. Chapter 13 takes a brief intermission from the appeal process to discuss court-specific briefing and special types of briefs, such as petitions for certiorari and amicus curiae or "friend of the court" filings.

Those chapters aside, the rest of the book's sequence is your appellate work sequence, from notice of appeal to briefing to oral argument. We break down the appeal process into three distinct phases: (1) the planning and learning phase; (2) the writing phase; and (3) the oral argument phase. The planning and learning phase is the subject of Chapters 4 through 6. These chapters deal with internal mastery—how to become fluent in the facts and law of your own appeal and start developing argument paths. In these chapters, you will apply the appellate doctrines and procedures identified in Chapters 2 and 3 as you strategically review your appellate record, spotting the most promising issues. You will also learn how to conduct preliminary strategy research, and acquire an expert approach to researching the appeal's merits. Near the end of this phase you will begin sifting and categorizing your raw legal and factual material into potential arguments. You will end the planning and learning phase by performing a candid assessment of your appellate case's strengths and weaknesses, so that you enter the next stage—the writing phase—with a collection of arguments and a clear-eyed view of their potential.

Turning from internal mastery to external persuasion, Chapters 7 through 12 cover the writing phase. This phase kicks off with a chapter devoted to developing a personal writing process, crucial for effective time management and avoiding writer's block. The next chapter shifts to knowing and influencing your judicial audience using sophisticated tools of rhetoric, persuasion theory, and applied storytelling. Armed with that knowledge, you can begin writing, and that is the focus of the remaining writing phase chapters. Those chapters focus on the theory and theme of your appeal, the issue statements, the statement of the facts, and the argument, because they are the heart of your brief. Here we aim to take what you know about these components of the brief and bridge you to a more advanced understanding. In Chapter 9, you will learn how to craft a nimble theory and theme, and devise issue statements that anchor your brief. You will also learn how experts tell their clients' stories in fact statements, the sails that propel the theory and theme. Most important, in Chapter 10, you will learn to shed beginner argument organizational paradigms like IRAC[3]—which stands for Issue-Rule-Application-Conclusion—and replace them with a more sophisticated approach. Chapter 11 then spotlights expert persuasive framing techniques to round out your appellate writing portfolio. The writing phase ends with Chapter 12, which adds the bells and whistles: specialized brief sections, targeted revision techniques, developing voice and style, using visuals to persuade, and filing the brief.

After Chapter 13's discussion of specialized briefs and court writing, Chapter 14 brings you to the oral argument phase. Although you will have thought about the oral argument all along, this chapter tracks what you must do when argument preparation ramps up. Here, too, you will go beyond what you have learned before. Chapter 14 exposes you to expert preparation techniques and insider strategies for handling hostile and friendly questions from the panel. This chapter then adds the layers of nonverbal persuasion and developing a personal oral argument style.

The Appeal Process at a Glance

- Appellant files Notice of Appeal and Docketing Statements.
- Both parties review the record, issue-spot, research, and develop arguments.
- Appellant writes and files opening brief.
- Appellee writes and files response brief.
- Appellant writes and files reply brief.
- Both parties prepare for and deliver oral argument.
- Parties prepare post-argument filings ordered or needed.

In every chapter, we offer concrete explanations of each phase, along with expert tips that will help you scale the novice-expert learning curve. You will engage with the material through reflection, challenge, and discussion questions and by deconstructing expert brief excerpts laid out in the text. These materials are enriched by our text's online companion, which houses Practice Alerts in the form of: (1) short exercises that develop key skills; (2) additional examples of briefs and working documents; (3) video and audiotaped interviews with prominent appellate practitioners; and (4) argument dissection classes taught by co-authors Carter Phillips and Jeff Green. Ultimately, we want you to walk away from this text equipped with a high-level understanding of appeals and the ability to win them, using the expert's tools.

REFLECTION, DISCUSSION, AND CHALLENGE QUESTIONS

The Appeal Process

- What kinds of writing have you done in your pre-law life and as a law student? What are your writing strengths and weaknesses?
- What have you learned about appeals in law school so far? What are your biggest knowledge gaps?
- What do you hope to learn from the appellate course you are taking? How does appellate work factor into your career goals?

Endnotes

1. David A. Rasch & Meehan Rasch, *Overcoming Writer's Block and Procrastination for Attorneys, Law Students, and Law Professors*, 43 New Mexico L. Rev. 193, 194-95, 239 n.1 (2013).
2. *Compare* Admin. Office of the U.S. Courts, Federal Court Management Statistics tbl.S-1 (2002), *available at* http://www.uscourts.gov/uscourts/Statistics/JudicialBusiness/2002/tables/s01sep02.pdf (reporting 32.9 percent of federal appeals terminated on the merits were granted oral argument in 2002), *with* Admin. Office of the U.S. Courts, Federal Court Management Statistics tbl.S-1 (2012), *available at* http://www.uscourts.gov/uscourts/Statistics/JudicialBusiness/2012/tables/S01Sep12.pdf (reporting only 18.8 percent of federal appeals terminated on the merits were granted oral argument in 2012).
3. IRAC has many variants in law school classrooms. *See, e.g.*, George D. Gopen, *Keynote Address: IRAC, REA, Where We Are Now, and Where We Should Be Going in the Teaching of Legal Writing*, 17 Legal Writing: J. Legal Writing Inst xvii, xviii (2011). For example, some professors use "CRAC" to reflect the firm conclusion that begins arguments, while others use "TREACC," where "T" refers to the topic sentence and "E" adds the component of explaining an authority before applying it to the facts.

2 Getting to and Staying in Appellate Court

Before an appellate court allows you through its doors, it will confirm that you belong there and that you will play by its rules. An appellant must fulfill a variety of doctrinal and procedural requirements before the court will review a case. On the doctrinal side, there are appellate access doctrines designed to ensure that the appellate court is the appropriate place for your case. Section 1 explains the major access doctrines and their impact on getting (or not getting) a case into an appellate court: finality and its exceptions, jurisdiction and timeliness, and standing and mootness. Section 2 shifts to the assorted procedural requirements embodied in the rules of pre-briefing procedure. These rules dictate what information an appellate court must receive before it can or will consider a case, and how that information must be communicated to the court. Noncompliance with these rules can end your appeal before a panel of judges even reviews the merits of your arguments, so they too act as gatekeepers in certain respects. Finally, rules that do not appear to address preliminary matters on their face — such as settlement — require a close look early on because they impact the unfolding and progress of your appeal.

Armed with the information in this chapter and the next, you can decide whether to bring an appeal. We use the federal doctrines and rules as our default, but keep in mind that state appellate courts impose their own prerequisites.

Section 1 Appellate Access Doctrines

The first step in an appeal is making sure that your case belongs in the appellate court. The primary doctrines governing appellate access are: (1) finality; (2) jurisdiction and timeliness; and (3) standing and mootness. Although these doctrines do not arise in every case, you must be familiar with them and keep them in mind all the way through the appeal. Finality, jurisdiction, timeliness, mootness, and standing may arise at any point — and do so midway or at the end of an appeal with alarming frequency.[1]

1.1 Finality and Its Exceptions

In appellate courts, the general rule is that only final orders — those that end litigation on the merits and leave nothing for the court to do but execute the judgment — are appealable.[2] The finality rule eliminates piecemeal review. Appellate review before trial litigation ends will inevitably fail to capture all of the potentially appealable issues in a case. Moreover, jumping back and forth between two court levels is inefficient and time-consuming. For example, if a trial court denies a defendant's motion to dismiss under Federal Rule of Civil Procedure 12(b)(6) but ultimately grants summary judgment to the defendant, interlocutory review of the 12(b)(6) denial would have proven premature and wasteful. In federal civil cases, finality is governed by Rule 58, which defines a final order as the entry of judgment on the docket.[3] If the trial court fails to issue a Rule 58 order, the responsible advocate will ask the trial court to enter it; otherwise, there may be no final order from which to appeal.[4] In criminal cases, the final order is the trial court's entry of the judgment of conviction and sentence.[5] Likewise, the dismissal of federal criminal charges constitutes a final judgment.[6]

**Practice Alert #1
Annotated Brief: Disputes
over Appellate Court
Jurisdiction**

Here you will find a sample brief highlighting the parties' arguments over the finality and timeliness of an appeal.

These finality rules have three important exceptions: (1) interlocutory appeals; (2) the collateral order doctrine; and (3) extraordinary writs. In federal court, the first and third exceptions are creatures of statute, while the second is a judicially created exception to finality. All three represent methods of reaching the appellate court before the trial court issues a final order. But as we discuss below, each method has its own rationale, substantive requirements, and procedural hurdles. You must be sure to choose the right method at the right time and to follow the right procedures.

Interlocutory appeals. An interlocutory appeal is the most common method of reaching an appellate court before the trial court is finished with the case. Interlocutory appeals challenge pretrial or trial rulings that are important enough to a party and to the judicial process to interrupt the trial proceedings.[7] In federal court, interlocutory appeals are governed by statute or rule, with some differences between civil and criminal cases.

1 — Civil cases. In federal civil cases, interlocutory appeals are governed by 28 U.S.C. § 1292. That statute is divided into two categories: interlocutory appeals as of right and permissive interlocutory appeals. Subsection (a) covers the first category, triggered by three types of trial court rulings: (1) preliminary or permanent injunctions; (2) orders concerning receivership; and (3) certain orders in admiralty cases. For example, if a trial court enters a preliminary injunction against a defendant in a trademark infringement suit, the defendant can use § 1292(a) to ask the appellate court to review that order immediately by filing a notice of appeal with the trial court.[8] She need not make any other showing nor wait to appeal until after trial on the merits of the infringement claim.[9]

Subsection (b) covers the second category, permissive interlocutory appeals. Unlike subsection (a), this subsection does not identify specific types of appealable orders but instead operates on a case-by-case basis. To garner permissive interlocutory review, each case must meet three requirements that are subject to approval by both the trial court and the appellate court — often referred to as a "two key" system. First, the district court must certify that: (1) the appeal involves a controlling question of law; (2) on which there is a substantial ground for difference of opinion; and (3) immediate appeal would materially advance the termination of the case.[10] After that, the appellate court must approve review of the certified question.[11] As the first two requirements suggest, § 1292(b) appeals typically raise unsettled or novel questions of law, such as whether a statute implies a private right of action or whether certain types of damages are available under a source of law.[12] In keeping with the policy against delaying litigation through appeal, subsection (b)'s third requirement demands that any permissive interlocutory appeal have at least the possibility — though not the certainty — of ending the litigation. Substantially shortening the time or decreasing the cost of the litigation may be enough.[13] Section 1292(b) review has been granted sparingly, prompting on average just over 100 applications per year, slightly less than half of which are granted.[14]

Aside from § 1292, the Federal Rules of Civil Procedure provide some avenues for interlocutory appeals. The first, Rule 23(f), allows a party to appeal a class certification ruling within 14 days of its entry, but the appeal will not stay trial proceedings unless the trial judge or appellate court orders otherwise. The other mechanism, Rule 54(b), is not technically an interlocutory order but it operates like one in multiparty, multiclaim litigation. Under this rule, the court may enter final judgment for a single party or on a single claim even if other claims or parties remain in the case. That order becomes immediately appealable if the trial court determines that there is "no just reason" to delay the appeal. For example, when a trial court grants summary judgment against one of multiple claimants to an insurance policy, it will often certify 54(b) review because that ruling ends the litigation for that claimant.[15]

State Court Comparison

State court systems vary in their treatment of interlocutory appeals, but in general they are permitted more generously than in the federal system. For instance, New York statutes authorize a broad range of interlocutory appeals ranging from trial rulings on the constitutionality of state statutes to provisional remedies. One factor influencing the breadth of interlocutory appeals may be the state legislature's assessment of the state judiciary. More appeal opportunities result in more checks on trial court decisions. But just as in the federal system, fairness, efficiency, and resource constraints drive state legislative choices as well.[16]

2 — Criminal cases. Courts are particularly sensitive to finality concerns in criminal cases because of the constitutional safeguards at play, so interlocutory appeals are even less common than in civil cases. For example, the finality rule helps prevent double jeopardy because it can be used to thwart piecemeal litigation that would, in essence, retry the defendant for the same crime.[17] For that reason, the government's avenues for interlocutory appeal are narrowly defined by statute,[18] and most issues that a defendant might wish to raise on appeal must await sentencing, which signals the end of the case at the trial level.

Although most criminal orders are not final and not appealable through interlocutory review, a select few are. These orders raise especially critical issues and rarely cause undue delay. Orders concerning whether to try a defendant as an adult or juvenile fall into this category, as do orders regarding pretrial detention and relief. Interlocutory appeals in criminal cases may arise under 28 U.S.C. § 1292(a),[19] or under 18 U.S.C. § 3731, if the government appeals.[20] The following chart summarizes which routine criminal rulings are subject to interlocutory review and which are not:

Type of Order	APPEALABLE or NONAPPEALABLE
Denial of motion to dismiss due to incompetency to stand trial	NONAPPEALABLE[21]
Trying the defendant as an adult or juvenile	APPEALABLE[22]
Denial of motion to dismiss indictment	NONAPPEALABLE[23]
Denial of motion to suppress made after indictment or information	NONAPPEALABLE[24]
Denial of motion to disqualify a judge	NONAPPEALABLE[25]
Denial of motion to dismiss on grounds of prior jeopardy	APPEALABLE[26]
Denial of speedy trial motion	NONAPPEALABLE[27]
Order relating to return of property entered after indictment or information	NONAPPEALABLE[28]
Granting of defendant's motion to exclude evidence	APPEALABLE[29]
Denial of motion challenging sentencing proceedings after conviction or guilty plea, but prior to sentencing	NONAPPEALABLE[30]
Denial of motion to postpone	NONAPPEALABLE[31]
Mistrial orders	NONAPPEALABLE[32]

Collateral order doctrine. The collateral order doctrine is another type of permissive interlocutory appeal. But in contrast to § 1292(b) appeals, this doctrine is judicially created, and review is not driven by novel legal questions vital to the merits of the case. Rather, the collateral order doctrine allows review of orders that are *unrelated* to the case's merits (hence the word "collateral"), but that if made in error, would cause real harm that could not be undone by appealing the final judgment.[33] A three-prong test governs the appealability of this small set of orders, which must: (1) "conclusively determine the disputed question"; (2) "resolve an important issue completely separate from the merits of the action"; and (3) be "effectively unreviewable . . . [after] final judgment."[34]

Unlike § 1292(b)'s requirements, whose application is case-dependent, the collateral order requirements apply more predictably to certain types of rulings. Commonly appealed collateral orders include those denying absolute, qualified, and sovereign immunity; double jeopardy decisions adverse to a criminal defendant; denials of motions to protect privileged documents; and orders denying an attorney's motion to withdraw.[35] Consider an order denying a party immunity. Immunity is not merely a defense to liability — it protects a party from the suit itself. Moreover, the party's immunity is often unrelated to the merits of the case. Forestalling a definitive answer on immunity until final judgment would subject a party to continued litigation when it is possible that she should not be there at all.[36] For the same reason, a refusal to appoint an attorney may be an appealable collateral order. The decision whether to appoint an attorney to an indigent defendant is separate from the case's merits, but has a drastic and lasting effect on the defendant's rights.[37]

Conversely, the following orders have been deemed nonappealable under the collateral order doctrine: the refusal to disqualify opposing counsel in a civil case; the denial of a stay pending similar state litigation; and the imposition of discovery sanctions under Federal Rule of Civil Procedure 37.[38] In many cases, these orders fail the third prong of the collateral order doctrine because they can be reviewed effectively after final judgment. In fact, these orders' full effect often remains unclear until the case ends.[39] For example, a speedy-trial violation must be assessed in light of prejudice to the defendant, which will be apparent only after trial.[40] As with all interim appeals, courts have narrowly construed the collateral order doctrine, reinforcing the final judgment rule's preeminence.

The following chart summarizes the appealability of several routine civil rulings that satisfy the collateral order doctrine:

Type of Order	APPEALABLE or NONAPPEALABLE
Denial of absolute, qualified, and sovereign immunity	APPEALABLE[41]
Denial of motion to protect privileged documents	APPEALABLE[42]
Denial of attorney's motion to withdraw	APPEALABLE[43]
Refusal to appoint an attorney	APPEALABLE

Type of Order	APPEALABLE or NONAPPEALABLE
Refusal to disqualify opposing counsel in a civil case	NONAPPEALABLE[44]
Denial of a stay pending similar state litigation	NONAPPEALABLE[45]
Imposition of sanctions under FRCP 37	NONAPPEALABLE[46]
Otherwise nonappealable, nonfinal orders that are "inextricably entwined" with appealable ones	PROBABLY APPEALABLE[47]

Extraordinary writs. The narrowest exceptions to the final judgment rule are the extraordinary writs, which include the writs of mandamus, prohibition, and coram nobis. The "extraordinary" circumstances meriting these writs are present only when no other legal remedy is available — that is, when the matter must be heard immediately and no other appellate avenues are open.[48] Writs are obtained by petitioning the court of appeals under the federal All Writs Act, 28 U.S.C. § 1651, which permits a court to issue any writ that is "in aid of" its jurisdiction. For example, in extreme circumstances an appellate court may issue a writ to avoid district court action that could thwart the appellate court's ability to exercise its eventual, rightful jurisdiction, such as when a district court repeatedly refuses to adjudicate an issue at all.[49] In such cases litigants are entitled to petition courts of appeals[50] even when there is no final judgment, because the typical appeals process will not redress the wrong. But this is a high bar to meet, and it is universally recognized that these writs are no substitute for appeal.[51] Practice reflects this narrow purpose: writs are issued only rarely, but the appellate lawyer should know when such relief is at least potentially available:[52]

> A few situations regularly recur in which [a] writ will issue: when a trial court has improperly denied a jury trial; when an allegation of district court misconduct raises a general procedural matter of first impression; and when a district court has acted improperly to remand a case previously removed from state court.[53]

The two most commonly used writs are mandamus and prohibition. They have been said to be "functionally interchangeable," but technically mandamus is used to compel performance of an act,[54] while prohibition is designed to prevent a lower court from exceeding its jurisdiction.[55] For example, a party might seek a writ of mandamus to vacate an order that exceeds the court's authority,[56] while a writ of prohibition might be used to prevent a court from improperly hearing a case at all. Despite this distinction, in federal court parties often request these writs in the alternative, and courts may treat a request for one as a request for the other.[57]

One other writ is worth mentioning. The writ of coram nobis exists to correct fundamental factual or legal errors[58] that render the proceeding "irregular and invalid."[59] This writ has been abolished in the civil context, but remains available in federal criminal cases.[60] Coram nobis is most often invoked when the statutory habeas corpus mechanisms — § 2254 for state prisoners and § 2255 for federal prisoners — simply do not apply.[61] The most common example is when a criminal defendant seeks to challenge her conviction but is no longer "in custody," a prerequisite to seeking relief under § 2254 and § 2255.[62] For example, a writ of coram nobis was used to overturn Fred Korematsu's conviction during World War II, decades after his sentence was served.[63]

REFLECTION, DISCUSSION, AND CHALLENGE QUESTIONS

Finality

- Are dismissals without prejudice appealable? Under what circumstances might such an order become appealable?
- What purpose does the finality rule serve? For the courts? For the parties? Under what circumstances might it operate unfairly?
- The exceptions to the finality rule are narrowly drawn. Would you draw them less narrowly?

1.2 Jurisdiction and Timeliness

In addition to the finality restrictions on appeals, appellate courts have limited subject matter jurisdiction. In the federal system, subject matter jurisdiction is conferred by Article III of the Constitution and by statutory jurisdictional grants.[64] A court cannot decide a case if it lacks jurisdiction, and parties can neither stipulate to nor waive subject matter jurisdiction.[65] Appellate courts take this limited jurisdictional grant seriously, and nearly every single circuit employs screening procedures to ensure that a case before it actually belongs there.[66] Nonetheless, jurisdictional problems can evade the preventive screenings and often are raised sua sponte[67] by the court very late in an appeal,[68] sometimes even during oral argument.[69] Telling a client who may have spent up to $100,000 or more on your appellate services that the case is going to be dismissed for lack of jurisdiction is not a conversation that any practitioner wants to endure. For this reason alone, advocates must be vigilant about assessing and ensuring appellate jurisdiction at all stages of the appeal.

Even if the appellate court has jurisdiction, the case may be barred if it is filed too late. A notice of appeal is the only document needed to initiate the appeal, but it must be filed within the time limits set by the Federal Rules of Appellate Procedure.[70] In civil cases, parties must file the notice of appeal within 30 days of the date the judgment is entered on the docket; if the United States is a party, however, the time limit is 60 days. Timeliness is a jurisdictional requirement in civil cases, meaning that it determines whether a court has authority to hear the case.[71] In criminal cases, a defendant has 14 days to file his notice of appeal.[72]

This requirement acts as a claim-processing rule in criminal cases,[73] meaning that it can be waived or forgiven by a court.[74] Paradoxically, the notice of appeal must be filed in the court of first instance rather than the appellate court. It divests the district court of jurisdiction and allows the case to move up to the appellate court.[75] A district court may extend the filing deadline for up to 30 days for good cause,[76] but the appellate court cannot grant extensions.[77]

The time available to file a notice of appeal may be affected by post-trial motions that toll the time to appeal, including motions seeking a new trial, acquittal, or some other modification of the judgment.[78] Caution is required when such motions are in play, as they are governed by their own time limits that may have serious implications for an appeal. Consider the interplay in the following example:

> A plaintiff loses his § 1983 civil rights claim of excessive force by state police officers following a jury trial. The district court enters judgment based on the verdict on February 10. Believing that certain evidentiary rulings and jury instructions led to an erroneous verdict, the plaintiff files a Rule 59 motion for a new trial challenging those rulings on March 14. The district court denies the motion and enters its order on April 20. The plaintiff then files his notice of appeal on May 10. Is his appeal timely? If your answer is yes, what is the scope of that appeal?

The answer is that his appeal is timely, but only as a challenge under Federal Rule of Civil Procedure 60(b), not as an appeal from a Rule 59 motion.

Here's why. Federal Rule of Civil Procedure 59 allows civil litigants to file motions for a new trial raising any trial court error. A properly filed Rule 59 motion will also toll the time to appeal. But Rule 59 sets a 28-day deadline for filing new trial motions following entry of judgment. Here, the plaintiff's Rule 59 motion was four days late: Judgment was entered on February 10 and the motion was filed on March 14.[79] Moreover, by rule, late Rule 59 motions are not stricken or denied; they are treated as an entirely different type of post-trial motion — a Rule 60(b) motion for relief from judgment.[80] A Rule 60(b) motion is a very different animal from a Rule 59 motion. Rule 60(b) does not challenge general trial errors but rather requests relief from a judgment on narrow grounds, such as mistake, inadvertence, surprise, or neglect. Rule 60(b) motions also do not toll the running of the notice-of-appeal clock for purposes of getting a new trial. In this example, the plaintiff's appeal clock began on February 10, when judgment was entered, not on April 20, when the court ruled on the motion. As a result, the plaintiff's notice of appeal, filed on May 10, is nearly two months late. As a practical matter, the plaintiff's lawyer not only forfeited the right to ask the district court for a new trial but the right to appeal the denial of a new trial as well. And although the district court will still

**Practice Alert #2
Jurisdiction and Timeliness
Exercises**

For additional practice, in the online companion you will find a series of factual scenarios requiring you to determine whether the court has jurisdiction and whether the appeal is timely.

decide the Rule 60(b) motion, and that decision could be separately appealed,[81] the grounds for granting a party relief under Rule 60(b) are so narrow that the losing party is not left with much — if anything — to appeal.

REFLECTION, DISCUSSION, AND CHALLENGE QUESTIONS

Jurisdiction and Timeliness

- At what point may a court of appeals dismiss an appeal for lack of jurisdiction?
- Why can't the appellate court extend the time for filing a notice of appeal? Why is this right reserved exclusively to the trial court?
- What if a civil plaintiff fails to file a notice of appeal within the specified time limits? Can the district court excuse this failure? What about the appellate court?
- What if a criminal defendant fails to file a timely notice of appeal and the government objects? What now?
- What if a district court erroneously entertains an untimely motion for reconsideration? Does that extend the time to file a notice of appeal?
- What if the trial court denies a civil party's motion for reconsideration on April 1, but fails to enter judgment under Rule 58. Is the party's notice of appeal filed on May 15 timely or untimely?

1.3   Standing and Mootness

Stemming from Article III's case-or-controversy requirement, standing to sue is another jurisdiction-based access requirement that cannot be waived or forfeited.[82] Standing focuses on the party seeking to get into court, in contrast to subject matter jurisdiction, which focuses on the issues the party seeks to raise. In order to have standing to sue, a plaintiff must have both a sufficient injury and a sufficient stake in the outcome to ensure that the court is deciding a concrete case or controversy.[83] The familiar three-part test requires an injury in fact, causation, and redressability of the alleged injury.[84] But while standing to sue requires one party to have injured the other, standing to appeal focuses on an injury caused by a trial court's errors. In most cases, appellate standing is immediately apparent. A losing civil plaintiff may be injured by the denial of damages, while a losing criminal defendant may be injured by a loss of freedom. Even a party that wins in the trial court may be aggrieved in some way by the judgment and have standing to appeal. For example, a plaintiff who wins a lawsuit but receives merely nominal damages or limited equitable relief may be aggrieved by the judgment in her favor. Further complexities arise when analyzing standing in the context of nonparties, amici, cross-claims, and interpleader actions. Some of these parties may not be aggrieved enough by a given ruling to have standing to appeal. Moreover, appellate courts generally do not find standing where one litigant seeks to assert another's rights. It would be impossible for an amicus, for example, to prove it has been injured by a decision that directly affects only the losing party.

Although the related doctrine of mootness is often conflated with standing,[85] the two are different. Standing must exist at the outset of the appeal and must relate to the injury alleged. It is supported by the rationale that judicial resources should be expended only on concrete controversies, not hypothetical disputes.[86] Mootness on appeal, by contrast, is about timing. If a harm to a party ends while the appeal is pending, or if it is too soon or too late for the appellate court's action to redress that harm, the appellate court should not expend resources deciding a matter that has resolved itself. Mootness often arises late in a case, because unlike standing, it is triggered by changed circumstances. Although the plaintiff bears the burden of showing standing, the defendant bears the burden of showing mootness, and these burdens are not coextensive.[87]

Practice Alert #3
Standing and Mootness Exercises

Here you will find a series of factual scenarios requiring you to determine whether appeal is barred by mootness or standing issues.

REFLECTION, DISCUSSION, AND CHALLENGE QUESTIONS

Standing and Mootness

- Is the standing to sue doctrine grounded in constitutional concerns or prudential concerns or both? What are these concerns?
- What are some differences between standing to sue and standing to appeal?
- If a mother is deported following a divorce, a court orders that the child accompany the mother, and both fly to the mother's home country, may the father appeal this decision in U.S. courts, or is the controversy moot?
- What if the petitioner in a case pending before the Supreme Court dies after oral argument? May the Court issue its decision? What if the defendant dies before his appeal is resolved?

Section 2 Pre-Briefing Appellate Procedure and Motion Practice

Assuming you've reviewed the various access doctrines and are certain that your case belongs in appellate court, it is now time to make sure that you properly get it before the court. The primary procedural requirements at play here are: (1) filing an adequate notice of appeal; (2) filing a proper appearance and other disclosures (often related to conflicts and jurisdiction); and (3) perfecting the record. This section provides a basic overview of these steps under the Federal Rules of Appellate Procedure. The requirements vary by jurisdiction, and court-specific rules may alter the timelines. This section also briefly covers appellate motion practice, because many of these procedural steps require motions. And although they are typically handled before any briefing on the merits, these motions can arise at any time. Finally, we discuss settlement and panel assignment mechanisms because those issues often arise early in the appeal.

2.1   Previewing the Rules to Prevent Surprises

Various sets of rules govern the procedure that must be followed in initiating and carrying forward your case. In federal courts, this includes the Federal Rules of Appellate Procedure, the rules of the circuit, and the court's own internal operating procedures. Similarly, appeals in state courts are governed by multiple sets of rules. Many circuits and individual courts prepare practice guides and post them on their websites; these are invaluable resources and should be consulted early and often.[88] Indeed, the minor variations in rules between courts are traps for the unwary. A brief or motion that is formatted properly in one court may be rejected by another court. The following table demonstrates just a few variations in court rules on the form of briefs:

	United States Court of Appeals for the 7th Circuit	Illinois Supreme Court	Supreme Court of the United States
Form of a Brief	Brief must be on 8½- by 11-inch paper with margins of at least one inch on all sides[89]	Brief must be on 8½- by 11-inch paper with 1½-inch margins on the left and 1-inch margins on all other sides[90]	Briefs must be in 6⅛- by 9¼-inch booklet format with margins of at least ¾ inch on all sides[91]
Filing of a Brief	Opening brief must be filed within 40 days after the record is filed, running from the date the appeal is docketed[92]	Opening brief must be filed 35 days after the record on appeal is filed with the appellate court[93]	Brief on the merits must be filed within 45 days of the order granting the petition for a writ of certiorari[94]

A lack of familiarity with the rules can have grave consequences — a court will not take an appeal that is improperly filed, and may reject noncompliant motions or briefs. Having a filing or brief rejected because of improper formatting means additional work and expense in the long run, and also can damage your credibility with the court. It is far better to know the rules and get the details right the first time.

2.2   Pre-Briefing Procedures

STEP 1 — File the Notice of Appeal. The first step in perfecting your appeal is to file the notice of appeal. The notice of appeal must be filed by an attorney who has entered an appearance in the trial court. As explained earlier, it must be filed in the district court, not the appellate court, and must be filed on time. Despite its importance, the notice of appeal is a relatively simple document that contains three pieces of information: (1) the party or parties appealing; (2) the judgment or order appealed; and (3) the court to which the appeal will be taken.[95] Notices of appeal are liberally construed, and courts will often treat a different document as a notice of appeal, so long as it contains the required information.[96]

STEP 2 — Fees; Docketing Statements; Disclosures; and Counsel of Record. When you file the notice of appeal in a federal case, you should also pay the filing fee in the district court[97] or move to proceed *in forma pauperis* (i.e., as an indigent who cannot afford the fee), also in the district court. You will next file and serve on all parties a docketing statement, which identifies the parties, the judge below, and any pending issues or similar cases that the appellate court should know about. For example, if you know that a codefendant in your client's trial has already appealed and the appeal is still pending, you should alert the appellate court so that it may consolidate the appeals. Also, it may be in your client's interest to have the same panel review two cases from different courts if their facts or legal issues overlap. By identifying the other case as "related," you increase the likelihood that the clerk's office will couple the cases for purposes of oral argument.

You must also file the required disclosures or jurisdictional statements as soon as possible. These include corporate disclosure statements under Federal Rule of Appellate Procedure 26.1, which identify parent companies or other financially interested parties related to a business entity litigant. You must also file a jurisdictional statement setting forth the basis for jurisdiction in the trial court as well as the basis for appellate jurisdiction. Disclosures and jurisdictional statements will be discussed more in Chapter 12, which covers required appellate brief sections. Finally, it should go without saying, but the lead attorney, who becomes the counsel of record when identified on the docketing statement or whatever document is first filed, must be admitted to practice in the court.[98] Fulfilling these preliminary requirements allows the court to decide whether it can hear the appeal, and whether all of the correct parties will be able to participate.

STEP 3 — Preparing the Record on Appeal. Once you have taken care of the filing formalities, you should immediately turn to compiling the record on appeal. An appellate court may review only what is on the record, and parties cannot refer to facts outside the record, so it is essential to ensure that yours is complete. The record on appeal consists of: "(1) the original papers and exhibits filed in the district court; (2) the transcript of proceedings, if any; and (3) a certified copy of the docket entries prepared by the district clerk."[99] The federal and local rules set guidelines for district courts to transmit the record. Some portions of record, however, will not automatically be included, and that's where the advocate must step in. Transcripts, for example, are not made part of the appellate record in federal court. Instead, the parties must order the relevant transcripts from the court reporter, who then files them so that the appellate court also has access to them.[100] The process of ordering and obtaining transcripts often causes delay due to backlogs in the court reporters' or trial court clerks' offices. As a result, the appealing advocate must take care to ask for extensions or even request a stay of appellate proceedings pending completion of the transcripts.

Some jurisdictions do not require or even allow parties to file copies of their trial exhibits; they are instead retained by the parties after the verdict.[101] A party who wishes to rely on an unfiled trial exhibit must first move in the district court to supplement the record on appeal,[102] and should file the motion well before his appellate brief is due to give the trial court time to rule on the motion. Additionally, some documents are routinely sealed by the district court, and some of these — like the Presentence Investigation Report in criminal cases — are potentially important to issues on appeal. If you want sealed documents to be part of the record, you must file a motion in the district court.

These ministerial matters take time — and can cause distractions from concentrating on the merits — so you must be proactive in putting the record in order. If you must supplement the record or access sealed documents, take these steps with plenty of time before the brief-filing deadline to allow for a thorough review of these additional record materials.

2.3   The Fundamentals of Appellate Motion Practice

Some of the procedural steps addressed in this section require motions, and failing to meet motion requirements can cause a court to refuse your appeal. To avoid this drastic result, an appellate advocate must be well versed in motion practice from the beginning. Though appellate motion practice varies from circuit to circuit,[103] certain core principles are universal. First, motions in federal courts of appeal are governed by three separate sets of rules: the Federal Rules of Appellate Procedure, the circuit's local rules, and the court's internal operating procedures. Second, motions in the appellate courts must be in writing[104] and are limited to 20 pages.[105] Third, motions are decided on the papers, without oral argument, unless the court orders otherwise.[106] Finally, though a single judge[107] or even

**Practice Alert #4
Drafting Exercise**

In the online companion you will find an exercise requiring you to draft a routine motion.

appellate staff may rule on a whole host of motions, only a three-judge panel may decide a motion that potentially ends a case.[108] For example, in the Seventh Circuit routine motions may be decided solely by staff attorneys, whereas a motions judge must consider the rarer, nonroutine motions.[109] Ordinarily, non-routine motions must first be filed in the district court, but can be initiated in the court of appeals if it would be impracticable to first move in the lower court or if the lower court has denied the motion.[110] The following chart lists several routine and non-routine motions at the appellate level:

Substantive Motions at the Appellate Level[111]

Routine Motions	Nonroutine Motions
To expedite appeal	For bond pending appeal
To supplement the record	For a stay pending appeal
To dismiss appeal by agreement	To dismiss appeal generally
To extend time	For leave to file an oversized brief
To consolidate appeals	To stay or recall the mandate
To withdraw as counsel in a civil case	For leave to file an amicus curiae brief

2.4   Settlement on Appeal

Even if your case meets all threshold requirements for an appeal, taking an appeal may not be in the best interests of your client. In civil cases, lawyers have ethical and professional obligations to discuss settlement with the client and opposing counsel, even at the outset of the appeal.[112] If settlement discussions are ongoing, counsel should keep the court updated on them.[113] Nearly every federal court of appeals has a mediation or settlement program in place.[114] These programs' goals include not only case resolution, but also helping litigants obtain outcomes not otherwise available through the appellate process, along with conserving judicial resources through efficient case management.[115] These programs vary court to court in their scope and formality. No circuit opens its program to criminal cases; however, some programs are available to parties in habeas corpus or mandamus proceedings.[116] Some circuits limit their programs to specific categories of civil cases, while other programs are open to the majority of civil cases coming before the court.[117] The Ninth Circuit even opens its program to cases being heard in other circuits.[118] If a case is program eligible, all but a few circuits make participation mandatory. But even in those circuits, the parties can agree that no purpose would be served by mediation, and typically their position is respected by the court's mediator.[119]

At least for civil litigants on appeal, the appellate settlement mechanisms provide an additional avenue of advocacy and case resolution. To achieve the best possible results for their clients, appellate practitioners should be prepared to engage in these kinds of negotiations.

2.5 Panel Assignment Mechanisms

Procedural rules are not the only early variables to consider. You must also know your audience. You will learn more about researching appellate judges and courts in Chapter 4, but for now we simply note that it is sound practice to learn as much as possible about the court and the judges who will decide the merits of your appeal. Individual judges inevitably bring their own experiences and approaches to each case they decide, and courts as a whole develop different personalities and reputations.[120] You cannot control who ultimately decides your case, but you should know how and when the court assigns your panel.

In federal courts, appeals granted oral argument are generally heard by a panel of three judges.[121] The composition of panels is random; cases are scheduled so that each judge will sit approximately the same number of times in a year. This randomized process is subject to very few exceptions. For example, judges will be recused from a case if there is an ethical conflict, and subsequent appeals are often reheard by the same panel that decided the first appeal in the case. Each court sets its own procedures for disclosing the panel's composition. The only federal court in which the panel is revealed long before oral argument is the D.C. Circuit, which discloses panels for merits hearings in the order setting the case for oral argument.[122] In civil cases, this takes place before briefs are filed.[123] By contrast, in most other courts the panel composition is not revealed until after the briefs have been filed. In some courts, attorneys do not learn the identities of the judges who will hear the appeal until the day of oral argument.[124] The following table lists when each circuit announces its panels:

Disclosure of Panel Composition in Federal Courts[125]

Court	Time of Disclosure
First Circuit	1 week before oral argument
Second Circuit	Thursday before oral argument
Third Circuit	10 days before oral argument
Fourth Circuit	Day of oral argument[126]
Fifth Circuit	1 week before oral argument[127]
Sixth Circuit	2 weeks before oral argument[128]
Seventh Circuit	Day of oral argument
Eighth Circuit	Approximately 1 month before oral argument
Ninth Circuit	Monday of the week before oral argument
Tenth Circuit	1 week before oral argument
Eleventh Circuit	1 week before oral argument
Federal Circuit	Day of oral argument
District of Columbia Circuit	1 month before oral argument[129]

As the chart shows, you will rarely know your judges' identities until after your briefs are filed, so this information is unlikely to influence briefing. But in some courts — like the D.C. Circuit and the Eighth Circuit — you may have the information before a reply brief is filed and, as noted above, the composition of your panel likely will impact oral argument preparation.

Endnotes

1. *See, e.g.*, Bender v. Williamsport Area Sch. Dist., 475 U.S. 534, 540-41 (1986); Hollingsworth v. Perry, 133 S. Ct. 2652, 2668 (2013).
2. 28 U.S.C. § 1291 (2006).
3. Fed. R. Civ. P. 58; Brown v. Fifth Third Bank, 730 F.3d 698, 700 (7th Cir. 2013).
4. *See* Fed. R. Civ. P. 58(d); *see also, e.g.*, Brown v. Columbia Sussex Corp., 664 F.3d 182, 185 n.5 (7th Cir. 2011).
5. *See* United States v. Moussaoui, 333 F.3d 509, 514 (4th Cir. 2003); U.S. Dept. of Justice, Practitioner's Handbook for Appeals to the United States Court of Appeals for the Seventh Circuit 24 (2014) [Hereinafter Practitioner's Handbook for the Seventh Circuit], *available at* http://www.ca7.uscourts.gov/Rules/handbook.pdf; 20 Charles Alan Wright & Mary Kay Kane, Federal Practice and Procedure: Federal Practice Deskbook § 108, n.3 (2d ed. 2011).
6. 18 U.S.C. § 3731 (2006).
7. *See* Dana Livingston Cobb, *Interlocutory Appeals and Mandamus in Federal Court*, Fourteenth Annual Conference on Federal and State Appeals, Univ. of Texas Law Sch., June 3 & 4, 2004, at 18.
8. Fed. R. App. P. 3(a).
9. Cobb, *supra* note 7, at 18.
10. 28 U.S.C. § 1292(b).
11. *Id.*
12. McFarlin v. Conseco Servs., LLC, 381 F.3d 1251, 1259 (11th Cir. 2004) (collecting cases). For more examples of orders deemed reviewable under 28 U.S.C. § 1292(b), *see* Cobb, *supra* note 7, at 26-27.
13. Sterk v. Redbox Automated Retail, LLC, 672 F.3d 535, 536 (7th Cir. 2012); McFarlin v. Conseco Servs., LLC, 381 F.3d 1251, 1259 (11th Cir. 2004).
14. 16 Charles Alan Wright et al., Federal Practice and Procedure § 3929, n.3 (3d ed. 2012).
15. *See* New Orleans Assets, LLC v. Woodward, 363 F.3d 372, 374 n.2 (5th Cir. 2004).
16. Daniel John Meador, Appellate Courts in the United States 33-34 (2d ed. 1994).
17. Thomas E. Baker, A Primer on the Jurisdiction of the U.S. Courts of Appeals 73-74 (2d ed. 2009); *see also, e.g.*, Loera v. United States, 714 F.3d 1025, 1030 (7th Cir. 2013); Boughton v. Cotter Corp., 10 F.3d 746, 748 (10th Cir. 1993).
18. Di Bella v. United States, 369 U.S. 121, 130 (1962). For a discussion of the types of interlocutory orders the government may appeal by statute, *see* Baker, *supra* note 17, at 78-81; *see also* 18 U.S.C. § 3731 (2006).
19. *See, e.g.*, United States v. Kaley, 579 F.3d 1246, 1252 (11th Cir. 2009) (reasoning that a protective order to preserve forfeitable assets in a criminal case operates like an injunction for purposes of 28 U.S.C. § 1292(a)).
20. *See, e.g.*, United States v. Ali, 718 F.3d 929, 934 (D.C. Cir. 2013).
21. 15B Charles Alan Wright, Federal Practice and Procedure § 3918.3 (2d ed. 1992) [Hereinafter 15B Federal Practice and Procedure].
22. *Id.*
23. *Id.*
24. *Id.*
25. *Id.*
26. *Id.* at § 3918.5.
27. *Id.* at §§ 3918.3-3918.5.
28. *Id.* at § 3918.4.
29. *Id.* at § 3918.3.
30. *Id.* at § 3918.7.
31. *Id.* at § 3918.6.
32. *Id.* at § 3918.3.
33. *See* Adam N. Steinman, *Reinventing Appellate Jurisdiction*, 48 B.C. L. Rev. 1237, 1247-51 (2007); *see also* Cohen v. Beneficial Indus. Loan Corp., 337 U.S. 541 (1949); United States v. Ryan, 402 U.S. 530, 533 (1971).
34. Coopers & Lybrand v. Livesay, 437 U.S. 463, 468-69 (1978) (setting forth this 3-prong test).

35. Gregory A. Castanias and Robert H. Klonoff, Federal Appellate Practice and Procedure in a Nutshell 86-87 (2008); *see also* Brad D. Feldman, *An Appeal for Immediate Appealability: Applying the Collateral Order Doctrine to Orders Denying Appointed Counsel in Civil Rights Cases*, 99 Geo. L.J. 1717, 1722-25 (2011).
36. *See, e.g.*, Lazy Y Ranch Ltd. v. Behrens, 546 F.3d 580, 587 (9th Cir. 2008).
37. *See* Robbins v. Maggio, 750 F.2d 405 (5th Cir. 1985).
38. Baker, *supra* note 17, at 44.
39. Firestone Tire & Rubber Co. v. Risjord, 449 U.S. 368, 377 (1981).
40. *See* United States v. MacDonald, 435 U.S. 850, 859 (1978).
41. Brad D. Feldman, *An Appeal for Immediate Appealability: Applying the Collateral Order Doctrine to Orders Denying Appointed Counsel in Civil Rights Cases*, 99 Geo. L.J. 1717, 1722-25 (2011).
42. *Id.*
43. *Id.*
44. *Id.*
45. *Id.*
46. *Id.*
47. U.S. Dept. of Justice, Practitioner's Handbook for Appeals to the United States Court of Appeals for the Seventh Circuit 47 (2014), *available at* http://www.ca7.uscourts.gov/Rules/handbook.pdf; Atwell v. Gabow, 311 Fed. Appx. 122, 123-24 (10th Cir. 2009); Thornton v. Gen. Motors Corp., 136 F.3d 450, 453-54 (5th Cir. 1998).
48. *In re* Avantel, S.A., 343 F.3d 311, 317 (5th Cir. 2003) (*citing In re* Dresser Indus., Inc., 972 F.2d 540, 543 (5th Cir. 1992)).
49. Will v. Calvert Fire Ins. Co., 437 U.S. 655, 661-62 (1978).
50. Baker, *supra* note 17, at 61.
51. *Id.* at 66.
52. *Id.* at 68 n.350 (citing Allied Chem. Corp. v. Daiflon, Inc., 449 U.S. 33, 35 (1980) (per curiam); Will v. Calvert Fire Ins. Co., 437 U.S. 655, 661-62 (1978)).
53. Baker, *supra* note 17, at 68; an analysis conducted by the authors indicates that, between September 2012 and September 2013, the federal circuit courts of appeal denied all but 7 of 207 petitions for writ of mandamus or prohibition considered.
54. *See* Black's Law Dictionary 1046-47 (9th ed. 2009).
55. *Id.* at 1331.
56. *E.g.*, Cheney v. U.S. Dist. Court for the Dist. of Columbia, 542 U.S. 367, 376 (2004).
57. *In re* Atlantic Pipe Corp., 304 F.3d 135, 138 n.1 (1st Cir. 2002).
58. United States v. George, 676 F.3d 249, 253 (1st Cir. 2012).
59. United States v. Mayer, 235 U.S. 55, 69 (1914).
60. United States v. Morgan, 346 U.S. 502, 505 n.4 (1954).
61. The writ is available only for criminal defendants. *See* United States v. Morgan, 346 U.S. 502, 503-04, 506-13 (1954).
62. Chaidez v. United States, 133 S. Ct. 1103, 1106 n.1 (2013).
63. Korematsu v. United States, 584 F. Supp. 1406 (N.D. Cal. 1984).
64. *See* Bender v. Williamsport Area Sch. Dist., 475 U.S. 534, 541 (1986).
65. *See, e.g.*, Weaver v. Hollywood Casino-Aurora, Inc., 255 F.3d 379, 384-85, 388 (7th Cir. 2001).
66. Laurel Hooper et al., Fed. Judicial Ctr., Case Management Procedures in the Federal Courts of Appeals 16-17, 49-214 (2d ed. 2011), *available at* http://www.fjc.gov/public/pdf.nsf/lookup/caseman2.pdf/$file/caseman2.pdf; Fed. R. App. P. 28(a)(4); 7th Cir. R. 3(c); U.S. Dept. of Justice, Practitioner's Handbook for Appeals to the United States Court of Appeals for the Seventh Circuit 17-18 (2014), *available at* http://www.ca7.uscourts.gov/Rules/handbook.pdf.
67. *See, e.g.*, Weaver v. Hollywood Casino-Aurora, Inc., 255 F.3d 379, 381 (7th Cir. 2001).
68. Shaw v. Dow Brands, Inc., 994 F.2d 364, 366 (7th Cir. 1993).
69. *See, e.g.*, Weaver v. Hollywood Casino-Aurora, Inc., 255 F.3d 379, 381 (7th Cir. 2001).
70. Fed. R. App. P. 3.
71. *Id.*
72. Fed. R. App. P. 4(b).
73. Claim-processing rules are those that "seek to promote the orderly progress of litigation by requiring that the parties take certain procedural steps at certain specified times." Henderson v. Shinseki, 562 U.S. 428, 435 (2011). *See also* Eberhart v. United States, 546 U.S. 12, 15 (2005); Kontrick v. Ryan, 540 U.S. 443, 456 (2004).
74. U.S. Dept. of Justice, Practitioner's Handbook for Appeals to the United States Court of Appeals for the Seventh Circuit 51 (2014), *available at* http://www.ca7.uscourts.gov/Rules/handbook.pdf; United States v. Neff, 598 F.3d 320, 322-23 (7th Cir. 2010).
75. Griggs v. Provident Consumer Disc. Co., 459 U.S. 56, 58 (1982)
76. Fed. R. App. P. 4(a)(5); *see also* Bowles v. Russell, 551 U.S. 205, 209-10 (2007).
77. Fed. R. App. P. 26(b).
78. Fed. R. App. P. 4.
79. Fed. R. Civ. P. 59(b).

80. Justice v. Town of Cicero, 682 F.3d 662, 665 (7th Cir. 2012).

81. *Id.*

82. *See* Lujan v. Defenders of Wildlife, 504 U.S. 555, 560 (1992).

83. Harry T. Edwards & Linda Elliott, Federal Standards of Review: Review of District Court Decisions and Agency Actions (Practitioner Edition), 13 (1st ed. 2007). [Hereinafter Edwards].

84. Lujan v. Defenders of Wildlife, 504 U.S. 555, 560-61 (1992).

85. Friends of Earth, Inc. v. Laidlaw Envtl. Servs. (TOC), Inc., 528 U.S. 167, 189-90 (2000).

86. *Id.* at 191-92.

87. *Id.* at 190.

88. *See, e.g.*, Clerk's Office, United States Court of Appeals for the Fifth Circuit, Practitioner's Guide to the U.S. Court of Appeals for the Fifth Circuit (2014), *available at* http://www.ca5.uscourts.gov/clerk/docs/pracguide.pdf; U.S. Dept. of Justice, Practitioner's Handbook for Appeals to the United States Court of Appeals for the Seventh Circuit 51 (2014), *available at* http://www.ca7.uscourts.gov/Rules/handbook.pdf; Lisa B. Fitzgerald, United States Court of Appeals for the Ninth Circuit, Appellate Jurisdiction in the Ninth Circuit (2012), *available at* http://cdn.ca9.uscourts.gov/datastore/uploads/guides/appellate_jurisdiction_outline/Appellate%20Jurisdiction%20Outline%202012%20update.pdf.

89. Fed. R. App. P. 32; 7th Cir. R. 32.

90. Ill. Sup. Ct. R. 341(a).

91. Sup. Ct. R. 33.

92. Fed. R. App. P. 31(a); 7th Cir. R. 31(a).

93. Ill. Sup. Ct. R. 343(a).

94. Sup. Ct. R. 25.

95. Fed. R. App. P. 3; U.S. Dept. of Justice, Practitioner's Handbook for Appeals to the United States Court of Appeals for the Seventh Circuit 56 (2014), *available at* http://www.ca7.uscourts.gov/Rules/handbook.pdf.

96. *See, e.g.*, Marmolejo v. United States, 196 F.3d 377, 378 (2d Cir. 1999) (per curiam); Wells v. Ryker, 591 F.3d 562, 565 (7th Cir. 2010); *See also* U.S. Dept. of Justice, Practitioner's Handbook for Appeals to the United States Court of Appeals for the Seventh Circuit 59 (2014) *available at* http://www.ca7.uscourts.gov/Rules/handbook.pdf.

97. United States Courts, Court of Appeals Fee Schedule, http://www.uscourts.gov/FormsAndFees/Fees/CourtOfAppealsMiscellaneousFeeSchedule.aspx (last visited Jul. 31, 2014).

98. Fed. R. App. P. 46(a).

99. Fed. R. App. P. 10(a).

100. Fed. R. App. P. 10(b)(1).

101. *See, e.g.*, D. Mass. Local R. 79.1(a); N.D. Ill. Local R. 26.3.

102. Fed. R. App. P. 10(e).

103. Thomas E. Baker, A Primer on the Jurisdiction of the U.S. Courts of Appeals 33 (2d ed. 2009).

104. Fed. R. App. P. 27(a)(1); 27(a)(2)(A).

105. Fed. R. App. P. 27(d)(2).

106. Fed. R. App. P. 27(e).

107. Fed. R. App. P. 27.

108. Fed. R. App. P. 27(c).

109. *Id.*

110. Fed. R. App. P. 8(a).

111. United States Court of Appeals for the Seventh Circuit, Operating Procedures 2-3 (2000), *available at* www.ca7.uscourts.gov/iops00.pdf.

112. U.S. Dept. of Justice, Practitioner's Handbook for Appeals to the United States Court of Appeals for the Seventh Circuit 78 (2014), *available at* http://www.ca7.uscourts.gov/Rules/handbook.pdf.

113. *Id.*

114. Laurel Hooper et al., Fed. Judicial Ctr., Case Management Procedures in the Federal Courts of Appeals 41, table 13 (2d ed. 2011), *available at* http://www.fjc.gov/public/pdf.nsf/lookup/caseman2.pdf/$file/caseman2.pdf.

115. Robert J. Niemic, Fed. Judicial Ctr., Mediation & Conference Programs in the Federal Courts of Appeals: A Sourcebook for Judges and Lawyers 5-6 (2d ed. 2006), *available at* www.fjc.gov/public/pdf.nsf/lookup/MediCon2.pdf/$file/MediCon2.pdf.

116. *Id.*; Laurel Hooper et al., Fed. Judicial Ctr., Case Management Procedures in the Federal Courts of Appeals 41, table 13 (2d ed. 2011), *available at* http://www.fjc.gov/public/pdf.nsf/lookup/caseman2.pdf/$file/caseman2.pdf.

117. Laurel Hooper et al., Fed. Judicial Ctr., Case Management Procedures in the Federal Courts of Appeals 15-16 (2d ed. 2011), *available at* http://www.fjc.gov/public/pdf.nsf/lookup/caseman2.pdf/$file/caseman2.pdf.

118. *Id.* at 16.

119. *Id.* at 41, table 13.

120. *See* Richard L. Revesz, *Litigation and Settlement in the Federal Appellate Courts: Impact of Panel Selection Procedures on Ideologically Divided Courts*, 29 J. Legal Stud. 685 (2000).

121. 28 U.S.C. § 46.

122. UNITED STATES COURT OF APPEALS FOR THE DISTRICT OF COLUMBIA CIRCUIT, HANDBOOK OF PRACTICE AND INTERNAL PROCEDURES 8 (2013), *available at* http://www.cadc.uscourts.gov/internet/home.nsf/Content/VL%20-%20RPP%20-%20Handbook%202006%20Rev%202007/$FILE/HandbookNovember2013WITHTOCLINKS22.pdf.

123. *Id.*

124. U.S. DEPT. OF JUSTICE, PRACTITIONER'S HANDBOOK FOR APPEALS TO THE UNITED STATES COURT OF APPEALS FOR THE SEVENTH CIRCUIT 10 (2014), *available at* http://www.ca7.uscourts.gov/Rules/handbook.pdf.

125. Reeves, *supra* note 121, at 688-89.

126. *Oral Argument Calendar*, UNITED STATES COURT OF APPEALS FOR THE FOURTH CIRCUIT, http://www.ca4.uscourts.gov/oral-argument.

127. *Rules and Internal Operating Procedure*, UNITED STATES COURT OF APPEALS FOR THE FIFTH CIRCUIT, 32 (2013), http://www.ca5.uscourts.gov/clerk/docs/5thcir-iop.pdf.

128. *Federal Rules of Appellate Procedure*, UNITED STATES COURT OF APPEALS FOR THE SIXTH CIRCUIT, 92 (2004), http://www.ca6.uscourts.gov/internet/rules_and_procedures/pdf/rules2004.pdf.

129. The D.C. Circuit appears to have changed this rule as of June 1, 2015. *See Revisions to the Handbook of Practice and Internal Procedures*, UNITED STATES COURT OF APPEALS FOR THE DISTRICT OF COLUMBIA, 6 (2015), http://www.cadc.uscourts.gov/internet/home.nsf/Content/Announcement%20-%20May%206%202015%20-%20Handbook%20Revisions/$FILE/2015HandbookRevisions%20Extracts%20May2015.pdf.

3 The Standards and Scope of Review

Once you have determined that your appeal clears the doctrinal hurdles discussed in Chapter 2 and have carefully reviewed the preliminary procedures, your next task is to figure out whether to appeal, and then what issues to raise. As you will see below, these issues overlap. Assuming that nonfrivolous issues exist,[1] you must consider the expense of an appeal vis-à-vis the likelihood of success, a question that is not simply tethered to the merits of the legal issue.[2] As a result you will engage in a sometimes complicated matrix of decisionmaking that marks one of the most important strategic points in an appeal, so much so that the next four chapters are devoted to exploring the topic from all angles: the substantive-strategic angle (Chapter 3), the process-based angle (Chapters 4 and 5) and the argument-development angle (Chapter 6). We first dive into the substantive-strategic arena, where if you are the appellant, you must decide on the best issues to raise on appeal. For appellees, the question is simpler: How do you defeat your opponent's issues or alternatively defend the judgment on grounds better than those offered by the trial court? Standards of review are a good threshold salvo for appellees, as is offering alternate grounds for affirmance. No matter which party you represent, then, you must be well versed on issue preservation, scope of review, and standards of review.

Section 1 Issue Preservation

Issue preservation requires alerting the trial court to its errors at or near the time they are committed. Appellants generally cannot raise issues that were not flagged at the trial level. Courts do not want to encourage the gamesmanship and waste of resources involved in sandbagging[3] opponents by raising errors for the first time on appeal when the trial court could have corrected them on its own.[4] Issue preservation requires an objection or motion on the record that enables the trial court to consider and rule on the question in the first instance.[5] A variety of procedural vehicles are used to preserve issues. Parties can file pretrial motions, raise verbal (or written) motions during the course of the trial, and file post-trial motions. The chart below summarizes issue preservation techniques and requirements for common federal court rulings.

Summary: Assessing Preserved Error in Federal Court

Issue	Proper Response	Time Constraints for Raising Error	Additional Considerations
Lack of Federal Subject Matter Jurisdiction	Can be raised in any manner by any party or the court.	Can be raised any time.[6]	Acting without jurisdiction is always harmful error.
Lack of Personal Jurisdiction	Must be raised in an answer or in a motion to dismiss.	Waived if not raised in a responsive pleading or answer.[7]	
Error in Admitting Evidence	Motion *in limine* (civil or criminal).	Must be made before a witness testifies at trial.[8]	Strict harmless error rule: may be raised only if it "affects a substantial right."[9]
	Motion to suppress (criminal).	Must be made pretrial, before the filing date set by the court.[10]	
	Trial objection.	Need a "timely" objection (immediately after the question) or motion to strike (immediately after the answer). No need to renew later.[11]	Objection must identify a specific evidentiary problem unless apparent from the context.[12]
Error in Excluding Evidence	Motion *in limine* (requesting advance ruling on admissibility).	Must be made before a witness testifies at trial.[13]	Strict harmless error rule: evidentiary ruling error may be raised only if it "affects a substantial right."[14] Must offer the document, summarize the testimony, or elicit what the testimony would have been.[15]
The Opposing Party's Claims are Legally Insufficient	Motion for Summary Judgment. OR	Must be filed before 30 days after discovery ends, unless court orders otherwise.[16]	
	Motion for judgment as a matter of law.	Must be made at the close of evidence; may be renewed up to 28 days after judgment.[17]	

Issue	Proper Response	Time Constraints for Raising Error	Additional Considerations
Civil or Criminal Trial Ends in Finding of Liability or Conviction, respectively*	Motion for a new trial.	Must be filed no later than 28 days after judgment in civil cases[18] and within 14 days in criminal cases (unless the basis is newly discovered evidence, which allows 3 years).[19]	
The Parties' Submitted Instructions are Inaccurate	Objection during jury charge conference.	If given the opportunity, must object before jury instructions are given and offer an alternative.[20]	Must state "distinctly" the matter objected to and the grounds.[21]

A single objection or motion usually preserves an issue without having to renew it during trial or in a post-trial pleading.[22] However, in federal court, some objections and motions do not carry forward post-trial (for example, a denial of a motion to dismiss or a motion for summary judgment), on the theory that they are mooted by the ultimate trial of the case. Federal court litigants must understand the difference or face dire consequences on appeal. Below is a non-exhaustive checklist of the major issue preservation pitfalls in both civil and criminal trials:

Issue Preservation

Provisional Rulings	When a trial court makes a conditional ruling on a motion (one that could change depending on how things play out later), counsel should make sure to obtain a final ruling.[23]
Formal Entry of Judgment	If the court fails to formally enter its judgment pursuant to Federal Rule of Civil Procedure 58, the appellate court may opt to dismiss the appeal.[24]
Evidence Exclusion	Appellate courts will often refuse to review evidence-exclusion challenges unless they were accompanied by an adequate offer of proof.[25]
Jury Instructions	Failure to object to jury instructions affirmatively waives review on appeal; even defense counsel's rote "no objection" recitation can result in a full waiver, though courts are willing to review for plain error if manifest injustice would result.[26]

Motions to Suppress	Suppression issues raised for the first time on appeal are barred unless good cause is shown.[27]
Fed. R. Civ. P. 50	In a jury trial, a failure to file a Federal Rule of Civil Procedure Rule 50(a) JMOL motion at the close of all the evidence waives the right to file a Rule 50(b) renewed JMOL motion after the judgment as well as any insufficiency arguments on appeal.[28]
No Actual Ruling	An evidentiary objection is deemed waived when the trial court did not rule on it and the objecting party fails to follow up and request a ruling.[29]
Fed. R. Crim. P. 29	A failure to make a Federal Rule of Criminal Procedure 29 insufficiency motion in the trial court precludes the defendant from raising insufficiency arguments on appeal.[30]
Evidence-Sufficiency Motion	If a party objects only to a specific ground on which the evidence was insufficient, she waives other grounds not raised. A nonspecific, blanket insufficiency motion, however, preserves all insufficiency claims.[31]
Sentencing Objection	A sentencing court must provide an adequate explanation of its sentence. Failure to do so can be reversible error, *but only* if the defendant objects to the district court's inadequate explanation.[32]
Plea Waivers	If a defendant's plea agreement includes an appeal waiver, then he cannot raise any challenge to his plea or sentence on appeal, unless the plea was involuntary or involved a miscarriage of justice.[33]

In truth, a primary challenge in appellate practice is dealing with imperfect (or entirely absent) issue preservation. Although it may seem that a trial lawyer would object to anything and everything that does not play out in her client's favor, the reality for an appellate practitioner who inherits a case is often one of spotty, partial, or missing objections. These unpreserved errors can take the form of judicial rulings or inappropriate testimony or argument met with total silence by the advocates. They can also be errors "hinted at" but not properly preserved because the motions or objections are made too late, raise the wrong grounds, or state the grounds so generally that the precise error is hard to detect. The explanations for such failures are many, and do not always indicate a lapse of judgment. The speed and demands of trial can make it difficult for a trial lawyer to catch every issue. Sometimes, the lawyer is trying to maintain a rapport with the trial judge or the jury or — at a minimum — trying not to signal to a jury with too many objections that her side may be weak or that she seeks to win on a technicality. There is nothing you can do but separate these potential plain errors from the harmful preserved errors, and assess them within the narrative of reversal that

**Practice Alert #1
Issue Preservation
Exercises**

Refer to the online companion for a series of hypotheticals on issue preservation.

we will discuss in Chapter 4. In any event, a keen understanding of the hurdles raised by unpreserved issues should inform your assessment of the costs and benefits of pursuing those issues on appeal.

REFLECTION, DISCUSSION, AND CHALLENGE QUESTIONS

Issue Preservation

- What fairness concerns are implicated by issue preservation? To the parties? To the courts?
- If a criminal defendant has been appointed counsel who failed to make crucial objections, and is now facing a 20-year sentence, who should bear the burden of this failure?
- Can you see any tension between a trial lawyer's role in front of the jury and an appellate lawyer's need for issue preservation? How can that tension be minimized?

Section 2 Standards of Review

Once you've determined which issues have been preserved (and those issues that were not), your next step is to match those issues with appellate standards of review. The standard of review is the lens through which an appellate court reviews a given issue on appeal. Though often overlooked by both trial practitioners (who sometimes fail to assiduously object to all errors) and appellate lawyers (who often treat them as nothing more than boilerplate), standards of review are among the most important — if not *the* most important — threshold considerations on appeal. For appellants, the standard of review dictates both the selection and ordering of issues on appeal — even more than the issues' merits in many cases. If an otherwise strong issue was unpreserved or is subject to a highly deferential standard of review, it will often take a backseat to issues that were preserved or are subject to a more searching standard of review. For appellees, standards of review are the first line of defense,[34] and courts are highly attuned to them as well.[35] The Federal Rules of Appellate Procedure, many local rules, and state courts' rules all require parties to state the applicable standard of review in their briefs. Therefore, a thorough understanding of the standards is an absolute prerequisite for any appellate practitioner.

Standards of review are generally pegged to the question of which judicial body is in the best position to decide the issue. Some issues' standards are easy to identify. Questions of first impression or disputes over the meaning of statutory terms or the correct legal test are purely legal, reviewed anew on appeal under the rationale that an appellate court can interpret the law as well as the trial judge. At the other end of the spectrum are witness-credibility determinations, which fall squarely within the trial court's domain, because it viewed the witnesses firsthand.[36] The corresponding standard of review for such issues is far more deferential. A trial court's discretionary rulings that manage the case pretrial (such as discovery rulings) or during trial (such as allowing leading questions) are also easy to peg for deferential review. Other issues are less clear cut, and are thus amenable to being framed favorably using creativity and judgment. Below we discuss the most common standards of review, their application, and their framing.

**Practice Alert #2
Annotated Brief — Disputes
Over the Applicable
Standard of Review**

In the online companion, you will find an annotated brief highlighting parties' opposing arguments over the applicable standards of review.

2.1 The De Novo Standard

Many appeals raise questions of law that were preserved below. When that magical confluence occurs, the best standard of review for an appellant applies: de novo review.[37] Under this standard, the appeals court reviews the issue independently, with no deference to the trial court's decision.[38] For example, when a trial court gives an erroneous jury instruction, which is supposed to explain the law that the jury must apply to the evidence, the appellate court reviews that issue de novo. Similarly, when an appellant claims that the lower court erroneously construed a statute, he is raising a pure question of law, which the appellate court will consider afresh. Other questions that routinely trigger de novo review include: (1) constitutional questions; (2) issues of jurisdiction or standing; (3) motions to dismiss for failure to state a claim or for other legal infirmity; (4) motions for summary judgment; and (5) issues testing the legal sufficiency of evidence in civil jury trials.[39]

This last question, sufficiency of the evidence, is more nuanced than it first appears. If a party moves for judgment as a matter of law under Federal Rule of Civil Procedure 50(a), claiming that the evidence was insufficient to meet the law's requirements, he can effectively convert what would otherwise be an unreviewable jury verdict under the Seventh Amendment into a question of law subject to the most lenient standard of review.[40] But do not get too excited here. De novo review in this context bears little resemblance to the version used to review pure questions of law. The appellate court's power to reverse a jury's verdict is constrained by another layer of deference to the factfinder's role: The court gives the benefit of all reasonable inferences to the prevailing party below and asks whether the record would allow *any* reasonable juror to find for the nonmoving party.[41] Similarly, in criminal cases, a court's power to enter a judgment of acquittal despite the jury's verdict is technically a question of law. But the appellate court is again constrained by a second deferential layer. Under the Supreme Court's decision in Jackson v. Virginia, the appellate court will affirm if "after viewing the evidence in the light most favorable to the prosecution, *any* rational trier of fact could have found the essential elements of the offense beyond a reasonable doubt."[42]

Aside from these sufficiency-of-the-evidence issues, the appellant should prioritize and pursue issues carrying de novo review, because it is the only time in the appellate process that the court will work with a relatively blank slate. A de novo-reviewed issue's ultimate strength will depend entirely on its substantive merits, undiminished by a reviewing lens. The appellee, by contrast, should resist the de novo standard if she can. Was the trial attorney's objection too vague or too late? If so, the issue jumps from the appellant-friendly de novo standard to the appellee-friendly plain error standard. Can the trial court's decision be framed as a ruling on the facts, not the law? If so, the appellee can transform de novo review into the deferential clear-error standard discussed below.

2.2   The Clearly Erroneous Standard

Appellate courts apply the deferential "clearly erroneous" standard of review to judge-made factual findings.[43] These include findings made by the judge observing witnesses during pretrial proceedings or a bench trial, as well as the findings of fact underlying the judge's sentencing in a criminal case. The prevailing wisdom is that the trial court is in the best position to evaluate witness credibility and to weigh the evidence, so the judge's findings on those matters are presumed correct.[44] Appellate courts will overturn these factual findings only if they are "left with the definite and firm conviction that a mistake has been committed."[45] As a practical matter, this means that if there are two acceptable takes on the evidence, the appellate court will not find clear error — even if it might see the facts differently.[46] But remember that the clear error standard applies only to a judge's factfinding, not the jury's. A jury's findings are afforded much more deference under the Seventh Amendment, governed by the lenient sufficiency review discussed in the previous section.[47]

2.3   The Abuse of Discretion Standard

Abuse of discretion is another deferential standard of review; it applies primarily to a trial court's evidentiary and case-management decisions.[48] At bottom, these are legal rulings, not factual findings governed by clear error. But they are often made on the spot, without the benefit of written submissions by the parties and unlimited time to ponder the result. Thus, unlike pure issues of law subject to de novo review, legal rulings governed by the abuse-of-discretion standard are accorded substantial deference. So long as the judge's decision rests within a range of acceptable choices, it will not be disturbed.

Decisions reviewed for an abuse of discretion (assuming they are part of a final, appealable order defined in Chapter 2) include:

- Most evidentiary rulings
- Rulings on leave to amend a complaint
- Discovery rulings
- Class certification motions
- Sanctions decisions
- Attorneys' fee applications

- Sentencing Guidelines application decisions arising after the Supreme Court's decision holding the United States Sentencing Guidelines to be advisory rather than mandatory[49]
- Rulings on new trial motions under Federal Rule of Civil Procedure 59(a)
- Motions to vacate judgments under Rule 60(b)
- Whether to grant a permanent or preliminary injunction.

As you can see, these kinds of rulings gain credence from the trial judge's firsthand experience, which is grounded in the entire course of the proceedings and in her ability to view the lawyers and witnesses in action.

2.4   The Plain Error Standard

The toughest standard of review to satisfy — plain error — applies when a party fails to object properly below. When you confront an unpreserved issue, your first task is to determine whether the issue was waived or forfeited. Waiver is the intentional abandonment of an appealable issue, which prevents the party from raising it at all.[50] In contrast, an inadvertent failure to preserve is called a forfeiture rather than a waiver. Only forfeited issues receive plain error review; waived issues are nearly always ignored by appellate courts.

Sometimes the record does not make clear whether a failure to preserve stems from waiver or a forfeiture. Assume, for example, that during the course of a pretrial hearing yielding a 30-page transcript, a trial lawyer primarily pressed one basis to obtain evidence from the other side (Theory 1), but then mentioned fleetingly an alternative basis (Theory 2) — the basis that you, as appellate counsel, have deemed more viable. The trial lawyer wrapped up the hearing emphasizing that he "only" wanted relief that seems to fit Theory 1. Using this statement, your opponent will undoubtedly argue for waiver of Theory 2, so you must be prepared to address waiver before you commit to raising the issue in your opening brief. And, of course, if you are the appellee, you will be looking carefully at each issue to see if you can mount a waiver challenge. Moreover, some federal rules and statutes, as well as the cases interpreting them, identify situations where a failure to object constitutes a waiver *even though* counsel did not affirmatively state that he was abandoning the claim. Failure to file motions to suppress,[51] to move to dismiss on speedy-trial grounds,[52] or to object to jury instructions[53] are just a few of the preservation mistakes that will be treated as full waivers, placing issues beyond appellate review. As you can see, navigating the plain error landscape is tricky and must be approached with deliberate planning and care.

If an issue was merely forfeited, and not intentionally waived, an appellate court may review the issue for plain error.[54] Plain error is usually invoked in criminal cases; though technically available in civil cases, it is rarely used there for a few reasons. First, in civil cases, Federal Rule of Civil Procedure 52 allows a party to challenge fact findings in *bench* trials regardless of whether objections were preserved below.[55] Therefore, an entire set of findings that would be deemed forfeited on the criminal side are preserved for review in civil cases, making it unnecessary to argue plain error. In civil *jury* trials, Federal Rule of Civil Procedure 50 imposes a full waiver—not merely a forfeiture that would allow plain error review—whenever a lawyer does not make a properly preserved and renewed Rule 50 motion for a judgment as a matter of law.[56] Therefore, plain error review simply isn't available in a large category of civil cases.[57] It arises mostly in the context of evidentiary decisions and jury instructions.[58] But even for those issues, when civil litigants weigh the high costs of appeal against the significant hurdle of overcoming plain error review, they often opt not to pursue them.[59]

When reviewing for plain error, courts apply a four-pronged test—one that is extremely difficult to satisfy. The court asks whether: (1) the trial court made an error; (2) the error was plain; (3) the error affected the party's substantial rights; and (4) overlooking the error would undermine the integrity of the judicial proceedings.[60] Issues are tossed out at every step. Courts routinely find no error at all, just as they do with the many preserved issues on review. In addition, courts often rely on splits of authority to find that the error was not "plain," but rather subject to interpretation.[61] Even if she meets the first two prongs, the appellant still must prove a high degree of prejudice—that the error affected her substantial rights.[62] In one of the author's cases, for example, the appellate court found that the trial court committed a plain error in allowing jurors to freely question witnesses on the stand.[63] The court nonetheless affirmed the defendant's conviction because these colloquies were fairly neutral and could not have influenced the verdict, given, in the court's view, the overwhelming evidence of the defendant's guilt. Finally, even if a party meets the first three prongs, the appellate court is free to overlook the error if it does not affect the fairness, integrity, or reputation of the judicial proceedings. Though rarely referenced in the case law,[64] prong four offers courts an additional escape hatch to affirm a prejudicial error, confirming the free rein of appellate decisionmaking under this standard of review.

2.5 Harmless Error and Structural Error

Even if a litigant has preserved an issue, and even if the appellate court decides that the trial court has committed an error, the appellate court will not reverse if the error is deemed "harmless."[65] Technical mistakes are not enough; the mistake must have caused some prejudice to the appealing party. Thus, the harmless error doctrine requires appellate courts to ignore errors that do not affect the parties' "substantial rights."[66] Dispositive rulings short of trial (such as motions for dismissal or summary judgment) are by their nature harmful because they end the case. Accordingly, no separate harmlessness inquiry is required. But for cases that proceed to trial, the Supreme Court has, over a series of decisions, defined the harmless error standard in both constitutional and nonconstitutional cases. These definitions have proven notoriously slippery in the hands of the circuit courts.[67]

Harmless and structural error in criminal cases. For nonconstitutional errors in criminal cases, the standard announced in Kotteakos v. United States almost always applies.[68] Under *Kotteakos*, an error that "did not influence the jury, or had but very slight effect" does not require reversal. If, however, after viewing the error embedded in the whole fabric of the proceeding, the court cannot rule out the possibility that the error swayed the judgment, reversal is required.[69] Once the defendant-appellant demonstrates an error, the burden is on the government to prove harmlessness. When a criminal defendant's constitutional rights are at stake, the burden shifts. The Supreme Court made clear in Chapman v. California that the government must prove harmless error beyond a reasonable doubt.[70] And though *Chapman* requires courts to determine what effect the error had on the guilty verdict in that particular case (as opposed to a more generalized effect on a nebulous "reasonable jury"), courts of appeals have come up with an array of definitions for meeting that standard.[71] For example, a minority of federal appellate courts will find an error harmless if the evidence of guilt is overwhelming,[72] while the majority rule examines the prejudicial effect of the error on the jury itself.[73] What this means is that under the majority rule, reversal will be required even if there is overwhelming evidence of guilt so long as there is some indication that the jury could have relied on the error in reaching its verdict.[74]

A few errors so infect the whole trial process that the Supreme Court has held that no showing of harmlessness is required before reversal.[75] Reversal is automatic for this small set of "structural errors": (1) total deprivation of right to counsel at trial;[76] (2) biased trial judge;[77] (3) unlawful exclusion of members of the defendant's race from a grand jury;[78] (4) deprivation of the right to self-representation at trial;[79] (5) denial of the right to a public trial;[80] and (6) defective reasonable-doubt instruction that effectively deprived the defendant of the right to a jury trial.[81] You should always keep an eye out to see if your case presents one of these structural errors because it secures your client an automatic reversal, but — not surprisingly — it is rare for a district court to commit such a profound error.

Harmless error in civil cases. In civil cases, the harmless error doctrine is slightly modified. Courts hearing civil cases generally apply the *Kotteakos* standard, but unlike in their criminal case counterparts, they place the burden of proving harmlessness on the party claiming error.[82] Regardless of the context, the harmless error doctrine is thought to be linked to high affirmance rates.[83] The bottom line is that after a full trial, appellate courts are extremely reluctant to reverse, and will do so only when convinced that they are reviewing a genuinely unfair result.

To summarize this section's discussion of the standards of review, the chart below displays them on a continuum that runs from less deferential to more deferential review. Harmless error is not displayed because it is not a product of deference, but rather an additional hurdle to clear once an error has been found.

STANDARD OF REVIEW CONTINUUM

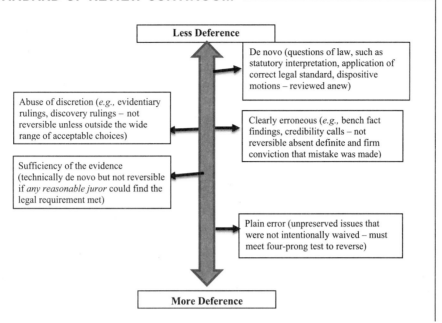

Section 3 **The Practical Impact of Standard of Review on an Appeal**

Now that you know the range of potential reviewing standards, the next question is, "So what"? Though these standards may seem little more than boilerplate, they can and do play a significant role in an appeal's trajectory. First and foremost, when the standard of review is not clear-cut, the parties must advocate for the standard that favors them. An appellant should look for ways to cast an issue as purely legal rather than as the product of factfinding, while appellees should take the opposite approach.[84] For instance, a bench trial finding of intentional employment discrim-

**Practice Alert #3
Standards of Review
Exercise**

The online companion contains a series of factual scenarios that require you to determine which standard of review should apply.

ination would be reviewed for clear error if premised on a constellation of employer conduct proven through documents and trial testimony. If the judge's opinion rests primarily on that factual analysis, then the appellee is well-positioned to argue this deferential standard. But de novo review would apply if the trial judge's discrimination ruling turned on one of two competing legal standards defining "intent." If the record reveals this basis for the ruling, then the appellant is in the driver's seat. Furthermore, an issue normally reviewed deferentially might be framed as a de novo legal question. A trial court's exclusion of expert evidence is usually reviewed for an abuse of discretion, which favors the appellee.[85] But if this evidentiary ruling turns on an unsettled question of law — say, a novel application of the *Daubert* test for admitting scientific expert testimony[86] — then the appellate court may review the same ruling de novo, a boon for the appellant.[87]

The standard of review can also take center stage in an appeal that raises mixed questions of law and fact. Mixed questions are those with roughly equal legal and factual components, each of which the trial judge had to adjudicate in issuing its ruling. A single mixed question can carry multiple standards. For example, in denying a motion to suppress, a trial judge will have made credibility findings about the police officers who testified during the suppression hearing, and those will be reviewed for clear error. The judge will also have applied the relevant legal standards under the Fourth Amendment, which will be reviewed de novo. These mixed questions require advocates to think critically about the issue's legal and factual components, and then argue them accordingly. Can those components be untangled? If not, where does the error *really* lie — in resolving evidentiary conflicts or in apprehending the law?

If an issue was raised using multiple procedural vehicles below, the advocate must decide which vehicle will garner the most favorable standard and frame it accordingly. Consider a case where the trial lawyer moved for judgment as a matter of law at the close of evidence under Federal Rule of Civil Procedure 50(a), then later moved for a new trial under Federal Rule of Civil Procedure 59, challenging the verdict as "against the weight of the evidence." These motions address the same core evidentiary problem — the facts somehow don't measure up to the law's requirements. But they are subject to different standards of review. The Rule 59 motion's denial will get abuse-of-discretion review, and will be affirmed as long as the denial was within a wide range of acceptable judicial choices. The Rule 50(a) ruling will receive the now-familiar sufficiency-of-the-evidence review, drawing all reasonable inferences in favor of the nonmoving party and affirming if "any reasonable juror" could have found the law's requirements met.[88]

Moreover, standards of review can intersect with arguments about preservation. For example, whether a party's trial objection encompassed a particular line of arguments is often hotly debated on appeal because it means the difference between plain error and de novo review.[89] What if a defendant moves for an acquittal, claiming that the government did not adequately prove his role in the conspiracy? Does he need to specify the type of conspiracy — chain versus hub-and-spoke — when making his objection in order to argue both on appeal? If he identifies one but not the other, can he raise both on appeal? These kinds of issue preservation questions arise frequently and result in extended briefing on standards of review.

Finally, even when the applicable standard of review is unambiguous, it still plays an important role in selecting which issues to raise on appeal. Take the following example of an appeal with six potential issues:

Issue	Standard of Review
Whether the expert's testimony violated the defendant's Confrontation Clause rights, because an expert cannot testify about factual evidence adduced from a different witness in order to establish essential facts.	PLAIN ERROR
Whether, even if expert testimony is permissible, the court's failure to instruct the jury that the witness was in fact an expert violated the Confrontation Clause because it blurred the line between the role of experts and fact witnesses.	PLAIN ERROR
Whether the government waived any forfeiture defense by failing to argue that the defendant did not preserve his Confrontation Clause arguments and by addressing the question on the merits.	DE NOVO
Whether the defendant was entitled to an evidentiary hearing on his pretrial motion to suppress to present evidence that he was entrapped.	ABUSE OF DISCRETION
Whether the defendant is entitled to resentencing under the Fair Sentencing Act of 2010, which the Supreme Court held to apply to all defendants convicted after its effective date.	PLAIN ERROR, but in this sentencing context such errors are automatically reversible, so functions as DE NOVO review
Whether the district court erred in finding that the defendant was a career offender.	CLEAR ERROR

Based on the standards of review, how would you rank these issues from strongest to weakest? If you were to choose only three issues, would you pick the top three or some other combination of issues? What other factors would you consider alongside the standard of review?

Practice Alert #4
Battles over Standards of Review Drafting Exercise

This exercise in the online companion divides you and your classmates into two groups: defense and prosecution. Both sides draft a short (1-2 pages) argument, advocating for their preferred standard of review.

REFLECTION, DISCUSSION, AND CHALLENGE QUESTIONS

Standards of Review

- Given the deference that appellate courts give trial court factfinding, should an advocate ever ask the appellate court to make its own factual findings, rather than issuing a remand?[90] What policies counsel for or against such an approach?

- Assume a district court imposes a two-level sentencing enhancement for obstruction of justice because the defendant was convicted of attempted escape from a law enforcement officer when fleeing out of fear for his safety. Is that a question of law (an inappropriate application of the Sentencing Guidelines) that the appeals court reviews de novo? Or is it a question of fact (a determination that fleeing for safety does not overcome the objective obstructionism of his overall behavior) subject to clearly erroneous review?

- Generally, courts are instructed to ignore "harmless" errors that do not affect the party's substantial rights. Consider a defendant convicted based on DNA evidence showing only a 1 in 10 trillion chance that a person unrelated to the defendant would match the DNA profile. Would that render a separate due process error harmless?

- What if an appellee concedes that a trial court's decision was both erroneous and not harmless? Is the appellate court entitled to overlook that concession and hold that the error is, nonetheless, harmless? What constitutional or prudential concerns might arise from such an approach?

- What makes an error "plain" for purposes of plain error review? If there is a circuit split, does that prevent a circuit that has definitively taken a side on the question from finding plain error? What if the circuits were split at the time of the trial but the issue is resolved by the Supreme Court during the appeal? Would that error be deemed plain?

- What is the interplay between plain error and harmless error, and how does it change between civil and criminal cases, and constitutional and nonconstitutional cases? What if a criminal defendant raises an unpreserved constitutional issue on appeal? Which standard (*Kotteakos* or *Chapman*) would apply and who would bear the burden of proving harmlessness?

- In criminal cases, evidence sufficiency issues carry nearly insurmountable standards. If preserved, they are governed by the Jackson v. Virginia standard, which requires affirmance if *any* rational juror could have found the defendant guilty. If unpreserved, they are governed by the plain error standard, which requires a *defendant*—rather than the government as is usual—to prove that he was prejudiced and that the error affects the integrity of the judicial system. Is there any difference? Which standard is more exacting?

Section 4   The Scope of Review

Scope of review and standard of review are often, mistakenly, used interchangeably. Standard of review addresses how an appellate court examines an issue at the front end — that is, the scrutiny with which it examines lower court error — while scope of review addresses the court's power and the remedies available to it in resolving the case at the back end.[91] Courts of appeals may impose a variety of remedies: affirmance, modification, vacatur, reversal, or remand with direction for a particular result or for further proceedings.[92] These technical terms of art simply reflect the court's power to order a wholesale reversal with no possibility for retrial, to order a partial reversal on issues that require more trial-level proceedings, or to affirm the lower court and end the case. An appellate court's scope of review is sweeping, limited only by the requirements that it rest on adequately preserved issues and facts contained in the record, and be confined to what the trial court actually did.[93]

Given these minimal constraints on scope of review, you should recognize the immense power that the appellate courts hold in fashioning a remedy, and should tailor requests for relief in the most appropriate way for the client and the court. For example, if your issue is one that the appellate court can decide itself, binding the parties and ending the appeal in your favor, then ask for that relief, rather than asking for a reversal and remand to the judge that ruled against you originally. On the other hand, if additional factfinding is required, the appellate court should not make the final determination, and you should ask for a remand with particular instructions to the trial court. In essence, you must show the appellate court that when the case ends on appeal, you know where it should go and what should happen next.

REFLECTION, DISCUSSION, AND CHALLENGE QUESTIONS

Scope of Review

- What might a lawyer consider in fashioning a proposed remedy that takes into account (1) the court's scope of review and (2) how that court might define its scope in that specific appeal?

Section 5   Client Counseling on Appeal

Just because you can bring an appeal with nonfrivolous issues does not mean you should. A number of prudential and ethical concerns come into play when counseling an appellate client. Naturally, appellate counseling involves assessing the likelihood of success; that alone encompasses a range of factors. You and your client must also discuss the development of the law, the client's wishes, and the court to which the appeal will be made. Finally, you have ethical obligations to both the court and to the client, and sometimes those obligations conflict. You must resolve those conflicts as you decide whether to appeal. The appellee's lawyer must also counsel her client and conform to ethical standards when, for example, advising the client to settle rather than to pursue an appeal to its end.

5.1 Advising the Client

The core question underlying a decision to appeal is the likelihood of success. Unfortunately, many clients overestimate their chances of securing reversal, largely because they do not understand the standard of review and its importance. In federal appellate courts, the average rate of reversal hovers right around 8.5 percent. And though the highest rate of reversal in the period ending in September 2014 was almost 15 percent, the vast majority of circuits affirm about 93 percent of the time.[94]

Low reversal rates reflect the many institutional hurdles erected before would-be appellants. First, as we explained earlier, most standards of review are designed to give deference to the lower court's decisions. Second, as you now know, even if an appellate panel finds that the lower court committed an error, it will ignore that error if it was harmless — a very common outcome. Third, appellate courts generally retain the power to affirm on any ground in the record. So, again, even if the district court erred in its decisionmaking, if there is an independent ground on which to affirm, appellate courts often will do so.

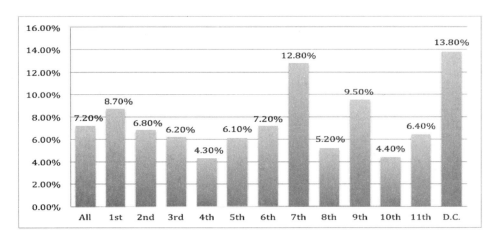

Once a case is eligible for appeal to the U.S. Supreme Court, the prospects are even more grim. In the October 2013 term, of the 7,376 cases filed seeking review in the Court, only 74 — or about 1 percent — were granted.[96] Notably, if you do get your foot in the door at the Supreme Court, you have a strong chance of obtaining a reversal, which the Court did in about 73 percent of the cases in the October 2013 term.[97]

Likelihood of success aside, other strategic factors must be discussed with the client. The possibility of creating bad law for future cases or engendering a circuit split are but a few considerations that loom large in civil cases for a large company or an entire industry. For example, if a large national firm like Wal-Mart, which has employees in every state, loses an employment case in the Seventh Circuit, it may think twice before appealing that decision to the U.S. Supreme Court. It runs the risk that the bad outcome from that single circuit could apply to all its employees nationwide. On the criminal side, lawyers must communicate to their clients that a successful sentencing challenge on appeal could result in an even higher sentence on remand. For example, what if a district court imposed a below-guidelines sentence but made a threshold procedural error by failing to adequately explain her reasoning for the sentence?[98] The appellant would likely win a resentencing due to the procedural error, but when the case returns to the district court, it could opt to impose a guidelines-range sentence that would be presumed reasonable if appealed once again. Clients must be apprised of such Pyrrhic victories so that they don't end up worse off for having won their appeals.

One final consideration in an appeal is the character of the court and the eventual composition of the panel. As Chapter 2 explained, circuits have their own personalities and reputations,[99] and even though circuit courts characterize their opinions as those of a single, unified court, it can scarcely be disputed that different judges and different panel compositions can and do influence the outcome of a case.[100] And remember that in several circuits the identity of the panel is not released until very late in the process.[101] Therefore, litigants must consider the known and unknown risks associated with the court to which they appeal in deciding whether to pursue it.[102] Chapter 4 explains how to research your court to make these judgments.

5.2   Ethics on Appeal

As an appellate lawyer, you have dual ethical responsibilities: one to your client, discussed above and embodied in the principle of zealous representation;[103] and one to the court. As an officer of the court, you have a duty of candor, which includes an ethical obligation not to file frivolous appeals or raise frivolous arguments.[104] Sometimes these two duties collide. The client may wish to appeal when there are no viable issues to raise, or she may insist on raising a frivolous issue alongside meritorious ones. Below we discuss how this tension plays out in criminal and civil contexts.

Anders briefs in criminal cases. A lawyer on direct appeal in a criminal case has the ultimate authority to decide to omit a frivolous issue on appeal. As for whether to appeal at all, the _Anders_ mechanism in criminal cases aims to ameliorate the inherent tension between the lawyers' two core duties. As a result of the Supreme Court's 1967 decision in Anders v. California, counsel who has reviewed a client's record but finds nothing to raise on appeal may file an "_Anders_" brief. In that brief, counsel analyzes all potential appeal issues, explains why an appeal would be frivolous, and makes a request to withdraw.[105] If the court agrees, it issues an order granting the motion to withdraw and dismissing the appeal. The _Anders_ procedure protects lawyers who must fulfill their duty of candor to the court, but it should not be invoked lightly. If any appeal issue is viable, the lawyer should raise it in zealous representation of his client, whose liberty is on the line.[106] Criminal defense lawyers also must be cognizant of their ethical duties to preserve issues for future appeal, including not only Supreme Court review, but also post-conviction and habeas relief after the direct appeal has ended. These post-conviction avenues are often subject to strict preservation rules that require the parties to have consistently raised the issue all the way throughout the litigation. Therefore, even if a lawyer does not believe a particular issue will succeed in the present appeal in the current court, he should be looking ahead in the client's interest to keep these avenues available if the direct appeal does not yield immediate relief.

Civil case considerations. By contrast, in the fee-paying, civil context, conflicts between lawyers and clients about raising borderline appeal issues are less common, because an individual's liberty is not at stake and because in the typical case a rational actor will not want to spend her money on a frivolous appeal. More salient in the civil context is a different duty to the client: to counsel him on the best course of action.[107] Such advice must take into account not only the expense and likelihood of success, but a candid assessment of the worst possible outcome from the appeal, both for the client[108] and the broader impact on the law.[109] For example, even if an appeal to the intermediate court would be prudent, an appeal to the United States Supreme Court might be a waste of client money. That Court is governed by its own set of rules and discretionary review.[110] If the case contains neither a split of authority nor a conflict with established Supreme Court precedent, then certiorari is not appropriate, no matter how wrong the appellate court's decision appears to be. The inverse also arises as it relates to the development of the law; some scholars have argued that the chase for Supreme Court litigation has led many lawyers to petition cases that are poor vehicles and create bad law.[111] Given that criminal defendants are entitled to a direct appeal until the certiorari stage,[112] however, appeals to the Supreme Court are inevitable on the criminal side at least. In any event, you must weigh these competing considerations in each case.

Appellate specialists. A related ethical consideration is whether the trial lawyer should continue on appeal or step aside for an experienced appellate practitioner. Clients who have established a rapport with their trial court lawyers are loyal to them, but that well-intended and fully understandable loyalty may not always garner the best results on appeal. First, using a specialist may be more efficient, require fewer hours of work, and, therefore, be less costly to the client.[113] Second, unlike the lawyers who tried the case below, appellate lawyers may take a more dispassionate view on the merits of the issues during their independent review of the case.[114] In a similar vein, appellate practitioners are better able to narrow and select issues because they are not wedded to arguments made below.[115] There is also evidence that appellate specialists improve appellate win rates.[116] One scholar conducted an empirical analysis of United States Supreme Court decisions between 2004 and 2010.[117] He found that "providing specialist counsel to non-corporate criminal defendants and individual civil plaintiffs significantly enhances those litigants' chances of success."[118] Specialists are able to combine substantive expertise with a deep knowledge of the specific appellate court, something that the trial lawyer may not have.[119] A good appellate lawyer will have established a rapport and credibility with the court because she has appeared there before and will likely return to the court again. To analogize to medicine, one would not visit a general practitioner for open-heart surgery, nor would one see an orthopedist for a cardiac problem. The same principle applies in the law. The lawyer's job is to counsel the client towards the best result; if that result does not require the lawyer's services, then she should speak up and excuse herself.

Delay and settlement. Finally, it should go without mention, but ethical issues arise when a lawyer pursues an appeal solely for purposes of delay or to encourage settlement. These ulterior motives may violate the lawyer's duty of candor to the court.

REFLECTION, DISCUSSION, AND CHALLENGE QUESTIONS

Counseling a Client and Ethics in Bringing an Appeal

- What basic tensions do you see between the lawyer's ethical duty of candor to the court and the duty to zealously represent the client?
- Assume a case presents a viable, but probably losing, issue for a criminal defendant, and that losing the case will create bad law in the circuit. In deciding whether to appeal, how does a lawyer balance his duties to his client and the general interest in proper development of the law?
- What if a criminal defendant loses on appeal in a unanimous, well-reasoned opinion but the defendant wishes to pursue rehearing and certiorari? How should a lawyer handle this conundrum?
- Courts of appeals routinely caution appellants to raise only their best two or three issues rather than taking a kitchen-sink approach to an appeal. What if a criminal client wants to raise eight other issues in the appeal? What should the lawyer do?
- What if the client wants to raise an issue that is clearly foreclosed by circuit precedent because he believes that the issue will ultimately be overturned by the Supreme Court. How should the lawyer handle that situation?
- What about settlement discussions after the case has been briefed and argued, but before the court issues the decision? Assume that oral argument questions hinted at how the panel was likely to rule. Is it appropriate to settle the case at this point to avoid the bad result or bad law?

Endnotes

1. Model Rules of Prof'l Conduct R. 3.1 (1983).
2. Criminal defendants are entitled to a government-funded direct appeal, so expense does not factor into the decisionmaking. *See* 18 U.S.C. § 3006A(c) (2012); Douglas v. California, 372 U.S. 353 (1963); Lissa Griffin, *The Right to Effective Assistance of Appellate Counsel*, 97 W. Va. L. Rev. 1 (1994).
3. Sandbagging is "[t]he act or practice of a trial lawyer's remaining cagily silent when a possible error occurs at trial, with the hope of preserving an issue for appeal if the court does not correct the problem." Black's Law Dictionary 1542 (Bryan A. Garner, ed., 10th ed., Thomson Reuters 2014).
4. 20 Charles Alan Wright & Mary Kay Kane, Federal Practice and Procedure: Federal Practice Deskbook § 111 at 964 (2d ed. 2011).
5. *See* Noreen Slank & Rosemary Gordon, *Pleading for Mercy: Dealing with Unpreserved Error*, 77 Mich. B.J., Jan. 1998, at 42; *American Bar Association Guidelines for the Appointment and Performance of Defense Counsel in Death Penalty Cases*, 31 Hofstra L. Rev. 913, 1031 (2003).
6. Fed. R. Civ. P. 12(h)(3).
7. Fed. R. Civ. P. 12(h)(1)(B)(ii).
8. Luce v. United States, 469 U.S. 38, 40 n.2 (1984).
9. Fed. R. Evid. 103(a).
10. Fed. R. Crim. P. 12(b)-(c).
11. Fed. R. Evid. 103(a); Fed. R. Civ. P. 46.
12. Fed. R. Evid. 103(a); Fed. R. Civ. P. 46.
13. Luce v. United States, 469 U.S. 38, 40 n.2 (1984).
14. Fed. R. Evid. 103(a).
15. Fed. R. Civ. P. 43(c).
16. Fed. R. Civ. P. 56(b).
17. Fed. R. Civ. P. 50.
18. Fed. R. Civ. P. 59.
19. Fed. R. Crim. P. 33.
20. Fed. R. Civ. P. 51(b).
21. Fed. R. Civ. P. 51(c)(1).
22. Fed. R. Evid. 103(a)(2). Some state courts require all claims of error to be collected and raised in post-trial briefings in order to preserve for appeal. *See, e.g.*, Mo. Sup. Ct. R. 78.07; Ill. Sup. Ct. R. 366(b)(2)(iii).
23. Crowe v. Bolduc, 334 F.3d 124, 133 (1st Cir. 2003); Gregory Silbert & Andrey Spektor, *A Primer on Preserving Objections and Arguments for Appeal in Federal Court*, N.Y. L.J., Aug. 27, 2012.
24. Hanson v. Town of Flower Mound, 679 F.2d 497, 502 (5th Cir. 1982); Theriot v. ASW Well Serv., Inc., 951 F.2d 84, 87 (5th Cir. 1992).
25. *See* Silbert & Spektor, *supra* note 23; Fed. R. Evid. 103.
26. Fed. R. Crim. P. 30; Fed. R. Civ. P. 51(c)(1); United States v. Olano, 507 U.S. 725, 737 (1993); United States v. Natale, 719 F.3d 719, 730 (7th Cir. 2013); United States v. Tyson, 653 F.3d 192, 211 (3d Cir. 2011).
27. Fed. R. Crim. P. 12; United States v. Berrios, 676 F.3d 118, 130 (3d Cir. 2012).
28. Hayer v. University of Medicine, 490 Fed. App'x 436, 438 (3d Cir. 2012).
29. Ramirez v. City of Buena Park, 560 F.3d 1012, 1026 (9th Cir. 2009).
30. *See* Fed. R. Crim. P. 29; United States v. Miller, 527 F.3d 54, 60-61 (3d Cir. 2008). *But cf.* United States v. Delgado, 256 F.3d 264, 274 (5th Cir. 2001).
31. United States v. Brown, 727 F.3d 329, 335 (5th Cir. 2013).
32. United States v. Gantt, 679 F.3d 1240, 1247 (10th Cir. 2012).
33. United States v. Tanner, 721 F.3d 1231, 1233 (10th Cir. 2013).
34. *See* Andrea Ambrose, *Making the Best of Being an Appellee*, Litigation, Spring 2012, at 26, 27; David E. Sorkin, *Persuasive Issue Statements*, 83 Ill. B.J. 139, 139 (1995); Mark Herrmann, *Inside Straight: "Standard of Review Decides Cases,"* Above the Law (Mar. 3, 2011, 10:14 am), http://abovethelaw.com/2011/03/inside-straight-standard-of-review-decides-cases.
35. *See* Fed. R. App. P. 28; Amanda Peters, *The Meaning, Measure, and Misuse of Standards of Review*, 13 Lewis & Clark L. Rev. 233, 235 (2009); Randall H. Warner, *A Crash Course in Appellate Standards of Review*, 36 Ariz. Att'y 30, 31 (1999).
36. Harry T. Edwards & Linda Elliott, Federal Standards of Review: Review of District Court Decisions and Agency Actions (Practitioner Edition), 13 (1st ed. 2007).
37. Paul R. Michel, *Appellate Advocacy — One Judge's Point of View*, 1 Fed. Cir. B.J., no. 1, Summer 1991, at 1, 3.
38. Edwards & Elliott, *supra* note 36, at 5; *see also, e.g.*, Bose Corp. v. Consumers Union, 466 U.S. 485, 514 n.31 (1984).
39. *See generally* Edwards & Elliott, *supra* note 36, at 26-50.
40. *Id.* at 50.
41. *Id.* at 51; *see also, e.g.*, United States v. Hinojosa, 728 F.3d 787, 789 (8th Cir. 2013).

42. 443 U.S. 307, 319 (1979).

43. Edwards & Elliott, *supra* note 36, at 21; Fed. R. Civ. P. 52(a)(6).

44. *Id.* at 22 (internal citation omitted); Robert Anderson IV, *Law, Fact, and Discretion in the Federal Courts: An Empirical Study*, 2012 Utah L. Rev. 1, 7-8 (2012).

45. Anderson v. City of Bessemer, 470 U.S. 564, 573 (1985) (*quoting* United States v. United States Gypsum Co., 333 U.S. 364, 395 (1948)) (internal quotation marks omitted).

46. *Id.* at 574.

47. Daniel John Meador, Appellate Courts in the United States 43 (2d ed. 2006).

48. Henry J. Friendly, *Indiscretion About Discretion*, 31 Emory L.J. 747 (1982); Anderson, *supra* note 44, at 8; Peters, *supra* note 35, at 243-44.

49. United States v. Booker, 543 U.S. 220 (2005).

50. United States v. Olano, 507 U.S. 725, 733 (*quoting* Johnson v. Zerbst, 304 U.S. 458, 464 (1938)) (1993); *see also, e.g.*, Stern v. Marshall, 131 S. Ct. 2594, 2608 (2011) United States v. Laslie, 716 F.3d 612, 614-15 (D.C. Cir. 2013); United States v. Natale, 719 F.3d 719, 729-31 (7th Cir. 2013); *but see* Williams v. Dieball, 724 F.3d 957, 961 n.2 (7th Cir. 2013). Remember, though, that some issues — like jurisdiction and standing — can never be waived. Edwards & Elliott, *supra* note 36, at 6.

51. Fed. R. Crim. P. 12(b)(3)(C), 12(e); *see, e.g.*, United States v. Burke, 633 F.3d 984, 989 (10th Cir. 2011).

52. 18 U.S.C. § 3162(a)(2) (2012); *see, e.g.*, United States v. Loughrin, 710 F.3d 1111, 1121 (10th Cir. 2013).

53. Fed. R. Civ. P. 51(c)(1); Fed. R. Crim. P. 30(d); *see, e.g.*, United States v. Collins, 684 F.3d 873, 878 (9th Cir. 2012).

54. Edwards & Elliott, *supra* note 36, at 6; Robert G. Boliek, Jr., *Appellate Practice and Procedure*, 59 Mercer L. Rev. 1075, 1089 (2008).

55. Fed. R. Civ. P. 52(a)(5).

56. Fed. R. Civ. P. 50; Edwards & Elliott, *supra* note 36, at 6.

57. *See, e.g.*, Fed. R. Civ. P. 51 n. on 2003 amendments; Jackson v. Parker, 627 F.3d 634, 640 (7th Cir. 2010) ("As such, while the plain error doctrine is often applied in criminal cases, it is rarely applied in civil cases."); Ledford v. Peeples, 657 F.3d 1222, 1257 (11th Cir. 2011) (noting the plain error doctrine "rarely applies in civil cases"); Richison v. Ernest Group, Inc., 634 F.3d 1123, 1130 (10th Cir. 2011) (stating that the plain error standard is an "extraordinary, nearly insurmountable burden" (quoting Employers Reinsurance Corp. v. Mid-Continent Cas. CO., 358 F.3d 757, 770 (10th Cir. 2004)) (internal quotations omitted)). *See also* Tory A. Weigand, Esq., *Raise or Lose: Appellate Discretion and Principled Decision-Making*, 17 Suffolk J. Trial & App. Advoc. 179, 200-04, 217 (2012).

58. *See* Fed. R. Civ. P. 51(d)(2) ("A court may consider a plain error in the [jury] instructions that has not been preserved as required by Rule 51(d)(1) if the error affects substantial rights."); Fed. R. Evid. 103(a) ("A court may take notice of a plain error [in an evidentiary ruling] affecting a substantial right, even if the claim of error was not properly preserved.")

59. Edwards & Elliott, *supra* note 36, at 26-50; D. Randall Johnson, *Giving Trial Judges the Final Word: Waiving the Right to Appeal Sentences Imposed Under the Sentencing Reform Act*, 71 Neb. L. Rev. 694, 722 (1992).

60. United States v. Olano, 507 U.S. 725, 736-37 (1993). *See also* United States v. Marcus, 560 U.S. 258, 262 (2010); Puckett v. United States, 556 U.S. 129, 129 (2009).

61. United States v. Carthorne, 726 F.3d 503, 516 (4th Cir. 2013).

62. *See, e.g.*, United States v. Sykes, 614 F.3d 303, 309-10 (7th Cir. 2010).

63. United States v. Sykes, 614 F.3d 303 (7th Cir. 2010).

64. *See, e.g.*, United States v. Escalante-Reyes, 689 F.3d 415, 425 (5th Cir. 2012); United States v. Dazey, 403 F.3d 1147, 1178 (10th Cir. 2005).

65. The concept of harmless error also is subsumed within the plain error test's third prong, which requires the complaining party to prove that the error affected her substantial rights. Unpreserved errors, therefore, simply apply *Olano*'s four-prong test; they are not subjected to the separate harmless error review conducted for errors reviewed under the de novo, clearly erroneous, or abuse of discretion standards.

66. Edwards & Elliott, *supra* note 36, at 5, 89; 28 U.S.C. § 2111 (2012); Fed. R. Crim. P. 52(a); Fed. R. Civ. P. 61.

67. *See, e.g.*, Virgin Islands v. Martinez, 620 F.3d 321, 337-38 (3d Cir. 2010); Wilson v. Mitchell, 498 F.3d 491, 503-04 (6th Cir. 2007).

68. 328 U.S. 750 (1946). There are a handful of so-called structural errors that so infect the entire trial process that they cannot be assessed for harmlessness. Neder v. United States, 527 U.S. 1, 7 (1999). These structural errors are: (1) total deprivation of right to counsel at trial, *Neder*, 527 U.S. at 8 (*citing* Johnson v. United States, 520 U.S. 461, 468 (1997), *in turn citing* Gideon v. Wainwright, 372 U.S. 335 (1963)); (2) biased trial judge, Tumey v. Ohio, 273 U.S. 510 (1927); (3) unlawful exclusion of members of the defendant's race from a grand jury, Vasquez v. Hillery, 474 U.S. 254 (1986); (4) deprivation of the right to self-representation at trial, McKaskle v.

Wiggins, 465 U.S. 168 (1984); (5) denial of the right to a public trial, Waller v. Georgia, 467 U.S. 39 (1984); and (6) defective reasonable-doubt instruction that effectively deprived the defendant of the right to a jury trial, Sullivan v. Louisiana, 508 U.S. 275 (1993). These constitutional violations affect the framework within which trials proceed, Arizona v. Fulminante, 499 U.S. 279, 310 (1991), and deprive defendants of basic protections that are necessary to ensure that criminal trials fairly and reliably determine guilt or innocence, *Neder*, 527 U.S. at 8-9. If one of these errors occurs, automatic reversal is required.

69. Kotteakos v. United States, 328 U.S. 750, 763-65 (1946).
70. 386 U.S. 18, 24 (1967).
71. *See* David A. Shields, *Note, East vs. West—Where Are Errors Harmless? Evaluating the Current Harmless Error Doctrine in the Federal Circuits*, 56 St. Louis U. L.J. 1319, 1322 (2012).
72. *See, e.g.,* Virgin Islands v. Martinez, 620 F.3d 321, 337-38 (3d Cir. 2010); Wilson v. Mitchell, 498 F.3d 491, 503 (6th Cir. 2007); United States v. Boling, 648 F.3d 474, 481 (7th Cir. 2011); Wilson v. Sirmons, 536 F.3d 1064, 1121 (10th Cir. 2008); United States v. Malol, 476 F.3d 1283, 1292 n.7 (11th Cir. 2007).
73. *See, e.g.,* United States v. Ofray-Campos, 534 F.3d 1, 36-37 (1st Cir. 2008); Gray v. Klauser, 282 F.3d 633, 655 (9th Cir. 2002), *vacated on other grounds*, 537 U.S. 1041 (2002); Smith v. Smith, 166 F.3d 1215, No. 97-1834 at *4-9 (6th Cir. 1998); United States v. Cunningham, 145 F.3d 1385, 1392-94 (D.C. Cir. 1998).
74. *See* Gregory Mitchell, *Against "Overwhelming" Appellate Activism: Constraining Harmless Error Review*, 82 Cal. L. Rev. 1335, 1358 (1994).
75. Arizona v. Fulminante, 499 U.S. 279, 309 (1991).
76. Neder v. United States, 527 U.S. 1, 8 (*citing* Johnson v. United States, 520 U.S. 461, 468 (1997), *in turn citing* Gideon v. Wainwright, 372 U.S. 335 (1963)).
77. Tumey v. Ohio, 273 U.S. 510 (1927).
78. Vasquez v. Hillery, 474 U.S. 254 (1986).
79. McKaskle v. Wiggins, 465 U.S. 168 (1984).
80. Waller v. Georgia, 467 U.S. 39 (1984).
81. Sullivan v. Louisiana, 508 U.S. 275 (1993).
82. Edwards & Elliott, *supra* note 36, at 96-98.
83. Steven H. Goldberg, *Harmless Error: Constitutional Sneak Thief*, 71 J. Crim. L. & Criminology 421, n.3 (1980).
84. *See* Ambrose, *supra* note 34, at 26.
85. *See, e.g.,* Toole v. Baxter Healthcare Corp., 235 F.3d 1307, 1312 (11th Cir. 2000).
86. Daubert v. Merrell Dow Pharmaceuticals, Inc., 509 U.S. 579, 593-95 (1993) (establishing five-factor test for measuring reliability of scientific evidence).
87. *See, e.g.,* United States v. Call, 129 F.3d 1402, 1405 (10th Cir. 1997).
88. *See, e.g.,* Nimely v. City of New York, 414 F.3d 381, 389-90 (2d Cir. 2005).
89. *See, e.g.,* United States v. Williams, 602 F.3d 313, 315 (5th Cir. 2010); United States v. Sturm, 673 F.3d 1274, 1281 (10th Cir. 2012).
90. *See, e.g.,* Pullman-Standard v. Swint, 456 U.S. 273, 291-92 (1982).
91. Lu-in Wang, *Morrison v. Department of Public Welfare and the Pennsylvania Revolution in Scope and Standard of Review*, 47 Duq. L. Rev. 609, 615-16 (2009).
92. 28 U.S.C. § 2106 (2012).
93. *See* Robert J. Martineau, *Considering New Issues on Appeal: The General Rule and the Gorilla Rule*, 40 Vand. L. Rev. 1023, 1061 (1987).
94. Admin. Office of the U.S. Courts, Appeals Terminated on the Merits, By Circuit tbl.B-5 (2014), *available at* http://www.uscourts.gov/statistics/table/b-5/judicial-business/2014/09/30.
95. *Id.*
96. *Statistics*, Supreme Court of the United States § II (October Term 2013), http://www.supreme-court.gov/orders/journal/jnl13.pdf
97. Kedar Bhatia, *Final Stat Pack for October Term 2013 and Key Takeways: Circuit Scorecard*, SCOTUSblog (June 30, 2014, 12:47 PM), http://sblog.s3.amazonaws.com/wp-content/uploads/2014/07/SCOTUSblog_scorecard_OT13.pdf
98. *See* Gall v. United States, 552 U.S. 38, 46 (2007).
99. Michael E. Solimine, *Judicial Stratification and the Reputations of the United States Courts of Appeals*, 32 Fla. St. U. L. Rev. 1331 (2005).
100. *See, e.g.,* Frank B. Cross & Emerson H. Tiller, *Judicial Partisanship and Obedience to Legal Doctrine: Whistleblowing on the Federal Courts of Appeals*, 107 Yale L.J. 2155 (1998); Joshua B. Fischman, *Estimating Preferences of Circuit Judges: A Model of Consensus Voting*, 54 J.L. & Econ. 781 (2011); Jonathan P. Kastellec, *Panel Composition and Judicial Compliance on the U.S. Courts of Appeals*, 23 J. L. Econ. & Org. 421 (2007).
101. *See generally* Richard L. Revesz, *Litigation and Settlement in the Federal Appellate Courts: Impact of Panel Selection Procedures on Ideologically Divided Courts*, 29 J. Legal Stud. 685 (2000).
102. Although trial-level litigation also contains this element of randomness in the case-assignment process, because litigants know their judge from the beginning of the case, they can account for

the impact of that assignment before major briefing occurs and the concomitant expenses are incurred.

103. MODEL RULES OF PROF'L CONDUCT Preamble ¶ 9 (1983).

104. MODEL RULES OF PROF'L CONDUCT R. 3.1, 3.3 (1983); John D. King, *Candor, Zeal, and the Substitution of Judgment: Ethics and the Mentally Ill Criminal Defendant*, 58 AM. U. L. REV. 209, 215-23 (2008); *see, e.g.*, MODEL RULES OF PROF'L CONDUCT R. 3.1 (1983).

105. *See* Anders v. California, 386 U.S. 738 (1967); *see also, e.g.*, United States v. Youla, 241 F.3d 296, 299-301 (3d Cir. 2001)

106. *See, e.g.*, United States v. O'Neil, 118 F.3d 65, 71 (2d Cir. 1997); Eng v. Cooley, 552 F.3d 1062, 1069 n.3 (9th Cir. 2009); United States v. Rodriguez, 627 F.3d 1372, 1380 (11th Cir. 2010); *see also How to File an* Anders *Brief*, U.S. CT. OF APP. FOR THE 2D CIR., http://www.ca2.uscourts.gov/clerk/case_filing/appealing_a_case/Anders_brief/how_to_file_an_anders_brief.html (last visited July 24, 2014) ("This Court has set a high standard for determining what constitutes a satisfactory Anders brief.").

107. *See* Roe v. Flores-Ortega, 528 U.S. 470, 480 (2000).

108. As discussed above, a lawyer should confer with the criminal client before appealing his sentence to ensure that the client is fully aware that a remand for resentencing could potentially result in a *higher* sentence. *See, e.g.*, United States v. Cong Van Pham, 722 F.3d 320, 325, 327 (5th Cir 2013); Thompson v. United States, 504 F.3d 1203, 1208 (5th Cir. 2007); *see also* United States v. Goldberg, 406 F.3d 891, 895 (7th Cir. 2005).

109. *See* Jules Lobel, *Courts as Forums for Protest*, 52 UCLA L. REV. 477, 547 (2004); Ralph Nader & William B. Schultz, *Public Interest Law with Bread on Table*, ABA J., Feb. 1985, at 74, 76; Theodore M. Shaw, *The Race Convention and Civil Rights in the United States*, 3 N.Y. CITY L. REV. 19, 35 (1998).

110. SUP. CT. R. 10.

111. *See* Nancy Morawetz, *Counterbalancing Distorted Incentives in Supreme Court Pro Bono Practice: Recommendations for the New Supreme Court Pro Bono Bar and Public Interest Practice Communities*, 86 NYU L. REV. 131 (2011).

112. UNITED STATES COURT OF APPEALS FOR THE SEVENTH CIRCUIT, CRIMINAL JUSTICE ACT FREQUENTLY ASKED QUESTIONS, http://www.ca7.uscourts.gov/cja/cja_faqs.pdf (last visited July 25, 2014).

113. Thomas G. Hungar and Nikesh Jindal, *Observations on the Rise of the Appellate Litigator*, 29 REV. LITIG. 511, 523 (2010)

114. *Id.* at 532-33.

115. *Id.* at 533.

116. *See* Jeffrey L. Fisher, *A Clinic's Place in the Supreme Court Bar*, 65 STAN. L. REV. 137, 201 (2013).

117. *Id.* at 201.

118. *Id.*

119. *Id.* at 174-75.

4 The Planning and Learning Phase: Digesting the Record and Spotting Issues

Chapters 2 and 3 introduced you to the nuts and bolts of appellate practice with a primer on what you must know before you embark on your first appeal. You learned how to get a case into appellate court, the procedures you must follow to keep your case on the docket, and the limits on appellate authority to fix lower court errors. You have also become conversant in the considerations that bear on whether and what issues to appeal. Now the book shifts focus, taking you along the path of a real-life appeal, where you apply this knowledge and begin your own appellate process.

Assume that you have just agreed to take or defend against an appeal, and you need to figure out what your case is all about and what your best appellate issues will be. This process demands that you digest reams of raw material with the goal of mastering your own case. Once you master the case, you can use your intellectual and creative skills to transform what you have learned into a persuasive (and winning) external communication. Alas, too many students and inexperienced advocates spend too little time on internal mastery, resulting in poorly thought-out or superficial appellate briefs. Moreover, taking advantage of trial counsel's expertise is a must. A few well-spent hours talking face to face with the attorney who tried the case below can supply a quick primer and ensure a more efficient record review.

Expert appellate advocates know how to become fluent in their cases by building a legal and factual universe that tells them what the appeal is all about. Experts have so internalized this "knowledge construction" process that its performance is nearly automatic. But because that process is not intuitive for less experienced writers, this section will guide you. It covers three specific tasks: (1) digesting the record; (2) issue spotting and strength assessment; and (3) conducting issue-strength and court research.

Section 1   Digesting the Record

The first step is to become fluent in the appellate record. As you know from Chapter 2, the record consists of "(1) the original papers and exhibits filed in

49

the district court; (2) the transcript of proceedings, if any; and (3) a certified copy of the docket entries prepared by the district clerk."[1] In short, the record is a textual representation of the entire case. The specific documents in the record vary by type of appeal. The charts below offer two examples: One lists typical documents in a civil summary judgment record; the other lists typical documents in a criminal trial record.

Typical Civil Appeal Record for Summary Judgment

- Docket entries
- Pleadings
- Pretrial motions and briefs (including the summary judgment briefs)
- Deposition excerpts
- Affidavits
- Documents, such as records and correspondence
- Lower court rulings and opinions on pretrial motions and on summary judgment
- Lower court's Rule 58 entry of judgment

Typical Criminal Appeal Trial Record

- Docket entries
- Grand jury testimony and exhibits
- Indictment
- Testimony from pretrial hearings (e.g., suppression hearings)
- Pretrial motions and briefs
- Lower court rulings and opinions on pretrial motions
- Trial testimony
- Trial exhibits
- Oral motions, arguments, and court rulings at trial, reflected in the trial transcript
- Jury charge proceedings, reflected in the trial transcript
- Judgment of conviction
- Presentence investigation report
- Sentencing hearing transcript
- Sentencing order

A record that spans thousands of pages, as many do, can be daunting to review. But if you perform a targeted quick look at the record before you start the in-depth review for preparing a record digest, you will grasp the fundamentals more quickly.

1.1 The Targeted Quick Look

Start your targeted quick look by reviewing the court's docket entries — you will get a bird's eye view of the procedural history and learn where to find key documents. From here, locate the parties' motion briefs and any trial court orders and opinions.

The motion briefs and trial court orders and opinions are excellent starting points; they typically explain what the case is about, offer pithy summaries of the evidence, and include citations to useful authorities. The briefs will also tell you what actions the trial court was asked to take and why. A careful review of these briefs will help you discern the nature and scope of potential appeal issues. Likewise, a critical read of the trial court's opinions can alert you to appealable error.

Then turn to the transcripts. The transcripts could reflect deposition testimony, trial testimony, or pretrial hearings. Make sure you know which of these you are looking at. As you review the transcripts for the targeted quick look, do a rapid review that focuses on finding the following: pretrial hearings and rulings; opening statements and closing arguments (to see what the lawyers thought was most important); evidentiary objections and rulings; offers of proof; oral trial motions; oral trial rulings; the charge conference; jury instructions; and post-trial motions and rulings. These are the top contenders for appealable issues.

Key Record Documents for the Targeted Quick Look

CIVIL CASE	CRIMINAL CASE
Docket entries	Docket entries
Motion to dismiss	Motion to dismiss
Motion in limine	Motion in limine
Motions for summary judgment	Motions to suppress, and *Brady/Giglio* motions
Post-trial motions	Post-trial motions
	Sentencing memoranda
Trial court orders and opinions on the above	Trial court orders and opinions on the above
Transcript segments: • Pretrial hearings on motions and rulings • Evidentiary objections, rulings, and offers of proof • Oral trial motions and rulings • Charge conference • Jury instructions • Post-trial motions and rulings • Opening and Closing Statements	Transcript segments: • Pretrial hearings on motions and rulings • Evidentiary objections, rulings, and offers of proof • Oral trial motions and rulings • Charge conference • Jury instructions • Post-trial motions and rulings • Opening and Closing Statements

After you have the basic lay of the land, it is time to generate a powerful information management tool. That tool is the record digest.

1.2 Preparing a Record Digest

A well-prepared record digest is an annotated summary of the record for use throughout the appeal. It should isolate key facts and legal rulings, register your first impressions, peg appeal issues, and tell you where to find everything at a glance. Your deep and active engagement with the record facilitates thinking and absorption in ways that passive reading will not. Through the digest process, you will internalize the evidence, develop storylines, spot strengths and problem areas, and develop research plans and argument ideas. Later on, as you write the brief, your record digest will be a reference guide to ensure that your facts are accurate and cite the correct record pages. The digest will also speed your preparation of any index required by court rules.

Here is what an effective record digest should reveal:

- The case's procedural history
- Important facts and their sources (pleadings, exhibits, affidavits, witness testimony)
- The parties' arguments and objections (oral or written in motion briefs)
- The court's rulings and reasoning (oral rulings or written opinions)
- Where to find this information, with page spans for each pleading, ruling, proceeding, exhibit, and witness
- Your impressions about:
  - Appealable errors
  - Conflicts in the evidence, and their importance
  - Strengths and weaknesses
  - Argument and storyline ideas

You can record this information in rows and columns in a Word table, an Excel spreadsheet, or any other format you like. Whatever format you use, make sure that it has word-searching capabilities so that you can locate information efficiently.

The first few rows in a record digest for a criminal trial appeal might look something like this:

RECORD PG. NOS.	DOC./ TESTIMONY/ DATE	DESCRIPTION & COMMENTS	OBJECTIONS/ RULINGS
R1-2	Indictment - 09/15/12	Charging Mutombo under Ill. law with (1) Attempt Making a Terrorist Threat; and (2) Unlawful Possession or Storage of Weapons in a Public Supported Building	
R3-66	**Record of Proceedings re: Motion to Suppress**	**Motion appears to preserve 4th Amendment issue — unlawful warrantless search or lawful inventory?**	
R4-19	Direct Examination of Officer Salles	Officer Salles only reports on part of note he considers threatening . . . the rest of it doesn't make sense (R12). Salles doesn't take CDs or other items in car (R14). D's atty. tries to classify inventory as "search," but Salles corrects him (R15). D's atty. distinguishes btw search for protection and inventory to secure valuables (R17). Salles admits he knew there was an ongoing investigation of Mutombo (R18). Salles doesn't recall if he knew car was Mutombo's when Sgt. told him to tow it (R19).	(R15): People's atty., objects when D's atty. asks if policy is to inventory cars to protect what might be valuable? Says calls for speculation of Chief's intent when created policy. **Sustained (R15).**
R19-33	Cross Examination of Officer Salles	People's Ex. 2: towing policy, admitted without objection (R20-21). People's Ex. 8: Photo of car parked partially in grass on side of road. Admitted without objection (R21). Salles was aware Mutombo was potential safety threat; he had read a memo from a detective (R23). Salles was aware that Mutombo had attempted to buy firearms (R24). During inventory, Salles found six rounds of .25 caliber ammunition in car center console (R25-26). After finding bullets, Salles felt alarmed; he notified his Sgt., who notified other officers at the NMU Police Dept. (R31).	People's atty. moves to introduce People's Ex. 12, a safety alert (R32). D's atty. objects on foundation/ hearsay (R32). People's atty. argues hearsay exception b/c it shows why Salles acted the way he did when he found the bullets. (R32). **Admitted (R33).**

This digest excerpt, from the same case, spots an evidentiary conflict:

RECORD PG. NOS.	DOC./ TESTIMONY/ DATE	DESCRIPTION & COMMENTS	OBJECTIONS/ RULINGS
R39-55	**Direct Examination of Sgt. Melvin Bowman**	Sgt. did not work Wed. or Thurs. (found Mutombo's car on Fri.) (R41). Policy is that car cannot be parked for more than 24 hours (R42). Another officer told Sgt. Bowman the car had been there two days (R42). Bowman not asking officer to search for criminal activity (R45). Other papers and pads in car (R46). Sgt. looked in trunk and saw speaker (R48-49). D's atty. asks Bowman about potential lyrics (R50). **Bowman's testimony seems inconsistent re: what he told Salles when he initiated the tow (R51).**	D's atty. asks Bowman if he thought note was in a condition where he was attempting to give it to someone (R53). People's atty. objects; calls for legal opinion; **Overruled (R53).**

Here, the digest records the writer's thoughts about strengths and storyline:

RECORD PG. NOS.	DOC./ TESTIMONY/ DATE	DESCRIPTION & COMMENTS	OBJECTIONS/ RULINGS
R177-209	Trial Testimony of Simi Washington	Asst. Prof. Criminology Law & Society at UC Irvine. Classifies Mutombo as an "aspiring gangster rapper," genre that is very violent. Notebook writings glorified guns, violence, being a G. Says the note's last line, "this is not a joke" was a cautionary statement. Discusses stages of development in writing songs, saw all stages in notebooks. Early stages of writing may not rhyme, could just be an idea. Concludes that the note's six lines blue ink was intro/outro. **Note: This is creative lawyering and good expert testimony. Story becomes more believable here.**	

In this excerpt, the writer forms impressions about another appealable issue:

RECORD PG. NOS.	DOC./ TESTIMONY/ DATE	DESCRIPTION & COMMENTS	OBJECTIONS/ RULINGS
R76-78	Motion to Dismiss Count I	**Defense**: 1st Am. rights violated by Count I; statute is unconstitutional as applied to Mutombo. (1) Note contains "rap lyrics" which are protected speech. (2) Rap lyrics not part of any illegal conduct, thus protected.	Motion to Dismiss Denied
		Court's Rationale: (1) Two parts of note are separate. Part of the note contains lyrics in black ink. Threat is in blue ink and does not rhyme. Note found with ammo and ski mask. Not protected artistic speech. (2) Arrested not just on basis of note, but also because he owned a gun, was awaiting guns ordered, and had ammo in his car. (3) True threats don't have to be communicated.	
		Note: Key here seems to be about definition of "true threat." This argument is much more developed on the record at trial and renewed through post-trial motion.	

After you have prepared the digest, review it right away. Reviewing your freshly prepared digest will give you a 5,000-foot perspective of the case: the story of what happened below, the most important witnesses, the key documents, and the most notable rulings.

**Practice Alert #1
Sample Digests**

The online companion contains two full-length sample digests that use different approaches and formatting choices. One is derived from a simulated record and the other is based on a real appellate record.

REFLECTION, DISCUSSION, AND CHALLENGE QUESTIONS

Digesting the Record

- Think about the appeal you are working on. What do you know about it already? What do you need to learn from your record review and digest?
- What record digest format will work best for you — Word table, Excel spreadsheet, or something else? Where and how will you record your own impressions?
- (After the digest is done): What surprised you about the lawyers' and trial court's actions? Would you prepare the digest differently next time? If so, how?

Section 2 **Spotting the Appeal Issues and Discerning Their Strength**

As you spot potential appeal issues during your record digest preparation, make three preliminary judgments. First, assess jurisdictional and finality requirements. Second, discern what issues the record supports appealing. Third, prioritize those appellate issues according to strength.

2.1   Jurisdiction and Finality

As a threshold matter, you must judge whether the appeal meets the finality and jurisdictional requirements discussed in Chapter 2. The most important practical check for jurisdiction is whether the notice of appeal is timely, especially if post-judgment motions have tolled the time period.

Next, look at the lower court's orders in the case's trial docket. As you learned in Chapter 2, a criminal case docket should contain a judgment of conviction and a sentencing order. Likewise, a civil case docket should end with a Rule 58 entry of judgment. If you do not see these final orders, then assess whether a finality exception applies.

In civil cases, any order that does not meet 28 U.S.C. § 1292(a)'s requirements for interlocutory appeal as of right bears a close look. Nonparty appeals often fall into this category, for example. Assess whether the order meets 28 U.S.C. § 1292(b)'s permissive interlocutory appeal test or the elements of the collateral order doctrine. Check, too, whether the order meets rule-specific, nonfinal appeals, such as Federal Rule of Civil Procedure 54(b) allowing for final judgment on less than all claims or parties, or Rule 23(f) permitting interim class certification review. Finally, if the appeal takes the form of a writ, review it for compliance with the rules governing that writ.

Any appeal with post-judgment motions in the record should be studied carefully. Sometimes parties appeal prematurely, before the court has ruled on all pending motions. Generally, the appeal is not ripe if any party's claim remains live.[2] But filing too early is always preferable to filing too late.

Jurisdiction and Finality

- ☑ Check to see if notice of appeal is timely and filed with the right court.
- ☑ In criminal cases, check for the judgment of conviction and sentencing order.
- ☑ In civil cases, check for the trial court's Rule 58 entry of judgment.
- ☑ If the appeal is from a nonfinal order, check whether it meets statutory, rule-based, or common law exceptions to finality.
- ☑ If the appeal is by writ, check for compliance with writ requirements.
- ☑ Check whether any party's claim or argued issue remains unresolved, especially if the record contains post-judgment motions.

2.2 Appealability and Strength — The Basics

Barring finality or jurisdictional problems, the next task is to discern the strongest appeal issues from those flagged in your record digest. Keep top of mind the appellate court's institutional roles — error correcting and law declaring.[3] As you've learned, appellate courts review judgments — not facts — so they will not address issues or arguments never brought to the trial court's attention unless the issues meet the stringent test for nonwaived plain error.[4] And remember that, irrespective of the standard of review, appellate courts are reluctant to reverse. So whatever appellate issues your record review uncovers, temper your enthusiasm or concern with this institutional and attitudinal context. With these principles in mind, the appeal issue assessment breaks down into these inquiries:

- Appealability
  - ○ What issues have been preserved?
  - ○ Are the preserved issues harmless errors or did they have real consequences for a party?
  - ○ If not preserved, what issues involve errors so egregious that they are "plain errors" that the lawyer did not intentionally waive?[5]
- Strength
  - ○ What standard(s) of review might apply, and how amenable are those standards to persuasive framing?
  - ○ Are these otherwise "good" appellate issues — that is, primarily legal in nature and important enough to merit the court's close attention?[6]

○ What relief will your client receive if the court of appeals agrees that there was error? Outright reversal or just a vacatur and remand? And on all of the case or on just part of the case?

2.3   How to Spot Appeal Issues

The preservation rule, as you learned in Chapter 3, is designed to give the trial court and opposing counsel fair notice of an error and the opportunity to correct it at the trial level.[7] Chapter 3's harmless error teachings also apply to your record review. Errors that do not affect a party's "substantial rights" are not reversible.[8] As such, your first priority should be spotting expressly preserved errors that really hurt a party, especially errors that motivated an advocate to make an extended written or oral argument. Some errors are not particularly well argued below, but that does not mean that they are not preserved. So long as the essence of the issue was before the court below, you may raise and develop it more fully on appeal. Using your record digest as a key, evaluate the lawyers' motions, their objections and offers of proof in hearing or trial transcripts, and the trial court's rulings. Then zero in on the *best* candidates for preserved error: issues raised in a *timely manner*, *distinctly enough*, using the *correct vehicle*, generating a *decision on the record* that was *harmful*.[9] Use the charts in Chapter 3, section 1 to help you assess preserved error.

**Practice Alert #2
"Judges Judging Judges"
Exercise**

In the online companion you will find two appellate opinions with robust discussions of lower court errors. This exercise asks you to reflect on the errors, discern how and why they caught the appellate court's attention, and rank them in order of magnitude.

Your second issue-spotting priority is to identify unpreserved plain errors that were not intentionally waived. As Chapter 3 explained, getting appellate review of a plain error is a serious uphill battle. If you encounter unpreserved errors that, in your judgment, are obvious and devastating to a party, judge them against the rare successful plain errors in controlling precedent. Absent a compelling analogy to plain errors that appellate courts have been willing to review, focus your efforts on preserved, harmful errors, and move to the next step—determining strength.

2.4   Prioritizing by Strength

Once you have identified the appeal issues, you must ascertain their strength. A preliminary strength assessment will help you choose (if appellant) or anticipate (if appellee) the issues to raise and brief on appeal. It will also help you prioritize issues and allocate your research and thinking time. Your strength assessment will be ongoing, of course, but at this early stage, use these criteria:

- The likely standard of review—strict or deferential
- The issue's amenability to favorable framing
- Legal and important in nature vs. factual and ordinary in nature

Above all, your strength assessment must be both pragmatic and strategic. From a pragmatic standpoint, consider how each issue fits the lower and appellate courts' respective institutional roles. Trial judges are well situated to make decisions that promote efficient litigation management. As factfinders in bench trials, they see witnesses and evidence firsthand, in real time, and so are best suited to rate credibility and evidentiary weight. But if your issues fall equally within the trial and appellate courts' zone of competence — deciding what the law is or how to apply it — the case for appellate intervention is more compelling. Even better, if you are the appellant, your issues may hit the appellate court's sweet spot, crying out for doctrinal coherence or presenting a novel legal question. From this pragmatic perspective, issue strength often boils down to who is in the best position to decide the issue, whether it is likely to recur in the same way, and whether it is amenable to standard setting.

But you must think strategically as well. And where pragmatics and strategy conflict, you should prioritize strategy. For example, if you represent the appellant, you might be deterred from raising too many issues on the theory that including relatively weak issues can and will detract from the appeal's overall strength.[10] But this is too simplistic a view. Issues that you deem weak in isolation might actually gain force if presented when joined with other issues that contribute to a "narrative of reversal." Multiple issues script a narrative of reversal when they hit on one central problem from different angles, creating an overwhelming sense of injustice. Finally, you have to consider the impact of your decision on the future (either via further appeal to higher courts or subsequent proceedings in habeas corpus, for example). You can and should preserve issues for the future if there is a possibility that they will yield dividends to your client, but you need not fully present (i.e., brief) each one of those issues in order to preserve them.

Consider a college student convicted of attempting to make a terrorist threat in state trial court. His conviction was based on writing provocative rap lyrics that he stashed between the driver's seat and console in his car. Police found the writing when they conducted a warrantless "inventory" search after finding the young man's locked car on a roadside. At trial, the government contended that this writing was a "true threat," not lyrics.[11] As the young man's appellate lawyer, you could raise issues ranging from facial and as-applied First Amendment challenges (because your client was convicted for alleged artistic expression) to a due process attack on the statute's vagueness (after all, what is an "attempted" terrorist threat?) to a sufficiency-of-the-evidence challenge based on a lack of intent to communicate a threat. You could also mount a Fourth Amendment challenge to the warrantless car search for failing the requirements of an inventory search. Were you to consider these issues in isolation, you might think the First Amendment too sweeping a basis for a state appellate decision, and sufficiency of the evidence a loser for its more deferential standard of review. But because the First Amendment and sufficiency issues help tell the story of overreaching government officials persecuting a citizen for a writing they find distasteful, both issues may be worth raising. And they complement the Fourth Amendment issue because they add bold brush strokes to the picture of overzealous law enforcement.

A related strategic component of issue strength is to consider fallback issues: those that may not effect a change in the law but whose narrowness might entice a cautious appellate panel. Cast within a narrative of reversal, the fallback issue will not only look stronger, but also offer the court a more restrained route to correcting your client's injustice. In the real-life appeal that is the basis for this example, the Illinois Appellate Court reversed the young man's conviction for insufficient evidence. Though subject to a more deferential standard of review than the First and Fourth Amendment issues, this narrower question carried the day.

If you represent the appellee, you must beware the power of this strategy. You can highlight aspects in the reversal narrative that don't "fit," undermining its fidelity or coherence. Or you can construct a competing "affirmance" narrative, one that reflects the appellate court's ability to affirm on any ground supported by the record. Whatever your strategy, your goal will be to whittle down both the number and strength of appellate issues in the court's eyes.

Practice Alert #3
Issue Assessment Practice Spotlight

In the online companion you will find a set of briefs that argue multiple appellate issues with varying standards of review and varying proportions of law and fact. The briefs are accompanied by questions that prompt you to consider the advocates' issue selection and prioritization strategies in light of this section's discussion.

REFLECTION, DISCUSSION, AND CHALLENGE QUESTIONS

Spotting Appeal Issues and Discerning Their Strength

- Review the appealable issues that you've flagged in your record digest. Which ones would the appellate court be most likely to scrutinize, and why? Which ones are least likely to get a close look on appeal?
- Find an issue from your record digest that has both legal and factual components. Without doing any research, make the best argument you can for de novo review on that issue. Then make the best argument you can for a more deferential standard of review.
- Based on the issues you have spotted in the record digest, can you begin to form a narrative of reversal? A competing narrative of affirmance?

Section 3 Conducting Issue-Strength and Court Research

Many expert appellate attorneys use their own judgment to make initial assessments about appealable issues and their strength. They will confirm or adjust those assessments as they learn more about the appeal. Less experienced advocates cannot make good judgments about appealable issues and strength without jumping directly into the research. Either way, both experienced and inexperienced lawyers must conduct research for a pragmatic and strategic assessment of the strength of various issues, and that process must be ongoing. This section offers guidance on how to conduct three main categories of issue-strength research: (1) the standard of review; (2) jurisdiction-specific preservation rules and error doctrines; and (3) the court and its handling of appeals.

3.1 Researching the Standard of Review

Standard of review research is especially important for errors that fall into complex categories, such as mixed law-fact questions, discretionary decisions with legal components, and legal questions that implicate the jury's role. Vital to your research process for these more malleable issues is brainstorming around the central problem that can anchor a narrative of reversal or affirmance. Think about how the relationships among the issues in your record digest can be framed to fit favorable standards of review and to coalesce around a central problem. This assessment should be a work in progress, open to rethinking as your research uncovers new cases and new ways of conceiving each issue. Indeed, you may go through multiple research cycles focused on standards of review until you can see clearly how they make the issues converge on the central problem. Ultimately, once you decide on the most advantageous and viable standard for each issue, you must support it with authority in your brief.

Standards of review are judicial doctrines housed in case law, but they are also discussed in secondary sources. Either place is a good starting point. If you are in a state appellate court, you might start with state practice manuals and bar journal articles to learn the range of jurisdiction-specific standards. You may even find that the classic standards of review have different names in state jurisdictions — "against the manifest weight of the evidence" instead of "clear error," or "arbitrary and capricious" instead of "abuse of discretion." For federal appeals, appellate practice treatises and practitioner-oriented manuals are invaluable resources.[12] In fact, many government appellate law offices post their practice manuals on the Web.[13] If your appellate issue is statutory, the annotated statute's case summaries on standards of review can be very helpful. These secondary sources will yield both content and case citations that you can use to pursue further research.

Ultimately, you will need to find controlling precedent, using authorities found in the record, in secondary sources, or through database searching. Use your jurisdiction and the substantive law to anchor your searches in the source you are using. Then, target commonly used standard-of-review language and concepts to dig deeper. If precedent does not yield a helpful standard, you can still use the case law to generate standard-of-review analogies to your appellate issue.

Example. Your client has been convicted of "constructively" possessing cocaine under a federal drug law, and you are appealing that conviction to the Eighth Circuit.[14] Both before and after the jury's verdict, the defense attorney moved for a judgment of acquittal under Federal Rule of Criminal Procedure 29. The trial court denied both motions and let the verdict stand. After a thorough review of the record, you conclude that these rulings were error because the evidence of possession is too thin. Though you would prefer to raise a purely legal issue on appeal, you find no other errors in the record. And you are not sure what the standard of review will be. At bottom, you are challenging the jury's verdict, though the issue was raised below through a legal vehicle — an acquittal motion.

To research the standard of review, you pull up the statute of conviction in the U.S.C.A., go to the Notes of Decisions, and skim the case summaries under the topic labeled "Standard of Review." Even if you do not find Eighth Circuit summaries, you will learn other circuits' approaches to drug possession convictions challenged via acquittal motions. For example, the case summaries will tell you that Rule 29 rulings are reviewed de novo because they ask for judgment as a matter of law. At the same time, because these motions challenge the sufficiency of the evidence, courts add the deferential Jackson v. Virginia layer to their review, viewing the evidence in favor of the government and the jury's verdict, and reversing only if no reasonable juror would have convicted.[15] Much the same information would appear in an appellate practice treatise or practitioner manual, should you choose to start there. Whatever your starting point, with the basic standard-of-review language in hand, you can shift to database searching to find Eighth Circuit cases. Combine the standard-of-review language with search terms crafted from "constructive possession" or from the statutory section itself, and you will discover the Eighth Circuit's approach in cases with the same substantive and procedural issue.

SUMMARY

> ### Researching the Standard of Review
>
> *Goal*: To find case law with the standard of review for issues comparable to yours, keeping in mind the central problem and narrative of reversal.
>
> *Search parameters*: Your jurisdiction, the procedural vehicle used to raise the issue below, the substantive law, and standard-of-review language that you know or think might apply.
>
> *Good sources*: Appellate practice treatises, practitioner manuals or articles, law journal articles, statutory notes of decisions, case law databases.

found in her drug dealer-boyfriend's apartment, sitting across the room at eye level from a small amount of the drug, a putty-like cocaine precursor.[1] The Eighth Circuit has established a common law test for constructive possession, which requires the government to prove that the defendant had: (1) knowledge of the drugs; (2) the ability to control them; and (3) the intent to control them.[2] Thinking about how these elements might apply in this scenario, you identify several merits research questions. Notice that the facts are framed broadly enough to reach analogous precedent on the same legal issue. The bold, italicized words are good candidates for generating further research terms:

- Does the federal statute shed any light on the breadth of the term *"possession"*?
- What general rules has the court articulated to define *knowledge, ability to control, and intent*? Are any of them subdivided into further rules or tests?
- How do courts discern *knowledge*? Must the drugs be in the defendant's *plain sight* for her to know about them? What if *drug paraphernalia* is in plain view but the drugs are not? Does the court consider a defendant's own *history with drugs*, or her knowledge of the *homeowner's prior drug dealings*?
- What proves *ability to control*? Mere *proximity to the substance*? *Words or actions* suggesting the defendant *intended to deliver* the substance? Part *ownership of the premises* where the drug was found? Or just frequenting the place? A key or *easy access* to the house? A *close relationship* with the *homeowner*?
- What shows *intent to control*, aside from the above? How much does the intent element overlap with the knowledge and control inquiries?
- Is possession easier or harder to show in a case with *multiple defendants*?
- How does the *sufficiency of the evidence* posture play into the question of possession? How about the *motion for acquittal* vehicle?

Once you draft these research questions, prioritize them. Which questions will yield answers with the biggest influence on your argument's strength and direction? Which questions are subsidiary to others? Rank them accordingly.

After you prioritize, devote the next section of your research plan to search terms. These terms will become more sophisticated and accurate as your research progresses, so add to this section of your plan as your research progresses. Using the constructive possession example, the record may yield a plentiful crop of legal language that shows how lawyers and judges talk about and conceptualize this issue. Use those words and phrases as a starting point. Beyond that, generate search terms by category of information using key words and phrases from your research questions. For example, think of words that reflect the general area of law (criminal law, drug crimes), the important people and their relationships (police, bystander, girlfriend), the specific legal issues (constructive possession), and the places, things, and actions at the forefront of the case (*e.g.*, cocaine, drug dealing, proximity, plain sight, relationship to dealer and residence). In each category, use the ladder of abstraction to brainstorm both more general and more specific concepts, as well as synonyms and related words, for each word or phrase. The chart below illustrates ladders of abstraction for conduct and location:

Sample Ladders of Abstraction: Conduct and Location

Conduct	Location
Criminal activity	Premises
Drug dealing	Residence
Drug distribution	Home
Cocaine distribution	Apartment

In the last section of your research plan, identify the sources likely to give you the most on-point and authoritative answers to your research questions. It helps to imagine the "dream authorities" that could tell you everything you need to know. In this example, the possession with intent to distribute statute may be an untapped source whose wording or structure could be used to construe possession broadly or narrowly. But it is the Eighth Circuit's constructive possession cases that will give you the most bang for your buck. The Eighth Circuit has probably decided comparable knowledge, control, or intent issues on specific facts that may resemble yours. Circuit precedent can also tell you much about the constructive possession element's meaning, even in cases whose facts have nothing to do with yours. Because the constructive possession issue is about the meaning of a legal element, circuit precedent has likely sorted out how the sufficiency and motion for acquittal postures affect the substantive analysis — finding those cases should be high priority, too. A lower, but still important, priority in this example would be persuasive precedent from other circuits using the same constructive possession elements with dead-on facts.

1.2 Research Plan: Unsettled Nonstatutory Law Issue

The next example follows the same core research plan, but the goal is different. Here, your focus changes from locating cases that define existing law and offer analogous facts to authorities that will help you argue competing legal standards in an unsettled area of the law.

Example— You represent a client who unsuccessfully sued police officers and their city employer for violating his Fourth Amendment rights. Originally, your client was arrested for burglary under Pennsylvania law. Pursuant to regular police procedure, the arresting officers immediately took a buccal (cheek) swab to extract your client's DNA, and ran it through local and national DNA collection databases. The databases turned up a match between your client's

DNA and DNA found at the crime scene of a two-year-old unsolved murder. After your client was tried and acquitted of this murder in state court, he brought this civil suit in federal court under 42 U.S.C. § 1983. He contended that the city's warrantless buccal swab program was an unreasonable search because arrestees (unlike convicted felons) maintain a reasonable expectation of privacy in their identities — an expectation that the blanket swabbing program violates. Granting summary judgment for the defendants, the district court held that that warrantless DNA profiling of arrestees does not violate the Fourth Amendment, applying a "totality of the circumstances" test that balanced your client's privacy expectations against the city's interest in the program.

From the record, you learn that most circuits apply the totality balancing test to warrantless DNA extraction challenges.[3] But a minority impose a "special needs" requirement on top of that test, upholding warrantless extractions only when they are justified by exceptional circumstances beyond typical law enforcement needs — that is, beyond mere incrimination purposes.[4] As applied to your client, the "special needs" gloss seems more advantageous, in part because it imposes an additional requirement on law enforcement and in part because the city's swab program appears to be motivated by typical law enforcement needs. The Third Circuit, which will decide your appeal, has never addressed which test applies in the DNA extraction context, and so you have an opening. You identify several preliminary merits research questions:

- How does the special needs requirement alter the pure totality balancing test? Is the special needs version likely to produce a favorable result in your client's case?
- Has the Third Circuit opined on the relative merits of a special needs versus totality balancing approach in other Fourth Amendment contexts — perhaps other criminal identification or testing contexts? How amenable is the court to each approach, and under what circumstances?
- In the circuits that apply the special needs requirement to DNA extractions, does their Fourth Amendment jurisprudence differ in any significant way from the Third Circuit's? Does anything else distinguish these jurisdictions in a way that suggests the Third Circuit would be unlikely to adopt their approaches?
- What rationales have these circuits used for imposing a special needs requirement on top of the totality balancing test? Have these courts said anything about cases like this one that would rule out applying the special needs requirement here?
- In applying their respective tests, do the circuits distinguish between random, suspicionless DNA extractions, and extractions from arrestees, parolees, probationers, convicted felons, or any other relevant grouping?
- What do other disciplines have to say about the efficacy and accuracy of blanket DNA testing programs and their related technology?

● What are the policy norms driving the majority-adopted totality
balancing test? How would grafting a special needs requirement onto
this test affect those norms?

After drafting these research questions, the next segment of your research plan
would generate search terms using the record, factual and legal categories, the
ladder of abstraction, and related and synonymous terms. You would then proceed
to the final section of your research plan, identifying the authorities most likely to
answer your research questions productively and authoritatively. But the unsettled nature of this issue makes the most promising sources very different from the
constructive possession example. Here you are not looking for settled legal definitions or factually similar cases in the jurisdiction. Rather, you are scouting out the
different Fourth Amendment tests and what they are trying to accomplish.

The two best starting points will be: (1) Supreme Court and Third Circuit
precedent on warrantless searches in the criminal identification context; and
(2) the decisions from each side of the circuit split. These authorities will tell
you more about the policy norms animating each test, their precise contours,
and the pros and cons of each one. You'll also want to zero in on cases where
choosing one test over the other either did make — or would make — a difference
in the Fourth Amendment outcome. Because your appeal issue is the subject of a
circuit split, it is also likely to be the subject of scholarly debate, which makes law
journals a rich source of ideas and arguments. These articles will also point you to
additional persuasive authority. DNA testing has been analyzed in nonlegal disciplines as well, and so the scientific and social science literature — and even
primers on advocacy organizations' websites — could be a goldmine on the two
tests' relative merits.

1.3 Research Plan: Statutory Interpretation Issue

The next example resembles the last in that it deals with an unsettled legal
question, but the debate is over statutory language, not a judicial test. The
core approach remains the same, but the goal changes again. This time, you
are searching for the best evidence of statutory meaning. Case law is still important but no longer decisive; the statute's language, purpose, and structure take
center stage.

Example — Your client is a company found liable in a Texas federal district
court in a Title VII case for retaliating against an employee who admitted that he
had sexually harassed a subordinate. Normally, Title VII, which outlaws workplace discrimination, protects harassment victims, not their harassers. But the
statute shields from retaliation "any employee" who has "participated in any
manner in an investigation."[5] You know that "investigation" means official investigations conducted by the Equal Employment Opportunity Commission,[6] the federal agency that enforces antidiscrimination laws. It was in response to an EEOC
investigator's questions that the employee confessed to harassing behavior, and
that confession led to his termination.

In the Fifth Circuit, which will hear your appeal, the open legal question is whether the employee's admission qualifies as "participating in any manner." That phrase fits testifying and providing information, but does it include admitting to the very conduct that the statute outlaws? In its summary judgment opinion before trial, the trial court answered "yes." The court relied on the broad sweep of the phrase "participated in *any* manner" to reason that the company was not entitled to judgment as a matter of law just because the plaintiff was the harasser. From the record, you see that the circuits are split on this issue, but the Fifth Circuit has never addressed it. Several merits research questions spring to mind:

- Besides "participation," what other activities does Title VII shield from retaliation, and where are those activities listed — in the same section or a different one?
- What is the purpose and focus of Title VII? Does it operate to punish and deter entities, or does it reach individual employees who have perpetrated discrimination?
- Why did Congress enact the retaliation provision? Does the legislative history shed any light on its scope? Does any post-enactment legislative activity reveal anything?
- What has the Fifth Circuit said about the meaning of "participate in any manner" in other contexts? Has the phrase received a broad or narrow construction?
- For circuits on both sides of the split, what rationales do they use? Are those rationales consistent with the way your circuit approaches Title VII and statutory interpretation in general?
- What other behaviors have courts deemed to be "participation," and which behaviors fall outside of its reach? Can any of those behaviors be compared to harassment admissions?
- What about the EEOC? Do its regulations or other publications take a stance on this issue? If so, what is the authoritative value of those pronouncements?
- What would happen if courts uniformly adopted one interpretation or the other? Would the result be in line with Title VII's goals or impede them?
- How have other antidiscrimination statutes' retaliation provisions been construed?

After drafting these questions, you will still move to the next step: generating a full complement of search terms. But the sources you prioritize at the third step will be different. The most direct answers to your questions will lie in Title VII itself and in the cases that comprise the circuit split. Those cases will offer insightful arguments construing the "participated in any manner" language and articulating why Title VII's purpose comports with their interpretation. But do not rely blindly on the cases. Your own assessment of the statutory language, structure, and purpose may ultimately be as compelling as the circuits' rationales.

The sources next most likely to answer your questions are legislative history, statutes with parallel language, and administrative regulations. And because circuit splits often generate scholarly reactions, law journal articles will be fruitful sources, both for finding authorities and generating policy arguments. Another priority, more on weight of authority than direct relevance, is Fifth Circuit retaliation case law. Mandatory precedent is a powerful force, even when precedent addresses your issue more generally than specifically.

The table below pulls together the core characteristics of an expert appellate research approach, no matter what your ultimate goal. Adapt the approach to guide your research on your appeal.

Template: Expert Research Plan

Law-Fact Application Goal:	To find controlling and persuasive authorities that define the legal standards and present analogous facts.
Unsettled Nonstatutory Law Goal:	To find persuasive authorities that adopt your test or rule, and controlling authorities that ground your argument or support your test or rule by analogy.
Unsettled Statutory Law Goal:	To find statutory support for your interpretation, persuasive authorities that adopt your interpretation, and controlling authorities that ground your argument or support your interpretation by analogy.
First Section	✓ Draft research questions whose answers you must know to advocate your side of the case. ✓ Frame the questions broadly enough to capture a range of authorities whose facts or subject matter can be analogized to yours.
Second Section	✓ Generate search terms with language in the record used by the parties, the court, or cited authorities. ✓ Generate more search terms with key words and phrases from your research questions. ✓ Brainstorm more general and more specific words, synonyms, and related words. ✓ Categorize your search terms to cover the general area of law; the specific legal issue on appeal; and important people and their relationships, places, things, and actions.
Third Section	✓ Ranked by efficiency and probable yield, list the sources that will either answer your questions directly, or will lead you to authorities with the answers. ✓ Within the ranking, identify what answers you are likely to find in controlling authority, and what answers you are likely to find in persuasive authority.
Ongoing	✓ Keep the plan dynamic by adding questions, search terms, and source ideas as your understanding improves.

REFLECTION, DISCUSSION, AND CHALLENGE QUESTIONS

Devising an Evolving Research Plan

- What are the research goals for your appellate issues? How do your issues line up with the example research plans discussed here?
- Pick one of your appellate issues and write down as many questions as you can about it in 30 minutes. Review those questions and see what information gaps they leave. Spend another 30 minutes writing questions to fill those gaps.
- Draft a research plan for your appeal.

Section 2 Executing the Plan to Be Efficient

2.1 Finding Your Jumping Off Point

To execute your research plan, you must start in the right place. That starting point will depend on whether: (1) you already have or know where to find relevant citations, and know the background law enough to dive in; or (2) you need background reading to become familiar with the area of law and find citations to relevant authority. The constructive possession example illustrates the difference between these two starting points. The first starting point makes sense if the parties' arguments or lower court rulings cite Eighth Circuit precedent on constructive possession. You would start by reading those authorities. Similarly, the record will cite the statute outlawing drug possession with intent to distribute, so you could (and probably should) start by finding and reading that statute. From there, you can browse the statutory annotations, which are case summaries organized by circuit and topic, looking under the topic of constructive possession.

The second starting point works well if you do not feel comfortable diving into the cases and statute until you better understand the concept of constructive possession and generate more vocabulary about it. Then you might start with a general secondary source like a treatise or practice manual. Internet searching for commentary can also give you a primer concerning the legal issue. State and federal agencies' websites, advocacy organizations' websites, news articles, blogs, and op-eds are among the many sources that can deepen your knowledge. At the same time, view those sources with a critical eye, taking into account their inherent biases and the reality that these types of searches can be a major time-sink. In the constructive possession example, you could prioritize by looking at the practice resources published by federal defender organizations or the websites of organizations devoted to fairness in drug sentencing.

2.2   Using Vertical and Horizontal Research Strategies

From these "jumping off" points, use the methods that match your research plan's top priorities and that will give you the most direct hits. These finding methods fall into three general categories: (1) "forward vertical" search methods like citators, which update a source with more recent authorities; (2) "backward vertical" search methods, such as locating earlier authorities within a source you are reading; and (3) "horizontal" database search methods, such as term searching or using topics and subtopics to find other sources categorized under the same point of law. The vertical strategies will give you the most direct hits — authorities that consider your source relevant enough to cite, and on the flip side, authorities so important that your source saw fit to rely on them. The horizontal methods are important supplements to improve the breadth of your search. They can round out your vertical research, locate authorities that supply analogies from other areas of the law, or unearth persuasive authority when your appellate issue presents a question of first impression.

Forward vertical searching. Because it is direct and efficient, most expert researchers start with a forward or backward vertical method, updating their source or mining the nuggets within it. The expert researcher will be savvy about using each method. For example, when an expert uses a citator's forward vertical method to find citing references, he will *always* limit the citing reference results by headnote, topic, jurisdiction, or type of authority. If he is feeling light on controlling authority or substantive knowledge at the moment, he will go right to the citing references' law journal articles. If the results are restricted by headnote, these articles will address the precise legal topic that the researcher is interested in. The journal articles not only reveal legal nuances that can help build arguments, they provide scads more relevant authority. If the researcher has already found several good mandatory authorities, he may use the citator to smooth out the edges of his research in the jurisdiction. Or if he is not satisfied with the mandatory authority he has found, he may then use the citator to find persuasive authority. That persuasive authority might be used to prop up mandatory authorities that are less on point, or they might supply a compelling factual analogy.

If your issue has a statutory basis, another forward vertical method is to use the statutory annotations. Most annotations are representative rather than comprehensive — and so must be supplemented with citators or other techniques — but they are especially valuable for gathering a stable of relevant authorities early on. The efficiency point here is to narrow the annotations by both topic and jurisdiction. That will keep you from going astray with cases that cite different sections of the statute or address irrelevant points of law.

Backward vertical searching. When experts use the "backward" vertical method, locating authorities within a source they are reading, they will do that work efficiently too. When they read a good case, for example, they don't read just any authority within it; they isolate the most relevant sections of the opinion and then read the cases that the court cites in those sections. When expert researchers find a treatise or practice manual's most on-point section, they go right to the footnotes to scan for mandatory or persuasive authority. The point is to read with a dual purpose — to absorb content and to find leads.

Horizontal searching. The most efficient "horizontal" method involves searching databases using topics and subtopics tied to the point of law being researched. Whether the expert launches a horizontal search using a link in a case headnote or by directly running the topic and subtopic through a database, she will limit that search by jurisdiction and with very focused search terms. Although this horizontal search will yield more false positives than the vertical searches, it offers coverage beyond authorities that have some direct citation connection to your source. The expert may even find new bodies of case law that can buttress her argument in creative ways, especially if the topic or subtopic extends her search to analogous areas of law.

> **Practice Alert #1**
> **Horizontal & Vertical Research Exercise**
> This exercise in the online companion compares vertical and horizontal search results using a case of your choice. It asks you to identify pressing questions about the case, pursue the answers with both vertical and horizontal research methods, then compare the results.

Notice what the expert researcher will *not* do. The expert researcher will not jump into a for-pay database with her search terms without first using the more direct, efficient, and cost-effective vertical and horizontal searches. Blind term searches often yield countless irrelevant authorities without a built-in relevance sorting mechanism. Instead, experts will use field restrictions (*e.g.,* author, title, headnote, judge) to narrow the database term search. And when a database term search yields too many results, the expert will correct for that by using narrower search terms to locate the most useful authorities

Summary: Vertical and Horizontal Research Methods

	VERTICAL Method	**HORIZONTAL Method**
Type	• Citators	• Database searching with headnote links
	• Statutory annotations	• Using legal topics and subtopics to run database searches
	• Reading authorities cited within other authorities	• Term searching in databases
Pros & cons	• Yields the most direct hits	• Adds breadth to vertical research
	• Efficient and easy to exclude irrelevant results	• Can unearth analogous bodies of law and novel legal approaches
	• Not a complete strategy; may not capture related bodies of law or sources that support a change in the law	• Poses high risk of irrelevant results, especially if used too early

within that bunch. Neither will the expert jump into a law journal database with search terms or without field restrictions. By far the most efficient way to find narrow secondary sources like law journals is through citing references to key cases, in statutory annotations, or in other secondary sources.

2.3   The Special Case of Statutory Construction Research

When your appellate issue goes beyond basic statutory analysis and involves disputed meaning of terms, like our third example research plan, a more in-depth legislative research process is in order. Specifically, you will need to locate: (1) all relevant sections of the statute; (2) relevant legislative history; (3) pertinent administrative regulations; (4) predecessor statutes from which the statute was derived or other statutes with parallel language; and (5) interpretive case law via vertical and horizontal searching.

Start with the statute's table of contents. Pay attention not only to the provision raised on appeal, but also to sections containing a preamble or statement of purpose, rules of construction, or definitions, along with sections that spell out the avenues of relief. Examine the statute's structure closely so that you understand how the legislature fit the puzzle pieces of different sections together into the whole. As Chapter 6 will explain, statutory interpretation arguments extend beyond the precise words or provision you are quibbling about. Context is crucial. Statutory interpretation arguments derive from how the words are circumscribed in definitional sections,[7] how they are used in other sections of the statute,[8] what words the legislature chose to include and omit in the provision,[9] the grammatical or syntactic structure of the provision,[10] and its place within the overall statutory scheme.[11] For some statutory construction arguments, the substantive provisions must be considered in tandem with the relief they provide.[12]

After thoroughly reviewing the statute's table of contents and extracting the relevant provisions, you will need to check for legislative history. Annotated statutes provide citations to relevant legislative history, and case law will often cite it too. You can then find the content of this legislative history in free online sources, such as the government's Thomas©[13] and GPO Access©,[14] or in for-pay databases. Likewise, compiled legislative histories in print, such as the U.S.C.C.A.N., are comprehensive and cost-effective sources of legislative history. The advantage of compiled histories is that they house in one browseable place all of the key legislative documents underlying the statute's passage.

If the statute is administered by a state or federal agency, you will need to find the governing regulations and documents promulgated by that agency. If you already know the name of this agency, the search is easy — you can simply find the agency website, which will link you to regulations and other agency guidance. As an example, the website of the Equal Employment Opportunity Commission, the agency responsible for enforcing federal antidiscrimination laws, provides links to its regulations, organized by statute and by topic within the statute.[15] The EEOC's website also links researchers to a wide variety of explanatory documents, such as its Enforcement Guidance and Compliance Manual. In addition to finding relevant regulations through agencies' websites, you can locate relevant regulatory citations in the annotated statutes. Ultimately, you will need to research the authoritativeness of all regulatory documents — some agency regulations are binding, others are persuasive only, and manuals have only minimal persuasive value[16] — but as tools for informing you about the law, they are invaluable.

Next, check for statutes that preceded your law or statutes with parallel language. One example of a predecessor law is the Rehabilitation Act, whose disability discrimination provisions for federally funded entities were the model for the Americans With Disabilities Act's private sector disability discrimination provisions.[17] The ADA's discrimination provisions likewise mirror older parallel statutory enactments: Title VII and the Age Discrimination in Employment Act.[18] As a result, decisions interpreting provisions in one statute are often highly relevant to interpreting the other. In some instances, it will be clear that the legislature modeled the subsequent statute on a predecessor provision and that previous judicial interpretations of that provision are also incorporated into the subsequent statute. Predecessor statutes can be found in the statutory annotations, but most times you will find references to predecessor and parallel statutes in secondary sources like law journals, treatises, and practice manuals.

Finally, locate cases that interpret your statute and link it to other laws. Those cases can be found in the statutory annotations, or by using a citator to update the relevant statutory provision. These cases can also be researched in a database, running a search using the statutory citation and targeted search terms. And once you have a handle on the key statutory concepts, you can use both vertical and horizontal search methods to flesh out your authority.

2.4   Knowing When to "Stop"

The word "stop" resides in quotation marks because the reality is that expert researchers will pause, not stop, when they gather enough authorities to write a draft. As Chapter 7 will explain, the writing process is recursive, because writing creates meaning and stimulates thinking. When you are writing and a question occurs to you that you cannot answer, that is probably a good time to go back to the research drawing board, both to find the answer and to determine how important it might be for the outcome of your case. Such an approach may reveal a newfound meaning to your statute, which will stimulate thinking that can generate new research questions and ideas, leading you to update your research plan and perform a focused mini-research cycle that informs your writing. These cycles may continue into later drafts. And, of course, you must keep updating the authorities in your brief using a citator until the day the brief is filed. Critically, you must check again before oral argument, to ensure that the law has not changed in a way that drastically changes or moots your appeal.

Aside from that, the most reliable sign that you have completed your research is discovering that all of your authorities refer back to one another. In other words, you find that you are not developing any new leads despite trying new research angles. If this experience of redundancy accompanies your thorough use of both vertical and horizontal research techniques in a wide variety of sources, then your research is comprehensive.

REFLECTION, DISCUSSION, AND CHALLENGE QUESTIONS

Executing Your Research Plan

- What will be your "jumping off" point for researching each appellate issue? What factors influence that choice?
- Why do you think so many novice researchers make the mistake of jumping too quickly into database searching? What guideposts will you use to decide when to move from vertical to horizontal searching?
- Think about the times when you stopped researching too early or spent too much time on research. What criteria will you use now to determine when to "stop"?

Section 3   Managing Your Research

The expert appellate researcher carefully tracks where she has been; she does not waste time performing the same searches over again. In addition, she slots and orders authorities according to their relevance and importance as she is researching and reading. Simultaneously, she analyzes these authorities and thinks about how to build arguments around them. The expert performs these cognitive tasks on an ongoing basis, so that no thought is forgotten, no idea is missed. In short, the expert excels at research management. Below are tips for approaching the major facets of research management: tracking progress, sorting authorities, and analyzing and synthesizing authorities to cultivate argument ideas.

3.1   Tracking Your Progress

Mark your path. First, make sure to check off your research questions as you answer them and cross off your high-priority sources as you find them. Second, keep a record of every search you perform and every lead you follow. Note which authorities you have searched vertically, both backwards and forwards. To track your horizontal research, jot down the topics, subtopics, and search terms you have used and the databases in which you have used them. For-pay research services have sophisticated and comprehensive research trails that show what searches you have run, and can even take you back to those search results. But do not depend on these research trails alone — after all, much of your electronic research will extend beyond those services, and you will use print sources too. Whether in handwritten or typewritten form, be sure to keep fastidious track of all your steps.

Record new research leads. Reserve space in your research plan or elsewhere to record new ideas for research leads. You can follow only one lead at a time, and you may not be able to pursue some leads for several days. To record vertical research leads when you read a book or an article, highlight or write down the promising cases and secondary sources it cites. When you read a case, highlight or record other promising cases cited within it. To keep your horizontal research on track, write down new topics and subtopics that you wish to pursue from your reading of cases, annotated statutes, and secondary sources.

Read now, read actively, and think critically. Do not wait to read book sections, articles, or cases until you have a large stack of papers sitting in front of you or a bevy of electronic folders staring you in the face. If you commit to a systematic method of recording where you have been and the leads you want to follow, you need not worry about "losing" ideas or information each time you pause to read and analyze what you have found. Take regular breaks from the finding process to read your sources, so that you don't become overwhelmed with the volume that awaits you, a common cause of paralyzing procrastination. Regular reading also boosts your understanding and allows you to refine and improve your research as you go.

When you turn to these sources, do not read passively. Instead, read authorities actively and with a critical mind focused intently on why you are reviewing that source and what you hope to gain from it. When you are reading cases, for example, record your impressions of their relevance, and write down the rules they develop, along with their key facts and notable reasoning. If you run across a powerful quotation, write it down and think about it. But avoid writing case briefs that just summarize the decision's content. Make direct connections to your case. Jot down whether the case looks promising for a rule, for reasoning by analogy, or for supporting a policy rationale. If the case is unfavorable, capture your immediate impressions for distinguishing or minimizing it. These impressions will help you decide whether the case is one you need to address in your opening brief or whether it can wait until the other side relies upon it. You can hand-write this information on the front of the case or electronically using margin notes. Alternatively, you can insert these impressions directly into standing documents. Along with these notations, circle or highlight relevant headnotes so that you can use citators and their restrictions efficiently.

3.2 Sorting Your Authorities

Novice researchers often make the mistake of printing out or electronically saving everything, but sorting nothing. They also tend to pass up authorities that seem unhelpful at first but later prove useful. But if you have been vigilant about critically reading your authorities as you go, you will also have a basis for

**Practice Alert #3
Critical Analysis Exercise**

This exercise in the online companion asks you to select two cases with opposing results on one of your appellate issues. Based on this section's tips, this exercise requires you to capture your impressions of each case, make direct connections between them and your appellate issue, and reconcile their disparate results.

sorting them intelligently. Experts sort authorities using some or all of the following techniques.

Sort with electronic folders. Electronic folders are excellent research repositories. They can reside on your hard drive, in the cloud, or within for-pay legal research services. You can label these folders with descriptive names and organize them by topics and subtopics keyed to your appellate issues, and by type of source. If one authority seems relevant to multiple issues or sub-issues, simply paste that case into multiple folders. In addition, create a separate folder for sources that you are not sure how to categorize or that do not seem helpful at first. These cases may blossom into useful authorities as your research and understanding progress. If they do not, you will at least know which cases to ignore if you encounter them in later research.

Especially if you are researching or writing collaboratively, cloud storage is an efficient way to share information and to let collaborators see each other's research in real time. Popular folder and document-sharing options include Dropbox© and Google Drive©. Once you choose a platform, you and your collaborators will need to agree on an organizational and naming approach. For example, you might divide folders by issue, topic, and subtopic, and then further by type of source. Sources should also be named uniformly. For example, file names for cases could consist of a party name and a shorthand word or phrase that conveys the case's relevance. Within each document, use electronic comments or annotations to mark the most relevant sections and comment on their significance. You will want to record more than your good finds, though. You also need a way to communicate which sources are unhelpful and sources whose use is not yet clear, so that you don't duplicate wasted reading efforts. To that end, you may want to create folders named "discarded sources" or "sources to be investigated." In addition to posting sources in a cloud-based platform, you can post collaborative documents like a joint research plan, which can be updated by any collaborator to show what work has been completed and what still must be done.

Sort in physical form. If you prefer "old school" methods, use folders with labels or a binder with tabs to sort printed research materials. As with the electronic folders, major tabs and folders can be organized by topic, subtopic, and type of source with subfolders or subtabs divided according to subtopics. But you should know that this method will be less efficient. Altering physical folders to reflect your research progress is cumbersome, and printing is expensive and time-consuming.

3.3   Analyzing and Synthesizing Authorities to Cultivate Arguments

As an appellate advocate, your legal research endgame is to build winning arguments. To cultivate those arguments, you must start bringing related authorities together and building argument ideas with them *as you are researching.* Chapter 6 will guide your argument development, but you must lay the foundation by analyzing and sorting authorities, and discerning the connections among them. Electronic tables or spreadsheets are research-management tools that will keep your ideas organized and centralized, and they will stimulate this thought process.

When you do not yet know how the authorities fit together into the bigger argument picture, use the authorities you've found as your organizing principle. Your columns could identify each authority; your rows could be impression categories that you fill in with shorthand analysis from your active critical reading, such as specific elements/factors/language addressed, policy norms developed, whether the authority is favorable or unfavorable, and how you might use or deal with it (*e.g.*, "for analogy," "to define rule," "to bolster policy argument," "to distinguish," "to attack"). If your descriptions are careful and consistent, and your software has a sorting function, you can sort by impression category (*e.g.*, sort primarily by element addressed and secondarily by favorable authorities to see all the authorities that favor your argument on element X).

> **Practice Alert #3**
> **Sample Research**
> **Management Tools**
>
> The online companion contains two sample research management tools that demonstrate different methods of centralizing, organizing, and synthesizing research results.

So sorted, these authorities' relationships will emerge. As you will see from the examples in Practice Alert #3, you will begin to make sense of them in groups. Which authorities can be reconciled and synthesized to form one or more premises of your argument? Which authorities can support broad points, and which of them deal with more nuanced propositions? Which authorities are diametrically opposed to each other and must be explained in some sensible way? This is nascent argument cultivation that can bloom into your Argument Assessment memo, discussed in Chapter 6.

Alternatively, you could organize the data by appellate issue. If you do, your columns would identify the issue, and your rows, any legal points related to that issue. You would fill in those rows with authorities that address those legal points. Because some authorities might be relevant to more than one appellate issue — or even more than one legal point — those authorities might appear in your spreadsheet multiple times. The advantage of this organization is that it ventures closer to the organization of your argument, which will slot authorities into issues, not address authorities seriatim. At the same time, this organizational method requires more analytical work up front. You must first conceive of discrete legal points underneath each issue and then fit authorities into those legal points, rather than using the spreadsheet as a way to discover what the legal points should be. As such, this organization works best if you already have experience with the types of issues involved in your appeal, if the issues are analytically straightforward, or if it is your second-generation information-management tool, prepared after you have gleaned what you can from the authority-driven table or spreadsheet.

REFLECTION, DISCUSSION, AND CHALLENGE QUESTIONS

Managing Your Research

- As you conduct research, how will you mark your path and keep track of your leads? How might you be able to centralize this information so that you can find it fast?
- What techniques will you use to force yourself to pause and read? Will you use a time-management tool, note taking, or some other active reading technique?
- What kind of research management tool best fits your project and your preferences? What information do you want to gain from that tool? What do you think it will look like?

Endnotes

1. 21 U.S.C. § 841(a)(1) (2012).
2. *See* U.S. v. Lee, 356 F.3d 831, 837 (8th Cir. 2003); U.S. v. Jackson, 610 F.3d 1038, 1043 (8th Cir. 2010).
3. Charles J. Nerko, *Assessing Fourth Amendment Challenges to DNA Extraction Statutes After* Samson v. California, 77 Fordham L. Rev. 917, 930 (2007).
4. *Id.; see also* New Jersey v. T.L.O., 469 U.S. 325, 351 (1985) (Blackmun, J., concurring) (coining the phrase "special needs doctrine").
5. 42 U.S.C. § 2000e-3(a) (2012).
6. Townsend v. Benjamin Enters., Inc., 679 F.3d 41, 47-49 (2d Cir. 2012).
7. *See* William N. Eskridge, Jr. & Phillip P. Frickey, *Statutory Interpretation as Practical Reasoning,* 42 Stan. L. Rev. 321, 355 (1990).
8. *Id.*
9. *See id.* at 355, 368.
10. *Id.* at 354-55.
11. *Id.* at 355.
12. *See* William N. Eskridge, Jr., *The New Textualism,* 37 UCLA L. Rev. 621, 661-62 (1990).
13. The Library of Congress Thomas, http://thomas.loc.gov/home/thomas.php.
14. U.S. Government Printing Office, http://www.gpo.gov/fdsys/.
15. U.S. Equal Employment Opportunity Commission, http://www.eeoc.gov/laws/index.cfm.
16. *See* U.S. v. Mead Corp., 533 U.S. 218 (2001); Chevron, U.S.A., Inc. v. Natural Res. Def. Council, 467 U.S. 837 (1984); Skidmore v. Swift & Co., 323 U.S. 134 (1944).
17. *Compare* 29 U.S.C.A. § 794 (2012) *with* 42 U.S.C. §§12111-12, 117, 12181-12, 189 (2012).
18. *Compare* 42 U.S.C. §§ 2000e-2000e-17 (2012) *with* 29 U.S.C. §§ 621-34 (2012).

6 The Planning and Learning Phase: Selecting and Refining Issues and Developing Arguments

This chapter marks the home stretch of your planning and learning phase. You should be working your way through the merits research, devoting your energy to sorting, analyzing, and synthesizing your authorities. If you have followed Chapter 5's advice, you have been diligent about connecting these authorities to your case and thinking about how to use them. What is the focus of your work now? As we discuss below, the answer depends on how well defined your appellate issues are. But for that discussion to make sense, we must first define some argument terminology.

As we define them, *issues* are global questions a brief poses as grounds for reversing or affirming the lower court. Each issue, in turn, has supporting *arguments*. Arguments are stand-alone conclusions that work together or alternatively to support an outcome on the issue. Arguments must be distinguished from *reasons*. Reasons are what each argument puts forward to support its conclusions. Rather than standing alone, as arguments do, reasons work in a progression, leading the court through the writer's logic to the argument's conclusion.

EXAMPLE

ISSUE Whether the district court abused its discretion in denying Wilke's motion for new counsel.

Main arguments

A. The district court abused its discretion in refusing to grant Wilke's motions.

B. The district court's abuse of discretion requires reversal.

Alternative arguments under section B

1. Wrongful denial of new counsel is structural error requiring automatic reversal, just as in the analogous context of wrongful denial of choice of counsel.

2. Even if this error is not structural, the correct test for reversal is *Chapman*'s harmless error test, not *Strickland*'s ineffective assistance test.

3. If this Court does apply *Strickland*, the test is met here and requires reversal.

Reasons supporting B.2's argument

- *Chapman*'s harmless error test maintains the important distinction between new counsel and ineffective assistance claims.

- *Chapman* avoids shoehorning a post-conviction test into a direct appeal proceeding, which would conflate the burdens on collateral and direct review.

- *Chapman* strikes the right balance between the rights of defendants to appointed counsel and retained counsel.

Depending on your appeal, your work right now might center on selecting and refining *issues*, or it might be geared towards sketching out ideas for *arguments*. For example, in many appellate clinics, the issues are not defined at the outset. Professors and students must dig for them, and then go through an iterative process of refining the issues until they reflect the most promising grounds for affirming or reversing. Committing to arguments before defining the issues would be too limiting. So intensive is this process that specific arguments might not be settled until the brief's first draft. On the other hand, if your issues are more clearly defined, your central task right now may be to sketch out potential arguments. This is often true of summary judgment and interlocutory appeals, especially if the lower court's opinion was clear about its grounds. Similarly, if you are writing to the U.S. Supreme Court, your outer universe of issues will be defined by the appellate litigation below. Finally, in a simulation course, some professors may even define the issues for you. Then your central task may be not only to sketch out argument ideas, but also to start working up supporting reasons.

This chapter's sections are tailored to this diversity of experience. Section 1, selecting and refining issues, is for appeals with ill-defined issues. Sections 2 through 4 are all directed towards developing arguments; these sections address the process that takes place after the issues are defined. Keep in mind that both issues and arguments may continue to be developed and revisited as you write. Some may wither under the scrutiny of your writing process, while new ones may emerge as writing sharpens your thinking. Nonetheless, this chapter will lay a strong foundation for the brief-writing enterprise that lies ahead.

Section 1   Selecting and Refining Issues

If your course or case requires you to select your issues, then you have the opportunity to engage in one of the most difficult, strategic, and interesting parts of your appeal. Assume you've digested the record and come up with a laundry list of potential issues, and—as discussed in Chapter 2—assigned the applicable standards of review. You will have a number of discrete errors that are open to challenge. As we explained in Chapter 4, you will also often find that your case presents a central problem. Perhaps the other side routinely mischaracterized the facts or the law. Perhaps the trial judge limited witness testimony, or excluded evidence altogether. Several issues in your case will loosely coalesce around this central problem, which will ultimately be worked into your appeal in a thematic way. Thematic value aside, you may be surprised to learn that issues are not always static or fixed; if you identify the central problem, there will be a number of angles from which to approach it. The key is to frame the issue in the most favorable way, given the law in your jurisdiction, the facts of your case, and the standard of review. For this, you will likely turn to your Argument Assessment memo assigned at the beginning of Section 4. This memo—like everything in your appeal—is part of a recursive process, and you will take many passes before you settle on the correct framing of your issue.

To start with a simple example, let's say your client was convicted of attempted bank robbery "by force and violence, or by intimidation."[1] From your record review, you know that your client donned a disguise and walked up to the door of the bank, but then got cold feet, turned around, and fled. As he ran away, he bumped into a customer and hurled expletives at him; he also was spotted by a concerned citizen who alerted the police, which led to his discovery. Your gut tells you that there is something not quite right about convicting a person for attempted bank robbery when he did not even enter the bank, and thus lacked any opportunity to engage in force, violence, or intimidation. You frame the issue, then, as one of evidence insufficiency, and turn to your legal research. What you discover, though, is that: (1) the standard of review for insufficiency challenges is, according to most cases, "nearly insurmountable";[2] and (2) several courts have upheld bank robbery convictions in similar circumstances, such as when the police have an informant on the inside and stop the car on the way to the bank.

At this point, some lawyers give up, label the issue as a nonstarter, and focus instead on the other issues in the case. But that intuitive question remains. Rather than discard the issue, it is time to creatively reframe it. Where else in the trial did this issue arise? Have any other courts recognized the problem that troubles you? You go back to the record and see that, of course, the elements of the offense are contained in the jury instructions. You note that the district court accepted the government's proposed jury instruction over your client's objection. You then pull the circuit's pattern instruction on the elements of bank robbery and notice that the government's proposed instruction altered the language of the pattern slightly to smooth over the very anomaly that has been gnawing at you. You dive back into legal research and discover that preserved jury instruction issues are reviewed de novo. You also find that at least one other circuit has interpreted the bank robbery statute as requiring actual force and violence or intimidation, rejecting the other courts' approach of upholding convictions premised on arrests made on the way to the bank. Suddenly your "insurmountable" issue has transformed into a winner on the facts, the standard of review, and the law. The lesson here is that you must be dogged and creative in your framing of the issues, and you must be willing to go back to the well.

Finally, once you've finalized and narrowed your list to the top five to seven issues, you will need to consider what number and combination of issues will be most likely to lead to your preferred outcome: affirmance or reversal. As a threshold matter, you do not want to take a kitchen-sink approach of arguing every preserved issue because doing so: (1) sends the signal to the panel that you have no confidence in any of your arguments, including those relevant to your strongest issues; and (2) dilutes your ability to spend adequate time and space in your brief developing your best arguments.[3] As a general rule, you will want to identify your top two to four issues. If you are having trouble narrowing them, consider once again your central problem. Often the central problem will impact several different parts of your appeal. For example, in a three-issue brief, you can use issues in concert to explain how and why the jury reached its unfavorable verdict based on insufficient evidence (Issue 1) because critical evidence was omitted (Issue 2) and because the jury instructions contained the wrong law (Issue 3). If you can select your issues in such a way that they complement your narrative, your appeal will be that much more powerful. With your issues finally in hand you now must flesh them out with powerful arguments, the subject of the rest of this chapter.

Section 2   Identifying Arguments and Relationships

No matter what the substantive or procedural issues on appeal, those issues will break down into one or more arguments, each with stand-alone conclusions. At this developmental prewriting stage, your goals should be modest: (1) generate potential arguments (Section 2.1); (2) think about how those arguments relate to each other and to the issue as a whole (Section 2.2); (3) sketch out a tentative blueprint of each argument's reasons (Section 3); and (4) start spotting potential weaknesses (Section 4).

2.1   Generating Potential Arguments

Your first task is to generate potential arguments to support your desired outcome on each issue. This work is a creative endeavor with as many different approaches as there are appellate advocates. The only sure guidance we can offer is that discerning arguments is the product of deep and considered thought about why the lower court was wrong or right on the issue, drawing on your research, record facts, logic, and common sense. Get those ideas about "why right" or "why wrong" down on paper, and then think about how they can work together or separately to drive the outcome you want.

Some issues will be simple and narrow with only one or two stand-alone arguments. For example, assume the issue is whether the lower court erred in admitting an unduly suggestive and unreliable photo array, violating your client's due process rights by creating a substantial risk of misidentification at trial. If the law is settled, this issue might break down into two arguments on why the lower court was wrong to let the evidence in: (1) the array was unduly suggestive; and (2) the array was unreliable.

Others issues will be more complex, meriting several arguments that themselves subdivide into arguments. For example, assume that on top of the arguments above, you've devised another rationale for reversal—the jurisdiction's current test for assessing suggestiveness and reliability is flawed because it ignores modern social science. That expands the universe of potential arguments, generating some alternatives, for example: (1) This court should revisit the test for deciding what makes a photo array suggestive and unreliable; (2) that test, applied here, shows the array was suggestive and unreliable; (3) even if this court retains the current test, the lower court erred because under that test: (a) the array was suggestive; and (b) the array was unreliable. Each of these arguments has a stand-alone conclusion and will have its own reasons as well, but all of them support reversal on the issue.

2.2 Discerning Argument Relationships

Once you have identified a range of arguments for each issue, think about their relationships to each other and to the issue as a whole. This relationship assessment will reveal which arguments are really part and parcel of others and which arguments are substantial enough to stand on their own. Thinking about argument relationships will also help you sketch out where and how those arguments should be made in relation to others. Arguments can bear many different kinds of logical and legal relationships to each other and to an issue, defying a comprehensive list. But here are some common argument relationships: (1) conjunctive; (2) alternative; (3) threshold/primary merits arguments; (4) totality; and (5) balancing.

Conjunctive arguments. First, argument relationships can be conjunctive—that is, the court must agree with each and every argument's conclusion for you to win the issue. In the first example above, the two arguments on suggestiveness and reliability are conjunctive. Both must be met for a favorable outcome on the issue. The same is true of any argument based on conjunctive requirements of the common law or a statute. For example, assume that you are an appellee defending the sufficiency of the evidence on a constructive drug possession conviction. Your arguments would be conjunctive contentions about each element: (1) the record shows the defendant knew about the contraband; *and* (2) abundant facts support the defendant's control over the contraband; *and* (3) the evidence reflects the defendant's intent to control the contraband. For you to prevail, the court must agree with all three.

Alternative arguments. Argument relationships can also be alternative, where any argument's conclusion standing alone would warrant reversal. In the expanded version of the photo array example above, arguments (1) and (2) work conjunctively to support a reversal, while argument (3) is an alternative, or "fallback" argument in case the court is not ready or willing to overrule the test. Argument (3) then splits into the same two conjunctive requirements as the first photo array example. Likewise, switching sides on the constructive possession issue would make the arguments alternative. The defendant would assert that the evidence was insufficient on (1) knowledge, *or* (2) control, *or* (3) intent (or just two of these or all three). Should the court agree with any one of these arguments, it would reverse.

Alternative arguments might be the product of a single legal framework, or they might arise from completely different tests or areas of law. Below is an argument whose legal framework expressly provides alternative routes for winning an issue.

ISSUE	**The district court correctly admitted prior-crime evidence under Federal Rule of Evidence 404(b).**
Alternative argument #1	The evidence was admissible to show the defendant's intent.
Alternative argument #2	The evidence was admissible to show the defendant's identity.
Alternative argument #3	The evidence was admissible to show the defendant's modus operandi.

The next example also presents arguments with alternative relationships, but this time, stemming from different areas of law. Because it pulls from diverse sources, this kind of argument collection is often more the product of an advocate's ingenuity than a structure inherent in the law.

ISSUE	**The district court erred when it allowed the trial to proceed without testimony from the confidential informant.**
Alternative argument #1	Admitting a videotape of an alleged drug transaction in lieu of the confidential informant's testimony violated the defendant's Confrontation Clause rights.
Alternative argument #2	The district court should have issued a material witness warrant for the confidential informant to appear.
Alternative argument #3	At a minimum, the district court should not have allowed the police officer to narrate the video in lieu of the confidential informant's testimony.

Threshold/primary merits arguments. Some arguments must clear initial hurdles to get to the merits — that is, the substantive meat of your appeal. These threshold arguments come in many forms. They range from arguments about whether a party or case is properly before the court at all (Chapter 2's finality, jurisdiction, standing, and moot-ness doctrines) to arguments more closely related to the merits, such as definitional or statutory coverage requirements. For example, if you are filing a permissive interlocutory appeal under section 1292(b), as a thresh-old matter you must argue that the issue involves a con-trolling question of law breeding a substantial difference of opinion and whose resolution would advance the case. After that, you would argue the substantive merits of your appellate issue. Likewise, if your appeal argues that your client was a victim of discrimination under the Americans With Disabilities Act, you may first need to argue the threshold requirement that your client is dis-abled under the Act — a definition that itself has three requirements. After that, you would argue the merits of the discrimination claim. A final example is an appeal that argues a violation of First Amendment free speech rights. Sometimes it is not obvious that a party has engaged in speech at all, and if that is the case, the brief would first make the threshold argument on speech before addressing the govern-ment's deprivation of speech rights.

> **Practice Alert #1**
> **Practice Spotlight on Argument Relationships**
>
> This exercise in the online companion presents excerpts from four appellate briefs, and asks you to identify the argument relationships in each, along with reflection questions prompting you to consider why the advocates ordered and structured their arguments as they did.

Totality arguments. Some arguments work together to form a "totality," that, when viewed as a whole, warrants reversal on the issue. One example is the Fourth Amendment's totality test for determining when an informant's tip estab-lishes probable cause for a search warrant. That test requires an issuing magis-trate to consider the informant's reliability, credibility, and basis of knowledge, with no single factor assigned more weight than any other.[4] Thus, if you are challenging a client's conviction because the search warrant used to find incrim-inating evidence was based on a flawed informant tip, your arguments would **not** be independent alternatives like this: (1) the warrant was invalid because it was based on an unreliable informant; (2) alternatively, the warrant was invalid because the informant lacked credibility; (3) the warrant was independently invalid because the informant lacked sufficient knowledge. Nor would they be conjunctive, asserting that because the informant was unreliable, lacked credi-bility, and lacked sufficient knowledge, therefore the warrant lacked probable cause. Instead, your arguments on each totality factor would contend how each one contributes — perhaps in differing amounts — to a big-picture, com-monsense conclusion that the warrant lacked probable cause.

Balancing arguments. Finally, some appellate issues demand balancing argu-ments, especially in constitutional cases. The constitutional right to privacy is one example, assessing violations by weighing an individual's privacy expectations against the government's interest in conducting the search.[5] Assume you represent a state office worker whose government employer hacked into her personal email on a work computer. To win on the privacy violation issue, your arguments must show how, on balance, your client's expectation of privacy outweighed the government employer's interests in hacking into her email account. You might make separate arguments with stand-alone conclusions on the strength of your client's privacy interest and the weakness of her employer's interest. But these are not conjunctive, alternative, or totality arguments. Instead, these arguments are two components that must be balanced against each other to show that their corresponding weights tilt to the violation side.

Common Argument Relationships

Relationship Among Arguments and to the Issue	Definition
Conjunctive	The court must agree with each argument for you to win the issue.
Alternative	You win the issue if the court agrees with any one of your arguments.
Totality	No argument is sufficient alone for you to win the issue, and conversely, proving all arguments is no guarantee of success. Rather, each argument contributes to a big picture that, viewed as a whole, favors you.
Balancing	Each argument establishes its weight in the balancing, and winning depends on showing the scale tips in your favor.

REFLECTION, DISCUSSION, AND CHALLENGE QUESTIONS

Argument Relationships

- Pick the most challenging issue in your appeal, and sit down with your record digest, your research management document, and some method of recording your thoughts. Based on what you have read and what you think, write down all your ideas for why the lower court was wrong on that issue (for appellants) or all your ideas for why the court was right on that issue (for appellees).
- As you review these ideas, ask yourself the following questions. Where are these ideas coming from? Are any of them essentially the same idea in different words? Which ideas might stand on their own, and which are just one part of a larger idea?

> ● Now start to assess relationships in greater depth. Which arguments
> are conjunctive? Which are alternatives? Must you clear any thresh-
> olds to get to the merits? Do you have any totality arguments? How
> about balancing arguments? Aside from these, what other relation-
> ships might connect your arguments?

Section 3   Sketching a Tentative Blueprint for Each Argument

Once you have identified a range of arguments for each issue, you can sketch a
tentative blueprint for each one. The goal is not to create a full-fledged outline for
your brief's argument section, but rather to give yourself, your supervisor, or your
professor a sense of each argument's direction and the reasons you might use to
build the argument. You can then conduct focused rounds of research and thinking
to give these ideas more definitive shape. If time and resources permit, you may also
elect to write — or your professor may assign you to draft — an Argument Assessment memo that records your frank evaluation of the arguments for each issue and
which ones might serve you best. That assignment is discussed in section 4.

Start your blueprint by defining, as precisely as possible, each argument's
overall conclusion. Then spend some time discerning the distinct reasons the
court must accept to reach each argument's conclusion. During this exercise,
you must make preliminary judgments about how to connect and sequence
those reasons along the argument pathway. For just as arguments have relationships to each other and to an issue, reasons have relationships to each other and
to an argument's conclusion. The rest of this section guides your reason-generating and sequencing work. It describes two major factors that influence the selection of reasons and their relationships: (1) where your argument falls on a fact-
law continuum; and (2) whether your argument requires statutory construction.
At the end, this section helps you apply these factors to your own work.

The first major factor defining the scope of available reasons is the fact-law
continuum. That continuum has two variables: (1) whether your argument
skews more factual or more legal; and (2) whether your argument applies settled
law or poses an unsettled legal question.[6]

3.1   Fact-Intensive Arguments

At one end of the spectrum, your argument might be intensely factual.[7] We have
emphasized that appellate courts typically decide questions of law, but facts are
powerful drivers of decisions as well. One accomplished appellate lawyer
explained that fact-intensive arguments can work in appellate briefs because
they appeal to common sense:

> If facts can be clarified to the degree that the barber, the grocer, and the shoemaker would consider that a certain result should follow as a matter of common sense, the probabilities are that the judge will arrive at the same conclusion. True, the judge will listen attentively to protracted oral arguments, will diligently read monumental briefs, will spend precious hours in making personal investigations of the evidence and the law — and notwithstanding all that, his carefully considered judgment will concur with that pronounced by the barber, the grocer, and the shoemaker. There is this difference, however: the judge, because of his specialized training, can express the rationale of the decision in profound language that fits into the juristic scheme.[8]

Fact-intensive arguments typically target a lower court action or interpretation of the record. The legal framework usually lacks detail, and the standard of review tends to be deferential. For example, you might contend that the lower court committed clear error in its factfinding following a breach of contract bench trial. You must overcome a difficult standard of review and show precisely how the lower court got the evidence wrong. Many of your reasons, then, will stem from grouping, characterizing, and adding up the facts relevant to breach in a way that undermines the lower court's findings. On the other side of the appeal, your opponent's reasons would be equally fact intensive, but the favorable standard of review would lighten her load.

Below is a set of reasons supporting a fact-intensive argument in an expert appellate brief. This brief defended a trial court's rejection of child abuse and neglect charges based on an assessment of the record facts. As you can see, the reasons focus not on establishing or defining legal standards, but rather on how one or more aspects of the evidence show that the court was right or wrong in its factual determinations.

EXAMPLE

Fact-Intensive Argument and Reasons[9]

ARGUMENT | The trial court correctly held that J.N.'s parents did not medically neglect him by refusing to consent to a central line (a tube inserted into a large vein to deliver medicine and fluids).

Reason #1 | The evidence shows the parents consented because their signed consent form is in the record.

Reason #2 | The trial court found the parents' trial testimony supporting consent to be credible, and that determination should not be disturbed on appeal.

Reason #3 | No evidence supports the state's theory that the parents revoked their consent by "whisking" their son away from the hospital before doctors could insert the central line.

3.2   Law-Fact Application Arguments

Closer to the middle of the spectrum are arguments that apply settled common law or undisputed statutory language to the facts.[10] The task here is different. You need not scale the mountain of a tough standard of review, nor can you hang your hat on deference; more often than not, these law-fact application arguments are subject to de novo review. Moreover, your objective is to illustrate how the lower court went wrong somewhere in its interpretation or application of the law to the facts, or, conversely, that it was right on the law and its application — not to show that it got the facts right or wrong.[11] As such, your blueprint will craft reasons using the governing legal framework, your own interpretation of the statute and case law, and your contentions about how the law properly applies to the record facts.

The next example is a classic law-fact application argument, where the reasons first establish the legal standard and then show how the record facts fail that standard. In this case, argued to the New York Court of Appeals, tobacco companies defended an appellate court's decision to vacate a judgment in favor of the plaintiffs, who had sued on negligent design defect theory. The reasons and their sequence reflect the governing legal framework — the requirements of a design defect claim — and then apply that framework to the record.

EXAMPLE

Settled Law-Fact Application Argument and Reasons[12]

ARGUMENT	Appellants failed to prove that Defendants' cigarettes are defectively designed.
Reason #1	To prove a design defect claim under New York law, a plaintiff must offer an alternative feasible design.
Reason #2	An alternative design is "feasible" only if it retains the functionality of the original.
Reason #3	No facts at trial showed that cigarettes with less tar and nicotine would perform the function that causes consumers to purchase cigarettes in the first place.

3.3   Unsettled Law or Law Change Arguments

At the other end of the spectrum are arguments about unsettled law or advocating for a change in the law. These purely legal arguments might ask the court to decide between competing common law tests, to adopt a new test or rule, or to overrule precedent.[13] Here the task is different still. Although review is likely de novo, the novelty of your question adds an extra hurdle: You cannot depend on stare decisis. You must instead prove the worth of your legal position in the absence of (or up against) the law of the forum in which you are located. Accordingly, your blueprint of reasons will draw on very different sources. For example, instead of being grounded primarily in binding authority, your reasons might revolve around the logic of persuasive precedent, analogies to other areas of the law, the good consequences of adopting your position, or the bad consequences of adopting your opponent's.[14]

Below is an argument from the Petitioners' Brief in the landmark case of Lawrence v. Texas, which overruled Bowers v. Hardwick's longstanding holding against same-sex couples' right of privacy in consensual sexual relations.[15] Petitioners were not just unable to rely on stare decisis; their argument flew in its face. So their reasons needed to find a way around this formidable obstacle. And they did, by drawing analogies to existing rights; fitting their position within a broader framework of Supreme Court precedent; and arguing good and bad consequences. Notice, too, that the reason sequencing is not deductive, but inductive. The reasons progress based on what persuasion theorists call the "foot in the door" technique, which starts with uncontroversial reasons that "prime" the reader to accept increasingly more debatable reasons along the path to the argument's conclusion.[16] Professor Kathryn Stanchi has coined this an exercise in taking the court up a high-dive ladder, rung by rung, and making the court comfortable enough to take the leap off with you into the pool of new law you propose.[17] We discuss this technique in more depth in Chapter 10.

EXAMPLE

Petitioners' Unsettled Law Argument and Reasons[18]

ARGUMENT	Well-established protections for intimate relationships, bodily integrity, and the privacy of the home converge in this vital freedom.
Reason #1	All adults have the same fundamental liberty interests in their private consensual sexual choices; there is no exception for same-sex couples.
Reason #2	This Court has recognized that the choices to enter into and maintain certain intimate human relationships must be secured from undue State intrusion.
Reason #3	The freedom to structure one's own private sexual intimacy with another adult is an essential associational freedom.
Reason #4	State regulation of sexual intimacy also implicates the liberty interest in bodily integrity.
Reason #5	The liberty interest here also involves the deeply entrenched interest in the privacy of the home.
Reason #6	Denying the existence of a liberty interest in private consensual adult sexual activity would give constitutional legitimacy to the grossest forms of intrusion into the homes of individuals and couples.
Reason #7	The core liberty interests at stake in this case are a bulwark against an overly controlling and intrusive government.

Below we see the flip side of this broader reasoning process, where a party is arguing *against* a change in the law. This example, from the tobacco design defect brief described in the law-fact application segment above, characterizes the plaintiffs' position as one that departs from existing product liability law. The reasons reflect that characterization, first defending the lower court's legal moves, then undercutting the plaintiffs' legal authority, and then following up with the good consequences of its legal position and the bad consequences of the opponent's.

EXAMPLE

Respondents' Unsettled Law Argument and Reasons[19]

| ARGUMENT | Appellants' efforts to avoid or eliminate the consumer acceptability requirement should be rejected. |

Reason #1   The trial court did not shift the focus of a design claim away from the manufacturer's conduct or adopt an industry-practice standard.

Reason #2   *Scarangella* does not relieve appellants of their burden to prove a feasible alternative design that is acceptable to consumers.

Reason #3   Requiring proof of an alternative design acceptable to consumers does not immunize cigarette manufacturers from liability.

Reason #4   The court should not create an exception for "highly dangerous" products.

The examples above are designed to help you discover the nature of your own arguments and their conclusions, and to focus your reason-generating and reason-sequencing processes during this developmental prewriting phase. Keep in mind that these examples do not represent the universe of legal argument. Rather, they are points along an argument continuum that runs from factual to legal, and from settled to unsettled law, as the diagram below illustrates:

Argument Continuum

| Intensely factual/ deferential standard of review. | Applying settled law to facts/mixed or de novo review. | Unsettled or novel legal questions, unresolved statutory interpretation/de novo review. |
| (more FACTUAL) | (more LEGAL) | (more UNSETTLED) |

In addition, remember that multiple arguments underlying a single issue might hit different points in the continuum. To draw on our earlier example, if your issue charges lower court error in admitting an unduly suggestive and unreliable photo array, you might support that issue with: (1) an unsettled law argument that advocates for a new suggestiveness and reliability test; and (2) a fallback settled-law argument that applies the current test to the facts. But of course if you are confident that the settled-law argument is stronger, then you should run that one first and offer the change in the law as an alternative. Most courts are incremental in their approach and would prefer to rule on settled-law grounds if possible. If you think the court also erred in assessing the underlying facts about the photo array, you might also add a fact-intensive clear error argument to the issue. Likewise, the above examples from the tobacco design defect appeal show how an advocate can mount both an affirmative law-fact application argument and a defensive unsettled law argument to prevail on an appellate issue.

3.4   The Special Case of Statutory Interpretation Arguments

One type of argument — statutory interpretation — merits separate treatment. Though they land on the law side of the continuum, these arguments are unique because they are built by selecting from a fairly standard set of interpretive tools, and those tools combine to form their own types of reasons and reasoning. Chapter 5 provided guidance on how to research statutory interpretation issues; this segment takes the next step and addresses how to justify a law's interpretation.

Generating reasons from statutory text. The statutory text is your go-to source for generating reasons in favor of your interpretation, because the text is considered the best evidence of statutory meaning.[20] The first step is to determine which parts of the statute apply to your appeal issues. Your issues may implicate threshold statutory coverage questions, questions about the elements of the statutory cause of action and its exceptions, or questions about defenses, remedies, or enforcement. You must isolate each potentially applicable section and carefully consider the language and structure of every one of those provisions. Eventually, these provisions will dictate your large-scale structure, anchoring your arguments and reasons.

The next step is to determine the range of meaning for each potentially applicable provision. It is rare for the text to resolve your appeal issue in a straightforward manner — the case would not have reached the appellate level otherwise. For example, the legislature may never have considered the scenario raised in your appeal, or times may have changed enough to render the text ambiguous.[21] Your task is to glean meaning from ambiguous language, or to fix the range of plausible interpretations of that language.[22] Once you have determined the range of meanings, you must decide which meaning best furthers your argument and then develop reasons to support it. Textual meaning can be deduced from many sources: (1) statutory definitions; (2) statutory scheme; (3) ordinary usage; (4) statutes with parallel language; (5) statutory context, aided by canons of construction; (6) statutory statements of purpose; (7) legislative history; and (8) administrative regulations.[23] We discuss each textual meaning tool in turn.

Statutory definitions and scheme, ordinary usage, and statutes with parallel language. The statute itself is always the starting point for gauging a term's meaning. Start with the definitions section. If the legislature saw fit to articulate what a word or phrase means right there in the law, that definition must be heeded. Likewise, if your disputed statutory term has been used elsewhere in the same statute, any meaning you assign to that term must be consistent with its usage throughout the statutory scheme.[24] Along the same lines, you must consider your disputed term in light of the law's entire structure — its physical placement and logical relationship to other sections.[25] Title VII's employment discrimination provisions are a good example of how statutory scheme informs meaning. For decades, the words "because of" (as in, an employer shall not discriminate against an employee "because of race") have prompted debate about just how much a decisionmaker's discriminatory state of mind must influence an employment action. Must discriminatory intent be the primary driver of the action, or is it enough if the decisionmaker harbored both a discriminatory mindset and a legitimate motive for the action? "Because of" was used in two different Title VII provisions: its discrimination and retaliation sections.[26] Normally, under the principle of consistent usage, these words would connote the exact same causation standard. But because the discrimination provision was modified by a remedies section elsewhere in the statute and the retaliation provision was not, the Supreme Court read them to set different causation standards.[27]

If a term is not explicitly defined in the statute, or informed by its consistent usage in the law or its place in the overall statutory scheme, advocates often turn to ordinary usage. Ordinary usage or meaning refers to the way an ordinary or reasonable person would interpret the language.[28] If you are lucky, persuasive case law will already have done the work of determining ordinary usage in a way that favors you. But more often than not, in an appellate statutory construction argument the cases are either split or silent on ordinary usage. So you must dig deeper to clear up the ambiguity or to discern the range of meanings. Dictionary definitions are a common ordinary meaning source and should always be consulted, if for no other reason than to see how expert lexicographers have synthesized ordinary usage.[29] But dictionaries themselves often produce dueling definitions, and so they are rarely sufficient to establish meaning by themselves. Moreover, many statutes deal with technical or specialized subjects whose use of terminology differs from ordinary usage.[30] In that case, case law or authoritative nonlegal sources from those technical areas can be important sources of meaning. Finally, as Chapter 5 explained, even if the statute in your appeal has not received a definitive (or even helpful) construction, chances are that courts have interpreted parallel language in related statutes, predecessor statutes, or even unrelated laws that have the same words.[31] These, too, can be brought to bear in establishing statutory meaning.

Statutory context using canons of construction. Textual meaning can also be gleaned from a set of interpretive tools called canons of construction. Some statutes — and even entire codes — come with built-in rules of construction.[32] On top of that, courts and scholars have, over time, devised interpretive maxims that use contextual clues to determine the meaning of a statutory word or phrase.[33] A full rendering of the canons of construction is beyond the scope of this text,[34] but we discuss four common ones here: *noscitur a sociis, ejusdem generis, expressio unius*, and the rule against surplusage. We illustrate their application with a broadly worded obstruction of justice provision in the Sarbanes-Oxley Act, the law passed to combat financial fraud in the wake of the Enron scandal:

> Whoever knowingly alters, destroys, mutilates, conceals, covers up, falsifies, or makes a false entry in any record, document, or tangible object with the intent to impede, obstruct, or influence the investigation or proper administration of any matter within the jurisdiction of any department or agency of the United States . . . shall be fined under this title, imprisoned not more than twenty years, or both.[35]

This law was used to convict a commercial fisherman who ordered a crew member to throw his fish back into the water in an effort to conceal that he had harvested an undersized red grouper.[36] Relying on multiple canons of construction, the fisherman contended that fish are not encompassed within the phrase "tangible object."[37] The first canon he used, *noscitur a sociis*, holds that an ambiguous word can gain meaning from the company it keeps — that is, the words surrounding it.[38] As applied to the fisherman's case, that canon required reading "tangible object" in context with the verbs and nouns preceding it. Because those verbs and nouns all referred to objects used to record and preserve information — and given the statute's overall financial fraud context — reading the phrase to cover fish would have created a contextual anomaly.[39] Likewise with the second canon of construction, *ejusdem generis*, which holds that a list of specific words preceding a more general phrase limits that phrase to objects which resemble those specific words.[40] Under this canon, it would be absurd to presume that when Congress wrote "record" or "document," it intended the next phrase, "tangible object," to embrace objects as disparate as fish — rather than, say, some other type of physical evidence.[41]

A third core canon is *expressio unius*, which dictates that a statutory list should be read exclusively; that is, other unmentioned words cannot be read into it.[42] This is an offshoot of the basic principle that the legislature says what it means and means what it says. For example, assume the fisherman did not challenge the interpretation of "tangible object" to include fish, nor did he have the grouper thrown overboard. Instead, with the aim of protesting the fishing laws, he kept the fish and displayed it prominently for all to see. That may have been illegal for other reasons, but not under section 1519, which requires the defendant to "alter[], destroy[], mutilate[], conceal[], cover[] up, falsif[y], or ma[ke] a false entry." The statute does not prohibit the acts of preserving or displaying, and the *expressio* canon would preclude reading those acts into the statute no matter what the fisherman's intent may have been. Even if the act of catching (and killing) a fish might be characterized as altering, destroying, or mutilating, in this scenario the fisherman would not have acted to impede, obstruct, or influence a government investigation, the next statutory requirement. A fourth commonly used contextual canon is the rule against surplusage. That canon holds that every single word in a statute has meaning and must be given effect, rather than ignored.[43] With respect to section 1519, every verb capturing the illegal conduct must be given independent meaning. "Falsify," for example, must be read to cover behavior distinct from the actions contemplated by the separately listed, more specific act of "making a false entry." If "falsify" is read so broadly that it swallows up "making a false entry," the latter phrase would become superfluous.

Along with these contextual canons come others that reflect more general legal norms. These include the rule of lenity, the practice of construing remedial statutes liberally, and the practice of strictly reading statutes that cover common law topics, among many others.[44] The rule of lenity provides that an ambiguous criminal law should be interpreted in favor of the defendant.[45] That canon underscored the interpretive result in the fisherman's case, where it was presumed that Congress would have been much clearer had it intended "tangible object" to encompass living things like fish, particularly given the 20-year sentence facing statutory violators.[46] Similarly, courts often give generous readings to remedial laws like Title VII's employment discrimination provisions, interpreting ambiguities to favor employees.[47] As for statutes that occupy historically common law territory, a statute must clearly state that it is supplanting the common law before a court will read it that way.[48] Such is the case with many states' trade secret misappropriation statutes, which occupy different roles in relation to common law misappropriation formulations, depending on the legislature's explicitly stated intent.[49]

Legislative purpose, legislative history, and administrative regulations. Aside from the text itself, meaning can be derived from statutory statements of legislative purpose, from legislative history, and from administrative regulations.[50] Just as you must isolate the statute's key provisions, you must find the purposes, pieces of history, and regulations pertinent to those provisions and mine them to help resolve ambiguities and determine the range of meanings. A statute's preamble section may articulate precisely why the legislature enacted it, and that purpose can be used to clarify, expand, or limit your disputed statutory term. For example, the Age Discrimination in Employment Act's preamble, which states the law's purpose to "promote employment of older persons based on their ability rather than age,"[51] has been a double-edged sword. Some judges have used this language to read the law expansively in favor of the protected age class,[52] while others have relied on it to cabin age claims to those arising from particular ability-based age stereotypes.[53] Legislative history is another source of legislative purpose. Notwithstanding the enduring judicial and scholarly debate on the proper uses of legislative history,[54] advocates can and do rely on it to clear up ambiguity and fix meaning in appellate arguments. The key, of course, is to know your judicial audience and to tailor your use of legislative history accordingly. The chart displayed later in this section ranks legislative history sources in order of their authoritative weight.

Finally, as Chapter 5 mentioned, administrative regulations may also clear up statutory ambiguities. But be cautious here. Not every administrative regulation has authoritative weight. Generally, the Congressional delegation of power to the agency will be spelled out in the statute, but the agency's use of that delegated power is subject to judicial review, using standards from a complex set of Supreme Court decisions.[55] Suffice it to say that it is unwise to rely on a regulatory interpretation to edify statutory meaning without thoroughly understanding its force.

Policy arguments and practical considerations. A final set of meaning-generating tools are policy arguments and practical considerations. If your interpretation would produce positive real-world results or further the essential purposes of the statute, for instance, you can argue that your interpretation is one Congress would have intended.[56] Conversely, if your opponent's interpretation would produce untenable real-world results or undermine the statute's goals, you can argue that Congress would not have signed on to that meaning. We defer a detailed discussion of policy arguments until Chapter 10, but for now, be aware that statutory meaning can be informed by the law's predicted future applications.

Practice Alert #3
Practice Spotlight on Statutory Interpretation Arguments

The online companion contains examples of two statutory interpretation arguments. One is improperly driven by case law, while the other employs the full complement of statutory construction tools. The examples are accompanied by reflection questions.

The hierarchy of statutory interpretation. Now that you have a grasp on the range of meaning-generating tools, you must prioritize them. Not all interpretive tools are created equal in the eyes of the law. The well-established hierarchy places the disputed text's language and statutory scheme—often informed by canons of construction—at the top, with express statements of legislative purpose just below it.[57] The weight of legislative history depends on its source—and, of course, how willing your court is to accept it as evidence of statutory meaning.[58] Products of consensus like committee reports, for example, carry more weight than isolated statements of legislators in floor debates.[59] Statutory amendment history may also shed light on meaning, but its thrust is far more circumstantial.[60] As explained above, administrative interpretations merit different levels of deference, depending on the agency's

delegated power and what kind of interpretive activity the agency is engaged in.[61] Finally, policy arguments that turn on the good or bad consequences of a particular interpretation must establish a strong link between those anticipated consequences and a given reading of the statute. The Supreme Court is fond of pointing out that no statute pursues a policy at all costs. Needless to say, your process of sketching out reasons in a statutory interpretation argument must be well-informed by the weight of each tool.

SUMMARY

Tools for Generating Reasons in a Statutory Interpretation Argument

- The language of the disputed statutory provisions, as elucidated by:
  - Statutory definitions and statutory scheme
  - Ordinary meaning, including dictionary definitions
  - Parallel language in other statutes
  - Canons of statutory construction
- Statutory pronouncements of legislative purpose (preamble and purpose clauses)
- Legislative history (in order of authoritative value)
  - Committee reports
  - Alternate versions of the law from the legislative process
  - Presidential signing statements
  - Floor debates
- Statutory amendment history
- Administrative regulations and interpretations
- Policy consequences of adopting one interpretation or another

Transforming meaning into arguments and reasons. Below is an outline of a statutory interpretation argument and reasons challenging the Environmental Protection Agency's Clean Air Act (CAA) authority to overturn a state permitting authority's decision. The case involved the Clean Air Act's "Prevention of Significant Deterioration of Air Quality" program, which requires states to determine the "Best Available Technology" (BACT) for an emissions source. Alaska's statutory interpretation argument was that the EPA had no power to second-guess the state's BACT determination. As you can see, the reasons supporting this argument invoke the unique tools of statutory interpretation, not case law or common law frameworks. In Chapters 10 and 11, you will see more fleshed-out examples of statutory construction arguments.

EXAMPLE

Statutory Interpretation Argument[62]

ARGUMENT | The EPA has no authority under the CAA to invalidate a state BACT determination that is based on consideration of the statutory factors.

Reason #1 The plain language of the CAA makes clear that BACT is a determination to be made by the states on a case-by-case basis.

Reason #2 The legislative history of the CAA confirms that BACT is "strictly a state and local decision."

Reason #3 The EPA's recourse in this case was not to unilaterally overturn the State's BACT determination, but to challenge it through available review processes.

Applying the fact-law continuum. Now it is time to apply the fact-law continuum concepts to your argument blueprints. Based on the reflection, discussion, and challenge questions on page 94, you should already have a rudimentary blueprint of your arguments; that process is reflected in the first bullet of the review chart below. Using the second bullet as your process guide, develop some reasons for each potential argument. Step away from your authorities and facts for now and work intuitively. Which is your favorite argument and why? Is it strongest because of a sense of justice, because of authority, because of likelihood of success? Where does each argument fall on the law-fact continuum? Are your arguments common law or statutory in nature? How does the nature of your arguments or the legal framework governing them shape the reasons available to you? As you review your nascent reasons, consider their sequencing as well.

After you have exhausted ideas from intuitive brainstorming, turn to your research management tool. As Chapter 5 explained, this tool should capture your impressions of authorities and make sense of how they relate to your case, revealing how they can band together or be used individually to support specific arguments. Draw on this tool's analytical work to craft more reasons or refine the ones you have. At the end of this process, you should have a series of reasons that can anchor each argument's blueprint, as well as a plan for sequencing.

REVIEW

Overall Argument Development Process

- Argument development and sequencing
  - Generate your own ideas about why the lower court was right or wrong.

- o Think about these ideas and their relationships to each other.
- o Factor in the legal framework, which might dictate those relationships (*e.g.*, conjunctive, alternative, threshold/merits, totality, balancing).
- o Sketch a blueprint of your arguments showing their preliminary sequence.
- Reason development and sequencing
- o Determine whether you are making a statutory interpretation argument; if so, use the tools of statutory interpretation to make a rough sketch of each argument's reasons and their preliminary sequence.
- o If you are not making a statutory interpretation argument, decide where your argument falls on the law-fact continuum.
- o Based on the argument's placement on the continuum and its legal framework, make a rough sketch of each argument's reasons and their preliminary sequence.[^62]

Section 4 Identifying and Confronting Weaknesses

As you sketch the blueprint for your arguments and engage in the additional research and intensive thinking that this process requires, you are bound to encounter some weaknesses. At this point, you don't need to decide whether the weaknesses are intractable or to settle on a method for dealing with them. You just need to learn more about those weaknesses and to start formulating some strategies.

Spotting weaknesses is a vital part of argument development, for if you skip it, you run the risk of two extremes: overconfidence or excessive doubt. Overconfidence leads to arguments that skim over weaknesses, while excessive doubt rejects potentially good arguments before they reach maturity. Both tendencies can undermine a brief, but they also pose ethical problems. Ultimately, the advocate who masks weaknesses in a brief may run afoul of Model Rule of Professional Conduct 3.3(a)(2), which requires attorneys to disclose directly adverse authority.[^63] The doubting advocate may not be providing the zealous representation called for in Rule 1.3.[^64] However, if you pay attention to potential weaknesses now, you will lay the foundation for a well-developed weakness-handling strategy in your brief.

Practice Alert #4
Argument Assessment
memo Drafting Assignment

The online companion contains directions for drafting an argument assessment memo that is designed to push your thinking about arguments and reasons. Two sample memos are included for guidance.

4.1 Finding the Weaknesses

To tease out weaknesses, review the arguments and reasons in your blueprint, and think about which aspects strike you as weak. Then return to your record digest and your research management tool, and collect the bad facts and bad law that could undermine those arguments. Next, consider how those weaknesses fit categories of common argument problems.[65] Below are some of those problems, tailored to an argument's placement on the fact-law continuum.

Arguments on the fact-intensive side of the continuum

- You are up against a clear error standard of review (if appellant).
- The law is sparse and doesn't clearly cut one way or the other on the record facts.
- The record conflicts with important parts of your desired evidentiary picture.
- The record is ambiguous at crucial points.

Law-fact application arguments

- Your precedent's best language is dicta.
- Your precedent is primarily persuasive, not controlling.
- Your favorable precedent is poorly or superficially reasoned or out of step with the jurisdiction's current approach.
- Your precedent can be factually distinguished or overcome with more analogous unfavorable precedent.
- You must use precedent whose rationale does not easily fit your case.
- The rules require some interpretive work to fit your case.
- Your record facts must be generalized up several levels to compare favorably to the precedent.

Arguments on the unsettled law side of the continuum

- Your position on the law is held by only a minority of jurisdictions.
- Your favorable precedent addresses distinguishable legal issues.
- Your jurisdiction's case law has general language that undercuts your reasoning or is inconsistent with the rationale in your favorable persuasive precedent.
- Your favorable precedent is poorly or superficially reasoned or out of step with your jurisdiction's approach in analogous areas of the law.

- Your proposed view of the law is out of step with emerging knowledge in other fields (*e.g.*, social science).
- Your proposed view of the law conflicts with current norms.
- Your proposed view of the law would produce negative real-world results, or your opponent's view would produce better real-world results.
- Your proposed outcome is simply unfair.

Statutory interpretation arguments

- Your statutory text has conflicting plain meanings.
- Your interpretation of the text undermines a coherent statutory structure.
- Your interpretation of the text does not square with the legislature's stated objectives or would harm the law's intended beneficiaries.
- Your interpretation of the text clashes with the same words' construction in other statutes.
- Your interpretation of the text does violence to settled rules of statutory construction.
- Your interpretation of the text conflicts with legislative history.
- Legislative action or inaction casts doubt on your interpretation.
- Your administrative regulations are not entitled to deference.
- Your favorable legislative history is not the product of consensus.
- Your interpretation would produce negative real-world results, or your opponent's interpretation would produce better real-world results.

4.2   Pushing Past the Weaknesses

With potential weaknesses identified, you can start to see whether you can push past them. For example, if your best case is persuasive precedent whose comparable and distinguishable facts are in equipoise, but you have controlling authority with favorable reasoning (though irrelevant facts) that can drive your argument, then the weakness could be manageable. A major weakness could take the form of persuasive authority with perfectly analogous facts, but whose rationale runs squarely against controlling case reasoning, undermining that case's pull. For unsettled-law arguments, a major weakness might be that only one jurisdiction has adopted your proposed test, while five jurisdictions stand steadfastly against it. If, on top of that, your test would produce negative real-world results that your jurisdiction has condemned in other contexts, then you are up against a major weakness. On the other hand, if your statutory interpretation argument rests on a convincing plain language interpretation that is contradicted by one legislator's statement in a floor debate, that may be a minor weakness. As you might imagine, the strength/weakness combinations are nearly infinite. It is up to you to put in the time and thought to discover them.

At this point, you may find yourself wanting to give up too easily, especially if you don't have much experience working on appeals. Resist the temptation to throw your hands up, and draw on your perseverance and creativity. Below are illustrative scenarios where major weaknesses demanded attorneys' ingenuity and grit.

Overwhelming authority rejects your unsettled law arguments. The urge to retreat is greatest in arguments that fall on the unsettled law side of continuum, where you are asking the court to take a position that peer courts may have rejected — or that the court itself has eschewed. Keep in mind that the Model Rules of Professional Conduct allow lawyers to advocate for legal change. Under the rules, lawyers can push for change when they have a "good faith argument for an extension, modification, or reversal of existing law."[66] A "good faith" argument might rest, for example, on a narrower interpretation of the negative cases. Perhaps, on a second read, you see that none of those cases directly addressed the argument you are making. Or maybe their language is qualified in a way that creates an opening for you. Or the legal issues might be distinct enough not to foreclose your position in this appeal. In addition to reading more closely, you might push your research. Your jurisdiction's most recent case law in related areas could suggest that the tide is changing, signaling receptivity to your arguments.

Moreover, judicial opinions must be considered in the context in which they were written, giving you an opportunity to limit seemingly adverse language. A sentence that meant one thing in the context of one case might not directly translate to your case, no matter how applicable the language seems to be on its face. Consider a Supreme Court opinion with a bold footnote whose language seems to preordain a negative result in your case. Upon a closer look, you discover that the language is actually dicta. And if the decision was unanimous, chances are that the value of unanimity trumped any Justice's desire to object to the footnote's dicta. One or more Justices might be willing to revisit the footnote's dicta in the context of your appeal.

Consider the classic law-change cases, such as how equal protection doctrine finally changed after a half-century from "separate but equal" to a true equality principle.[67] Compare Bowers v. Hardwick's statement that the right to privacy does not confer "a fundamental right to homosexuals to engage in acts of consensual sodomy"[68] with Lawrence v. Texas's pronouncement, 17 years later, that the right to privacy "gives them the full right to engage in [consensual sexual conduct] without intervention of the government."[69] Changing norms contributed to both legal shifts, but at their core were astute lawyers who spotted the bellwether of change and had the perseverance and creativity pursue it. The stakes in your appeal may be less lofty, but if you face the same uphill precedent battle, the lawyering task is no different.

The controlling case law favors your opponent and credible distinctions elude you. This scenario often confronts appellants in criminal cases, where reversal rates trend even lower than in civil cases.[70] Assume you represent a defendant convicted of bank robbery based on evidence that he had robbed a gas station in the past. The rules of evidence prohibit introducing earlier crimes to show that the defendant has a "propensity" to commit robberies.[71] But this evidence can be used for other reasons, such as to show that the defendant's method of committing both crimes was so distinctive that it suggests he was the perpetrator of both.[72] If your jurisdiction's cases ruling on prior crimes evidence have all sided with the government, you are in a tough spot, but you have some options.

First, you can revisit those cases and your facts to look harder for a way to distinguish this precedent. At first, your record review left the impression that the prior robbery evidence was, in fact, offered to show the perpetrator's identity, not the defendant's own propensity to rob. But after further analysis, you can see that the gas station and bank robberies are quite different.

Although both perpetrators brandished Swiss pocket knives, wore hoodies, and used similar words to coerce their victims, those are surface similarities that many robbers might share. A deeper evaluation illuminates the differences; robbing a gas station is a much smaller endeavor, with different objectives, than robbing a bank. You begin to see, in contrast, how the precedent's prior crimes' similarities run deeper, pointing more definitively to a single perpetrator. Moreover, you have an extra fact that isn't in the precedent. Whatever his initial impetus, the prosecutor's closing argument explicitly tagged the gas station robbery as propensity evidence when he called the defendant a "career thief." Aside from revisiting the case and fact comparisons, you might be able to reposition the standard of review. Normally, evidentiary questions are reviewed for abuse of discretion. But if you keep digging and thinking about the case law, you might find that the line

Practice Alert #5
The "Bad Case" Exercise

This exercise in the online companion puts you in the role of an appellant's attorney. You will read a short fact pattern and three cases, one of which is squarely against your client. Using the techniques you learned in this section, you will in work small groups to generate specific strategies for neutralizing this case's effect on your argument.

between propensity and identity evidence has sparked an appellate debate with opposing rules of law. If the choice of rule would affect the outcome in your case, you may be able to garner a de novo standard of review.

4.3 Strengthening Strategies

These scenarios are but a sample of weaknesses that, once examined, are not the roadblocks they first seemed. Although pushing past potential weaknesses is hardly a check-the-box affair, here are some strategies to consider:

- Strengthen analogies and distinctions by considering deeper comparisons or changing their level of abstraction.
- Revisit the unfavorable authorities to search for narrowing or broadening possibilities or other "outs."
- Juxtapose on-point persuasive case law with more general controlling precedent, searching that precedent for encouraging trends or language.
- Use context to reframe bad law or bad facts.

- Push your research into analogous areas of law from which you might import more favorable rationales or principles.
- Reframe the issue from a different angle, and see if it can be viewed in a way that draws in more favorable precedent and legal standards.

Bear in mind that, at this stage, you are merely laying a foundation for handling weaknesses — one that is subject to further thinking and research. To that end, make sure to record ideas for additional research and exploration so that you can begin pursuing them.

Endnotes

1. 18 U.S.C. § 2113(a) (2012).
2. *See, e.g.,* United States v. Villasenor, 664 F.3d 673, 679 (7th Cir. 2011).
3. *See* Symposium, *What Appellate Advocates Seek from Appellate Judges and What Appellate Judges Seek from Appellate Advocates,* 31 N.M. L. Rev. 255, 257 (2000) ("[M]ake only sound arguments and eliminate the weaker ones. Justice Frankfurter, reflecting on this point, once said that it's like a clock striking thirteen. It puts all the other ones in doubt.") (quoting Judge Murphy).
4. Illinois v. Gates, 462 U.S. 213, 233 (1983).
5. City of Ontario v. Quon, 560 U.S. 746, 756-57 (2010).
6. For discussions of how arguments differ based on factual versus legal components, *see generally* Larry Alexander, *The Banality of Legal Reasoning,* 73 Notre Dame L. Rev. 517 (1998); Wilson R. Huhn, *Teaching Legal Analysis Using a Pluralistic Model of Law,* 36 Gonz. L. Rev. 433 (2001); Morley Witus, *A Checklist for Legal Argument,* 90 Dec Mich. B.J. 26 (2011).
7. *See, e.g.,* Mortimer Levitan, *Confidential Chat on the Craft of Briefing,* 4 J. App. Prac. & Process 305, 314 (2002) ("The most persuasive arguments are factual rather than legal.").
8. *Id.* at 314.
9. Derived from Brief of Respondents-Appellees at 42-46, In Re J.N., No. 95-1958 (Ill. App. Ct. 1996) (written by Kirkland & Ellis and Thomas M. Ryan).
10. *See* Huhn, *supra* note 6, at 476-78.
11. *See, e.g.,* Leonard I. Garth, *How to Appeal to an Appellate Judge,* 21 Litig. 20, 23 (1994) ("Most judges are familiar with the relevant cases and law, but have to be educated as to how those cases and law are to be applied to the facts of the appeal before them. . . . What I do want to know is, how the facts of this case fall, if they do, within the *Brady* doctrine, and whether the facts of this case satisfy each of the *Brady* requirements.").
12. Derived from Brief of Defendants-Respondents at 14-20, Rose v. Brown & Williamson, No. 101996/02 (N.Y. 2008) (written by Mayer Brown, Chadbourne & Parke, Arnold & Porter, and Winston & Strawn).
13. *See* Huhn, *supra* note 6, at 458-67. In this section, Huhn outlines several types of legal arguments and discusses competing precedent issues in depth.
14. *See id.* at 446-50; Ellie Margolis, *Closing the Floodgates: Making Persuasive Policy Arguments in Appellate Briefs,* 62 Mont. L. Rev. 59, 70-79 (2001); Michael R. Smith, *The Sociological and Cognitive Dimensions of Policy-Based Persuasion,* 22 J.L. & Pol'y 35, 62-89 (2013).
15. Lawrence v. Texas, 539 U.S. 558 (2003); Bowers v. Hardwick, 478 U.S. 186 (1986).
16. Kathryn M. Stanchi, *The Science of Persuasion: An Initial Exploration,* 2006 Mich. St. L. Rev. 411, 417-19 (2006).
17. *Id.* at 415-16.
18. Derived from Brief of Petitioners at 11-16, Lawrence v. Texas, No. 02-102 (2003) (written by Jenner & Block, Lambda Legal Defense & Education Fund, and Williams, Birnberg & Andersen).
19. Derived from Brief of Defendants-Respondents at 29-39, Rose v. Brown & Williamson, No. 101996/02 (N.Y. 2008) (written by Mayer Brown, Chadbourne & Parke, Arnold & Porter, and Winston & Strawn).
20. William N. Eskridge, *The New Textualism,* 37 UCLA L. Rev. 621, 621 (1990).
21. Katherine Clark & Matthew Connolly, *A Guide to Reading, Interpreting and Applying Statutes,* The Writing Center at GULC 2 (2006).
22. *Id.*
23. *Id.* at 2-9.
24. Antonin Scalia & Bryan A. Garner, Reading Law: The Interpretation of Legal Texts 170-73 (2012); Clark & Connolly, *supra* note 21, at 6-7.
25. Scalia & Garner, *supra* note 24, at 167.

26. 42 U.S.C. § 2000e-2(a) (discrimination provision); 42 U.S.C. § 2000e-3(a) (retaliation provision).

27. University of S.W. Texas Med. Ctr. v. Nassar, 133 S. Ct. 2517 (2013).

28. WILLIAM N. ESKRIDGE, JR., PHILIP P. FRICKEY, & ELIZABETH GARRETT, CASES AND MATERIALS ON LEGISLATION: STATUTES AND THE CREATION OF PUBLIC POLICY 820 (3d. ed. 2001); SCALIA & GARNER, *supra* note 24, at 69-70.

29. For guidance on using dictionaries to inform statutory interpretation, see SCALIA & GARNER, *supra* note 24, at 415-24.

30. SCALIA & GARNER, *supra* note 24, at 73-77; Clark & Connolly, *supra* note 21, at 5.

31. SCALIA & GARNER, *supra* note 24, at 252.

32. *See, e.g.*, Americans With Disabilities Act, 42 U.S.C. § 12102(4); Pennsylvania Statutory Construction Act, 19 Pa. Cons. Stat § 1921 *et seq.*

33. Clark & Connolly, *supra* note 21, at 7.

34. For a comprehensive discussion of statutory canons and statutory construction, *see generally* SCALIA & GARNER, *supra* note 24.

35. 18 U.S.C. § 1519.

36. Yates v. United States, 135 S. Ct. 1074 (2015).

37. *Id.* at 1080.

38. *See* SCALIA & GARNER, *supra* note 24, at 195-98; Clark & Connolly, *supra* note 21, at 7.

39. Yates, 135 S. Ct. at 1085-86.

40. *See* SCALIA & GARNER, *supra* note 24, at 199; Clark & Connolly, *supra* note 21, at 8.

41. Yates, 135 S. Ct. at 1086-87.

42. *See* SCALIA & GARNER, *supra* note 24, at 107; Clark & Connolly, *supra* note 21, at 8-9.

43. *See* SCALIA & GARNER, *supra* note 24, at 174; Clark & Connolly, *supra* note 21, at 6.

44. For a complete canon list, *see* SCALIA & GARNER, *supra* note 24, at xi-xvi.

45. *See id.* at 296.

46. Yates, 135 S. Ct. at 1088.

47. *See, e.g.*, Pantchenko v. C.B. Dolge Co., 581 F.2d 1052, 1054-55 (2d Cir. 1978); Bailey v. USX Corp., 850 F.2d 1506, 1509 (11th Cir. 1988).

48. *See* SCALIA & GARNER, *supra* note 24, at 318.

49. *Compare* 765 Ill. Comp. Stat. Ann. 1065/1-9 (statute preempting the common law) *with* Mass. Gen. Laws Ann. ch. 93, § 42 (statute co-existing with common law).

50. Eskridge, *supra* note 20, at 658-59.

51. 29 U.S.C. § 621(b).

52. *See, e.g.*, EEOC v. Cosmair, Inc., 821 F.2d 1085, 1088-89 (5th Cir. 1987).

53. *See, e.g.*, Hazen Paper Co. v. Biggins, 507 U.S. 604, 610-11 (1993).

54. *See* Eskridge, *supra* note 20, at 641.

55. *See* Michael P. Healy, *Reconciling* Chevron, Mead, *and the Review of Agency Discretion: Source of Law and the Standards of Judicial Review*, 19 GEO. MASON L. REV. 1, 3 (2011).

56. William N. Eskridge & Philip P. Frickey, *Statutory Interpretation as Practical Reasoning*, 42 STAN. L. REV. 321, 332-33 (1990) (explaining the "purposivism" theory of statutory interpretation).

57. *Id.* at 353-54.

58. *Id.* at 356-57.

59. *See id.* at 327.

60. *Id.* at 356-58.

61. U.S. v. Mead Corp., 533 U.S. 218 (2001); Chevron, U.S.A., Inc. v. Natural Res. Def. Council, 467 U.S. 837 (1984); Skidmore v. Swift & Co., 323 U.S. 134 (1944).

62. Derived from Brief for Petitioner at iii-iv, State of Alaska v. EPA, No. 02-658 (2003) (written by the State of Alaska and Hogan & Hartson).

63. MODEL RULES OF PROF'L CONDUCT R. 3.3(a)(2) (2013) ("A lawyer shall not knowingly . . . fail to disclose to the tribunal legal authority in the controlling jurisdiction known to the lawyer to be directly adverse to the position of the client and not disclosed by opposing counsel.").

64. MODEL RULES OF PROF'L CONDUCT R. 1.3, 1.3 cmt. 1 (2013).

65. Huhn, *supra* note 6, at 458-67; Witus, *supra* note 6, at 28; J. Thomas Sullivan, *Ethical and Aggressive Appellate Advocacy: Confronting Adverse Authority*, 59 U. MIAMI L. REV. 341, 354-81 (2005).

66. MODEL RULES OF PROF'L CONDUCT R. 3.1 (2013).

67. Plessy v. Ferguson 163 U.S. 537 (1896); Brown v. Bd. of Educ. of Topeka, 347 U.S. 483 (1953).

68. Bowers v. Hardwick, 478 U.S. 186, 192 (1986).

69. Lawrence v. Texas, 539 U.S. 558, 578 (2003).

70. UNITED STATES COURTS, STATISTICAL TABLES—U.S. COURTS OF APPEALS, TABLE B-5 (Sept. 2013), http://www.uscourts.gov/uscourts/Statistics/JudicialBusiness/2013/appendices/B05Sep13.pdf (showing the percentage of appeals reversed on the merits in all circuits for a 12-month period ending September 30, 2013).

71. FED. R. EVID. 404.

72. *See, e.g.*, United States v. Puckett, 405 F.3d 589, 596-98 (2004).

7 The Writing Phase: Developing a Personal Writing Process

By now, you have worked through the planning and learning phase of your appeal. You have spotted the issues, researched their merits, and selected your arguments. You have a keen sense of the case's strengths and weaknesses and have thought deeply about both. Naturally, you are anxious to tell the court about it. But before you start to transform your internal thoughts into an external communication, you must settle on a personal writing process.

This chapter will guide you in developing that process — a process that will stay with you through many years and many appeals. It first explains how to immerse yourself in the writing mindset, and then discusses how to craft a writing process that separates distinct cognitive tasks but honors the recursive nature of writing. The chapter ends with advice on navigating the waters of collaborative writing, a reality in appellate practice, where you will write with coworkers, co-counsel, and attorneys representing other parties. Along the way, you will encounter suggestions for overcoming writer's block and for working through writing snags. You will also see examples of how appellate writers employ a writing process that ensures deep exploration and works recursively to sharpen thinking and perfect writing. But the starting point is to put yourself in a writing state of mind.

Section 1 Adopting the Expert Writing Mindset

The expert writing mindset stems from a particular outlook and daily dedication to the craft of writing. Expert writers across fields attribute writing success to the following expert writing habits:[1]

- Deliberate practice
- Total open-mindedness about critiques from peers and mentors
- Talking to others about your writing
- Analyzing good appellate writing
- Reading great works on writing and excellent writing of any kind

1.1 Deliberate Practice

K. Anders Ericsson, a leading researcher on expertise, says that expertise results not from years of experience, but from deliberative practice, which requires concentrated and sustained effort while performing more and more complex tasks.[2] In other words, the sheer number of appellate briefs you write does not make you an effective appellate writer. You will move towards mastery only if you take a running inventory of both strengths and weaknesses—then craft strategies for ferreting out those weaknesses. Some of your weaknesses will be *writing process oriented*; you may be approaching the writing process with faulty strategies or no strategies at all. Other weaknesses will center on your *writing tendencies*. For example, your natural writing "voice" may be objective and academic rather than pointed and argumentative. Whatever your writing flaws, you must deal with them head on if you want to get better faster. Take stock both as you write and afterward, when you have time to reflect on the project.

Practice Alert #1
Deliberate Practice
Inventory

The online companion contains a Deliberate Practice Inventory, which prompts you to confront your writing strengths and weaknesses, and gives you a space to record expert techniques that you wish to try.

1.2 Open-Mindedness About Critiques

Capturing the angst of writers around the world, author Anne Lamott still dreads writing critiques:

> My first response if [my reader has] a lot of suggestions is never profound relief that I have someone in my life who will be honest with me. . . . [My] first thought is, "Well, I'm sorry, but I can't be friends with you anymore because you have too many problems."[3]

The writing professor Peter Elbow offers a sober response: "You often learn the most from reactions to words that you loathe. Do you want to learn how to write or protect your feelings?"[4] Appellate writers work in a world of high intellectual demands, unforgiving deadlines, and discerning consumers in the form of supervising attorneys, clients, and judges. On top of that, appellate practice is a highly structured discourse community with accepted conventions. As a novice seeking to enter that community, you will learn best if you approach your work as an open-minded apprentice, who wants to learn from the masters but develop her own style.

If the critique is unspecific or unkindly delivered, you can still learn from it in two ways. First, you can ask neutrally phrased, factual questions. You might query, "When you say _____, can you be more specific?" or pose "what" questions that prompt the critic to be more concrete.[5] Second, you can dig for the underlying truth, which is present in all critiques.[6] If you're told that your writing is unclear, diagnose the potential causes. A lack of clarity could stem from not knowing what you want to say, from trying to say too much all at once, or from trying to impress with complex syntax and fancy words rather than simple, lucid prose. Or you might be told that your writing is unpersuasive. Take a fresh look with a reader's eyes and see whether your writing simply tells what you know and makes the reader work out her own conclusion, rather than conveying specific reasons that compel the reader to reach a conclusion. It is worth the effort: Empirical evidence shows that taking criticism well fuels creativity at work and improves the flow of communication with superiors.[7] It is a core component of successfully "managing up." Hard as it is in the moment, you will come away a better writer by extracting future value from current critiques, and adding them to your Deliberate Practice Inventory.

1.3 Talking to Others About Your Writing

Talking about your writing makes it better, so within ethical and pedagogical constraints, find a trusted pair of ears. As you talk, ideas you have never had or connections you have never made may emerge spontaneously. Your listener might suggest new directions for arguments, offer a new perspective, or help you find your theme and story. Whether senior associates in practice or peers in a law school course, these knowledgeable and invested listeners can help you sharpen your thinking more efficiently than hours of individual planning. One further benefit of these conversations is that you must often be very concise because your "volunteers" don't have a lot of spare time. Speaking about your case in a time-constrained fashion always helps you decide what really matters. And, after you have these conversations, don't wait to write. Sit down and record the best ideas right away.

1.4 Analyzing Good Appellate Writing

Expert appellate writing, carefully deconstructed, has much to teach us. Carry this book's approach to analyzing top-shelf briefs with you in practice. Make it your job to know who the best appellate brief writers are and where you can find their work.[8] When you read these writers' briefs, think about why the writing works. Did the writer find a way to tell a compelling story that extends through a legal argument's rigorous logical structure? And how did the writer accomplish this — through an abiding theme, a unique large-scale structure, or by strategically placing and crafting individual sentences? How did the writer find a way to make a regulatory scheme relatable and interesting? Maybe she accomplished this feat with simplicity of words, or rhetorical techniques such as personification and metaphor. Identify the expert techniques that you find most arresting, then add them to your Deliberate Practice Inventory.

1.5   Reading Great Works on Writing and Great Writing of All Kinds

According to Chief Justice John Roberts, "The only way to learn about good writing is to read good writing."[9] He marvels at good writing's power of suggestion:

> Your mind structures the words and it sees them, and when you try to write them again, they tend to come out better because your mind is thinking of what was a pleasing sentence to read and remembers that when you try to write.[10]

Justice Ginsburg agrees. Her writing inspiration comes from the "strong" style of Tolstoy, the "word pictures" of Jane Austen, and her former professor Vladimir Nabokov, whose writing she can "hear" on the page.[11] So do not limit yourself to reading appellate briefs. Continue to read the work of essayists and news writers, literary classics and award-winning biographies. Note their techniques, too, on your Deliberate Practice Inventory for your own work. And finally, supplement your collection with great works on *how* to write.[12]

REFLECTION, DISCUSSION, AND CHALLENGE QUESTIONS

Adopting an Expert Writing Mindset

- Which expert writing habits have you already formed, and which ones can you add?
- Whose writing do you admire most? Pick a passage from this writer and critically assess what you like about it. Pick two features to incorporate in your appellate brief.
- Have you ever responded poorly to criticism of your writing? What could your critic have done to generate a more positive response? In hindsight, how could you have managed the interaction to gain value from it?
- What sets you up for a productive day of writing and what, in turn, sabotages your writing? Record these impressions on your Deliberate Practice Inventory.

Section 2   Elements of an Expert Writing Process

2.1   Why Have a Writing Process?

The writing mindset gives you a metacognitive approach to writing; that is, a way of thinking about how you think about writing. But it must be combined with a functional writing process. For appellate lawyers, a writing process is a professional necessity. Inexperienced writers of all kinds struggle to produce writing. Add to the usual writing challenges the demands of written appellate advocacy, and even writers with years of experience can be confounded about where to begin and how to move from point *A* to point *B*. On top of that, so much is riding on the writing—a client's freedom, a person's livelihood, a billion dollar deal, entire ways of doing business. There is no room for writer's block or procrastination, but these are ideal conditions for breeding both.

The antidote is to develop a *workable, dependable, but flexible* writing process that spans the length of the appeal. Your process should account for how experts approach complex writing tasks, but it must also account for your strengths and weaknesses. The chart below lists the many advantages of using a writing process in appellate work.

Benefits of Using a Writing Process

- It helps you allocate your time up front.
- It promotes focus in your writing.
- It prevents writer's block by breaking out distinct cognitive tasks.
- It allows you to develop connections among ideas and to discover what is most important, making writing less daunting.
- It eases frustration by reassuring you that a recursive process and large-scale revisions are vital to excellent work product.
- It ensures that you "own" your writing because you decide the process that works best for you.

2.2 What Is an Expert Writing Process?

At their core, all expert writing processes share two basic features: (1) They separate distinct cognitive tasks, rather than merging tasks or starting too soon on a late-phase task (like worrying about word choice); and (2) they are recursive in nature, open to discovery and conceptual rethinking all along the way.[13]

We start with the first core feature of a successful writing process: breaking up distinct cognitive tasks. Put simply, the brain shifts modes during the process of composition. Each mode is taxing in its own way, and does not work well when forced to multitask with others. Each mode also has a time and place within a writing project; a writer who invokes these modes haphazardly will find that her work product is chaotic. Critically, these modes are recursive and symbiotic. When one mode stalls, the brain jump-starts it by switching back to another. In many ways, these modes, and their relationships to each other, can be captured in the metaphoric food service roles in a fine dining restaurant:[14]

Roles in Food Service	Cognitive Modes in Writing
Executive Chef: generating the vision for the restaurant and its menu; problem solving in the kitchen; overseeing the big picture of food preparation, service, and ambiance	*Executive Chef mode*: generating ideas, problem solving in the writing process, overseeing the writing project's big picture
Sous Chef: prioritizing, structuring, and directing the kitchen operations	*Sous Chef mode*: prioritizing and structuring arguments, achieving focus
Line Cook: efficiently executing the food order to the chef's and diner's specifications	*Line Cook mode*: efficiently executing a draft to sous chef specifications with audience in mind
Expediter and Server: assessing the food's presentation and taste and the overall dining experience with an exacting eye, each from a different perspective	*Expediter and Server mode*: assessing the work product with an exacting eye and revising over many rounds, each with a different perspective

These modes do have a general progression. You will spend more time in Executive Chef mode at the beginning, and hold off on Expediter/Server mode until after you have written a full draft. The modes also have a pecking order. As the word "executive" connotes, whenever a writer hits a snag in another mode, her first line of defense is to check in with the Executive Chef, who can troubleshoot the problem. Proportionally, you should spend far more time in Expediter/Server mode than anywhere else, for that mode is what affects the audience most directly, just as a Server has the most influence on a diner's experience. Finally, these modes do not happen strictly in order, nor just once in the writing process. For expert appellate writers, these modes recur in "mini-cycles" over time. This is called a "recursive writing process" — the second core feature.[15]

Each recursive mini-cycle is more focused than the original, conducted to remedy a specific problem. For no matter how accomplished the appellate writer, she simply cannot catch everything the first time around. Moreover, appellate writing is "epistemic," meaning that the act of appellate writing is the act of *constructing law* by synthesizing, framing, reasoning, and applying.[16] Because appellate writing actually creates new legal substance, at any point in time a writer must be willing to engage in large-scale rethinking to reconcile earlier work with newly discovered meaning. The diagram below illustrates the modes' recursiveness:

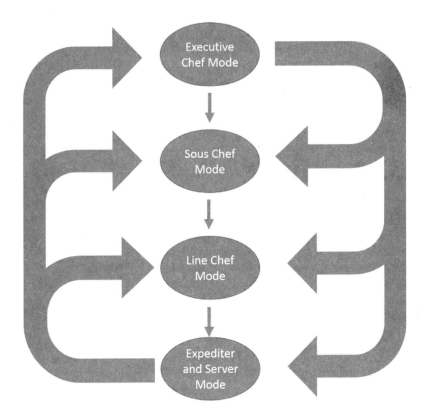

2.3 Honoring Distinct Recursive Modes

Executive Chef mode. Every restaurant has an Executive Chef, the creative and intellectual force who plans the menu and oversees the restaurant's theme, the overall food preparation, and the service experience. When you are in Executive Chef mode in your writing process, you must become adept at both broad and deep thinking, and be prepared to inject plentiful, fresh concepts into the appellate writing project, both at the beginning and whenever other modes have stalled. The consummate brainstormer, the Executive Chef excels at conjuring and connecting big ideas. Conversely, the Executive Chef cannot be burdened with selecting or ordering those ideas or with any sort of detail work. Others modes are better designed for that.

For an appellate writer, Executive Chef mode runs in full throttle at the outset as the writer is reading and digesting the record, researching and synthesizing authorities. As you know from the planning and learning phase, reading and reflecting on these sources generates connections between authorities, argument paths, and potential weaknesses in the appeal. Staying in Executive Chef mode during this phase helps you harness these powerful global thoughts. But don't make the mistake of shifting out of this mode too quickly at the beginning. If you do, your thinking will be stunted and your approaches artificially limited. You may never dive deep enough to find the winning argument.

When you are in Executive Chef mode during the planning and learning phase, before you have started to write, the challenge lies in capturing its genius in a systematic way. Here are four options:

1. Freewriting and zero drafts.[17] Freewriting means simply writing whatever is on your mind about your writing project, helping you to generate new ideas and begin connecting them. This method works well for writers who find the creative process difficult. This writing is not a "draft" in the usual sense — it is for you to tell thoughts to yourself, not to any reader. So, when your mind begins filling with ideas from a session of reading, start writing in prose every thought that comes to mind. This isn't about sentence structure, word choice, or even paragraphing. In fact, your entire freewrite may be a single, giant paragraph, full of awkward constructions and imprecise words, and that is okay.

The zero draft is for writers who need even more help generating ideas. Instead of spitting out your own ideas, in a zero draft, you write what you know about what you have read. A zero draft may be bullet-point summaries of law review articles, treatise sections, cases, or statutory sections, for example. This is a valuable project, not only because you generate summaries that you can draw on later when writing the brief, but also because you can — just by the act of writing — stimulate thought that breeds new ideas.

2. Dictation or voice recognition software. If you speak more fluently than you write, use dictation or voice recognition software to record your work in Executive Chef mode. Just as talking about your ideas to a trusted listener can spur the creative process, talking aloud to yourself can crystallize concepts and generate fresh connections.

**Practice Alert #2
Executive Chef Exercise**

This exercise in the online companion prompts you to analyze a short fact pattern and two cases exclusively in Executive Chef mode, generating as many ideas and connections as possible without switching cognitive tasks.

3. Mindmapping programs. These programs, many free on the Internet, allow you to set up visual diagrams of thought by clicking on an electronic canvas. They are especially helpful to visual, nonlinear thinkers. Concepts reside in boxes or ovals that can be connected by lines that represent myriad relationships among ideas. The advantages of mindmapping programs are that they facilitate nonlinear thinking, they are easy to manipulate and change over time as you learn more about your appeal, and they allow you to see the big conceptual picture and many potential relationships at a glance. The disadvantage is that the concept boxes or ovals do not hold much text, and so don't allow much elaboration.

4. Oversized paper or large whiteboard. If you prefer low-tech methods of recording ideas, or just prefer to work in a physical rather than virtual medium, invest in oversized construction paper or a large whiteboard. Here, you can draw your own nonlinear representation of concepts and potential relationships. The paper version cannot be manipulated in the same way as an electronic mindmap, but you can use multiple sheets of paper to create several maps that each flesh out ideas about a particular concept. A whiteboard is easier to change and manipulate than paper, but its space is finite; however, if you take digital photos of your whiteboard maps, you can create a permanent record.

Below are two examples that show how Executive Chef mode can contribute both at the beginning and again later in the writing process, using the idea-capturing methods above.

Example 1 — freewriting in Executive Chef mode to generate new ideas.

You represent a journalist who refuses to testify in a civil proceeding, invoking First Amendment and state law journalist's privileges against divulging her sources. You are appealing the lower court's interlocutory decision ordering the journalist to name these sources. The First Amendment doctrine in this area is complex, and it overlaps with the state law privilege in some ways but diverges from it in others. After a sustained period of researching, reading, and synthesizing, you still do not see the makings of an argument. So you freewrite everything you have learned or can think about in a "zero draft." You make no effort to impose order on this draft, or even to rein in your thoughts. Now, with this zero draft in hand, connections and argument ideas begin to emerge. You begin to discover what this project is all about, and how you can build around that focus. From here, you create an outline that lays out points and progression, then produce a new draft that makes good on the elements of the outline.

Example 2 — shifting back to Executive Chef mode to rethink focus and theme.

Because the Executive Chef has the broadest vision, the appellate writer often switches back to this mode after the planning and learning phase is done. In fact, she shifts back whenever she needs to reset her focus or come up with new ideas — even in the midst of a draft. In a restaurant, the Executive Chef is on site, wandering among the various line chefs and periodically diving in whenever he sees a problem or simply for quality control. He also often will station himself at the end of the line to spot-check the final plate — to make sure it is perfect — before it is handed off to the server. In the same way, Executive Chef mode is ideal for reworking a theme, revisiting your arguments, or filling in legal or factual gaps. A recursive shift to Executive Chef is also in order if you find yourself writing endlessly around the issues instead of hitting them head on. And should you ever run into a dead end, you can return to the Executive Chef's creative well to search for a new direction.

As an example, assume you represent a toy company, the plaintiff-appellant in an intellectual property case, claiming rights in a product shaped like a small plastic computer tablet filled with jelly beans. In the trial court, the client, which markets and sells the product, moved for a preliminary injunction against the contract manufacturer, which designs and manufactures the product. The district court denied the preliminary injunction, finding no likelihood of success because: (1) the product is not intellectual property of any kind; and (2) the product belongs to the contract manufacturer anyway. This ruling prompted your interlocutory appeal. Your early drafts focus intently on the first issue — pages and pages argue that the product merits protection through trade dress, copyright law, and a design patent. You send a draft to the partner, who balks. She calls you into her office and tells you to write up the brief with a different theme and focus — " we own it, they stole it, this court should give it back." She wants much less on what "it" is, and much more on the manufacturer's wrongful taking.

You need to check back with the Executive Chef to generate arguments that achieve this new focus. To that end, you conduct some limited research, taking care not to exceed the scope of the arguments below. Your critical and creative reassessment of the case law leads you to a new focus that emphasizes the other side's bad behavior. Now you plan to spend only a quarter of the argument on what "it" is, with the rest devoted to wrongful taking.

Sous Chef mode. No matter how brilliant and astute the Executive Chef's ideas and plans, the kitchen will grind to a halt without someone to implement the ideas and plans at a more granular level. In the restaurant world, that is the job of the Sous Chef, who works directly under the Executive Chef to realize the Executive Chef's ideas through structuring, prioritizing, and directing the kitchen's work. The Sous Chef ensures that all of the menu ingredients are on hand in the right amounts and the right quality; she manages the line cooks and ensures that each station for the evening's service is appropriately and fully staffed; she makes sure that each station has completed its *mise en place* — the food prep work — well in advance of the dining hour. Similarly, in writing, after spending quality time in the more generative and creative Executive Chef mode, a writer needs to decide what is important and impose order on her thinking. To make that shift, the writer must switch to Sous Chef mode, an entirely different cognitive task that is more logical than it is creative.

In Sous Chef mode, you select and organize ideas and start to plan their progression. Working from your mindmap, your freewrite, or dictated notes, you can focus your energy on pulling related material together and separating the important from the unimportant. You can put your mind to figuring out which of the many relational lines between concepts on a mindmap is most logical — or which chunk on page 2 of the freewrite really fits with that chunk on page 25. From there, you can begin to see how legal concepts and facts can form distinct arguments. The product of Sous Chef mode is a linear outline, one that is centered on a focal thematic point or storyline, and that elevates certain concepts to "main points" and slots others as "sub-points" underneath.

Sous Chef mode is a solitary, supervisory one that does not mix well with other cognitive modes. To tap into its power, you must dial down Executive Chef's creativity and work with the ideas you have. Staying in Sous Chef mode also means that you are still concerning yourself with the big picture, and not with distracting details such as how to put paragraphs and sentences together.

An appellate writer needs Sous Chef mode at many points during a recursive writing process. The Sous Chef must first step in after the initial output of the Executive Chef. The next time is after you build a first draft. An outline that seems to put legal and factual relationships in the right place before you write a draft may need to be revisited. Because the act of writing creates new meaning, you are bound to discover better ways of organizing as you are writing. In the restaurant context, let's say that two of your line cooks get ill at the last moment and must go home. As Sous Chef, your job is to handle that problem and readjust your staffing to account for this new problem. The

**Practice Alert #3
Sous Chef Exercise**

The online companion contains an exercise in which you will assess contrasting point-heading examples while operating in Sous Chef mode.

same process applies during this mode of your writing process; as Sous Chef, you are the ultimate project manager, and you must redouble your organizational efforts to solve the problem. This does not mean that your first time in Sous Chef mode was a waste; it was a good starting place that helped you find a more effective progression.

Example — returning to Sous Chef mode when your original structure fails.

Consider a criminal case involving a theft conviction based on eyewitness testimony. The issue on appeal is whether the testimony should have been excluded because it was tainted by a suggestive photo array. Researching this testimony's admissibility on appeal, you read several cases that give you the basic analytical structure — a five-factor totality test that determines whether the eyewitness testimony has "independent origins" from the tainted photo array. You think the five-factor structure in all the opinions you have read will work pretty well. So you prepare an argument outline that envisions separate point headings for each factor, following the same order that those factors have appeared in every case.

But when you start writing a draft, you realize that this organizational framework does not work well for your argument. As it turns out, factor #1 doesn't even come into play. You did not catch this earlier because it was during the act of writing that the light went on. You suddenly realized that facts that you thought matched up with factor #1 actually fit more logically under factor #5. It also became clear that factor #3's argument is so straightforward that you can dispense with it at the outset; you needn't blindly adhere to the factor's #3 placement just because judicial opinions address it there. Finally, you realize how much the factors overlap as they apply to your case. This has resulted in a redundancy problem—you see now that you are saying the same thing several times. A switch back to Sous Chef mode is in order so that you can re-see where everything fits. With the new insights you gained from writing, you can call on that mode for a dispassionate and logical assessment of how the factors should be organized to best advance your argument—not a generic judicial opinion.

Line Cook mode. In Line Cook mode, the brain shifts again, working to execute the Sous Chef's orders with a first draft. This mode returns the writer to a more creative orientation, but on a smaller scale and within the Sous Chef's organizational strictures. Distinct from the Executive Chef's freewriting or zero drafts, which are meant for the writer alone, the Line Cook's work begins to consider the writing audience, just as a restaurant Line Cook must work to the diner's specifications along with the chef's. For example, the Line Cook must often adapt the Executive Chef's recipe to account for what the suppliers have brought and the diners' preferences. Though the Executive Chef may prefer his rack of lamb to be served medium-rare, if the diner will not eat it prepared that way, then the Line Cook must make the necessary adjustments. The Line Cook thus operates with just a bit of autonomy within the confines of the original structure; he could not unilaterally substitute veal for lamb in the recipe without going back to consult the Executive Chef, for example.

Example—going back to Executive Chef mode when Line Cook mode reveals problems.

On behalf of your employer client, you are appealing a jury verdict holding your client liable for wrongful termination. The plaintiff's legal theory was that the employer duped him into working for the company by misrepresenting the prospects for his job and promotion potential, when in fact the company never intended to give him these opportunities, and terminated him a year later in a reduction in force. The trial-level arguments focused on how the evidence failed to prove the technical elements of promissory fraud and promissory estoppel. You find these arguments well-grounded in the law, and believe the appellate court will be more amenable to them, and so you plan and outline the arguments, then switch to Line Cook mode to write a draft of the brief. But something is missing. The brief is dry and boring, and never seems to drive to the heart of the dispute.

It is time to go back to Executive Chef mode. To analogize to a restaurant, let's say that — despite the Sous Chef's best efforts — you discover as Line Cook that of the 60 pounds of scallops that the seafood purveyor sent, 40 are spoiled. You can no longer execute your assigned entree: Coquille St. Jacques. So it is back to the Executive Chef for guidance; he will suggest that you quickly defrost the lump crabmeat from the freezer and prepare deviled crab instead. You can use most of the same ingredients that you have on hand to prepare the substitute dish, which will allow the dining service to continue on schedule. In Line Cook mode in your writing project you would do the same thing: revisit the case law and read it from a different angle. You realize that your jurisdiction's courts are especially hostile to "my job didn't live up to recruiting promises" claims when the plaintiff actually got the job, worked for some time in the position, and looks to be manufacturing job security he never bargained for. This theme squarely fits the record facts, and so you begin a new, concentrated round of research, revisiting the record, brainstorming ideas about the new focus, then revising your brief so that the theme gives life to the legal arguments.

Making the most out of Line Cook mode. Unless a problem arises — like the scallop example used above — Line Cook mode should be fast and furious, leaving very little room for judgment or writer's block to creep in. In the words of one accomplished appellate advocate, you just have to "bang out a draft," ideally in one block of uninterrupted time. Line Cooks must produce their assigned dish with skill and speed and pass it along to the next station; they have no time to worry about an extra splash of sauce ending up on the plate's rim. Ultimately, the expediter and server will take care of that final polishing. It is possible that your Line Cook mode writing may be as awkward and unrefined as the freewrite, but you are executing the core of your assigned task and moving the project ahead towards its final step. At the end of Line Cook mode, you may also be many pages or words over the court's limit. Be comfortable with that. You should be able to fix it in Expediter/Server mode.

Line Cook mode is especially hostile to any tendency to slow down to fix the small cosmetics. Though you may be tempted to do so, combining a generative mode with an evaluative one, you must resist. A Line Cook would never walk away from his station to place a sprig of parsley on a plate as it leaves the kitchen; if he did, his own orders would begin to pile up and he would effectively shut down the well-functioning system at work in the kitchen. As a writer, then, you also must resist the temptation to find the perfect word or tweak a turn of phrase, because the result is a slow, frustrating, and inefficient drafting process. As you turn to the thesaurus and search for the right words and begin to refine syntax, for example, you lose valuable time generating text, taking hours or even days more than it should to complete a draft. Stymied this way, you also lose the ability to discover meaning through writing; few writers can simultaneously make meaning and perfect its expression.

Expediter/Server mode. After your stopover in Line Cook mode, it is time to view your work with a critical eye. You enter Expediter/Server mode, whose hallmark is perfecting the presentation through revision, revision, and then more revision. The Expediter in a kitchen is a non-cooking job. Her only role is to make sure the plates match the orders and to finalize and garnish the dishes before handing off to the Server. The Server also evaluates the dish before taking it to the table for the ultimate audience: the diner. This mode marks another cognitive shift away from creativity and towards cold, hard, evaluation. It takes the near-automatic work of Line Cook mode and makes it pristine. The proportion of time you spend in Expediter/Server mode relative to your overall timeline should be quite high — *as high as 40 percent*. This is because the Expediter/Server's work is complex and itself has numerous tasks.

We reserve a more detailed discussion of the Expediter/Server mode and its tasks for Chapter 12, the point in your writing process when you will be ready to shift into this mode. Unlike other modes, which can be triggered at various points in the writing process, you should stay out of Expediter/Server mode until you have completed at least one full round of Executive Chef → Sous Chef → Line Cook. That is because the Expediter/Server's judgmental temperament can hamper and artificially limit these bigger-picture and creative modes. For now, what's important is to set aside enough time for Expediter/Server as you plan your writing process.

Review Expert Writing Process Modes

Mode	Cognitive Task	Techniques & Tools
Executive Chef	• Brainstorming ideas • Finding a focus • Problem solving the writing process	• Freewriting • Zero drafts • Dictation • Mindmapping
Sous Chef	• Transforming legal concepts and facts into arguments • Prioritizing arguments and sifting main points from subpoints	• Pull together related ideas from freewrite, zero draft, dictated work, or visual map • Draft a linear outline
Line Cook	• Write to Sous Chef specifications with audience expectations in mind	• Draft quickly without editing
Expediter & Server	• Revise and perfect the brief with an exacting eye	• Revision techniques discussed in Chapter 12

REFLECTION, DISCUSSION, AND CHALLENGE QUESTIONS

Expert Writing Process Elements

- Which elements of the expert writing process have proven most difficult for you in the past? How can you overcome those difficulties as you write this brief?
- Have you ever encountered a writing process challenge that resembles the examples in this section? Think back to that experience. Knowing what you do now, how might you have separated cognitive tasks or moved recursively to solve the problem?
- Have you received writing feedback that critiques a weakness that you can trace back to a writing process problem? What deliberate practices can you adopt to strike a better balance among cognitive tasks?

2.4 Putting It All Together into a Personal Writing Process

Beyond incorporating the elements of an expert writing process, your writing process must work for you. A personal writing process should fit your own strengths, weaknesses, working style, and the nature of the appellate project. For example, you may be a natural Executive Chef, comfortable brainstorming and able to see the big picture at all times. So you may not need to consciously think about what happens in this mode, because it will occur naturally. Your weakness may instead lie in putting off Expediter/Server mode for too long — all that time spent brainstorming leaves little room for multiple revisions, stopping you short at an unrefined draft.

On the other hand, if you have trouble summoning your Executive Chef, you not only may need to set aside time for it, but you also may need to avoid writing a draft for a while to force deep thinking to exhaust ideas and connections. Still other writers are stymied by Sous Chef mode, and have trouble creating structured outlines. Those writers can benefit by moving right to Line Cook mode after Executive Chef mode, then entering Sous Chef mode by crafting a "reverse outline" from that text.[18] And if your trouble is Line Cook mode, and you get blocked turning an outline into prose, use Sous Chef mode to create a much more detailed outline, making the step from outline to draft much smaller.

Your working style may also dictate how and when you perform these cognitive tasks. Perhaps some are easier for you at night; others, in the morning. In addition, use the writing tools that work well for you, whether it is note-taking software, word-processing software, whiteboards, handwritten notes, or voice recognition software — or even strong coffee, good lighting, and the right room temperature. You may work more efficiently in sustained blocks of time, cycling through many cognitive tasks, or do your best work handling fewer cognitive tasks in two-hour bursts each day.

Finally, the appellate project's nature will shape your writing process. A denser record with hefty authorities may demand several cycles: one for each complex sub-issue in the brief, followed by more focused recursive mini-cycles. In contrast, a short appellate motion brief may require only one major cycle and just a few mini-cycles over a day or two.

REFLECTION, DISCUSSION, AND CHALLENGE QUESTIONS

The Writing Process

- What sets you up for a productive day of writing and what, in turn, sabotages your writing? Do you get carried away by reactive tasks like responding to non-urgent emails or phone calls? What sleep habits or dietary choices sap your energy rather than fuel your brain for writing? Record these impressions on your Deliberate Practice Inventory.
- Sketch out a personal writing process for yourself. Make sure it has the expert elements of distinct cognitive tasks and recursiveness. Then add elements that specifically address your writing process challenges. Try it out on a short writing assignment, and record your impressions on your Deliberate Practice Inventory.

Section 3   The Joys and Travails of Collaborative Writing

The notion of the appellate lawyer holed up in her office cranking out a brief in solitude is generally a fiction. Large writing projects like an appellate brief are more often than not group projects. Unless you are a solo practitioner, you will almost always be reporting to a superior or supervising a younger attorney on your writing projects. These, too, are collaborations, though they differ in some ways from a collaboration among peers. And even if you generally fly solo, you will still have appeals with co-counsel, or appeals where you must garner amici support, or consolidated appeals where you must work with other parties whose cases were consolidated with yours. Given these realities, too little attention is spent on the benefits of collaborative writing, its potential pitfalls, its unique writing process, and other strategies that can be used to make this experience rewarding and productive. These are discussed in turn below.

3.1   The Benefits of Collaboration

Collaborative writing at its best pays many dividends. It stimulates creative thinking and questioning of long-standing paradigms and consideration of new approaches. It facilitates the open debate of ideas, generates heightened interest in a project, and can ultimately lead to the best solutions.[19] In the law school context, students accrue additional benefits from collaborative writing projects with their peers: (1) improved legal writing and reasoning skills; (2) additional feedback; (3) a shared workload; (4) new problem-solving techniques; (5) new, deepened relationships with peers; and (6) greater ownership over the learning process.[20] Though the benefits are many, the grumbling about group work persists, resulting in large part from the potential problems that can arise when several people bear joint responsibility for a single final product.

3.2 The Challenges of Collaboration

Collaborative writing is fraught with potential pitfalls. Appellate briefs are complex documents that could be revised almost infinitely.[21] Group dynamics can be tricky, and personality differences and emotions can interfere with the work at hand. Researchers have identified many specific concerns that arise among group members during collaborative writing projects:

- **Poor task definition**: If a team member focuses too heavily on one task, the finished product will be imbalanced. Conversely, sometimes there are simply too many cooks in the kitchen, all focusing on the same task, which makes the project unwieldy.[22]
- **Personality and motivation differences**: Some people simply want to get the project finished, while others see it as a vehicle for making a statement about their abilities. Some people boldly take and receive criticism, while others are easily offended.[23]
- **Poor conflict management or conflict avoidance**: If conflicts remain unresolved, team members become pitted against each other; if members avoid conflict, then decisions on which all seemed to agree — simply to avoid conflict — will lead to ambivalence and reduced commitment later on.[24]
- **Emergent leadership and power issues**: A leader may naturally emerge early in the process who may not be well suited to the task in the long term, or a team member who is not well suited for the job may vie for the role, creating internal conflict.[25]
- **Freeloading, commitment issues, and inequitable work distribution**: These issues not only lead to hard feelings but may also lead to delays in finishing the project.[26]
- **Distance, technology, and other physical barriers**: Sporadic, unstructured meetings, the lack of a centralized meeting place, conducting meetings via email when they could take place in person, and inefficient use of time all contribute to a less-than-optimal collaboration.[27]
- **Version control and unifying the parts into a whole**: Inefficiencies and confusion arise when multiple versions are circulated at the same time. Members may fight for control of the document, and the ultimate product may sound disjointed for lack of a coherent voice and style.

Given these very real issues that arise in collaborative writing, it is essential to go into a project with open communication and a plan to maximize the benefits and minimize the downsides. We suggest some strategies in the following section.

Practice Alert #4
Using your Deliberate
Practice Inventory to Create
a Team Writing Plan

For this exercise in the online companion, you will bring the practice inventory that you created at the beginning of the chapter (where you identified your writing strengths and weaknesses) to a group of three or more people. As a group, assess your writing strengths and weaknesses, along with any relevant personality and leadership traits, and set up a plan for your appellate writing project based on that information.

3.3   Strategies for Successful Collaboration

Approached deliberately and thoughtfully, the pros of collaboration can far outweigh the cons. Awareness, planning, and minimizing distance are the three most important components for successful collaboration.

Awareness includes three distinct sub-parts. First, you have to be aware of your members' strengths and limitations, which means you have to take the time to get to know each other before diving into the brief. Second, you have to be aware of—and agree on—the rhetorical context and audience.[28] Without this crucial step, your brief will focus on the wrong information or deliver it in a less than effective way, leading to inefficiency and group dissatisfaction. Third, you have to be aware of the nuances of the group writing process. You know now how to create your own personal writing process that is recursive, not linear. In a collaborative writing context, you must do the same thing for your group, and adapt your writing process to accommodate the group's needs as well. As a threshold first step at the beginning of a writing project, set up an in-person meeting. Candidly discuss who should play what roles in the drafting process, and make sure that everyone is on board with the proper tone and approach for the client and the specific court. In a law firm, these roles will probably shake out more naturally due to varying levels of seniority on the team. But in law school when you are working with peers, or when you must collaborate with other lawyers outside your firm, taking the time for this frank discussion will pay dividends later.

The second component—planning—can also be broken down into steps. First, create a task list. Because you now know your members' strengths and weaknesses, you can assign tasks that take them into account. You also need to assign tasks to avoid duplicating efforts. Here is a task list one of the authors routinely uses at the end of the editing process. It facilitates feedback from many contributors in a compressed time frame:

TO: Appellate Clinic Students
FROM: Sarah Schrup
RE: Brief Crunch Week
DATE: November 30, 2013

We are entering a brief crunch week. This is the time we all need to pull together to give the brief the final push to perfection. To that end, please take the time over the next couple of days to give the brief a final proofread and to offer any final comments or suggestions. In addition to the global proofreading and editing of the facts and argument, there are a number of tiny, individual tasks that need completion. I have assigned each one of you one additional task that you should complete on your own. Hopefully this will prevent any little mistakes from falling through the cracks but also will allow the class as a whole to work more efficiently by not repeating these smaller tasks. **So, unless you happen to notice something glaring, you do not need to concern yourself with any menial task but your own.** Give your task the same attention that you would on your own brief so that we can rely on each other's work.

McDONNELL BRIEF: Please return your edits and proofing no later than December 3.

TASKS and ASSIGNMENTS:

1. Confirm that there is one (and only one) space between the end of each sentence and the next sentence as well as between the end of a sentence and any citation (including record citations). GREG

2. Check the record citations to make sure they are in proper Bluebook format, including periods on the inside of the parentheses unless they include an additional explanatory parenthetical at the end, proper embedded cite form, and proper abbreviation of court documents. Make sure it is consistent throughout the document. (*i.e.,* Hr'g instead of Hearing; no "at" with trial transcript cites). PETER

3. Check case citations for Bluebook format. BOBBY

4. Case and statute cite checking. MARCIA

5. Cross-reference the pagination for the TOC, making sure the brief sections are accurate in the TOC. Make sure the headings in the TOC match those in the brief and are properly indented. Make sure the capitalization, underlining, and bolding are consistent among the headings and in the TOC. JAN

6. Double check that the same font (Century Schoolbook), size (12 pt), margin (1 inch), spacing (double except for block quotes), justification (left) is consistent throughout the whole paper. CINDY

7. Double-check each record cite for accuracy. MIKE

8. On a separate hard copy, do one final line-by-line edit to find typos and grammatical mistakes. CAROL

Second, you need to create a realistic timeline, one that accounts for the natural inefficiency in group work and allows ample time for everyone to revise the document. Group work takes longer because you must coordinate and exchange drafts, individually review each other's work, and then meld it into a cohesive whole. One person should be designated "master" of the brief at various points in the process so that different versions do not float around simultaneously. And the final "master" of the document should be made responsible for smoothing over voice differences among sections. The group must also decide who will be responsible for the final push to file (final proofreading, preparing the appendices and cover letters, arranging for copying and mailing, and e-filing), which can take several hours.

The third component of effective collaboration revolves around reducing physical (and virtual) barriers. Experts repeatedly emphasize the importance of proximity and informal, live interaction for optimal collaboration.[29] Indeed, "[t]he point is to have the most active lines of communication be the shortest in physical length."[30] The advent of technology has made legal research, writing, and editing much easier in certain ways; collaboration software allows users to centralize the project, its drafts, timelines, research, task list, and communications.[31] But problems arise when technology substitutes for face-to-face meeting time. If you live and work near your teammates, set up weekly meetings, and try to have a central war room if you can.[32] Only when distance is inevitable — your partners live in a different city or even around the world — does meeting via technology become a boon. Use technology deliberately and to efficiently manage your project, not as an excuse to stay on your couch in your living room.

Practice Alert #5
Unifying Voice in a Single Draft

This exercise in the online companion casts you as master of a brief written by three people with contrasting writing styles and voices.

3.4   Court-Mandated and External Collaborations

Appellate courts have the power to consolidate cases that raise the same or related questions, and parties sometimes file joint appeals.[33] Additionally, as you will learn in Chapter 13, parties routinely solicit amici to support their respective sides in circuit courts of appeals and the United States Supreme Court. These court-mandated and external writing partnerships present unique collaboration challenges. After all, you may not know these lawyers well, you did not necessarily choose to work with them, and distance may complicate your interactions. For example, if two cases are consolidated for briefing, freeloading may become a problem if one party simply decides to piggyback on the other's work. On the flip side, parties joined together on appeal may disagree on whether to raise an issue or how to frame it, or — if they are writing their own briefs — may take conflicting positions. If you are tasked with coordinating amici, a process discussed in Chapter 13, you will need not only to find them but also to make sure that their positions do not undermine your client's case. Optimally, the amicus effort will be coordinated so that each brief touches on a different, but important, aspect of the issue before the court.[34] Finally, multiple parties can mean divided oral argument time; because these minutes are few and precious, disagreements may arise on how to allocate it. Interpersonal skills are really important here, as is honesty, early communication, and task definition. With care and attention, though, these collaborative relationships can run smoothly.

Endnotes

1. *See* Roy Peter Clark, Writing Tools: 50 Essential Strategies for Every Writer pt. 4 (2006).
2. K. Anders Ericsson et al., *The Role of Deliberate Practice in the Acquisition of Expert Performance*, 100 Psychol. Review 363, 367-69 (1993).
3. Anne Lamott, Bird by Bird: Some Instructions on Writing and Life 166 (First Anchor Books ed. 1995).
4. Peter Elbow, Writing Without Teachers 78 (25th Anniversary ed. 1998).
5. Sue Shellenbarger, *How to Take Criticism Well*, Wall St. J. (June 18, 2014, 6:41 am), http://online.wsj.com/articles/how-to-take-criticism-well-1403046866.
6. *Id.*
7. *Id.*
8. For example, the U.S. Solicitor General's Office website has a brief bank. Commercial publishers rank appellate practices, and top law firm appellate practices post winning briefs on their firm websites. SCOTUSblog, federal and state appellate courts' websites, and for-pay research services are also good sources of appellate briefs.
9. Bryan A. Garner, *Interviews with United States Supreme Court Justices*, 13 Scribes J. Legal Writing 1, 39-40 (2010) (interview with Chief Justice Roberts).
10. *Id.*
11. *Id.* at 135, 139-40 (2010) (interview with Justice Ginsburg).
12. *See, e.g.*, Clark, *supra* note 1; Annie Dillard, The Writing Life (Harper & Row 1989); Stanley Fish, How to Write a Sentence and How to Read One (2011); Lamott, *supra* note 3; William Zinsser, On Writing Well (30th Anniversary ed., Collins 2006).
13. *See, e.g.*, Christopher M. Anzidei, *The Revision Process in Legal Writing: Seeing Better to Write Better*, 8 Legal Writing: J. Legal Writing Inst. 23 (2002); Linda L. Berger, *Applying New Rhetoric to Legal Discourse: The Ebb and Flow of Reader and Writer, Text and Context*, 49 J. Legal Educ. 155 (1999); Patricia Bizzell, *Cognition, Convention, and Certainty: What We Need to Know About Writing*, in Cross-Talk in Comp Theory 387 (Victor Villanueva ed., 2d ed., 2003); Linda Flower & John R. Hayes, *A Cognitive Process Theory of Writing*, 32 C. Composition & Comm. 365 (1981); Paul Kei Matsuda, *Process and Post-Process: A Discursive History*, 12 J. Second Language Writing 65 (2002); Sondra Perl, *Understanding Composing*, 31 C. Composition & Comm. 363 (1980); J. Christopher Rideout & Jill J. Ramsfield, *Legal Writing: A Revised View*, 69 Wash. L. Rev. 35 (1994); Nancy Soonpaa, *Using Composition Theory and Scholarship to Teach Legal Writing More Effectively*, 3 Legal Writing: J. Legal Writing Inst. 81 (1997); Adam Todd, *Neither Dead Nor Dangerous: Postmodernism and the Teaching of Legal Writing*, 58 Baylor L. Rev. 893 (2006).
14. Experts in the composition field have come up with a wide variety of roles and metaphors for the cognitive tasks involved in the writing process. Composition theorist Betty S. Flowers created a paradigm with memorable characters: Madman–Architect–Carpenter–Judge. *See* Betty S. Flowers, *Madman, Architect, Carpenter, Judge: Roles and the Writing Process*, 58 Language Arts 834 (1997). Legal writing expert Bryan Garner has adapted the paradigm to the legal writing process. *See, e.g.*, Bryan Garner, The Winning Brief: 100 Tips for Persuasive Briefing in Trial and Appellate Courts (Oxford Univ. Press, 2d ed. 2004); Bryan Garner, Legal Writing in Plain English: A Text with Exercises (U. Chi. Press, 2d ed. 2013). And Roy Peter Clark, Senior Scholar at the Poynter Institute for journalists, uses a metaphorical stair-step model to describe writing's distinct cognitive steps. *See* Clark, *supra* note 1, pt. 4.
15. *See* Berger, *supra* note 13, at 162; Flower & Hayes, *supra* note 13, at 375; Nancy Soonpaa, *supra* note 13, at 90; *see generally* Anzidei, *supra* note 13.
16. Philip C. Kissam, *Thinking (By Writing) About Legal Writing*, 40 Vand. L. Rev. 135, 138-41 (1987).
17. For an explanation of freewriting and zero drafting, *see* Berger, *supra* note 13, at 175-79.
18. *See, e.g.*, Clark, *supra* note 1, at 119-23.
19. Mary M. Lay, *Interpersonal Conflict in Collaborative Writing: What We Can Learn from Gender Studies*, J. Bus. & Tech. Comm., Sept. 1989, at 5.
20. Elizabeth L. Inglehart et al., *From Collaborative Learning to Collaborative Writing in the Legal Writing Classroom*, 9 Legal Writing: J. Legal Writing Inst. 185, 193-95, 214-16 (2003).
21. Paul Benjamin Lowry et al., *Building a Taxonomy and Nomenclature of Collaborative Writing to Improve Interdisciplinary Research and Practice*, J. Bus. Comm., January 2004, at 66, 70.
22. Mary M. Lay & William M. Karis, *Theoretical Overview of the Collaborative Process*, in Collaborative Writing in Industry: Investigations in Theory and Practice, 9 (Lowry & Karis eds., Baywood Publishing 1991); Janis Forman & Patricia Katsky, *The Group Report: A Problem in Small Group or Writing Processes?*, J. Bus. Comm., Oct. 1986, at 23, 28.
23. Lay, *supra* note 19, at 5.
24. *Id.* at 23, 25.
25. *Id.*
26. *Id.* at 23, 28.
27. *Id.*; Geoffrey Cross, *Collective Form: An Exploration of Large-Group Writing*, J. Bus. Comm., Jan. 2000, at 77, 94-95 ("A human-made physical setting . . . promotes power relationships we suppress or ignore in verbal communication" [so a centralized war-room is a good way to increase prestige and

visibility of a multimember project.] "The point is to have the most active lines of communication be the shortest in physical length.").

28. Janis Forman & Patricia Katsky, *The Group Report: A Problem in Small Group or Writing Processes?*, J. Bus. Comm., Oct. 1986, at 23, 29-31.

29. Robert E. Kraut et al., *Understanding Effects of Proximity on Collaboration: Implications for Technologies to Support Remote Collaborative Work in* Distributed Work 137 (Pamela J. Hinds and Sara Kiesler eds., MIT Press 2002), *available at* http://www.psychology.sunysb.edu/sbrennan-/papers/kraut.pdf; Cross, *supra* note 27, at 77, 94.

30. Cross, *supra* note 27, at 77, 95.

31. *See e.g.*, Jill Duffy, *Basecamp*, PCMag.com, (April 11, 2013), http://www.pcmag.com/article2/ 0,2817,2372953,00.asp (reviewing free Basecamp project management software).

32. Geoffrey Cross, *supra* note 27, at 77, 95 ("A dedicated room made the project more tangible than the previous ephemeral email messages and meetings in anonymous conference rooms. . . . Virtual teams that congregate in technological space may be dehumanizing[.]") (internal quotations omitted).

33. Fed. R. App. P. 3(b),15(a); Sup. Ct. R. 27.3.

34. Mary-Christine Sungaila, *Effective Amicus Practice Before the United States Supreme Court: A Case Study*, 8 S. Cal. Rev. L. & Women's Stud. 187, 189-90 (1999).

The Writing Phase: The Basics of Judicial Audience, Rhetoric, and Persuasion

Chapter 6 taught you about the logical side of argument, introducing analytical argument relationships and the fact-law continuum and its influence on argument structure. Chapter 7 then switched gears from the internal process of planning and learning to the external process of communicating, offering a template for constructing a personal writing process. This chapter moves the writing phase forward by shifting focus to your audience, with the goal of teaching you how to persuade discerning consumers of briefs. To that end, Section 1 teaches you more about the appellate audience and what its brief-writing needs are. Drawing on works as diverse as Aristotle's writings and social science studies, savvy brief writers have found ways to reach this tough judicial audience. To transfer that wisdom to you, Section 2 explains how appellate writing has been informed by three important disciplines: (1) rhetoric; (2) applied storytelling; and (3) cognitive psychology-based persuasion theory. Together, these disciplines tell us that logical reasoning is not the only arrow in the brief-writer's quiver. When logic pairs with narrative, and when the writer fosters credibility through a sound structure and measured appeals to emotion, then even the most skeptical readers can be persuaded. Because the power of "logic plus" sets the framework for writing the entire brief, we discuss it here, before you draft specific sections.

Section 1 Persuading a Judicial Audience

Legal advocacy and rhetoric are tightly joined, and rightly so, because rhetoric has much to say about persuasion.[1] Most notably, rhetoric teaches us that persuasive communication rigorously attends to occasion, purpose, and audience.[2] Cognitive psychology-based persuasion theory is in accord, and builds on the audience thread. It tells us that persuasion depends on gaining the audience's attention, then getting the audience to understand, accept, and retain your message.[3]

In appellate briefs, the occasion is well defined. A lower court has issued a ruling, and one or more parties wants it overturned, while other parties seek to defend it. As for the purposes of appellate writing, the ultimate goal is to persuade

137

the decisionmakers to act in a way that benefits a client. The most important rhetorical feature—the audience[4]—is also fixed. Though far from monolithic as individuals, as a group appellate judges are highly educated, experienced, and trained legal analysts and advocates.[5] They have staggering reading and writing burdens that inundate them with all manner of complex legal issues. With these personal qualities and external pressures, it is no small task to capture this group's attention. Faced with such a daunting endeavor, we need to learn as much as we can about what appellate judges want.[6]

1.1   Judicial Audience Characteristics and Preferences

In 2002 Georgetown Professor Kristen Robbins Tiscione gave us some answers: She conducted an empirical study of federal judges' brief-writing preferences. She surveyed all sitting federal judges at the district court, circuit court, and Supreme Court level, with a 46 percent response rate.[7] Many others have written anecdotally about how to persuade judicial audiences.[8] Together, these sources give us, in Professor Tiscione's words, "the inside scoop" on what judges really want from briefs.

Tiscione found that the four most important goals of persuasive brief writing from the court's perspective are: (1) identifying the legal issue for decision; (2) informing the court about controlling legal authority; (3) making the best arguments for the client; and (4) refuting the opponent's best arguments.[9] But the judges said lawyers regularly fall short of the third and fourth goals. About these failings, two themes stood out. First, the judges said high-quality legal analysis and good organization are the two most important aspects of brief writing, in that order—ahead of tone, style, and mechanics. Second, the judges said lawyers consistently fail to deliver on two particular aspects of legal analysis: (1) they do not consistently use the law to their advantage; and (2) they ignore weaknesses in their arguments.[10]

1.2   Writing Qualities Valued by Judges

These laments are troubling, but they also reflect an opportunity. Writers who can deliver a thorough, persuasive, and nuanced analysis via a well-organized and tightly written brief will have an edge. According to the judicial respondents, good legal analytical and organizational skills translate into five distinct qualities, each of which markedly increases your brief's influence:

- Using the law only as needed to advance your arguments
- Explaining what authorities mean in the context of your case
- Exploiting deeper connections between the precedent and your case and dealing with weaknesses head-on
- Focused, streamlined arguments
- Clear, concise writing devoid of redundancy and verbosity

First — Knowing how to use the law means discussing the law only as necessary to make your argument — no more, and no less.[11] Too many writers, especially less experienced ones, drone on about the law in a treatise-like fashion and don't end up using most of that law to argue for a specific result in their case.[12] Another version of this problem is the serial case-brief argument, where the writer simply describes the facts, holding, and reasoning of several cases and never synthesizes those cases into coherent legal principles.[13] In sum, the law should "set the stage" or lay the foundation for your argument, and authorities should be limited to that essential use.

Second — To make clear the law's import, you must explain what the authorities mean in a given context.[14] Be explicit about how and why the authorities dictate a result in your own case, rather than listing authorities and facts next to each other and hoping the court will tie them together. After all, just because you know in your head why the cases are good for you doesn't make that self-evident to the court. The best briefs, then, will marry the law and facts, showing how they work together to produce a favorable result.

Third — Sophisticated legal analysis goes beyond throwing precedent at the court.[15] High-level analysis uses the full range of pertinent authorities, extracts the purposes underlying their legal principles, and then exploits their deeper connections, not just their surface-level similarities.[16] Sophisticated legal analysts take these deep connections and thematic threads and fashion creative arguments and analogies from them.[17] A sophisticated analysis is also two-sided; it does not gloss over weaknesses, oversimplify, or overstate the law but deals head-on with these complexities, including the contrary arguments that they might support.[18]

Fourth — Judges want a tight, focused argument structure, with no extraneous points, paragraphs, sentences, or words knocking it off course.[19] Simply put, judges want the complex made simple and streamlined. They want to be able to follow your analytical trajectory with ease, for one point to lead effortlessly to the next, and for each step forward in the progression to answer their next natural question. In this respect, "you have to spoon-feed the judge,"[20] and it makes sense, given the cognitive and time demands of the appellate court's reading burden. For the same reason, other prized organizational qualities include introductory paragraphs, roadmaps that preview arguments, and starting off with the strongest argument.[21]

Fifth — Judges place a premium on clarity, conciseness, and clean writing.[22] Though we might have gleaned that without a study, the judges' responses yield a taxonomy of just how advocates' writing goes wrong in these respects. To begin with, advocates too often say the same thing in different words.[23] Redundancy not only adds length, it detracts from the tight argument quality that judges crave. Advocates also make unnecessary arguments.[24] This, too, results in long, unfocused briefs, and makes judges feel as though their time is being wasted.[25] Just as often, advocates fail to put in the revision time needed to crystallize their thinking. When this happens, advocates write around the issues and use imprecise words, missing what they really want to convey. They craft meandering prose unconstrained by the strong headings, topic sentences, and unified paragraphs needed to communicate their thinking efficiently.[26] Verbosity is the other culprit.[27] Too many lawyers just don't know how to (or won't) pare down their language. And so judges are assaulted by multiple prepositional phrases stacked up on one another, wordy sentences that take forever to make meaning, clunky phrases, hyperbolic adverbs, and all other manner of space-hogging clutter.

Practice Alert #1
Spotting Bad Brief Writing

In the online companion, you will find an excerpt from an appellate brief that exhibits some of the writing flaws discussed in Tiscione's study. Your task is to identify and improve on these flaws.

REFLECTION, DISCUSSION, AND CHALLENGE QUESTIONS

Judicial Audience

- Why do you think the problems cited in Tiscione's study persist even for writers who are law graduates, many of them experienced practitioners? Is it insufficient writing training, bad habits, lack of ability, fuzzy thinking, a lack of time, or unwillingness to sharpen their thinking? Or some combination of the above?
- Why do you think a judge wants to be "spoon fed" so that she doesn't have to work too hard to understand a brief? How does this quality set judges apart from other audiences you have written for? How have your other writing audiences been similar?
- Think about a "bad brief" that you have read or written. Why was it so ineffective? Was the analysis inadequate, the organization poor, or the writing unclear or bloated? Did the writing lose credibility because the work product was sloppy? In retrospect, how do you think that brief could have been improved?

Section 2   "Logic Plus" (Rhetoric, Applied Storytelling, Persuasion Theory)

Empirical studies and anecdotal observations of judicial preferences are not the sole sources of persuasion strategy. The disciplines of rhetoric, applied storytelling, and cognitive psychology-based persuasion theory have just as much to say about influencing a judicial audience. This section defines the major brief-writing contributions of each discipline, followed by expert brief examples that demonstrate their techniques.

2.1   Rhetoric: Persuasion Through Audience Connection

Lawyers use a very specific genre of rhetoric: the rhetoric of advocacy, whose aim is to sway a decisionmaking audience using the best available means of persuasion.[28] Rhetoric has shaped brief writing in many ways, each embedded in the chapters of this book:

- It conceived the three-way rhetorical situation of audience, purpose, and occasion.[29]
- It originated what we now think of as the major parts of a brief—issues, facts, summary of argument, argument, and conclusion.[30]
- It offered methods for discovering the available arguments.[31]
- It gave us reasoning and argument patterns.[32]
- It set the parameters for the formal style of legal brief writing.[33]
- It introduced the aesthetics of pleasing style, what we think of as rhetorical techniques.[34]

Here, we focus on rhetoric's best-known contribution to brief writing: the modes of persuasion.

According to Aristotle, persuasion's central goal is to create a "psychic connection" between speaker and audience.[35] A writer makes that connection through both artistic and inartistic means of persuasion. The inartistic means are what the outside world gives us—facts and law—while the artistic means are what we, as skilled advocates, add to the equation.[36] The artistic means break down into three modes of persuasion: pathos, ethos, and logos.[37]

Logos is the appeal to the mind; it is the brief writer's deployment of reasoning, proof, and structure to persuade with sound, consistent, and complete arguments.[38] Pathos is the appeal to emotion, although those appeals are never bald in appellate brief writing. Instead, briefs use pathos to put the reader in a certain mindset, appealing to the reader's beliefs and values about conduct and situations.[39] Brief-style pathos emerges in policy and equity arguments,[40] the use of narrative and metaphor,[41] and stylistic elements,[42] among other techniques. Ethos is the appeal through character, primarily the speaker's, but also the central players in the case.[43] Character is often thought of as credibility, defined by the core traits of personal goodness, likeability, knowledge, and authority.[44] An effective persuasive communicator must use all three modes, in a mix appropriate to the audience and occasion.[45]

In keeping with these teachings, brief writers use logos, ethos, and pathos in discrete sections and throughout the entire brief, sometimes separately, and sometimes in combination. Often, these appeals start with the writer's portrayal of the parties, as in this appellate brief from the well-known Facebook litigation saga:[46]

ARTISTIC MEANS OF PERSUASION

Portrayal of the Parties in Facebook v. Connect U

This appeal arises from the settlement of rancorous litigation on two coasts. On one side were Appellees Facebook, Inc., and its founder and CEO Mark Zuckerberg. On the other side were Appellants, who founded a failing competitor of Facebook called Connect U. The CU Founders claimed that they had the idea for Facebook first, and Facebook stole their idea. Facebook denied those claims, and for its part, accused Connect U and its founders of unlawfully infiltrating its systems, stealing millions of email addresses, and then spamming them. During a global mediation, the parties signed a "Term Sheet and Settlement Agreement." . . .

Surrounded by a bevy of lawyers, CU Founders signed the deal. Then they suffered a bout of settler's remorse. They ask this Court to relieve them of the deal they struck to plunge back into scorched-earth litigation.

Appealing to ethos, the writers use characterization to build up Zuckerberg and Facebook and to take down the CU Founders. Zuckerberg is the "founder and CEO" of Facebook — whose success needs no elaboration — while the CU Founders are not named or identified as executives; their notable trait is founding a "failing competitor." The CU Founders' claims and actions sound immature, from the playground-ish "they had the idea for Facebook first" to needing a "bevy of lawyers" to "suffer[ing] a bout of settler's remorse." In contrast, Facebook's claims and actions are portrayed as mature and substantial, from its detailed accusations against Connect U to standing by the settlement agreement. The writers also launch a combined pathos-logos-ethos appeal, counting on a negative reaction to CU's breach of the settlement agreement that prolonged the litigation, which cuts against both legal standards and judicial values. Notice that most of these factual details are not legally relevant to whether Connect U breached the agreement. They are there for motivation, rather than justification.[47]

Brief writers use the artistic means of persuasion not only to portray the parties in a certain light but also to influence the judges' views of the legal claims, apart from their logical soundness and legal validity. These appeals often run through multiple sections of the brief. As examples of this technique, below are three excerpts from a U.S. Supreme Court brief submitted by BMW of North America in a consumer fraud case.[48] This brief challenged a large punitive damage award arising from BMW's failure to disclose post-import refinishing on its automobiles before distributing them to dealers and consumers. Let's start with the issue statements:

ARTISTIC MEANS OF PERSUASION

Issue Statement in BMW v. Gore

Whether the Alabama Supreme Court, having found that the jury's $4,000,000 punitive damages verdict unconstitutionally punished petitioner for hundreds of transactions that occurred entirely outside of Alabama, was obligated, but failed, to provide a meaningful remedy for that violation.

Whether the $2,000,000 remitted punitive exaction, which is 500 times respondent's compensatory damages, is so excessive as to violate the Due Process Clause of the Fourteenth Amendment.

The precise damage amounts, spelled out in numerals rather than prose, have direct pathos value. Those are shocking numbers, even for federal judges. Likewise, describing the high punitive-to-compensatory ratio within the issue statement compounds the reader's sense of gross excess. In the first issue, the writers add an ethos and logos attack on the Alabama Supreme Court, making it look illogical and careless at the same time. Without these persuasive appeals, the first issue might read something like this: "Whether the state supreme court failed to provide a meaningful remedy for the jury's unconstitutionally large punitive damages award, which punished petitioner for transactions that occurred outside of Alabama." This issue fairly conveys the legal question, but fails to persuade.

Similar appeals to pathos and ethos run through the Statement of Facts:

ARTISTIC MEANS OF PERSUASION

Statement of Facts in BMW v. Gore

In their journey from the assembly line to the dealer's showroom, automobiles occasionally experience minor damage requiring repair or refinishing. The question then naturally arises whether, or in what circumstances, the fact of repair or refinishing should be disclosed to the dealer or to the retail purchaser of the automobile. . . .

[N]umerous states have adopted disclosure thresholds. The vast majority, including Alabama (which enacted its statute after the trial in this case), require disclosure only if any repairs or refinishing cost more than 3% (or some higher percentage) of MSRP. . . . In this case, a jury found that BMW's disclosure policy constituted fraud under Alabama law. . . .

In 1990, Ira Gore, a medical doctor specializing in oncology, purchased a 1990 BMW 535i from German Auto in Birmingham, Alabama, for $40,750.88. Dr. Gore drove his car for approximately nine months before taking it to Slick Finish, an independent automobile detailing shop. He was not dissatisfied with the car's overall appearance; nor had he noticed any problems with, or flaws in, the car's paint. He simply wanted to make the car look "snazzier than it would normally appear." The proprietor of the detailing shop, Leonard Slick, informed Dr. Gore that his car had been repainted.

It turned out that the automobile purchased by Dr. Gore had sustained superficial paint damage. . . . In keeping with its nationwide policy, BMW had not disclosed the repairs to German Auto because the cost of those repairs—$601—was substantially less than 3% of the MSRP for the vehicle. . . .

The jury . . . award[ed] Dr. Gore $4,000 in compensatory damages and $4 million in punitive damages. [The Alabama Supreme Court upheld the award of punitive damages but reduced the amount to $2 million.]

After reading these facts, one wonders why Dr. Gore should be getting so much money from BMW for imperceptible paint flaws. The writers establish BMW's ethos by showing it was ahead of the curve, conforming to the strictest state disclosure standards and adopting its 3% policy even before the State of Alabama did. Pathos comes in when the writers point out that Alabama later passed a law contrary to the jury's verdict, making the high punitive damages seem especially unfair. Compounding the unfairness is the seemingly trivial harm to Dr. Gore, who is portrayed as a high-maintenance, wealthy man trying to extract yet more money from a deep pocket. Our attention is diverted from the fact that the small magnitude of damage is legally irrelevant; only the lack of disclosure matters. But as a result of these appeals to pathos and ethos, the reader already has a favorable mindset before reading a word of logical argument.

The writers perpetuate the appeal to pathos when they reach their first overtly argumentative section. As with the issue statements, numerals are used for their affective punch, from describing the award to its juxtaposition with other figures:

ARTISTIC MEANS OF PERSUASION

Summary of Argument in BMW v. Gore

The $2 million punitive damages award must be set aside for the independent reason that it is grossly excessive in violation of the Due Process Clause. The punishment is a breathtaking 500 times the actual and potential harm allegedly suffered by Dr. Gore and is 35 times the harm to all 14 Alabama BMW owners. In addition, the punitive damages are 1,000 times the civil penalty for violating Alabama's repair disclosure statute and over 70 times the maximum penalty that could be imposed for 14 violations. . . .

Some cases do not lend themselves well to these sorts of pathos appeals, and the parties might lack natural ethos as well. This leaves the writers to rely on logos as the primary persuasive tool. They may also focus their ethos and pathos appeals away from the parties and onto the personas of nonparty actors and the authoritative sources for their arguments.

In the examples below, from U.S. Supreme Court briefs filed in Burrage v. United States, the parties argue over the proper causation standard for when "*death . . . results* from the use of [a controlled substance]" trafficked by a defendant.[49] The defendant was a heroin dealer, and the victim who purchased the drugs and died after taking them was a long-time drug user. Neither actor offers much pathos or ethos value. On top of that, the arguments were highly technical, parsing statutory language, medical testimony, and causation jurisprudence to argue whether the defendant's heroin dealing had to be merely a "contributing cause" or rise to the level of a "but-for" and proximate cause of the victim's death. The table below, which compares the parties' point headings, reveals the heavily logos-based nature of the arguments. They persuade through syllogistic structure and analytical break-downs of the statute and causation doctrine.

ARTISTIC MEANS OF PERSUASION

Logos in Burrage v. United States

Petitioner's (Defendant's) Brief[50]	Respondent's (Government's) Brief[51]
II. Contributing cause is not sufficient for a conviction for distribution of drugs resulting in death 　A. The text of § 841 does not support a contributing cause standard. 　B. If "death results" can be read as requiring only a contributing cause, then the statute is gravely ambiguous and the rule of lenity applies. 　C. But-for cause is required and is not satisfied by a contributing causation standard.	II. As a matter of causation in fact, death resulted from the use of the heroin petitioner distributed because that heroin was a contributing cause of the victim's death by mixed-drug intoxication. 　A. Like many criminal laws, the "death results" provision does not require strict but-for causation. 　　1. Criminal law generally does not insist on but-for causation. 　　2. "Contributing cause" is the appropriate test for causation in fact. 　　3. The "death results" provision is satisfied by a showing that use of the controlled substance contributed to the victim's death. 　B. Petitioner was properly convicted under the "death results" provision.

The briefs do make pathos and ethos appeals, but they center on Congress, society at large, and the testifying experts. The government's brief casts Congress in the ethos role, pointing out that the "death results" provision was passed in the mid-1980s in response to the "crisis and . . . plague" of America's drug problem.[52] The brief goes so far as to use a lawmaker's floor debate reference to basketball star Len Bias's drug overdose death.[53] The brief also relies on the ethos of the CDC and its statistics on current drug overdose deaths.[54] None of these facts is strictly legally relevant to the proper causation standard. But they set a compelling backdrop for motivating the court to choose a looser causation requirement.

In the defendant's brief, the writers exploit the ethos and logos value of medical expert testimony, even breaking down into bullet-point form the several factors that the medical examiner deemed to have contributed to the victim's death.[55]

Both parties invoke the inherent credibility of venerable criminal law scholar Wayne LaFave, using his commentary to support their respective causation standards.[56] The defense also relies on the authoritative ethos of the many cases and commentators deeming proximate cause a "bedrock rule of both tort and criminal law."[57] In its parry to this argument, the government points out that "the court below held to the contrary, as has every other court of appeals to consider the question."[58] Both are common techniques to show the weight behind the argument, separate from the validity of the argument itself.

Practice Alert #2
Using the Artistic Means of Persuasion

This exercise in the online companion asks you to analyze a brief excerpt that uses pathos, ethos, and logos appeals. You will identify those attributes and consider how they are effective or ineffective for the rhetorical situation.

2.2 Applied Storytelling and Cognitive Psychology: Persuasion Through Stories and Schemas

How applied storytelling and cognitive psychology inform appellate persuasion. Rhetoric's artistic means of persuasion complement another logic-plus approach that can win over judicial audiences: the use of stories. Storytelling, also called narrative reasoning, works through the same channels as pathos, ethos, and logos, influencing both emotion and cognition.[59] Whether examined through the lens of applied storytelling or cognitive psychology-based persuasion theory, the potential power of narrative on appellate decisionmaking is undeniable.[60] This subsection briefly introduces the applied storytelling and cognitive psychology disciplines as relevant to narrative reasoning, explains what narrative reasoning means in briefs — it extends far beyond a good statement of facts — and shows why narrative reasoning persuades. It ends with effective storytelling examples from expert appellate briefs.

An emerging discipline with roots in law and literature,[61] applied storytelling examines stories as persuasive devices.[62] This discipline aims to discern how storytelling influences audiences in the everyday practice of law,[63] and to unearth the deep structures and hidden themes that make stories so persuasive.[64] Cognitive psychology seeks to understand how stories persuade through schema.[65] Schema are cognitive structures in the mind that make sense of the world by folding new knowledge into an existing framework.[66] They are mental energy-saving devices that give us the ability to efficiently convert novel information and situations into scenarios that we already understand.[67] They operate largely under the radar, without conscious thought.[68]

As applied to appellate briefs, the narrative reasoning these disciplines refer to is not just the client's story told in the statement of facts, although Chapter 9 addresses the use of narrative in that section of an appellate brief. Here, we refer to narrative in a much broader sense, contemplating everything from a meta-narrative that pervades the entire brief to a micro-narrative that begins and ends within a single argument section.[69] These narratives may well tell the client's story, but they may also tell a story about the law or a much broader phenomenon within which the appellate case is situated.[70] Whatever the narrative's scope, it has defining features that set it apart from other persuasive devices. In the simplest terms, a narrative tells of "a character's struggles to overcome obstacles and reach an important goal."[71] Its central elements are character, conflict, theme, setting, and plot.[72] Setting in a brief is largely predetermined by place and time,[73] and we take up theme in Chapter 9. Here, we focus on the other elements that become malleable in the brief writer's hands: character, conflict, and plot.

Elements of narrative in appellate briefs. In almost every appeal, there is a protagonist, an antagonist, and conflict between them, requiring movement towards a resolution.[74] Depending on whom she represents, a lawyer will cast these roles and the conflict differently. Her client may be the little guy, a David confronting a Goliath.[75] Her opponent might portray the same parties as the revered leader and the interloper. The Facebook v. Connect U example in the previous section takes that tack against the upstart Connect U. The BMW v. Gore example in that section defines a different conflict: a successful law-abiding enterprise threatened by an opportunistic individual seeking to empty its deep pockets. But the featured characters need not be people. They can be institutions and reified ideas such as legal principles.[76] Constitutional amendments can be protectors, laws can be unyielding authority figures, and confusing common law developments can be the Keystone Cops. Nor are brief characters limited to predictable archetypes. For example, scholars have discussed how to cast domestic violence victims as heroes rather than victims,[77] and how to make the law the villain and the court the hero in post-conviction appeals.[78]

Just as important as character and conflict is the lawyer's construction of plot, or story structure.[79] Plot is concerned with what happens and in what order, and with cause and effect.[80] Brief-writing plots tend to begin either with chaos in search of resolution, or with a comfortable stasis that is suddenly thrown off, and seeks to be righted.[81] Recurring plotlines in brief writing include the quest, the rebirth, and the tragedy.[82] For example, Professor Linda Edwards makes a compelling case that the Petitioner's argument section in Miranda v. Arizona was structured as a birth story, telling the tale of "growing law" whose natural culmination was the right to counsel during an interrogation.[83] Analyzing the argument's structure, Edwards observes that it meticulously constructed the right-to-counsel doctrine from counsel at trial in federal court, to counsel at trial in state court, to counsel at arraignments and proceedings, to counsel at pre-arraignment investigations.[84] By then, the Court was predisposed to close the final gap in the law with the right to counsel during interrogations.[85] The birth story framework had made this holding seem the next logical step in the doctrinal evolution, not a radical new right.

As an example of a quest plotline, Professor Jennifer Sheppard points to the Petitioner's brief in Gideon v. Wainwright.[86] Here, pre-*Miranda*, the writers could not use the birth story motif. Instead, Gideon was portrayed as the everyman laboring towards the "distant, all-important goal" of the basic right to counsel, with the State of Florida cast as the antagonist.[87] Like Gideon, the state of the law was also in crisis, and the writers argued with urgency, using commonsense and policy appeals to convince the Court to join Gideon's quest and end the crisis once and for all by recognizing this vital right.[88]

Why narrative persuades on appeal. It is a fair question to ask why storytelling should work in appeals. After all, we are often told that judges are coldly logical and objective, immune to such so-called parlor tricks.[89] The answer is threefold. First, stories work because they appeal to schemas buried deep within our minds, outside the realm of conscious thought.[90] We organize stories into schema just like other information — in fact, humans are predisposed to translate their experiences into narrative terms.[91] We relate to stories far more than abstract principles.[92] Regulation writers and Restatement drafters recognize this; that is why their rules are often accompanied by narrative examples.[93] Brief writers who use stock stories well-known and established within the culture — such as birth, rescue, and quest — have an even greater advantage.[94] For once the reader recognizes that story, schemas take over and the reader forms judgments and resolutions consistent with that story, sometimes at the expense of the individual story's unique characteristics.[95] That can be used to the writer's advantage, or it can be a trap for the unwary. All of this counsels brief writers to carefully pair the deeper logic of storytelling with traditional logical argument.[96]

Stories also work because narratives are innate ways of understanding human experience.[97] As evolutionary psychologists have explained, humans are just as much feeling machines as thinking machines.[98] Indeed, we are adapted to benefit from narrative.[99] Intuitively, stories persuade because they are interesting, they have surrounded us from birth to adulthood, and they are imbued with strong emotions, values, and beliefs.[100]

Preliminary empirical evidence supports the power of story to influence judges and law clerks reading appellate briefs. Professor Ken Chestek conducted a small study in which he compared the persuasive effects of "narrativized" briefs to briefs making a purely logical argument.[101] He prepared briefs on both sides of a fictional dispute, one logos-based and one narrativized brief for each side.[102] The narrativized or story briefs used the story elements described above, while the logos briefs omitted or minimized them; Chestek kept all other aspects of the briefs constant.[103] Using a double-blind protocol, Chestek distributed the briefs and a survey to 95 participants, consisting of appellate judges, clerks, practitioners, and law professors.[104] Asked which briefs were more persuasive for the position being advocated, 64.2 percent of all respondents preferred the story briefs, and 57.6 percent of the appellate judges and clerks had this same preference.[105] On the other side, only 30.5 percent of respondents and 36.4 percent of the judge-clerk respondents preferred the pure logos briefs.[106] Although the small sample size begs further study, it is a starting point for confirming the persuasive benefits of narrative reasoning.

Contemporary examples of narrative briefs. Further evidence that narrative reasoning works is its common appearance in contemporary expert appellate briefs. A compelling example is the Appellees' submission to the Ninth Circuit in Perry v. Schwarzenegger, the case that challenged California's Proposition 8. Below is an excerpt from the introduction, which exemplifies the brief's approach.

STORYTELLING EXAMPLE ⎯⎯⎯⎯⎯⎯⎯⎯⎯⎯⎯⎯⎯⎯⎯⎯⎯⎯⎯⎯

Introduction in Perry v. Schwarzenegger[107]

This case is about marriage, "the most important relation in life," Zablocki v. Redhail, 434 U.S. 374, 384 (1978), and equality, the most essential principle of the American dream, from the Declaration of Independence, to the Gettysburg Address, to the Fourteenth Amendment.

Fourteen times the Supreme Court has stated that marriage is a fundamental right of all individuals. This case tests the proposition whether gay and lesbian Americans among us should be counted as "persons" under the Fourteenth Amendment, or whether they constitute a permanent underclass ineligible for protection under that cornerstone of our Constitution.

The unmistakable, undeniable purpose and effect of Proposition 8 is to select gay men and lesbians — and them alone — and enshrine in California's Constitution that they are different, that their loving and committed relationships are ineligible for the designation "marriage," and that they are unworthy of that "most important relation in life."

The characters and conflict in this story are sharply drawn and sagely cast. The narrative has relatable protagonists, the gay and lesbian Americans "among us," whose relationships are just as loving and committed and worthy of marriage as heterosexual partnerships. Proposition 8 (not the people of California, mind you) is the antagonist that has upset the stasis in which gay and lesbian Americans had the same marital rights as everyone else, creating a crisis in which gays and lesbians alone have suddenly become ineligible for that right, "the most important in life." The writers show that this insider/outsider designation is inaccurate, unfair, and downright cruel, not to mention against federal law. This sets up a persecution narrative, a stock story with many correlates in history, bringing with it the strong feelings and values that accompany the telling and hearing of those stories. But there are other important characters as well: the historical and legal benchmarks of our democracy mentioned in the first paragraph, all of which federal appellate judges hold in high regard and desire to maintain. In this narrative, Proposition 8 is just as serious a threat to those institutions as it is to gay and lesbian Americans. Stasis will be restored only if the Court recognizes that same-sex relationships are worthy of equal dignity under these well-established norms.

Another contemporary example, the Petitioner's brief in Lawrence v. Texas, took a page from the *Miranda* brief, using elements of a birth story plotline. The Petitioners were a same-sex couple prosecuted under Texas's "Homosexual Conduct" law for engaging in sexual relations in Lawrence's home. Arguing that the Texas law unconstitutionally infringed the Petitioners' due process rights to privacy and liberty, the first subsection is titled: "Well-Established Protections for Intimate Relationships, Bodily Integrity, and the Privacy of the Home Converge in This Vital Freedom." We surveyed this same section back in Chapter 6, analyzing its logos reason selection and sequencing. Now we can see how the writers paired traditional logical argument with the deeper logic of storytelling. Like the *Miranda* writers, the *Lawrence* writers tell the story of two strands of due process law — privacy and liberty — that have grown over time to become robust protectors against intrusive government actions. The chart below shows the structure of this story by reproducing the section's topic sentences.

STORYTELLING EXAMPLE

Topic Sentences in Lawrence v. Texas Argument[108]

- All adults have the same fundamental liberty interests in their private consensual sexual choices. This fundamental protection is rooted in three well-recognized aspects of personal liberty — in intimate relationships, in bodily integrity, and in the privacy of the home.
- The Court has recognized that "choices to enter into and maintain certain intimate human relationships must be secured against undue intrusion by the State because of the role of such relationships in safeguarding the individual freedom that is central to our constitutional scheme."
- The adult couple whose shared life includes sexual intimacy is undoubtedly one of the most important and profound forms of intimate association.

- Sexual intimacy is "a sensitive, key relationship of human existence, central to family life, community welfare, and the development of human personality."
- State regulation of sexual intimacy also implicates the liberty interest in bodily integrity.
- Control over one's body is fundamentally at stake in sexual relations, involving as they do the most intimate physical interactions conceivable.
- Even without physical entry by the police, Section 21.06 directly invades the privacy of the home by criminalizing the private intimate contact taking place there.
- Denying the existence of a liberty interest in private consensual adult sexual activity would give constitutional legitimacy to the grossest forms of intrusion into the homes of individuals and couples.
- The core liberty interests at stake in this case are a bulwark against an overly controlling and intrusive government.

The next topic sentence completes the growth arc. It reads: "There Is No Constitutional Exception to Liberty for Gay and Lesbian American Citizens."[109] From this argument we see that the liberty interest in private consensual sexual choices, the liberty interest in bodily integrity, and the privacy of the home are already all there in the law, and that sexual intimacy is and always has been vital to our social and psychological beings. All that remains is for the Court to take the next step in the growth trajectory and recognize how these protections and norms naturally "converge" in the right to engage in consensual same-sex relationships. The Petitioners offered this growth narrative as a powerful counterstory to the Respondents' contention that they were seeking an unprecedented fundamental right to sodomy.[110] And as we know, the Petitioners' strategy worked.

Our final example uses another narrative technique, introduced in Chapter 4: the narrative of reversal. In this story, the lower court has erred at every turn, the opposing party has gotten away with unacceptable behavior, and as a consequence, the client has suffered an unfairness that can be righted only with reversal. As you will see, this is not a strategy of throwing everything up on the ceiling and seeing what sticks; it is a restrained technique that demands careful selection of issues and arguments.

In this brief, whose organization we viewed from a structure perspective back in Chapter 6, the argument plotline centers on cause and effect rather than chronology. It tells the story of fundamental wrongs that caused a defendant's drug conviction. The three antagonists are the lower court, a police officer, and a confidential informant. The informant's dark, blurry video of alleged drug buys was narrated on the stand by the officer, who wasn't present but added his own "color commentary" to the video. This police-narrated video was admitted at trial even though the informant — the defendant's own nephew with whom he was feuding — never testified. Six months before trial, the informant had a change of heart and submitted an affidavit and a video stating he'd fabricated the whole story and admitting that he'd never captured his uncle dealing drugs on film. The court refused to admit this recantation, calling it hearsay. As the point headings below reveal, the brief's narrative of reversal has a central point of departure: the informant's absence from trial. The plot's other contributions are the trial court's refusal to appoint the defendant a new attorney, and its refusal to suppress a statement the defendant made without *Miranda* warnings.

STORYTELLING EXAMPLE

Point Headings in United States v. Wilke

I. The district court improperly admitted a video without requiring the testimony of the confidential informant who made it.
   A. The government's failure to call the confidential informant as a witness violated Wilke's Sixth Amendment right to confront his accuser.
      1. The video was a statement.
      2. The video was testimonial.
      3. The video was hearsay.
   B. The government failed to make reasonable efforts to locate the confidential informant, thereby violating Wilke's right to present a complete defense.
   C. Even if the video was properly admitted, allowing Officer Dudley to narrate it was more prejudicial than probative.
II. The district court's erroneous denial of Wilke's motions for new counsel merits reversal.
   A. The district court abused its discretion in refusing to grant Wilke's motions.
      1. Wilke's motions were timely.
      2. The district court's inquiry into Wilke's motions was insufficient.
      3. Wilke and his attorney suffered a breakdown in communication that prevented an adequate defense.
      4. Other factors evidence an abuse of discretion.
   B. The district court's abuse of discretion requires reversal.
      1. If this court requires a harmlessness showing, *Chapman* should apply.
      2. Reversal is warranted even under *Strickland*.
      3. If this Court does apply *Strickland*, the test is met here and requires reversal.
III. The statement Officer Dudley obtained from Wilke violated his *Miranda* rights.

In this narrative of reversal, the characters are all human, in contrast to the two previous examples, which revolved more around ideas and institutions. Here, the defendant's stasis was upset by his vindictive (but later regretful) nephew, and then the chaos was compounded by a trial judge and a complicit police officer who refused to right the nephew's wrong and whose actions suggest a desire to convict at constitutional cost. The point headings tell a story about each character's responsibility for fundamental trial errors: Section I narrates the confidential informant-created errors; Section II tells the story of an error for which the lower court is solely responsible; and Section III tells how the officer's actions merit reversal. Read together, these sections recall the stock "person vs. machine"[111] conflict and the stock "David vs. Goliath"[112] story, in which the government's immense power is joined with a vengeful person's vendetta to rob an unwitting man of his constitutional rights. Notice how the writers carefully pair this deeper storytelling logic with characteristic logical argument. The arguments and reasons center on legal elements and alternatives, even as they weave a narrative of reversal.

Storytelling is not without its pitfalls.[113] Brief writers must be attuned to the limiting and harmful effects of stock stories. The facts and law may not live up to the stock stories that the writer wishes to evoke.[114] Over-stated archetypes, ill-fitting formulaic structures, and oversimplified facts can also doom a brief's effectiveness.[115] A writer, intending to tell a favorable story, might even trigger unfavorable stock stories embedded within the judges' minds.[116] Finally, no story is good enough to overcome failings in logic or to be effective with logic that does not fit the story's substance and structure.[117] As such, brief writers must be cautious when deploying narrative reasoning's powerful force.

Practice Alert #3
Storytelling Techniques

In the online companion, you will find excerpts from opposing briefs, each of which casts the parties' dispute in different storytelling terms. You will identify the storytelling elements in each brief and evaluate the strengths and weaknesses of each side's approach.

2.3 Metaphor: A Prized Tactic of Rhetoricians, Storytellers, and Persuasion Theorists

The subject of increasing study in legal advocacy scholarship,[118] metaphors are a persuasive tool whose power finds collective support in the disciplines of rhetoric, storytelling, and persuasion theory. Metaphors are figures of speech that use a word or phrase that applies to one thing to refer to something else, suggesting a resemblance between the two.[119] Law is full of conceptual metaphors. For example, balancing tests, elements, and long-arm statutes all speak of legal ideas in figurative terms.[120] Indeed, metaphors are used so often in legal writing that we barely notice them: the law as a seamless web, cases with progeny, corporations with veils, and constitutions with penumbras,[121] and even the marketplace of ideas.[122] These examples may now seem trite or overused.[123] But when these metaphors were first introduced, they had real persuasive power.[124]

Many classical rhetoricians found metaphors attractive because they are subtle, concise, and engaging, facilitating insights that logic alone could not achieve.[125] These rhetoricians also recognized that metaphors are downright pleasing.[126] From a cognitive science perspective, metaphors work just as stories do, by creating mental shortcuts.[127] Metaphors draw on embedded knowledge in our existing schemas to help us grasp new concepts or think about a known concept in a different way.[128] Metaphor, then, is not just a pleasing figure of speech, but helps the reader reason through categorization and inference, drawing on her ability to see one thing as another.[129]

Metaphor works in appellate advocacy for several reasons. The most basic is that metaphors already pervade legal discourse; they are an accepted tool for communicating law's ideas. Metaphors also work in appellate advocacy because they reflect how we think about abstract ideas[130] and help to simplify; after all, the legal concepts in most appeals are abstract and complex. Moreover, law, especially at the appellate level, is an interpretive enterprise, and metaphors can aid interpretation by helping readers to see what pure logic might not reveal.[131] Finally, metaphor works on appellate audiences because of its stealth. Metaphors, unlike legal positions, are not explicitly announced. They derive power from their beneath-consciousness operation on our schemas.[132]

The Perry v. Schwarzenegger introduction we saw earlier in this section uses metaphors to advance its message and to make the abstract concrete. That introduction makes the Fourteenth Amendment a "cornerstone" of constitutional protection, then proceeds to explain how Proposition 8 "selects" gay men and women and "enshrines" their underclass status in the California Constitution.[133] These architectural metaphors, which evoke structural permanence, turn high concepts into tangible things. In doing so, they drive home that Proposition 8 would forever remove gay and lesbian Californians from the fundamental protections given to everyone else and consign them to a state-mandated rights dungeon. The writers also use metaphor to characterize their opponents' failure to make their record in the court below: "Proponents and their amici now attempt to *fill the evidentiary void* they left in the district court with an *avalanche* of non-record citations, distortions, and misstatements regarding the proceedings below...."[134] *Void* and *avalanche* imply a desperate, scattershot, last-minute scrambling, and this language appeals to its audience. Few audiences know and dislike belated and indiscriminate information dumps as much as federal judges.

Practice Alert #4
Evaluating Metaphors

This exercise in the online companion reprints short passages from several briefs, each of which uses metaphor in a different way. You will be asked to identify where the metaphors are, what comparisons they suggest, whether they are fresh or overused, and whether they are effective in advancing the writer's argument.

As with storytelling, metaphors should be used with caution. Their effectiveness depends on how well the metaphor corresponds to its subject.[135] Ill-fitting or far-fetched metaphors breed reader skepticism and detract from the writer's credibility and message.[136] In addition, metaphors can oversimplify rather than illuminate; they do not always fairly capture the ideas and abstractions to which they aim to bring vividness and clarity.[137] As Justice Cardozo wrote long ago, "Metaphors in law are to be narrowly watched, for starting as devices to liberate thought, they end often by enslaving it."[138] So keep your metaphors fresh and precise, don't let them box you into characterizations that can work against you, and think through the implied comparisons for accuracy and consistency with your arguments.[139]

REFLECTION, DISCUSSION, AND CHALLENGE QUESTIONS

"Logic Plus"

- When you read this section, were you surprised to learn that appellate lawyers use these logic-plus persuasion techniques? What do you think about these techniques? Is your viewpoint different now than it was before you read this section?

- Think about the best brief you have ever read. Pull up the brief if you can find it. Did the brief make appeals to ethos and pathos, in addition to logos? Did it tell a story, and if so what was that story? Did the brief writer use any metaphors, and if so, what was your reaction to them?

- Think about the appeal you are handling right now. Can you envision using any of these logic-plus techniques in your brief? If so, sketch out your ideas for them. What pitfalls might you encounter if you use these techniques?

Endnotes

1. *See, e.g.,* Jack M. Balkin & Sanford Levinson, *Law and the Humanities: An Uneasy Relationship,* 18 YALE J.L. & HUMAN. 155, 177 (2006); Linda L. Berger, *Studying and Teaching "Law as Rhetoric": A Place to Stand,* 16 LEGAL WRITING: J. LEGAL WRITING INST. 3, 5-6 (2010); Gerald Wetlaufer, *Rhetoric and Its Denial in Legal Discourse,* 76 VA. L. REV. 1545, 1560 (1990); James Boyd White, *Law as Rhetoric, Rhetoric as Law: The Arts of Cultural and Communal Life,* 52 U. CHI. L. REV. 684, 684 (1985).

2. Linda L. Berger, *Applying New Rhetoric to Legal Discourse: The Ebb and Flow of Reader and Writer, Text and Context,* 49 J. LEGAL EDUC. 155, 157-58 (1999); J. Christopher Rideout & Jill J. Ramsfield, *Legal Writing: A Revised View,* 69 WASH. L. REV. 35, 56-61 (1994); Nancy Soonpaa, *Using Composition Theory and Scholarship to Teach Legal Writing More Effectively,* 3 LEGAL WRITING: J. LEGAL WRITING INST. 81, 86-87 (1997).

3. DOUGLAS LAVINE, CARDINAL RULES OF ADVOCACY: UNDERSTANDING AND MASTERING FUNDAMENTAL PRINCIPLES OF PERSUASION 206-07 (2002) (discussing the Yale Attitude Change approach created by Carl Hovland).

4. Steven D. Jamar, *Aristotle Teaches Persuasion: The Psychic Connection,* 8 SCRIBES J. LEGAL WRITING 61, 70-71 (2002); Richard A. Posner, *Convincing a Federal Court of Appeals,* 25 No. 2 LITIG. 3, 3 (1999) ("A sense of audience is the key to rhetorical effectiveness.").

5. *See* Leonard J. Garth, *How to Appeal to an Appellate Judge,* 21 No. 1 LITIG. 20, 23 (1994); Posner, *supra* note 4, at 3; Antonin Scalia & Bryan A. Garner, *Making Your Case: The Art of Persuading Judges,* 94-MAY A.B.A. J. 41, 43, 47 (2008).

6. Michael Frost, *Ethos, Pathos & Legal Audience,* 99 DICK. L. REV. 85, 92-94 (1994).

7. Kristen K. Robbins Tiscione, *The Inside Scoop: What Federal Judges Really Think About the Way Lawyers Write,* 8 LEGAL WRITING: J. LEGAL WRITING INST. 257, 261 (2002). Although the study was not limited to appellate judges, trial and appellate judges' responses were largely consistent.

8. *See, e.g.,* Garth, *supra* note 5; Michael J. Higdon, *The Legal Reader: An Exposé,* 43 N.M. L. REV. 77 (2013); Susan H. Kosse & David T. ButleRitchie, *How Judges, Practitioners, and Legal Writing*

Teachers Assess the Writing Skills of New Law Graduates: A Comparative Study, 53 J. Legal Educ. 80 (2003); Posner, *supra* note 4; Scalia & Garner, *supra* note 5.

9. Robbins Tiscione, *supra* note 7, at 265 (80% of judicial respondents found these goals "essential or very important").

10. *Id.* at 264-72.

11. *Id.* at 278-82.

12. *Id.* at 268; Higdon, *supra* note 8, at 102.

13. Robbins Tiscione, *supra* note 7, at 268-69.

14. *Id.* at 268; Higdon, *supra* note 8, at 108.

15. Posner, *supra* note 4, at 4; *see* Robbins Tiscione, *supra* note 7, at 268-70.

16. Posner, *supra* note 4, at 62; Robbins Tiscione, *supra* note 7, at 268-70.

17. Robbins Tiscione, *supra* note 7, at 268-70; Scalia & Garner, *supra* note 5, at 44.

18. Higdon, *supra* note 8, at 118-19; Robbins Tiscione, *supra* note 7, at 269.

19. Robbins Tiscione, *supra* note 7, at 264, 273-74.

20. Posner, *supra* note 4, at 3.

21. Robbins Tiscione, *supra* note 7, at 273-74.

22. *Id.* at 278-82.

23. Higdon, *supra* note 8, at 104-05; Robbins Tiscione, *supra* note 7, at 281.

24. Higdon, *supra* note 8, at 103-04; Robbins Tiscione, *supra* note 7, at 281-82.

25. Higdon, *supra* note 8, at 105; Robbins Tiscione, *supra* note 7, at 281.

26. Higdon, *supra* note 8, at 98-100; Robbins Tiscione, *supra* note 7, at 280; Scalia & Garner, *supra* note 5, at 43.

27. Higdon, *supra* note 8, at 88; Robbins Tiscione, *supra* note 7, at 280.

28. Brett G. Scharffs, *The Character of Legal Reasoning*, 61 Wash. & Lee L. Rev. 733, 745 (2004); Wetlaufer, *supra* note 1, at 1557-58.

29. Rhetorical situation is also defined in terms of exigence, audience, and constraints. Linda Levine & Kurt M. Saunders, *Thinking Like a Rhetor*, 43 J. Legal Educ. 108, 116 (1993).

30. Frost, *supra* note 6, at 94-99.

31. Michael Frost, *Greco-Roman Legal Analysis: The Topics of Invention*, 66 St. John's L. Rev. 107, 113 (1992).

32. Kurt M. Saunders, *Law as Rhetoric, Rhetoric as Argument*, 44 J. Legal Educ. 566 (1994) (discussing Chaim Perelman & Stephen Toulmin); *see also* Frost, *supra* note 31, at 109; Levine & Saunders, *supra* note 29, at 109-11; Scharffs, *supra* note 28, at 744-45.

33. Wetlaufer, *supra* note 1, at 1557-58.

34. Frost, *supra* note 31, at 114; *see also* Steven D. Jamar. *Aristotle Teaches Persuasion: The Psychic Connection*, 8 Scribes J. Legal Writing 61, 61-62 (2002); Craig D. Tindall, *Rhetorical Style*, 50-Jun Fed. Law. 24, 24-25 (2003).

35. Jamar, *supra* note 4, at 62.

36. John W. Cooley, *A Classical Approach to Mediation–Part I: Classical Rhetoric and the Art of Persuasion in Mediation*, 19 U. Dayton L. Rev. 83, 89-92 (1993); Leigh Hunt Greenshaw, *To Say What the Law Is: Learning the Practice of Legal Rhetoric*, 29 Val. U. L. Rev. 861, 876 (1995).

37. Cooley, *supra* note 37, at 89-92.

38. *Id.* at 92; Scharffs, *supra* note 28, at 752 (citing Aristotle, On Rhetoric, *in* Aristotle on Rhetoric: A Theory of Civic Discourse (George A. Kennedy ed. & trans., Oxford U. Press 1991)).

39. Cooley, *supra* note 37, at 92.

40. Levine & Saunders, *supra* note 29, at 119.

41. Berger, *supra* note 1, at 38-43.

42. Frost, *supra* note 31, at 124-25.

43. Berger, *supra* note 1, at 38-43.

44. Cooley, *supra* note 37, at 92; Jamar, *supra* note 4, at 73.

45. Frost, *supra* note 6, at 86-87.

46. Brief of Appellees at 1, Facebook, Inc. v. Connect U., Nos. 08-16745, 08-16873, 09-15021 (written by Orrick, Herrington & Sutcliffe LLP).

47. Richard K. Neumann, Legal Reasoning and Legal Writing: Structure, Strategy, and Style 305 (5th ed. 2005).

48. Brief for the Petitioner, BMW of North America, Inc. v. Gore, No. 94-896 (written by Mayer Brown and Walston, Stabler, Wells, Anderson & Bains).

49. 21 U.S.C. § 841(b)(1)(C) (2012).

50. Brief for the Petitioner at iv, Burrage v. United States, No. 12-7515 (written by Dickey & Campbell and Sidley Austin).

51. Brief for the Respondent at 3, Burrage v. United States, No. 12-7515 (written by the Solicitor General's Office.).

52. *Id.*

53. *Id.* at 4.

54. *Id.* at 4-5.

55. Brief for the Petitioner at 6, Burrage v. United States, No. 12-7515 (written by Dickey & Campbell and Sidley Austin).

56. *Id.* at 34; Brief for the Respondent at 18-26, Burrage v. United States, No. 12-7515 (written by the Solicitor General's Office.).

57. Brief for the Petitioner at 19, Burrage v. United States, No. 12-7515 (written by Dickey & Campbell and Sidley Austin).

58. Brief for the Respondent at 18-26, Burrage v. United States, No. 12-7515 (written by the Solicitor General's Office).

59. Jennifer Sheppard, *Once Upon a Time, Happily Ever After, and in a Galaxy Far, Far Away: Using Narrative to Fill the Cognitive Gap Left by Overreliance on Pure Logic in Appellate Briefs and Motion Memoranda*, 46 Willamette L. Rev. 255, 256 (2009); J. Christopher Rideout, *Storytelling, Narrative Rationality, and Legal Persuasion*, 14 Legal Writing: J. Legal Writing Inst. 53, 55 (2008).

60. *See infra* notes 89-106.

61. *See generally* Ruth Anne Robbins, *An Introduction to Applied Storytelling and to This Symposium*, 14 Legal Writing: J. Legal Writing Inst. 3 (2008).

62. J. Christopher Rideout, *Discipline-Building and Disciplinary Values: Thoughts on Legal Writing at Year Twenty-Five of the Legal Writing Institute*, 16 Legal Writing: J. Legal Writing Inst. 477, 487 (2008).

63. Robbins, *supra* note 61, at 7.

64. Rideout, *supra* note 62, at 488.

65. *See, e.g.*, Robert P. Burns, A Theory of the Trial 159 (1999); Rideout, *supra* note 59, at 55, 58; *see also* Jerome Bruner, Acts of Meaning 45 (1990).

66. Sheppard, *supra* note 59, at 259 (citing Richard K. Sherwin, *The Narrative Construction of Legal Reality*, 18 Vt. L. Rev. 684, 700 (1994) and Linda L. Berger, *How Embedded Knowledge Structures Affect Judicial Decision Making: A Rhetorical Analysis of Metaphor, Narrative, and Imagination in Child Custody Disputes*, 18 S. Cal. Interdisc. L.J. 259, 265 (2009)).

67. Berger, *supra* note 66, at 265; Sherwin, *supra* note 66, at 700.

68. Berger, *supra* note 66, at 262-63. This chapter discusses cognitive psychology's brief-writing contributions through schema theory, while Chapter 10's section on counterarguments discusses the contributions of priming theory and inoculation theory, both methods of managing negative information.

69. Linda H. Edwards, *Once Upon a Time in Law: Myth, Metaphor, and Authority*, 77 Tenn. L. Rev. 883, 883-84 (2010).

70. *Id.* at 884.

71. Kenneth D. Chestek, *Judging by the Numbers: An Empirical Study of the Power of Story*, 7 J. Ass'n Legal Writing Directors 1, 8 (2010) (quoting Kendall Haven, Story Proof: The Science Behind the Startling Power of Story 3 (Libs. Unlimited 2007)).

72. Edwards, *supra* note 69, at 888; Sheppard, *supra* note 59, at 270.

73. Sheppard, *supra* note 59, at 279.

74. Edwards, *supra* note 69, at 886.

75. Sheppard, *supra* note 59, at 271-72.

76. *Id.* at 274-76 (2009); *see* Edwards, *supra* note 69, at 890.

77. *See* Ruth Anne Robbins, *Harry Potter, Ruby Slippers and Merlin: Telling the Client's Story Using the Characters and Paradigm of the Archetypal Hero's Journey*, 29 Seattle U. L. Rev. 767, 779-82 (2006).

78. Philip N. Meyer, *Are the Characters in a Death Penalty Brief Like the Characters in a Movie?*, 32 Vt. L. Rev. 877, 893-94 (2008).

79. Sheppard, *supra* note 59, at 280.

80. *Id.*

81. Edwards, *supra* note 69, at 886-87.

82. Sheppard, *supra* note 59, at 283.

83. Edwards, *supra* note 69, at 891-98.

84. *Id.* at 895-96.

85. *Id.* at 896.

86. Sheppard, *supra* note 59, at 284-95.

87. *Id.* at 283, 286 (citing Christopher Booker, The Seven Basic Plots: Why We Tell Stories (2004)).

88. *Id.* at 286-93.

89. *Id.* at 256-57 (quoting Robbins, *supra* note 77, at 769; citing Herbert A. Eastman, *Speaking Truth to Power: The Language of Civil Rights Litigators*, 104 Yale L.J. 763, 809 (1995)).

90. Edwards, *supra* note 69, at 891; Sheppard, *supra* note 59, at 263-64.

91. J. Christopher Rideout, *Storytelling, Narrative Rationality, and Legal Persuasion*, 14 Legal Writing: J. Legal Writing Inst. 53, 57 (2008) (quoting Jerome Bruner, Acts of Meaning 47 (Harv. U. Press 1990)).

92. Lea B. Vaughn, *Feeling at Home: Law, Cognitive Science, and Narrative*, 43 McGeorge L. Rev. 999, 1016-17 (2012).

93. *Id.*

94. Sheppard, *supra* note 59, at 261-63.

95. *Id.*

96. *Id.* at 264 (2009).

97. Rideout, *supra* note 91, at 55, 57-59.

98. Vaughn, *supra* note 92, at 1024.

99. *Id.* at 1028.

100. Chestek, *supra* note 71, at 3; Sheppard, *supra* note 59, at 264; Vaughn, *supra* note 92, at 1000-01, 1028.

101. Chestek, *supra* note 71, at 8.

102. *Id.* at 10-11.

103. *Id.* at 10-17.

104. *Id.* at 17-18.

105. *Id.* at 19-20.

106. *Id.*

107. Brief for Appellees at 1, Perry v. Schwarzenegger, No. 10-16696 (written by Gibson, Dunn & Crutcher and Boies, Schiller & Flexner).

108. Brief of Petitioners at 11–15, Lawrence v. Texas, No. 02-102 (written by Jenner & Block, Lambda Legal Defense and Education Fund, and Williams, Birnberg & Anderson).

109. *Id.* at 16.

110. Respondent's Brief at 13-14, Lawrence v. Texas, No. 02-102 (written by Charles A. Rosenthal, et al.).

111. Sheppard, *supra* note 59, at 270 (citing JOSIP NOVAKOVICH, FICTION WRITER'S WORKSHOP 74-75 (1995); Brian J. Foley & Ruth Anne Robbins, *Fiction 101: A Primer for Lawyers on How to Use Fiction Writing Techniques to Write Persuasive Fact Sections*, 32 RUTGERS L.J. 459, 469 (2001); JANET BURROWAY & ELIZABETH STUCKEY-FRENCH, WRITING FICTION: A GUIDE TO NARRATIVE CRAFT 263 (7th ed. 2007)); *see id.* at 273 (recognizing that it is not "difficult to imagine the government or a large corporation as an automaton that seeks to crush its smaller, weaker opponent under the weight of its might").

112. Sheppard, *supra* note 59, at 272.

113. *See generally* Steven J. Johansen, *This Is Not the Whole Truth: The Ethics of Telling Stories to Clients*, 38 ARIZ. ST. L.J. 961, 979-92 (2006); Steven J. Johansen, *Was Colonel Sanders a Terrorist?: An Essay on the Ethical Limits of Applied Legal Storytelling*, 7 J. ASS'N LEGAL WRITING DIRECTORS 63 (2010); Jeanne M. Kaiser, *When the Truth and the Story Collide: What Legal Writers Can Learn from the Experience of Non-Fiction Writings About the Limits of Legal Storytelling*, 16 LEGAL WRITING: J. LEGAL WRITING INST. 163, 169-72 (2010); Jennifer Sheppard, *What If the Big Bad Wolf in All Those Fairy Tales Was Just Misunderstood?: Techniques for Maintaining Narrative Rationality While Altering Stock Stories That Are Harmful to Your Client's Case*, 34 HASTINGS COMM. & ENT. L.J. 187, 193-94 (2012).

114. Sheppard, *supra* note 59, at 265; Sheppard, *supra* note 113, at 194-95.

115. Sheppard, *supra* note 59, at 264; *see* Kaiser, *supra* note 113, at 169-72; Sheppard, *supra* note 113, at 195; *see also* Steven J. Johansen, *supra* note 113, at 991-92.

116. Sheppard, *supra* note 59, at 267; *see also* Sheppard, *supra* note 113, at 189.

117. *See* Johansen, *supra* note 113, at 981-82; Kaiser, *supra* note 113, at 182; Sheppard, *supra* note 113, at 193-94 (2012).

118. *See, e.g.*, Berger, *supra* note 1, at 38-40; Linda L. Berger, *What Is the Sound of a Corporation Speaking? How the Cognitive Theory of Metaphor Can Help Lawyers Shape the Law*, 2 J. ASS'N LEGAL WRITING DIRECTORS 169, 172-73 (2004); Edwards, *supra* note 69, at 883-84; Thomas Ross, *Metaphor and Paradox*, 23 GA. L. REV. 1053, 1053-54 (1989); Michael R. Smith, *Levels of Metaphor in Persuasive Legal Writing*, 58 MERCER L. REV. 919, 919 (2007).

119. *See* MICHAEL R. SMITH, ADVANCED LEGAL WRITING: THEORIES AND STRATEGIES IN PERSUASIVE WRITING 199-200 (2d ed. 2008).

120. Smith, *supra* note 118, at 929.

121. Michael Frost, *Greco-Roman Analysis of Metaphoric Reasoning*, 2 LEGAL WRITING: J. LEGAL WRITING INST. 113, 113 (1996); *see also* Ross, *supra* note 118, at 1053.

122. Berger, *supra* note 118, at 171.

123. *See id.* at 180; Frost, *supra* note 121, at 113.

124. Berger, *supra* note 118, at 169.

125. Frost, *supra* note 121, at 118-19.

126. *Id.* at 121.

127. Berger, *supra* note 118, at 174-77.

128. Berger, *supra* note 1, at 39.

129. Berger, *supra* note 118, at 176.

130. Edwards, *supra* note 69, at 888 (2010) (citing GEORGE LAKOFF & MARK JOHNSON, METAPHORS WE LIVE BY 47 (1980)).

131. Berger, *supra* note 118, at 179-80.

132. *Id.* at 177.

133. Brief for Appellees at 1-2, Perry v. Schwarzenegger, No. 10-16696 (written by Gibson, Dunn & Crutcher, LLP & Boies, Schiller & Flexner, LLP).
134. *Id.* at 5.
135. Frost, *supra* note 121, at 122 (1996).
136. *Id.* at 134.
137. Smith, *supra* note 118, at 923.
138. Berkey v. Third Ave. Ry. Co., 155 N.E. 58, 61 (N.Y. 1926).
139. Frost, *supra* note 121, at 134.

9 The Writing Phase: Framing Your Client's Story

This chapter takes the lessons from Chapter 8 and applies them to critical initial brief sections: issue statements and fact statements. More than any other, these sections employ the "logic plus" tools of rhetoric, storytelling, and cognitive psychology to make a strong first impression on the court. Their collective goal is to communicate the story of the appeal from a distinct point of view or cognitive "frame" — a frame that will prime the court to receive the rest of your brief's message favorably, lingering through the court's decisionmaking.

Loosely defined, *framing* means influencing an audience to consume your message from a particular perspective.[1] Framing makes combined appeals to the artistic means of persuasion and draws on storytelling and cognitive psychology as well. Here's a simple example. An 18-year-old singing phenom who wants to pursue a lucrative recording contract instead of attending college might frame the issue as one of missed opportunity in the present: If he rejects the contract to attend college, he may lose his only opportunity to make it big in the industry. His parent may set a different frame, asking her son to take the long view. The music industry will still be there when he graduates. When he turns 40, will he be more likely to regret a college education or to view it as a short time period in which he gained the maturity and training to build a lasting music career? The related concept of *priming* means presenting early information in a way that influences the reader's reactions to later information.[2] Priming studies abound in the field of cognitive psychology: Wine shoppers primed with French music were more likely to buy French wine;[3] subjects primed with a pleasant cleaning scent were more likely to clean their messy eating space;[4] and game players primed with a briefcase (versus a backpack) played more competitively.[5] In the context of issue statements and fact statements, framing[6] and priming[7] have the same power. They allow advocates to make the most of early positioning and point of view when judicial attention is high and the judicial mind is motivated to learn and judge.[8]

Section 1 addresses the foundation for framing and priming in briefs — the appeal's theory and theme, which manifest early and run throughout the document. Section 2 discusses how to capture theory and theme in issue statements, along with a concise and precise expression of exactly what the court must decide in the appeal. Section 3 moves to fact statements. Here, we take Chapter 8's

161

discussion of narrative down to the micro level and discuss strategies for telling the client's story in a way that furthers your theory and theme but remains true to the record, complete, and well-organized.

Keep in mind that many advocates write the issues and fact statements last, after drafting the argument section and considering in depth the appeal's theory and theme. The writing sequence for these sections may also depend on your instructor and whether you are taking a simulation or clinic course. Whether you draft these sections early or late in the writing process, this chapter will guide you.

Section 1 Refining the Appeal's Theory and Theme

Earlier chapters have referred to theory and theme, but we have not yet defined them. That is because theory and theme development is an ongoing task whose seeds are sown in the record digest process, germinate in the planning and learning phase, and bloom in the writing phase. Theme, especially, is in constant flux, being shaped and reshaped as you learn more and think more about your appeal. It is refined and finalized in the writing process.

1.1 Defining Theory and Theme

The word *theory* refers to the *legal basis* underlying your arguments.[9] This includes not only your overarching theory — the narrative of reversal or affirmance — but also the discrete legal results you seek on each issue. The overarching theory is a big-picture concept; it results from the interplay of your separate issues.[10] Consider a criminal appeal where the defendant raises three issues: (1) The trial court curtailed the defendant's cross-examination of a prosecution witness on privacy grounds; (2) the trial court refused to allow the defendant access to potentially exculpatory evidence; and (3) prosecutorial misstatements occurred during closing arguments. The overarching legal theory would be one of due process, the denial of a fair trial. In turn, each legal issue has its own discrete theory that plays into the overarching theory. For example, the cross-examination issue's legal theory would incorporate the governing legal test: The witness's privacy interest was outweighed by the defendant's due process right to explore her potential bias.

Theme, too, is holistic, but it is much more akin to the storytelling examples analyzed in Chapter 8. It has no strict connection to the law or logic.[11] Theme stems from the emotional elements underlying your appeal that, when pulled together, communicate a central message and prompt a "visceral reaction that allows the reader to be immersed in the story."[12] It is useful to think of theme in the following terms: "This is a case about _____." or "My client wins because _____."[13] In the above example, in contrast to his due process theory, the criminal defendant's theme could be one of government over-reaching — a man who constantly tried to present his defense but was thwarted by the court and the prosecutor at each turn.[14] More examples are in the chart below, which distinguishes between the theory and the theme in three of Chapter 8's expert brief excerpts.

Examples: Theory vs. Theme

	Legal Theory	Theme
Facebook v. Connect U	The parties' settlement agreement was clear, complete, and enforceable, and Connect U breached that agreement by filing suit.	Sophisticated businesses must be held to their promises; settler's remorse is no ground for reneging on a deal.
Perry v. Schwarzenegger	Proposition 8's opposite-sex definition of marriage deprives gay and lesbian individuals of their fundamental right to marry and violates their equal protection rights.	This country has long rejected arbitrary discrimination; Proposition 8 is just discriminatory group subordination in another form and it must be rejected as well.
Lawrence v. Texas	Criminalizing adult consensual sex violates due process rights to liberty and privacy and equal protection of the law.	The government has no business regulating the intimate choices of consenting adults, much less singling out one group for worse treatment on that basis.

Theory works on judicial readers because it appeals to law and logic and imposes coherence on the brief.[15] Theme works on judicial readers because it appeals to the familiar and "ties all the complex analysis into an emotional trigger."[16] That, in turn, enhances both comprehension and retention — particularly retention of details.[17] Judges acknowledge as much, by expressing a clear preference for briefs that incorporate both of these unifying concepts.[18] As such, it is worth your time to devote effort to choosing and refining both theory and theme.

1.2   Choosing an Appellate Theory and Theme

As between theory and theme, the latter is more difficult to develop. Articulating a legal theory comes fairly naturally to advocates intensively trained in reading and applying law. But developing a theme requires the writer to think and communicate from two points of view — the client's and the court's — and to merge her own with the former.[19] It also requires her to think outside the law and back to more basic human motivations, skills that law school doctrinal courses rarely develop.[20] But if you have done the intellectual work that the planning phase requires, you should be well positioned to choose and refine your theme. It is now a matter of combining that work with the proper mindset. To tap into a thematic mode of thinking, consider the following checklist of ideas, adapted from the combined wisdom of two noted persuasion scholars:[21]

    ☑ What are my client's most powerful and memorable emotional facts?

    ☑ What specific emotions will they evoke in the judicial reader?[22]

☑ Can I frame the theme around an injustice requiring the court's intervention (appellants)?[23]

☑ Can I frame the theme around the concept that the legal system cannot remedy every wrong or that maintaining the status quo is the most desirable outcome (appellees)?[24]

☑ Can I frame the theme around results that will represent a significant gain or loss?[25]

☑ What human motivations and behaviors lie at the core of this appeal — redemption, resilience, courage, betrayal, greed, over-reaching, dishonesty, exclusion, intrusion, or something else? (The list is virtually infinite.)

☑ Can I frame a theme that accounts for all the facts — good and bad, details and all?

☑ Though not a law-based concept, is my theme consistent with the potential legal theories in my appeal?

☑ Putting aside the law and facts, can I frame a theme that is plausible and consistent with common sense?

The last three items reflect the risk of crafting a theme. The first six may generate lofty ideas about what went right or wrong and why, leading to overblown themes that generate skepticism rather than emotions that pair with reason to drive favorable decisions. At bottom, you are an officer of the court writing a legal document governed by the rules of ethics and evidence, and your credibility is at stake.[26] Your theme must be consistent with the cold hard facts and cannot selectively exclude those that don't fit it. So be wary of the overstated archetypes, the ill-fitting themes, and getting carried away by creativity and the fun of story crafting. The theme's objective is to form a cohesive unit of otherwise loosely connected events, not to exaggerate or appeal to emotion at accuracy's expense.[27]

1.3 Expressing Theory and Theme in Appellate Briefs

Once you have settled on theory and theme, you must consider how to express them in your brief. Communicating theory is the more overt exercise. The magic legal and factual words must surface in each section to make clear the driving legal theory, and the overarching theory must spring from your choice of legal issues and the argument's structure. The theme is more subtle. It is pervasively insinuated, not limited to particular sections or words. In fact, themes are rarely articulated verbatim in the brief's language, but are instead communicated through framing in multiple sections. Consider the following excerpts from the BMW v. Gore Petitioner's brief. We looked at these excerpts back in Chapter 8; now let's view them from a theory and theme perspective.

| EXAMPLE | Theory and Theme in BMW v. Gore |

Issue Statement

Whether the $2,000,000 remitted punitive exaction, which is 500 times respondent's compensatory damages, is so excessive as to violate the Due Process Clause of the Fourteenth Amendment.

Statement of Facts

In their journey from the assembly line to the dealer's showroom, automobiles occasionally experience minor damage requiring repair or refinishing. The question then naturally arises whether, or in what circumstances, the fact of repair or refinishing should be disclosed to the dealer or to the retail purchaser of the automobile. . . .

[N]umerous states have adopted disclosure thresholds. The vast majority, including Alabama (which enacted its statute after the trial in this case), require disclosure only if any repairs or refinishing cost more than 3% (or some higher percentage) of MSRP. . . . In this case, a jury found that BMW's disclosure policy constituted fraud under Alabama law. . . .

In 1990, Ira Gore, a medical doctor specializing in oncology, purchased a 1990 BMW 535i from German Auto in Birmingham, Alabama, for $40,750.88. Dr. Gore drove his car for approximately nine months before taking it to Slick Finish, an independent automobile detailing shop. He was not dissatisfied with the car's overall appearance; nor had he noticed any problems with, or flaws in, the car's paint. He simply wanted to make the car look "snazzier than it would normally appear." The proprietor of the detailing shop, Leonard Slick, informed Dr. Gore that his car had been repainted.

It turned out that the automobile purchased by Dr. Gore had sustained superficial paint damage. . . . In keeping with its nationwide policy, BMW had not disclosed the repairs to German Auto because the cost of those repairs — $601 — was substantially less than 3% of the MSRP for the vehicle. . . .

The jury . . . award[ed] Dr. Gore $4,000 in compensatory damages and $4 million in punitive damages. [The Alabama Supreme Court upheld the award of punitive damages but reduced them to $2 million.]

Summary of Argument

The $2 million punitive damages award must be set aside for the independent reason that it is grossly excessive in violation of the Due Process Clause. The punishment is a breathtaking 500 times the actual and potential harm allegedly suffered by Dr. Gore and is 35 times the harm to all 14 Alabama BWM dealership owners. In addition, the punitive damages are 1,000 times the civil penalty for violating Alabama's repair disclosure statute and over 70 times the maximum penalty that could be imposed for 14 violations. . . .

Point Headings

II. The $2 Million Dollar Punishment Is Grossly Excessive and Therefore Violates the Substantive Component of the Due Process Clause
   A. The $2 Million Dollar Punishment for What BMW Did to Dr. Gore, or Even for All of BMW's Alabama-Related Conduct, Far Exceeds an Amount Reasonably Necessary to Accomplish Alabama's Interests in Punishment and Deterrence
      1. The ratio of punitive damages to actual or potential harm to the plaintiff
      2. The nature of the alleged misconduct
      3. Civil penalties for comparable misconduct
      4. Financial condition
   B. The Fact That BMW's 3% Disclosure Threshold Affected Sales to Numerous Other BMW Owners Does Not Justify the $2 Million Punishment

Together, these brief sections establish an overarching legal theory: that the punitive damages award exceeded the Alabama court system's power to punish and deter corporations doing business there, in violation of the Due Process Clause. That theory first shows up in the issue statement's language naming the damage amounts and invoking the Fourteenth Amendment. It appears in the fact statement's characterization of the paint damage as minimal and the punitive damages as grossly excessive by comparison. The summary of argument and the point headings are more explicit about the legal theory, as they must be. The first sentence of the summary says precisely what the due process legal theory is, and then the point headings break down the analytical components of the due process violation using key legal terms — ratio, misconduct, comparison to civil penalties, and financial condition.

The theme tying into this legal theory is that awarding massive punitive damages for minimal product flaws is an unfair punishment — one that encourages greedy opportunism, rather than deterring consumer fraud. Notice how communicating theme is a more subtle endeavor. Not once do the writers call Dr. Gore greedy or opportunistic, or say outright that it was unfair to make BMW pay $2 million for barely perceptible paint flaws. Rather, those thematic messages are communicated by framing. The issue statement carries this theme by using numerals and a mathematical equation to highlight the disparity between the compensatory and punitive damage awards. In the statement of facts, Dr. Gore's greedy opportunism is communicated through his medical specialty and the brand and cost of the car he chose, as well as his strange insistence on — and delay in pursuing — a "snazzier" coat of paint. The

Practice Alert #1
Theory and Theme Exercise

This exercise in the online companion presents excerpts of several sections in a brief, and asks you to identify the theme and theory expressed, and to assess their effectiveness.

excessive punishment message comes through in the facts emphasizing BMW's adherence to most states' disclosure thresholds and Alabama's revised one, along with the superficial nature of the undisclosed paint damage. The summary of argument picks up on the theme by expanding on the issue statement's math equations, as well as using detail and loaded words like "breathtaking" to contrast the maximal punitive award with the minimal damage. The point headings then translate that theme into more overtly legal language, complemented by framing techniques such as the repeated phrase "$2 million punishment" (which appears three times) and calling out Dr. Gore by name.

REFLECTION, DISCUSSION, AND CHALLENGE QUESTIONS

Theory and Theme

- Identify the overarching legal theory in your appeal, and write it out in a sentence. How can you communicate that theory with language, structure, and choice of issues and arguments?
- Write out your answers to the questions in the checklist of theme ideas on page 5. Use those answers to generate at least two plausible themes.
- Now put yourself in your opponent's shoes and answer the same questions from your opponent's perspective. Generate at least two plausible opposing themes.
- Now think deeply about the risks of your theme. As currently framed, is it too hyperbolic, inviting judicial skepticism? Does it conveniently ignore bad facts or bad law? Does it reflect common sense?

Section 2 The Anchor of Your Brief: Issue Statements

Now that you understand theme and theory and have seen how they translate in briefs, it is time to incorporate them into your own drafting process, starting with the issue statements, a term synonymous with questions presented. The issue statement is often the judges' first glimpse into your case. The Question Presented section in a U.S. Supreme Court brief falls on the very first page, even before the table of contents. With its compressed character and up-front placement, the issue statement is an ideal framing and priming vehicle.[28] Nowhere else will the court encounter such an advantageously positioned, concentrated expression of what your case is about. So it is worth drafting and redrafting your issue statements until you perfect them, even if the time spent on them seems disproportionate to their length.[29]

Viewing the issue statements as an anchor in your brief is a helpful metaphor to keep in mind as you set out to draft them. First, issue statements are the first place that a reader turns when she wants to get oriented within your case, using this section to quickly grasp what will follow in the next 50 or so pages of the brief. For that reason, issue statements should be thematic and subtly persuasive. Second, like an anchor, your issue statements will immobilize you, staking out your legal theory and limiting the scope or the breadth of the question that the court will review and decide.[30] Therefore, crafting the issue with precision is vitally important. It cannot be so narrow that it hampers your ability to make effective arguments or so broad that it becomes meaningless. Third, in this compact space, clarity and conciseness are at a premium.[31] This section will explore each issue attribute — thematic and subtly persuasive, precise, clear and concise — in greater depth.

We speak in terms of attributes rather than rules or conventions because aside from these attributes, there is no single right way to craft an issue statement for every brief and every audience.[32] To illustrate this diversity, we first discuss two basic types of issue statements: the traditional one-sentence issue and a form that is gaining momentum in intermediate appellate courts — the multi-sentence issue statement.[33]

2.1   Single-Sentence vs. Multi-Sentence Issue Statements

Choosing a form. The one-sentence issue statement is a familiar form to most. It is a self-contained interrogatory beginning with "whether," "can," "does," "under," or a host of other common verbs or prepositions.[34] After that, the issue typically proceeds from general to specific, identifying the controlling law and then key facts or more specifics about what the court must decide about the law.[35] (Some move in the opposite direction if the facts are especially compelling.) In contrast, A multi-sentence issue typically builds up to the interrogatory with a declarative sentence or two of favorably framed law or facts. The single-sentence issue's advantage is its relative brevity and well-accepted format.[36] The multi-sentence issue's advantage is its ability to avoid syntactical complexity and over-compression that can confuse and distract.[37] To see the difference, consider these two forms of the same issue statement:

Example: Issue Statement Comparison

Single-Sentence	Multi-Sentence
Whether the undefined term "cocaine base" in the five-year mandatory minimum sentencing provision under the 1986 Controlled Substances Act should be expanded to punish all chemically similar formulations of cocaine base as harshly as crack, even if they are less dangerous than crack.	In the Controlled Substances Act, Congress mandated a five-year minimum sentence for defendants convicted of possessing "cocaine base." The Act does not define cocaine base, but Congress passed the statute in 1986 to curb an epidemic spread of crack. Should the Act's mandatory minimum sentencing provision extend to all chemical cocaine bases — even those less dangerous than crack?

One author presents these competing examples to her students each year. Their reactions vary. Some students find the single-sentence issue easier to grasp because it has fewer words and comparatively less detail. This one-sentence format also emphasizes the connections among ideas, expressed through grammatical relationships.[38] Those who disagree remark that the single-sentence issue packs in way too much information for the reader to grasp at once. They say it requires too much setup in the early clauses, whose prepositions must be carefully chosen to express the right relationships, and that the rest of the issue's effort to be precise assaults the reader with detail and no corresponding pause for the reader to absorb it. These students comment that the multi-sentence issue makes plain the underlying logic, allows for a thematic appeal, and packs more punch with the ending question as a result. Indeed, when the legal question is especially complex or requires more background to understand, the multi-sentence format almost always will be the best choice.

But in other appeals, a single-sentence issue may be more effective. Consider the BMW v. Gore issue statement, and what it might look like if converted to the multi-sentence format:

Example: Issue Statement Comparison in BMW v. Gore

Single-Sentence	Multi-Sentence
Whether the $2,000,000 remitted punitive exaction, which is 500 times respondent's compensatory damages, is so excessive as to violate the Due Process Clause of the Fourteenth Amendment.	The Due Process Clause prohibits state courts from imposing punitive damage awards that are excessive and disproportionate to the harm caused. Here, the Alabama Supreme Court affirmed a $2,000,000 punitive damage award that was 500 times the respondent's compensatory damages. Did that award violate the Due Process Clause of the Fourteenth Amendment?

Here, the multi-sentence format's utility is dubious. The legal question is so straightforward, and the facts so arresting, that the first sentence defining due process comes across as "master of the obvious," without any real persuasive weight. In contrast, the single-sentence issue jumps right into its messaging, and loses nothing in comprehension or clarity by pushing the legal hook to the end. Its juxtaposition of law and facts implies the desired result with greater impact and efficiency.

Before you decide on an issue form, you must know your audience. Briefs to the United States Supreme Court nearly always use the one-sentence "whether" format, most likely a product of convention and big-picture legal questions' amenability to that format.[39] Trends in state courts can also implicitly reveal a court's format preference.[40] So, be sure to check court rules and become familiar with the issue conventions in your court. And whichever format you choose for one brief, don't let that choice blindly dictate what you do in perpetuity. Using this section's guidance, think carefully about which format fits the audience, purpose, and occasion of that particular appeal.[41]

REFLECTION, DISCUSSION, AND CHALLENGE QUESTIONS

Single-Sentence vs. Multi-Sentence Issues

- What are your reactions to the single-sentence and multi-sentence issue examples in this section? Do you have a natural aversion to or preference for one over the other?
- Think about your appellate issues and what you want the reader to glean from them. Do your issues lend themselves best to a single sentence or multiple sentences? Why?
- Pick one issue and draft it in both formats. Which one is more effective? Why?

2.2 Thematic and Subtly Persuasive

Acting as anchors, issue statements should ground your brief's theme. An issue devoid of thematic content may be accurate and helpful, but ultimately unpersuasive. At the same time, you must tread softly in comparison to the summary of argument and argument sections. You may not overtly argue in your issue statements; they should be written in a way that suggests your preferred resolution.[42] So you must find a way to generate a high persuasive impact with a low argumentative volume. You can accomplish this with proper framing techniques, such as strategic word choice (particularly vivid and concrete nouns and verbs), sentence structure, and artful selection and description of the law and facts.[43] You will miss the mark if the issue falls back on abstract language, if it essentially answers the question to be decided, or if it uses hyperbolic language.

Consider the following three student examples from the appeal introduced back in Chapter 4, which challenged the conviction of a college student for attempting to make a terrorist threat. One issue was whether a warrantless police search of the student's car exceeded the scope of an inventory, an exception to the warrant requirement permitted only for "caretaking purposes," such as preventing loss of valuables. The issue broke down into two subpoints: (1) Was the inventory of the student's car a pretext for an investigatory search, which requires a warrant? (2) Assuming no pretext, did police exceed the inventory's scope by examining items that lacked obvious value? With this context in mind, decide which issue you find most persuasive, and why. Then read the analysis that follows them.

EXAMPLES

> ### Assessing Issue Persuasiveness
>
> A. Does the Fourth Amendment's inventory exception allow police to conduct an investigatory automobile search without a warrant?
> B. Does the Fourth Amendment's inventory exception allow police to enter the locked car of a person under investigation, search the car, and pick up and read the person's private thoughts written on the back of a loose paper?
> C. Does the Fourth Amendment's inventory exception allow police to conduct a pretextual warrantless automobile search designed to incriminate the owner and to exceed the scope of an inventory by intrusively reading the owner's private writings?

Example A uses such abstract language that it presents a question the law has already answered. If the search is investigatory, by definition a warrant is required; if it is conducted with inventory objectives, then a warrant is not required. The real question is what motivated the officers here — a desire to investigate the owner or to protect his valuables? To convey that focus, the issue needs more concrete language. On top of that, Example A lacks any thematic elements. The tone is even; there is no viewpoint or suggested answer. The nouns and verbs are neutral and nondescript. Nor do we know what drives the writer's legal conclusion that the search was "investigatory," so we are not inclined to agree with it.

Example C represents the other extreme; it is hyperbolic and argumentative. We are told that the search was pretextual, designed to incriminate, and that it exceeded the inventory's scope. What, then, is there for the court to decide? Moreover, we do not know what lies behind those three characterizations; the issue fails to drill down beneath them to expose the concrete facts. Furthermore, the words "designed to incriminate" and "intrusively" go too far. The issue should let the court see through the writer's artful description *how* a desire to find evidence motivated the police and *why* their behavior was so intrusive, instead of being told what to think by use of pejorative labels.

Example B strikes the right balance. It never argues, it only describes and shows with vivid, concrete language, and artful selection, and suggests an answer rather than supplying it. The words "locked car of a person under investigation" suggest that the police had no value-protecting objective (the car locks would take care of that) and that they were too tempted by the ongoing investigation to limit their search to inventory objectives. Likewise, the "private thoughts written on the back of a loose paper" language undermines the police's ostensible value-protecting motive. Notice, too, how the issue mentions only three facts. The goal is not to be comprehensive, but to emphasize the facts that fit the theme and drive the result. Altogether, this issue pushes the court towards the conclusion the advocate seeks (the search was pretextual and excessive in scope) as well as towards a "no" answer to the question (the inventory exception doesn't allow this conduct). But the issue never once veers into argumentative language, abstractions, or conclusory assertions.

Review: Thematic Persuasive Issue Framing

DO	DON'T
Frame the issue to suggest an answer favorable to your client.	Assume the issue to be decided by overtly stating your legal conclusion.
Be selective rather than comprehensive—focus on what fits the theme and drives the result.	Insert details that don't fit the theme or drive the result.
Use strategic word choice and artful description to show rather than tell.	Use argumentative or hyperbolic language or intensifying adverbs.
Use juxtaposition and parallelism to highlight law-fact matchups.	Use abstract or conclusory words that mask their factual backing.

2.3 Precise

Just as the issue statements anchor your theme, they immobilize you by limiting the scope or the breadth of the question that the court will review and decide.[44] Therefore, the issues must be precise, written carefully with an eye towards striking the correct balance between broad applicability and the questions specific to the case facts and the jurisdiction's law. For example, take the issue statement from a recent Supreme Court case, Kingsley v. Henderson:

EXAMPLE

Issue Precision in Kingsley v. Hendrickson

Whether the requirements of a 42 U.S.C. § 1983 **excessive force claim** brought by a plaintiff who was a **pretrial detainee** at the time of the incident are satisfied by showing that the state actor **deliberately used force** against the pretrial detainee and that the use of force was **objectively unreasonable**.

The bold portions reflect crucial decisions in framing the issue to tee up a very precise question. The authors began by limiting the issue to excessive force claims, not all types of § 1983 actions brought by pretrial detainees. Though it might have been tempting to broaden the issue's scope to generate a more sweeping rule, the facts of the case and the Court's preference to make incremental changes in the law necessitated this modifier. The second bold portion—"pretrial detainee"—likewise was an important signal to the Court. It showed that the case was not going to engender a sweeping rule that encompassed all prison civil rights cases. Rather, the case was limited to pretrial detainees, those who are being held awaiting trial, and not convicted prisoners. Because the Court had previously distinguished between these two groups of inmates, it was an important factual distinction to make.

The third and fourth bold portions conveyed the heart of the legal issue: the mental state, if any, that a civil rights plaintiff must prove the jailers harbored. Notice, though, that this portion of the issue is more broadly worded.[45] It neither specifies the constitutional basis for the rule nor catalogues the ways that a plaintiff would make this showing. One of the debated questions in the case was which constitutional provision governed the inquiry: the Fourth Amendment or the Fourteenth. Thus the authors did not commit to a specific constitutional hook in the question presented, leaving room to argue both in the brief. Additionally, some members of the Court had expressed hesitation to expand the scope of the Fourteenth Amendment's substantive due process right, so the authors chose not to specify the precise contours of that right. Finally, notice how the authors used subtle persuasion, suggesting only their side's preferred result: an objective standard, rather than the subjective mental state requirement adopted by the appellate court below.

Consider how even slight changes in the wording or structure of the Question Presented completely alter its meaning, scope, and force, illustrated in three variations:

Original

Whether the requirements of a 42 U.S.C. § 1983 **excessive force claim** brought by a plaintiff who was a **pretrial detainee** at the time of the incident are satisfied by showing that the state actor **deliberately used force** against the pretrial detainee and that the use of force was **objectively unreasonable**.

Variation #1: Whether the requirements of a 42 U.S.C. § 1983 claim are satisfied by a showing that the state actor deliberately used force against the pretrial detainee and the use of force was objectively unreasonable.

Variation #2: Whether the requirements of a 42 U.S.C. § 1983 excessive force claim brought by a plaintiff who was a pretrial detainee at the time of the incident are satisfied by a showing that the state actor deliberately used force against the pretrial detainee and the use of force was objectively unreasonable in violation of the Fourteenth Amendment right to substantive due process.

Variation #3: Whether the court below erred in holding that a plaintiff who is a pretrial detainee must prove that the defendants acted with at least a reckless state of mind when applying force to him in order to prevail in a 42 U.S.C. § 1983 excessive force claim.

Variation 1 omits the excessive force limitation, making the issue's scope unclear, particularly given the wide variety of constitutional violations that § 1983 encompasses. Relegated to a less prominent position in the issue, the important pretrial detainee limitation is deemphasized as well. Variation 2 commits to a Fourteenth Amendment substantive due process legal theory, which is strategically unwise. Variation 3 is too neutral and suggests nothing about the preferred result. It merely criticizes the lower court's rule rather than offer the correct legal standard.

The precision lesson is clear: Make the issue statement's anchoring function work for you rather than against you. Draft carefully and deliberately so that you are not locked into a formulation that fails to capture your desired rule and result.

2.4   Clear and Concise

Notwithstanding its persuasiveness and precision, an issue statement will accomplish nothing if the court cannot understand it.[46] Understanding the issue is a function of its clarity and conciseness. This section discusses both in turn.

Clarity. Several drafting techniques promote issue clarity. These techniques work at three levels: (1) the structural level; (2) the sentence level; and (3) the word level. At the structural level, a clear issue should be ordered logically, putting context before detail. A multi-sentence issue accomplishes this with syllogistic or chronological structure. Consider the following examples of the inventory search issue discussed in Section 2.2.

Example: Issue Clarity — Structure

Clear Version	Unclear Version
The Fourth Amendment protects car owners from unlawful searches by requiring officers to inventory for valuables only, not as a pretext to find incriminating evidence. In this case, a police officer entered Maurice Mutombo's locked car and seized a scrap of paper containing his private musings while Mr. Mutombo was under investigation. Did the officer violate Mr. Mutombo's Fourth Amendment rights?	Mr. Mutombo's private writings on a piece of scrap paper were seized by police officers who entered his locked car and then searched it. Inventory searches, which are conducted to protect valuables, are only allowed when conducted in good faith and without investigatory motives. Did law enforcement violate Appellant's Fourth Amendment rights?

The second issue lacks clarity at all three levels, but its fundamental problem is structural. The factual minor premise comes before the law's major premise, putting detail before context. The reader must literally transpose the first two sentences in her mind to grasp the suggested conclusion. Even the first sentence's chronology is inverted, explaining the seizure before the search. The clear version, by contrast, uses syllogistic structure to lay bare its deductive processes, and tracks the sequence of events.

To maintain clarity at the sentence level, an issue should ideally keep subjects and verbs close together and near the beginning, followed by the sentence's remaining elements. This pushes syntactical complexity towards the sentence's end, after the reader has already grasped the two grammatical elements that hold the most meaning.[47] Although most issues need modifying clauses to achieve precision, too many complex clauses can bog the reader down. If precision or persuasion demands multiple clauses, then use parallel sentence structure to make them manageable for the reader. Also avoid stacked-up prepositional phrases, which tend to string the reader along rather than efficiently conveying the meaning.

Clarity also stems from word choice. In addition to using vivid and strategic words, be as concrete as you can. Keep the actors in your sentences, even if those actors are conceptual or institutional rather than human. Use either proper names or strategic labels for those actors — employer/employee, buyer/seller, company/consumer, government/defendant — rather than appellate procedural labels (Appellant/Appellee), which don't communicate relationships or hold strategic meaning.[48] And watch out for excessive detail or language that assumes reader knowledge about the case. The next example illustrates these sentence- and word-level clarity problems.

Example: Issue Clarity — Sentence and Word Level

Clear Version	Unclear Version
Does the Fourth Amendment's inventory exception allow police to enter the locked car of a person under investigation, search the car, and pick up and read the person's private thoughts written on the back of a loose paper?	When a police officer with investigative motives enters a car that is locked and searches the car, including reading private thoughts on the back side of a loose piece of paper between the front seat and the console, is the Fourth Amendment's inventory exception violated?

The unclear version unnecessarily separates its main subject and verb. We know right away that the issue is about a police officer, but we don't know what the officer did — enter and search — until after we hear about the officer's motive. That motive is a detail that should follow the verb; otherwise the reader must hold on to this information until she figures out what the officer actually did. After that comes yet another clause ("including") with stacked-together prepositional phrases, full of unnecessary details. Finally, notice how two important actors are buried in the unclear version. The Fourth Amendment is a key conceptual actor, but isn't mentioned until the end. The person whose car was searched isn't mentioned at all — and that is the writer's own client. The clear version avoids all of these problems by making every actor concrete, naming those actors near the beginning, and keeping those actors close to concrete parallel action verbs (allow, enter, search, pick up).

For strategic reasons, some issues must depart from the sentence structure orthodoxy. Review the BMW v. Gore issue statement from Section 2.1: "Whether the $2,000,000 remitted punitive exaction, which is 500 times respondent's compensatory damages, is so excessive as to violate the Due Process Clause of the Fourteenth Amendment." Here, the writers use an interrupting clause and push the key legal actor to the end in the name of persuasion. If the reader knows early on that the punitive damages were 500 times the compensatory damages, she encounters the Due Process question ready to rule in BMW's favor. At 22 words, the issue is extraordinarily succinct and free of unnecessary verbiage or detail. So, too, the *Kingsley* issue in Section 2.3, which splits up the statutory subject (§ 1983 requirements) and verb (are satisfied) to capture the key limiting principles early on. Such streamlined, strategically crafted issues can depart from the "rules" without sacrificing clarity.

Practice Alert #2
Issue Statement Drafting Exercise

The online companion contains excerpts of briefs for which you must draft appropriate and persuasive issue statements. It also contains a series of poorly drafted issues and asks you to rewrite them.

Conciseness. The same drafting strategies promote another core attribute: conciseness. A concise issue statement immediately delivers the crucial information that the reader needs to get a handle on the issue and no more; it does not ramble, build up, meander, or dive into detail.[49] By and large, you will accomplish all of these objectives if you keep subjects and verbs together up front, minimize prepositional phrases, use concrete language and active verbs, and make sure that every word counts. But as a backstop, you can target the most common word-wasting culprits directly. After drafting your issue statements, perform a focused edit to weed out the following: (1) passive voice (unless used strategically); (2) double negatives; (3) legalese; (4) verbs turned into nouns (e.g., "conduct an investigation of instead of" "investigate"); and (5) adverbs and adjectives whose meaning can be captured in a more precise noun or verb.

SUMMARY

Drafting Issues with Clarity and Conciseness

- Structural Techniques
  - Use syllogistic or chronological ordering for multi-sentence issues.
  - Sequence to answer the reader's next natural question.
  - Put context before detail.
- Sentence-Level Techniques
  - Keep subjects and verbs close together up front.
  - In general, limit clauses and prepositional phrases to those necessary for precision.
  - Use parallel sentence structure.
- Word-Level Techniques
  - Keep the actors in your sentences, designating them with proper names or meaningful labels.
  - Use concrete, specific words rather than general, abstract words.
  - Use strong active verbs whenever you can.
  - Avoid details that aren't crucial for context or necessary to the result.
  - Perform a focused edit for common verbosity culprits.

Section 3   Priming and Framing in the Fact Statement

If the issue statements are your anchor, the fact statement represents your sails: It should propel your theme and your client's story in a visually arresting way. More than any other section in an appellant's brief, the fact statement is where you have the ability to convey the sense of injustice arising from the decision below, but you must do this without turning the facts into an argument section. And if you are the appellee, you will use this section to cast the appellant in a poor light, undeserving of relief. Whether appellant or appellee, you have two common goals here: to accurately report what happened below and, just as with issue statements, to frame and prime with subtle persuasion. The following pages walk you through the strategies that will allow you to accomplish both.

3.1   Translating Theory, Theme, and Issues into a Compelling Narrative

The fact statement cannot be drafted without keen attention to your theories, themes, and issues. These elements will influence everything from your fact statement's large-scale organization down to precise word choice. And just as with the issue's suggested answer, the fact statement should motivate the court to write a favorable ending to the story—all while remaining free of argument or hyperbole.[50] But knowing that the facts should persuade is one thing; figuring out how to present them to accomplish that objective is another. The first step is to get a handle on the fact statement's three most important narrative components, which were introduced in a broader context back in Chapter 8:[51] conflict, character, and plot.[52] We begin with pre-drafting strategies designed to stimulate your thinking about how to develop each component.

Conflict. The first pre-drafting strategy is to define the basic conflict in your appeal.[53] The conflict drives the theme and maintains the reader's interest in the story, taking advantage of the natural human desire for resolution.[54]

OVERVIEW ————————————————————————————

Basic Conflict Types[55]

- Person vs. Person
- Person vs. Self
- Person vs. Society
- Person (little guy) vs. State (government) or Machine (institutional big guy)
- Person vs. Nature
- Person vs. God

The following chart shows how these stock conflicts can drive expert briefs' themes:

Examples: Conflict Definition in Briefs

	THEME	TYPE OF CONFLICT
Facebook v. Connect U	Sophisticated businesses must be held to their promises; settler's remorse is no ground for reneging on a deal.	(Honest) Person vs. (Dishonest) Person
Perry v. Schwarzenegger	This country has long rejected arbitrary discrimination; Proposition 8 is just discriminatory group subordination in another form and it must be rejected as well.	Person vs. Society
Lawrence v. Texas	The government has no business regulating the intimate choices of consenting adults, much less singling out one group for worse treatment on that basis.	Person vs. State

Keep in mind that defining conflict is not as simple as slotting in the two parties and their legal dispute. The real conflict may be between your client and a law or other force not embodied in a party, such as an addiction. If your client is not naturally sympathetic, it may also be advantageous to frame one side of the conflict as a proxy for your client — perhaps a value, such as individual rights or a free market economy.

After defining your conflict, the next step is to pull it together with your theme, theory, and issue. It is helpful to prepare a chart that tracks all four. Here is an example based on the due process/denial of fair trial appeal example that illustrated theory and theme back in Section 1.1:

Theory, Theme, Issue, Conflict
(Narrative of reversal: due process/denial of fair trial)

	ISSUE 1: CIRCUMSCRIBED CROSS-EXAMINATION	*ISSUE 2*: DENIAL OF ACCESS TO EXCULPATORY EVIDENCE	*ISSUE 3*: PROSECUTORIAL MISCONDUCT DURING CLOSING ARGUMENT
Theory	The trial court unjustifiably invoked a witness's privacy interests as a basis for preventing the defendant's full inquiry into her potential bias.	The trial court violated the defendant's due process rights when it denied him access to probative, impeaching evidence, which was not rendered inadmissible by any other rule of evidence.	The prosecutor's repeated references to the defendant as a predator who should be convicted in order to protect the community violated the defendant's right to a fair trial.

	ISSUE 1: CIRCUMSCRIBED CROSS-EXAMINATION	*ISSUE 2:* DENIAL OF ACCESS TO EXCULPATORY EVIDENCE	*ISSUE 3:* PROSECUTORIAL MISCONDUCT DURING CLOSING ARGUMENT
Theme	Government over-reaching — a man who constantly tried to present his defense but was thwarted by the court and the prosecutor at each turn.	Government over-reaching — a man who constantly tried to present his defense but was thwarted by the court and the prosecutor at each turn.	Government over-reaching — a man who constantly tried to present his defense but was thwarted by the court and the prosecutor at each turn.
Conflict	Person vs. State	Person vs. State	Person vs. State

Character. After you gain this holistic view of how your theory, theme, issue, and conflict interact, the next step is to think more deeply about the characters who generated the conflict — your client or her proxy and the opposing party or whichever force stands on the opposite side of the conflict. This requires translating the stock conflict actors into three-dimensional characters.[56] The objective is to think strategically about their roles, goals, and motivations. Chapter 8 offered several examples: the revered leader protecting his turf against the interloper (Facebook v. Connect U); a successful law-abiding enterprise threatened by an opportunistic individual seeking to empty its deep pockets (BMW v. Gore); and outsider citizens fighting a villainous, repressive law (Perry v. Schwarzenegger) or beseeching the law as hero to combat an overbearing and intrusive government (Lawrence v. Texas).

To develop character roles, you must consider what makes your client (or her proxy) likeable and sympathetic, a person, institution, or concept with good and relatable goals. You must also think about what makes the actor on the other side of the conflict unlikable and unsympathetic, a person, institution, or concept with distasteful goals.[57] Think in particular about how each actor behaved both before and during the conflict, along with their deeper struggles and drives and the means they have used to attain their goals.[58] The supporting players may merit similar character development, depending on how large they loom in the case.[59]

For example, the statement of facts in the due process/denial of fair trial example above developed the defendant's character as an admirable person with impressive goals and achievements. The writers began with the appellant's generosity and work ethic, his lack of criminal history, his close-knit family, and his academic and professional achievements. The alleged victim's character, by contrast, was not developed, save for highlighting inconsistencies and deficiencies in her testimony. Because the theory of the case turned on procedural facts and the theme of government over-reaching, the fact statement also developed the court's and prosecutors' negative traits and goals by detailing their overzealous actions (cutting off cross-examination, refusing to disclose exculpatory evidence, closing argument misconduct). Each character's qualities were present in the record, of course; drafting the fact statement is not a fiction-writing exercise. Nonetheless, this pre-drafting thought about character development will ease your work in collecting and framing the emotionally significant facts discussed below in Section 3.2, as well as in shaping the drafting process.

Plot. Your fact statement does not merely string facts together[60] but presents a cogent and persuasive account of what happened and why. To accomplish this, you must give thought to plot. Usually, in a statement of facts, the plot starts with chaos in search of resolution, or with a comfortable steady state that is suddenly thrown off and seeks to be righted.[61] Beyond that, as Chapter 8 explained, plots can take many forms, including stock plotlines such as the quest, the rebirth, the tragedy, the birth story, the rescue story, overcoming the monster, or rags to riches.[62] But you needn't select any of these stock plotlines, and you shouldn't if none fits your facts. In the due process/denial of fair trial appeal, for example, the fact statement plot began with a paragraph of comfortable stasis, telling the story of a hard-working child of first-generation immigrants rising above his circumstances to earn a law degree from a selective law school, and then building a thriving law practice. This paragraph was followed by an abrupt shift to the chaos — a chance encounter with a woman who later accused him of sexual assault. The chaos extended to the man's arrest, charging, and fundamentally unfair trial. By the end of the fact statement, the court was primed to offer a favorable resolution — reversal of the man's convictions. Ultimately, as we discuss below, your fact statement's plot will be expressed through organization, point of view, and techniques that emphasize and de-emphasize information. But having the plot elements in mind before you write will make for a more effective and efficient drafting process.

Practice Alert #3
Fact Statement Narrative Exercise

The online companion contains fact statements from opposing briefs in the same appeal. This exercise asks you to identify each side's theme, as well as describe the writers' approaches to the narrative components of character, conflict, and plot.

3.2 Compiling and Categorizing the Facts

Next comes the work of compiling the facts. Keep in mind the universe you are dealing with: facts memorialized and entered into the record below, which is unlikely to include everything that actually occurred. For example, as noted in Chapter 2, in some courts the exhibits admitted at trial are not automatically included in the record on appeal. You must move to supplement the record before you may rely on them. Similarly, sometimes sidebars or conferences in chambers are not transcribed. If you were counsel below, you may know about an opponent's representation or a court ruling that was not recorded, but neither can be mentioned in your brief. Finally, each sentence in the statement of the facts must be supported (or at least supportable) by a citation to the record, which not only serves as a helpful check on your fact selection, but also shows the court that you are thorough and accurate.

Once you have defined the factual universe, you must further cull and categorize those facts.[63] The governing law, your theme-driven narrative, and the brief's space constraints will collectively drive this fact selection, resulting in a more defined set[64] of facts that settle into four categories: (1) legally significant facts (both good and bad); (2) emotionally significant facts (only good); (3) other important background facts; and (4) procedural facts.[65]

Legally significant facts. Your first priority is to gather the legally significant facts: those essential to understanding and deciding the issues on appeal. If you are arguing that police officers conducted an illegal search, for instance, then you must include all the baseline facts surrounding that incident—favorable *and* unfavorable. A favorable fact about the search might be questionable circumstances prompting the traffic stop, recorded on the officer's dashboard camera. Or perhaps the officer said something indicating that he did not believe he had authority to conduct the search. But what if your client, the defendant-appellant, was acting suspiciously in a high-crime neighborhood when the officer pulled him over? Or suppose he was merely the passenger, and the driver consented to the search? Though they tend to support the search's legality (and not your argument), those facts are just as crucial to resolving the Fourth Amendment issue, so they must be disclosed, not ignored.[66] Later we will discuss strategies for minimizing those facts' impact; for now, just compile them.

Emotionally significant facts. The next category includes "emotionally significant" facts. These are the facts you need for conflict and character development, for theme expression, and for plotline cogency and continuity. They are not essential to deciding the legal issues, but they help the court understand your client and the other actors and provide much-needed context. To continue with the illegal search example, several facts could be emotionally significant. Was your client driving home late at night because he had just been taking care of his elderly grandmother? Was this his first ever run-in with the police? Had there been media reports of pretextual police stops in recent months? In the due process/denial of fair trial appeal, recall that the defendant challenged a trial ruling circumscribing his cross-examination of a witness. Assume the record revealed more rulings where the trial court limited the defendant's presentation of evidence, but because trial counsel did not object, they were not pursued on appeal. Those rulings are "emotionally significant" facts as well. They can't speak directly to the cross-examination issue that was preserved and raised, but the pattern is favorable context supporting a thematic contention that the defendant did not receive a fair trial.

Background facts. The third batch of facts supplies another form of context. "Background facts" set the historical, cultural, or physical scene,[67] promoting a deeper understanding of what happened and why.[68] Below is an example of background factual information that segues into client-specific facts in a mortgage fraud case. Notice how the historical context suggests that the real culprits in the story are bank lenders, not the borrower, who was himself a victim.

EXAMPLE ————————————————————————————

Background Facts Leading into Narrative

In the last decade the housing market was fraught with subprime lenders that granted mortgages at high interest rates to unlikely borrowers — borrowers who often had credit ratings too low to qualify for ordinary mortgages. The banks issuing these loans, including the bank involved here — Long Beach Mortgage Company — profited from this business, making money from high interest rates and awarding commissions to encourage underwriting loans in high volume. This phenomenon created an atmosphere in which lenders issued mortgages with impunity and then transferred the high risk of default to investors through mortgage-backed securities.

Lenders did not always (or often) verify the information stated on mortgage applications, and it became common for borrowers to misstate their financial situations in order to receive loans, which they were often unable to pay back. Former bank employees, including a woman who authorized some of the mortgages in this case, have testified that they signed thousands of mortgage assignments each day, spending only a few seconds on each document. For a time, this approach was profitable for banks, but a combination of failing loans and the depressed housing market led lenders such as Long Beach Mortgage Company to collapse. Other lenders managed to stay afloat, but are now being investigated for dubious loan practices and may be on the line for millions or billions of dollars in fines.

As for the borrowers, scores ultimately faced prosecution and imprisonment for the alleged misrepresentations contained in the very mortgage applications that banks had accepted without question.

One such borrower was James Winter. In 2005 and 2006 Winter bought and sold several properties. . . .

Next is an example of background facts embedded into the client-specific narrative. Here, those facts set a compelling physical scene in a Section 1983 conditions-of-confinement case:

EXAMPLE ————————————————————————————

Background Facts Mixed into Narrative

Like the residents in other divisions of the Hinton County Jail, Mr. Swint was subjected to intolerable living conditions in Division Five. Insects infested his cell. (A.4.) He found cockroaches and mice in his food. (A.4.) The water was contaminated and toxic. (A.11.) His cell was inadequately heated during the frigid winter months. (A.13.) He was never allowed to go outside for recreation or exercise. (A.4.) And Mr. Swint and those that worked with him were fed nutritionally inadequate meals: Every morning, the jail provided Mr. Swint only a single egg with a half cup of cereal with milk and a small packet of Kool-Aid for breakfast; every afternoon, the Kool-Aid came with a peanut butter sandwich and some cookies. (A.4.) Although Mr. Swint theoretically could have supplemented his diet at the commissary, the extreme price markups at the commissary kept him from doing so. (A.4; A.11) (alleging that commissary is overpriced, claiming that it charges $4.96 for 4.5 ounces of chicken and $0.92 for Ramen Noodles).

This should come as no surprise to anyone familiar with the Hinton County Jail. No stranger to civil rights suits, it has been subject to continuous injunction for the last seven years, and its unconstitutional conditions are well documented in Department of Justice reports. Letter from Grace Chung Becker, Acting Assistant Attorney General, U.S. Dep't of Justice, Civil Rights Div., to Cty. Bd. President, (Jul. 11, 2010) [hereinafter Jail Findings Letter] ("[E]nvironmental and sanitation deficiencies at HCJ result in unconstitutional living conditions for inmates. . . . It was rare to find hot water availability in a cell, and we observed many inmates locked in cells for as long as 26 hours with no access to drinking water. . . . The three major pest problems observed during our site visits involved mice, cockroaches and drain flies. . . . [In the kitchens, i]nmate workers were not utilizing gloves or hairnets, numerous sinks had clogged drains, and excessive garbage was piled on the floor.").

Procedural Facts. The final set of facts is procedural. Think of procedural facts as those that happen once the parties reach the courthouse. How was the lawsuit initiated? When did the prosecutors file the indictment? When did the plaintiff file her complaint? How did the court rule on potentially dispositive motions throughout the proceeding? When and how did the case end? Depending on the court, you may need to write a separate section that captures all of the procedural facts. That separate section is often called the Statement of the Case, and we discuss it in Chapter 12. When the procedural facts appear in their own section, the narrative facts are often housed in another section called the Statement of Facts. In many courts, however, there is just one section — also, confusingly, called the Statement of the Case — which includes the narrative facts as well as the procedural facts. Be sure to check the rules in your jurisdiction.[69]

Whether in a stand-alone section or woven into your comprehensive factual narrative, the procedural facts should cover all of the litigation events for every issue on appeal. Below is an example from the mortgage fraud case discussed above, addressing the procedural facts in a separate section. On appeal, the defendant raised a *Brady* claim,[70] argued that the evidence was insufficient to sustain his conviction, and challenged a jury instruction along with the restitution imposed in his sentence. The callout boxes show how each procedural event is keyed to a legal issue.

| EXAMPLE | Statement of the Case (Procedural Facts Only)

On January 4, 2011, the government indicted James Winter for an alleged mortgage-fraud and wire-fraud scheme. (R.1.) Winter moved pretrial for a subpoena to recover evidence that local police had illegally seized from his home and retained in their possession, (R.231), claiming in part that the evidence would be instrumental to his defense, (A.8–9). The district court denied Winter's motion to obtain the materials, (A.12), but ordered the government to produce a report detailing the status of the evidence, which it did on October 24, 2012 (A.38–42).

← *Procedural facts related to Brady claim*

After a three-day trial that began on January 14, 2013, the jury returned a guilty verdict against Winter on both counts. At the close of evidence, Winter timely moved for acquittal based on insufficiency of the evidence. (A.16.) On January 22, 2013, Winter filed a post-trial motion based on insufficiency of the evidence and the district court's failure to give his requested buyer–seller jury instruction. (R.282.) The district court denied Winter's motion to reconsider and his written motion for acquittal. (A.18.)

← *Procedural facts related to claim of insufficiency*

← *Procedural facts related to jury instruction issue*

The district court sentenced Winter on April 23, 2013. The court accepted the loss calculations suggested by the Probation Department. (Sentencing Hr'g Tr. 12.) The Probation report applied the U.S. Sentencing Guidelines Manual § 2B1.1, and found a base offense level of seven. Although the government did not present any evidence or witnesses related to the amount of loss at sentencing or in its version of the offense submitted to the Probation Office, (R.291), the district court accepted—with one modification proposed by the PSR (R.291 at 8)—the government's proposed loss amount. The district court found Winter responsible for $956,300 in losses. This corresponded to an increase of 14 levels in Winter's sentence. The court ultimately determined Winter's guideline range to be 70 to 87 months.

← *Procedural facts related to sentencing issue*

> The court sentenced Winter to 60 months of imprisonment
> and 3 years of supervised release. (A.2–3.) In addition, the
> court ordered restitution to be paid to JP Morgan and to the
> FDIC in the amount of $956,300. (A.5.) The district court
> entered judgment on May 24, 2013. (A.1.) Winter timely
> filed his notice of appeal on May 28, 2013. (R.327.)

Once you have categorized your facts, consider creating a chart to keep track of them. The digest that you prepared earlier will be incredibly helpful now if you were thorough and conscientious in preparing it. You can use that digest to extract the factual details and slot them into a chart that builds on the theory and theme chart you have already created.

3.3 Organizing the Statement of Facts

> **Practice Alert #4**
> **Example of Fact Chart**
>
> The online companion contains a chart that organizes the *Winter* facts by category and by issue, as well as by theory and theme.

Now that you have spent quality time thinking about your facts' narrative components and sorting the facts into the categories you need to develop that narrative, it is time to draft the statement of facts. You must first settle on an organizational scheme. That scheme will be driven in part by plot, but also by clarity and cogency. No matter how compelling a plot, if its expression confuses the court or leads the court to misunderstand what happened, it will have defeated its purpose. Most fact statements are organized in one of three ways: (1) straight chronology; (2) altered chronology; or (3) a mix of chronological and topical sequencing.

Straight chronology. If your client's story is best told by starting with the "steady state" and then moving to the disruption, then the basic scheme will likely be chronological.[71] Within the chronological sequence, you have choices. You may wish to start with your emotionally significant character facts, as in this example from the due process/denial of a fair trial appeal, which shows how the character facts discussed in Section 3.1 appeared in the narrative:

EXAMPLE

Starting with Character Facts

Andy Parchmann is, by all accounts from those who know him, a kind, generous, caring, supportive, and hard-working person. (A.499–500; A.503–04; 512–13.) He has no criminal history. (C00356.) He is a child of first-generation, immigrant parents who worked hard in blue-collar jobs to support Mr. Parchmann and his siblings. (A.504.) They have a close and supportive family, whom he strives to make proud. (A.514.) Through his hard work and studies, he attended the University

> of Virginia Law School and became a successful transactional lawyer. (Vol. 1, 8/28/12 Tr. A-10–11.) He shared the fruits of his hard work with his friends and family, lending support and financial assistance whenever he saw the need. (C00411) (noting that Mr. Parchmann "has helped many friends find jobs, provided financial assistance to friends in need, and consistently gone above and beyond to help those close to him"); *see also* (C00426).

Alternatively, you could start the chronology with background facts as backdrop for the client-specific facts, as the mortgage fraud appeal example did by detailing the mortgage crisis before mentioning the defendant. A chronological organization can also start later in time, diving right into the chaos. An example of this organization is the earlier conditions of confinement example, which began with facts describing the atrocious prison conditions, and then continued moving forward.

The main advantages of a chronological organization are clarity and reader comprehension. Because chronological sequence is the reader's default expectation, readers can process it well.[72] But as with any organizational scheme, be wary of using it mindlessly.[73]

Altered chronology. Your plot may instead lend itself to an altered chronology. A linear structure can be confining and may not focus the reader's attention as intently on theme or theory.[74] Nonlinear fact statements take two primary forms. The first and most common kicks off with a persuasive summary preceding the detailed narrative.[75] Much like a summary of argument or an overview paragraph in an argument, a narrative summary brings the legal issue into sharp focus and more deliberately primes the reader for the facts that follow. A summary start is also useful for tying together long and complex narratives. Take this example from a Supreme Court brief arguing in favor of a "direct threat" defense under the Americans With Disabilities Act. The "direct threat" defense applies when a worker's health condition poses a threat to himself or others in the workplace, relieving the employer of discrimination liability for employment actions based on that health condition.[76]

EXAMPLE

Starting with a Persuasive Summary[77]

Chevron, U.S.A., Inc. (Chevron) withdrew an offer to employ respondent Mario Echazabal in a refinery job in which he inevitably would have been exposed to liver-toxic substances after Chevron's physicians determined that respondent had a "history of a long-term liver problem, [a] diagnosis of chronic active Hepatitis C, and significantly elevated liver enzymes over a period of years." (J.A. 39.) Chevron's physicians concluded that the "exposure to hepatotoxic chemicals" involved in the job "would further damage [respondent's] already reduced liver capacity," "seriously endanger his health," and "potentially cause [his] death." (J.A. 39-40.) Respondent's own doctor advised Chevron that respondent should not be exposed to hepatotoxins. (J.A. 98, 163-164.)

The question in this case is whether the Americans With Disabilities Act permits an employer to refuse employment to a person who it determines, based on the individualized and objective conclusions of physicians, would face a substantial risk of significant harm or death in carrying out the essential functions of the job.

Notice how compressed this summary is. It captures the entire plotline in one short paragraph without falling victim to excessive detail — the main risk that accompanies this technique. The writers also persuade without engaging in argument. They never say, "Mario Echazabal posed a direct threat to himself," or "Echazabal's ADA claim is defeated by the direct threat defense." As we will explore in the next section, the writers *show* all of that through factual description, using detail, juxtaposition, and word choice to paint a compelling picture.

A second, less common nonlinear structure is to start *in media res* — Latin for starting in the middle of the action. This structure works well if your plot benefits from starting with the chaos and then moving back in time to capture the key background or emotionally significant character facts.[78] The advantage of this structure is that it snags the reader's attention and primes the reader to receive the favorable character facts and anything else that happens in the narrative.[79] But it takes considerable skill to pull off. The writer must be able to transition backwards from the chaos and then jump forward in time again.

Mixed chronological and topical organization. Some appeals require discussion of topics that lack a time-based element, necessitating a mixed chronological and topical organization. Topical facts run the gamut from contract provisions to business processes and policies to expert testimony to descriptions of property. These facts are often covered in a brief interlude from the chronological narrative. For example, in the Facebook v. Connect U appeal, the facts moved chronologically from the parties' competing lawsuits to a mediation proceeding, and then paused to describe the settlement agreement arising out of that proceeding. The parties' entry into that agreement was part of the chronology, but the agreement's terms were not. After explaining the terms, the writers picked up on the chronology, moving into Connect U's breach of the agreement and Facebook's efforts to enforce it.[80] Along the same lines, appeals governed by complex statutory regimes might narrate key statutory or regulatory provisions before or along with the events in the fact statement. This approach is common in Supreme Court briefs with statutory interpretation arguments.[81]

Two final points about organization warrant attention: the first is a technique to use and the second is problem to avoid. Fact statements benefit from topical headings that move the reader through the statement of facts. These headings are not only educational, they promote flow and reader comprehension.[82] Consider the following series of fact statement headings from the Facebook v. Connect U brief:

EXAMPLE

Headings in a Statement of Facts

- The Parties Litigate High-Stakes Disputes on Two Coasts
- The District Court Orders Mediation in the Heat of Discovery
- The CU Founders Develop Settlers' Remorse
- Facebook Moves to Enforce the Settlement Agreement in California
- The California District Court Enforces the Settlement Agreement
- The District Court Orders Specific Performance

These headings ferry the reader through a long and complex narrative involving multiple lawsuits in different courts. At the same time, the headings persuade without arguing. The writers do not say, "CU Breaches the Settlement Agreement," but instead say, vividly and descriptively, "The CU Founders Develop Settlers' Remorse." Indeed, the headings resemble news headlines, drawing the reader in and conjuring powerful visuals with phrases like "High Stakes Litigation on Two Coasts" and "in the Heat of Discovery."

Now, the problem to avoid: a witness-by-witness organization. Too many novice writers, neglecting to consider plot and theme, string together snippets of testimony, making the fact statement read like a mini trial transcript. This is an ineffective organizational approach. Not only do serial summaries obscure what happened and why, they prevent character, conflict, and theme development. Moreover, as the next section will explain, adopting a distinct point of view is a vital component of persuasion in a fact statement. Testimonial summaries that simply describe what each witness said lack any viewpoint at all.

REVIEW

Statement of Facts Organization

- Straight chronology variations:
  - Start with character facts
  - Start with background facts
  - Start with chaos
  - Then move forward in time
- Altered chronology variations:
  - Start with a plot summary

- o Start *in media res*
- o Then go backward to capture character and background facts
- A chronology with topical interludes is useful for:
  - o Describing writings
  - o Describing processes
  - o Describing expert testimony
  - o Describing property
  - o Narrating a statutory regime
  - o Explaining anything else that lacks a time component
- DO use newspaper-like topical headings to promote flow and comprehension.
- DON'T organize witness by witness.

3.4 Using the Statement of Facts as a Tool of Persuasion

Overt argument and legal conclusions are not only inappropriate and unwelcome in fact statements, they are outright barred by many courts' rules.[83] As such, your fact statement must find other ways to persuade, namely with: (1) point of view; (2) fact positioning; (3) fact description; and (4) and word choice. The basic objective of all these tools is to *show* through description rather than *tell* through argument,[84] influencing the reader to form her own opinions rather than telling her what to think.

Point of view. Point of view—"through whose eyes the reader views the action"[85]—is a core narrative component.[86] In a fact statement, the lawyer's point of view is subsumed into the client's; the lawyer is simply the "medium of expression." A client-centered viewpoint persuades by transforming a two-dimensional party into a three-dimensional character that the court can care about.[87]

Point of view often comes through first in character development, as in Section 3.3's example developing Andy Parchmann's background in his due process/denial of fair trial appeal. But institutions can have character-driven viewpoints too. In the Facebook v. Connect U appeal, for example, the opening paragraphs in the statement of facts detail how founder Mark Zuckerberg "steered Facebook to become an enterprise that now serves over 400 million users worldwide, and is probably the hottest start-up in the world."[88] Meanwhile, the Connect U "rivals" waited until "after Zuckerberg launched Facebook" to found a competing business—one with "the much more mundane mission of helping Harvard students find dates with each other and land jobs with Harvard alumni."[89] The fact selection, details, and vivid word choices[90] emphasize Connect U's insularity and relatively modest aims, using point of view to make it a much less appealing character than Facebook.

Characterizing alone is not enough. To achieve a point of view, the fact statement should make the court see, feel, and hear exactly what the client did—almost as if a video camera were strapped to the client, revealing the client's unfiltered experience.[91] The due process/denial of a fair trial brief artfully accomplishes this in the following excerpt describing Mr. Parchmann's encounter with the alleged victim and his subsequent arrest.

EXAMPLE

Point of View in a Statement of Facts

On August 6, 2012, a chance encounter changed lives forever. On a warm summer evening, Mr. Parchmann took some friends sightseeing and out to dinner near Washington, D.C.'s Georgetown neighborhood. (A.322–23.) Afterwards, around 9:00 p.m., his friends moved on to a new locale, while Mr. Parchmann decided to walk towards his home in the DuPont Circle neighborhood. (A.324–25.) As he walked down P Street, he tripped on the sidewalk. (A.326.) A woman who was walking in the same direction noticed his gaffe, so Mr. Parchmann covered his embarrassment by making a joke at his own expense. (A.326.) The woman laughed and the two engaged in a brief conversation. (A.327.) When Mr. Parchmann asked her where she was heading, she told him that she was going to the Jaxx Hotel—where she was staying—to have a drink at the bar with her friends. (A.327.) She told him that the rooftop bar had a great view and that he should stop by. (A.328.) Mr. Parchmann told her that he lived just across the street and that she should come have a drink at his apartment, number 341. (A.328.) The woman parried, telling him that she was in room 312. (A.328.) The two then parted ways. (A.328–29.)

* * *

Mr. Parchmann was in police custody for at least five to six hours. (Vol. 7, 2/27/14 Tr. 131.) Although the officers asserted at trial that they did not permit him to use the restroom during the entirety of this period, (Vol. 7, 2/27/14 Tr. 127), Mr. Parchmann testified that he did use the bathroom, and it was filthy, (A.349–50, A.352). Being a self-professed "son of a germaphobe," Mr. Parchmann put lip balm on his hands after using the bathroom because it was the only thing available to him and he believed it could serve to clean his hands. (A.353–54.) While at the station, Mr. Parchmann also spoke with Detective Miller, who asked Mr. Parchmann if he could take a hand swab. (A.355.) Eager to get home, Mr. Parchmann asked Detective Miller if agreeing to the hand swab would help him leave any sooner. (A.356.) When Detective Miller said no, Mr. Parchmann declined the hand swab. (A.356.)

The writer conveys point of view through details that only Mr. Parchmann would have known at the time, such as having dinner in Georgetown, and the fact that he took his friends sightseeing. Likewise, only Mr. Parchmann would have known his feelings of embarrassment after tripping on the sidewalk in front of a woman passing by. That same viewpoint holds in the second paragraph about Mr. Parchmann's arrest. We experience the long period in police custody with unpalatable conditions as the defendant did, and gain insight into his mindset through the description of his conversation with the detective.[92] But notice the writer's careful attention to accuracy. Though told through a distinct viewpoint, all of these facts have objective evidentiary support in the record.

Of course, a fact statement cannot tell only the facts that the client knew at the time; it must also cover the legally relevant, emotionally significant, and background facts that appear in the record — everything that you culled using the guidance from Section 3.2. Those facts can be conveyed with a viewpoint in the same way, through the characters' traits or actions. Take this example from the Fourth Amendment inventory search scenario discussed back in Section 2.2, describing the police search of Mr. Mutombo's car. Even though he did not personally witness the search, it is nonetheless described from Mr. Mutombo's viewpoint, in a way that advances the theory and theme of the appeal.

EXAMPLE

Point of View in a Statement of Facts

When the Glen Lake police discovered that the car belonged to Mutombo — the very person they were investigating in connection with the weapons sale — they notified NMV campus officers, who in turn sent out a safety alert to all NMV officers and began to monitor Mutombo's car closely to gather evidence of activity "going on" around the car. (08/22/2008 Suppression Hr'g Tr. 67-71.)

* * *

Officers were dispatched to search the car in advance of the tow. (08/22/2008 Suppression Hr'g Tr. 5, 44-45.) Officer Tom Salles was tasked with this job. (08/22/2008 Suppression Hr'g Tr. 5-6.) After forcing entry into the locked car, Salles testified that he began to inventory the car's contents. (08/22/2008 Suppression Hr'g Tr. 8-9, 37.) Salles's search, however, turned to gathering evidence when he noticed bullets in the center console of the car. (08/22/2008 Suppression Hr'g Tr. 25-26.) Salles also noticed a crumpled piece of paper shoved between the center console and the driver's seat. (08/22/2008 Suppression Hr'g Tr. 10, 27.) He picked it up and saw that it was a piece of paper advertising asthma inhalers. (08/22/2008 Suppression Hr'g Tr. 10-11.) He determined quickly that the paper was not of medical significance. (08/22/2008 Suppression Hr'g Tr. 11-13.) Nonetheless, he continued to read, concluding immediately that what was written on the front page of the paper did not make sense to him.

Fact positioning. Fact positioning is a powerful tool for emphasizing good facts and de-emphasizing less favorable facts. Fact positioning triggers the primacy and recency effects, in which readers recall best what they heard first and last, with more muddled recollections of what came in between.[93] Fact positioning can happen at the paragraph level and the sentence level. At the paragraph level, starting or finishing with a sentence of favorable facts can cause them to linger in the reader's mind.[94] Sentences that use active voice naturally slot facts into important subject, verb, and object positions, where they attract more attention. Short sentences have the same attention-catching effect.[95] By contrast, sentences that place facts in the middle of a longer sentence with multiple clauses make those facts harder to pull out.[96] Another classic de-emphasis technique is to put bad facts in a dependent clause, followed by an independent clause that contains context or more favorable facts.[97] The independent clause is where the reader's attention fixes naturally, implicitly discounting the dependent clause's content. Writers who wish to downplay unfavorable information about an actor or to highlight what happened to someone will use the passive voice, which tells the reader how something was acted upon, not who did what.[98] Below are simple illustrations of various fact positioning techniques.

Example: Fact Positioning

To emphasize/highlight	To de-emphasize/lowlight
Use active voice, simple sentence structure. Defendant ran a red light and crashed into Plaintiff.	**Use passive voice (sparingly).** Plaintiff was struck in the intersection.
Place facts prominently, at the beginning or end of paragraphs and at the beginning or end of sentences. Respondent's own doctor advised Chevron that respondent should not be exposed to hepatotoxins [end of paragraph].	**Bury facts in the middle of paragraphs, in clauses in the middle of a sentence, or in dependent clauses.** Although Mr. Echazabal's doctor suggested that he avoid prolonged exposure to hepatotoxins, the doctor never analyzed the specific exposure that respondent would face in the plant.
Use shorter sentences in shorter paragraphs; use active voice. The defendant shot the victim.	**Use longer sentences in longer paragraphs; use passive voice.** Ms. Sabatini and her assailant struggled over his gun, and in the process the assailant was shot and loosened his grip on her, allowing Ms. Sabatini to escape with her life.

The next example from the *Mutombo* appeal employs multiple forms of fact positioning in a single fact statement. Recall that Mr. Mutombo's attempted terrorist threat conviction was premised on a note, which he claimed was a First Amendment-protected draft of rap song lyrics. To advance that theory, the brief emphasized Mr. Mutombo's genuine, artistic interest in rap, while downplaying a gun collection pastime that, in the State's view, corroborated Mr. Mutombo's terroristic aims.

EXAMPLE Fact Positioning

Mutombo's interest in gangsta rap was artistic. In all other respects he was a peaceful person, and he was viewed that way by both friends and professors at the university. (C576-613; R898.) According to friends and fellow rappers, Mutombo—like most successful musicians—created lyrics constantly, scribbling them wherever and whenever inspiration struck. (RI 101-1102.) He would use scrap paper, napkins, notebooks, and computer programs to record his song ideas. (RI 131-40.) Similarly, Mutombo drew inspiration for his lyrics from everywhere—from television shows to current events to his own relationships. (RI 104.) One evening Mutombo and his friend, Thad Parsons, were watching an episode of *Law and Order* that dealt with a person who had sent a ransom note demanding money in order to avert something bad happening to a character on the show. (RI 106.) Mutombo told Parsons that he thought that this would make a good topic for a rap composition or a skit to accompany a rap song. (RII 06-07.)

← Short, active voice sentence at beginning of paragraph emphasizes artistic rap interest.

← Ending sentence highlights best fact – an alternative explanation for the note's language

Another of Mutombo's interests was buying and selling guns on the Internet. These transactions were legal and above board, as Mutombo had a firearms owner identification card and used a federal firearms licensee to

← Topic sentence structure emphasizes Mutombo's interest more than his actions.

facilitate his transfer of guns from his Internet transactions. (R717; 733-34.) He *Early sentences highlight the legality of these transactions.* also legally possessed his own handgun, although he never registered it with NMV, which was a misdemeanor violation of Illinois law. (R593.) Federal Agents, in coordination *Less favorable facts about not registering the gun are buried mid-paragraph in a dependent clause.* with the Glen Lake Police Department and the NMV campus police, began investigating in mid-July 2007 Mutombo's possible purchases and sale of guns. (08/09/2007 Grand Jury Tr. 10; 08/22/2008 Suppression Hr'g Tr. 17-18; R709-716.) Through this investigation, officers learned that Mutombo had ordered four other guns but had not *Two sentences at the end highlight that Mutombo never had guns in his possession.* received them from the federal firearms licensee. (R644-49; R733-34.) In fact, it is undisputed Mutombo never possessed any of these four weapons. (R733-734.)

REVIEW

Fact Positioning Techniques

- Paragraph Level
  - First and last sentences emphasize
  - Middle sentences de-emphasize
- Sentence Level
  - Active voice emphasizes
  - Passive voice deemphasizes
  - Short sentences emphasize
  - Long sentences with multiple clauses de-emphasize
  - Independent clauses emphasize
  - Dependent clauses de-emphasize

Fact description. The same objective facts can be described in entirely different ways, depending on how much detail surrounds them, how they are characterized, whether they are contextualized, and whether they are paraphrased or quoted.[99] To emphasize good facts, writers build out factual details that evoke images.[100] These details slow the reader's pace, focusing her attention on the passage, and help her to form a clear picture in her mind—one that is both memorable and affecting. Below are some simple examples of strategic fact description.

Example: Fact Description

To emphasize/highlight	To de-emphasize/lowlight
Provide context and detail; "describe." Respondent had a history of long-term liver problems, had been diagnosed with chronic, active Hepatitis C, and had significantly elevated liver enzymes over a period of years.	**Characterize; provide minimal context.** Respondent had a diagnosed liver disease.
Juxtapose facts to emphasize them. Defendant ignored impairment warnings on the Benadryl label, choosing to get behind the wheel of his car just an hour later.	**Place facts far away from each other.** Defendant took Benadryl to combat his allergic reaction. . . . About an hour later, he had to get in the car to pick up his son from soccer practice.
Quote directly. Respondent's doctor opined that working in Chevron's refinery "would seriously endanger his health."	**Paraphrase – accurately but not colorfully.** Respondent's doctor acknowledged that prolonged hepatotoxic exposure in the refinery could compromise his health eventually.

The next example reproduces the first paragraph of the conditions of confinement fact statement discussed in Section 3.2, now examining its use of detail.

EXAMPLE

Using Vivid Details to Persuade

Like the residents in other divisions of the Hinton County Jail, Mr. Swint was subjected to intolerable living conditions in Division Five. Insects infested his cell. (A.4.) He found cockroaches and mice in his food. (A.4.) The water was contaminated and toxic. (A.11.) His cell was inadequately heated during the frigid winter months. (A.13.) He was never allowed to go outside for recreation or exercise. (A.4.) And Mr. Swint and those that worked with him were fed nutritionally inadequate meals: Every morning, the jail provided Mr. Swint only a single egg with a half cup of cereal with milk and a small packet of Kool-Aid for breakfast; every afternoon, the Kool-Aid came with a peanut butter sandwich and some cookies. (A.4.) Although Mr. Swint theoretically could have supplemented his diet at the commissary, the extreme price markups at the commissary kept him from doing so. (A.4; A.11) (alleging that commissary is overpriced, claiming that it charges $4.96 for 4.5 ounces of chicken and $0.92 for Ramen Noodles).

The writers do not stop at characterizing the living conditions as "intolerable." Instead, they use image-evoking detail to show precisely how intolerable the conditions were. Reading this passage, one would be hard-pressed not to summon images of scurrying vermin, miniscule food portions, and frigid small spaces. Everyone has seen that movie. Choosing to specify the types of critters in the cell, along with the one egg and half-cup of cereal meal, supplemented by the worst kind of junk food, is what gives this passage its vividness, and therefore its impact on the reader.

At the opposite end of the spectrum is summary,[101] a form of fact description whose power lies in adding up key facts that, in turn, tee up arguments. Take this example from the Google v. Oracle appeal, a copyright infringement action contending that Google copied Oracle's software source code and then used the pilfered code to undercut Oracle in the smartphone market.[102]

EXAMPLE

Summarizing to Persuade

As is evident from those client lists, Sun/Oracle—a significant force in personal computers, servers, and web-based applications, A133, 141—was already a strong presence in mobile devices and poised to be a major force in smartphones, A22,237.

Until Google entered the picture.

The Google juggernaut rests on a grand bargain. A21, 631. Google, famously, does not directly charge users. Instead, Google collects information about its users and makes money selling advertising targeted at them. Advertisers pay large sums for that targeting. A7898, 7902-04, 7916-18, 7922, 7979.

The first sentence uses summary to characterize Oracle's market stature. No one person said explicitly, "Oracle was poised to be a major force in smartphones;" rather, it is a fact the writer gleaned from several discrete pieces of evidence, strategically packaged for the reader. Adding up these market facts also tees up the writer's later legal arguments, which center on Google's commercial use of the source code and the financial harm thereby imposed on Oracle. The third paragraph then summarizes Google's business model as a "grand bargain," and follows up with the supporting specifics. Later, the brief capitalizes on this characterization by showing how Google's hemmed-in business model made it desperate to infringe. But be aware that summarizing comes with the risk of veering into argument. For example, had this writer said, "Google's desperate and deliberate copying of Oracle's source code undercut Oracle's market share and irreparably harmed its financial position," he would have crossed that line.

Two more fact description techniques are context and juxtaposition.[103] Context can explain away or minimize a seemingly bad fact, especially if that context immediately surrounds the bad fact.[104] For example, the *Mutombo* appeal's paragraph addressing Mr. Mutombo's purchase of guns used context to soften that information's impact. Specifying that the transactions were "legal and above board" and that Mutombo "had a firearms owner identification card and used a federal firearms licensee" made them seem inconsequential, or at least less likely to raise the reader's hackles. And it is undoubtedly better for the court to hear the gun facts first from Mutombo than from the government.

Writers also juxtapose one fact against another to cast actors or events in a favorable or unfavorable light. The introductory paragraph from the Chevron v. Echazabal appeal, reproduced in Section 3.3, uses this technique:

EXAMPLE

Using Juxtaposition to Persuade

Chevron, U.S.A., Inc. (Chevron) withdrew an offer to employ respondent Mario Echazabal in a refinery job in which he inevitably would have been exposed to liver-toxic substances after Chevron's physicians determined that respondent had a "history of a long-term liver problem, [a] diagnosis of chronic active Hepatitis C, and significantly elevated liver enzymes over a period of years." (J.A. 39.)

By pulling together Chevron's decision not to hire Echazabal together with two more facts — the refinery's hepatotoxic environment and the medical testimony about Echazabal's liver condition — the writers cast the employment decision in a much more understandable and nondiscriminatory light.

Finally, a writer can show instead of tell by using direct quotations rather than paraphrasing. Quotations, like detail, highlight facts by attracting attention to them.[105] Some direct quotations serve the simple purpose of emphasizing the favorable information in the quotations, as the example above does by quoting the medical testimony in Chevron's favor. Others build or undermine the speaker's credibility.[106]

Word choice. For such a small unit of speech, words have disproportionate power to emphasize and de-emphasize information.[107] To emphasize favorable facts, use vivid, concrete words — particularly nouns and verbs — that conjure images in the mind's eye. Avoid mushy legalese, as well as adjectives and adverbs that strain rather than enhancing descriptive value.[108] Conversely, to de-emphasize unfavorable facts, use bland language devoid of emotional connotations. Word choices should also be strategic in a big-picture sense. They should be made deliberately to further your theory and theme, and should avoid playing into the opposing theory and theme.[109]

Example: Word Choice

To emphasize/highlight	To de-emphasize/lowlight
Use precise, power-packed words charged with meaning. Defendant ran a red light and crashed into Plaintiff.	**Use bland, colorless words.** Plaintiff was struck in the intersection.

Always Avoid: Using terms that play into the other side's theory and theme; overusing adjectives and adverbs; and veering into legal conclusions.

This next excerpt from the *Facebook* brief uses several vivid word choices that advance the writer's theory and theme that Connect U breached the settlement agreement as a result of settler's remorse:[110]

EXAMPLE

Persuading Through Word Choice

After a period of negotiations, Connect U retreated into radio silence. ER 512, 703. Then Connect U abruptly fired its lawyers, alleging that they had committed malpractice in negotiating the Settlement Agreement, SER 37-41, and set out to scuttle the deal.

The phrase "retreated into radio silence" colorfully suggests that Connect U was scheming behind closed doors to find a way out of the settlement agreement. "Abruptly fired" is an effective adverb-verb pairing, connoting the sudden nature of Connect U's about-face. The vivid verb in "*scuttle* the deal" to describe Connect U's breach packs more punch than would a bland phrase "get out of the deal."

A final word choice strategy comes in the form of selective repetition. A well-crafted label or turn of phrase for a key concept can be used throughout a fact statement in a way that becomes so entrenched in the reader's mind that he or she always thinks of that fact in just that way. An example from the BMW v. Gore brief, as we saw in section 1.3, is the repeated phrase "$2 million punishment." Another example appears in the Oracle v. Google brief. Here, the writers wanted to emphasize Oracle's philosophy to write source code that could be used in any platform, benefiting consumers and the market, while making clear that Google's strategy was to make its source code run only on the Android platform, benefitting only itself. The Oracle

Practice Alert #5
Fact Statement Analysis

The online companion contains two sets of competing facts from an Appellant's and Appellee's brief. It prompts you to analyze the persuasive fact-writing techniques employed by each party.

philosophy was captured in the pithy phrase, "write once, run anywhere" — a phrase that appears seven times in the statement of facts. Google's contrasting philosophy was characterized as "write once, run only on Android."

REVIEW

Fact Description and Word Choice Techniques

- Develop favorable facts with detail that evokes images.
- Summarize to add up events and tee up arguments.
- Contextualize bad facts to downplay or explain them away.
- Juxtapose two or more facts to elicit negative or positive reactions to an event or actor.
- Use direct quotes instead of paraphrasing to highlight favorable facts or zero in on key testimony.
- Choose vivid, precise words that produce compelling images and further your theory and theme.
- Use bland language to downplay negative information.
- Use selective repetition to underscore themes.

3.5 Avoiding Fact Statement Pitfalls

We end this section by discussing the ways in which the statement of facts can go wrong. There are several: (1) veering into argument; (2) exaggerating or misstating the record; (3) omitting legally relevant facts; (4) going outside the record; (5) failing to cite the record; (6) using excessive detail; and (7) reflexively quoting the lower court's language if you are appellant or petitioner.

The first five reflect directly on the writer's credibility and in turn, the facts' believability. We have already discussed avoiding argument. But missteps relating to factual accuracy will just as surely cause the court to discount what you are saying and kill your credibility as an advocate — and may even lead to sanctions.[111] No matter how fervently you wish away negative facts or hope for better facts, you must stay true to the record. It is fine to point out the absence of evidence in the record, and in fact that is a good persuasive technique, but you cannot rely on evidence that exists outside of it (unless it is evidence amenable to judicial notice). Equally important is meticulous use of record citations. You can see what that looks like in every example this chapter uses. In each example, nearly every sentence is followed by at least one record citation. It may not look pretty, but it is a necessity, for the court and its clerks will rely on those citations to look for proof that what you are saying is correct. When you draft those citations, make sure to follow any local court rules and conventions about what form they should take. And make absolutely sure that the citations in fact support the asserted facts.

Excessive detail can also sink a fact statement. If you include a name, date, or place, the reader is going to assume that she needs to remember it. If those details never make another appearance in the brief, the reader will become annoyed and frustrated for having expended mental energy needlessly. And although you must include in your statement any facts on which you later rely, you need not — and indeed should not — simply repeat the same facts in the same way between your fact statement and your argument section. Make smart choices about where the detail matters most. It may make most sense to simply alert the reader at the 10,000-foot level during the statement of facts, and then dive into the nitty-gritty details down in the argument section. For example, in the mortgage-fraud example we have used in this chapter, you might opt to describe the restitution loss calculations more generally in the statement of facts ("In arriving at its restitution amount to JP Morgan, the district court merely totaled the outstanding mortgages without considering the defendant's loan payments or that many of the mortgage loans had been negotiated downstream to successor lenders. (Tr. 330.)"), but with more detail later during the argument ("With respect to the 14th Street property, it is undisputed that Mr. Winter made 18 successive mortgage payments (Tr.330), which should have been subtracted from the total restitution amount. And as for the Kensington Street property, JP Morgan had sold the mortgage downstream, so it should not have been awarded the $63,000 in restitution arising from that loan. (Tr.330-33.)").

Finally, all too many appellants and petitioners fall into the habit of reflexively using direct quotes from the lower court's opinion in fact statements that blend in procedural history. As with any other negative fact, adverse lower court reasoning should be lowlighted, not highlighted. So direct quotes, which catch the reader's eye, should be avoided. Moreover, adverse statements that are not germane to the appeal but are otherwise harmful to the appealing party can be omitted altogether. As for adverse statements that cannot be avoided because they directly impact the appeal, simply paraphrase them, and use the other persuasive fact-writing strategies you have learned to downplay their significance.

Endnotes

1. Judith A. Fischer, *Got Issues? An Empirical Study About Framing Them*, 6 J. Ass'n Legal Writing Directors 1, 2-3 (2009) ("The framing effect occurs when a speaker's emphasis on certain considerations affects what others focus on in forming opinions.") (citing E. James N. Druckman, *On the Limits of Framing Effects: Who Can Frame?*, 63 J. Pol. 1041, 1042 (2001)).
2. Kathryn M. Stanchi, *The Power of Priming in Legal Advocacy: Using the Science of First Impressions to Persuade the Reader*, 89 Or. L. Rev. 305, 306 (2010) ("People judge quickly and tend to cling to those judgments."). Stanchi describes a study in which students formed immediate impressions of an instructor from watching the instructor for just minutes on video. Those impressions remained when the instructor went live in the classroom and held for the entire semester. *Id.*
3. Adrian C. North, David J. Hargreaves & Jennifer McKendrick, *The Influence of In-Store Music on Wine Selections*, 84 J. Applied Psychol. 271, 271-76 (1999).
4. Rob W. Holland, Merel Hendriks & Henk Aarts, *Smells Like Clean Spirit: Nonconscious Effects of Scent on Cognition and Behavior*, 16 Psychol. Sci. 689, 689-93 (2005).
5. Aaron C. Kay, S. Christian Wheeler, John A. Bargh & Lee Ross, *Material Priming: The Influence of Mundane Physical Objects on Situational Construal and Competitive Behavioral Choice*, 95 Org. Behav. & Hum. Decisions Processes 83, 83-96 (2004).

6. Fischer, *supra* note 1, at 3. Synthesizing framing scholarship, Fischer explains that "frames affect[] what others focus on in forming opinions . . . frames affect how people see issues."

7. Stanchi, *supra* note 2, at 311.

8. *Id.* at 310 (explaining that the issue and fact statements "can prime the reader to see the case in a particular way by pushing the theme of the case and evoking particular emotions in the reader").

9. Kenneth D. Chestek, *Judging by the Numbers: An Empirical Study of the Power of Story*, 7 J. OF THE ASS'N OF LEGAL WRITING DIRECTORS 1, 14-15 (2010).

10. Mary Ann Becker, *What Is Your Favorite Book? Using Narrative to Teach Theme Development in Persuasive Writing*, 46:3 GONZ. L. REV. 575, 581 (2010) (a theory pulls the law and facts together into a "coherent and credible whole") (internal citations and quotations omitted); *see also* Chestek, *supra* note 9, at 14 (defining "theory of the case" as "'the legal theory': the logical, law-based reason why a particular result is desired") (citing Antonin Scalia & Bryan A. Garner, MAKING YOUR CASE: THE ART OF PERSUADING JUDGES 41, 59 (Thomson West 2008)); Stanchi, *supra* note 2, at 312 (differentiating between theme and theory).

11. Becker, *supra* note 10, at 580 (noting that the theme "has no independent legal weight" but gives legal arguments their force by "reveal[ing] well-known familiar, and intriguing story lines, such as love, greed, and revenge") (quoting STEVEN LUBET, MODERN TRIAL ADVOCACY: ANALYSIS AND PRACTICE 9 (3d ed. 2004)).

12. *Id.* at 579.

13. Jennifer Sheppard, *Once Upon a Time, Happily Ever After, and In a Galaxy Far, Far Away: Using Narrative to Fill the Cognitive Gap Left by Overreliance on Pure Logic in Appellate Briefs and Motion Memoranda*, 46 WILLAMETTE L. REV. 255, 274 (2009).

14. ROBERT P. BURNS, A THEORY OF THE TRIAL 36 (1999). Becker's article, *supra* note 10, offers more theme examples: "This is a case about loyalty and betrayal." "This is a case about keeping promises." "This is a case about a wealthy man's abuse of an employee."

15. SCALIA & GARNER, *supra* note 10, at 59.

16. Becker, *supra* note 10, at 579. Studies in neuroscience confirm a strong and surprising link between emotions and decisionmaking; in the brain, "emotional and cognitive/rational pathways overlap." Stanchi, *supra* note 2, at 313-14. As such, "we are more likely to make wise decisions when the rational parts of our brain, i.e., the frontal cortex, work in concert with the emotional parts of our brain. . . . [O]ur brains work best when we engage in 'whole brain' thinking." Steven J. Johansen, *Was Colonel Sanders a Terrorist? An Essay on the Ethical Limits of Applied Legal Storytelling*, 7 J. OF THE ASS'N OF LEGAL WRITING DIRECTORS 63, 81-82 (2010) (citing JONAH LEHRER, HOW WE DECIDE 248-49 (Houghton Mifflin Harcourt 2009)).

17. Stanchi, *supra* note 2, at 315.

18. Susan Hanley Kosse & David T. ButleRitchie, *How Judges, Practitioners, and Legal Writing Teachers Assess the Writing Skills of New Law Graduates: A Comparative Study*, 53 J. LEGAL ED. 80, 85-86 (2003) (reporting that 71.4% of responding judges and attorneys deemed the absence of a theme or theory a "basic writing problem" and ranked the theme or theory as the most important element of legal style); *see also* Chestek, *supra* note 9, at 19-20 (reporting a marked judicial preference for thematic "story briefs").

19. Becker, *supra* note 10, at 586 (theme is "where the client's voice and point of view are present").

20. *Id.* at 576; Stanchi, *supra* note 2, at 312.

21. Stanchi, *supra* note 2, at 315-24; RICHARD K. NEUMANN, JR., LEGAL REASONING AND LEGAL WRITING, STRUCTURE, STRATEGY & STYLE 296-97 (6th ed. 2009) (citations omitted).

22. Stanchi, *supra* note 2, at 322-25 (discussing the impact of themes that evoke anger or sadness in the reader).

23. This approach harnesses the power of negative emotions. *Id.* at 318.

24. This approach takes advantage of "omission bias," the "preference people have for inaction over action." *Id.* at 319.

25. Decisionmakers are more motivated to act to avoid losses than to effect gains, the result of a cognitive bias called "loss aversion." *Id.* at 320-21.

26. *See* Ian Gallacher, *Thinking Like Nonlawyers: Why Empathy Is a Core Lawyering Skill and Why Legal Education Should Change to Reflect Its Importance*, 8 J. OF THE ASS'N OF LEGAL WRITING DIRECTORS 109, 120 (2011).

27. *See* Becker, *supra* note 10, at 604 (responding to Alan Dershowitz's critique of narrative in legal argument).

28. Stanchi, *supra* note 2, at 325; Fischer, *supra* note 1, at 2; Wayne Schiess & Elana Einhorn, *Issue Statements: Different Kinds for Different Documents*, 50 WASHBURN L.J. 341, 341 (2011).

29. Schiess & Einhorn, *supra* note 28, at 341. These writers sum up the importance of issue statements and the corresponding effort to perfect them:

> According to one expert, "no point is more important in persuasive and analytical writing than the issue statement." One judge has asserted that that the issue statement is one of the most important parts of briefs and memoranda. In light of this importance, successful lawyers can spend hours crafting an issue statement for an appellate document. One has

said that "the statement of issues in a brief or memorandum requires more effort than any other section."

Id. (internal citations omitted).

30. *See, e.g.,* Sup. Ct. R. 14 (limiting the Court's review to the questions presented and "every subsidiary question fairly included therein"). The Court will not entertain attempts to shoehorn additional, perhaps unpreserved, issues or arguments into the briefs.

31. Fischer, *supra* note 1, at 225-26 (study concluding that issue "clarity and succinctness are of the highest importance").

32. Schiess & Einhorn, *supra* note 28, at 353.

33. *Id.* at 342; Judith A. Fischer, *Got Issues? An Empirical Study About Framing Them,* 6 J. Ass'n Legal Writing Directors 1, 26 (2009).

34. Schiess & Einhorn, *supra* note 28, at 43-44.

35. *See* Fischer, *supra* note 1, at 12.

36. *Id.* at 11.

37. *See id.*; Schiess & Einhorn, *supra* note 28, at 342 (summarizing critiques of the single-sentence issue statement).

38. *See* Fischer, *supra* note 1, at 11.

39. *See id.* at 12 n.75 (citing Bradley S. Coleman et al., *Grammatical and Structural Choices in Issue Framing: A Quantitative Analysis of Questions Presented from a Half Century of Supreme Court Briefs,* 29 Am. J. Trial Advoc. 336 (2005)); Schiess & Einhorn, *supra* note 28, at 351-52.

40. *See* Fischer, *supra* note 1, at 12.

41. *See* Schiess & Einhorn, *supra* note 28, at 353.

42. *See* Fischer, *supra* note 1, at 22.

43. *Id.* at 24; *see also* Stanchi, *supra* note 2, at 325-26.

44. *See supra* note 30.

45. *See* Schiess & Einhorn, *supra* note 28, at 354-55 (recognizing the need for broader issue statement components in briefs to courts of last resort).

46. *See* Fischer, *supra* note 1, at 9 ("A judge should not have to struggle to decode an issue statement, and if asked to do so probably will not.") (internal quotations and citations omitted).

47. Roy Peter Clark, Writing Tools: 50 Essential Strategies for Every Writer, 11-14 (2006).

48. *See* Fischer, *supra* note 1, at 17-18.

49. *Compare Id.* at 5-9 (2009) (analyzing the faults of over-long issues) *with* Schiess & Einhorn, *supra* note 28, at 348, 350 (same).

50. Brian J. Foley & Ruth Ann Robbins, *Fiction 101: A Primer for Lawyers on How to Use Fiction Writing Techniques to Write Persuasive Facts Sections,* 32 Rutgers L.J. 459, 472-73 (2001).

51. Jennifer Sheppard, *Once Upon a Time, Happily Ever After, and In a Galaxy Far, Far Away: Using Narrative to Fill the Cognitive Gap Left by Overreliance on Pure Logic in Appellate Briefs and Motion Memoranda,* 46 Willamette L. Rev. 255, 270-83 (2009); Elizabeth Fajans & Mary R. Falk, *Untold Stories: Restoring Narrative to Pleading Practice,* 15 Legal Writing: J. Legal Writing Inst. 3, 23-46 (2009); Foley & Robbins, *supra* note 50, at 465-80. While Chapter 8 explored those storytelling components on a much larger scale (the entire brief) — here, we focus on how they work in the statement of facts.

52. Carolyn Grose, *Storytelling Across the Curriculum: From Margin to Center, from Clinic to the Classroom,* 7 J. of the Ass'n of Legal Writing Directors 37, 39 (2010) ("Construction is the act of building: putting together the elements that comprise the story and then writing it down. Performance of the story — reading it, telling it, enacting it — comes later.").

53. Sheppard, *supra* note 51, at 270 ("When developing a story to explain the case, a lawyer should begin by defining the conflict.").

54. *Id.* at 270 (internal quotations and citations omitted).

55. *See id.*; Foley & Robbins, *supra* note 50, at 469.

56. Foley & Robbins, *supra* note 50, at 468 (Characters "have needs and goals. . . . Odysseus tries to get home. Scarlett O'Hara decides never to go hungry again."); Fajans & Falk, *supra* note 51, at 30.

57. *See* Phillip N. Meyer, *Vignettes From a Narrative Primer,* 12 Legal Writing: J. Legal Writing Inst. 229, 268 (2006) ("The cast of characters determines how the theme is developed into the plot.").

58. Foley & Robbins, *supra* note 50, at 470.

59. Meyer, *supra* note 57, at 268.

60. Fajans & Falk, *supra* note 51, at 17 (quoting Anthony Amsterdam & Jerome Bruner, Minding the Law at 111 (Harvard U. Press 2000)).

61. *See* Grose, *supra* note 52, at 42 (outlining the typical plot elements as the steady state, the disruption, the characters' handling of disruption, and resolution) (citing Anthony Amsterdam & Jerome Bruner, Minding the Law at 113-114 (Harvard U. Press 2000)); *see also* Fajans & Falk, *supra* note 51, at 18 (2009) (citing Anthony Amsterdam & Jerome Bruner, Minding the Law at 113-14 (Harvard U. Press 2000)); Sheppard, *supra* note 51, at 280-83 (describing the same elements as introduction, rising action, climax, falling action, resolution).

62. Sheppard, *supra* note 51, at 283.

63. Grose, *supra* note 52, at 45 ("[S]torytellers . . . construct the stories by sorting through what is out there and figuring out both what to say and how to say it, based on the storyteller's own perspective about what matters.").
64. *See id.* at 44 (describing the fact selection process as "pick[ing] and choos[ing] from the available facts to present a picture of what happened that most accurately reflects our sense of what matters").
65. LAUREL CURRIE OATES & ANNE ENQUIST, THE LEGAL WRITING HANDBOOK at 387-88 (4th ed., 2006); *see also* Sheppard, *supra* note 51, at 268-83 (discussing all four categories in explaining how to draft a persuasive narrative in a brief); Fajans & Falk, *supra* note 51, at 23-47 (discussing four categories in explaining how to draft a persuasive narrative in a complaint).
66. Sheppard, *supra* note 51, at 280 ("A lawyer cannot ignore aspects of the factual or legal setting that may impede his or her arguments on behalf of his client . . . without sacrificing credibility and plausibility.").
67. Fajans & Falk, *supra* note 51, at 39; Sheppard, *supra* note 51, at 278-79.
68. Sheppard, *supra* note 51, at 279.
69. The Federal Circuit's local rules provide for separate procedural and factual sections in this manner. *See* FED. CIR. R. 28(7), (8). The Second and Eleventh Circuits contemplate a single Statement of the Case, which begins with the procedural facts and then moves to the factual narrative. *See* 2D CIR. R. 28.1; 11TH CIR. RULE 28-1(i). The remaining circuits either do not differentiate between procedural and other facts, or require them to be in a single Statement of the Case section. *See, e.g.,* 1ST CIR. R. 28; 3D CIR. R. 28.1; 4TH CIR. R. 28(F); 5TH CIR. R. 28.3(G); 6TH CIR. R. 28; 7TH CIR. R. 28; 8TH CIR. R. 28A; 9TH CIR. R. 28-2; 10TH CIR. R. 28; D.C. CIR. R. 28. Absent a specific rule prohibition, though, many attorneys choose to write separate Statement of the Case and Statement of Facts sections, with the procedural facts confined to the former.
70. *See* Brady v. Maryland, 373 U.S. 83, 86 (1963) (describing how this type of claim arises when prosecutors refuse to turn over potentially exculpatory evidence in their possession).
71. Fajans & Falk, *supra* note 51, at 24.
72. *Id.*
73. *Id.* ("'Defaults can be quite dangerous. . . . Habitual chronology can distract us from telling an effective story that complements and enhances our legal argument.'") (quoting Stephen V. Armstrong & Timothy P. Terrell, *Organizing Facts to Tell Stories,* 9 PERSPECTIVES 90, 90 (2001)).
74. *Id.*
75. *Id.* at 25 (referring to this technique as "compressing time").
76. *See, e.g.,* 42 U.S.C. § 12113(b) ("The term 'qualification standards' may include a requirement that an individual shall not pose a direct threat to the health or safety of other individuals in the workplace."); 29 C.F.R. § 1630.15(b)(2) ("[T]he term 'qualification standard' may include a requirement that an individual shall not pose a direct threat to the health or safety of the individual or others in the workplace.").
77. Brief for the Petitioner at 1-2, Chevron U.S.A., Inc. v. Echazabal, No. 00-1406 (written by Mayer Brown and Hawkins, Schnabel, Lindahl, & Beck).
78. Fajans & Falk, *supra* note 51, at 25 (describing this structure as "starting at a critical point in the story and then drawing back in time to describe the characters in the story and the events that brought them to that critical point").
79. *Id.* at 24-25.
80. Brief for the Appellees at 5-15, Facebook, Inc. v. Connect U, Nos. 08-16745, 08-16873, 09-15021 (written by Orrick, Herrington & Sutcliffe LLP).
81. *See, e.g.,* Brief for the Petitioner at 3-6, University of Texas Southwestern Medical Center v. Nassar No. 12-484 (written by King & Spalding LLP).
82. Sarah E. Ricks & Jane L. Istvan, *Effective Brief Writing Despite High Volume Practice: Ten Misconceptions That Results in Bad Briefs* 38 U. TOL. L. REV. 1113, 1125-26 (2007) ("Use topical (not argumentative) headings to break up a long story into digestible chunks and to focus on the narrative.").
83. *See* ILL. SUP. CT. R. 341(e)(6) ("Statement of Facts, which shall contain the facts necessary to an understanding of the case, stated accurately and fairly without argument or comment . . ."); MO. SUP. CT. R. 84.04(c) ("The statement of facts shall be a fair and concise statement of the facts relevant to the questions presented for determination without argument.").
84. Philip N. Meyer, *Teaching Writing and Teaching Doctrine: A Symbiotic Relationship?,* 12 LEGAL WRITING: J. LEGAL WRITING INST. 229, 242-44 (2006).
85. Fajans & Falk, *supra* note 51, at 27.
86. *See* Becker, *supra* note 10, 582-94; Sheppard, *supra* note 51, at 268-69.
87. Becker, *supra* note 10, at 585; Foley & Robbins, *supra* note 50, at 478 ("[R]eaders often root for the character they identify with or like or know.").
88. Brief for the Appellees at 1, Facebook, Inc. v. Connect U, Nos. 08-16745, 08-16873, 09-15021 (written by Orrick, Herrington & Sutcliffe LLP).
89. *Id.* at 5.

90. Meyer, *supra* note 84, at 263-64 ("Effective characterization captures appropriate traits in images, or in careful descriptions, often through the selection of vivid details.").
91. Fajans & Falk, *supra* note 51, at 38.
92. Foley & Robbins, *supra* note 50, at 479 ("Through a person's [point of view], a writer can learn, and then set forth, the person's reasoning behind, and motivation for, his actions.").
93. Stanchi, *supra* note 2, 346-47.
94. Oates & Enquist, *supra* note 65, at 393.
95. *Id.* at 394.
96. *Id.*
97. *Id.* at 395-96.
98. *Id.* at 395.
99. Grose, *supra* note 52, at 44.
100. Meyer, *supra* note 84, at 241 (discussing the narrative functions of detail and summary); Fajans & Falk, *supra* note 51, at 40 ("Details elicit emotion, create mental pictures, stimulate associations, and lend coherence and fidelity to narratives.").
101. Meyer, *supra* note 84, at 241 (discussing the narrative functions of detail and summary).
102. Brief for the Appellant at 16, Oracle America, Inc. v. Google Inc., Nos. 2013-1021, 2013-1022 (written by Orrick, Herrington & Sutcliffe, Oracle America, and & Kirkland & Ellis).
103. *See* Oates & Enquist, *supra* note 65, at 389-90.
104. Sheppard, *supra* note 51, at 280; Ricks & Istvan, *supra* note 82, at 1125-26.
105. Meyer, *supra* note 84, at 234-44.
106. *See id.* at 234-44.
107. Oates & Enquist, *supra* note 65, at 396; Fajans & Falk, *supra* note 51, at 44-46.
108. Fajans & Falk, *supra* note 51, at 44.
109. Oates & Enquist, *supra* note 65, at 396.
110. Brief for the Appellees at 10, Facebook, Inc. v. Connect U, Nos. 08-16745, 08-16873, 09-15021 (written by Orrick, Herrington & Sutcliffe).
111. Johansen, *supra* note 16, at 64-86; *see* Meyer, *supra* note 84, at 230 ("Legal storytelling is a carefully circumscribed business.").

10 The Writing Phase: Structuring Arguments Beyond IRAC

With draft issues and fact statement in hand, you are ready to turn to the Argument section. By now you should be eager to write it. In the planning and learning phase, you settled on two to four issues that coalesce around a central problem and that offer the best chance of affirmance or reversal. You identified and sketched out a tentative blueprint of supporting arguments and reasons. And you became intimately familiar with the law, the record, and areas of vulnerability.

In writing process terms, your argument work has thus far been a collaboration between the Executive Chef and Sous Chef. Now the Sous Chef should rise to a more prominent role, working out a more definitive argument order and reason sequence. After that, you'll don the Line Cook hat, and efficiently execute a draft without small-scale judgment. But before you can tap into the Line Cook's quick and bloodless drafting mode, you must understand two core tasks of drafting arguments: (1) structuring the argument to explain and persuade; and (2) framing the argument to convey your client's viewpoint and story. The former relies heavily on law and logic while the latter leans more heavily on Chapter 8's "logic plus" rhetoric and storytelling techniques.

Chapters 10 and 11 break down an expert approach to these structuring and framing tasks. Our goal in these chapters is ambitious. We aim to wean you from IRAC or CRAC or any other acronym-driven organizational paradigm that served you well as a neophyte legal writer, and to replace those paradigms with a more sophisticated and flexible approach to building arguments. As you read, keep in mind that you may need more than one Sous-Chef/Line Cook collaborative pass to incorporate these structuring and framing principles. Moreover, understand that these chapters describe structure and framing from the standpoint of the ideal — a perfected structure, a compelling frame. Particularly at this stage of your writing career, it will not be until you reach the Server/Expediter phase that you will achieve these nuanced results.

This chapter kicks off the expert argument-building process with structure. No matter how persuasively framed or stylistically appealing, an ill-structured argument will lose your appeal. If the court is unable to follow your line of reasoning, your arguments will be written off. Section 1 begins the structure discussion with larger-scale questions of argument order. Section 2 covers the smaller-scale work of sequencing and developing the reasons supporting each argument. Section 3 shifts gears, turning from what to do to what to avoid. It discusses common legal reasoning errors, including logical fallacies. Section 4 offers a complementary method of testing your arguments: mooting and round-tabling during the drafting process. By this chapter's end, you will be equipped with the tools to build every argument in your brief into a streamlined, airtight product. You will then be ready for Chapter 11's argument-framing techniques.

Section 1   Ordering Arguments

Recall our definition of issues and arguments from Chapter 6. Issues are global questions a brief poses as grounds for reversing or affirming the lower court, while arguments are stand-alone conclusions that work together or alternatively to support an outcome on each issue. Here we are concerned with which arguments come first, second, or third underneath each issue — and what factors drive those decisions. The three main drivers for argument ordering are: (1) the logical and legal relationships among arguments; (2) argument strength; and (3) appellate strategy. As we'll explain, one driver may trump the others, depending on the nature of your arguments and your objectives.

1.1   The Role of Argument Relationships

The large-scale ordering baseline is argument relationship, both logical and legal. Recall the typical relationships from Chapter 6: conjunctive, alternative, threshold/primary merits arguments, totality, and balancing. Arguments with multiple conjunctive requirements, disjunctive alternatives, or totality or balancing tests must break down those components into subarguments. Thus, an argument that a defendant "constructively possessed" drugs must subdivide into the elements of that crime, and an argument that turns on either an intentional or reckless state of mind would split into those alternatives. Threshold arguments, such as juris-diction or standing, must precede arguments on the merits.[1] The same is true of coverage or qualification questions, such as whether an employer is a "covered entity" under the Americans With Disabilities Act, which must be dealt with before primary arguments, such as whether the employer discriminated under the Act. In the special case of statutory construction arguments, plain meaning must precede purpose-oriented arguments.[2] And both of these should precede consequentialist policy arguments. After these baseline placement principles, strength and strategy factor into the mix.

1.2   The Role of Argument Strength

One argument may get the pole position over another because of its strength on the merits. Indeed, the textbook approach is to make the strongest argument first.[3] In the main, judges say they prefer this arrangement.[4] As an example of strength-based ordering, take the case of an appellee-employer who won summary judgment in a federal court diversity case on a former employee's defamation claim. That claim arose from a supervisor's statement to someone outside the company, remarking that the employee was a sub-par performer. Assume the lower court granted summary judgment on three alternative grounds: (1) the statement was not defamatory; (2) it was not false; and (3) and in any event, the supervisor had a qualified privilege to make the statement. On appeal, one of these alternative grounds could have stronger legal or factual footing than another. If apposite authority holds categorically that "sub-par performer" is a statement of opinion, not fact, then the "not defamatory" argument is strong and worthy of a featured placement. But even stronger may be the qualified privilege argument, which, given the precedent, is typically more amenable to legal determinations and avoids the judgment calls that accompany fact versus opinion distinctions.[5] The falsity argument may be more tenuous because a statement's veracity is often a question of fact.[6] Many advocates would order the arguments accordingly, first asking for affirmance outright on the qualified privilege defense, then alternatively arguing that the claim fails as a matter of law because: (1) The statement was not defamatory; and (2) also alternatively, the statement was true.

1.3 The Role of Strategy

But strategy can trump pure strength. In this example, the defamatory and falsity elements' failings may unite around a central theme, creating a narrative of affirmance. Perhaps the employer's appellate strategy is to paint the employee's case as one that attempts to subvert an at-will employment relationship (in which an employer can terminate without any reason) — and only by stretching the defamation elements beyond recognition. In that sense, defending the appeal is about the integrity of defamation claims and the restrained institutional role of a federal appellate court reviewing state law issues. The qualified privilege argument may be demoted or omitted if it does not fit into that theme. Moreover, qualified privilege is an affirmative defense on which the employer bears the burden of proof. That, too, could weaken the employer's appellate position, favoring a less prominent spot for that argument. A contrasting strategy that views the qualified privilege argument as the strongest could dictate putting it at the end, but in either a clean-up or fallback role. In a clean-up role, the qualified privilege argument finishes on a point of strength; this argument's recency effect might then influence the court's view of the others.[7] Or, putting the qualified privilege argument last may be a judgment that it is a safe fallback position, with the more malleable defamatory and falsity elements representing a bigger ask.[8] Cognitive psychologists call this the "door in the face"[9] strategy, in which these riskier but still reasonable element-based arguments prime the audience to accept the qualified privilege argument's relatively meager request.[10]

For still different strategic reasons, some advocates might dispense with the falsity argument altogether in the quest for affirmance. If the appellate court reverses and remands along with an unfavorable legal determination on falsity — for example by defining it broadly — then raising this argument may do more harm than good in the long run.[11] Although the appellate court has the power to address falsity if the lower court relied on it and the appellant raised it,[12] the appellee's strategic decision to exclude it may lead the court to rest its decision on the fully briefed points.

Practice Alert #1
Argument Ordering
Exercise

The online companion contains an exercise using Tables of Contents from two appellate briefs, along with a basic description of the legal issues on appeal. For each, you will be asked to discern what likely motivated the advocates' ordering choices.

1.4   The Role of Preservation Arguments

Preservation arguments are longer shots that typically reside at the end of an appellate brief to preserve an issue for review in a court of last resort.[13] While an appellate court may be unwilling to address a constitutional issue when a statutory holding would end the matter, or be wary of adopting a new legal test when the existing test would yield the same result, a supreme court might view the case as the perfect vehicle to decide such bold questions. If the advocate does not raise the constitutional argument or new test in his brief to the intermediate appellate court, however, that opportunity is lost. Because courts of last resort will not address an argument that the appellate court has not had the opportunity to review,[14] those arguments must be made at the intermediate level first. This is the exception to the rule against raising weaker arguments.[15] An argument that looks tenuous at the intermediate level may actually be a winner at the supreme court level.

SUMMARY

Large-Scale Argument Ordering Principles

STEP 1 — For each issue, determine the logical and legal relationships of your supporting arguments. Mark them as threshold/primary, conjunctive, alternative, totality, balancing, or statutory construction arguments. Make preliminary ordering decisions on this basis.

STEP 2 — Rank these arguments from strongest to weakest. Remember to consider the standard of review, the burden of proof, and the ease of legal determination, not just substantive strength. Adjust your preliminary order accordingly.

STEP 3 — Consider your appellate strategy. Does your preliminary order fit thematic or storytelling objectives? Does it make sense to put any "big ask" arguments up front? Would any of your stronger arguments perform well in a "cleanup" or "fallback" role? Does your preliminary ordering pose any remand risks?

STEP 4 — Determine whether you have any preservation arguments, and whether you might pursue the appeal past the intermediate level.

1.5 Argument Placement Pitfalls

On the flip side of these ordering principles are organizational traps to avoid. The most common is reflexive acquiescence to others' organizational schemes. Avoid the rut of placing arguments in the order that most courts address them. This risk runs high with conjunctive and totality arguments because their legal frameworks limit your flexibility. One order may make logical sense for the opinion — the negligence elements of duty, breach, causation, and damage follow a temporal line, for example — but a different arrangement may further your own arguments. Multi-factor tests, too, tend to appear in the same monotonous sequence opinion after opinion. Do not use that arrangement unless it serves your objectives. Moreover, factors that seem distinct in the abstract may overlap in the context of your appellate record. If it fits your appeal and improves efficiency, design a single argument around multiple factors, rather than addressing each factor separately. In short, let the core ordering principles of logic, strength, and strategy dictate your arrangement, not rote adherence to what has come before.

Another trap is uncritically tracking your opponent's ordering scheme. Many advocates eschew their opponent's argument organization, which will be strategically designed to further the opponent's case, not their own. These advocates prefer to craft their own organizational framework, so that the court encounters the arguments from their client's vantage point, and through their own narrative of reversal or affirmance. As long as the advocate includes directly responsive counterarguments, the organizational disparities should not impede the court's comprehension. In contrast, some advocates shadow their opponent's organization, reasoning that the court can better track the arguments — and more importantly, their responses — if the order remains consistent throughout briefing. Both schools of thought have this in common: strategic reasons drive their decisions. Whichever approach you adopt, it should involve the same critical thought.

REFLECTION, DISCUSSION, AND CHALLENGE QUESTIONS

Argument Ordering

- Consider what has guided your argument ordering in the past. What new strategies did you learn in this section?
- Do you think an advocate's strongest argument should always come first? Why or why not?
- Think about the appeal you are working on. What will dictate your ordering of arguments? Using the principles from this section, write a few short paragraphs describing your argument ordering strategy.

Section 2   Beyond IRAC: Building a Reason-Based Argument Structure

With argument placement squared away, the next structural step is to build the arguments themselves. At its most basic level, argument structure is a function of logic and reason.[16] That's what judges say drives their decisions,[17] despite the obvious influence of the "logic plus" tools covered in Chapter 8.[18] Reasons move in a progression, doing the work of spelling out how the advocate gets from Point A (a set of existing legal and factual circumstances) to Point B (the advocate's winning conclusion).[19] This is where organizational paradigms like IRAC and CRAC fall short, as narrow and incomplete expressions of argument structure.[20] The basic units of argument are not abstract rules (R), nor are they some combination of rules and facts (A). Indeed, some arguments do not even turn on the facts. Instead the units of argument are the advocate's own ideas about *why* the court should accept the argument's conclusion, gleaned from processing the authorities and facts and forming those raw materials into the advocate's own propositions.

2.1   IRAC Structure vs. Reason-Based Structure

Two student-written examples reproduced below show the difference between an IRAC-based argument and a Beyond IRAC, reason-based argument. These examples stem from the *Mutombo* appeal, where, as you'll recall, Mr. Mutombo argued that the writing forming the basis for his attempted terrorist threat conviction should have been suppressed. He contended that the warrantless automobile search that produced the writing failed the Fourth Amendment's inventory exception because the search was conducted for investigatory purposes, not caretaking objectives.

Review these two examples, carefully comparing their structure and progression. As you do, notice how the IRAC-based example treats the rules and facts in separate blocks, making the writer's reasons hard to discern, while the Beyond-IRAC example is structured around the writer's three distinct reasons for why the search had no caretaking purpose.

EXAMPLE #1 **IRAC-Based Structure**

A. By Seizing and Reading the Composition in Mutombo's Car, Police Exceeded the Scope of a Valid Inventory Search.

Officer Salles violated the Fourth Amendment when he examined the piece of paper stuck between the front seat and console of Mutombo's   ⟵ *Issue* car. Salles's action went well beyond the scope of an inventory and did nothing to further a valid caretaking purpose.

Because personal papers found during an inventory retain a heightened expectation of privacy, *see D'Antorio*, 926 P.2d at 1163, police can examine them only if there is a compelling caretaking purpose. Courts recognize three caretaking purposes: (1) to protect the owner's property; (2) to safeguard officers from danger; and (3) to protect police from claims of lost or ⟵ *Rules* damaged goods. Colorado v. Bertine, 479 U.S. 367, 371-72 (1987); People v. Gipson, 786 N.E.2d 540, 544 (Ill. 2003). Seizing personal documents triggers none of these caretaking purposes. *See Seng*, 766 N.E.2d at 504 ("Generally speaking, none of the legitimate purposes of a custodial search will justify reading the accused's papers. . . ."); *D'Antonio*, 926 P.2d at 1164 (same). Just as unconnected to caretaking purposes — and even more intrusive — is an officer's in-depth review of a personal document's contents. *Compare D'Antonio*, 926 P.2d at 1165 (finding patrolman's recording of info on front of bank card reasonable to protect owner's property and guard against claim of malfeasance) *with Seng*, 766 N.E.2d at 504 (holding an officer's recording of information on the reverse side of a bank card unsupported by any caretaking purpose). **Aside from requiring a caretaking purpose, an inventory search can extend "only to where an officer can reasonably conclude that valuable property may be located." U.S. v. Edwards, 577 F.2d 883, 894-95 (5th Cir. 1978). Permitting officers to examine documents for purposes other than identification or value, or to look beyond where valuable items are likely to appear, risks turning an inventory search into a "general means of discovering evidence." Bertine, 479 U.S. at 367 (Blackmun, J., concurring).**

The search of Mutombo's vehicle exceeded the scope of an inventory because Officer Salles read over his personal paper for reasons other than ⟵ *Application* determining its identity or value. *Salles testified that he pulled the paper from between the seat and console only because he thought it had medical value.* He noticed the image of an inhaler on the paper and initially believed it to be a prescription. **Aside from the fact that nothing of value is likely to be located between a seat and console**, *even this initial review exceeded a caretaking purpose because a paper reflecting a prescription has no inherent value. Rather, the value lies in the prescribing physician's order, and that order can be replicated.* Moreover, Salles's further examination proved too much. After reading over the paper's front side, he realized it was not a prescription and thus lacked medical value. R. 12. Nonetheless, he turned the piece of scrap over and examined its reverse side—finding Mutombo's handwritten composition. R. 11-12. Officer Salles's conduct thus violated the Fourth Amendment and contents   ⟵ *Conclusion* of the paper should have been suppressed.

EXAMPLE #2 **Reason-Based Structure**

A. Bradley Police exceeded the scope of an inventory search because inspecting a loose piece of paper does not serve any inventory objectives.

Inventory searches are a narrow exception to the Fourth Amendment's warrant requirement, legal only if officers inspect a car's contents for "caretaking purposes": to protect the owner's   ⟵ *Conclusion and Roadmap* valuables, to ensure officer safety, or to avoid claims of lost or damaged goods. Colorado v. Bertine, 479 U.S. 367, 371-72 (1987); South Dakota v. Opperman, 428 U.S. 364, 380 (1976) ("[U]pholding searches of this type provides no general license for the police to examine all the contents of such automobiles.") (Powell, J., concurring). The piece of paper stuffed between the front seat and center console of Mr. Mutombo's locked, abandoned car was not valuable, at risk of theft, or dangerous to police. Absent these caretaking purposes, Officer Salles was not authorized to scrutinize the paper's contents—or even catalog it in the first place.

Officer Salles violated Mr. Mutombo's Fourth Amendment rights the moment he picked up the loose piece of paper containing Mr. Mutombo's lyrics because that paper posed no threat to police and had no obvious value. The safety rationale does not apply here because it is undisputed that the paper itself posed no risk of harm. **As for the valuables justification, an inventory search extends "only to where an officer can *reasonably* conclude that valuable property may be located." U.S. v. Edwards, 577 F.2d 883, 894-95 (5th Cir. 1978) (emphasis added). In *Edwards*, the defendant challenged a police search of loose carpet flaps in his car, contending that no reasonable officer could believe anything valuable would be hidden there. *Id.* The court upheld the search's scope because the carpet flap had been displaced, supporting a reasonable belief that valuable property might be stored beneath. *Id.* But it refused to "condone searching under the carpeting in every case, much less the ripping apart of an automobile, or any part thereof, under the guise of an inventory search." *Id.* at 895.**

Just like a glove compartment, trunk, or console, the area beneath unsettled carpet flaps might be a reasonable place to check for a vehicle owner's valuables. But it is unreasonable to assume that anything contained in a handwritten, loose paper stuffed between a car seat and console would be valuable enough to require inventorying. Officer Salles claimed that he picked up and inspected the paper because he believed it might contain a medical prescription. *Even if the paper had contained a prescription, it would not have been valuable in the inventory sense. Failure to log a written prescription would neither jeopardize the security of the prescription nor give rise to liability for the police department.*

Even if Officer Salles could justify a quick glance to determine the paper's value, he went well beyond that. Personal papers trigger heightened privacy expectations, *see D'Antorio*,

← **Reason 1** *(safety)*

← **Reason 2** *(valuables)*

← **Reason 3** *(alternative basis— privacy)*

926 P.2d at 1163, and Officer Salles's careful study of both sides of the handwritten document in Mutombo's car took the search beyond any ostensible value purpose. *See* U.S. v. Khoury, 901 F.2d 948, 949 (11th Cir. 1990) (distinguishing between flipping through notebook pages to rule out anything of value hidden between its pages and reading the notebook, for which the officer "had no purpose other than investigation") (emphasis added); *see also Seng,* 766 N.E.2d at 504 (holding that an officer's transcribing information on the back side of an ATM card had an improper investigatory purpose). Officer Salles's thorough reading of the paper, including all text on both sides, was purely investigatory and illegal in the absence of a search warrant. The lower court erred in refusing to suppress this evidence.

← *Conclusion*

Notice how Example 1 combines all the rules on caretaking purposes, then treats all the facts together afterwards. Even though the writer uses signposting and transitions to connect the facts back to the rules — and covers much the same substantive ground as Example 2 — the rule and fact "blocking" obscures the progression of reasons supporting the conclusion that Officer Salles acted without a caretaking purpose.

In contrast, Example 2 is explicitly organized around and progresses through three separate reasons, each relating to a caretaking purpose, and each framed as the advocate's own proposition. The first reason quickly eliminates danger as a rationale for examining the paper. The second reason attacks the officer's asserted value-protecting purpose, focusing on the paper's location in a place where a driver would not keep valuables. The third reason is framed as an alternative ground: Even assuming a value-protecting purpose, the officer exceeded that purpose by reading much more than necessary to assess the writing's value.

Example 1's IRAC structure splinters and conceals these distinct reasons, as shown by the bold face text in its second and third paragraphs. Although the bold face text at the end of the second paragraph cover a relevant rule of law on protecting valuables and the bold face clause midway through the next paragraph applies it, this information is never presented as a coherent, self-contained reason. Example 2's bold face text integrates the law and facts on the valve-protecting purpose making their connection much more directly and efficiently.

Example 1 also misses an opportunity to preempt opposing arguments. As we explain in Chapter 11, the most effective arguments are two-sided;[21] they not only advance their affirmative positions but also cut off opposing positions—sometimes in the same breath. Review the italicized text in Example 2's third paragraph. Here, as part of Reason 3, the writer refutes the argument that the officer's motive was to protect valuables because he first believed the note was a prescription. That same content appears in the italicized text in Example 1's third paragraph, but it is presented defensively at the beginning of the application section, where a strong *affirmative* reason would normally appear.

REFLECTION, DISCUSSION, AND CHALLENGE QUESTIONS

Reason-Based Argument Structure

- What is your reaction to the IRAC-based and reason-based examples? What advantages do you think a reason-based structure offers over IRAC? Are you wary of using a reason-based structure, and if so, why?
- Find a sample of legal writing from your first year of law school. Evaluate its structure. Did you use IRAC or some other ordering principle?
- If you used IRAC, how would this sample look if you changed it into a reason-based structure?

2.2 Building Reason-Based Arguments with Reasoning Chains

Now that you have a basic understanding of what it means to build arguments around reasons rather than IRAC, you must build a reason-based structure for your own appellate arguments. Chapter 6 proposed that you draft a tentative blueprint for your arguments, devising the distinct reasons the court must accept in order to agree with each argument's conclusion. If you drafted an Argument Assessment memo, you may even have gone so far as to map out a preliminary sequence of those reasons. Now it is time to define and develop those reasons into ironclad arguments with seemingly inexorable conclusions.

A word about this section's teaching method: We do not aim to replace IRAC or CRAC with another paradigm, for paradigms oversimplify argument structure. As such, this section does not offer a "how to" manual with organizational boxes to check. Instead, it describes an expert approach, one based on universal principles of organization and logic, and demonstrates how the approach works in common argument contexts. The goal is for you to internalize the approach and to use the expert examples to inform your work, which must be tailored to your own appeal's demands.

In briefs, the reasons supporting each argument are sequenced and connected in a chain[22] that develops the reasons and builds progressively towards the argument's conclusion. The chain metaphor captures the reasons' strength of connection and their fluid course to the result the writer seeks.[23] Often, the reasoning chain's core component is the syllogism. In the first year of law school (or earlier), you probably learned that a syllogism proves a conclusion based on two premises.[24] The syllogism starts with a general proposition (the major premise), moves to a more specific proposition (the minor premise), and ends with a conclusion. A good example is the old saw involving Socrates' mortality:

EXAMPLE

Basic Syllogism

All humans are mortals.   ← *Major premise*
Socrates is human.   ← *Minor premise*
Therefore, Socrates is mortal.   ← *Conclusion*

A syllogism's power comes from the principle that what is true of the universal is true of the particular. In this example, the human Socrates' mortality is undeniable given the universal truth that all humans are mortal. In legal argument, the syllogism makes an equally compelling match of the universal to the particular. If an advocate can set up a universal legal "bucket" into which falls a particular facet of his case, then the resulting conclusion has great force, as shown here:

EXAMPLE

Legal Syllogism

Title VII's concept of discrimination includes racially hostile work environments "*permeated* with discriminatory intimidation, ridicule, and insult."[25]

The plaintiff, an African American employee, endured a work environment in which his supervisor continuously directed racial epithets at him and frequently mocked his racial identity.

Therefore, the plaintiff suffered discrimination under Title VII.

Now, within this broad syllogism, a reasoning chain must be embedded to prove the discrimination conclusion. Its major premises would break down the legal definition of a racially hostile work environment, such as how long must it go on and what kind of conduct qualifies as harassing. Its minor premises would fold in the time span, frequency, and severity of the supervisor's racial epithets. Together these premises would force the hostile environment conclusion. This type of reasoning chain, which builds reasons in the form of successive syllogisms on the way to an argument's conclusion, is called a "polysyllogism."[26] To illustrate, if the Beyond IRAC example argument's reasons were translated into polysyllogistic form, its reasoning "chain" would look like this:

Roadmap of the argument:	Inventory searches are valid only if the searching officer has a caretaking purpose.
	Officer Salles had no caretaking purpose when he searched Mutombo's car and examined the note within it.
	Therefore his search was invalid.
Reason #1's chain link:	One caretaking purpose is protecting officer safety.
	The note itself posed no safety risk. **(Reason 1)**
	Therefore, Salles's review of the note cannot be justified on safety grounds.
Reason #2's chain link:	The remaining two caretaking purposes relate to protecting the owner's valuables.
	If an officer's search reaches areas where no reasonable owner would store valuables, the search is not designed to protect them.
	It is unreasonable to assume that Mutombo would store valuables in the crevice between his front car seat and console. **(Reason 2)**
	Therefore, Salles's search of that area cannot be justified as a search for valuables.
Reason #3's chain link:	An officer's leeway to examine personal papers, which enjoy heightened privacy protections, is limited to the bare minimum needed to discern value.
	Officer Salles's front-and-back examination of the paper exceeded the quick look needed to assess value. **(Reason 3)**
	Therefore, Salles's thorough reading of the paper exceeded the scope of a value-protecting inventory search.

The formal syllogism is not the only way to build a reasoning chain. Reasons and their progression must account for law's indeterminate nature and the advocate's interpretive role; legal argument cannot be reduced to a math equation.[27] For example, reasons do not always prove conclusions in a linear manner but can operate in a "confluence" to drive the argument's conclusion.[28] In addition, reasoning by analogy may be needed along the way to communicate what a syllogism cannot.[29] Still other arguments call for the less absolute form of inductive reasoning, which derives a general conclusion from many particulars.[30]

The sections below address these variations on how to build a reasoning chain, using expert examples that focus on: (1) the argument's placement on the law-fact continuum; and (2) whether the argument involves statutory interpretation. Introduced back in Chapter 6, these two factors drive an argument's core goals, whether it is to sell the advocate's assessment of the record, the advocate's application of the law to the facts, or a new rule of law or interpretation of a statute. Just as these goals vary, so too does the most effective makeup of the reasoning chain.

REVIEW

Reasoning Chain Concepts

Reasons: The justifications for an argument's conclusions.

Reasoning chain: A sequential progression of reasons that builds towards the argument's conclusion.

Major types of reasoning chains: Syllogistic, inductive, confluence. Analogical reasoning may be integrated into any type of chain.

Factors that influence reasoning chains: Where an argument falls along the law-fact continuum and whether the argument requires statutory interpretation.

2.3 Fact-Intensive Reasoning Chains

Perched on one end of the law-fact argument continuum, fact-intensive arguments arise when the standard of review is deferential and the legal framework lacks detail. As Chapter 6 explained, these arguments typically target a lower court action (*e.g.*, imposition of sanctions, denial of a continuance) or interpretation of the record (*e.g.*, clearly erroneous view of the facts, arbitrary and capricious administrative determination). The resulting reasoning chain must then link the lower court's finding or action to the writer's conclusion that it was right or wrong under the applicable standard of review. The reasoning chain progressions are as infinite as the facts that prompt the argument, but all boil down to some version of: (1) grouping, characterizing, or adding up the facts; and then (2) explaining why the lower court did right or wrong by them.

Example — *Facebook v. Connect U.*[31] In this appeal to the Ninth Circuit, discussed in earlier chapters, Appellant Connect U contended that the lower court abused its discretion in enforcing the parties' settlement agreement because the agreement's terms were too indefinite. Below is Appellee Facebook's fact-intensive argument defending the lower court's action; the links in the reasoning chain are marked on the right.

EXAMPLE Fact-Intensive Reasoning Chain

1. **The Settlement Agreement recites specific obligations capable of enforcement.**

     The Settlement Agreement is enforceable as a contract so long as its terms are "sufficiently certain." *Elite Show Servs.*, 14 Cal. Rptr. 3d at 188. All the parties had to do to fulfill their intention to be bound was to state the terms clearly enough to enable a court to discern the parties' "obligations thereunder and determine whether those obligations have been performed or breached." *Id.*; *see also* Holmes v. Lerner, 88 Cal. Rptr. 2d 130, 141 (Ct. App. 1999). The district court had no trouble discerning the parties' respective obligations under the Settlement Agreement as written. The Settlement Agreement specifies:

     ⟵ *Malleable legal standard forcing argument on the facts*

     ⟵ ***Link 1**: adding up and characterizing the facts*

     - how much stock Facebook would issue
     - exactly what kind of stock Facebook had to turn over ("common shares")
     - what special rights the stock would carry (they would "be subject to the same anti-dilution protections afforded to Series D preferred stock")
     - what proportion of outstanding Facebook shares the transferred shares would represent
     - what else Facebook would pay
     - what the CU Founders had to give in return (all Connect U stock); and
     - the basic contours of Facebook's "acquisition" of Connect U ("consistent with a stock and cash for stock acquisition").

     In light of all these details, it was easy for the district court to determine whether Connect U and its Founders had "performed or breached" their "obligations thereunder." *Elite Show Servs.*, 14 Cal. Rptr. 3d at 188. All it needed to know was that Facebook stood ready to transfer $XX and XX[32] shares and to dismiss its case against the CU Founders, but the CU Founders refused to transfer their stock—in any form at all—or dismiss their case against

     ⟵ ***Link 2:** why the lower court handled these facts correctly*

> Facebook. It was equally easy for the district court to enforce the Settlement Agreement. All it had to do was order each party to dismiss their respective suits and to turn over the agreed-upon consideration, without adjustment, warranty, embellishment, or modification. ER 48-60. It did not have to supply missing detail. The simplicity of the enforcement mechanism — and the ease with which the parties consummated the transaction when ordered to do so — proves that the Settlement Agreement's terms were "sufficiently certain," and, therefore, enforceable. *Elite Show Servs.,* 14 Cal. Rptr. 3d at 188.

← ***Link 3:*** *another reason why the lower court handled these facts correctly*

← ***Conclusion:*** *pulling the links together*

Without much legal guidance on what constitutes "sufficiently certain" contract terms, the debate's locus shifts to the settlement facts. The reasoning chain connecting the lower court's finding (terms specific enough to be enforceable) to the advocate's conclusion (this finding was not an abuse of discretion) has three links: (1) what the key terms are; (2) why those terms make breach and performance easy to assess; and (3) why those terms are easy to enforce on their face, without the court having to fill in details.

Notice how this argument fully develops the reasoning within each chain link, putting every step that is in the writer's head onto the paper, answering the reader's next natural question. If the writer had skipped from the statement, "the district court had no trouble discerning the parties' respective obligations," to the next paragraph's contentions that Facebook stood ready to transfer shares and money and dismiss its case while CU refused to transfer its stock or dismiss its case — without first laying out the key settlement terms — the result would be an incomplete reasoning chain. Because the reader would have no proof of what the parties' respective obligations actually were, she would have no reason to care about what Facebook or CU were ready to do or why the performance terms were specific. Likewise, if the writer had skipped from the settlement terms to bare conclusions that the agreement was "detailed" and the enforcement mechanism "simple," that, too would leave the link incomplete. The court would have to fill in the "why" behind those conclusions, independently assessing what makes the terms detailed enough and the enforcement mechanism so simple. Either misstep would violate the writer's directive to "spoon-feed the judge" by providing the "essential materials for following [the] argument."[33] Spelling out both the "what" in the form of settlement terms and the "why" behind their definiteness, this writer forges sturdy chain links of steel.

Practice Alert #2
Practice Spotlight on Fact-Intensive Reasoning Chains

This exercise in the online companion presents another fact-intensive reasoning chain, and asks you to assess the reasons' development and progression.

Example — United States v. Worku.[34] Flipping to the appellant's side, the next fact-intensive reasoning chain challenges a lower court's sentence for identity theft and immigration fraud. Mr. Worku's conviction was based on his assuming an ailing Kenyan man's identity to help the man's children gain entry to the United States. On appeal to the Tenth Circuit, Appellant Worku argued that the lower court impermissibly enhanced his sentence by finding that he fled to the United States to conceal alleged human rights offenses in Ethiopia in the 1970s.

| EXAMPLE #2 | Fact-Intensive Reasoning Chain |

A. There Was No Evidence of an Intent to Conceal Past Actions.

The district court's sentencing decision relied heavily on the court's finding that "Worku concealed his true identity and sought to avoid further prosecution and punishment for his participation in Ethiopia of the crimes of torture and murder." (Sent. Order, Dkt. # 140, ROA p. 502.) The court added: "I find that the nature of Worku's conduct in Ethiopia and the lies he employed to cover up that sordid conduct take this case out of the heartland of § 1425 prosecutions." (*Id.* p. 503.) The court likewise referred to Mr. Worku as "a person fleeing another country on the basis of convictions for human rights violations." (*Id.,* p. 513.)

← *Link 1: characterizing the district court's factual findings*

But those were not plausible findings, because there was no evidence that Mr. Worku came to the United States to conceal his Ethiopian conduct, whatever that might be. Instead, the PSR stated that Mr. Worku moved to Kenya in 1992, six years after his release from prison in Ethiopia and eight years before the Ethiopian conviction *in absentia*, and there is no record evidence that he did so to "conceal" anything. (PSR, Dkt. # 131, Restr. ROA p. 110.) Instead, the PSR notes that he did so after a change in the controlling political party that caused Mr. Worku to be worried about political persecution. (*Id.*) Mr. Worku was then granted refugee status and political asylum by the Kenyan government. (*Id.,* p.111.) There was no evidence at all that Mr. Worku was facing deportation to Ethiopia from Kenya.

← *Link 2: one reason the record contradicts these findings — Worku's asylum-motivated move to Kenya, not flight to conceal torture*

Instead, Mr. Worku lived peacefully in Kenya until he was contacted by a broker to assist the family of Habteab Berhe Temanu with their refugee application. The Government's evidence on this point was that Mr. Worku assumed the identity of the father because he was so ill that he would be unable to successfully complete an immigration interview. Through Mr. Worku's efforts, that family immigrated with Mr. Worku to the United States in 2004. (*Id.*, p. 111.)

Link 3: another reason the record contradicts this finding — Worku's motive to help family

In sum, there was no evidence supporting the district court's conclusion that the reason Mr. Worku came to the United States was to conceal his alleged role in torture in the Higher 15 Prison. . . . The district court's findings as to intent to conceal torture were clearly erroneous in light of the Government's evidence that Mr. Worku came to the United States and misrepresented himself not to "conceal" his past but to assist another family.

Conclusion: pulling the links together

As with the *Facebook* example above, the *Worku* writer constructs a reasoning chain between the lower court's findings (Worku fled to U.S. to conceal his role in torture) to the advocate's conclusion (this finding was clearly erroneous). The chain links do the same kind of work, articulating: (1) what the lower court's findings were; (2) why one piece of evidence refutes those findings; and (3) why another piece of evidence refutes those findings. Here, too, the writer leaves nothing for the court to unravel. The reasoning chain does not stop at an assertion that Mr. Worku moved to Kenya and was transparent about his reasons for doing so; instead the writer engages the specific facts proving when and why Worku made the move. Similarly, the writer does not baldly assert that Worku came to the United States to help a Kenyan family; the writer lays out the specific record facts proving that motive. Finally, the writer ties everything together in the concluding sentences, explaining why these pieces of evidence belie a torture concealment motive, making the court's finding on that point clearly erroneous.

REFLECTION, DISCUSSION, AND CHALLENGE QUESTIONS

Fact-Intensive Reasoning Chains

- Consider the arguments in your brief. Are any of them fact intensive? If so, what makes these arguments fact intensive?
- Construct a skeletal reasoning chain for each fact-intensive argument. Be sure that the chain incorporates these components: (1) grouping, characterizing, or adding up the facts; and (2) explaining why the lower court handled them correctly or incorrectly.

- Once you have a fact-intensive argument draft, reverse engineer the underlying reasoning chain to test its logic and strength. Make sure the chain links are distinct reasons for your argument's conclusion, that each link explains the "what" before the "why," and that each link moves the argument forward.

2.4   Law-Fact Application Reasoning Chains

Another notch down the law-fact continuum are settled law-fact arguments. As Chapter 6 explained, these arguments add a layer of complexity to fact-intensive arguments in the form of a more detailed legal framework, and typically trigger a de novo standard of review. Because these arguments revolve around settled—if malleable—legal principles, those principles must anchor the reasoning chain. Moreover, because these arguments require slotting facts inside or outside of those existing legal principles, a syllogistic reasoning chain is usually the most effective approach.

Example—Oracle v. Google.[35] This Federal Circuit appeal, discussed back in Chapter 9, arose from a copyright infringement fight over Oracle's software code. Oracle claimed that Google infringed by copying Oracle's code verbatim and using it in a competing mobile platform—Android. Following a jury verdict in Oracle's favor, Google won a judgment as matter of law (JMOL) ruling denying copyright protection, and Oracle lost a JMOL on Google's fair use defense. Below is a segment of Oracle's argument against fair use. The federal copyright statute defines fair use with four nonexclusive factors, one of which is "the purpose and character of the use, including whether such use is of a commercial nature."[36]

EXAMPLE   **Law-Fact Application Reasoning Chain**

A. **Google's Copying Was Commercially Motivated, Not Transformative, and Illicit.**

Google's use of Oracle's code is purely commercial. *Id.* at 562. Android is one of the most lucrative endeavors of the past decade. Google's counsel conceded that "the fact that it's a commercial use is not in dispute . . . . The evidence is pretty clear that they created it to provide a platform on which other Google product[s] could do better." A21,591. The district court agreed: "Google's internal documents show[] how many billions of dollars they expected to make off of [Android]. . . . This was intended for commercial purposes with large amounts of money at stake and, therefore, it was not fair use. It was copying." A21,594.

⟵ ***Link 1:*** *Google's use is commercial.*

In considering the first factor, courts also ⟵ **Link 2:** *Google's use was not transformative.*

inquire whether the copied material substitutes for the original or, instead, adds or changes the purpose of the original, thereby "transform[ing]" it in a meaningful way. *Campbell*, 510 U.S. at 579. Google's use of Java declaring code was anything but transformative. Mere alteration is not transformation. A use of copied material is not transformative unless the material is used "in a different manner or for a different purpose from the original." Hon. Pierre Leval, *Toward a Fair Use Standard*, 103 Harv. L. Rev. 1105, 1111 (1990); *see Campbell*, 510 U.S. at 579.

Google's use of the declaring code was exactly the same as in Java: to call upon prewritten packages to perform the same functions. The packages also serve the identical purpose: solving the same complex problems and performing the same often-needed functions programmers desire. While using the declaring code in exactly the same way as the original, Google deployed that purloined code in Android to compete directly with commercially licensed derivatives of Oracle's work. Oracle licenses Java in the mobile market and licensed it for smartphones specifically, including RIM's Blackberry, Nokia's Series 60 phones, and Danger's Sidekick/Hiptop. *Supra* at 15-16.

Such superseding use is "*always*" unfair. *Harper & Row*, 471 U.S. at 550 (emphasis added); *id.* at 569 ("[A] use that supplants any part of the normal market for a copyrighted work would ordinarily be considered an infringement." (citation omitted)). Copying work to use for the same purpose simply cannot be fair use. *See* Peter Letterese & Assocs. v. World Inst. of Scientology Enters., Int'l, 533 F.3d 1287, 1311, 1318 (11th Cir. 2008) (book about sales techniques superseded the original even though it "adopt[ed] a different format, incorporate[d] pedagogical tools . . . , and condense[d] the material in the [original] book"); Elvis Presley Enters., Inc. v. Passport Video, 349 F.3d 622, 628-30 (9th Cir. 2003) (documentary containing "significant portions" of video clips supersedes original and is not fair use); Twin Peaks Prods., Inc. v. Publ'ns Int'l, Ltd., 996 F.2d 1366, 1375-77 (2d Cir.

Link 3: *Google's use supplanted part of Oracle's market.*

1993) (holding that a comprehensive guide to the characters and plot of a television show supersedes the show and is not fair use).

Finally, "[f]air use presupposes good faith and fair dealing." *Harper & Row*, 471 U.S. at 562 (internal quotation marks omitted). Google considered, negotiated, and ultimately rejected the opportunity to license the packages, deciding to "[d]o Java anyway and defend our decision, perhaps making enemies along the way." A1166. That Google knew it needed a license, and then sought but did not obtain one, weighs heavily in showing "the character of the use" was not fair. Los Angeles News Serv. v. KCAL-TV Channel 9, 108 F.3d 1119, 1122 (9th Cir. 1997). Google "knowingly . . . exploited a purloined work for free that could have [otherwise] been obtained." *Id.*

← **Link 4:** *Google's use was not in good faith.*

The reasoning chain is a series of syllogisms propelled by legal principles that define the commercial use factor. And that chain is reason-based, not IRAC-driven: each legal principle anchors a distinct reason. Pared to its essence, the syllogistic chain looks like this:

Settled legal principles:	First factor of the fair use test — was the use commercial?
Reason #1's link:	Commercial use strongly suggests unfair use. Google copied and used Oracle's Java source code to increase its stake in the market and make millions in profits, and for no other reason. Because Google's use was purely commercial, it weighs against a fair use defense.
Reason #2's link:	Commercial use may be fair if it is truly transformative. Google used the source code in exactly the same way that Oracle had, in the same market. Therefore, Google's use was a pure substitution, not a fair transformative use.
Reason #3's link:	A "superseding use" that supplants the original work's market is always unfair. Google's use supplanted the use of Oracle's licenses in the mobile and smart phone markets. That superseding use alone makes Google's use unfair.
Reason #4's link:	Fair use requires good faith and fair dealing. Google knew it needed a license to use Java but went ahead and copied the code without Oracle's permission anyway. This knowledge demonstrates bad faith and eliminates the fair use defense.

One more quality makes this reasoning chain stand out. The links are not only organized logically and consistently with the law, they are organized strategically and efficiently. The first link addresses what is sure to be a pressing reader question: How was Google's use commercial? The second addresses a more defensive point, but one that's likely to enter the reader's mind next: Mightn't Google's use qualify as transformative? The writer then leans on the same set of facts to bridge efficiently to the next link — Google's use was not only identical to the copyrighted work, it went so far as to reduce Oracle's market share. Had the writer ordered the links differently, he would have courted factual repetition. This ordering choice also sandwiches a defensive point between two affirmative points, injecting the pathos of stolen market share to boot. The final link on good faith and fair dealing bolsters the argument with a fairness/equity point. This link is not strictly necessary to prove the conclusion. But it is a strategically wise storytelling choice that paints Google in a negative light, attacking its ethos while offering the court more impetus to rule in Oracle's favor.

Practice Alert #3
Practice Spotlight on Law-Fact Application Reasoning Chains

This exercise in the online companion presents another law-fact application reasoning chain, and asks you to reverse engineer its underlying reasons and assess the reasons' development and progression.

REFLECTION, DISCUSSION, AND CHALLENGE QUESTIONS

Law-Fact Application Reasoning Chains

- Consider the arguments in your brief. Do any apply law to facts? If so, what is the governing legal framework?
- Determine the legal framework's core principles. Work on processing those principles and the record facts into your own reasons for the argument's conclusion.
- Once you have the reasons, try drafting a syllogism for each one. Build those syllogisms into a reasoning chain.
- After you've drafted the argument, reverse engineer the underlying reasoning chain to test its logic and strength. Make sure the chain links are distinct reasons for your argument's conclusion, that each link explains the "what" before the "why," and that each link moves the argument forward.

2.5   Unsettled Law Reasoning Chains

On the far side of the law-fact continuum stand appellate arguments that operate outside of settled law. As Chapter 6 explained, these arguments often propose new rules or tests or novel applications. They use reasoning chains, too, but of a different sort — in two ways. First, as we discussed in Chapter 6, the reasons are different in kind. Rather than being constructed from settled legal principles, unsettled law argument reasons revolve around the logic of persuasive precedent, analogies to other areas of the law, the good consequences of adopting the advocate's position, and the bad consequences of adopting the opponent's position.[37] Second, the logical progression of the reasons is different. The syllogistic logic that works in settled-law arguments won't work here—or at least not as a starting point.[38]

As an example, take Lawrence v. Texas, the landmark case holding Texas's criminal sodomy law unconstitutional. Recall from Chapter 6 that Petitioners argued that Texas law unconstitutionally infringed their due process rights to privacy and liberty. With a straight syllogism at its core, the reasoning chain would have looked something like this:

EXAMPLE

Syllogistic Reasoning Chain

The constitutional rights to privacy and liberty include the right to engage in same-sex sexual relations.

The Texas statute makes that conduct criminal.

Because the Texas statute criminalizes conduct protected as a liberty and privacy right, it is unconstitutional.

As we saw in Chapter 6, the writers did not do this, and the reason is clear. The major premise was, at the time, untrue—Bowers v. Hardwick said so. Instead, the *Lawrence* writers had to work by induction, piecing together a host of existing privacy and liberty rights (intimate relationships, bodily integrity, and the home) to create their own major premise establishing the breadth of the existing right.[39] After clearing that hurdle, the argument could proceed syllogistically (and quickly), showing how the Texas law violated that right.

This inductive process of generalizing from legal principles not directly on point—but spot-on when collectively and strategically framed—plays a critical role in unsettled law arguments.[40] The reasoning chains actively construct the advocate's desired rule or test—what Professor Kathryn Stanchi calls the target rule—proceeding from principle to principle and building proof and momentum along the way.[41] The inductively produced target rule lacks the firmness of a syllogism, yielding only probable results.[42] But a well-ordered reasoning chain can overcome this weakness by using a sequential request strategy, which presents a "series of persuasive messages . . . in a certain order."[43] The right order can make up for inductive reasoning's relative uncertainty, especially if it proceeds in the foot-in-the-door or high-dive sequence introduced in Chapter 6. Recall that the advocate using this sequence starts with the most agreeable proposition and builds up to ever-more controversial propositions, until the desired rule is just a baby step away.[44] Referred to as the halo effect, the original proposition's power to induce ultimate reader agreement is profound: "[O]nce the message recipient starts nodding 'yes,' it is likely that she will continue to nod 'yes.'"[45]

Example — People v. Mutombo. As you may recall from earlier chapters, the Fourth Amendment inventory search was not the only issue in the *Mutombo* appeal. The case also presented pure questions of law involving Mutombo's writing, which the government deemed an attempted terrorist threat under Illinois law, but Mutombo contended was a rap song composition. Wedged between the front seat and console of Mutombo's car, this writing was never shared with and its contents never communicated to anyone. That undisputed fact raised a legal question under a then-new attempted terrorist threat law: What does it mean to *attempt* to make a threat? Does the attempt lie in producing the writing itself, or does it lie in trying, but failing, to get the writing to its intended recipient? The excerpt below, which comes from the Appellant's brief filed in the real appeal (not the simulated case), argues the latter.[46] Accordingly, the writers argue, Mutombo's unsent writing was an insufficient evidentiary basis for his attempted terrorist threat conviction.

EXAMPLE   **Unsettled Law Reasoning Chain**

A. Without evidence of communication, the State cannot prove that Mutombo was guilty of attempting to make a terrorist threat

Communication to a target audience is the *sine qua non* of the crime of attempting to make a terrorist threat. Thus, the State was required to prove it as an element of its case. Yet it failed to do so, a fact the State readily concedes. Although the crime of attempt with which Mutombo was charged has its own statutory elements of intent and substantial step, the State also needed to prove the element of communication from the underlying substantive offense in order to establish the threat. Communication is the sole touchstone for gauging whether the statutory elements of intent and substantial step are met. *Cf.* Stansberry v. State, 954 N.E.2d 507, 512 (Ind. Ct. App. 2011) (finding that the defendant could not be convicted of "attempted resisting law enforcement" when the state offered only proof that the defendant acted with force, but no evidence that he resisted, obstructed, or interfered with the officers, as the substantive offense required). That is, the State cannot establish the defendant's intent unless there is an object of that intent, which in this case is a threat.

⟵ *Target Rule*

⟵ *Link 1's easy sell: attempt crimes incorporate the underlying offense's elements*

⟵ *Link 2's easy sell: the underlying offense requires a threat*

In criminal law, a threat is a very particular type of conduct, where the perpetrator communicates to the victim that she will take an additional harmful action in the future. *Black's Law Dictionary* at 1480 (6th ed. 1990) (defining threat as "a communicated intent to inflict physical or other harm on any person or on property. A declaration of an intention to injure another."); *see also* Illinois Pattern Instructions, Criminal, No. 13.33F (defining threat as "a menace, *however communicated*") (emphasis supplied). Thus, as a threshold matter, this Court must distinguish between conduct in furtherance of a *threat* and conduct in furtherance of *other types of criminal activity.* To that end, the State offered only two pieces of evidence to support its contention that Mutombo had attempted to make a *threat:* (1) the sheet of lyrics discovered under the center console of Mutombo's car; and (2) a Movie Maker file that Mutombo had deleted from his computer. Among all of the evidence presented, these are the only two things that could conceivably be conduct relating to a threat, versus conduct related to some other type of criminal activity.

⟵ **Link 3:** *a threat communicates a promise of future harm, as opposed to communicating for some other criminal purpose*

But neither of these things was evidence that Mutombo made a threat or that he had attempted to make a threat because, quite simply, an action (or an activity, writing, or statement) only becomes a threat once it has been communicated in some manner. Communication is the absolute prerequisite to proving either a completed threat or an attempted threat. A completed threat is conduct by which the perpetrator communicates to the *intended victim* that additional harmful action will occur in the future; an attempted threat is the same conduct communicated in a way that it *does not* reach the victim but instead reaches a *third party.*

⟵ **Link 4:** *words do not become threats until they are communicated to someone; until then, they are just private musings*

The paradigmatic examples of attempted threats all include, at a minimum, an act by which the person attempting to threaten communicates his or her message to *some person,* even if the communication does not ultimately reach its intended audience. Alec Walen, *Criminal Statements of Terrorist Intent: How to Understand the Law Governing Terrorist Threats, and Why It Should be Used Instead of Long-Term Preventive Detention*, 101 J. CRIM. L. & CRIMINOLOGY 803, 803 & n.2 (2011) (describing the "paradigmatic kind of threat" as one "in which the person making the threat tries to communicate the threat to one or more victims") (citing Corpus Juris Secundum on Threats, 86 C.J.S. THREATS § 3 (2010)). One example is the person who writes the threatening message and sends it in the mail to the intended victim, only to have a postal carrier intercept the message and deliver it to the police. The message has not reached its intended recipient, but it has been communicated and so the attempted threat has occurred. The same would be true, for example, if a prisoner made a threatening phone call from the jailhouse phone to a witness who will testify in his case, only to discover that the person on the other end of the call is a police officer rather than the witness. In that case, too, the message does not reach the victim, but it has been communicated to someone and so the attempted threat is complete.

A third example would be the employee who writes a threatening email to her coworkers and hits the send button, only to have the email intercepted by her corporate office technology department before it reaches the in-boxes of its intended recipients. In each of these examples — whether the communication ultimately reaches the intended victim or the perpetrator attempts to communicate the message to the victim but fails, communicating the threat instead to a third party — there is some communication that occurs. That communication is what distinguishes a threat or attempted threat from a mere private musing.

The fact that there was no evidence of communication in this case shows that the State failed to meet its burden of proof. The State did not offer any evidence of communication. Indeed, the State conceded that it could not and did not prove

← *Link 5:*
application of target rule to facts

> communication, and it went further to say that there was in fact no communication of either piece of evidence—the sheet of paper and the Movie Maker file—that it had advanced in support of its case that Mutombo had attempted to make a terrorist threat. *See supra* at 7. Without evidence of communication, the State's case necessarily falters, the evidence is insufficient to demonstrate attempt to make a terrorist threat, and Mutombo's conviction must be reversed.

This reasoning chain orchestrates a careful inductive march to the target rule. It starts with two simple, agreeable propositions about the elements of attempt and the elements of the underlying offense. But the supporting authority establishes these basic propositions in the context of attempted resisting arrest, not attempted terrorist threat. So the writers have more work to do.

To start building the definition of threat-as-communication, the next inductive link narrows the universe of what is and what is not a threat. Here, the writers must rely on secondary sources that do not address attempted threats, but that simply set the basic parameters of the word "threat" as requiring a communication. That allows the writers to narrow down the relevant "threat" facts to two pieces of evidence, neither of which Mutombo tried to communicate to anyone. Having nailed down the communicative aspect of "threat," next comes the toughest sell, establishing what "communication" means in the context of an *attempted* threat—a thwarted effort to reach the recipient, not just the act of writing words with no effort to put them out into the world. Here, the writers have only secondary source support, and they mainly reason by example, using vivid illustrations to show how their definition of attempted threat still distinguishes the "attempt" version of the crime from the completed version.

Had the writers tried a standard syllogistic chain, they would have failed to persuade. The major premise they needed—attempted threats mean thwarted efforts to communicate and nothing less—did not exist in the statute or case law. It had to be built from other legal principles. Notice, too, that the writers did not stop after the first two links establishing the basic requirement of proving an attempted threat. This was a good "halo effect" starting point. But ending there would have stopped the proof short, for it would

Practice Alert #4
Practice Spotlight on Unsettled Law Reasoning Chains

This exercise in the online companion presents another unsettled law reasoning chain, and asks you to reverse engineer its underlying reasons and assess the reasons' development and progression.

have left "attempted threat" undefined. The writers needed more links to define the contours of this phrase to fit the target rule. Finally, notice how the writers were careful to keep the argument tied into their case. Each link makes clear its significance for the threat evidence in the record, rather than simply stating the legal principles and letting the court figure out how they might apply to the appeal. Just as important, the final paragraph closes out the writers' reasoning with the only deductive link in the chain, applying the fully established target rule to the case fact.

REFLECTION, DISCUSSION, AND CHALLENGE QUESTIONS

Unsettled Law Reasoning Chains

- Consider the arguments in your brief. Do any of them deal with unsettled law?
- Identify your "target rule" and your opponent's "target rule." What inductive pieces must you pull together to bridge between existing law and your target rule?
- Once you have the inductive pieces, try drafting a "foot in the door" reasoning chain that sequences these pieces from agreeable to controversial propositions, all the way up to your target rule.
- If you need to apply the target rule to a set of facts to complete the argument, add a syllogistic reasoning chain at the end.
- After you've drafted the argument, reverse engineer the underlying reasoning chain to test its logic and strength. Make sure the chain links are distinct reasons for your argument's conclusion, that each link explains the "what" before the "why," and that each link moves the argument forward.

2.6 Statutory Interpretation Reasoning Chains

Occupying a unique space on the law side of the continuum, statutory interpretation arguments fashion their reasons from the standard interpretive tools discussed in Chapter 6. The reasoning chain forming those arguments has unique elements, too. A statutory interpretation reasoning chain must not only honor the established text-purpose-policy hierarchy, it must also proceed inductively to establish the advocate's reading of the text as the best one. In this way, the chain's progression parallels selling a new common law test or rule. The difference is that the interpretive tools, rather than common law principles, do the selling. And those tools work in confluence with each other,[47] building "cumulative strength as they are woven together."[48] As Chapter 6's example from the Alaska v. EPA brief showed,[49] this confluence occurs when the text, the purpose, and the policy all point in one direction.[50]

Example — University of South Texas Medical Center v. Nassar.[51] This appeal to the Supreme Court produced a landmark employment discrimination decision on the causation standard for Title VII retaliation claims. It inspired our statutory structure example back in Chapter 6. Recall that Title VII, along with nearly every other federal employment discrimination statute, outlaws employment actions taken "because of" a statutorily protected status or activity. For decades the words "because of" divided the lower courts and the Justices.[52] Judges disagreed on the role the discriminatory mindset must play in an employment decision — whether "because of" meant a but-for cause or some lower level of influence.

In 2009, the Supreme Court held that "because of" in the Age Discrimination in Employment Act requires but-for causation. But that holding was not the end of the story. Title VII is a separate law that prohibits status discrimination (race, sex, religion, color, national origin)[53] and retaliation[54] in two different sections. And unlike the ADEA, Title VII was amended in 1991 to add a new provision that makes an employment decision unlawful if "race, color, religion, sex, or national origin was a *motivating* factor."[55] Left unmentioned was retaliation, raising questions about whether this motivating factor standard applies only to status discrimination claims. The excerpt below argues that it does, subjecting retaliation to the higher but-for cause standard.

| EXAMPLE | **Statutory Interpretation Reasoning Chain**[56] |

I. *A Title VII Retaliation Plaintiff Must Prove That Protected Activity Was the "But-For" Cause of an Adverse Employment Action*

A. Title VII's Text Is Clear

    1. This case should *begin and end* with the statutory text. *See* Gross v. FBL Fin. Servs., Inc., 557 U.S. 167, 175-76 (2009). Title VII prohibits retaliation "because" the employee had engaged in protected activity. 42 U.S.C. § 2000e-3(a). "[B]ecause" means "by reason of: on account of." *Gross,* 557 U.S. at 176 (quoting 1 Webster's Third New International Dictionary 194 (1966)); *accord* 2 Oxford English Dictionary 41 (2d ed. 1989) ("for the reason that"); Random House Dictionary of the English Language 132 (1966) ("by reason; on account"). **Thus, retaliation must have been "the 'reason' that the employer decided to act."** *Gross,* 557 U.S. at 176; *see also* Hazen Paper Co. v. Biggins, 507 U.S. 604, 610 (1993).

←— *Link 1 (text):* ordinary meaning of "because of" = but-for cause

←— *Core reasoning*

Under that ordinary meaning, "the phrase 'because of' conveys the idea that the motive in question made a difference to the outcome," *Price Waterhouse*, 490 U.S. at 281 (Kennedy, J., dissenting), *i.e.*, was its "'but-for' cause." *Gross*, 557 U.S. at 176-77; *accord Price Waterhouse*, at 262-63 (O'Connor, J., concurring in judgment). . . . If an employer took the same action it would have taken regardless of any retaliatory or discriminatory animus, it did exactly what the civil rights acts seek to achieve — equal treatment of all employees, regardless of whether they engaged in protected activity or belonged to a particular class. *See Price Waterhouse*, 490 U.S. at 282 (Kennedy, J., dissenting). [citations omitted]

⟵ ***Link 2*** *(purpose): Title VII's equal treatment goal is furthered by but-for causation*

2. The common law backdrop confirms the statute's plain meaning. Unless it clearly indicates otherwise, Congress intends its legislation to incorporate traditional tort principles. *See, e.g.*, Meyer v. Holley, 537 U.S. 280, 285 (2003). Thus, "[c]onventional rules of civil litigation generally apply in Title VII cases." [citations omitted] Under the common law, **"[a]n act or omission is not regarded as a cause of an event if the particular event would have occurred without it."** *Gross*, 557 U.S. at 176-77.

⟵ ***Link 3:*** *common law confirms that "because of" means "but-for"*

Core Reasoning

*   *   *

3. [In the Civil Rights Act of 1991] Congress . . . specifically authoriz[ed] mixed motive claims for discrimination under 42 U.S.C. § 2000e-2(a) *but not for retaliation* under 42 U.S.C. § 2000e-3(a). Under the 1991 amendments, "an unlawful employment practice is established when the complaining party demonstrates that race, color, religion, sex, or national origin was a motivating factor for any employment practice, even though other factors also motivated the practice." 1991 CRA, § 107(a), 105 Stat. at 1075 (codified at 42 U.S.C. § 2000e-2(m)). **Critically, those prohibited motivating factors — "race, color, religion, sex, or national origin" — are the prohibited bases for discrimination under 42 U.S.C. § 2000e-2(a). They**

⟵ ***Link 4*** *(statutory structure): read in context with the original provisions, the amendment confirms but-for causation*

⟵ *Core reasoning*

do not include retaliation under 42 U.S.C. § 2000e-3(a), the provision at issue here. Congress underscored that point by enacting this new mixed-motive prohibition as an amendment to Title VII's general discrimination provision, 42 U.S.C. § 2000e-2, and not to its retaliation provision, *id.* § 2000e-3(a).

This differential treatment is all the more notable because retaliation is itself a type of discrimination under Title VII. Section 2000e-2 forbids "discriminat[ion]" based on membership in the five protected classes noted above. *Id.* § 2000e-2(a). Title VII's retaliation provision, 42 U.S.C. § 2000e-3(a) — which is entitled "[d]iscrimination for making charges, testifying, assisting, or participating in enforcement proceedings" — prohibits employers from "discriminat[ing]" against two other categories of employees: those who opposed a practice made unlawful under Title VII or those who participated in an investigation into allegedly unlawful conduct. **Thus, the 1991 amendments specifically single out one of the two types of Title VII "discrimination" for special, mixed-motive treatment. Because that differential treatment must be given effect,** the courts of appeals have repeatedly held that the 1991 mixed-motive amendments do not apply to retaliation claims. [citations omitted]

⟵ *Core reasoning*

Congress's specific authorization of mixed-motive claims for a subset of Title VII claims *confirms that Title VII's more general language* prohibiting discrimination and retaliation "because of" improper factors does not authorize mixed-motive claims. If it did, § 2000e-2(m)'s specific motivating-factor provision would be surplusage, and its exclusion of retaliation would be inexplicable. *See Gross,* 557 U.S. at 178 n.5. The 1991 amendments therefore give rise to the "strongest" of inferences that mixed-motive claims are available only to the extent specifically authorized by § 2000e-2(m). *See id.* at 175.

*   *   *

4. In contrast to its clear statutory text, Title VII's legislative history contains something for everyone, as the *Price Waterhouse* opinions demonstrate. *Compare Price Waterhouse,* 490 U.S. at 243-44 (plurality opinion), *with* 490 U.S. at 262 (O'Connor, J., concurring in judgment), *with* 490 U.S. at 286-87 & n.3 (Kennedy, J., dissenting). Read as a whole, however, the legislative history of the 1964 Civil Rights Act "bears out what its plain language suggests: a substantive violation of the statute only occurs when consideration of an illegitimate criterion is the 'but-for' cause of an adverse employment action." *Price Waterhouse,* 490 U.S. at 262 (O'Connor, J., concurring in judgment). Indeed, the interpretive memorandum submitted by the bill's sponsors provided that a Title VII "plaintiff, *as in any civil case,* would have the burden of proving that discrimination had occurred." 110 Cong. Rec. 7214 (Apr. 4, 1964) (emphasis added).

The legislative history of the 1991 amendments does not disturb that conclusion for Title VII retaliation claims. Nothing in that legislative history states that Congress intended its mixed-motive amendments to govern such claims. Even if it did, legislative history could not modify the plain statutory text. *See* Milner v. Dep't of Navy, 131 S. Ct. 1259, 1266 (2011).

⟵ ***Link 5***: *legislative history is consistent with but-for causation for retaliation claims*

This example constructs an inductive chain, stronger with each link, showing how the interpretive tools coalesce around the "but-for" reading. In this chain, the writer centered on two core pieces of text—the original language and the amendment—and linked them to his conclusion. The original language generates links 1 through 3, the amendment link 4, and the legislative history of both generates link 5. Each link's reasons reflect the statutory construction hierarchy: (1) the "because of" text; (2) buttressed by statutory purpose; (3) buttressed by the common law backdrop; and then (4) the statutory structure of the original and amended language; and (5) Title VII's legislative history. And all five links point in one direction—that motivating factor causation applies to status discrimination, while but-for causation applies to retaliation. The bold face text in each link shows how the writer articulated the core reasoning to support communicated this confluence.

Notice that the writer does not stop at Link 3. Proving that "because of" equals "but-for" causation solves only half the equation, because it addresses only half of the relevant text. The writer must also deal with the 1991 amendment, and whether its "motivating factor" language maps onto the status provision only, or onto both status and retaliation. As Link 4 illustrates, that is no small task. The writer must not only parse the amendment's text, but also relate it back to the original status and retaliation provisions. This is painstaking work; the writer digs deep into the language and employs canons of construction. Then, at the end, the advocate turns to legislative history. Because the history is not directly supportive, the best the writer can do is to show that it is at least consistent with the other tools.

As in the other examples, this writer leaves nothing to the court's imagination. Every reasoning step in the writer's head makes it onto the page — both the "what" and the "why." To see how, take a look at the example's three bold face "core reasoning" areas. Link 1's first paragraph does not end after establishing the definition of "because of" means "on account of" or "for the reason that." It finishes the thought by explicitly tying that definition back to the retaliation provision. Likewise, in the third paragraph, Link 3 doesn't stop with the general assertion that background tort principles are relevant; it articulates precisely what the relevant tort causation principles are.

> **Practice Alert #5**
> **Practice Spotlight on Statutory Interpretation Reasoning Chains**
> This exercise in the online companion presents a statutory interpretation reasoning chain from another appellate brief, and asks you to reverse engineer its underlying reasons and assess the reasons' development and progression.

Link 4's complex statutory structure reasoning is also fully developed. To cover the "what," the writer weaves in the language of each relevant provision, rather than assuming that the court will recall that language from some earlier section in the brief. As for the "why," the writer supplies that, too. Contrasting each section's language and juxtaposing it with the 1991 amendments, the writer shows why the amendment's "motivating factor" language wasn't meant to apply to retaliation claims. The need for these "what" and "why" components seems obvious to the reader, but often escapes the writer. Meticulous attention to both ensures a complete reasoning chain.

REFLECTION, DISCUSSION, AND CHALLENGE QUESTIONS

Statutory Interpretation Reasoning Chains

- Consider the arguments in your brief. Do any of them deal with statutory interpretation?
- For each disputed statutory term, gather the interpretive tools that best support your position on statutory meaning. Use the tools to form links in your reasoning chain.

- Order the chain links according to two principles: (1) the accepted hierarchy of statutory interpretation; and (2) the "foot in the door" sequence moving from agreeable to controversial propositions, leading to your desired interpretation.
- If you need to apply your desired interpretation to the facts to complete the argument, add a syllogistic reasoning chain at the end.
- After you've drafted the argument, reverse engineer the underlying reasoning chain to test its logic and strength. Make sure the chain links are distinct reasons for your argument's conclusion, that each link explains the "what" before the "why," and that each link moves the argument forward.

Section 3   Avoiding Common Legal Reasoning Problems

No matter how well sequenced, a reasoning chain link with just one fissure can cause an entire argument to fall apart. This section illustrates the most common reasoning defects. It assumes that the argument's interpretations of law and facts are defensible — *i.e.*, that there are no false premises — and focuses on how the process of reasoning with those interpretations can go awry. The potential missteps fall into three basic categories: (1) missing pieces; (2) jumping to conclusions; and (3) shifting focus. Some can be classified as formal logical fallacies; others are just variations on poor legal reasoning.

3.1   Missing Pieces

An argument with a missing piece omits a core component of legal reasoning.[57] The absent component could be the law, in the form of a missing major premise.[58] Or the minor premise might be absent, forcing the reader to supply the link between the law's general proposition and the writer's specific conclusion.[59] Still other chains stop the reasoning process short; they contain the premises but omit the conclusion,[60] requiring the reader to complete the thought.

Consider how the reasoning chain from the Beyond IRAC example earlier in the chapter might look if it were missing pieces, such as the law's major premise:

| EXAMPLE   Missing Major Premise |

Inventory searches must have valid aims. U.S. v. Edwards, 577 F.2d 883, 894-95 (5th Cir. 1978) (emphasis added). In *Edwards*, the defendant ← *Missing major* challenged a police search of loose carpet flaps in   *premise* his car, contending that no reasonable officer could believe anything valuable would be hidden there. *Id.* The court upheld the search's scope because the carpet flap had been displaced, supporting a reasonable belief that valuable property might be stored beneath. *Id.* But it refused to "condone searching under the carpeting in every case, much less the ripping apart of an automobile, or any part thereof, under the guise of an inventory search." *Id.* at 895.

Just like a glove compartment, trunk, or console, the area beneath unsettled carpet flaps might be a reasonable place to check for a vehicle owner's valuables. But it is unreasonable to assume that anything contained in a handwritten, loose paper stuffed between a car seat and console would be valuable enough to require inventorying.

This passage leaves out the major premise that anchors the reasoning chain; it never defines an inventory's scope as limited to places where an officer can reasonably hope to find valuables. The topic sentence is too general to communicate that point, while the *Edwards* explanation is too detailed for the reader to glean it without considerable effort.[61] A more carefully reasoned passage would define the major premise at the same level of specificity as the minor premise and the conclusion.

Now consider how the passage would read with the major premise but without the minor premise:

| EXAMPLE | **Missing Minor Premise**

As for the valuables justification, an inventory search extends "only to where an officer can *reasonably* conclude that valuable property may be located." U.S. v. Edwards, 577 F.2d 883, 894-95 (5th Cir. 1978) (emphasis added). In *Edwards,* the defendant challenged a police search of loose carpet flaps in his car, contending that no reasonable officer could believe anything valuable would be hidden there. *Id.* The court upheld the search's scope because the carpet flap had been displaced, supporting a reasonable belief that valuable property might be stored beneath. *Id.* But it refused to "condone searching under the carpeting in every case, much less the ripping apart of an automobile, or any part thereof, under the guise of an inventory search." *Id.* at 895. Because it was unreasonable for Officer Salles to look for valuable items between the front seat and console of Mutombo's car, he exceeded the scope of an inventory.   ⟵ *Missing minor premise*

Here the problem lies in the writer's failure to connect the major premise — where an officer may reasonably search — to the conclusion that the officer exceeded that scope here. The reader is left wondering exactly why the front seat-console space was an unreasonable place to look when the underside of a displaced carpet flap was a perfectly reasonable place to search. Overall, the reasoning strikes the reader as conclusory.[62]

In this example, this missing piece is the conclusion:

EXAMPLE **Missing Conclusion**

As for the valuables justification, an inventory search extends "only to where an officer can *reasonably* conclude that valuable property may be located." U.S. v. Edwards, 577 F.2d 883, 894-95 (5th Cir. 1978) (emphasis added). In *Edwards,* the defendant challenged a police search of loose carpet flaps in his car, contending that no reasonable officer could believe anything valuable would be hidden there. *Id.* The court upheld the search's scope because the carpet flap had been displaced, supporting a reasonable belief that valuable property might be stored beneath. *Id.* But it refused to "condone searching under the carpeting in every case, much less the ripping apart of an automobile, or any part thereof, under the guise of an inventory search." *Id.* at 895.

Just like a glove compartment, trunk, or console, the area beneath unsettled carpet flaps might be a reasonable place to check for a vehicle owner's valuable items. But here, Officer Salles pulled the loose piece of paper from the space between the front seat and console.   ⟵ *Missing conclusion*

Without an explicit conclusion about the reasonableness of Salles's action, the argument simply trails off. The reader is saddled with the analytical work of piecing together why this space was an unreasonable place to look for valuables, particularly as compared to the space in *Edwards*.[63] The hole in the reasoning is not just unsatisfying, it is confusing.[64]

A final missing pieces problem is the circular argument, also known as "begging the question."[65] Circular arguments assert repetitive conclusions without support, for example: "The belief in God is universal because everybody believes in God."[66] This exchange is also circular: "Gino's East pizza is the best pizza in the city of Chicago." "Why?" "Because it's made at Gino's East." A circular legal argument might look like this:

EXAMPLE **Circular Argument**

As for the valuables justification, an inventory search extends "only to where an officer can *reasonably* conclude that valuable property may be located." U.S. v. Edwards, 577 F.2d 883, 894-95 (5th Cir. 1978) (emphasis added). In *Edwards*, the defendant challenged a police search of loose carpet flaps in his car, contending that no reasonable officer could believe anything valuable would be hidden there. *Id.* The court upheld the search's scope because the carpet flap had been displaced, supporting a reasonable belief that valuable property might be stored beneath. *Id.* But it refused to "condone searching under the carpeting in every case, much less the ripping apart of an automobile, or any part thereof, under the guise of an inventory search." *Id.* at 895.

The area beneath unsettled carpet flaps might be a reasonable place to check for a vehicle owner's valuables. But in this case Officer Salles's search ⟵ *Circular* exceeded the scope of an inventory because *Argument* inventorying officers cannot search places unlikely to contain valuables.

This argument's thrust is that Salles's search was unreasonable in scope because inventory searches cannot extend to areas where it is unreasonable for officers to look. It essentially restates the legal rule, and begs the question of *why* Salles's search was unreasonable.

3.2 Jumping to Conclusions

This reasoning flaw has an obvious marker: The conclusion does not follow from what the writer has already said. For example, the writer's premises might have something in common, but that commonality does not logically produce the conclusion that the writer urges.[67] A fictitious example from the government's perspective in the *Mutombo* appeal illustrates the point. In the sufficiency argument, the government contended that Mutombo's writing was an attempted threat by virtue of its reduction to writing and its menacing content — even if he never tried to send it to anyone. If it had contained this type of flaw, the government's argument might proceed in this fashion:

- Unsent menacing writings can be attempted threats.
- The note found in Mutombo's car was a menacing writing promising a Virginia Tech-style campus massacre.
- Therefore the note was an attempted threat, even if no one received it.

This conclusion is too hasty. Just because some unsent menacing writings *can* be attempted threats doesn't mean that *all* unsent menacing writings are. This example lacks what the actual brief contained — an explanation of why Mutombo's note is the *type* of unsent menacing writing that falls into the attempted threat bucket.

A variation on this problem appears when the two premises have a shared quality, but that quality does not produce any definitive conclusions. An example (assuming the premises are valid) might read:

- Mutombo's note promised a future harm to a specific population.
- Threats promise future harm to a specific person or population.
- Therefore, Mutombo's note was a threat.

The problem here is that even though Mutombo's note and threats share a common promise-of-harm feature, that feature does not alone make them fully equivalent.[68] Mutombo's note and threats may also have many distinguishing features — for example, musical stanzas — and those unmentioned distinctions might so outweigh the similarities that they refute the conclusion.

A corollary reasoning flaw accompanies negative propositions. It shows up most often as two negatives producing a positive conclusion — a logically impossible phenomenon.[69] The reasoning chain in the government's sufficiency argument in *Mutombo* would contain this flaw if it made the following leap, even if the premises themselves were well founded:

- Mere unwritten thoughts are not threats.
- Mutombo's note is not a mere unwritten thought.
- Therefore, Mutombo's note is a threat.

This example strains to make something out of courts' negative conclusions on distinguishable facts. But just because a court deems one scenario to fail the rule does not mean the advocate's distinguishable facts meet the rule. Likewise, the mission of equating Mutombo's writing to a threat gains nothing from the fact that unwritten thoughts cannot be characterized that way. "It is like saying in the world of shapes that an unidentified object must be a circle because it is definitely not a square."[70]

3.3 Shifting Focus

When a reasoning chain shifts focus midstream, it is bound to skip logical steps. One version of this problem comes into play when the writer must prove two or more separate points on the way to a conclusion.[71] Instead of methodically building each chain link seriatim, the writer fuses those links together, as in this fictitious government argument in *Mutombo*.[72]

- An attempt crime is proven when the defendant takes a "substantial step" towards completing the crime.
- A completed threat is proven when a defendant uses menacing words.
- Therefore, a defendant is guilty of an attempted threat when he takes the step of writing down menacing words.

There is virtually no connection between the premises or between the premises and the conclusion. In the first place, the premises talk past each other rather than working in tandem. Between the first and second, the writer abruptly shifts gears, moving from one point about attempt crimes to a different point about completed threats. In addition, the conclusion does not follow from the premises. The writer needs to clarify the definition of "substantial step" and develop the relationship between attempt crimes and completed crimes, as well as between attempted threats and completed threats. Only then can the reader begin to see how these multiple concepts work together to establish the target rule for proving an attempted threat.

A meta-version of focus shifting happens when a writer overcompresses his reasoning writ large. This problem manifests in "packed paragraphs" that cram multiple syllogistic or inductive links into a small space without fully developing any of them.[73] The writer takes on too much instead of taking the time to develop each link one at a time.[74] Tight word limits do not justify this sort of compressed reasoning; the solution is to be more selective with the reasons in the first place.

A third shifting problem stems from imprecision. When the meaning or connotation of words shifts between premises, the result is the "fallacy of equivocation."[75] Take this example, a flawed hypothetical rewriting of the Facebook v. Connect U settlement agreement syllogism:

- An otherwise valid settlement agreement is enforceable if its terms are sufficiently certain.

- This settlement agreement spelled out the parties' obligations in great detail.
- Therefore, the settlement agreement was sufficiently certain.

The fallacy lies in equating certainty with detail. Detailed provisions are not inherently certain, for too much detail can be confusing, conflicting, and overwhelming — leaving the interpretation decidedly *uncertain.*

This section's examples are but a sampling of all possible fallacies and reasoning flaws. Yet they are representative problems that surface again and again in advocates' writing.[76] The frequency with which these errors are committed underscores the importance of not just building a well-sequenced reasoning chain, but testing the underlying logic of each link. So, when you activate the Server/Expediter's keen vision as discussed in Chapter 12, spend at least one revision round looking for and rooting out these problems in your own work. And when you get your opponent's brief, look for the same mistakes.

Practice Alert #6
Legal Reasoning Flaws
Exercise

This exercise in the online companion reproduces an argument from an appellate brief, and asks you to identify and label its reasoning flaws. It then asks you to choose one flaw and remedy it.

Section 4   Using Roundtables and Moots to Test Arguments, Improve Thinking, and Sharpen Writing

If you act alone as argument drafter and tester, chances are you will overlook problems — even glaring ones. Your intimate familiarity with the work may rob you of perspective and dull your instincts. So use peers and colleagues as a sounding board for the validity and efficacy of your arguments. Better yet, workshop your arguments on each issue during the drafting phase. A workshop can take many forms, depending on your time constraints. At a minimum, set aside two or three hours to get feedback from your team or other trusted colleagues. Do this well before you begin the Server/Expediter revisions; you will be less inclined to discard or alter arguments once you've spent time polishing them.

If time allows, try what one author calls "Appeal in Reverse." The Appeal in Reverse exercise helps you achieve early on the clarity that normally arrives much later in the appellate process. Naturally, your thinking crystallizes as your appeal progresses. For example, writing a reply brief brings your arguments into sharper focus because you must confront and defend weaknesses. Preparing for oral argument forces you to distill your case to its essence and to simplify your arguments so that they can be presented to and understood by a listening audience. Not one advocate has written a reply brief or delivered an oral argument without thinking afterward, "I wish I had included that in the opening brief."

To accelerate this process, select your most difficult issue early on, perhaps shortly after you have finalized your appellate issues. Spend one or two days furiously researching and organizing the issue's arguments. If you cannot generate a draft, create a detailed bullet-point outline with citations, and enlist a colleague to play your opponent. She will spend two days doing the same work on her side. Shortly afterwards, hold a moot court where you and your opponent present the issue and field questions just as if you were preparing for oral argument. Then follow it with a robust roundtable discussion. This exercise is rigorous and time intensive, but it focuses your arguments and exposes their weaknesses in a way that is virtually impossible to achieve otherwise. Optimally you would repeat the exercise with every issue, but the reality of deadlines and the press of other work will likely foreclose a reprise. If nothing else, carve out the time to "Appeal in Reverse" your toughest issue. Your brief will be all the stronger for it.

Endnotes

1. Sarah E. Ricks & Jane L. Istvan, *Effective Brief Writing Despite High Volume Practice: Ten Misconceptions that Result in Bad Briefs*, U. Tol. L. Rev. 1113, 1119 (2007).
2. William N. Eskridge, Jr. & Philip P. Frickey, *Statutory Interpretation as Practical Reasoning*, 42 Stan. L. Rev. 321, 340 (1990).
3. *See, e.g.*, Girvan Peck, Writing Persuasive Briefs 133-34 (1984); Ruggero J. Aldisert, Winning on Appeal: Better Briefs and Oral Argument 243-55, 117, 139-40, 211 (rev. 1st ed. 1996); *see also* Ricks & Istvan, *supra* note 1, at 1119; Ruggiero J. Aldisert, *Perspective from the Bench on the Value of Clinical Appellate Training of Law Students*, 75 Miss. L.J. 645, 655 (2006); Kathryn M. Stanchi, *The Science of Persuasion: An Initial Exploration*, 2006 Mich. St. L. Rev. 411, 421 ("The persuasive writer wants to create an argument chain that leads the judge to start nodding 'yes' to her arguments.").
4. Kristen K. Robbins Tiscione, *The Inside Scoop: What Federal Judges Really Think About the Way Lawyers Write*, 8 Legal Writing: J. Legal Writing Inst. 257, 264 (2002).
5. Boyd v. Nationwide Mut. Ins. Co., 208 F.3d 406 (2d Cir. 2000); Frakes v. Crete Carrier Corp., 579 F.3d 426 (5th Cir. 2009); Babb v. Minder, 806 F.2d 749 (7th Cir. 1986).
6. Boyd v. Nationwide Mut. Ins. Co., 208 F.3d 406 (2d Cir. 2000); Frakes v. Crete Carrier Corp., 579 F.3d 426 (5th Cir. 2009); Babb v. Minder, 806 F.2d 749 (7th Cir. 1986).
7. Katherine Stanchi, *Teaching Students to Present Law Persuasively Using Techniques from Psychology*, 19 Perspectives: Teaching Legal Res. & Writing 142, 147 (2011); H. Mitchell Caldwell, L. Timothy Perrin, Richard Gabriel & Sharon R. Gross, *Primacy, Recency, Ethos, and Pathos: Integrating Principles of Communication Into the Direct Examination*, 76 Notre Dame L. Rev. 423, 437-40 (2001).
8. Stanchi, *supra* note 3, at 427-31 (Cognitive science confirms that this "door in the face" approach has had some success.).
9. *Id.* at 430-31.
10. *Id.*
11. United States v. Bartsh, 69 F.3d 864, 866 (8th Cir. 1995); Oladeinde v. City of Birmingham, 230 F.3d 1275, 1288 (11th Cir. 2000); Michael A. Berch, *We've Only Just Begun: The Impact of Remand Orders from Higher to Lower Courts on American Jurisprudence*, 36 Ariz. St. L.J. 493, 496-97 (2004).
12. Feliciano v. City of Miami Beach, 707 F.3d 1244, 1251-52 (11th Cir. 2013); Box v. A & P Tea Co., 772 F.2d 1372, 1376 (7th Cir. 1985); Joan E. Steinman, *Appellate Courts as First Responders: The Constitutionality and Propriety of Appellate Courts' Resolving Issues in the First Instance*, 87 Notre Dame L. Rev. 1521, 1593 (2012).
13. Hon. Robert R. Baldock, Hon. Carlos F. Lucero & Vicki Mandell-King, *What Appellate Advocates Seek from Appellate Judges and What Appellate Judges Seek from Appellate Advocates Panel Two*, 31 N.M. L. Rev. 267, 270 (2001) (Preservation arguments are especially important in criminal cases).
14. Robert F. Parsley, *Litigating Waiver of Issues for Appeal and On Appeal in Federal Courts, in* Strategies for Appellate Litigation: Leading Lawyers Examine the Unique Differences Between Appellate and Trial Practice (2013).
15. *See e.g.*, David M. Ebel, Michael R. Murphy & Andrew G. Schultz, *What Appellate Advocates Seek from Appellate Judges and What Appellate Judges Seek from Appellate Advocates Panel One*, 31 N.M. L. Rev. 255, 257 (2001).
16. *See* Ruggero J. Aldisert, Stephen Clowney & Jeremy D. Peterson, *Logic for Law Students: How to Think Like a Lawyer*, 69 U. Pitt. L. Rev. 1, 3 (2007); Mary Massaron Ross, *A Basis for Legal Reasoning: Logic on Appeal*, 3 Journal of the Ass'n of Legal Writing Directors 177, 180 (2006); Wilson Huhn, *The Use and Limits of Syllogistic Reasoning in Briefing Cases*, 42 Santa Clara L. Rev. 813, 815-16 (2002).
17. Ross, *supra* note 16, at 179.

18. Debra Cassens Weiss, *Connecticut Justice Apologized to Kelo Plaintiff at a Private Gathering*, ABA JOURNAL, Sept. 20, 2011, http://www.abajournal.com/news/article/connecticut_justice_apologized_to_kelo_plaintiff_at_a_private_gathering/.

19. Stanchi, *supra* note 3, at 415; ALDISERT, *supra* note 3, at 243-55; Michael Burgoon et al., *Language Expectancy Theory*, in THE PERSUASION HANDBOOK: DEVELOPMENTS IN THEORY AND PRACTICE 117, 121 (James Price Dillard & Michael Pfau, eds., 2002); *see* Aldisert et al., *supra* note 16, at 3.

20. Joel R. Cornwell, *Legal Writing as a Kind of Philosophy*, 48 Mercer L. Rev. 1091 (1997); *see* Tracy Turner, *Finding Consensus in Legal Writing Discourse Regarding Organizational Structure: A Review and Analysis of the Use of IRAC and Its Progenies*, 9 LEGAL COMM. & RHETORIC: JALWD 351, 354 n.10 (2012); Sarah O. Schrup & Susan E. Provenzano, *The Conscious Curriculum: From Novice Towards Mastery in Written Legal Analysis and Advocacy*, 108 NW. U. L. REV. COLLOQUY 80, 92-93 (2013).

21. Kathryn M. Stanchi, *Playing with Fire: The Science of Confronting Adverse Material in Legal Advocacy*, 60 RUTGERS L. REV. 381 (2008).

22. Stanchi, *supra* note 3, at 416-17; Ross, *supra* note 16, at 185; Aldisert et al., *supra* note 16, at 8-9.

23. Stanchi, *supra* note 3, at 411; Aldisert et al., *supra* note 16, at 5-6; Huhn, *supra* note 16, at 849-52.

24. Aldisert et al., *supra* note 16, at 3; Ross, *supra* note 16, at 183.

25. Harris v. Forklift Sys., Inc., 510 U.S. 17, 21 (1993) (quoting Meritor Sav. Bank, FSB v. Vinson, 477 U.S. 57, 65, (1986) (internal quotations omitted)).

26. *See* Aldisert et al., *supra* note 16, at 9; Huhn, *supra* note 16, at 820, 861.

27. *See* Aldisert et al., *supra* note 16, at 9; Huhn, *supra* note 16, at 843.

28. Huhn, *supra* note 16, at 820.

29. *See* Ross, *supra* note 16, at 180-81; Stanchi, *supra* note 3, at 454-45; Aldisert et al., *supra* note 16, at 18-19.

30. Ross, *supra* note 16, at 180-81; Aldisert et al., *supra* note 16, at 12-14.

31. Brief for the Appellees at 23-24, Facebook, Inc. v. Connect U., Nos. 08-16745, 08-16873, 09-15021 (written by Orrick, Herrington & Sutcliffe).

32. The dollar and share amounts are blacked out in the briefs to protect confidential information.

33. Richard A. Posner, *Convincing a Federal Court of Appeals*, LITIGATION, 1991, at 3.

34. Brief for the Appellant at 17, United States v. Worku, No. 14-1218 (written by Snell & Wilmer).

35. Brief for the Appellant at 69-72, Oracle v. Google, Nos. 2013-1021, 2013-1022 (written by Orrick, Herrington & Sutcliffe).

36. 17 U.S.C. § 107 (2015).

37. *See* Wilson R. Huhn, *Teaching Legal Analysis Using a Pluralistic Model of Law*, 36 GONZ. L. REV. 433, 446-50 (2001); Ellie Margolis, *Closing the Floodgates: Making Persuasive Policy Arguments in Appellate Briefs*, 62 MONT. L. REV. 59, 70-79 (2001); Michael R. Smith, *The Sociological and Cognitive Dimensions of Policy-Based Persuasion*, 22 J.L. & POL'Y 35, 62-89 (2013).

38. Aldisert et al., *supra* note 16, at 13 ("Where an issue of law is unsettled, and there is no binding precedent to supply a major premise for your syllogism, deductive logic is of no use to you.").

39. *Id.* ("When there is no clear statute — no governing authority — to provide the major premise necessary for a syllogism, the law student must build the major premise himself.").

40. *Id.* Ross, *supra* note 16, at 180-81; Stanchi, *supra* note 3, at 425.

41. Stanchi, *supra* note 7, at 143.

42. Aldisert et al., *supra* note 16, at 13.

43. Stanchi, *supra* note 3, at 415.

44. *Id.* at 419.

45. *Id.*

46. Although the argument centers on a statute, we classify it as an unsettled law argument because it advocates for a new legal principle rather than using the standard interpretive tools to justify the law's reading.

47. Huhn, *supra* note 16, at 820. To reflect the "confluence" relationship, Huhn refers to legal arguments as a "cable" rather than a chain. Although "a chain is only as strong as its weakest link," "a cable's strength relies not on that of individual threads, but upon their cumulative strength as they are woven together." *Id.* at 849-50.

48. *Id.* at 850 (2002); *see also* Katherine Clark & Matthew Connolly, *A Guide to Reading, Interpreting and Applying Statutes*, THE WRITING CENTER AT GULC 1 (2006); *see also* William N. Eskridge, Jr., *Dynamic Statutory Interpretation*, 135 U. PA. L. REV. 1479, 1481 (1987).

49. *See supra* Chapter 6 at 105-06.

50. *Supra* note 16, at 849. *See also* William N. Eskridge, Jr., *Dynamic Statutory Interpretation*, 135 U. PA. L. REV. 1479, 1479 (1987).

51. Brief of the Petitioner at 14-21, Univ. of Tex. Sw. Med. Ctr. v. Nassar, No. 12-484 (written by King & Spalding and the state of Texas).

52. *See, e.g.*, Price Waterhouse v. Hopkins, 490 U.S. 228 (1989) (overruled by Gross v. FBL Fin. Serv., Inc., 557 U.S. 167 (2009)).

53. 42 U.S.C.A. § 2000e-2(a)(1).

54. *Id.*

55. Civil Rights Act, 42 U.S.C. § 2000e(m) (1991).

56. As indicted by the ellipses and brackets, this excerpt omits small portions of text for space and pedagogical reasons.
57. *See, e.g.,* Kristen K. Robbins Tiscione, *Paradigm Lost: Recapturing Classical Rhetoric to Validate Legal Reasoning,* 27 Vt. L. Rev. 483, 498-509 (2003); Ross, *supra* note 16, at 188.
58. *See, e.g.,* Robbins Tiscione, *supra* note 57, at 498-505.
59. *Id.* at 498-99.
60. *Id.* at 505-09.
61. *Id.* at 498. Robbins Tiscione labels this problem the "Book Report." She elaborates: "In this context, the 'rule' or major premise is usually intuited by the writer but not made explicit in the writing. Instead, the writer jumps immediately to the application of the rule by simply narrating or 'reporting on' the salient facts and sometimes, but not always, including the holding of the cited case." *Id.*
62. *Id.* at 499.
63. *Id.* at 505; Robbins Tiscione calls this the "Fear of Commitment," where "the writer feels uncomfortable drawing a conclusion from the premises she has laid out and simply fails to include one." *Id.*
64. *Id.*
65. Ross, *supra* note 16, at 188-89.
66. Example from S. Morris Engel, With Good Reason: An Introduction to Informal Fallacies 114 (2d ed. 1982).
67. In logic lingo, this problem is "the fallacy of the illicit major term or illicit minor term." Ross, *supra* note 16, at 186. This fallacy reaches a conclusion about a whole class "when the class was not referred to in its entirety in the major premise." Aldisert et al., *supra* note 16, at 11.
68. Logicians call this "the fallacy of the undistributed middle." Ross, *supra* note 16, at 185; *see also* Robbins Tiscione, *supra* note 57, at 494.
69. Edward P. J. Corbett, Classical Rhetoric for the Modern Student 23, 54 (3d ed. 1990). This is called the "fallacy of exclusive premises." Ross, *supra* note 16, at 186. Robbins-Tiscione coins this as the "Negative Proof." Robbins Tiscione, *supra* note 57, at 526-31.
70. Robbins Tiscione, *supra* note 57, at 529.
71. Aldisert et al., *supra* note 16, at 13.
72. *Id.* The logicians' term for this problem is "the fallacy of four terms," as it tackles four separate concepts without sufficiently connecting any of them. Ross, *supra* note 16, at 185.
73. Robbins Tiscione, *supra* note 57, at 509-12, 530.
74. *Id.* at 509.
75. Ross, *supra* note 16, at 185; Aldisert et al., *supra* note 16, at 14.
76. *See generally* Aldisert et al., *supra* note 16; Ross, *supra* note 16; Robbins Tiscione, *supra* note 57.

11 The Writing Phase: Framing Arguments Beyond IRAC

This chapter continues the argument-drafting process, shifting gears from logically structuring arguments to framing them. As Chapter 9 explained in the context of issues and fact statements, framing means influencing an audience to consume your message from a particular perspective.[1] Framing operates on multiple levels in an argument section; it is not a one-dimensional approach.[2] This section breaks down expert argument framing methods into four strategies: (1) frontloading and priming in overview paragraphs, point headings, and topic and concluding sentences; (2) strategically presenting the law; (3) managing opposing arguments; and (4) crafting policy arguments. After completing this chapter's work, you should be primed and ready to add the "bells and whistles" of style, voice, and revising to perfection — covered in Chapter 12.

Section 1 Frontloading and Priming

Frontloading, also called "point first" writing, means stating the upshot of your argument or persuasive message at the outset.[3] Busy judicial readers crave these spoilers[4] because they establish a clear focus and a definitive direction, both of which help the judge to follow and assess the argument.[5] As Chapter 9 explained, the related concept of "priming" means presenting early information in a way that influences the reader's reactions to later information.[6] In the argument section, priming works by establishing a baseline favorable impression of the advocate's position that colors judicial perceptions of the entire argument.[7] Used together at critical argument junctures, frontloading and priming create first impressions that last not only the duration of the judge's reading time but remain long afterwards.[8] Those critical junctures are where judicial attention is at its peak — overview paragraphs, point headings, and topic and concluding sentences.[9]

1.1 Overview Paragraphs

Overview paragraphs appear at the beginning of argument sections and subsections. They have educational and persuasive purposes. From an educational

249

standpoint, overview paragraphs accomplish three things: (1) They state the section's big-picture conclusions; (2) they supply its driving legal principles; and (3) they roadmap the reasons that support the writer's conclusion. Judicial preference for overview paragraphs[10] is not the only reason to include them. Educational psychologists have found that these advance organizers offer a knowledge base for the reader's later use, and facilitate recall by helping the reader understand relationships among subtopics.[11]

At the same time that these paragraphs educate, they prime the reader, making her ready to rule without even having read the argument. Two priming strategies achieve this persuasive effect: (1) selecting advantageous big-picture principles; and (2) characterizing the law to fit the theme and the facts to fit the law. Characterization is a technique that presents a fresh angle on the law or facts, one that is different from the opponent's.[12] Of course, the characterization must be accurate to be effective.

Overview paragraphs for main sections. To illustrate each of these educational and priming principles, let's look at an exemplary student-drafted set of overview paragraphs, written in the *Mutombo* appeal challenging a college student's conviction for attempting to make a terrorist threat, discussed in earlier chapters. These paragraphs, housed under a main section heading, introduce the entire argument challenging the scope of the officers' inventory search.

EXAMPLE   **Main Section Overview Paragraph**

II. The Trial Court Erred by Denying Defendant's Motion to Suppress Evidence Seized During an Unconstitutional Search of Defendant's Car.

The Fourth Amendment exists "to safeguard the privacy and security of individuals against arbitrary invasions by government officials." South Dakota v. Opperman, 428 U.S. 364, 377 (1976) (Powell, J., concurring). Consequently, the Supreme Court has interpreted the Constitution to require that police obtain a warrant before they conduct any investigatory search of a criminal suspect's property. *See* Chambers v. Maroney, 399 U.S. 42, 51 (1970). Warrantless searches are per se unreasonable, and the Supreme Court has established that so-called inventory searches only escape Fourth Amendment prohibition if they are both

← *Priming with selection of advantageous big-picture principles and characterization of law to fit theme*

narrowly tailored to achieve police's community caretaking function and not administered for ulterior motives. *See* Colorado v. Bertine, 479 U.S. 367, 372 (1987); Illinois v. Lafayette, 462 U.S. 640 (1983).

The purported "inventory" search of ⟵ *Big picture conclusion* Maurice Mutombo's car was neither *(substantive)* executed in good faith nor tailored to achieve the legitimate goals of a proper inventory search. Police entered Mr. Mutombo's car to conduct an "inventory" pursuant to their established tow policy, but did so merely as ⟵ *Roadmap of reasoning* a pretext to search for incriminating *chain and* evidence in a criminal suspect's car. *characterization of* Furthermore, by picking up, turning over, *facts to fit law* and thoroughly reading Mr. Mutombo's private, handwritten thoughts, Officer Salles exceeded the scope of a constitutionally permissible inventory search. Engaging with the words written on a sheet of paper that poses no imminent danger to police and possesses no intrinsic value does not further any of the legitimate objectives of an inventory. Evidence gathered as a result of such activity cannot, therefore, serve as the basis of a criminal charge or conviction.

Illinois appellate courts review de novo trial court decisions regarding the legal question of ⟵ *Big picture conclusion* whether suppression of evidence is warranted. *(procedural)* People v. Gipson, 203 Ill. 2d 298, 304 (Ill. 2003). Here, the trial court committed harmful error when it denied Mr. Mutombo's motion to suppress evidence uncovered by the NWU Police Department in the course of conducting a warrantless investigatory search of his locked disabled vehicle. Accordingly, this Court should overturn Mr. Mutombo's conviction for Attempt Making a Terrorist Threat.

These paragraphs cover the three core educational components. First, the reader immediately sees the section's main substantive and procedural conclusions: The police violated the Fourth Amendment by conducting an excessive and pretextual inventory search, and the lower court's refusal to suppress the evidence from that search was harmful error. Second, the reader learns the driving legal principles—inventory searches must further caretaking purposes and must be conducted in good faith. Third, the next paragraph roadmaps the reasoning chain with an overview of how the facts fit those legal principles to drive the conclusion. Impressively, this writer covers both the "what" and the "why" in short order: (1) no good faith here, *because the officers were looking for evidence of a crime*; (2) no caretaking purposes here, *because words on a sheet of paper have no value and present no danger.* A less effective version would be conclusory, and simply assert that the officers acted in bad faith and without a caretaking purpose, omitting the reasons why. Or it would be too elaborate, with loads of factual detail. This version plays it just right.

As it educates, this overview segment primes the reader to agree with its conclusion by using both selection and characterization. The first paragraph selects big-picture defendant-friendly Fourth Amendment principles to set the stage for the rest of the argument. One can imagine the opposing overview paragraphs calling the court's attention to the competing principles of the police's discretion and protective role. This paragraph characterizes too, ordering and phrasing sentences from a distinctly defense viewpoint. Front and center is the default rule that "the Constitution *require[s]*" the police to get a warrant for investigatory searches. Inventory searches are then painted as narrow exceptions that are "per se unreasonable" *unless* they are "narrowly tailored" and lack "ulterior motives." The opposing brief might not even mention the default warrant rule, focusing exclusively on when an inventory search is valid and emphasizing the permissible rationales. But this writer's selection and characterization invite the court to view the officers' motives and actions with skepticism and suspicion—before the argument has even begun.

Overview paragraphs for subsections. Moving in a level, overview paragraphs that precede subsections have parallel but pared-down components. As much as judges want overviews, they are anxious to get to the meat of the argument. To meet that need, subsection overview paragraphs are shorter on big-picture principles and the "why" behind the advocate's conclusions. Here's a sample introducing the pretext argument.

EXAMPLE **Subsection Overview Paragraph**

A. **The search of Mutombo's car was pretextual because it took place during an ongoing criminal investigation and deviated from the police's written tow policy.**

An inventory search of a vehicle is pretextual when the police have an ulterior motive to discover ← *Driving legal principles* incriminating evidence. *See* Florida v. Wells, 495

U.S. 1, 4 (1990) ("An inventory search must not be used as a ruse for a general rummaging in order to discover incriminating evidence."). The fact that the NWU police were assisting the Glen Lake Police and the A.T.F. with an ongoing investigation into Mutombo—and deviated from their tow policy to further the investigation—shows the "inventory search" was actually a pretext for gathering evidence. ← *Conclusion and roadmap*

Having read the main section introduction, the reader already knows the basic legal principles and facts that drive pretext, so the writer doesn't belabor them here. Instead, she moves immediately to new information: Pretext encompasses ulterior investigatory motives. She then efficiently combines the subsection's conclusion and roadmap in a single sentence. Priming still plays an important role. The first sentence emphasizes when a search *is* pretextual—not when it could be or when it isn't. The second sentence characterizes the facts as an easy fit with the law; it is not a big step to infer pretext when police "deviate" from "policy."

Keep in mind that overview paragraphs—like all legal writing conventions—should not be written without a purpose. It is always fair to ask what persuasive and educational goals overview paragraphs would accomplish in any given part of the argument, especially if you have already written a lengthy section introduction. The keys remain education and persuasion. If the court doesn't need any more context to understand the subsection and the persuasive benefits are outweighed by brevity concerns, then jump into the argument. On the other hand, if the reasoning chain is complex or you can get some priming mileage from legal or factual context that hasn't yet been provided, then the overview paragraphs will accomplish something and are worth including.

SUMMARY

Overview Paragraphs

- Overview paragraphs educate by frontloading and persuade by priming.
- Main section introductions should frontload by: (1) stating the section's big-picture conclusions; (2) articulating the section's driving legal principles; and (3) roadmapping the section's supporting reasons.
- Main section introductions should also prime by: (1) selecting advantageous big-picture principles; and (2) characterizing the law to fit the theme and the facts to fit the law.
- Subsection introductions should be less elaborate, focusing more on the basic conclusion and reasons than on big-picture principles and the "why."
- Use your judgment to decide whether you need overview paragraphs at any given point in the brief.

1.2 Point Headings

Point headings appear in two places: the Table of Contents and the Argument section. They serve distinct frontloading and priming purposes, educating and persuading in a more condensed manner than overview paragraphs. When viewed in the Table of Contents, point headings present a meta-structure of the Argument that reveals big picture relationships at a glance, which in turn improves reader recall.[13] Situated in the Argument section, point headings improve recall in a second way—by helping the reader chunk information so that it is consumed in manageable bites and remembered more effectively.[14] Finally, point headings improve reader comprehension by providing transitions and reading breathers. They help the reader track the argument's flow and allow her to catch her breath before the next reasoning chain.

But point headings won't yield these comprehension and recall benefits unless they are well drafted. Well-drafted point headings excel in three ways: structure, content, and style.

Point headings—Structure. As an integrated part of the Argument, the point headings should reflect Chapter 10's argument ordering and reasoning chain principles. If you have thoughtfully sequenced your issues, arguments, and reasons, and considered how each fits underneath the other and in what order, then the headings' organization—the ordering of points and subpoints—takes care of itself. Compare the following examples from the competing Supreme Court briefs in Lawrence v. Texas:[15]

Point Heading Comparison in Lawrence v. Texas Due Process Arguments

Petitioners' Brief	Respondent's Brief

I. Section 21.06 Violates Constitutional Rights to Liberty and Privacy Possessed by All Americans
  A. American Adults Have Fundamental Liberty and Privacy Interests in Making Their Own Choices About Private, Consensual Sexual Relations
    1. Well-Established Protections for Intimate Relationships, Bodily Integrity, and the Privacy of the Home Converge in This Vital Freedom
    2. There Is No Constitutional Exception to Liberty for Gay and Lesbian Citizens
    3. Objective Considerations Support Recognition of Fundamental Interests Here
	I. Substantive Due Process Under the Fourteenth Amendment
	  A. The appellate record is inadequate to support the recognition of the limited constitutional right asserted by the petitioners
	  B. The Court has adopted a historical approach to the recognition of liberty interests protected under the Due Process Clause
	  C. This nation has no deep-rooted tradition of protecting a right to engage in sodomy
	  D. No tradition of protection exists at any level of specificity of designation of an asserted liberty interest
	  E. Principles of stare decisis counsel against recognition of a new protected liberty interest

---

Petitioners' Brief	Respondent's Brief
B. Texas Cannot Justify Section 21.06's Criminal Prohibition of Petitioners' and Other Adults' Private Sexual Intimacy C. *Bowers* Should Not Block Recognition and Enforcement of These Fundamental Interests	

The Petitioners' headings honor the baseline ordering principles of argument relationship, strength, and strategy. Section I's main heading announces the overall due process argument — Texas law violates constitutional rights to liberty and privacy. In a logical, strategic order, sections A through C present arguments *why* the law violates those rights. Section A affirmatively explains how, then sections B and C attack opposing justifications. Critically, Section A does not repeat what the reader has learned from Section I's main heading; it adds a layer of detail.

Within Section A's argument, the reason sequencing is equally effective, with sections 1 through 3 each adding layers of detail about the liberty and privacy rights at stake. These sections also reflect strategic sequencing: Section 1 affirmatively establishes these rights' breadth while Section 2 seals off this contention by pointing out the lack of exceptions.

In contrast, the Respondent's headings float adrift. Section I's main heading announces the due process topic, but then the subheadings indiscriminately — and repetitively — survey that topic rather than communicating specific arguments in a logical progression. Indeed, Section A's point could be a threshold argument about problems with the record, or it could be a merits argument about how the law applies to the facts. If the latter, then it should not be a stand-alone argument but a subpoint under some other section. Section B announces a jurisprudential approach, but never connects that approach to the due process rights asserted in the case. Section C articulates the only case-specific argument, but Section D sounds as though it covers the same ground in more general terms. Overall, these headings lack a clear hierarchy and are too general for effective reader "chunking."

Point headings — Content. To promote recall and comprehension, point heading content must be precise, pithy, and argumentative — not topical and objective. A precise and pithy heading is specific enough to capture the ensuing argument, but short and simple enough to convey it quickly. Each subheading should add a layer of detail or reasoning to the main heading, rather than repeating it in different words. But there is a balance; too much detail impedes reader comprehension and slows the reader's pace. For instance, some writers draft long headings believing that every heading needs both a conclusion and a reason. Certainly every heading must identify a conclusion; but let the surrounding context dictate the need for reasons. Keep in mind that in the Table of Contents, for example, a reader encounters the headings in context with each other. That means a very short main heading can be followed by more elaborate subheadings and vice versa without confusing the reader. To account for context in the Argument, a sparser heading can be followed by a more detailed topic sentence without sacrificing clarity.

Argumentative headings are the product of vivid nouns and active verbs, rather than abstract nouns and linking verbs. Those core nouns and verbs usually appear in the heading's first few words. Take the contrasting *Lawrence* examples. In the Petitioners' headings, the "who" and the "what" are clear from the start: "American Adults" have "Fundamental Privacy and Liberty Interests," for example. The Respondent's headings obscure the who and the what, with oblique statements like "no tradition of protection exists at any level of specificity of designation of an asserted liberty interest." This near-complete absence of actors and actions, along with the serial prepositional phrases, make this heading both objective and impenetrable.

Here are more effective point headings from Chapter 10's expert brief excerpts. These headings' colorful, concrete language leaves no doubt about the writer's conclusion or the "who" and "what" involved. Their high precision obviates the need for extra wording and detail. And they are decidedly argumentative, taking firm positions rather than announcing topics.

- The Settlement Agreement Recites Specific Obligations Capable of Enforcement[16]
- Google's Copying Was Commercially Motivated, Not Transformative, and Illicit[17]
- A Title VII Retaliation Plaintiff Must Prove that Protected Activity Was the "But-For" Cause of an Adverse Employment Action[18]
- Title VII's Text Is Clear[19]

Point headings — Style. Aside from their structure and content, headings should use style and formatting techniques that meet judicial expectations.[20] Main headings should reflect the issues on appeal. They should be left-justified and preceded by a roman numeral.[21] Subheadings should capture the arguments underneath the issues. They should be indented one level and preceded by a capital letter.[22] Sub-subheadings, if used at all, should be indented one more level, and preceded with an Arabic numeral. As for typeface, choose options that accelerate reading rather than slow it. Chapter 12 addresses this topic in more depth, but for now you should know that all caps headings are the worst choice, followed closely by italics and underlining.[23] Bold headings, by contrast, do not appear to affect reading speed.[24] The point here is to be judicious, and to consider typeface along with heading length.[25] The longer the heading — and we recommend that no heading ever span more than three lines — the more typeface will affect reading speed.

Practice Alert #1
Point Headings Exercise

This exercise in the online companion presents a flawed set of point headings from an appellate brief. It asks you to redraft those headings' structure, content, and style using this section's guidance.

Finally, a word about the number of headings and subheadings. Rarely should a brief have more than four headings at any level. If your headings exceed this number, chances are that your points are repetitive or you are offering too many arguments or reasons. It's a sign that you need to refine or consolidate. By the same token, a brief with more than three heading levels (*i.e.*, beyond I. . . . A. . . . 1. . . .) risks choppiness, hampering reader retention and recall. At this micro-level, use strong topic sentences to convey your points instead of adding a heading level.

SUMMARY

Point Headings

- Point heading structure is argument structure; use Chapter 10's ordering principles to discern main headings (I), subheadings (A), and sub-subheadings (1).
- Reevaluate your argument structure and selection if your headings at any level number more than four.
- To avoid disjointedness, don't create headings at the fourth level of indentation; use topic sentences instead.
- To be persuasive, point headings should state clear, affirmative conclusions in economical language — and never in more than a single sentence or more than four lines.
- Put vivid nouns and verbs near the beginning of headings to show who is doing what; limit prepositional phrases, which drag out the point.
- Use your judgment to decide whether a heading needs a supporting reason in addition to a conclusion; let context be your guide.

1.3 Topic and Concluding Sentences

Topic sentences. Topic sentences frontload and prime in much the same way as point headings, preparing the reader for what comes next, but at the paragraph level. Relative to their size, topic sentences are responsible for a large share of an argument's forward momentum. But if they are weak, topic sentences create more than their share of comprehension and stalling problems. Effective topic sentences share three qualities: (1) they launch the point that the paragraph makes — no more and no less; (2) they launch that point argumentatively, not objectively; and (3) they move the reader forward from one link to the next.

These three qualities mark a series of topic sentences in successive paragraphs from the United States v. Worku Appellant's Brief, discussed in Chapter 10:[26]

- The district court's sentencing decision relied heavily on the court's finding that "Worku concealed his true identity and sought to avoid further prosecution and punishment for his participation in Ethiopia of the crimes of torture and murder."

- **But** those were not plausible findings, because there was **no evidence** that Mr. Worku came to the United States to conceal his Ethiopian conduct, whatever that might be.
- **Instead**, Mr. Worku lived peacefully in Kenya until he was contacted by a broker to assist the family of Habteab Berhe Temanu with their refugee application.
- **In sum**, there was no evidence supporting the district court's conclusion that the reason Mr. Worku came to the United States was to conceal his alleged role in torture in the Higher 15 Prison.

These sentences leave no doubt about what each paragraph will cover. And, as the full excerpt in Chapter 10 shows, they do not stray from what the rest of their paragraph contends. These topic sentences are advocacy pieces as well. Each sentence's language is argumentative, not descriptive, taking firm positions on everything: The lower court findings "were not plausible"; there was "no evidence" that Mr. Worku acted to conceal; he "lived peacefully" in Kenya; and thus "no evidence" supports the lower court's conclusion. Notice the bold faced directional words, linking the reader from old to new information. The content is directional, too; each sentence's substance moves the reader forward one step in the reasoning chain. Even in isolation, these topic sentences tell much about the argument's structure and content.

A topic sentence that immediately follows a point heading presents an added challenge — how to make it accomplish something new? Instead of repeating the heading in the same or different words, use the topic sentence to add a layer of reasoning, or conversely to take on a chunk of the heading's promise, as this heading-topic sentence pairing does:

- Google's Copying Was Commercially Motivated, Not Transformative, and Illicit [Heading]
- Google's use of Oracle's code is purely commercial. [Topic sentence][27]

A topic sentence can also be a framing device, designed for an arresting effect. This next series, also from Chapter 10's Oracle v. Google excerpt, illustrates the power of the short topic sentence:[28]

- Google's use of Oracle's code is purely commercial.
- In considering the first factor, **courts also inquire** whether the copied material substitutes for the original or, instead, adds or changes the purpose of the original, thereby "transform[ing]" it in a meaningful way.
- Google's use of the declaring code **was exactly the same** as in Java: to call upon prewritten packages to perform the same functions.

- **Such superseding use** is "*always*" unfair.
- **Finally**, "[f]air use presupposes good faith and fair dealing."

These sentences vary in length, but the first, fourth, and fifth sentence average just 7.66 words. Though shorter, they launch each paragraph's point just as surely as the longer *Worku* examples; the "why" comes in the rest of paragraph. Concentrated in a smaller space, their argumentative tone is even more intense. And despite their modest length, these sentences still incorporate the bold faced directional language. The takeaway is that good topic sentences can be short or long. When the goals are to inform and persuade, sometimes less is more.

**Practice Alert #2
Topic Sentences Exercise**

This exercise in the online companion presents a series of paragraphs with weak topic sentences. It asks you to add or redraft the topic sentences with the qualities discussed in this section.

Concluding sentences. Concluding sentences do not frontload or prime as much as they account for what has been said in a new and compelling way. Some concluding sentences pull together multiple reasoning strands and tie them into the writer's conclusion in a final "money sentence," as in this Facebook v. Connect U paragraph from Chapter 10:[29]

EXAMPLE

Paragraph with Concluding "Money Sentence"

In light of all these details, it was easy for the district court to determine whether ConnectU and its Founders had "performed or breached" their "obligations thereunder." *Elite Show Servs.*, 14 Cal. Rptr. 3d at 188. All it needed to know was that Facebook stood ready to transfer $XX and XX[30] shares and to dismiss its case against the CU Founders, but the CU Founders refused to transfer their stock — in any form at all — or dismiss their case against Facebook. It was equally easy for the district court to enforce the Settlement Agreement. All it had to do was order each party to dismiss their respective suits and to turn over the agreed-upon consideration, without adjustment, warranty, embellishment, or modification. ER 48-60. It did not have to supply missing detail. The **simplicity of the enforcement mechanism** — and the **ease with which the parties consummated** the transaction when ordered to do so — proves that the Settlement Agreement's terms were "sufficiently certain," and, therefore, enforceable. *Elite Show Servs.*, 14 Cal. Rptr. 3d at 188.

The boldfaced words harken back to the simplicity and ease of performance reasons, pulling these chain links together and tying them explicitly to the "sufficiently certain" conclusion. A lesser writer may have simply said "therefore" or "for the reasons above," "the Settlement Agreement terms were sufficiently certain." A money sentence like this one does a lot more intellectual and persuasive work in a compact space.

Other concluding sentences take a different tack. They may conclude a build-up to the paragraph's strongest point or communicate a powerful message, techniques this same writer used in other passages.

EXAMPLE

More Concluding Sentences[31]

This is an uncommon copyright case. Usually, the accused infringer has created a work — whether a visual work, work of literature, or computer program — that bears *similarities* to the plaintiff's work. And the court's role is to determine whether the two are sufficiently similar to amount to plagiarism. **Here, we have admitted plagiarism — at least 7,000 times over — and the jury found infringement.**

*   *   *

Here, again, the district court reached the wrong conclusion because it dissected the work too minutely — fixating on the individual line of code rather than the larger arrangement of which it was a part. *Supra* at 50-51. Moreover, applying "short phrases" as the district court did would invalidate practically any computer program. Virtually every line of the typical program is a short phrase. If each were unprotectable without regard to its relation to the larger whole, there would be nothing left of the program. **And nothing left of *Atari*.**

Whatever approach you take, make sure the final sentence does not simply repeat the topic sentence in the same or different words. That wastes the court's time as well as a persuasive opportunity.

REFLECTION, DISCUSSION, AND CHALLENGE QUESTIONS

Topic Sentence Edit

At a late stage in your drafting process, isolate all the topic sentences in your brief and put them in a separate document. Then assess how well they communicate the structure and flow of each argument. Ask yourself these questions:

- Does each topic sentence articulate a clear starting point, or does it begin in the middle of your reasoning?
- Does each topic sentence articulate its point argumentatively, not objectively?
- Does each topic sentence use directional language to move the reader forward?
- Viewed as a whole, do the topic sentences reflect a logical reasoning chain?

Section 2   Framing and Using the Law

Framing and using the law are among appellate advocacy's most significant challenges. Law students often leave the first year with rigid and inaccurate understandings of how to handle law in an argument. They may present the law too objectively, worried that framing and characterization amount to improper "spin." Just as unproductive are students' overblown discussions of the law going far beyond what is needed to support the argument. Or they may assume that every argument needs a full-blown discussion of the cases and corresponding analogical reasoning. As Professor Tiscione's federal judges study revealed, even practicing lawyers struggle to use authority well.[32] Accordingly, this section is devoted to expert appellate strategies for framing and using the law in an argument.

2.1   Framing Rules and Tests

Judges do not read the law in your briefs for general edification, but rather to make a legal ruling in your appeal. They expect candor, but they also expect advocacy. Thus, whether gleaned from one case or synthesized from several, legal rules and tests should always be framed to: (1) reflect your advocacy position; and (2) smoothly apply to the facts. You needn't sacrifice accuracy or credibility along the way. Framing rules and tests is not about altering substance. It is about using your interpretive powers to dig into the law and call the court's attention to the ways in which it supports your position. And that, in turn, is a matter of marshaling the most critical and favorable parts of your authorities, as well as using sentence structure and word choices to set high or low standards, broad or narrow rules — whichever works in your favor.

Compare these competing expressions of the legal tests for a valid inventory search:

Appellant's Test	Appellee's Test
Inventory searches are a narrow exception to the Fourth Amendment's warrant requirement, legal only if officers inspect a car's contents for "caretaking purposes": to protect the owner's valuables, to ensure officer safety, or to avoid claims of lost or damaged goods.	A vehicle inventory is "a well-defined exception" to the Fourth Amendment's warrant requirement. These inventories "serve to protect an owner's property while it is in the custody of the police, to insure against claims of lost, stolen, or vandalized property, and to guard the police from danger."

According to the Appellant, inventory searches are a "narrow exception" to the warrant requirement, but the Appellee characterizes them as a "well-defined exception." Neither is inaccurate, each just reflects a different framing perspective. On one hand, if courts recognize only three justifications for a warrantless inventory, the exception does seem narrow. On the other hand, a narrow exception can legitimately be "well-defined" — and that quote happens to come from a Supreme Court case. These examples not only characterize how inventories fit within Fourth Amendment doctrine, they also frame the inventory standards to fit their advocacy positions. For example, to downplay the inventory search justifications, the Appellant paraphrases them, while the Appellee defines them with an elaborate, police-friendly direct quote.

In the *Mutombo* appeal, a section challenging Mutombo's conviction on First Amendment grounds contends: "*Unless* a person communicates his or her *private, written* thoughts in a manner that removes them from constitutional protection, the *Constitution prohibits* the States from punishing criminally those thoughts." This rule frames First Amendment protections broadly, in a way that easily encompasses Mutombo's short handwritten note stashed between a car seat and console. It also shows how positive rules can be extracted from bad-result cases. The cited cases rejected First Amendment protections for statements expressing a desire to commit specific crimes. But both opinions signed onto the "freedom of mind" principle expressed in the rule, and that is what the advocate emphasizes.[33] The brief then favorably frames that principle with word choice and sentence structure. With the "unless" clause, protection is made the rule and punishment the exception, and only when a person "communicates . . . thoughts" in a certain way. The adjectives "private, written" are rhetorical, framing such thoughts to suggest that most people wouldn't go around revealing them, and insinuating that the First Amendment exception should be even narrower. In the main clause, the subject-verb-object "the Constitution prohibits" draws on the founding document's ethos and turns it into an actor that definitively and broadly bans criminal punishment in these circumstances.

Conversely, the Oracle v. Google fair use argument frames a narrow rule in response to Google's defense contending that its use of Oracle's source code was transformative. "A use of copied material is *not* transformative *unless* the material is used 'in a different manner or for a different purpose from the original.'"[34] This narrow rule favors Oracle, because it undermines Google's position that it used source code in a fundamentally different way than Oracle did. The writer accomplished this framing with nothing more than sentence structure and word choice leading into the rule. The "not" and "unless" language emphasizes that transformative use is the exception rather than the rule. Were Google to frame the same rule, it might say, in contrast, "A use of copied material *is* transformative *whenever* the material is used in *either* 'a different manner' or 'for a different purpose from the original.'"

Statutory interpretation arguments frame rules too. Chapter 10's *Nassar* brief excerpt, which advocated "but-for" causation for retaliation claims, framed a favorably broad rule in this topic sentence-rule Title VII pairing: "The common law backdrop confirms the statute's plain meaning. Unless it clearly indicates otherwise, Congress intends its legislation to incorporate traditional tort principles. *See, e.g.*, Meyer v. Holley, 537 U.S. 280, 285 (2003)."[35] This statement carries a much firmer tone than the *Meyer* case's actual — but substantively identical — language: "[W]hen Congress creates a tort action, it legislates against a legal background of ordinary tort-related vicarious liability rules and consequently intends its legislation to incorporate those rules." The framing lies in switching up the sentence structure and choosing the words leading into the rule. Together, the introductory clause's "unless" and "clearly indicates" give the remaining language the feel of a broad tort law default rule — one that will easily apply to the retaliation provision.

2.2 Strategic Use and Presentation of Case Law

Effective appellate advocates not only frame the law well but know how to use it strategically. In an argument, the law has two basic purposes: (1) it supplies the governing legal principles; and (2) it drives the specific appeal's result.[36] So, to use the law well, the advocate's first order of business is to limit discussion of authority to these essential uses. For example, the student advocates who briefed the inventory search examples in Chapter 10 did not start by quoting the Fourth Amendment. They did not even start by laying out general Fourth Amendment principles on police searches. Rather, they focused their legal discussions on a few favorable big-picture principles to set the foundation for their arguments and then jumped into the rules governing the inventory exception. Even then, the writers did not cover the universe of inventory rules — only those vital to making their arguments or defending against their opponent's.

So constrained in their legal discussions, advocates must make the best use of them. In an argument, authorities are framed and used in one of three ways: (1) with direct quotes or paraphrasing; (2) as full-text discussions; or (3) in explanatory parentheticals. At any given point, the most effective choice depends on the nature of the argument and your specific goal for using the authority.

Quoting and paraphrasing authority. In legal argument, paraphrasing is almost always preferable to quoting. Yet few things are more tempting than the perfect quote. It is immensely satisfying to discover a choice nugget of judicial language and then drop it directly into your argument. Sometimes this proclivity produces good results, but more often it does not. Generally, it is best to directly quote authorities only when they say something much better than you could in the context of your specific argument — words that eloquently express a core point or communicate with uncommon efficiency.[37] Other good quotation candidates are statutory or common law language vital to resolving the issue on appeal.[38]

But quote too often and the brief starts to sound like a bunch of parroted opinions, unconnected to the advocate's positions or argument. Paraphrasing is the antidote, especially when the authority does not merit a full-text discussion. As explained above, writers paraphrase authorities when they frame rules and tests. Writers also paraphrase when they write synthesized rules from multiple cases. In that sense, paraphrasing is really the default rule of presenting authorities. It allows the writer to frame strategically, to be efficient, and to integrate what outside authorities say directly into the writer's own arguments, promoting flow and persuasion.

Full-text discussions. Not every argument — or even every brief — needs a full-text case discussion or extended analogies to the record facts. Indeed, of all the expert excerpts in Chapter 10, only one has a full-blown case discussion. This may surprise you if the IRAC model has governed your writing, for that model typically assumes a case explanation and analogy for every rule. Not so with argument. Simply put, some arguments are not amenable to analogical reasoning because the case law is not factually on point. In that situation, taking the time to highlight an inapposite case and to stretch the corresponding analogy weakens your argument[39] and wastes words.[40] A case merits fuller discussion only when it directly furthers your argument in some way. Below we discuss the most common strategic reasons.

In its most common form, a full-text discussion bolsters syllogistic or inductive reasoning with an on-point example or a convincing distinction from opposing authority.[41] In essence, the full-text explanation becomes a compelling story about how a legal concept has worked in a parallel way in the past.[42] Consider how a full-text discussion of United States v. Edwards accomplishes these objectives in this student's law-fact application argument from the *Mutombo* appeal.

EXAMPLE **Effective Full Text Case Discussion**

As for the valuables justification, an inventory search extends "only to where an officer can *reasonably* conclude that valuable property may be located." United States v. Edwards, 577 F.2d 883, 894-95 (5th Cir. 1978) (emphasis added). In *Edwards*, the defendant challenged a police search of loose carpet flaps in his car, contending that no reasonable officer could believe anything valuable would be hidden there. *Id.* The court upheld the search's scope because the carpet flap had been displaced, supporting a reasonable belief that valuable property might be stored beneath. *Id.* But it refused to "condone searching under the carpeting in every case, much less the ripping apart of an automobile, or any part thereof, under the guise of an inventory search." *Id.* at 895.

Just like a glove compartment, trunk, or console, the area beneath unsettled carpet flaps might be a reasonable place to check for a vehicle owner's valuables. But it is unreasonable to assume that anything contained in a handwritten, loose paper stuffed between a car seat and console would be valuable enough to require inventorying.

The vague concept of limiting searches to where valuables may "reasonably" be found begs illustration. So the writer provides one with *Edwards.* Now, *Edwards* is really an unfavorable precedent in disguise, for it upholds an inventory search rather than striking it down. But the writer's explanation turns *Edwards* in the appellant's favor by highlighting and explaining the distinguishing carpet flap displacement facts, then highlighting dicta that easily applies to the appellant's own case. The second paragraph's *Edwards* distinction does important work too. It takes the opinion's reasoning and uses it to widen the gulf between places reasonably likely to hold valuables and places where no reasonable person would store them — then characterizes the space between the car seat and console as the latter. Together, the case explanation and analogical reasoning increase the basic syllogism's force. The advocate would get far less mileage from a quote, paraphrased rule, or explanatory parenthetical.

These full-text explanations needn't be long, and they don't have to be followed by analogical reasoning, especially when the analogy is obvious from the explanation itself. Take this three-sentence example in the Google v. Oracle Appellant's Brief, used to fend off Google's argument that Oracle's source code lost copyright protection because it became the "industry standard."[43]

EXAMPLE **Short Full-Text Case Discussion**

The Ninth Circuit agrees. In *PMI*, it rejected the argument that everyone could copy the plaintiff's medical coding system because the system had become the "industry standard." 121 F.3d at 520 n.8. Like Google here, competitors remained free to "develop comparative or better coding . . . and lobby" for their adoption. *Id.* Copyright "prevents wholesale copying of an existing system." *Id.*

Well-placed full-text discussions also have a role in unsettled law arguments, as in the next example from the *Mutombo* appeal. Here, the writers ran up against the "true threat" exception to First Amendment protection, an unsettled area of the law. To advance a narrow reading of that exception, the writers delved into a persuasive authority, Porter v. Ascension Parish School Board:

EXAMPLE **Unsettled Law Full-Text Case Discussion**

The Supreme Court in Virginia v. Black defined the category of "true threats" as encompassing "those statements when the speaker means *to communicate* a serious intent to commit an act of unlawful violence to a particular individual or group of individuals." 538 U.S. at 359 (emphasis added). It is no exaggeration to say that in each and every published decision in which American courts have found that speech can be punished as a "true threat," the threat at issue has been communicated to a victim or to a third party. In Porter v. Ascension Parish Sch. Bd., 393 F.3d 608 (5th Cir. 2004), for example, the Fifth Circuit applied Virginia v. Black and held that if a speaker does not "intend[] to communicate a potential threat," then it is not a "true threat." *Id.* at 616-17. There a student had made a drawing depicting a violent event, but he had left that drawing in his closet and had not communicated it to another person. *Id.* at 611-12. The Court explained the requirement that speech must be communicated in order to be a "true threat":

> [T]o lose the protection of the First Amendment and be lawfully punished, the threat must be intentionally or knowingly *communicated* to either the object of the threat or a third person. Importantly, whether a speaker intended to communicate a potential threat is a threshold issue, and a finding of no intent to communicate obviates the need to assess whether the speech constitutes a "true threat."

Id. at 616-17 (citations omitted).

This paragraph's chain link can be forged only if the advocate sells the idea that "true threats" have to be communicated like any other threat. The *Porter* explanation furthers that goal. The work begins in the topic sentence, which emphasizes the word "communication" in the Supreme Court's true threat definition. In the ensuing *Porter* explanation, the writer highlights the communication requirement and illustrates it with *Porter*'s facts. The violent drawing stowed in a closet vividly demonstrates how critical it is to import a communication requirement into the true threat analysis, lest people be punished for their thoughts. And the court's reasoning captures precisely why, in language very favorable to the appellant. This deeper explanation of the true threat concept could not be captured in a quote or parenthetical.

Notwithstanding this example, analogical case law explanations should be used with care in unsettled law arguments. The typical analogies that drive law-fact applications — these facts are like my facts, therefore we win under the same rule — do not advance a novel reading of the law or new legal rules. To strategically further these arguments, a full-text explanation must draw a deeper analogy, one that captures the law's animating principles or underlying goals. For example, the Lawrence v. Texas Petitioners lingered for a half-paragraph[44] on the Supreme Court's decision in Griswold v. Connecticut, which struck down state criminalization of contraceptives. Their argument was not the bare idea that contraceptive use is like same-sex consensual relations. Instead the analogy rested on the underlying liberty principle against state regulation of intimate relationship choices.

Other strategic justifications for full-text explanations have nothing to do with facts or analogical reasoning. In unsettled law arguments, for example, case explanations may lay out the holding and reasoning of persuasive precedent that adopts the rule of law that the advocate is proposing. In that case, it is the reason behind the rule or test that persuades, rather than a fact-to-fact comparison. Or the advocate may use a full-text explanation to show how the law has evolved closer to her proposed test. Even law-fact application arguments may use full-text explanations for the sole purpose of explaining how the law works apart from any factual context — especially if the legal concept is complex or counterintuitive.

Explanatory parentheticals. As a device for synthesizing authorities and illustrating legal concepts, explanatory parentheticals far outpace full-text explanations in federal appellate filings.[45] The reasons are varied. One is pragmatic; parentheticals compress several examples into a small space, a prized commodity in appellate briefs. And those examples are disproportionately powerful. Because judicial readers are so familiar with parentheticals as a supplement to and illustration of legal concepts, a writer can, with just one sentence, cause the judicial reader to form a complete story in her mind.[46] Aside from their efficiency advantages, parentheticals have educational and persuasive benefits. By showing how the law has worked multiple times in the past instead of in just one case, parentheticals can convey weight of authority and offer a wider array of examples.[47] Parentheticals are best used in three ways: (1) to substantiate; (2) to synthesize; and (3) to illustrate.

For example, the *Mutombo* brief writers substantiated First Amendment protections for artistic expression with a series of direct parenthetical quotes from Supreme Court cases:

EXAMPLE **Parenthetical with Direct Quotes**

This protection of speech extends to artistic expression, such as the rap lyrics found in Mutombo's car. National Endowment for the Arts v. Finley, 524 U.S. 569, 602 (1998) ("It goes without saying that artistic expression lies within this First Amendment protection."); Ward v. Rock Against Racism, 491 U.S. 781, 790 (1989) (noting that "[m]usic is one of the oldest form of human expression"); *see also* Hurley v. Irish-American Gay, Lesbian and Bisexual Group of Boston, 515 U.S. 557, 569 (1995) (remarking that examples of painting, music, and poetry are "unquestionably shielded").

Rather than substantiating a legal proposition, synthesizing parentheticals show how a range of cases supports the writer's assertion. The point is not what these courts explicitly said about a legal principle, but rather what they did to make the writer's assertion viable. The next example from the Google v.

Oracle Appellant's Brief uses multiple vivid parentheticals to support a bold proposition in response to Google's fair use argument:[48]

EXAMPLE   Synthesizing Parentheticals

Copying work to use for the same purpose simply cannot be fair use. *See* Peter Letterese & Assocs. v. World Inst. of Scientology Enters., Int'l, 533 F.3d 1287, 1311, 1318 (11th Cir. 2008) (book about sales techniques superseded the original even though it "adopt[ed] a different format, incorporate[d] pedagogical tools . . . , and condense[d] the material in the [original] book"); Elvis Presley Enters., Inc. v. Passport Video, 349 F.3d 622, 628-30 (9th Cir. 2003) (documentary containing "significant portions" of video clips supersedes original and is not fair use); Twin Peaks Prods., Inc. v. Publ'ns Int'l, Ltd., 996 F.2d 1366, 1375-77 (2d Cir. 1993) (holding that a comprehensive guide to the characters and plot of a television show supersedes the show and is not fair use).

These parentheticals show that the writer got the rule from reading the cases together. They also tell miniature case stories that spell out examples of an original use — like a book, video clips, and TV show — and a superseding use — like a book in a different and condensed format, a documentary using the clips, and a comprehensive show character guide. With these examples in hand, it is much easier for the reader to understand how Google's competing use of source code was unfair because it superseded Oracle's original use of the code. In a sense, these kinds of synthesizing parentheticals are horizontal, providing concrete examples of the spectrum of activities or objects covered by the rule.

In contrast, parentheticals that illustrate have a vertical focus. They do not show the rule's range but rather elaborate more deeply on the writer's point. Consider this example from an appellate brief in which the writer elaborates on how courts have struggled to classify art as speech:

EXAMPLE   Illustrating Parentheticals[49]

Ruling on the first appeal, this Court referenced some of the difficulty federal courts have experienced in determining the extent of constitutional protection afforded objects loosely referred to as art. *Cressman*, 719 F.3d at 1154 n.14. *See, e.g.,* Kleinman v. City of San Marcos, 597 F.3d 323, 326 (5th Cir. 2010) (discounting the speech component of a car used as a cactus planter); Mastrovincenzo v. City of New York, 435 F.3d 78, 92-93 (2d Cir. 2006) (noting the complexity of supplying constitutional protection to sale items merely because they are called "art").

Two caveats about drafting parentheticals. First, they should never run more than one sentence.[50] Lengthy parentheticals beg to be skipped just as block quotes do. Second, check to make sure your parentheticals do not say the same thing as the preceding sentence in different words.[51] Because they aim to illustrate, parentheticals must be more specific than anything you are saying in the text. They should move your argument forward rather than treading water in one place.

Using case law in statutory construction arguments. Our final point on framing and use of case law applies to statutory interpretation arguments — specifically, arguments that advance competing readings of the law. The bottom line is that case law should be integrated into these interpretive arguments, not featured front and center.[52] The reason lies in the goal of statutory construction. To prove the merits of your statutory reading, you must marshal the best supporting evidence for it. That best evidence lies in interpretive tools such as textual analysis, canons of construction, and legislative purpose, not in the case law.[53] If binding authority had established the correct reading, you would not be litigating the issue, so by definition, your court's case law will not be the best evidence.[54] Your court's case law may have interpreted other language in the statute, analyzed the law's purposes, discussed its legislative history, or read parallel statutory language elsewhere in a supportive way, and, of course, you would bring those cases to bear in your statutory analysis. But that case law is just another interpretive tool, not definitive evidence of the right reading.

As for persuasive authorities that adopt your reading of the law, those cases are not the best evidence of your proposed statutory reading either. They are not legislative products.[55] Just because another court agrees with your reading of the statute does not, by virtue of its authority, establish that reading as the best one. In fact, most statutory interpretation arguments have competing "he said, she said," persuasive case law behind them.[56] Your use of case law must reflect these realities. Full-text explanations will rarely be appropriate because facts and analogies don't further interpretive positions. The most efficient way to convey persuasive authorities' agreement and the judicial rationales behind it is to slot them into your reasoning chains for each interpretive tool — most typically in direct quote or parenthetical form.[57] For example, a case that concurs with your textual analysis would be cited in that part of the reasoning chain. A case that analyzes the legislative history of the law should be seamlessly integrated into that part of the chain. As we will see in the next section, policy arguments sometimes feature more fulsome case discussions, but only as an example of the good or bad results flowing from your reading or your opponent's reading.

Practice Alert #3
Practice Spotlight on Use and Presentation of the Law

This exercise in the online companion contains excerpts from three appellate briefs, each of which use and present case law in contrasting ways. The exercise asks you to identify each distinct strategy behind the writer's use of case law, and to evaluate whether it is effective.

SUMMARY

Framing and Using the Law

- Rules and tests should favor your advocacy position and undercut your opponent's. Frame high or low standards and broad or narrow rules using your interpretive powers and word choices leading into and characterizing the rule.

- When presenting the law, quote sparingly and paraphrase liberally.
- Be strategic about full-text discussions; use them only when they further your argument in a definable way.
- Full-text discussions can supply analogical reasoning that supplements an argument's syllogistic and inductive reasoning. Aside from their analogical role, full-text discussions can also explain the law's rationale and development.
- Be wary of using full-text discussions in unsettled law arguments, where standard factual analogies will not persuade.
- Make case law a "supporting actor" to the best interpretive evidence in statutory interpretation arguments.
- Parentheticals are efficient and persuasive methods of framing the law. They can be used to economically express substantive points, synthesize authorities, and illustrate ideas.

Section 3   Crafting Policy Arguments

3.1   Definition and Purpose of Policy Arguments

Policy arguments are a singular method of framing the law. Relying more heavily on pathos than logos,[58] they persuade not by framing the governing law itself, but instead by framing the law's effects.[59] Working from the premise that a rule or interpretation is legally tenable, they focus instead on results.[60] Although policy arguments can buttress settled law-fact application arguments, they play a larger role in unsettled law and statutory interpretation arguments, which dispute what the law is or should be.[61] To show that one rule, test, or reading is superior to another is, in part, to demonstrate its probable effects on people and institutions in the future.[62]

Given that objective, the label "policy argument" is a misnomer — the very words invite the reaction, "Courts are not policy makers!" But litigation policy arguments do not implicate the legislative task of making policy choices in the first instance. Rather, policy arguments work from a universe of existing — but competing — values that are already reflected in the law but that will be activated by the court's choice of one legal rule over another.[63] For example, a brief may contend that adopting a lenient standard for fraud in commercial disputes will transform ordinary contract cases into tort damage vehicles. This preference for a "wall" between contract and tort is already engrained in the common law,[64] but the court's choice of a fraud standard could reinforce or weaken that wall. Arguing that a high bar for defamation's qualified privilege in employment cases will chill important personnel communications reflects a value that the privilege itself encompasses: a balance between the freedom to run one's business and the dignity interest in one's reputation.[65] Conversely, arguing that a private sector employee's termination for bad-mouthing his employer impinges on freedom of expression implicates policies that have nothing to do with private-sector employment law.[66] Effective policy arguments, then, do not choose from a random grab bag of values. They work within an existing legal universe, and in that way, respect the unique roles of courts and legislatures.[67] Effective policy arguments have three basic components: (1) the value(s) at stake; (2) the cause — which is the court's choice of one legal reading over another; and (3) the effect — how likely is the legal reading to cause a result that impacts the value.[68]

3.2 Constructing Policy Arguments

Identifying and establishing the value(s) at stake. The values present in law roughly break down into three categories: (1) effects on law and the legal system; (2) effects on the parties and others like them; and (3) effects on third parties.[69] Values related to the legal system's workings include:

- Adopting firm rules that promote certainty and are easy and efficient to administer[70]
- Adopting flexible rules that can be adapted to a wide range of scenarios and evolving norms[71]
- Adopting rules that do not encourage excessive litigation ("closing the floodgates")[72]
- Adopting rules that won't spiral out of control by expanding to growing numbers of cases[73]
- Adopting rules that best reflect the competencies of governmental branches (judicial, legislative, executive) or decisionmakers within that branch (*e.g.*, judge or jury).[74]

Values that relate to current or future litigants or third parties (whether people or institutions) include:

- **Normative values**, such as:
  - Public safety
  - Transparency

     ○ Antipaternalism
     ○ Fair distribution of resources
     ○ Entrepreneurialism
     ○ Correcting power imbalances
     ○ Holding people to promises
     ○ Choosing between the lesser of two evils
     ○ Imposing costs on the party best able to bear them[75]
- **Purely economic arguments**, such as:
     ○ Promotion of free markets
     ○ Efficient (as opposed to fair) distribution of resources
     ○ Obtaining the greatest benefit at the least cost.[76]

Thus, in constructing a policy argument, the advocate's first order of business is to identify the range of values implicated by her proposed reading of the law. This is usually a straightforward matter. The relevant values can be found in case law addressing related questions or in analogous areas of the law; in secondary sources; in constitutional provisions; or in statutory sources such as a preamble or purpose section or legislative history.[77]

Establishing cause and effect with reasoning and authority. The second and third components—proving cause and effect—present a greater challenge. To contend that any given rule of law will have a predictable effect on the legal system, people, or institutions is an audacious statement. Although the rule's impact on the parties may be fairly predictable on the record, its future effects are speculative. The effects are not just attenuated in time, they are based on suppositions about future behavior and facts not before the court—usually the province of social scientists, not lawyers.[78] But a skilled advocate can make the rule-result connection seem not just possible, but probable.[79] This is a joint feat of reasoning and authority.

    1. Policy argument reasoning. Concerning reasoning, the advocate must clearly identify the cause—that is, the interpretation she or her opponent is proposing—and methodically explain how that cause is linked to a value and how that value will play out for good or ill in the real world. As with any other argument, the writer must form distinct reasons and forge chain links between them along the way to the conclusion. But these chain links are not syllogistic or inductive; they are cause and effect oriented. Consider this excerpt from the *Nassar* Petitioner's brief discussed in Chapter 10, which argues that a but-for retaliation causation standard (cause) will further (effect) the value of a firm, workable rule:[80]

| EXAMPLE | **Policy Argument Reasoning—Positive Effects of Advocate's Rule** |

B. *Gross* Established a Bright-Line, Easily Administrable Rule

The complexity of *Price Waterhouse* stands in stark contrast to the simplicity of *Gross*. In individual cases, *Gross* is easy to apply. A plaintiff must prove that an improper factor was the but-for cause of an adverse employment action, and the familiar *McDonnell Douglas* framework governs that proof. There are no questions about whether to apply *McDonnell Douglas* or some other standard, no shifting in the burden of persuasion, and thus none of the uncertainties that dogged *Price Waterhouse*.   ← *States the value, asserts that the but-for standard will serve it. The rest explains why.*

← *Link 1: But-for uses a familiar framework and that framework is well-established and easy to apply.*

Under *Gross*, it is also easy to determine whether a plaintiff may proceed under a mixed-motive framework. Apart from the 1991 amendments to Title VII discussed above, all of the other major employment discrimination and retaliation statutes require a plaintiff to prove but-for causation.

Title VII retaliation, the ADEA, the Americans with Disabilities Act, and the Genetic Information Nondiscrimination Act of 2008 all prohibit actions taken "because" of an improper motive. [citations omitted]. Some of these statutes also prohibit discrimination "on the basis of "a protected category or discrimination "based on" a protected activity. [citations omitted]. As *Gross* held, the "statutory phrase, 'based on,' has the same meaning as the phrase, 'because of.'" *Gross*, 557 U.S. at 176.

Because Congress has not separately authorized mixed-motive claims for any of those statutes, they all require a plaintiff to prove but-for causation under *Gross*. [citations omitted] The Rehabilitation Act of 1973 similarly prohibits discrimination "solely by reason of [an individual's] disability," 29 U.S.C. § 294(a), which is at least as strict a standard as but-for causation. *See Lewis*, 681 F.3d at 314-15; *Palmquist*, 689 F.3d at 73-74.   ← *Link 2: In discrimination law, but-for causation is the rule, not the exception.*

> Especially considering the relative simplicity of this statutory structure, resurrecting *Price Waterhouse* as an additional alternative would introduce an unwarranted amount of confusion and disparity in the system. If Congress wished to amend the employment laws in this respect, it could easily and accurately express its intent so long as the drafting rules were clear, as they are under *Gross*. Instead, Congress has rejected proposals that would have abrogated *Gross* by authorizing mixed-motive claims under all of the major employment acts. [citations omitted]

← **Link 3:** *Leaving it to Congress, not Courts, to alter the causation rule promotes uniformity and certainty.*

In drafting this passage, the writer considered precisely how a but-for standard would promote the bright-line rule value and settled on four distinct reasons. His argument links cause and effect by explaining *what* comes with but-for causation and *why* that quality promotes ease and clarity. The "what" and "why" appear in the chain links as follows: (1) The *McDonnell Douglas* framework incorporates but-for causation (what) and that framework is well established (why); (2) all major discrimination laws use the same "because of" language (what) and a but-for interpretation would promote uniformity among them (why); (3) leaving any causation changes to Congress rather than one-off judicial interpretations (what) would promote clarity and certainty (why).

The next passage from the *Nassar* Petitioner's brief turns the tables and argues the bad results of the opposing mixed-motive standard. Rarely will a court be convinced by a one-sided argument that speaks only of the good achieved by an interpretation without addressing the opposing interpretation's impact. Moreover, cognitive psychology research suggests that this type of "bad results" policy argument triggers "loss aversion" and "negativity bias," making it more powerful than arguments turning on the promise of future positive consequences.[81] In this passage, the values to avoid—litigation abuse and unfairness to employers—combine normative, economic, and legal system administration appeals. The chain links then tie the mixed-motive cause to the effects on those values.

EXAMPLE	Policy Argument Reasoning—Bad Results of Opponent's Rule[82]

C. Burden Shifting Invites Abuse and Unfairness.

[Overview paragraph omitted]

1. Mixed motives are easy to allege—any "stray remark" or hint of discriminatory animus might suffice. *Price Waterhouse,* 490 U.S. at 291 (Kennedy, J., dissenting). But they are difficult for defendants to disprove, in part because many employment decisions are inherently subjective.

States the value, asserts that the mixed-motive standard threatens it. The rest explains why.

Thus, "there is no denying that putting employers to the work of persuading factfinders that their choices are reasonable makes it harder and costlier to defend than if employers merely bore the burden of production." *Meacham,* 554 U.S. at 101. Empirical evidence confirms that plaintiffs recover "significantly more often" when courts give a "so-called motivating factor instruction" to the jury. David Sherwyn & Michael Heise, *The* Gross *Beast of Burden of Proof: Experimental Evidence on How the Burden of Proof Influences Employment Discrimination Case Outcomes,* 42 Ariz. St. L.J. 901, 944 (2010).

Link 1: Mixed motives are easy to allege and hard to disprove.

The difficulty of disproving subjective intent is compounded by the difficulty of securing summary judgment in mixed-motive cases. *See* Burns v. Gadsden State Cmty. Coll., 908 F.2d 1512, 1519 (11th Cir. 1990). Mixed-motive claims are generally not susceptible to summary judgment because the plaintiff's burden is "so light." David A. Cathcart & Mark Snyderman, *The Civil Rights Act of 1991,* SF41 ALI-ABA 391, 432 (2001); *see also* White v. Baxter Healthcare Corp., 533 F.3d 381, 402 (6th Cir. 2008); Staten v. New Place Casino, LLC, 187 F. App'x 350, 361-62 (5th Cir. 2006). Absent summary judgment, an employer must incur the full costs and risks of trial, where outcomes are uncertain. *See also* Katz, *Fundamental Incoherence, supra,* at 493. As

Link 2: The same quality makes summary judgment hard to obtain and imposes unfair employer costs.

such, employers face tremendous financial pressures to settle even meritless mixed-motive suits; failing to do so can be even more wasteful.

Instead of being a limited exception, moreover, mixed-motive suits could become the norm. Employment decisions "are almost always mixed-motive decisions turning on many factors." *See* Cathcart & Snyderman, *supra,* at 432. Thus, "every plaintiff is certain to ask for a" mixed-motive instruction. *Price Waterhouse,* 490 U.S. at 291 (Kennedy, J., dissenting); *see also Smith,* 602 F.3d at 333. Plaintiffs have little reason to shoulder the burden of proving "pretext" under *McDonnell Douglas* when they could instead rely on the "easier burden of persuasion" that allows "plaintiffs [to] win more." Zimmer, *supra,* at 1922 n.152, 1943.

    ⟵   **Link 3:** *The same quality unfairly favors plaintiffs at trial and hamstrings employer decisionmaking.*

This argument's reasoning is explicit and urgent. It casts the mixed-motive standard as one that will allow plaintiffs to sail through the litigation process with retaliation claims of questionable merit, and that will saddle employers with costly and burdensome defenses and hold hostage their personnel processes. As with the writer's positive effects argument, the connection between the mixed-motive cause and these undesirable effects is methodically formed with both the "what" and the "why."

2. Policy argument authority. This argument also makes excellent use of authority, which, aside from quality reasoning, is the most significant contributor to a policy argument's strength.[83] Policy argument authorities have two main purposes: (1) establishing the importance of a value or its effects; and (2) establishing the probability between an interpretive cause and its effects.[84] In the *Nassar* excerpt, the advocate's authority does both. To establish the values and their significance, the writer turns to case law and secondary sources. The citation to *Meacham* shows that the Supreme Court cares about the fair allocation of proof burdens, particularly as it impacts an employer's personnel decisions. The Katz journal article establishes the downsides of trials, while the Cathcart & Snyderman piece captures the pervasiveness of multi-motive personnel decisions. None of these sources directly addresses retaliation or causation. Instead, they establish the values on which the retaliation causation standard will have a real-world impact.

To establish the cause-effect probabilities, the *Nassar* passage combines an empirical study on plaintiffs' success rate in mixed-motive instruction cases with a law journal article substantiating the uphill summary judgment battle in mixed-motive cases, and folds in a dissenting Justice's prediction of how mixed-motive instructions would proliferate were it the default causation rule. None proves to a certainty that a retaliation mixed-motive standard will force trials, reward nonmeritorious claims, or hamstring personnel decisions. But this passage illustrates how marshaling these seemingly disparate authorities causes the reader to perceive the cause-effect as probable, not just possible.

The use of nonlegal authority in policy arguments deserves special mention; although advocates are often reluctant to use it, judges are more willing to invoke it.[85] These sources, particularly those with empirical backing, are often the most direct proof of cause and effect, because they are designed to measure precisely that phenomenon.[86] There is no legal bar to introducing these materials at the appellate level.[87] Nonlegal materials suited to this purpose include scientific or social science studies, history scholarship, economic data, medical reports, and even news articles reporting on current trends.[88] Drawing on these materials' probability power, a later policy argument in the *Nassar* brief adds a second nonlegal source, citing EEOC charging statistics to support "the recent proliferation of retaliation claims."[89] Not every policy argument has such legislative-like data to support it, though, so case law must often suffice, usually in the form of persuasive opinions from the same or related areas of law that have used the same cause-effect rationale to justify rule choice.[90] A perfect illustration of this use of persuasive authority is the Kennedy dissent cited in the *Nassar* passage's last paragraph.

3.3 Policy Argument Rhetorical Strategies

Rhetorical strategies aid policy arguments as well. Two in particular are well established. The first is combining more extreme, less likely consequences with less extreme, more likely consequences.[91] The second strategy is to use vivid examples or otherwise make policy arguments memorable.[92]

The first strategy has its roots in the "conjunction fallacy," which occurs because people are naturally more skeptical of extreme results than moderate results.[93] In addition to addressing both the upside of the advocate's interpretation and the downside of the opponent's, the two *Nassar* excerpts, read together, do just this. The first excerpt predicts a less extreme consequence — a bright-line easily administered rule versus a malleable, confusing rule — while the second forecasts a much more serious and wide-ranging set of burdens on employers and the litigation process. By pairing these arguments (the first directly precedes the second in the brief), the writer reaps the benefits of the conjunction fallacy.

The second rhetorical strategy is vividness. A policy argument can be made vivid in any number of ways, ranging from a striking precedent example, to using record facts as an example of results, to an advocate's self-created example, to a metaphor, to a literary reference.[94] Let's look at how some expert briefs use vividness to their advantage in policy arguments. In this passage, the *Nassar* writer uses his client's facts as an exemplar of how the mixed-motive standard would undermine employer personnel practices generally.[95]

EXAMPLE Client Facts as Prototype

Mixed-motive retaliation claims pose an especially serious problem where, as here, an employer took action based on a straightforward and nondiscriminatory written policy, but an employee claims that one of his or her supervisors felt some improper animus. *Cf.* Staub v. Proctor Hosp., 131 S. Ct. 1186, 1193-94 (2011). Activity protected by the retaliation statutes may well upset some of the people involved. Indeed, in the modern workplace, "it will often be possible for an aggrieved employee or applicant to find someone whose input into the process was in some way motivated by an impermissible factor." Cathcart & Snyderman, *supra* at 432. But Title VII does not prohibit feelings (which are generally protected by the First Amendment); it prohibits actual acts of retaliation. 42 U.S.C. § 2000e-3(a); *see Price Waterhouse,* 490 U.S. at 262 (O'Connor, J., concurring in judgment); *id.* at 282 (Kennedy, J., dissenting).

This next passage from a Supreme Court brief spotlights a Seventh Circuit case, using descriptive detail and colorful language to magnify its impact. The writer's tactic is to show how the case would have been decided if it had applied the Ninth Circuit's lenient definition of "disability" under the Americans with Disabilities Act.[96]

EXAMPLE Illustrative Precedent Case

The Ninth Circuit's "difference" test creates a perverse incentive to misrepresent nonlimiting impairments when convenient to secure employment. A good example of this is Roth v. Lutheran Gen. Hosp., 57 F.3d 1446 (7th Cir. 1995), in which a would-be pediatrician claimed that he had been discriminated against during the selection process for a residency program due to his poor vision. Dr. Roth was born with eye impairments that altered his ability to fuse images and to sense depth. *Id.* at 1449. He alleged that these problems prevented him from pursuing his chosen profession because he could not work for more than eight to ten hours at a time and all residency programs require long shifts. *Id.* at 1454.

   On school and job applications, however, Dr. Roth either failed to list his visual condition when specifically asked about "handicaps" or characterized himself as "cured." *Id.* at 1448. He completed pharmacy and law degrees — earning the latter full time while working as a pharmacist — and served as a faculty lecturer and defense attorney/consultant while attending medical school, all without accommodation. *Id.* at 1455-56. The Seventh Circuit denied Dr. Roth's request for a preliminary injunction ordering his admission to the residency program, holding that he was not substantially limited in seeing or learning. Dr. Roth's impairment may have "affected" his major life activities, but it did not "ris[e] to the level of a disability." *Id.* at 1454.

The application of the Ninth Circuit's "difference" test to these facts would produce an absurd and unjust result. Dr. Roth's diagnosed eye conditions and the evidence that they had some effect on his sight would render him disabled. Ignored would be the contrary evidence that he could perform lengthy, uninterrupted, eye-straining work, and the fact that he had informed employers and educators that he suffered no limitations. In short, Dr. Roth would be permitted to use his impairment "when it was beneficial and opportune"—to get him the job of his choice. 57 F.3d at 1456. But as the Seventh Circuit observed, "there is a clear bright line of demarcation between extending the statutory protection to a truly disabled individual (so that he or she can lead a normal life . . .) and allowing an individual with marginal impairment to use disability laws as bargaining chips to gain a competitive advantage." *Id.* at 1460.

The last example, from the Oracle v. Google Appellant's Brief, uses a vivid metaphor of the advocate's own creation to drive home the absurd results of the lower court's decision refusing to hold Google accountable for copying Oracle's source code. The metaphor actually starts in the Introduction section and is woven thematically throughout the brief.[97]

EXAMPLE Vivid Metaphor

Ann Droid wants to publish a bestseller. So she sits down with an advance copy of *Harry Potter and the Order of the Phoenix*—the fifth book—and proceeds to transcribe. She verbatim copies all the chapter titles—from Chapter 1 ("Dudley Demented") to Chapter 38 ("The Second War Begins"). She copies verbatim the topic sentences of each paragraph, starting from the first (highly descriptive) one and continuing, in order, to the last, simple one ("Harry nodded."). She then paraphrases the rest of each paragraph. She rushes the competing version to press before the original under the title: *Ann Droid's Harry Potter 5.0*. The knock-off flies off the shelves.

J.K. Rowling sues for copyright infringement. Ann's defenses: "But I wrote most of the words from scratch. Besides, this was fair use, because I copied only the portions necessary to tap into the *Harry Potter* fan base."

Obviously, the defenses would fail.

Defendant Google Inc. has copied a blockbuster literary work just as surely, and as improperly, as Ann Droid—and has offered the same defenses. . . .

3.4 Policy Argument Placement

A final (and recurring) question about policy arguments is where to put them. There is no firm answer. Some policy arguments are robust enough to reside in their own section, under their own point heading. A separate section works well for policy arguments that require several chain links to develop the value, cause, and effect. The primary risk that accompanies these stand-alone policy arguments is veering off course. When a writer isolates policy arguments away from rule-based arguments, the temptation to inject irrelevant values is much greater. Without the rule-based argument to discipline the writer's focus, these sections can also end up stretching cause and effect beyond credulity. For that reason and others, some policy arguments — particularly shorter ones — work best when integrated directly into rule-based arguments. That is especially true if the rule-based argument would be dry and technical without the immediacy of a pathos-laden policy argument. These integrated policy arguments may be as short as a sentence or a paragraph. But they should still contain a compressed version of the three components — value, cause, and effect.

Review

Policy Arguments

- Policy arguments have three basic components: (1) the value; (2) the cause; and (3) the effect.
- In basic terms, legal values encompass: (1) effects on law and the legal system; (2) effects on the litigants and others like them; and (3) effects on third parties. The value must be substantiated with authority.
- Establishing a legal interpretation's probable effect in the real world is a bigger challenge. Nonlegal sources can supply evidence of probability, but persuasive authorities combined with meticulous reasoning can also suffice.
- To strengthen your policy arguments, combine arguments predicting more extreme consequences with arguments predicting less extreme consequences.
- To make your policy arguments memorable, use a striking precedent example, use your facts as a prototype, create your own example, or employ a metaphor or literary reference.
- Use your judgment to decide where to house your policy arguments. Beware of the tendency to veer off course when a policy argument stands in its own section.

Summary

Building Policy Arguments

- Consider the policy arguments you are thinking about making. Identify a range of underlying values for each one. Identify your opponent's competing values as well.
- Locate authority to substantiate each value. Look to case law, secondary sources, constitutional provisions, statutory preambles or purpose sections, or legislative history.
- Locate authority to substantiate the probability. Consider using nonlegal sources in conjunction with legal sources.
- Rank the strength of each value and the extremity of each effect. Structure your policy arguments to take advantage of the conjunction fallacy.
- For each policy argument, sketch a rough outline that records the progression from cause to effect. Consider how your reasoning chain can be constructed to tighten the connection.
- Decide on at least one "vividness" strategy for each policy argument.

Section 4 Managing Weaknesses and Opposing Arguments

The task of framing arguments goes beyond making supportive points. It extends to effectively managing weaknesses and undercutting opposing arguments.[98] By now you should have a keen sense of your appeal's weaknesses and your opponent's likely arguments, especially if you have done Chapter 10's "Appeal in Reverse" exercise. In your brief, it can be tempting to pretend those weaknesses and arguments do not exist — especially if they have devastating potential — or to hope that the other side will never think of them. So engrained is the desire to press a client's cause affirmatively that lawyers have conjured injury metaphors to capture the experience of addressing negative law or facts: a "self-inflicted wound," "agonizing," and "painful."[99]

It is true that a purely responsive argument without any affirmative frame surrounding it is unpersuasive,[100] and it is equally unwise to "overeducate" your opponent or to make their arguments for them.[101] But to play the ostrich in legal argument is to cede your credibility, to waste a persuasive framing opportunity, and to abdicate your role as learned counselor to the court.[102] Moreover, the Model Rules of Professional Conduct impose ethical obligations to disclose "authority in the controlling jurisdiction known to the lawyer to be directly adverse."[103] The Rule has been interpreted to suggest a "broader duty to litigate forthrightly."[104] The most effective arguments, then, are neither polemic nor evenhanded. They are "two-sided."[105] Effective arguments not only advance affirmative positions but also cut off opposing positions — sometimes in the same breath.[106]

The specific drafting strategy varies depending on whether you are arguing in the first instance or responding to an opposing argument. If you are the appellant filing the opening brief, the most effective strategy is preemptive. If you are the appellee filing a response brief or the appellant filing a reply, you already know what the opposing arguments are, so, the most effective strategy is to be directly responsive. We discuss these preemptive and responsive strategies in turn.

4.1 Preemptive Strategies

Preemptive strategies for managing weaknesses are more subtle than directly responsive strategies. It is true that the parties have tipped their argumentative hands, at least in part, by the appellate stage. An appellant does not, however, know precisely which arguments the opponent will make, or the strategies that he will invoke concerning standards of review. Moreover, you won't know how your opponent has assessed argument strength and prioritized accordingly. So your brief must anticipate her arguments, as well as her approach to exposing your weaknesses, without overeducating her in the process. Your opening brief can achieve these goals by crafting "two-sided refutational messages" and "inoculating."

In the preemptive context, a two-sided refutational message makes the advocate's own arguments more resilient in the face of later opposing attacks.[107] Done well, this kind of message advances the client's position (one side) and in close proximity counteracts weaknesses or opposing arguments (the second side).[108] Cognitive science studies show that two-sided refutational messaging works by causing long-term attitude change that holds up against opposing arguments.[109] These effects stem from audience expectations that there are always two sides to every story and every argument. Acknowledging both sides makes the writer more credible and knowledgeable.[110] In addition, two-sided messages are attention grabbing and thought provoking. Stimulating the reader's thought by juxtaposing affirmative and defensive positions makes the reader more likely to agree with the message.[111] The related strategy of inoculation undermines the opponent's likely arguments.[112] By exposing the reader to a weakened version of opposing arguments in a way that simultaneously undercuts them, the writer makes the reader more resistant to accepting that upcoming opposing message.[113]

Both strategies can be used in the appellant's opening brief. To be effective, though, the refutational point must come after your strong, affirmative argument. Leading with weaknesses or responses makes you look defensive and invites the court to view law and facts from your opponent's standpoint, rather than your own strategically advantageous frame.[114]

Two-sided messaging examples. The Beyond IRAC example from Chapter 10 shows how to preempt an opposing argument by weaving a response directly into an affirmative argument:

EXAMPLE Two-Sided Messaging

Officer Salles violated Mr. Mutombo's Fourth Amendment rights the moment he picked up the loose piece of paper containing Mr. Mutombo's lyrics because that paper posed no threat to police and had no obvious value. The safety rationale does not apply here because it is undisputed that the paper itself posed no risk of harm. As for the valuables justification, an inventory search extends "only to where an officer can *reasonably* conclude that valuable property may be located." United States v. Edwards, 577 F.2d 883, 894-95 (5th Cir. 1978) (emphasis added). In *Edwards,* the defendant challenged a police search of loose carpet flaps in his car, contending that no reasonable officer could believe anything valuable would be hidden there. *Id.* The court upheld the search's scope because the carpet flap had been displaced, supporting a reasonable belief that valuable property might be stored beneath. *Id.* But it refused to "condone searching under the carpeting in every case, much less the ripping apart of an automobile, or any part thereof, under the guise of an inventory search." *Id.* at 895.

Just like a glove compartment, trunk, or console, the area beneath unsettled carpet flaps might be a reasonable place to check for a vehicle owner's valuables. But it is unreasonable to assume that anything contained in a handwritten, loose paper stuffed between a car seat and console would be valuable enough to require inventorying. Officer Salles claimed that he picked up and inspected the paper because he believed it might contain a medical prescription. **Even if the paper had contained a prescription, it would not have been valuable in the inventory sense. Failure to log a written prescription would neither jeopardize the security of the prescription nor give rise to liability for the police department.**

The boldfaced language in the second paragraph expresses the two-sided refutational message. After a paragraph and a half of arguing that the crevice between the front seat and console is an unreasonable place to search for valuables, the advocate anticipates that his opponent will contend that medical prescriptions are valuable, and the prescription pad image on the paper in this space is what caught Salles's eye. The writer simultaneously addresses and undercuts that argument by making this fact irrelevant under the law — a prescription is not valuable in an inventory sense.

Notice what the writer does not do. He does not say, "Appellee will likely argue that it was reasonable for Salles to search between the front seat and console because he thought the paper was a medical prescription, an item with value to the prescription recipient." That would have called undue attention to the opponent's argument and articulated the reasoning for the opponent. Rhetorically, the "Appellee will likely argue" phrasing sounds weak and defensive as well. Instead, the writer uses bold and affirmative language to knock down the opposing argument even as he raises it: "*it would not have been valuable* in the inventory sense." In effect, this language says, "Judge, don't believe them if they say this and here's why," rather than, "Judge, they might say this, and if they do, here is my response."

The next example's two-sided message refutes an opposing argument by preemptively showing that the facts don't fit the rule, rather than by establishing a fact's irrelevance.[115]

EXAMPLE **Two-Sided Messaging**

Google's use of Oracle's code is purely commercial. *Id.* at 562. Android is one of the most lucrative endeavors of the past decade. Google's counsel conceded that "the fact that it's a commercial use is not in dispute. . . . The evidence is pretty clear that they created it to provide a platform on which other Google product[s] could do better." A21,591. The district court agreed: "Google's internal documents show[] how many billions of dollars they expected to make off of [Android]. . . . This was intended for commercial purposes with large amounts of money at stake and, therefore, it was not fair use. It was copying." A21,594.

In considering the first factor, courts also inquire whether the copied material substitutes for the original or, instead, adds or changes the purpose of the original, thereby "transform[ing]" it in a meaningful way. *Campbell*, 510 U.S. at 579. **Google's use of Java declaring code was anything but transformative. Mere alteration is not transformation. A use of copied material is not transformative unless the material is used "in a different manner or for a different purpose from the original."** Hon. Pierre Leval, *Toward a Fair Use Standard*, 103 Harv. L. Rev. 1105, 1111 (1990); *see Campbell*, 510 U.S. at 579.

Google's use of the declaring code was exactly the same as in Java: to call upon prewritten packages to perform the same functions. The packages also serve the identical purpose: solving the same complex problems and performing the same often-needed functions programmers desire. While using the declaring code in exactly the same way as the original, Google deployed that purloined code in Android to compete directly with commercially licensed derivatives of Oracle's work. Oracle licenses Java in the mobile market and licensed it for smartphones specifically, including RIM's Blackberry, Nokia's Series 60 phones, and Danger's Sidekick/Hiptop. *Supra* at 15-16.

The transformative use point in the second paragraph is not one that Oracle must make to prove Google's use was commercial, not fair. The first paragraph alone meets that objective. Rather, the second paragraph is a product of anticipation — predicting that Google will contend that its use was fair even if it was commercial, because it dramatically transformed the original use. In the same affirmative tone as the previous example, the writer cuts off this argument with the bold face statements defining transformative use narrowly and showing how the facts fall outside of it. The third paragraph then finishes off the reasoning by marshaling the record support defeating transformative use.

Inoculation example. These paragraphs from the *Mutombo* appeal followed a section of affirmative argument contending that artistic expression and private thoughts are First Amendment-protected speech.

EXAMPLE   Inoculation

B. **Mutombo's conviction is unconstitutional because his handwritten words were never communicated to another person**

The only way that private, handwritten words on a piece of paper could leave the protected waters of the First Amendment is if they were a "true threat," one of the "well-defined and narrowly limited classes of speech" that the States may punish without violating the constitutional protections just discussed. *See* Virginia v. Black, 538 U.S. at 359 (deciding that the States can ban a so-called true threat). But private speech is only a true threat if it is **actually communicated** in some form to another person — either to its intended recipient or to a third party.

The Supreme Court in Virginia v. Black defined the category of "true threats" as encompassing "those statements when the speaker means *to communicate* a serious intent to commit an act of unlawful violence to a particular individual or group of individuals." 538 U.S. at 359 (emphasis added). **It is no exaggeration to say that in each and every published decision in which American courts have found that speech can be punished as a "true threat," the threat at issue has been communicated to a victim or to a third party.** In Porter v. Ascension Parish Sch. Bd., 393 F.3d 608 (5th Cir. 2004), for example, the Fifth Circuit applied Virginia v. Black and held that if a speaker does not "intend[] to communicate a potential threat," then it is not a "true threat." *Id.* at 616-17. There a student had made a drawing depicting a violent event, but he had left that drawing in his closet and had not communicated it to another person. *Id.* at 611-12. The Court explained the requirement that speech must be communicated in order to be a "true threat":

> [T]o lose the protection of the First Amendment and be lawfully punished, the threat must be intentionally or knowingly *communicated* to either the object of the threat or a third person. Importantly, whether a speaker intended to communicate a potential threat is a threshold issue, and a finding of no intent to communicate obviates the need to assess whether the speech constitutes a "true threat."

Id. at 616-17 (citations omitted). Stressing the fundamental principle discussed above — that "[p]rivate writings . . . enjoy the protection of the First Amendment" — the court stated, "[f]or such writings to lose their First Amendment protection, something more than their accidental and unintentional exposure to public scrutiny must take place." *Id.* at 617-18.

Every court to consider the issue has followed this rule. . . . [citations omitted]

The boldfaced sentences inoculate against the opposing argument that Mutombo's writing was a true threat as it stood on the piece of paper found in his car. The first two sentences frame a rule that will make it harder for the court to accept this opposing contention at face value, because they label true threats as a "narrowly limited" class of unprotected speech that still requires "actual communication." The third boldfaced sentence neutralizes *Virginia v. Black*, the seminal Supreme Court case validating the true threat doctrine, by highlighting the best part of its definition and putting it into context. Juxtaposed against *Porter* and the final sentence, which continued with a veritable citation-fest of cases imposing a communication requirement on true threats after *Black*, *Black*'s language looks more favorable. But notice how subtle this strategy is. The writer never overtly refers to an opposing argument nor explicitly acknowledges any weakness. These paragraphs have the same affirmative feel as the previous section did. But they operate to undercut rather than establish.

4.2   Responsive Strategies

Chapter 13 addresses response and reply briefs in full, but here we zero in on responsive argument strategies. Because the court has now heard the opposing arguments, the court expects a direct response, and you must be prepared to give one. But beware of the tendency to respond, respond, respond rather than weaving your responses into your affirmative frame. Just as you do not want to leave strong counterpoints unanswered, you do not want the court to keep viewing those counterpoints from the opponent's perspective.

This direct response integration strategy takes work, but it is persuasive. It contains three distinct components: (1) the affirmative frame, which briefly states or reprises the affirmative position; (2) the "setup," which targets and characterizes the opposing argument; and (3) the "takedown," which shreds the opposing argument by explaining its flaws. The challenge with the affirmative frame is to keep it short. As appellee, your affirmative points may need to be more compressed to allow space for refutation. In the appellant's reply brief, the key is to avoid repeating what your opening brief says in too much detail. There, your affirmative frame should be even more succinct, just detailed enough to produce reader recall of your main points.

Whether you are filing a response or reply, the second component—the "setup"—should avoid giving too much credence to the opposing argument. Keep it short and simple, not detailed; the goal is to trigger basic recall of the opposing point. The final component's "takedown" is what should consume most of the space and the reader's and writer's attention.

This responsive example comes from the *Facebook v. Connect U* Appellee's Brief. Recall from Chapter 10's excerpt that Facebook began by defending the lower court's ruling that the parties' Settlement Agreement terms were "sufficiently definite." This directly responsive section followed.[116]

| EXAMPLE | Responsive Two-Sided Messaging

2. The parties themselves agreed that terms the CU Founders now deem essential were not material to them when they signed the Settlement Agreement.

The CU Founders assert that this Court must override the parties' stated intention to be bound because the Settlement Agreement did not specify various additional terms, such as additional "representations and warranties," whether there would be "restrictions on transferability" of the Facebook stock, and the details of the releases. OB 7. The CU Founders insist that *this Court* must deem all these terms to be "critical economic and legal terms of the transaction," OB 54, which would mean that no party could ever voluntarily undertake an acquisition without including these terms. They are mistaken.

Contracting parties are entitled to decide whether a term is "critical" *to them*—at least so long as a court can be reasonably certain of what the deal was. *See* Copeland v. Baskin Robbins *U.S.A.*, 117 Cal. Rptr. 2d 875, 879 n.3 (Ct. App. 2002) ("Whether a term is 'essential' depends on its relative importance to the parties and whether its absence would make enforcing the remainder of the contract unfair to either party."). Here, the CU Founders stated their intention to be bound by the Settlement Agreement as written, even though these additional terms were not specified, and regardless of whether they executed "more formal documents." ER 482. More importantly, they agreed that *"Facebook will determine* the form & documentation of the acquisition of ConnectU's shares"—so long as the "form & documentation" were ultimately "consistent with a stock and cash for stock acquisition." ER 483 (emphasis added). In signing this contract, the CU Founders confirmed that they were so indifferent to the ancillary details described in their appellate brief that they were happy to let Facebook dictate them.

← Section 2 follows Section 1's affirmative frame—the terms were sufficiently definite.

← The "set up" briefly characterizes CU's opposing argument.

← The rest of this passage executes the "take down."

> In light of this explicit contractual stipulation, it does not matter that there might be circumstances in *other* deals where *other* sellers might consider some or all of these other terms to be "customary" or "'standard practice.'" OB 63 (citation omitted). "[N]either law nor equity requires that every term and condition of an agreement be set forth in the contract." [citations omitted] Parties to a contract are free to agree that certain terms that might be important to other parties in other circumstances are not material to them, or that it is more important to them to lock in a deal right now than it is to haggle over terms that they might negotiate under less exigent circumstances. [citations omitted]

The first paragraph expertly executes the "setup." From this paragraph, the reader can immediately tell which opposing argument is being addressed — the one that contends that the Agreement needs more terms to be enforceable. Even as the writer sets up this opposing point for a takedown, he is already undercutting it, communicating a two-sided refutational message. By directly quoting terms that sound picky and technical — but that CU contended needed to be in the Agreement — the writer makes these terms sound subsidiary from the get-go. The next sentence's reference to "this Court" lays the foundation for the takedown's point that parties, not courts, decide what contract terms are vital. Concluding the setup, the writer exposes the bad precedent the opposing argument would set and comes right out and says it is mistaken.

The "takedown" then finishes off the work in the next two paragraphs. The first paragraph uses authority and reasoning to show that the Court's role is to decide term certainty, and the parties' role is to decide which terms to include. Because CU acceded to the contract as written, it couldn't have thought the omitted terms were critical. The second paragraph then does away with the relevance of custom and practice, getting back to the core point that contracting is a two-party enterprise.

The final example takes us back to Chapter 8, which introduced the Appellees' Brief in Perry v. Schwartzenegger, one of the instrumental marriage cases that paved the way to the Supreme Court's decision in Obergefell v. Hodges. Perry challenged California's Proposition 8, a ballot proposition that amended the California Constitution to define marriage as an opposite-sex institution. This excerpt followed the Appellees' affirmative argument that Proposition 8 violates due process by impinging on the fundamental right of marriage.[117]

EXAMPLE **Responsive Two-Sided Messaging**

C. Allowing Same-Sex Couples to Marry Would Promote "Responsible Procreation."

Even if "responsible procreation" were the defining purpose of marriage—which it is not—marriage by individuals of the same sex would nonetheless further that purpose.

The "setup" briefly characterizes the opposing procreation argument.

Proponents' own definition of so-called responsible procreation centers on the welfare of children and the need for them to be "raised in stable family units." Prop. Br. 58. Indeed, Proponents attempt to distinguish Proposition 8 from antimiscegenation laws on the ground that, "by prohibiting interracial marriages, [those laws] substantially *decreased* the likelihood that children of mixed-race couples would be born to and raised by their parents in stable and enduring family units." *Id.* at 66. Therefore, Proponents contend, such laws were "affirmatively *at war* with" marriage's "central procreative purposes." *Id.* But by prohibiting same-sex couples from marrying and creating "stable and enduring family units," Proposition 8 is equally "at war" with these purposes and affirmatively harmful to the children of same-sex couples. *See Zablocki*, 434 U.S. at 390 ("the net result of preventing . . . marriage is simply more illegitimate children").

The rest of this passage executes the "takedown."

As the district court found, "The tangible and intangible benefits of marriage flow to a married couple's children." ER 106; *see also* SER 180-81 (Lamb: explaining that when a cohabiting couple marries, that marriage can improve the adjustment outcomes of the couple's child because of "the advantages that accrue to marriage"); SER 440-42 (American Psychiatric Association: marriage benefits the couple's children). Even Proponents' expert David Blankenhorn agreed that "children raised by same-sex couples would benefit if their parents were permitted to marry." ER 83 (citing SER 285); *see also* SER 291 (same).

Moreover, California law treats gay men and lesbians equally to heterosexuals with respect to the rights and obligations of parenthood, including the right to produce and raise children, the right to

> adopt children, the right to become foster parents, and the obligation to provide for children after separation. *See* Elisa B. v. Superior Court, 117 P.3d 660, 666 (Cal. 2005); Cal. Fam. Code § 297.5. More than 37,000 children in California are currently being raised by same-sex couples. SER 558-63. Allowing these couples to marry would plainly serve the purpose of "increasing the likelihood that children will be born to and raised in stable family units." Prop. Br. 58 [citations omitted]

Viewed within the affirmative frame that marriage is a fundamental right, the opposing argument that marriage's goal is "responsible procreation" already sounds weak. The "setup" then briefly summarizes and characterizes this argument. Using the opponents' miscegenation distinction against them, the second paragraph exposes its flawed premise and fundamental inconsistency at the same time as it describes that premise. This simultaneous set up/knock down is classic two-sided refutational messaging. The takedown's first paragraph then shows how the facts refute the opponent's "stable family" premise. The second paragraph then shows how the law refutes that same premise.

SUMMARY

Managing Weaknesses and Opposing Arguments

- Dealing forthrightly with weaknesses and counterarguments enhances the credibility and persuasiveness of your affirmative arguments.
- To avoid calling undue attention to weaknesses and opposing points, use the strategies of two-sided messaging and inoculation.
- Don't present the negatives without context and don't present the positives without acknowledging the negatives.
- In opening briefs, use preemptive strategies. Craft rules, frame cases, and anticipate arguments in a way that undermines their effectiveness before the judge hears them from the other side.
- Avoid the defensive language, "my opponent will likely argue."
- In response and reply briefs, be explicit and direct with your responses. Divide the response into three components: (1) the affirmative frame, which briefly states or reprises the affirmative position; (2) the "setup," which targets and characterizes the opposing argument; and (3) the "takedown," which shreds the opposing argument by explaining its flaws.

Endnotes

1. Judith D. Fischer, *Got Issues? An Empirical Study About Framing Them*, 6 J. Ass'n Legal Writing Directors 1, 2-3 (2009) ("The framing effect occurs when a speaker's emphasis on certain considerations affects what others focus on in forming opinions.") (citing E. James N. Druckman, *On the Limits of Framing Effects: Who Can Frame?*, 63 J. Pol. 1041, 1042 (2001)).

2. Stephen V. Armstrong & Timothy P. Terrell, *Why Is It So Hard to Front-Load?*, 18 Persp.: Teaching Legal Res. & Writing 30, 31 (2009) ("It is a cast of mind that applies everywhere, because it has to do with how we insert new chunks of information—whatever the size of the chunk—into the flow of information streaming through a reader's mind.").

3. Armstrong & Terrell, *supra* note 2, at 30.

4. Kristen K. Robbins Tiscione, *The Inside Scoop: What Federal Judges Really Think About the Way Lawyers Write*, 8 Legal Writing: J. Legal Writing Inst. 257, 273-74 (2002).

5. Armstrong & Terrell, *supra* note 2, at 31.

6. Kathryn M. Stanchi, *The Power of Priming in Legal Advocacy: Using the Science of First Impressions to Persuade the Reader*, 89 Or. L. Rev. 305, 306 (2010).

7. *Id.* at 311.

8. *Id.* at 307-33.

9. *Id.* at 307.

10. Robbins Tiscione, *supra* note 4, at 273-74.

11. Ruth Ann Robbins, *Painting with Print: Incorporating Concepts of Typographic and Layout Design Into the Text of Legal Writing Documents*, 2 J. Ass'n Legal Writing Directors 109, 124-25 (2004). Surveying the science behind roadmaps, Robbins explains why they work: "Advance organizers such as roadmaps or summaries create a learning base that the reader can call upon as pre-learned material when later introduced to the material in more depth. The information is learned the first time in the advance organizer and placed into the working (short-term) memory if the related text is read immediately afterwards." *Id.*

12. Laura E. Little, *Characterizations and Legal Discourse*, 6 J. Ass'n Legal Writing Directors 121, 125 (1996).

13. *See, e.g.*, Robbins, *supra* note 11, at 124-25.

14. *Id.* at 125.

15. Brief for the Petitioner at ii-iv, Lawrence v. Texas, No. 02-102 (written by Jenner & Block, Lambda Legal Defense and Education Fund, and Williams, Birnberg & Andersen); Brief for the Respondent at ii, Lawrence v. Texas, No. 02-102 (written by Charles A. Rosenthal, William J. Delmore III, and Scott A. Durfee).

16. Brief for the Appellees at ii-iii, Facebook, Inc. v. Connect U, Nos. 08-16745, 08-16873, 09-15021 (written by Orrick, Herrington & Sutcliffe).

17. Brief for the Appellant at iii-v, Oracle America, Inc. v. Google Inc., Nos. 2013-1021, 2013-1022 (written by Orrick, Herrington & Sutcliffe, Oracle America, Inc., and Kirkland & Ellis).

18. Brief for the Petitioner at ii-iii, University of Texas Southwestern Medical Center v. Nassar, No. 12-484 (written by King & Spalding).

19. *Id.*

20. *See, e.g.*, Practitioner's Handbook for Appeals to the United States Court of Appeals for the Seventh Circuit 121-22, 133-34 (2014). We use the Seventh Circuit Handbook to illustrate the default stylistic and structural expectations of most appellate courts. However, as with all other aspects of your appeal, you must look to your appellate court's specific rules. If those rules dictate the format and style of point headings, follow them instead.

21. *Id.* at 133-34.

22. *Id.*

23. Robbins, *supra* note 11, at 115-18.

24. *Id.* at 119.

25. *See* Practitioner's Handbook for Appeals to the United States Court of Appeals for the Seventh Circuit 134 (2014).

26. Brief for the Appellant at 30-31, United States v. Worku, No. 14-1218 (written by Snell & Wilmer).

27. Brief for the Appellant at 69, Oracle America, Inc. v. Google Inc., Nos. 2013-1021, 2013-1022 (written by Orrick, Herrington & Sutcliffe, Oracle America, Inc., and Kirkland & Ellis).

28. *Id.* at 69-72.

29. Brief for the Appellees at 24, Facebook, Inc. v. Connect U, Nos. 08-16745, 08-16873, 09-15021 (written by Orrick, Herrington & Sutcliffe).

30. *Id.*

31. Brief for the Appellant at 40-55, Oracle America, Inc. v. Google Inc., Nos. 2013-1021, 2013-1022 (written by Orrick, Herrington & Sutcliffe, & Oracle America, and Kirkland & Ellis).

32. Robbins Tiscione, *supra* note 4, at 264-72.

33. People v. Woodruff, 223 Ill.2d 386, 304-05 (2006).

34. Brief for the Appellant at 70, Oracle America, Inc. v. Google Inc., Nos. 2013-1021, 2013-1022 (written by Orrick, Herrington & Sutcliffe, Oracle America, Inc., and Kirkland & Ellis).

35. Brief for the Petitioner at ii-iii, University of Texas Southwestern Medical Center v. Nassar, No. 12-484 (written by King & Spalding and the state of Texas).

36. Richard A. Posner, *Convincing a Federal Court of Appeals*, 25 No. 2 Litig. 3, 4 (1999).

37. Sarah E. Ricks & Jane L. Istvan, *Effective Brief Writing Despite High Volume Practice: Ten Misconceptions That Results in Bad Briefs*, 38 U. Tol. L. Rev. 1113, 1122 (2007) (quoting Richard K. Neumann, Jr., Legal Reasoning and Legal Writing 275-80 (4th ed. 2001)).

38. *Id.* at 1122.

39. Michael D. Murray, *For the Love of Parentheticals: The Story of Parenthetical Usage in Synthesis, Rhetoric, Economics, and Narrative Reasoning*, 38 U. Dayton L. Rev. 175, 191 (2012) As Murray explains:

   Opaque or unsubstantiated reasoning, overworking or stretching an analogy to a precedent that is not closely aligned to the client's narrative and rhetorical situation, imposes a cost on the reader who must take the time to unpack the analogy, evaluate whether it is analogous, and still might have to invest the time to compare the analogy to other controlling authorities that also are on point."

   Id.

40. *Id.* at 191-92 (discussing the relative inefficiencies of case-to-case analogies).

41. Wilson Huhn, *The Stages of Legal Reasoning: Formalism, Analogy, and Realism*, 48 Vill. L. Rev. 305, 312 (2003) ("'The basic pattern of legal reasoning is reasoning by example. It is reasoning from case to case.'") (quoting Edward Levi, An Introduction to Legal Reasoning 1-2 (U. Chi. Press ed., 1948)).

42. Michael R. Smith, Advanced Legal Writing: Theories and Strategies in Persuasive Writing 46 (3d ed. 2012). In this way, case explanations — whether full-text or housed in an explanatory parenthetical — provide "an illustration of the abstract rule to help the reader understand the rule" and its importance to the case. As Smith points out, the "cognitive advantages of illustrations" are well documented. *Id.*

43. Brief for the Appellant at 65, Oracle America, Inc. v. Google Inc., Nos. 2013-1021, 2013-1022 (written by Orrick, Herrington & Sutcliffe, Oracle America, Inc., and Kirkland & Ellis).

44. Brief for the Petitioner at 12, Lawrence v. Texas, No. 02-102 (written by Jenner & Block, Lambda Legal Defense and Education Fund, Inc., and Williams, Birnberg & Andersen).

45. *See* Michael D. Murray, *The Promise of Parentheticals: An Empirical Study of the Use of Parentheticals in Federal Appellate Briefs*, 10 Legal Comm. & Rhetoric: JALWD 1, 3-5 (2013); Murray, *supra* note 39, at 179.

46. Michael R. Smith, Advanced Legal Writing: Theories and Strategies in Persuasive Writing 45 (2d ed. 2008).

47. Murray, *supra* note 39, at 182-88.

48. Brief for the Appellant at 71, Oracle America, Inc. v. Google Inc., Nos. 2013-1021, 2013-1022 (written by Orrick, Herrington & Sutcliffe, Oracle America, Inc., and Kirkland & Ellis).

49. Brief for the Appellant at ii-iii, Cressman v. Thompson, No. 14-6020 (written by Sturgill, Turner, Barker, & Moloney).

50. Smith, *supra* note 46, at 56.

51. *Id.* at 54.

52. William P. Statsky & R. John Wernet, Case Analysis and Fundamentals of Legal Writing 189 (4th ed. 1995) ("[Y]our presentation of case law is integrated into the analysis.").

53. Lisa S. Bressman & Abbe R. Gluck, *Statutory Interpretation from the Inside–An Empirical Study of Congressional Drafting, Delegation, and the Canons: Part II*, 66 Stan. L. Rev. 725, 743 (2014) ("[T]he particularly granular level on which many text-focused debates now take place in the case law seems disconnected from the way in which members and congressional policy staff engage in the drafting process."); Carlos E. Gomez, *Reinterpreting Statutory Interpretation*, 74 N.C. L. Rev. 585, 720 (1996) (stating that one ought to first use text, legislative history, and canons of construction when engaging in statutory interpretation); K Mart Corp v. Cartier, Inc., 486 U.S. 281, 291 (1988) (requiring statutory interpretation begins first with an examination of the language itself and "the language and design of the statute as a whole").

54. Hart v. Massanari, 266 F.3d 1155, 1175 (9th Cir. 2001) ("A district court bound by circuit authority, for example, has no choice but to follow it, even if convinced that such authority was wrongly decided."); Posner, *supra* note 36, at 3 ("[O]nly rarely is it effective advocacy to try to convince the judges that the case law compels them to rule in your favor. Just think: if the case law relating to the case at hand were one-sided, would the case have gotten to the appellate stage[?]").

55. Timothy Schwartz, Comment, *Cases Time Forgot: Why Judges Can Sometimes Ignore Controlling Precedent*, 56 Emory L.J. 1475, 1470 (2007) ("The touchstone of persuasive authority is that the deciding court is not required to follow [the] result or reasoning of the referenced authority.").

56. Julian W. Smith, *Evidence of Ambiguity: The Effect of Circuit Splits on the Interpretation of Federal Criminal Law*, 16 Suffolk J. Trial & App. Advoc. 79, 80 (2011) ("But federal courts of appeals sometimes interpret the same federal criminal statute differently, thus creating a judicial irony

dubbed the 'circuit split.' Circuit splits indicate that the law in question not only had the ability to be interpreted multiple ways, but that it was actually interpreted multiple ways.").

57. Murray, *supra* note 39, at 189 ("[P]arentheticals allow the elegant and efficient presentation of interpretive principles drawn from multiple samples of dispositions of similar cases to guide and persuade the audience as to the disposition of the present case.").

58. Ellie Margolis, *Closing the Floodgates: Making Persuasive Policy Arguments in Appellate Briefs*, 62 Mont. L. Rev. 59, 65-67 (2001).

59. Wilson R. Huhn, *Teaching Legal Analysis Using a Pluralistic Model of Law*, 36 Gonz. L. Rev. 433, 487 (2000-2001) (Huhn's apt metaphor for this difference is marker buoys (rules) and their unseen anchors (animating policies)); *see also* Margolis, *supra* note 58, at 70; Michael R. Smith, *The Sociological and Cognitive Dimensions of Policy-Based Persuasion*, 22 J. L. & Pol'y 35, 41-42 (2013).

60. Huhn, *supra* note 59, at 485 ("The distinctive feature of policy arguments is that they are consequentialist in nature. . . . [T]he core of a policy argument is that a certain interpretation of the law will bring about a certain state of affairs, and this state of affairs is either acceptable or unacceptable in the eyes of the law."); Smith, *supra* note 59, at 39-53.

61. Margolis, *supra* note 58, at 65 ("[P]olicy plays an especially important role in three types of cases: common law cases of first impression, constitutional cases raising novel application of constitutional provisions, and cases of first-time statutory interpretation."); Smith, *supra* note 59, at 39 (defining a policy argument as one "made by a legal advocate to a court that urges the court to resolve the issue before it by establishing a new rule that advances or protects a particular social value implicated by the issue").

62. Ellie Margolis, *Beyond Brandeis: Exploring the Uses of Nonlegal Material in Appellate Briefs*, 34 U.S.F. L. Rev. 197, 211 (2000); Huhn, *supra* note 59, at 486; Smith, *supra* note 59, at 37-63.

63. *See* Margolis, *supra* note 62, at 211-12; Smith, *supra* note 59, at 43 ("[D]ecision-making based on values is more often not a choice between either advancing or not advancing a particular value; it is more often a decision about which of the competing values to advance.").

64. *See, e.g.*, Pa. Glass Sand Corp. v. Caterpillar Tractor Co., 652 F.2d 1165, 1169 (3d Cir. 1981) ("Tort law rests on obligations imposed by law, rather than bargain. . . . On the other hand, contract law . . . protects expectation interests.").

65. O. Lee Reed & Jan W. Henkel, *Facilitating the Flow of Truthful Personnel Information: Some Needed Change in the Standard Required to Overcome the Qualified Privilege to Defame*, 26 Am. Bus. L.J. 305, 310-12 (1988).

66. *See* David C. Yamada, *Dignity, "Rankism," and Hierarchy in the Workplace: Creating a "Dignitarian" Agenda for American Employment Law*, 28 Berkeley J. Emp. & Lab. L. 305, 319-20 (2007) (noting that private employees are generally excluded from claiming protection of constitutional speech guarantees in the workplace as a matter of private-sector employment law); Huhn, *supra* note 59, at 488. Huhn presents more extreme examples, such as "racism, religious bigotry, and class bias," which "exist as powerful forces in society" but "do not form a part of any valid legal argument." *Id.*

67. *See* Huhn, *supra* note 59, at 486 (contending that "the value at stake" must be "one of the purposes of the law").

68. *See id.* at 486. Huhn suggests that advocates ask themselves a series of questions in the process of crafting policy arguments: "1. Is the factual prediction accurate? 2. Is the value at stake one of the purposes of the law? 3. Is the value at stake sufficiently strong? 4. How likely is it that the decision in this case will serve this value? 5. Are there other, competing values that are also at stake?" *Id.*

69. *See* Margolis, *supra* note 58, at 70-79 (2001); Smith, *supra* note 59, at 53-54.

70. Margolis, *supra* note 58, at 72.

71. *Id.*

72. *Id.* at 73.

73. *Id.*

74. *Id.* at 77.

75. *See id.* at 74-75.

76. *See id.* at 78-79.

77. *Id.*

78. *Id.*

80. Brief for the Petitioner at 28, University of Texas Southwestern Medical Center v. Nassar, No. 12-484 (written by King & Spalding and the state of Texas).

81. Smith, *supra* note 59, at 77-78.

82. Brief for the Petitioner at 30, University of Texas Southwestern Medical Center v. Nassar, No. 12-484 (written by King & Spalding and the state of Texas).

83. Margolis, *supra* note 58, at 68-82.

84. Smith, *supra* note 59, at 68-82.

85. Margolis, *supra* note 58, at 83; Margolis, *supra* note 62, at 207-08.

86. Margolis, *supra* note 58, at 81; Smith, *supra* note 59, at 68-70.

87. Margolis, *supra* note 62, at 202-06.

88. Smith, *supra* note 59, at 69.

89. Brief for the Petitioner at 33-34, University of Texas Southwestern Medical Center v. Nassar, No. 12-484 (written by King & Spalding and the state of Texas).

90. Margolis, *supra* note 58, at 80-81.

91. Smith, *supra* note 59, at 74.

92. *Id.* at 74-88.

93. *Id.* at 71-72.

94. *Id.* at 74-88.

95. Brief for the Petitioner at 34, University of Texas Southwestern Medical Center v. Nassar, No. 12-484 (written by King & Spalding and the state of Texas).

96. Brief *Amicus Curiae* for the American Trucking Associations, et al., in Support of Petitioner at 22, Albertson's, Inc. v. Kirkingburg, No. 98-591 (written by Mayer Brown and ATA Litigation Center).

97. Brief for the Appellant at 1, Oracle America, Inc. v. Google Inc., Nos. 2013-1021, 2013-1022 (written by Orrick, Herrington & Sutcliffe, Oracle America, Inc., Kirkland & Ellis).

98. Kathryn M. Stanchi, *Playing with Fire: The Science of Confronting Adverse Material in Legal Advocacy*, 60 Rutgers L. Rev. 381, 381 (2008) ("Confronting and defusing negative information is a critical aspect of the art of persuasion.").

99. *Id.*

100. *Id.* at 397.

101. Robin Wellford Slocum, Legal Reasoning Writing and Other Lawyering Skills 492 (3d ed. 2011).

102. *See* Stanchi, *supra* note 98, at 388-89. "In the words of Judge Posner, an advocate whose brief ignores weaknesses 'is made to seem foolish and worse, deceitful. He will have lost the court's confidence and will find it difficult to regain. . . . What is more, he will have created a situation in which the judges first encounter the weaknesses in his case in the opponent's version of them, and the opponent will try to magnify them.'" *Id.* (quoting Posner, *supra* note 36, at 62).

103. Model Rules of Prof'l Conduct R. 3.3(a)(2) (1983).

104. J. Thomas Sullivan, *Ethical and Aggressive Appellate Advocacy: Confronting Adverse Authority*, 59 U. Miami L. Rev. 341, 352 (2005).

105. Stanchi, *supra* note 98, at 395.

106. *See id.* at 394 (Stanchi refers to these as "two-sided refutational messages," a label coined by cognitive scientists.).

107. *Id.* at 392-93.

108. *Id.* at 394.

109. *Id.* at 395.

110. *Id.* at 397-98.

111. *Id.* at 398-99.

112. *Id.* at 393.

113. *Id.* at 399-408.

114. *Id.* at 397; Slocum, *supra* note 101, at 491.

115. Brief for the Appellant at 69, Oracle America, Inc. v. Google Inc., Nos. 2013-1021, 2013-1022 (written by Orrick, Herrington & Sutcliffe, Oracle America, Inc., and Kirkland & Ellis).

116. Brief for the Appellees at 24-25, Facebook, Inc. v. Connect U., Nos. 08-16745, 08-16873, 09-15021 (written by Orrick, Herrington & Sutcliffe).

117. Brief for Appellees at 50-51, Perry v. Schwarzenegger, No. 10-16696 (written by Gibson, Dunn & Crutcher and Boies, Schiller & Flexner).

12

The Writing Phase: Drafting Specialized Sections, Revising to Perfection, and Filing the Brief

As you near the end of the writing phase, you will be an expert on your appellate issues, having created and followed a research plan, developed your argument, brainstormed and organized your ideas, and written and assessed your draft multiple times. Each is essential in crafting a persuasive brief. But alone they are not enough to win over a panel of appellate judges. In addition to being well researched and persuasively written, your brief must make an impeccable first impression. To begin with, your brief must contain every section required by court rules, and those sections' content must heed the rules as well. Contrary to how many advocates approach them, specialized brief sections also present opportunities to persuade, and you must seize them.

The brief must also be written to satisfy the client and the court in a manner that facilitates easy reading. You'll need to keep both in mind as you revise. To transform your work into an audience-centered product that reads flawlessly, you must commit to multiple revision rounds, each with a distinct, deliberate purpose. This is also the time to cultivate style and voice, qualities that are easier to infuse in late-stage revisions. Just as important as perfecting your writing is taking advantage of technology and fine-tuning your formatting. Now more than ever, advocates are using technology and formatting not just reactively to meet the rules, but affirmatively to please and persuade.

One overarching point: Court rules are central to every aspect of late-stage brief preparation. In a federal appellate court, the rules you must know inside and out are the Federal Rules of Appellate Procedure and the circuit's own rules, which can vary significantly from circuit to circuit. Those rules must be consulted multiple times as you finalize your work, and you will see that we reference them often here. You must not leave room for your brief to be rejected on technical grounds. That means giving scrupulous attention to the rules' filing requirements, and allowing ample time to grasp and apply them to your brief.

Breaking down each late-stage preparation step into its component parts, this chapter guides you in the final push to filing.

Section 1 Drafting Specialized Sections and Compiling Appendices

Your completed brief is more than just a statement of issues, a statement of facts, and argument. Although most of your writing time and the judges' attention will be spent on these sections, courts require several specialized sections that serve specific purposes for the reader. Here is a sample table of contents from a Seventh Circuit brief, showing where those sections typically reside:

Table of Contents

In the federal system, three rules of appellate procedure govern these aspects of your brief: Rule 28 (specialized sections); Rule 30 (appendices); and Rule 32 (formatting). Circuit rules often require more detail or additional sections.[1] Therefore, although this section tracks the Federal Rules of Appellate Procedure, you must as always study local circuit rules, too. The federal circuits' practitioner handbooks are a good starting point for ensuring that your brief contains all required sections.

Before we dive into these specialized sections, we should say a word about introductions. Though not addressed in the federal rules, many believe that a succinct introduction is an essential first glimpse into your arguments and themes. Other practitioners, however, are skittish about inserting content outside of the required brief sections. And judges appear to have mixed feelings about the use of introductions.[2] You will need to decide for yourself whether the rules' list of brief sections is exclusive or whether the rules are flexible enough to accommodate an introduction.

If you opt to include an introduction, here are some tips for crafting it. A well-written introduction should accomplish three goals in a pointed and succinct way: (1) It should tell the reader why you should win; (2) it should give the reader some sense of what the case is about; and (3) it should convey your theme(s).[3] Thus, you must write the introduction to be both fact specific and thematic.[4] By this we mean you should refer to the people and places in your case rather than using abstract labels, and state exactly how your client was wronged or precisely why the lower court was right. Your language should not be overwrought and emotional, but it should not be staid or vanilla either. Evocative prose is especially important in the introduction's opening sentences. Read the kick-off sentences in the introductions below:

Example: Introduction Comparison

Brief #1	Brief #2
The district court erroneously dismissed Appellant Jenna R. Leffler's lawsuit on two separate occasions, once under 28 U.S.C. § 1915(e)(2)(B) and again under Federal Rule of Civil Procedure 12(b)(6). Both dismissals were the culmination of multiple errors.	Jenna Leffler did everything she could to properly preserve her claims in the district court: She filed two timely EEOC charges that explicitly alleged sex discrimination and retaliation; she then filed her First Complaint within Title VII's 90-day statute of limitations; finally, when the district court dismissed her First Complaint and told her she could file an amended complaint, Leffler promptly did just that.

Which version is more powerful? Which one makes you want to continue reading to find out what happened? Which one hints at the theme underlying the arguments in the brief? After your forceful opening sentences, lay out the big-picture concrete facts that will set the tone for what follows, and sketch out — but only in the most general terms — the legal bases for your arguments. Your introduction should not be a condensed summary of the argument. It serves a different purpose: to engage your reader and to connect her to your client's cause.

Your final decision with respect to the introduction is where to put it. Some practitioners are bold, placing it in a stand-alone section, which is then labeled in the table of contents as "Introduction." Others weave a short introduction directly into the brief's mandatory preliminary sections. Here is an example of a persuasive introduction woven into the Questions Presented akin to an elongated multi-sentence statement:

EXAMPLE

> Petitioner Pleasant Grove City owns and displays a number of monuments, memorials, and other objects in a municipal park. Respondent Summum sued in federal court, contending that because the city had accepted monuments donated by local civic groups, the First Amendment compels the city to accept and display Summum's "Seven Aphorisms" monument as well. The district court denied Summum's request for a preliminary injunction, but a panel of the Tenth Circuit reversed, holding that the city must immediately erect and display Summum's monument. The Tenth Circuit then denied the city's petition for rehearing en banc by an equally divided, 6-6 vote. The questions presented are:
>
> 1. Did the Tenth Circuit err by holding, in conflict with the Second, Third, Seventh, Eighth, and D.C. Circuits, that a monument donated to a municipality and thereafter owned, controlled, and displayed by the municipality is not government speech but rather remains the private speech of the monument's donor. . . .

And here is an introduction written as a stand-alone section in the Ninth Circuit Proposition 8 case Perry v. Schwarzenegger, first encountered in Chapter 8. It could just as well have launched the Statement of the Case:

EXAMPLE

> This case is about marriage, "the most important relation in life," Zablocki v. Redhail, 434 U.S. 374, 384 (1978), and equality, the most essential principle of the American dream, from the Declaration of Independence, to the Gettysburg Address, to the Fourteenth Amendment. Fourteen times the Supreme Court has stated that marriage is a fundamental right of all individuals. This case tests the proposition whether the gay and lesbian Americans among us should be counted as "persons" under the Fourteenth Amendment, or whether they constitute a permanent underclass ineligible for protection under that cornerstone of our Constitution. The unmistakable, undeniable purpose and effect of Proposition 8 is to select gay men and lesbians — and them alone — and enshrine in California's Constitution that they are different, that their loving and committed relationships are ineligible for the

> designation "marriage," and that they are unworthy of that "important relation in life." After an expensive, demeaning campaign in which voters were constantly warned to vote "Yes on 8" to "protect our children"—principally from the notion that gay men and lesbians were persons entitled to equal dignity and respect—Proposition 8 passed with a 52% majority, stripping away the state constitutional right to marry from gay men and lesbians. Proponents' stigmatization of gay and lesbian relationships as distinctly second-class thus became the official constitutional position of the State of California.

As you can see, these short paragraphs pack a persuasive punch to begin the brief. We turn now to the required specialized brief sections.

**Practice Alert #1
Drafting an Introduction**

Refer to the online companion for an exercise asking you to draft a persuasive introduction from a sample brief.

1.1 Cover Page

The first part of the brief that anyone will see is the cover. Composing a cover page is not as simple as it may seem: Its content is very specific and its format highly regulated. However, many appellate courts' websites post samples that show precisely how your cover page should look. In federal courts, the cover must contain the appellate court case number, the appellate court's name, the case title, the nature of the proceeding and the name of the court below, the brief title, and the attorney of record's contact information.[5] The type of brief you are filing determines what color the cover must be: For example, an appellant's opening brief cover is blue, and the appellee's response cover is red.[6] You must take care to ensure that all of the information is correct—a typo on the cover makes the wrong first impression.

1.2 Corporate Disclosure Statement

When an appeal is initiated, the court must know exactly who the interested parties are. If you represent a corporation, your brief will need a corporate disclosure statement, required by Federal Rule of Appellate Procedure 26.1.[7] This rule requires that nongovernmental corporate parties identify any parent corporation or corporation holding more than 10 percent of their stock, or state that no such corporation exists. Some circuits require a broader statement, in some cases identifying all parties with an interest in the matter.[8] In some courts this extends to every party, including amici, who appeared in the lower court; courts need this information to check for conflicts with the judging panel.[9] A judge's prior jobs, her affiliation with certain organizations, or even the stock she holds in her retirement accounts may all be grounds to recuse her from your case. Be sure to consult your court's rules to determine how much information the court requires regarding parties and corporate relationships.

1.3   Table of Contents

Though seemingly formulaic, the table of contents plays an important persuasive role. Consolidated in one place, your fact and argument headings provide a compelling narrative of your whole case. At a glance, the table also assures the court of your credibility and competence. It shows that you have included all the brief's required sections, and presented them in a format that eases the reader's navigation.

Federal Rule of Appellate Procedure 28, which addresses the table of contents, does not specify how detailed it must be, requiring only that you include page numbers.[10] Some circuit courts require more. For example, the Eleventh Circuit specifies that the table of contents should include page references to both headings and subheadings in the argument section.[11] Other courts require a section called "Points and Authorities," which combines the table of contents and table of authorities (discussed in the next section). This section typically lists the authorities cited in each section of the brief under each heading alphabetically or in order of importance. If your court does not specify what should be included in your table of contents, use your best judgment.

Practically speaking, you should wait to generate your table of contents until you have settled on your final argument headings and subheadings. When you are ready to tackle the table of contents, you may type it manually or use your word processing software's table of contents function. However, if you opt for the latter, do not forget to verify that all headings in the body of the brief match the headings in the table of contents, and that the page numbers are accurate, particularly when a new section begins near the top or bottom of the page. You must repeat this proofreading process every time you make changes to the brief, and update accordingly. Finally, make your tables visually appealing by incorporating enough white space and using consistent formatting. We devote more attention to visual rhetoric later in the chapter.

1.4   Table of Authorities

The clerks and judges who read your brief will need to assess the strength and quality of your legal arguments. Collecting your authorities in one place provides a jumping-off point for this process. Your table of authorities must list every source and the pages on which those sources appear, divided according to type of source.[12] Cases reside in their own section, as do statutes. If you rely on other types of authority, you can either house each type in its own section or consolidate them in a catch-all "Other Authority" section. These authorities could range from law reviews and treatises to statistical information, news articles, or sentencing guidelines. All cases and law review articles should be listed alphabetically, while statutes and regulations should appear in numerical order.[13] Use long-form citations without pin cites and identify each page where the authority appears in your brief. Use the word *passim* in place of page numbers for any authority cited more than five times. In some courts, such as the District of Columbia Circuit, you may need to select the sources on which you principally rely.[14] The guiding principle is to give the court an overview of the authorities that govern the appeal issues.

Like the table of contents, the table of authorities is best left until your brief is substantially complete, to minimize the rounds of revision. Although some software programs can recognize citations and assist you in compiling the table, those programs are far from foolproof. As such, part or all of your table may need to be manually constructed. This is a time-consuming process that demands attention to detail as you comb through "*id.*" references to find every place a source appears. And you must leave enough time before filing to accomplish this task; few gaffes impact an attorney's credibility more than preliminary pages riddled with typos that could have been avoided with just a few more hours' work. As with the table of contents, you must review and update the table of authorities every time you make a change to your brief. And be sure to perform one last citation check on any case that is vulnerable to appellate review. Indeed, this advice applies throughout the appeal; if you cite a case that is overturned while the appeal is pending, you must alert the court and opposing counsel. Although perfecting the table of authorities may seem tedious, when done well, it adds another dimension of credibility and persuasion to your brief.

1.5   Jurisdictional Statement

As discussed in Chapter 2, a court of appeals cannot take your case unless it has jurisdiction. To prove that you are appealing to the appropriate forum, your brief must include a jurisdictional statement covering four points: (1) the basis for the lower court's subject matter jurisdiction; (2) the basis for the appellate court's jurisdiction; (3) the filing dates demonstrating the timeliness of appeal; and (4) the finality of the order being appealed.[15] It does not suffice to declare that the court has jurisdiction; you must also state the supporting legal basis. In most cases that task is straightforward. You will cite the provisions for federal criminal, federal question, or diversity jurisdiction, along with 28 U.S.C. § 1291, which confers appellate jurisdiction over federal district court cases. To that you will add the notice of appeal's filing date and a citation to the rule that sets the filing deadline. For interlocutory appeals, the jurisdictional section will be more robust, incorporating the standards discussed in Chapter 2. No matter what the posture of your appeal, this section's importance cannot be understated. As you now know, jurisdiction is a threshold issue that cannot be waived. If this section does not establish that the appellate court has jurisdiction, you risk your appeal coming to an end before it begins.

1.6   Statement of the Case

You learned in Chapter 9 how to convey your client's story in a persuasive narrative. But these narrative facts tell only what gave rise to the trial court litigation; they do not explain what led to the appeal. The appellate court must understand what happened procedurally below in order to review the lower court's rulings. As Chapter 9 explained, in some courts narrative and procedural facts are combined into a single "statement of the case." In that chapter, we discussed how to integrate narrative and procedural facts in a single section. Here, we address the other common alternative: the statement of the case as a stand-alone section with only procedural facts.

So constituted, the statement of the case contains three basic elements: (1) the legal claims or charges that started the case; (2) the key procedural steps below; and (3) a summary of the lower court rulings to be reviewed.[16] Some courts impose more requirements. For example, in the Eleventh Circuit, a statement of the case must summarize the proceedings and their disposition, identify all facts that rely on inferences, and state the standard of review for each issue.[17]

Your approach to the statement of the case should parallel your approach to the statement of facts. Within the rules' bounds, consider which procedural aspects of the case below are most relevant to the issues on appeal. Do not waste words discussing collateral procedural issues that did not impact the orders being reviewed. It helps to compare your statement of the case to your argument section. If a procedural step does not appear in the argument and is not necessary to understand the case in its entirety, then omit it. You must also consider how to frame the procedural history of your case. For example, if you are the appellee, you will spend more time describing the lower court decision that you would like affirmed. As the appellant, you might highlight the lower court's procedural errors to begin calling those decisions into question. That said, you mustn't argue in this section. Stick to straight reporting of the facts (including those that do not favor you), but use the same subtle persuasive fact-writing strategies as you did in the statement of facts. The techniques of point of view, strategic fact placement, fact description, and word choice are just as appropriate to employ in this section.

1.7 Summary of the Argument

Your summary of the argument is one of the most important sections of the brief, and is usually one of the last things you write. It is the section that the judges often turn to first, and the very last thing they review before oral argument. Knowing the judicial attention this section will receive, don't give it short shrift by writing a terse, vanilla overview of the argument section. Instead, craft your summary to maximize its persuasive effect in a condensed space. The rule of thumb is that the summary should not exceed two pages—and some courts explicitly limit the length of this section. In that brief space, you must ably present the essence of your case, your theory and theme, and the crux of your arguments. You must not simply repeat the section headings that appear in your argument, and in fact the federal rules prohibit it.[18] Leave out case and record citations, which are not expected in this section and add unnecessary length.

The lead. The summary's most critical segment is its beginning, a "lead" that launches your opening salvo, captures the court's attention, and presents your case from a 5,000-foot view. The court should come away from the lead with three vital pieces of information: (1) your overall conclusion on the appellate issues; (2) your legal theory and theme; and (3) the result you want. The lead should also be stylistically arresting. Many summaries of argument start with aphorisms, metaphors, or memorable phrases. And all use vivid word choices and direct language to drive home what it is at stake in the appeal. The challenge is to accomplish all of this in a single paragraph. Below is an example of an effective lead in summary from a brief with almost 30 pages of argument.

EXAMPLE **Summary of the Argument**

Roger Short had just been released from prison into his parents' home when a ten-person S.W.A.T. team executed a search warrant for his brother. Finding Short's father's collection of hunting weapons, but not his brother, police opted to arrest Short instead. Despite Short's insistence on his innocence, his eager willingness to provide buccal swabs for a DNA analysis that he believed would exonerate him, and an administrative law judge's refusal to find that he possessed these guns or to revoke his probation, federal prosecutors steadfastly pursued their felon-in-possession charges. When Short insisted on going to trial and putting the government to its reasonable-doubt burden, the government filled the gaps in its case with a series of improper evidence, remarks, and instructions. In the end, though, the evidence simply did not satisfy the government's burden of proving Short's guilt beyond a reasonable doubt. This Court should either reverse Short's conviction or vacate the conviction and remand the case for a new trial for three reasons.

← *Using facts to set the stage; highlighting the theme of unfairness*

← *Previewing the arguments and the legal theory; gap-filling and insufficient evidence*

← *Overall conclusion and desired result*

The body. Next, the body of this section should succinctly summarize the argument for each issue on appeal. Think of the body of the summary as a closed accordion that will be expanded in your argument section. To condense your arguments in a meaningful way, extract the most important premises from your argument on each issue and transform them into strong conclusions. Then give the reader the "why" behind these premises, using one-step logic. One-step logic requires compressing each argument's "what" and "why" reasoning into a sentence or two. Follow up with a concluding sentence that wraps up the premise and transitions to the next one. The excerpt below, a continuation of the summary reproduced above, provides an example:

> First, there was insufficient evidence to convict Short of intentionally possessing the firearm or ammunition. The government proceeded on a constructive-possession theory, but it could neither establish his intent through a nexus connecting him to the firearms nor offer other satisfactory circumstantial evidence of Short's intent. Second and relatedly, the jury instructions confusingly failed to tell the jury that it had to separately find Short's intent to possess firearms or ammunition. By gratuitously defining the term *knowingly* while failing to define the term *intent*, the instructions unduly emphasized Short's knowledge and unmistakably implied that the jury could convict on that basis alone. Finally, during closing arguments the government asked the jury to make a propensity inference about Short's intent to commit the present crime based on his prior criminal record and, moreover, asked the jury during closing to protect the community from Short through its verdict. These remarks, founded on improper testimony, prejudiced Short and denied him a fair trial.

← *Succinct summary of the issues, providing just one powerful sentence of reasoning to support each issue*

← *Vivid terms add interest*

Common errors. Four common errors befall summaries of argument. First, when you condense your reasoning, you run the risk of making it opaque to the reader, leaving out context that the court needs. The summary of the argument must stand on its own without reference to the argument section. Stand squarely in the reader's shoes and force yourself to think about what the court does and doesn't know at this stage of reading your brief. Second, your one-step logic reasoning may be incomplete, failing to provide a bridge for the reader from the topic sentence to the concluding sentence wrap-up. As a check, ask yourself if your reasoning would prompt the court to say, "Huh?" or "So what?" If your reasoning elicits that response, revise and rephrase until your reasoning hits the right ratio of context to detail and prompts no more confused reactions. Third, some summaries of argument simply list the writer's conclusions without any supporting reasoning at all. Summaries bearing this flaw come across as conclusory and strident, so make sure you haven't left out the crucial "why." Fourth, many summaries of argument are too long, taking the reader deep into the woods with details that they can't yet appreciate. If you pay heed to the two-page rule of thumb and keep the reader's needs top of mind, you will avoid this problem.

Above all, focus on presenting your legal arguments in sharp, persuasive prose. Nothing promotes reader comprehension like vivid language, precision, and direct syntax. These qualities are more important than ever in the summary of argument, whose brevity exposes every word, and where first impressions can be made or lost.

1.8   Conclusion

After the argument section concludes, your brief does not end. You must add a very short conclusion section.[19] Do not provide a paragraph-long summary of the arguments you just presented. Here, the appellate panel is looking for one specific piece of information: the relief you seek. Accordingly, you must understand your goals and the potential remedies. Should the ruling from which you are appealing be reversed outright? Are you looking to have the case retried? If yours is a criminal case, should a conviction be overturned, or should the case merely be remanded for resentencing? Consider your client's goals in the context of the applicable law: What can you plausibly ask the court to do based upon the arguments that you made? The answers to these questions may impact how you make your arguments and structure your brief, so this section is a good check on your prior work. And again, review the rules to ensure that there are no other requirements in your jurisdiction. In the Tenth Circuit, for example, your conclusion must be followed by an explanation of why oral argument is requested, if you have asked for it.[20]

1.9   Certificate of Compliance

Your brief may need to include a certificate of compliance warranting that it meets the requirements of the court to which you are appealing. In federal appellate courts, you must certify compliance with type-volume limits, and must state the number of words or the number of lines in the brief.[21] A few courts require additional information, such as the name of the word processing software used to produce the document. Your certificate of compliance will be easy to create, but you must take it seriously. In courts such as the Fifth Circuit, a certificate of compliance containing a material misrepresentation may lead the court to strike the brief and even to issue sanctions.[22]

1.10   Appendix

Your appendix—or appendices, in some cases—permits you to highlight the most important aspects of your record and present it directly to the judges. Although the judges deciding your case will have access to the entire record on appeal, they will not sit down to comb through it the way that you must (though their clerks will). Therefore, your appendix must compile the most critical pieces of record evidence.

In federal court, Federal Rule of Appellate Procedure 30 governs the content of appendices, but you must also make some judgment calls. The rule states that the appendix to an appellant's opening brief must include:

> (A) The relevant docket entries in the proceedings below; (B) the relevant portions of the pleadings, charge, findings, or opinion; (C) the judgment, order, or decision in question; and (D) other parts of the record to which the parties wish to direct the court's attention.[23]

You must decide what is relevant and what merits the court's special attention. Although the appellant always compiles an appendix (and appellees do not necessarily have to do so), courts encourage the parties to agree on its contents.[24] The appendix should accordingly reflect information critical to both sides' arguments.[25] Several courts supplement or expand on these rules, requiring reproduced judicial decisions and findings or a transcript of reasons for the judgment;[26] the entire docket sheet from the proceedings below;[27] challenged jury instructions;[28] or any relevant magistrate judge's report and recommendation.[29] In short, many types of documents may be required, and if not, they may be included at your option.

To determine what should go into your appendix, look at the rules in conjunction with the record items that you cite most frequently. Look back at your record digest to identify documents or transcript pages that contain important information affecting the appellate issues, such as the lower court judge's explanation of her ruling. And use your common sense — look for the portions of the record that you find particularly compelling.

Of course, your appendix cannot contain the entire record; you must pick and choose the key excerpts. Because brief appendices are public records, you must also take care to avoid including anything that should not appear in a court filing, such as sealed documents. In a criminal case, for example, you must leave out the defendant's Pre-Sentence Investigation Report, no matter how interesting or relevant to your arguments. In civil cases, protective orders place confidential information under seal, and that must be left out as well. Note, however, that some courts will allow sealed documents to be filed in a separate volume.[30] Even if your appeal does not rely on sealed documents or other confidential information, keep in mind that you still mustn't inundate your audience with information. You need not include a record item in your appendix in order to cite to it in your brief. Brevity is desirable in an appendix not only for the sake of the reader, but also for practical reasons: The length of your appendix is likely to affect how it will be filed. Many courts will permit appendices below a certain page limit to be bound with the brief, but require an appendix that exceeds the limit to be bound separately.[31] Regardless of how your appendix is bound, be sure to follow all of the formatting rules required by your jurisdiction — at a minimum, it will need to include a table of contents and be paginated.

Summary: Key Rules Relating to Specialized Brief Sections

Federal Rule of Appellate Procedure	Specialized Brief Section and Rule
30(a)(2)	Cover Page: lists the case name and number, the names of the appeals and lower courts, the nature of the proceeding, the title of the filing, and the name and contact information of the attorney of record.
28(a)(1)	Corporate Disclosure Statement: for nongovernmental entities, identifies parent corporations or other publicly held companies owning more than 10 percent of the party's stock.
28(a)(2)	Table of Contents: lists each section of the brief and its corresponding page number.
28(a)(3)	Table of Authorities: lists, with corresponding page numbers, all cases in alphabetical order, all statutes in numerical order, and any other authorities cited in the brief.
28(a)(4)	Jurisdictional Statement: states the basis for the lower court's jurisdiction, the basis for the circuit court's appellate jurisdiction, the filing dates establishing timeliness, and the procedural facts showing finality or the basis for interlocutory appeal.
28(a)(6)	Statement of the Case: concise recital of the relevant facts, procedural history, and rulings to be reviewed.
28(a)(7)	Summary of the Argument: concise statement of the arguments made in the body of the brief.
28(a)(9)	Conclusion: concise statement of the relief sought.
32(a)(7)(C)	Certificate of Compliance: attorney's certification that the brief complies with the court's type-volume limitation, including the word count or number of lines, as appropriate.
30(a)	Required Appendix: preceded by its own table of contents, a compilation of relevant docket entries; relevant portions of the pleadings, charges, findings, or opinions; the judgment, order, or opinion being appealed; and other parts of the record to be considered by the court.

REFLECTION, DISCUSSION, AND CHALLENGE QUESTIONS

Drafting Specialized Sections

- The federal rules governing appellate briefs neither expressly approve nor prohibit introduction sections in a brief. Would you include an introduction in your brief? Why or why not?
- Most courts require or at least permit parties to supply an appendix with the brief. At what point in the process should the appendix be compiled? What should you consider when deciding whether to include record and transcript material in the appendix?

Section 2   Revising to Please the Client and the Court

In addition to setting aside time for the brief's specialized sections and appendices, you must spend many hours revising your brief's primary sections. This section addresses the work to be done after completing a full draft of your brief, tailoring it to two crucial parties: your client and the court.

2.1   Client-Centered Revisions

An appellate advocate's client contact will be less than that of a trial lawyer. Although a trial lawyer must spend significant time consulting with her client to build her case, an appellate lawyer's time will instead be devoted to research and brief writing. There is no need to conduct intensive fact investigation, as the record will be settled by the time the appellate process begins. But you have an ethical obligation to remain in contact with your client,[32] and in any event, your client will surely have an opinion on matters relating to his appeal. Your client can be a valuable resource, especially if you were not counsel in the court below, because he is likely to be intimately familiar with the proceedings and may have strong ideas about what ought to be addressed on appeal. At the same time, an unsophisticated client may have no idea that his pet issues cannot be addressed on appeal because they lack record support or are not legally sound. For this reason, crafting a brief that is pleasing to the client can be a difficult task.

In revising your brief to please the client, your guiding principle should be your ethical duty to provide zealous advocacy. You must balance the story that your client wants to tell with the legal argument that you can plausibly present to the court — and ensure that your client understands the balancing process. The scopes and standards of review can be difficult enough for some lawyers to understand, let alone for a client unfamiliar with the legal process. You may need to explain why you have chosen to address an issue that the client does not feel strongly about, while omitting one that the client is passionate about but that is not ideally suited for review. Similarly, your client may need your assistance in understanding the nature of the relief a successful appeal will provide. For example, if you are representing a criminal defendant who was convicted in the court below, you may decide that your best appellate issue challenges only the sentence and not the conviction. It is up to you to make sure the client understands that if you succeed, he will still have a conviction on his record, but may spend less time in jail.

Practice Alert #2
Sample Specialized Sections

The online companion contains samples of properly formatted and paginated briefs, as well as examples of the specialized sections discussed above.

2.2 Court-Focused Revisions

It is just as crucial to consider the court's perspective. Although appellate judges are far from monolithic, Chapter 8 makes clear that as an audience, they share certain characteristics — and those characteristics should inform your revision process. Remember, appellate judges are busy, intelligent generalists with staggering reading and writing burdens of their own. They are skeptical by nature and will turn a critical eye towards every argument, every paragraph, every sentence, and every word. As we saw from Professor Tiscione's study, judges crave brevity, clarity, relentlessly forward-moving arguments, and transparent organization. They want you to tell them why the law matters, not leave it up to them to figure out. They also find incivility distasteful, so temper any vitriolic impulses you may have toward the opposing party or the lower court. A brief that harps on the appalling misconduct of the opposing party or the woeful incompetence of the lower court judge may only serve to make its author look petty or unreasonable, particularly if these characterizations are exaggerated in any way. A better brief will use record facts to illustrate such problems without resorting to personal attacks.

Keep in mind that judges are human too, and wish to be drawn into a piece of writing. As Chief Justice Roberts puts it:

> Think of the poor judge who is reading, again, hundreds and hundreds of these briefs. Liven their life up just a little bit . . . with something interesting. . . . [I]f it's in the course of the narrative and it's not going to be distracting, I think they'll appreciate it.[33]

In short, appellate judges are critical thinkers with no time for drama, and who want to grasp your arguments quickly and without difficulty. But they are also intrigued by compelling stories and interesting writing and want to decide cases of unusual significance. As you enter the many-layered revision process, keep these judicial audience traits front of mind and let them guide your choices.

There is a final, important aspect of revision that matters to both the client and the court: having a clean, easy-to-read, and error-free brief. Achieving this goal, however, takes a lot of time and effort over several rounds of revision. Recall from Chapter 7 that the final stage of your writing process is your hybrid role as both restaurant Expediter and Server — the people charged with assessing the final product critically to meet the consumer's needs. Here we flesh out what that dual role really entails by breaking out the varied tasks that you must complete. The chart below delineates these tasks, each of which should be the focus of a separate revision round.

> ### Expediter/Server Tasks
>
> - Revising to say what you mean
> - Revising as a proxy for your audience
> - Revising for consistency and coherence
> - Revising to improve flow and continuity
> - Revising to cut unnecessary arguments, sections, paragraphs, sentences, and words
> - Revising for style and voice
> - Revising for grammar
> - Revising for mechanical errors

"Re-seeing" the project. The object of the first few rounds of revision should be to "re-see" your entire project.[34] Look both inward and outward to: (1) resolve dissonance between what you meant to say and what you actually said; and (2) revisit your original decisions and explore better ways to connect with the audience.[35]

The first objective, resolving dissonance, means accepting that what is in your head is not always on the paper. Rhetoricians call this honoring the "felt sense"—the writer's internal thoughts about what he wants to get across.[36] All brief writers have experienced reading a draft and feeling uneasy about it because we did not say what we meant. For instance, you may have written too abstractly about a concept that was concrete in your mind's eye, used a progression whose logic does not unfurl the way it did in your head, or written about something entirely different from what you meant to write about. The writing needs retrofitting to match your intent. To retrofit, you might turn back into Executive Chef to rediscover your overall purpose, or become the Sous Chef again to reconfigure your ideas.

The second objective of early revisions is audience centered. Draft in hand, the writer can now shift perspective and become the reader, thinking about what will please the audience. For example, an appellate writer may revise to reverse his by-the-book, text-first, legislative-history-second statutory interpretation argument. His revised version might start with what motivated Congress to pass the legislation, because he now realizes that this structure gives the court context crucial to grasping the textual analysis that follows—and is a more interesting way to start. A writer whose original arguments converged on a logic-oriented theme about the opposing side's inconsistency might, in revising, discover that a story-bound theme emphasizing the client's harms will resonate more with the court. To generate these audience-oriented ideas in the first place, the writer may shift back to Executive Chef mode.[37] The writer can then shift back to her Sous Chef persona to integrate these new discoveries with structure and content likely to improve the audience's reaction.

Larger-scale revisions. You must also embrace the need for large-scale changes. And you must not hold tightly to words, sentences, or even organization in this process. The mark of an expert writer is complete openness to changes of all magnitude, until the writing both reflects the writer's meaning and meets rhetorical goals. As D.C. Circuit Judge Patricia Wald explains, only then is the writer free to begin smaller-scale revisions of paragraphs, sentences, and words:

> **[Line Cook mode:]** My first draft wanders; it is full of irrelevancies and blind alleys. I am driven by this overwhelming desire to get it over with. I savor nothing. It is a crude beginning. But when I finish that draft, I at least have definite clues as to what I am trying to say, and it often surprises me. **[Shift back to Sous Chef mode:]** It is at that point that I must decide if it is worth saying. If so, I go back, fill in blanks, check sources, and write topic headings or sentences so I have an outline in my head. . . . **[Expediter/ Server mode:]** It's usually not until later drafts, sometimes a fourth or fifth, or even sixth draft—if I am lucky—that I begin actually to enjoy the writing process in any sense, to indulge myself with the prediction that a point has been made or a pitfall avoided. Meanwhile, through all the successive drafts, I am cutting frantically. I persist in underestimating my own ability to communicate or my readers' ability to comprehend, and I say the same thing too many times.[38]

Therefore, once you have passed through your draft at least twice and made all the revisions you need to capture your intended meaning and to achieve an audience orientation, you can begin a new revision round—one that starts big. That means spending time just on larger-scale revisions for consistency and coherence, continuity and flow. You might shift back into Sous Chef and Line Cook personas at this point, moving chunks of writing that interrupt flow or fit better elsewhere, removing slow or ineffective arguments, adding transition paragraphs, or rewriting to pull points together more effectively.

Cutting. Now that you have improved the content and organization, it is time to cut.[39] Follow William Strunk's maxim here: "A sentence should contain no unnecessary words, a paragraph no unnecessary sentences, for the same reason that a drawing should have no unnecessary lines and a machine no unnecessary parts."[40] Be ruthless. Start with arguments, sections, and paragraphs, then move to sentences and words. After all, if you spend an entire revision cutting at the sentence level, only to strike later the paragraphs that contained those sentences, you have wasted your time.

Practice Alert #3
Expediter/Server Exercise

In this exercise in the online companion, you will take a poorly written argument and revise it over several rounds, each with a distinct revision purpose.

Clarity and precision. When you have finished cutting, it is time to revise for clarity and precision, style and vividness. Now you should evaluate each sentence individually; try to trim down the words and replace bland ones with more evocative choices. Only after you are satisfied that your writing is as crisp and clear as it can be and reflects your style and voice should you consider the work of copyediting — proofreading and fixing grammar mistakes.

All told, how many revisions does it take to finish off your work as Expediter/ Server? Judge Wald says that she revises her opinions no less than five times. For Justice Scalia, no less than five redrafts will do either.[41] When Justice Breyer wrote his book *Active Liberty*, he rewrote the entire text between 10 and 20 times.[42] If these eminent writers need revisions in this quantity, most of us need many more.

Novice vs. Expert Approaches to Revision[43]

Novice revision approaches	Expert revision approaches
Allocate little time for revision	Allocate more time to revision than any other writing task
View revision as a one-dimensional single pass through the first draft	View revision as a dynamic tool, applied with different purposes through several drafts
Use revision to correct errors, such as grammar problems, spelling gaffes, or incorrect word choices	Use revision to discover meaning and fit rhetorical goals
Develop fixed attachments to organization, sentences, and words	Willing to revisit big-picture structure, focus, and progression
Consider revision a painful, necessary evil borne of first draft "failures"	Consider revision a "treat" that gives the writer the luxury of better expressing meaning

REFLECTION, DISCUSSION, AND CHALLENGE QUESTIONS

Revising

- Should the client contribute to the brief-writing process? How and when?
- How would you resolve a disagreement with a client about whether an issue should be addressed in the briefs?
- Were you surprised to learn that writers at the top of the legal profession spend so much time revising their writing? Why do you think these experts still need so many revisions to craft excellent work product? Compare Judge Wald's writing and revising process to your own — what can you take from it, and what would not work for you?

2.3 Writing with Style and Developing Voice

Developing style and voice is an ongoing project for every writer. Because you will continue to experiment for some time rather than fully realizing those qualities in your current writing project, we address style and voice separately here.

As you advance as a lawyer — becoming increasingly adept at sound writing and analysis — you will be able to pay more attention to legal style and to cultivating your professional voice. Just as earlier parts of this book encouraged you to go "beyond IRAC" in your analysis, you should do the same in your writing. Legal argument infused with an authentic, confident tone captures the reader's attention and interest, increases your credibility, and, as a result, increases the likelihood that what you are saying will persuade. And that's the whole point. Remember that you are still relative beginners, still new to the discourse of the law.[44] Law school begins by stripping away your personal voice in writing in order to acclimate you to the very different writing of the law. This process of stripping away and rebuilding takes time; you will probably find yourself imitating others, faking it for a while. Once you are firmly situated in legal discourse, though, you can start to reassert your authorial presence.[45]

Style. Developing style and voice first requires you to know the difference between the two. Legal style, as we define it here, describes the objective nuances and writing conventions used in law. The elements of legal writing style are the foundation on which you cultivate your voice. Without a solid understanding of them, your writing will fall short because it cannot meet the expectations of your reader, who seeks clear, on-point, and unfussy prose.[46] The writer who ignores these legal writing fundamentals will be viewed as self-indulgent and undisciplined. Lots of lawyers have their own style "dos and don'ts" and some of these reflect personal preferences. But certain style principles are well established in legal writing, and below we list several that often pose problems for new lawyers. As you'll see, the driving forces in legal style are simplicity and clarity.

Principles of Legal Style and Grammar

Legal Style Principle	Example
Adverb usage Clearly, obviously, patently, plainly, surely	*Ineffective*: Plaintiff has clearly stated a prima facie case. *Effective*: Plaintiff has alleged all three elements of the prima facie case: (1) _____; (2) _____; and (3) _____.
Active vs. Passive Voice Active voice is preferred in almost all circumstances.	*Ineffective*: The defendant was found guilty by the jury. *Effective*: The jury found the defendant guilty.

Legal Style Principle	Example
Although vs. While "Although" introduces counterargument. "While" indicates temporal spans.	Although courts in other jurisdictions have adopted the rule, the courts in this jurisdiction have not.
Because vs. Since "Because" shows causality. "Since" indicates the passing of time.	The court overruled counsel's objection because the witness's statement was relevant. Since last week the court has held several more trials.
Dates Use two commas when combining a date and a year but no commas when combining a month and a year.	On July 7, 2015, she filed a motion to dismiss. In July 2015 she filed a motion to dismiss.
Hyphens vs. Dashes A hyphen connects two words that function together as one concept; an en dash indicates a span; an em dash indicates a break in thought.	Court-appointed lawyer The witness's testimony is contained in the trial transcript on pages 23–34. A court reporter has one task—to create a record of each hearing.
Legalisms	*Avoid*: aforesaid, henceforth, herein, thereafter, etc. *Try instead*: previous, from now on, here, etc.
Nominalization Turning verbs into bloated nouns.	*Ineffective*: The judge made a determination of the issues. *Correct*: The judge determined the issues.
Parallelism Each item in a list must be grammatically identical.	*Ineffective*: To avoid collection proceedings, the debtor immediately made payments to his landlord, his bank, and to cover his credit card balance.
That vs. Which "Which" is used only after a comma to set off nonessential information; "That" is used the rest of the time.	The contract, which was signed in 2009, is enforceable. The delay that happened yesterday . . .

Once you have studied and internalized the elements of legal style, you may find that your writing is mechanical and sparse. But if it is for a time, it need not remain that way. Legal writing can be pleasing and interesting, elegant and fluid. Spartan and bare-bones prose is just a stepping-stone on the necessary path towards legal writing mastery. And that is where voice comes in.

Voice. Defining voice in writing is a slippery task. Some define voice solely in terms of language; others add in the author's analytical choices.[47] Scholars also subdivide the notion of voice between the personal/human and the professional.[48] For our purposes, a hybrid of these is your ultimate goal: to develop a voice that melds your own personal writing qualities with professional discourse principles. The voice of professional legal discourse is difficult to generalize, but in its ideal form is often described as formal but conversational, confident, precise, and direct. The elements that project the author's personal presence in the text have been described by Judge Posner as:

> not only vocabulary and grammar but also the often tacit principles governing the length and complexity of sentences, the organization of sentences into larger units such as paragraphs, and the level of formality at which to pitch the writing. These tools are used not just to communicate an idea but also to establish a mood and perhaps a sense of the writer's personality.[49]

In short, your legal writing voice encompasses both the writing skills you brought to law school and your internalization of the legal writing principles learned since.

Development strategies. Developing voice is a process. You will need time and practice, but the sooner you start, the sooner it will enter your muscle memory. First, you need to make sure you are comfortable with the professional discourse element, writing as a lawyer using the tools acquired during your law school experience. Then build your repertoire of professional discourse elements by reading different lawyers' and judges' writings and analyzing them—much as Chapter 7 advised as a technique for adopting the writing mindset. As you read, see if you can figure out what voice elements and techniques define these writers' briefs and opinions, and identify which ones resonate with you. After you feel comfortably steeped in the discourse of law, you can start the process of making it your own.

Your next task is to develop your personal authorial voice in the context of law. To begin that process, candidly and critically assess your pre-law-school writing style and voice, if indeed you had one. Even if you have historically been considered (or considered yourself) a "good" writer, you need to figure out precisely what qualities appealed to those who read your writing. If your strength was logical flow, keep that, but assess whether your writing might be too clinical or dry. If your writing was described as descriptive or imaginative, you'll want to maintain your rich vocabulary and interesting syntax, but watch out because you may be prone to repetition, wandering, and wordiness. If you do not know your pre-law writing style, do some reflective, nonlaw writing and analyze it. And ask others to read it as well. Once armed with the knowledge of the writing qualities you bring to the table, you are ready to develop them further in the context of the law. Take a judicial opinion and try to translate it into a different author's voice. Then take a stab at editing that same sample as if it were your own. Circle back to make sure that you are not violating the fundamentals of legal style and then continue on. Eventually your professional voice in the law will emerge, and you will spend the rest of your career honing and improving it.

Section 3   Looks Matter: Persuading Through Formatting and Technology

Your breif's overarching goal is to persuade, and aside from how the brief reads, your document's physical appearance plays a larger role than you might suspect. After you have spent hundreds of hours poring over the record, researching the law, and crafting your arguments, it would be a shame to have all of that work marginalized by your design choices. Thus, an integral part of late-stage brief preparation is to make your document visually easy and interesting to read; if you do that, the reader will find you more credible, will be grateful for your efforts, and will be more open to what you have to say. You can also employ visual techniques that make your arguments easier to remember. We explore below the two main components of visual presentation: (1) the typography and the text itself; and (2) the use of demonstrative visuals to increase the impact of your message. Finally, at the end of the chapter, we introduce you to the nascent issue of whether you can and should make your brief tech-friendly for tablet readers or through the use of hyperlinks and other conventions.

A caveat before we begin: Your formatting and organizational choices must always conform to the court's rules. For example, the Federal Rules of Appellate Procedure mandate double-spaced text in the body of a brief, margins of at least one inch on each side of the page, and 14-point or larger font.[50] Several circuits supplement or modify these rules,[51] so it is important to check those first, and if the court requires a certain font that you wouldn't otherwise use for the reasons we explain below, you obviously must defer to those rules.

3.1   Persuading Through Typography and Text

In her excellent article *Painting with Print*, law professor Ruth Ann Robbins exhaustively analyzes how a writer's formatting and organizational choices impact the document's overall effectiveness.[52] She first focuses on what she calls the legibility of the typed text, which includes capitalization, emphasis, font choice, text size, and spacing choices. Each of these things directly influences ease and speed of reading.[53] First, writers should avoid the use of all-caps, both in headings and in the text. Capitalization slows a reader down by 12-15 percent and creates extra work for the reader, the opposite of what you intend.[54] Bolding and italics can be useful for emphasis, if used sparingly. Second, for font choice, writers should opt for serif fonts, rather than the sans-serif variety, because the serifs provide continuity and lead the reader's eye more quickly and easily to the next letter and word.[55] Take a look at the following example, one in the classic serif font Garamond and the other in the sans serif Arial:

The district court erred in granting BigCorp's motion to dismiss.

The district court erred in granting BigCorp's motion to dismiss.

Other good serif fonts include Century Schoolbook, Times New Roman, and Georgia. Third, writers should use proportionally spaced fonts rather than mono-space fonts because they, too, are easier to read. See that the difference below between proportionally spaced Times New Roman and `Courier` font:

The district court erred in granting BigCorp's motion to dismiss.

```
The district court erred in granting BigCorp's motion to
dismiss.
```

It simply takes longer (exactly 4.7 percent longer, to be precise) to read the mono-spaced type.[56] Finally, don't neglect the white space on the page. Graphic artists recommend that no more than 50 percent of the page be covered with type.[57] As a result, margins, spacing, indentation, and justification all must be consciously considered when crafting the document. A word about justification: Although some courts adhere to the professional-printer convention of full justification, most design experts agree that left-justified is simply easier to read because it avoids the extra spacing between words and the resulting "rivers" of text within a paragraph.[58]

Once you've addressed these baseline legibility issues, you should examine your brief's organizational techniques to make sure you are maximizing the persuasive visual potential there as well. The essential component is the use of headings, which divide up what would otherwise be a daunting mass of text into easily digestible chunks.[59] Headings allow the reader to keep track of the overall structure of your argument and—if written well and persuasively—to remember the details contained within it as well.[60] As we discussed in Chapter 11, draw your reader's eye to your headings by single-spacing them, writing them in regular text (not all-caps), and then bolding them.

3.2 Using Demonstrative Visuals in Your Brief

Though more often used at the trial level in demonstrative exhibits, visual aids also work in briefs. If a picture is worth a thousand words, these "magazine briefs"[61]—a term coined by Peter Bensinger at Bartlit Beck Herman Palenchar & Scott LLP—persuade by powerfully delivering your arguments in shorthand and in a different, visual medium. Building on the work of such information-design visionaries as Edward Tufte, magazine briefs use several techniques to show a reader very quickly what would take pages to explain in text, ultimately less effectively.[62] Visual displays cater to a broader audience, and allow readers to understand the concepts more easily[63] Two of Tufte's techniques are particularly effective in the context of legal briefs and especially in factual narratives: (1) using small multiples and other demonstrative graphics that convey loads of information through a single image; and (2) using gray-scale and white space to minimize "noise" in your document.[64] At a minimum, appellate advocates should not shy away from integrating exhibits into the text of the brief, where they will be most effective, rather than relegating them to the appendix.

Small multiples are visuals that "work as efficient and convincing summaries of data or an argument, making the same point again and again by offering complementary variations on the major substantive theme."[65] One of the most iconic examples of this is Tufte's children's shirt collection, which as you can see, "move[s] to the heart of visual reasoning — to see, distinguish, choose . . . relying on an active eye to select and make contrasts rather than on bygone memories of images scattered over pages and . . . pages." As you can see, the eye immediately sorts and categorizes the differences among the shirts in an effective and efficient way something paragraphs of prose simply cannot accomplish:[66]

In the context of the law specifically, briefs, in a simple way. Reproduced below is a graphic timeline included in a brief by Barlit Beck Herman Palenchar & Scott LLP. Notice how it communicates, simply and easily, what would have taken pages of prose to describe:[67]

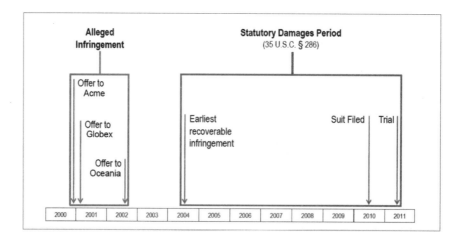

The second Tufte principle is to minimize stark black and white and integrate grays. Like the use of all-caps, overuse of bold black grid lines against the brief's white paper creates "noise" without adding information; it is tiring and hard to read.[68] See the following example:

Relevant sentencing ranges				
	Statutory section applicable to possession of 13 grams	Statutory sentencing range (years)	Relevant Guidelines range (months)	Minimum supervised release (years)
Pre-FSA	§ 841(b)(1)(B) (5–50 grams)	5–40	262–327	4
Post-FSA	§ 841(b)(1)(C) (0–28 grams)	0–20	210–240	3

Relevant sentencing ranges

	Statutory section RE: possession of 13 grams	Statutory Sentencing range (years)	Guidelines range (months)	Minimum supervised release (years)
Pre-FSA	§ 841(b)(1)(B) (5–50 grams)	5–40	262–327	4
Post-FSA	§ 841(b)(1)(C) (0–28 grams)	0–20	210–240	3

By eliminating unnecessary grid lines, the reader's eyes are drawn to the important information contained within the boxes, not to the boxes themselves.

Finally, even if you don't need fancy charts and grids in your brief, you may want to consider importing exhibits or other demonstratives into the text where they will be more effective. On the following pages we reproduce four brief excerpts that embed demonstratives within argumentative text.

EXAMPLE

The only other corroborating evidence that the defendant had crack was Wilbert's and Groning's respective visual observations of the substance, which are hardly conclusive because "powder" cocaine can in fact look rocky. *See Cocaine*, U.S. Drug Enforcement Agency, http://www.justice.gov/dea/pr/multimedia-library/image-gallery/images_cocaine.shtml (last visited Apr. 2, 2013) (depicting various images of cocaine and crack, two of which are reproduced below); *see also* United States v. Fuller, 532 F.3d 656, 660-61 (7th Cir. 2008) (recognizing that powder cocaine can be "rerocked").

Image of Powder Cocaine, available at http://www.justice.gov/dea/pr/multimedia-library/image-gallery/cocaine/cocaine_hcl3.jpg

Image of Crack Cocaine, available at http://www.justice.gov/dea/pr/multimedia-library/image-gallery/cocaine/crack_cocaine2.jpg

Absent any forensic analysis and given the contradictory presence of the straws, a *reasonable* jury could have concluded that these subjective visual observations did not prove beyond a reasonable doubt that the substance was indeed crack and not merely, say, cocaine.

EXAMPLE

The photo array was unduly suggestive. Police composed the photo array in a way that overemphasized the "freckle-ish, pale skin" that Thompson found so important to his identification. (*See, e.g.*, App. A. 10.) Further, the photo was then enlarged, skewing the contrast and emphasizing those features to an even greater degree.

EXAMPLE

The officer testified that one image—image 13A-33—depicted what "appear[ed] to be crack cocaine" being transferred from the defendant to the informant.

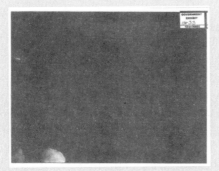

Government Exhibit 13A-33

Yet the video depicts nothing more than a momentary flash of white in the bottom corner of an otherwise black screen. Nothing about this image would lead one to independently conclude that it showed a transfer of crack cocaine.

Bartlit Beck has used similar graphic representations with considerable success. Here is a demonstrative from one of its briefs:[69]

The judge adapted and included the demonstrative in the court's final opinion.[70]

3.3   The Role of Technology in Brief Writing

In future editions of this book we expect this section to be much more extensive. As it stands now, the law simply has not caught up with technology. The United States Supreme Court is only now preparing to offer e-filing. So it should come as no surprise that neither courts nor the lawyers who practice before them are particularly savvy about using technology in briefing. What is more, tablet technology does not accommodate legal briefs particularly well. Hyperlinks take readers away from the primary document, note-taking is difficult, footnotes are hard to read, and the court may not have the programs to best access your electronic brief. Moreover, court rules generally do not account for — and may actually proscribe — formatting techniques that make e-reading easier.[71] For example, what if your brief hyperlinks to Lexis, but your court uses only Westlaw? Or what if your case law hyperlink requires the user to sign in with her personal password, thus making the task harder rather than easier?

We can envision a day in the not-so-distant future when technology will permit lawyers to file tablet-friendly briefs that contain embedded pop-up windows showing cited authority and record documents. For the time being, however, we merely need to account for the fact that most judges read electronic versions of briefs on their PCs, rather than hard copies, when electronic briefs are available.[72] Providing the court with a brief that is tailored to PC reading will lead judges and clerks to rely more heavily on your brief and to spend more time engaging with your arguments. As outlined in the chart below, paper briefs and electronic briefs should ideally be constructed differently to take into account the differences in how people read in each medium. Yet courts generally require that the electronic version be identical to the paper version.[73] Given this reality, we simply highlight the differences between paper reading, PC reading, and tablet reading, and hope that technology and court rules eventually catch up.

Differences Between Paper, PC, and Tablet Reading

	Paper Brief	PC Brief	Tablet Brief
How People Interact with the Brief	Immersed in single text and read it slowly and fully, one task at a time and immersed in the single text.	Read it fully but may engage in some multi-tasking.	Skim and multitask most.[74] Use the F-pattern, which means the reader focuses on the left side of the page and does not read everything.[75]
	Limited universe of information.	Unlimited information at fingertips (and distractions).	No windows in tablets discourages jumping away from the document.
	Must have physical brief with you to access.	Electronic version makes it accessible in many places, but access is not immediate (must sign in, connect to Internet, etc.).	Immediate access, which may result in reading in short spurts rather than prolonged interaction with the document.[76]
Formatting	Typical heading hierarchy used (I., A., 1., etc.)	Typical heading hierarchy used (I., A., 1., etc.)	Scientific numbering better (1.1, 1.2, etc.) Left-align headings to accommodate F-Pattern reading.
Structure	No bookmarks	Bookmarks to link to TOC and to prevent scrolling	Bookmarks to link to TOC and to prevent scrolling, but must be edited to be shorter[78]
	No hyperlinks	Some hyperlinks, but not too many[77]	Some hyperlinks, but not too many
	Prose, longer paragraphs with full explication of the arguments	Prose, longer paragraphs with full explication of the arguments	Visible structure, lists, bullets, topic sentences important to accommodate F-Pattern reading
	Standard text length	Standard text length	Shorter text is better

	Paper Brief	**PC Brief**	**Tablet Brief**
Footnotes	Easily accessible at the bottom of the page	Require scrolling	Hard to access
External Sources	Not easily accessible	Most easily accessible with multiple windows at fingertips	Somewhat accessible

REFLECTION, DISCUSSION, AND CHALLENGE QUESTIONS

Readability

- What writing habits do you already have that increase or decrease the readability of your writing?

Section 4 Filing and Serving the Brief

You have now researched your issues, written your brief, prepared the required special sections and appendix, and formatted the entire document to maximize its readability. The only thing left is putting the brief in front of the court to which you are appealing and serving opposing counsel. The manner of filing and the number of briefs that must be filed and served are governed by court rules. In federal courts, the default requirement is to provide 25 bound copies of the brief to the clerk of court, and two copies to unrepresented parties or to other parties' counsel, although many circuits require a different number of briefs to be filed at the court.[79] Many courts now permit or even require electronic filing in addition to hard copies of the brief, though the federal rules are silent about it.[80] The court's website will provide direction on whether electronic filing is required and how it is accomplished.

When a court allows for — or requires — electronic filing, do not take this as an opportunity to wait until a few hours before the deadline to file the brief. An Internet outage, missing or outdated court log-in information, confusion over how to properly classify the document, when electronically filing, general computer failure, and other unexpected circumstances can all foil the best-laid plan. If a brief is due at midnight, ensure that all the required information and resources are in place during normal business hours to avoid a last-minute scramble requiring technical or other support. An attorney who waits until the last minute to file puts undue pressure on herself and her team.

Do not forget the importance of properly serving opposing counsel. Courts that allow electronic filing may also require you to serve hard copies in addition to electronic service. Before filing, ensure that you have opposing counsel's proper contact information. After filing and serving, you may sit back, relax, and wait for a response.

Endnotes

1. MARIE LEARY, ANALYSIS OF BRIEFING REQUIREMENTS OF THE FEDERAL COURTS OF APPEALS 1 (2004).
2. Lance Curry, *No Introduction Needed? The Effectiveness of Introductions in Appellate Briefs*, THE RECORD, JOURNAL OF THE APPELLATE PRACTICE SECTION OF THE FLORIDA BAR 12-13 (Winter 2011).
3. David J. Perlman, *How to Write an Introduction*, APPELLATE ISSUES, COUNCIL OF APPELLATE LAWYERS 1 (Spring 2012).
4. *Id.* at 2.
5. FED. R. APP. P. 32(a)(2).
6. *Id.*
7. FED. R. APP. P. 28(a)(1).
8. *E.g.*, FED. CIR. R. 28(a)(1), 47.4.
9. D.C. CIR. R. 28(a)(1).
10. FED. R. APP. P. 28(a)(2).
11. 11TH CIR. R. 28-1(d).
12. FED. R. APP. P. 28(a)(3).
13. *Id.*
14. D.C. CIR. R. 28(a)(1)(C).
15. FED. R. APP. P. 28(a)(4).
16. FED. R. APP. P. 28(a)(6).
17. 11TH CIR. R. 28-1(i).
18. FED. R. APP. P. 28(a)(7).
19. FED. R. APP. P. 28(a)(9).
20. 10TH CIR. R. 28.2(C)(4).
21. FED. R. APP. P. 32(a)(7)(C).
22. 5TH CIR. R. 32.3.
23. FED. R. APP. P. 30(a).
24. FED. R. APP. P. 30(b).
25. *See* 10TH CIR. R. 30.1(A)(1) ("The appellant must file an appendix sufficient for considering and deciding the issues on appeal.").
26. *E.g.*, 7TH CIR. R. 30(a).
27. *E.g.*, 11TH CIR. R. 30-1(a)(1); FED. CIR. R. 30(a)(2)(A).
28. *E.g.*, 11TH CIR. R. 30-1(a)(9).
29. *E.g.*, 5TH CIR. R. 30.1.4(g).
30. 10TH CIR. R. 30.1(C)(4).
31. *See, e.g.*, 7TH CIR. R. 30(7) (permitting the appendix to be bound with the brief if it does not exceed 50 pages); FED. CIR. R. 30(d) (permitting the appendix to be bound with the brief if is does not exceed 100 pages).
32. MODEL RULES OF PROF'L CONDUCT R. 1.4(a) (1983).
33. Bryan A. Garner, *Interviews with United States Supreme Court Justices*, 13 SCRIBES J. LEGAL WRITING 1, 18 (2010) (interview with Chief Justice Roberts).
34. *See, e.g.*, Christopher M. Anzidei, *The Revision Process in Legal Writing: Seeing Better to Write Better*, 8 LEGAL WRITING: J. LEGAL WRITING INST. 23, 45-47 (2002).
35. *Id.* at 44.
36. *See, e.g., Id.* at 31-34; Sondra Perl, *Understanding Composing*, 31 C. COMPOSITION & COMM. 363, 365-69 (1980) (attributing "felt sense" to University of Chicago philosopher Eugene Gendlin).
37. Anzidei, *supra* note 34, at 48; Linda Flower & John R. Hayes, *A Cognitive Process Theory of Writing*, 32 C. COMPOSITION & COMM. 365, 375 (1981).
38. Patricia M. Wald, *"How I Write" Essays*, 4 SCRIBES J. LEGAL WRITING 55, 55-56 (1993) (bold alterations added).
39. ROY P. CLARK, WRITING TOOLS: 50 ESSENTIAL STRATEGIES FOR EVERY WRITER 50 (2006).
40. *Id.*
41. Garner, supra note 33, at 67 (Interview with Justice Scalia).
42. *Id.* at 145 (Interview with Justice Breyer).
43. *See* Anzidei, *supra* note 34, at 34-44; Nancy Soonpaa, *Using Composition Theory and Scholarship to Teach Legal Writing More Effectively*, 3 LEGAL WRITING: J. LEGAL WRITING INST. 81, 90-95 (1997).
44. J. Christopher Rideout, *Voice, Self and Persona in Legal Writing*, 67 J. OF THE LEGAL WRITING INSTITUTE 67, 80 (2009) ("[V]oicing occurs, not independently of the text, but through the text itself, and through the discourse in which the text is located.").

45. Andrea McArdle, *Teaching Writing in Clinical, Lawyering, and Legal Writing Courses: Negotiating Professional and Personal Voice*, 12 Clinical L. Rev 501, 512 (2006); *see also* Rideout, *supra* note 44, at 101.

46. Gerald Wetlaufer, *Rhetoric and Its Denial in Legal Discourse*, 76 Va. L. Rev. 1545, 1588-89 (1990) (A "lawyer's attention to clarity, order and relevance in discourse . . . appears to be an unmitigated virtue. . . . [W]e are less likely to wander or to waste time attending to matters that are irrelevant.").

47. Rideout, *supra* note 44, at 72, 78 (quoting Peter Elbow) (defining voice as "a sound, a texture, a rhythm" and "words that capture the sound of an individual on the page"); Richard A. Posner, *Judge's Writing Styles (And Do They Matter)*, 62 U. Chi. L. Rev. 1420, 1422 (1995) (suggesting that some adopt a broad definition that merges style with rhetoric).

48. Rideout, *supra* note 44, at 73, 81 (distinguishing between personal and professional voice) (internal citations omitted); Julius G. Getman, *Colloquy: Human Voice in Legal Discourse*, 66 Tex. L. Rev. 577, 582 (1988) (describing human voice as "language that uses ordinary concepts and familiar situations without professional ornamentation in order to analyze legal issues").

49. Posner, *supra* note 47, at 1422.

50. Fed. R. App. P. 32(a)(4)-(5).

51. *See, e.g.*, 5th Cir. R. 32.1 (permitting footnotes in 12-point or larger font); 7th Cir. R. 32(b) (permitting 12-point or larger font in the body of a brief and 11-point or larger in the footnotes).

52. Ruth Ann Robbins, *Painting with Print: Incorporating Concepts of Typographic and Layout Design into the Text of Legal Writing Documents*, 2 J. Ass'n Legal Writing Directors 108 (2004).

53. *Id.* at 114.

54. *Id.* at 115-16.

55. *Id.* at 119-20.

56. *Id.* at 120-21.

57. *Id.* at 124.

58. *Id.* at 130; Practitioner's Handbook for Appeals to the United States Court of Appeals for the Seventh Circuit 133 (2014).

59. Robbins, *supra* note 52, at 124-25.

60. *Id.* at 125-26.

61. Peter Bensinger, Jr., *Magazine Briefs*, Bartlit Beck Herman Palenchar & Scott LLP (2000), *available at* http://www.bartlit-beck.com/media/news/10_article_92800.pdf.

62. Edward R. Tufte, Envisioning Information (1990).

63. *Id.* at 31.

64. *Id.* at 30-31, 33, 59-63, 68.

65. *Id.* at 30.

66. *Id.* at 33.

67. Bartlit Beck Herman Palenchar & Scott LLP © 2014.

68. Edward R. Tufte, Envisioning Information 63 (1990).

69. Bartlit Beck Herman Palenchar & Scott LLP © 2014.

70. Memorandum Opinion & Order, Rolls Royce PLC v. United Technologies Corp., 2011 WL 1740143, at *9 (E.D. Va. May 4, 2011).

71. *Compare* 2d Cir. R. 25.1 (addressing how hyperlinks may be used in electronically filed documents) *with* 8th Cir. R. 25(a) (requiring only that electronically filed documents be in PDF format and addressing no other formatting issues).

72. Robert Dubose, *Writing Appellate Briefs for Tablet Readers*, Spring 2012 Appellate Issues 9, 10.

73. *See, e.g.*, 3d Cir. L.A.R. 113.1(c); 5th Cir. R. 25.2.

74. Dubose, *supra* note 72, at 12.

75. *Id.* at 11-12.

76. *Id.* at 12.

77. *Id.* at 15.

78. *Id.* at 14.

79. Fed. R. App. P. 31(b).

80. *See, e.g.*, Fed. R. App. P. 25; 7th Cir. R. 25(a); 7th Cir. R. 31(b); 11th Cir. R. 31-3.

13 Special Types of Briefs

Armed with the advanced appellate advocacy techniques from the preceding chapters, you can now apply the same principles to the wide variety of briefs that you will encounter as an appellate lawyer. This chapter tackles four specialized briefs: (1) response and reply briefs; (2) amicus briefs; (3) administrative agency appeals briefs, and (4) briefs seeking discretionary review, including certiorari petitions to the United States Supreme Court. Within each section we flag these briefs' similarities to the garden variety appellant's brief discussed in the preceding chapters More importantly, we flag their differences.

Section 1 Response and Reply Briefs

Responses (filed by the appellee) and reply briefs (filed by the appellant last in the trio of briefs in a typical appeal) share many of the same characteristics of the opening brief: (1) they have specialized sections and formatting requirements; (2) they pay careful attention to the standard of review; (3) they must be the result of a thorough investigation of the record and relevant authority; (4) they must convey your legal theory and theme; (5) they must be well organized and persuasively written; and (5) they must be revised to perfection. But these briefs are also different. The most obvious difference? Their fundamental purpose: to answer the other side's arguments.

The practical consequences of this distinction play out in a couple of ways. First, the issues have already been selected and framed. You cannot ignore or fail to address any nonfrivolous issue. You also cannot fundamentally change the appellant's arguments, though you may be able to steer the judge's attention in a different direction through standard of review or subtle re-tooling of the existing arguments. For example, in one case, an appellant relied on common law precedent to claim that the lower court erred in admitting certain evidence. But because the state supreme court had only recently codified its rules of evidence and explicitly patterned them after the federal rules, the appellee reframed the argument as rules based, rather than common law based, which in turn opened up a new world of precedent interpreting the applicable rule. Fundamentally, the question was the same — erroneous admission of evidence — but the angle from which the appellee approached it was different.

A second difference is that responsive briefs may be less burdensome than the appellant's opening brief. Much of the heavy lifting on the specialized sections and the required appendices falls on the appellant's shoulders, for court rules provide that the appellee does not need to include certain sections if he does not object to the appellant's version of them. That said, an appellee should never pass up an opportunity to persuade in one of these sections if appropriate. Reply briefs do not have any specialized sections beyond the table of contents, table of authorities, and the required end-of-brief certifications. Beyond these baseline similarities, though, responses and replies are very different creatures.

1.1 The Appellee's Response Brief

As the appellee, you have a strong arrow in your quiver: The trial court ruled in your favor below. This benefit is counterbalanced somewhat by the fact that your brief is sandwiched between two appellant's briefs, and the appellant gets the last word. Still, you should not underestimate the power of having the lower court on your side. Remember from Chapter 3 that the national affirmance rate in federal appeals is high; so too, then, is your chance of prevailing. To maximize those chances, your brief should: (1) play up the favorable procedural posture of having won below; (2) keenly focus on issue preservation and standards of review as your first line of defense; and (3) strategically respond to the appellant's arguments with your own affirmative theory, not a defensive one.

Identifying your arguments. But first things first. You should review the record completely before anything else, particularly if you were not counsel below. Even if you were, many months have passed since you last thought about this case and your memory of events may differ from what actually occurred. Ideally, you would complete this record review and digesting before you receive the appellant's brief and certainly before beginning any research or writing. Assuming you have completed all of the record review and process-based steps outlined in Chapter 4, your next step is to exhaustively analyze the other side's brief. This step takes the place of the argument development and assessment work for appellants discussed in Chapter 6, section 1. The appellant has selected the issues and arguments, so you must now turn your attention to dismantling them alongside your own affirmative case. One helpful approach is to create a brief analysis chart where you record the other side's arguments and authorities, your potential responses, relevant facts, and open research questions. Such a chart forces you to approach the appellant's brief slowly and methodically, and ensures that you don't miss anything. It looks something like this:

Appellant Argument	SOR Challenge?	Appellant Authority	Appellee Response	Appellee Authority	Research/ Comments
In deciding whether two statutory violations do, in fact, constitute separate offenses for Double Jeopardy purposes, the first step is to determine from the text and legislative history of the statute what Congress intended.	Claims de novo, but did not preserve this precise argument below. Focused instead on the reasoning of *Prince*, which is not a double-jeopardy case. Argue for plain error.	*Garrett*, *Albernaz*, *Simpson*	The question is not immediately one of double jeopardy but rather one of congressional intent to impose multiple punishments. The doctrine of constitutional avoidance and the rule of lenity could counsel a different result.	*Prince*, *Bell*, *Universal CIT*, *Gore*, *Gaddis*, *Simpson*	What is the background on double jeopardy and the interplay of *Blockburger* in that analysis? Does the State correctly frame up the test?
Blockburger is the test for constitutionality in Double Jeopardy inquiries.		*Dixon*	But only when the test actually applies.	*Jeffers*, *Ladner*	Get a copy of the statute at issue in *Blockburger*.

This analysis chart allows you to accomplish several things. First, you can pinpoint standard-of-review challenges that you might be able to mount. As you can see from this example, the appellee believes that the appellant may be asserting an argument that it did not pursue below, thus opening up an argument for plain error review. From this analysis chart, you can also begin to categorize arguments in a way that builds your own affirmative case. In the example above, you can see how the appellee has identified the appellant's argument, and is asserting her own framework to answer the question, rather than blindly accepting the appellant's premise. The appellant says that *Blockburger* is the governing test for all cases; the appellee says that there are other doctrines that apply before reaching *Blockburger*, and those may warrant a different result. What you should take from this is that although you must operate within the issues the appellant identifies, you are not completely bound to the appellant's structure or organization. As Chapter 10 explained, you can even address the issues in a different order than the opening brief, so long as you provide a good roadmap and rationale for doing so at the outset.

Practice Alert #1 Brief Analysis Chart

This exercise in the online companion allows you to take a stab at crafting an analysis chart for a response or reply brief with the supplied examples or your own appeal briefs.

Finally and relatedly, a chart can help you engage in a meta-analysis of the other side's brief, which will in turn help with developing your opposing theory and theme. Try to define, in plain language, what large-scale rhetorical tactic the other side is using and determine its weaknesses. Does the appellant ignore a threshold inquiry or try to recast unfavorable facts or law in a less than convincing way? Can you detect a pattern to the other side's approach? If so, tell the court what the other side is up to. This global assessment of the other side's brief simultaneously provides at least part of your theme, adds another compelling reason for your position, and leads the judges to question the strength of the opposing arguments. This approach works well for reply briefs as well.

Outlining and drafting your arguments. Once you have identified your affirmative arguments, you should draft an outline to ensure that you have organized your points in the most persuasive and effective way. Your organizational structure as the appellee must account for the variables particular to your responsive position in the appeal. You should start first with any challenges to the appellant's proposed standards of review. Argue forcefully for the reasons why the issues are not preserved or subject to a more deferential standard. Then, you can move onto the merits of your argument. When you do, remember Chapter 11, Section 4.2's responsive argument strategy to be affirmative, not defensive, while simultaneously undercutting the other side's position. Compare the following two examples:

The government states that the public interests in having alibi-notice statutes will "apply differently" in cases where a defendant testifies to an alibi on his own behalf as opposed to a witness testifying for the defendant. (Gov. Br. at 28.) However, in *Alicea*, this Court does not make this distinction. In the case, this Court states that it is reviewing the "history and purpose of alibi notice statutes" and does not specify that this review, and the public interests the court annunciates, are confined to alibi-notice statutes that apply only to defendants testifying on their own behalf. Alicea v. Gagnon, 675 F.2d 913, 916 (7th Cir. 1982).	The critical rationale of this Court's *Alicea* decision applies equally to a defendant's own testimony and a defense witness's testimony. Alicea v. Gagnon, 675 F.2d 913, 916 (7th Cir. 1982) (emphasizing the court's reliance on the public interests, history, and purpose of alibi-notice statutes but not distinguishing between types of alibi testimony). Therefore the government cannot prevail based on this facile distinction. (Gov't Br. 28 n.5) (claiming that there are "good reasons to believe . . ." but not explaining why or how those public interests might apply differently in the two contexts).

Notice how the first is less persuasive because it places the other side's argument right up front and forces the author to claw back her position from the other side's framing of the issue. The framing of the first example also requires additional explanation of the case in that long third sentence. The second example, however, packs more punch in a very economical way. The first sentence simultaneously affirms the client's position and undercuts the opponent's, while the parenthetical continues the takedown by delivering essential information in a strategic way. The second sentence is devoted to further dismantling of the other side's position.

Aside from directly integrating responses into your affirmative points, another valuable strategy in dismantling arguments is to point out their weaknesses. A smart appellant will have minimized these, so your job is to capitalize on them.[1] Did the appellant rely on marginal authority or shade the facts in a way not supported by the record? Did the appellant waive or concede any important points? Marshall all of these reasons into a cohesive whole and show them to the court as reasons why the appellant's position falls on the wrong side of the law and of good policy.

You also should take advantage of your best procedural weapon: The lower court found in your favor. Quote liberally from the memorandum opinion or order and devote lots of airtime to the trial judge's reasoning. A word of caution though: Sometimes the trial judge's reasoning is wrong; you must nonetheless defend the outcome, which can be a challenge. One strategy is to first mention and defend the trial court's faulty reasoning, and then follow up immediately with your own alternative and complementary reasoning that likewise merits affirmance. An appellate court can affirm on any basis evident from the record,[2] so you can use this to your advantage even when you are having trouble defending the trial judge's precise rationale.

**Practice Alert #2
Comparing the Structures Between Opening and Response Briefs**

In the online companion you will find sample point headings and summaries of arguments from opening and response briefs from the same case. Identify the differences in approach between the two.

Your final task is to account for the fact that another brief—the reply—will follow yours. Consider the appellant's likely response to your argument and, if you think it could be damaging, preemptively address and rebut it using the preemptive argument strategies discussed in Chapter 11, Section 4.1. For example, in the brief analysis chart above, you could anticipate based on your research that courts apply the rule of lenity rarely and only to grievous statutory ambiguities. You can expect that the appellant will seize on this line of authority, so better for you to take some of the sting out of it yourself. You should acknowledge that it is applied rarely, but then explain why your case justifies it. Dealing with opposing arguments head-on in your response brief will make it more powerful and compelling.

1.2 The Appellant's Reply Brief

The reply brief—when executed correctly—can be one of the most useful and important parts in an appeal. Sadly, these briefs are often neglected, and are therefore ineffective and even frustrating. Put yourself in the judges' (and their clerks') position: You have two briefs with polar opposite takes on the same issue. You want and need help figuring out who is correct. When a reply brief arrives that either fails to address the other side's key arguments or merely repeats in rote fashion the arguments in the opening brief, you have sorely disappointed those who were hoping for your help. Aside from the assistance you can provide to your ultimate audience, the reply carries significant strategic benefits. It is not only your sole chance to respond to the appellee's arguments, you get the last word, a powerful tool in your persuasive arsenal.

Replies are short, to the point, and must be completed very quickly. In federal court, appellants have 14 days to complete a reply and they are limited to half the words of the opening brief.[3] Unlike response briefs, which usually contain additional specialized sections, such as a statement of the case, statement of the facts, and a summary of the argument, reply briefs have no such window dressing. They are all argument. Even though the arguments are short, they must — like responses — address each important point raised by the other side. Do not neglect or ignore issues, especially the toughest ones. Acknowledge the difficulty and then go on to tell the court why you win anyway. Specifically, you should aim to accomplish two things in your reply brief.

Reply brief drafting strategies. First, echo the themes of the opening brief in a concise introduction. Your primary task is to interlace the themes you established in the opening brief with a statement that pinpoints the key legal issues.[4] You should concisely state the reasons why the trial court reversibly erred. The introduction is also a strategic location to list those arguments that your opponent has conceded or failed to address.[5]

After the introduction, the same strategies for appellees apply equally to appellants in reply: The brief should focus on the arguments that most effectively undermine the other side's position.[6] In responding to the appellee's arguments, you should (if you haven't already done so in the introduction) highlight those arguments that the appellee has conceded or not contested.[7] You should also weave in responses to the appellee's statement of facts if necessary, pointing out any significant factual misstatements or failures to comply with the requirement that parties submit an accurate, unbiased, and supported set of facts.[8] While you should refrain from attacking your opponent, you can use the opportunity to flag the error and (persuasively) restate the correct, yet unbiased, facts. You will gain credibility with the court, which will appreciate having an accurate recitation of the facts.[9] Also, be on the lookout for loopholes in the appellee's arguments, instances where the appellee has cited less than reputable legal authority, or has gaps in her analysis.[10] Finally, like the appellee, you must zero in on your most critical affirmative points while effectively rebutting the other side's arguments, again using Chapter 11's responsive argument strategies. Do not just repeat the appellee's argument. To illustrate this idea, consider the following two iterations of the same argument in a hypothetical contracts dispute.

The appellee argues that the contract at issue did not need to be in writing. Though the contract was for the sale of goods worth more than $500, the appellee argues, the contract qualifies for an exception to the Statute of Frauds because it was for the sale of specifically manufactured goods. This argument is erroneous. The parties contracted for the sale of Granny Smith apples, which are a common good. Thus, the contract is governed by the Statute of Frauds, and must be in writing to be enforceable.	The contract at issue is governed by the Statute of Frauds because it was for the sale of goods worth more than $500. Therefore, the contract must be in writing to be enforceable. Appellee's invocation of the exception to the Statute of Frauds for specifically manufactured goods fails: Granny Smith apples do not fall into that category. Therefore, the Statute of Frauds governs.

Notice how the second example strategically sandwiches the appellee's argument into the appellant's affirmative argument. The appellant's position occupies both the eye-catching first line of the paragraph as well as the conclusive last sentence. As such, the appellant maintains the first and last word on the matter.

Maintaining the proper scope. One of the most difficult tasks is to limit the reply brief to *responsive* points, not points made in the opening brief. Advocates are too often tempted to default to their original arguments. But this type of circular reasoning — "they're wrong because of what I already said" — is not only unhelpful, but also annoying to the court. No one wants to waste time rereading arguments, especially when they simply do not resolve the question facing the court. At times, you must hark back to an argument that you made in the opening brief in order to *build on* it in the reply. But that is different than the rote repetition that we are warning against here; your reply arguments must be narrowly tailored and operate as a cohesive whole with the other two briefs. Just as it is with response briefs, the brief-analysis chart is an invaluable tool for analyzing and organizing your arguments, and for avoiding repetition. For a reply brief, it would look like this:

Appellee Argument	Appellee Authority	Appellant Reply	Point from Opening Brief	Research/ Comments
Even pro se litigants are supposed to know the applicable statute of limitations.	Jackson v. Astrue, 506 F.3d 1349 (11th Cir. 2007).	Lay out nuances of finality doctrine.	Check p.14 for discussion about the triggering of the statute.	Cites re complexity in this area of law.

Consider the following two examples, which illustrate the difference between responsive and repetitive arguments.

Defensive opening sentence followed by repeating opening arguments:

The government maintains that under Taylor v. Illinois, it is not required to show willful misconduct or bad faith in order to preclude alibi testimony under Rule 12.1. (Gov't Br. 27-28.) Appellant reiterates the belief that *Taylor* stands for the proposition that the preclusion of alibi testimony for failure to give notice should not be available without evidence of willful misconduct. As stated in the opening

Affirmative opening defining the question for the court:

The government concedes the applicable standard (Gov't Br. 25) (citing *Taylor*, 484 U.S. at 414-15) (setting forth "guideposts, directing courts to balance the defendant's right to call favorable witnesses with 'countervailing public interests.'"), so its invocation of a "willful misconduct" threshold serves only to distract from the central question facing this Court: whether the district

brief, such an interpretation comports with the principles and policies underlying the rule: to deter bad faith. (Br. 18.)

court applied the governing standard. The district court did not, excluding the witness's testimony on the presumption that "Rule 12.1 favors not permitting an alibi witness." (App. A. 43.) Had the district court engaged in the required balancing it would not have found sufficient countervailing government interests to trump the defendant's right to present the only evidence in his defense. *See, e.g.,* United States v. Portela, 167 F.3d 687, 705 (1st Cir. 1999); United States v. Hamilton, 128 F.3d 996, 1002 (6th Cir. 1997).

The other major pitfall in reply briefs is to succumb to the temptation to introduce new arguments or issues. Courts routinely find such issues — first raised in a reply brief — waived,[11] and court rules often flatly prohibit them.[12] In any event, it is unethical and unprofessional. You cannot sandbag the other side by reserving an argument in your back pocket for the time when the other side no longer has the opportunity to respond in writing. Sometimes, however, there is a fine line between crafting a responsive argument, fleshing out an existing argument, and a inserting a "new" argument; even experienced practitioners sometimes struggle with the distinction. Inevitably your thinking about an issue crystallizes as the appeal progresses: A response from the appellee may spur you to express the core of your issue more cleanly or succinctly. That is ok; such refinements of existing arguments do not cross the line into "new" issues or arguments. Other times, though, you have just missed an argument, and you uncover it during your research for the reply. As difficult as it will be, you must simply leave it behind. One good benchmark is to examine the new authority you cite in your reply. You can rely on new cases in your reply, but only if they directly respond to an argument made by the other side. Another rule of thumb is to compare your statement of the issues and summary of the argument to the arguments you make in your reply. If the latter strays from the core of those opening brief components, then you should shy away from them. One final, related test is to make sure that any point in your reply brief could be supported by a citation from your opening brief.

Below are examples of permissible reply brief arguments, and ones that cross the line.

Reply Brief Example: Impermissible New Argument

Opening Argument	Appellee's Response	Reply Argument
The evidence was **insufficient to prove the defendant guilty of a conspiracy** to distribute drugs, when the evidence established only that Jackson sold drugs to some others with no evidence of an agreement to further distribute them, which is required for a drug-distribution conspiracy. These mere **buyer-seller transactions** between the defendant and assorted others were insufficient to prove the government's case.	The government must prove that two or more people joined together for the purposes of distributing unlawful drugs and that the defendant knew of and intended to join the agreement. Evidence of jointly undertaken activity is enough. For example, the **evidence showed that the defendant knowingly obtained drugs from a third party in order for witness X to sell them to others.**	The government's proof at trial **fatally varied** from the conspiracy it charged. The indictment charged a **hub and spoke conspiracy** where the defendant served as the central hub; at trial, the government proved only a **chain-link conspiracy** where the defendant was but one part but not the glue holding it together. Courts have reversed when the government changes the type of conspiracy charged.*

* Argument changes from insufficiency to a new fatal variance by distinguishing between types of conspiracies, a point not addressed in the opening brief.

Reply Brief Example: Permissible Refinement of Existing Argument

Opening Argument	Appellee's Response	Reply Argument
The warrantless search of the defendant's car was not a valid inventory search because although it satisfies the first of the three factors governing such searches, it fails to satisfy the other two. Specifically, under factor two, the search must not be pretextual. In this case, however, the search was pretextual because the police had already targeted the defendant and had been surveilling the car for criminal activity in the days leading up to the search. As for the third factor, according to department policy the purpose of the inventory search must be to protect the owner's property and the police from claims of theft. Here, the police did not inventory all of the valuable items in the car, so they did not satisfy the third factor.	The local police had not yet formally joined the federal investigation of the defendant. And the police inventory was sufficiently complete, though not exhaustive. Therefore, the search was not mere pretext.	The police failure to follow its own inventory search procedures — which expressly require that anything of value be inventoried — also supports the conclusion that its search was not conducted in good faith and was pretextual. *See* People v. Alewelt, 217 Ill. App. 3d 578, 581 (3d Dist. 1991) (affirming trial court's finding that the officer's incomplete inventory report supported the conclusion that the search was pretextual).*

* Discussion of policy mentioned mostly in third factor during opening brief but moved to second factor in reply brief as direct response to the appellee.

Reply Brief Example: Permissible Responsive Argument with New Case

Opening Argument	Appellee's Response	Reply Argument
The evidence of the defendant's prior drug deals fails the test employed under Rule 404(b) because the evidence was used to show that the defendant had a propensity for dealing drugs and not that he committed the sale of which he was accused. **Rule 404(b) prohibits the use of evidence of other bad acts to show that a defendant has a propensity to commit a crime** and that he acted in accordance with that propensity on the occasion in question. *See* United States v. Best, 250 F.3d 1084, 1090 (7th Cir. 2001).	The district court did not err by not excluding defendant's post-arrest statements because **those statements were inextricably intertwined with the charged conduct and they "arose out of the same transaction or series of transactions as the charged offense."** United States v. Lott, No. 05-1713, 2006 WL 760160, at *4 (7th Cir. Mar. 27, 2006). According to this Court, such evidence **"is not considered 'other crimes' evidence under Fed. R. Evid. 404(b)."** *Id.**	**The inextricably-intertwined doctrine does not apply** because the link between the defendant's statements about his drug-dealing past and the charged transaction was attenuated. **Cases applying this doctrine, including those involving drug offenses, have involved prior conduct that was directly and concretely related to explaining a specific aspect of the charged crime.** *See, e.g., Gougis,* 214 F.3d at 445 ([explanatory parenthetical omitted]); United States v. Johnson, 248 F.3d 655, 665 (7th Cir. 2001) ([explanatory parenthetical omitted]). None of the government's cases involved a single defendant engaging in a one-time, commonplace drug transaction.

* Appellee introduced new theory in its response that allowed the appellant's reply to develop a new argument with new cases.

**Practice Alert #3
Tone**

In the online companion you will find sample reply brief excerpts. Edit the samples to experiment with finding the best tone for a reply brief.

Once you have defined and refined your reply arguments, ensured that they fall within the scope of the first two briefs, and outlined your points in an organized whole that is affirmative rather than defensive, you should consider tone and theme. As discussed above, in your meta-analysis of the other side's brief, you will have discovered what logical fallacies and other mistakes define it. Part of your theme will incorporate a global description of these failings, as well as any fundamental errors by the lower court that define the appeal. It is appropriate, then, to adopt a pithier and more forceful tone in the reply. After all, you are an advocate and you must defend your position. Your tone should not, however, veer off into snarkiness or *ad hominem* attacks. Your many rounds of revisions will smooth out the rough edges in this regard, and you should not stop until you feel that you've struck the proper balance between zealous advocacy and lawyerly civility.

The "dos and don'ts" of reply briefs are summarized in the chart below:

The Reply Brief

DO	DON'T
Respond to other side	Fail to file a reply, even if it is optional
Answer the tough questions	Repeat your opening brief
Remain conscious of meta-analysis and theme	Introduce new issues or arguments not contained in the opening brief
Be affirmative, not defensive	Use a tone that "shouts" at the judges or is so snarky that it impacts your credibility
Employ a more forceful tone	

REFLECTION, DISCUSSION, AND CHALLENGE QUESTIONS

Response and Reply Briefs

- What are the primary similarities and differences between opening briefs, response briefs, and reply briefs?
- What would you do if your opponent introduced a new issue or argument in a reply brief?
- If you were the appellant and you discovered when writing the reply brief that you had not framed an issue in the optimal way, how would you communicate that to the client?

Section 2 Amicus Briefs

Amicus briefs, or "friend of the court" briefs, can be an invaluable resource to an appellate litigant. Such briefs add weight and persuasive power on your side of the appeal. At a minimum, they require courts to take another look at your side, and different language or creative theories may even carry the day. They also delight clients and offer you an opportunity to engage your colleagues in important legal work and perhaps find new clients of their own. Amicus briefs are briefs written not by a party, but rather by an independent entity in support of one of the parties (or, rarely, in support of neither party). Their purpose is to twofold: (1) to assist the court in understanding aspects of the case that may not be covered in the parties' briefs; and (2) to voice the position of a group that might be specially impacted by the ultimate disposition of the case. In a large financial case, for example, the American Bankers Association might hire a law firm to prepare an amicus brief. And in a federal criminal case, the National Association of Attorneys

General might weigh in with the collective states' interests in the issue. In theory, any court can accept amicus briefs, but they are filed most commonly in the U.S. Supreme Court and in some federal circuit courts of appeals. Given their prominence in appellate practice, we set forth a few essential pointers below. First, we cover the practical aspects of developing amici for your case, as well as the applicable rules and strategies for interacting with your amici. In the next section, we approach it from the other side — what to do when you are asked to write an amicus brief.

2.1 Developing Amici for Your Case

As in all other things, timing is important. If your case is one that might benefit from having an amicus brief on your side, you'll have to start working on that aspect of your case as soon as possible. As you might imagine, finding an organization, convincing them to get involved, obtaining the proper authorities, and finding an author all take time. And in federal circuit courts of appeal[13] and the United States Supreme Court[14] an amicus must submit its brief a mere seven days following the filing of the brief by the party they are supporting. Many appellate practitioners make the mistake of waiting too long to seek amicus assistance, most often because it takes a supporting organization some weeks to obtain internal approval.

Let's go back to the *Mutombo* appeal, challenging a college-aged rapper's conviction for attempted terrorist threats on First and Fourth Amendment grounds. Obviously, the case presents a number of interesting legal questions, and just as soon as you have identified those, you'll want to be asking the crucial question: Who else besides my client might really care about this? One obvious group would be criminal defense attorneys. Groups like the National Association of Criminal Defense Lawyers ("NACDL") often file in cases of first impression involving novel prosecution theories. Instructions on how to approach NACDL for amicus help can be found on its website.[15] Your case also has free speech implications and so you may want to approach a group like the American Civil Liberties Union ("ACLU"). Even if the ACLU is not in a position to help, they may know of other groups that may be interested. Here, you will have to be at your entrepreneurial best. And there is also the music industry itself; for example, you might approach labels like Outlaw Recordz and explain that this type of prosecution could threaten their artists, or you might try to find an organization like the Hip Hop Association,[16] and make a similar pitch about potential harm to their membership. Unless you happen to have a colleague that acts as general counsel or outside counsel to one of these groups, you can see that just getting your request heard is going to take some time and creative effort.

2.2 The Applicable Rules

If you do get agreement from a group to act as amicus, you must then pay close attention to amicus participation requirements in your appellate court. In the federal circuit courts and the United States Supreme Court, for example, an amicus can file a brief without seeking leave of the court if all parties agree. That means that you or your amicus will have to contact your opponent and seek their consent to filing. If your opponent refuses, then you will have to file a motion under Federal Rule of Appellate Procedure 29(a) or Supreme Court Rule 37.2(b).[17] It may seem surprising, but consent is usually given. The reason is that if an amicus files a motion for leave to file a brief, the brief will accompany that motion and the court of appeals will read the amicus brief and very likely grant leave to file. So all your opponent will have accomplished is exactly what they were trying to prevent in opposing your request; that is, having the amicus brief make an impact. Such opposition also makes your opponent look bad by being obstreperous and creating extra work for the court. Obviously, if the shoe is on the other foot, and your opponent comes to you with a request to consent to amici, you might take the opportunity to be especially gracious and civil, knowing full well what your opponent may not — that there really is little choice for you in the matter.

There are also important questions concerning timing. As explained above, an amicus must usually file its brief on the heels of the filing of the party it supports. But there are trickier situations — like supporting a petition for rehearing en banc in a federal circuit court. In those instances, the court is not required to call for a responsive brief, so if you wait seven days to file an amicus brief, the court may already have considered the petition. It is best in such instances to file on the same day, or the next business day, after the petitioner.

It is also best practice to notify the court of amicus participation as early as possible so that the court can check for panel conflicts. This practice is embodied in some courts' rules. The D.C. Circuit, for example, says in Rule IX (A)(4) ("Amici Curiae and Interveners") that: "The Court encourages those who wish to participate as amici . . . to notify the court as soon as practicable after a case is docketed in this court, by filing a notice of intent to participate, a representation of consent, or a motion for leave of court when necessary." Further explaining that the court is concerned about recusals, the rule then warns that: "Parties seeking leave to participate as amicus curiae after the merits panel has been assigned or at the rehearing stage should be aware that the court will not accept an amicus brief where it would result in a recusal of a member of the panel or recusal of a member of the en banc court."

There is also the question of costs. In the Supreme Court, for example, all amicus briefs must be printed. So take care to warn your amici that, even though you are participating pro bono, or your client is in forma pauperis and the brief is filed on regular paper, amici must file a professionally printed brief.[18]

Finally, federal district courts and other trial-level state courts are very different when it comes to permitting amicus participation. At the district court level, the "consent" rule does not apply and all potential amici must seek leave to file. Experience shows that such requests are seldom granted and, because you must file your brief together with the motion for leave to file, a denial of that motion represents a significant waste of time and resources. The reason for different treatment of amici at the trial court level likely has to do with the adversarial nature of the proceedings and the district court's need to carefully manage its docket. More parties at the trial level may well create more headaches for a district judge than for an appellate court with a more circumscribed set of proceedings. Thus, before you suggest that an amicus undertake such an effort at the district court level, you will want to very carefully assess whatever information you can about the individual judge's practices and the practices in that district.

2.3 Amicus Strategy

In addition to identifying and approaching groups, you'll want to give very careful attention both to what these groups will say and the likely impact on the court of appeals. Once you've approached a particular group and they have agreed to file, you will also lose a measure of control. These are independent groups. Some groups are more regular participants as amici — such as the ACLU — and so they are likely to be highly cooperative with you. But others may be strongly independent and you might, much to your chagrin, learn what they have to say only the day that you are served a copy of the filed brief.

The key to avoiding unpleasant surprises is to make a gentle, but specific, suggestion to your potential amicus during your first conversations of what points you would like them to address. So you might say to the record label in the *Mutombo* appeal that you'd like them to write about the history of gansta rap as a music genre and its artistic qualities. A brief that glorifies the "gangsta life," on the other hand, might send the judges and clerks in the wrong direction.

Court rules forbid parties' attorneys from directly authoring an amicus brief and often require that you — as appellant or appellee — certify that you have not authored or economically supported an amicus brief.[19] But even if the rules did not expressly forbid such direct authorship, it would be ethically suspect for you to write one. Amici curiae are independent and should not be exploited to provide you extra pages to write your brief. And even if that were somehow permissible, it would be a strategic mistake. First, you want to be as concise as possible within your own limits and aim for a brief that is shorter — and, hopefully, significantly shorter — than your allowable limit. Second, unless your amici have something different and compelling to say, their brief is likely to be of no effect on the court. Appellate judges even have a disparaging name for amicus briefs that just repeat, in different words, the arguments that the supported party has made in their own brief: "me too" briefs. Understandably, their effect is nil.

It is conceivable that the mere appearance of a particularly well known, non-legal organization — say, the American Medical Association — in support of your case may have some marginal impact on the law clerks and their judges. But just because the AMA agrees with you is no reason for you to win. And it may well be that curious judges and law clerks in the *Mutombo* appeal scenario would pick up the Outlaw Recordz brief for its novelty, but it is certain that the novelty will wear off quickly if the amicus brief doesn't say something interesting that contributes to the discussion surrounding the case.

2.4 Authoring an Amicus Brief

Let's suppose that your law school classmate has called you to assist with the Outlaw Recordz brief. She has gently suggested that it would be great to have a brief on the history of gangsta rap as a musical genre and its artistic qualities. Assuming that the client is on board, how do you approach your effort?

Two important realities face you and every writer of an amicus. First, you have to do something different — you have to offer a novel thought about the case. Second, you don't have a lot of time and can't afford to wait until your former classmate has filed the appellant's brief.

Amicus briefs are most persuasive in two situations: (1) when they offer empirical evidence to a court that might be uniquely offered by that amicus group;[20] and (2) when they offer creative and novel arguments that shed a different light on the legal question presented.[21] As noted, certain well-respected organizations that file often like the ACLU or the U.S. Chamber of Commerce might also garner attention — but often only because they satisfy one of the two basic criteria above. And, of course, the same would be true of other groups, no matter how high the celebrity quotient.

In many ways, amici who want to impact appellate process seek to offer their peculiar brand of expertise. Thus, a criminal defense group might file a brief on the impact that a resolution of the legal issue presented is likely to have on the plea bargaining process. Or, if you were representing Outlaw Recordz in our example, you may want to add to your argument a comparison of the lyrics in the defendant's supposed threats to popular songs to demonstrate the compatibility of the supposed threats with successes in the music genre. It's doubtful that the court of appeals is going to be able to turn to other authorities to assess the lyrics of gangsta rap songs. Here, your client, a record company who has retained you to write an amicus brief on its behalf, offers a unique and largely unchallengeable perspective.

As you proceed with the writing of your amicus brief, do not hesitate to share your thoughts and your drafts with the parties. There is no rule that prevents coordination between amicus and the party they are supporting. The only critical rule[22] is that the party cannot author or financially support your brief. Accordingly, if you choose to share drafts of your amicus brief, you should be wary of party attempts at rewriting. All comments, suggestions, and line-edits are up to you as the author and you should take them that way. In those instances where you and a party have a serious disagreement about the direction of a particular argument, you are often best served by suggesting that the argument be removed entirely rather than offering something that might be used by the other side as a "wedge" argument to divide the amicus and the party that she supports. Indeed, if you've reached that stage, it may well be that this is not a case for you and your client — a would-be amicus — to participate in anyway, given that the party that you support doesn't seem to want the arguments that you are making and vice-versa. As amicus, it is always better for you to "pull the plug" rather than make bad law.

Finally, while authoring an amicus brief may seem slightly less glamorous than participating on behalf of a party, amicus briefs are wonderful opportunities to exercise your writing skills in an area that is constrained by little more than your imagination. Indeed, amicus briefs are often utilized to present the more "radical" argument that a party may not be willing or able to make. Thus, arguing that the First Amendment supports a presumption against all prosecutions for threats (or other words) where no identifiable victim is present sets out a strong legal argument that the appellant may not want to make — either because it was not made below, or because the appellant wants to argue only that the district court's interpretation of the statute raises "constitutional questions" that ought to be avoided. You, on the other hand, get to make a full-throated constitutional argument. In just such cases lies the joy—and the challenge—of effective amicus practice.

Section 3   Administrative Agency Appeals

Until now, this book has focused on appellate review of decisions made by lower courts of general jurisdiction. But if your appeal arises from an administrative agency, different rules apply. You must first understand what must be done in front of the agency's board of decisionmakers before you initiate an appeal outside the agency. In particular, you may need to exhaust the agency's appeal procedure before you can even set foot in a federal court. And the agency's rules and standards of review can be very different from those described in the book thus far. Finally, even if your appeal takes to you federal court, the standards of review that these courts apply to administrative agency decisions are often extremely deferential.

Checking agency rules. That said, although agency appeals have their own specialized rules and standards of review, the general approaches to planning, learning, and writing discussed in the earlier chapters of this book apply equally here. As always, one of your earliest tasks will be to review the relevant rules to ensure that you are operating in the proper court and that your case meets all of the requirements necessary for review. A good starting place is the statute that creates and empowers the agency, as well as the regulations the agency has implemented regarding its own procedure. These rules will help you understand how the agency issues its orders and when they are final. Additionally, the statute will let you know when and to what judicial body appeals should be made. For example, if permitted by statute, federal agency decisions are reviewable by federal courts. The federal court that will hear your agency appeal depends on the agency involved. Some agency appeals will advance directly to the circuit court, while others can be heard in a district court. Social Security disputes or appeals from a bankruptcy court can generally be taken to a district court, but Board of Immigration Appeals decisions are usually reviewed by federal appeals courts.[23]

Checking court rules. You must also check the general rules governing appeals in your jurisdiction because they will explain how to proceed in an administrative appeal. Therefore, if your agency appeal is in federal court, you should refer to the Federal Rules of Appellate Procedure, the Federal Rules of Criminal or Civil

Procedure, and your court's local rules. For example, if you learned that your federal court venue was a circuit court of appeals, as in the immigration example discussed below, a review of the applicable federal rules would tell you that you need to file a document called a "petition for review" (rather than a notice of appeal), and that this petition must be filed with the clerk of court within a set amount of time.[24] Like the notice of appeal, the petition for review is a short and simple document that contains the name of each party seeking review, the name of the agency, and the order or part of an order to be reviewed.[25] Further review of the applicable federal rules would reveal that the rest of the process is similar to appealing a district court decision: You must pay any fees required by the court and begin to compile your record on appeal. In an agency appeal, the record is the same as it would be had proceedings occurred in a district court: It is limited to the order involved; any findings or report on which the order was based; and what occurred in the proceedings before the agency, including the pleadings and evidence presented.[26] As in an appeal of a district court decision, the record can be corrected or supplemented in the case of errors or omissions.[27] However, unlike an appeal of a district court decision, it is not necessarily the duty of the appealing party to order any transcripts or otherwise complete the record. The agency is required to file the original record, or a certified copy, with the clerk of court within 40 days of being served with a petition for review.[28]

Example: an immigration appeal. Although requirements vary due to the independence each agency is given to make its own rules, the following illustration shows how an appeal may progress in one specific field: immigration. The field of immigration law is reserved to the federal government through the Executive Office of Immigration Review, which has established a system of review for cases involving removal of immigrants. Immigration cases are first heard in specialized immigration courts, which render decisions that may be appealed to the Board of Immigration Appeals, the highest decisionmaking authority within the agency.[29] The Board of Immigration Appeals is, like a judicial court of appeals, tasked with rendering decisions that promote uniformity in the application of relevant laws.[30] Once you've filed the petition for review in the circuit court of appeals — which in the case of a Board of Immigration Appeals decision must happen within 30 days of the agency decision — the appeal will proceed much like any other appeal from briefing to argument to disposition.[31]

State administrative agency appeals. If your case proceeded before a state administrative agency, rather than a federal agency, that agency's rules will govern the appellate process. Generally, state agency decisions must be appealed to state courts. While some administrative orders must be heard by a state trial court, others are immediately appealable to a state appellate court. In Illinois, for example, only the final orders of agencies such as the Pollution Control Board, the Illinois State Labor Relations Board, the Illinois Educational Labor Relations Board, and certain orders of the Illinois Gaming Board are directly appealable to the Illinois Appellate Court.[32] In large part, these state agency appeals follow the same process as an ordinary appeal, with minor variations similar to federal agency appeals. The document required to file your appeal and the amount of time you have to file it may be different, and it will likely be the duty of the agency to file the record after it receives notice of the appeal. In Illinois, for example, a petition for administrative review rather than a notice of appeal must be filed within 35 days of a final administrative order, and the agency must prepare the record upon written request from the petitioner.[33] Though jurisdictional and procedural rules may vary, your approach in researching your appeal and constructing your argument will be the same.

PRELIMINARY CHECKLIST ───────────────────────────

Agency Appeal

- File a petition for review with the clerk of the court of appeals within the deadline prescribed by law.
- Pay any required fees.
- Compile agency record in accordance with Federal Rule of Appellate Procedure 16(a).
- Do NOT order transcripts or file the record with the court — this is the agency's duty to complete within 40 days of being served.
- If necessary, file a motion to stay with the agency, or with the appellate court if filing in the agency is impracticable.

Section 4 | Certiorari Practice in the United States Supreme Court and Discretionary Review in State Court

Until now, we have focused on appeals as of right, usually to intermediate appellate bodies. We turn now to courts of last resort and their discretionary review process, which is the method by which these courts choose the cases they hear. Although most courts of last resort retain some avenues of original and mandatory jurisdiction,[34] the bulk of a supreme court's caseload comes from the cases stemming from its discretionary review process.

4.1 Certiorari Practice in the United States Supreme Court

If you have lost in the federal court of appeals (or in the state court of last resort if your case involves an issue of federal law), your final potential avenue for review is the United States Supreme Court. Obtaining review by the Court, however, is rare. In 2013, for example, approximately 7,376 petitions for certiorari were filed in the Supreme Court, and 74 were granted.[35] That means that, on average, the Court accepts only about 1 percent of the cases filed. Given these odds, your chances of success will rise if your petition is crafted with an eye towards satisfying the Court's criteria for review, which are encapsulated in Supreme Court Rule 10.

In short, the Court will not accept your case merely to correct an erroneous result below. Rather, the Court accepts cases only when they present: (1) a conflict among lower federal and/or state courts on an important federal issue; (2) a conflict with existing Supreme Court law on an important federal issue; or (3) an issue that is otherwise of national importance despite the absence of extant conflict.[36]

Factors that influence a grant of certiorari. The first two categories are fairly self-explanatory, but the third category deserves a bit more attention. What makes a case one of national importance in the absence of a split? One thing would be cases that are important to the survival of an industry or carry other types of practical importance for the economy or well-being of the nation. For example, in Exxon v. Baker, the Supreme Court granted certiorari to review the Ninth Circuit's determination that the punitive damage award in the wake of the Valdez oil spill, the worst in the nation's history, did not violate Exxon's due process rights. The case did not involve a circuit split, but it was a case of national importance that the Court took to resolve on the merits. Other cases in this category are those in areas of the law in which uniformity of the law is particularly important. Some examples here include the workings of the class-action mechanism under Federal Rule of Civil Procedure 23 or cases arising under admiralty law. If an interpretive question arises about how class actions are to proceed, the Court may accept the case and resolve the question even if there isn't a split. Given the large number of class actions working through the courts at any given time, were the Supreme Court to wait for an actual split of authority, the delay could unnecessarily gum up the system in a huge part of most courts' dockets.

Not only must the case fall into one of these three categories, that category must have been outcome determinative in your particular case. That is, the court of appeals decision may note a split of authority in its decision, but if the Supreme Court determines that any error arising from it was harmless, if it finds that there is an alternate legal basis to reach the same result, or if it finds that the question in the cert petition isn't squarely presented by the case, then the Supreme Court is unlikely to take the case. The Court sees little point in deciding cases where the issue is not squarely presented; it knows that if the issue is important, another, cleaner version of it will come up sooner or later.

Relatedly, the issue presented in your case must be one that is likely to recur. The Court is unlikely to grant certiorari on an issue that simply won't arise frequently in future cases; it is a waste of time and space given the very few cases that the Court is able to hear each term. If you can show that the issue impacts a large number of litigants of a certain class, perhaps through case filing statistics, you will be on much firmer footing than merely baldly asserting that it will recur. Finally, the Court will often pass on a case if the split of authority is in its nascent stages. The Court often prefers to allow an issue to "percolate" among the courts of appeals for a period of time, which allows it to prioritize mature splits and also to weigh the views of more courts of appeals when it finally opts to decide an issue.

As you can see, the factors that the Court entertains in deciding whether to exercise its review are vastly different from the reason that an intermediate appellate court reviews a case: to ensure the correct result for that particular litigant.

The Court at this stage cares very little for the merits of the issue or in righting a wrong result.

Contents of a cert petition. Petitions for certiorari reflect these unique and specialized purposes. The brief must be structured to convey several essential pieces of information to the Justices (really, their law clerks) quickly and accurately, as they wade through the more than 7,000 petitions submitted each year and try to find the appropriate cases to review.

Supreme Court Rule 14 governs the nuts and bolts of the petition (Rules 12 and 13 govern logistics and timing). The Rule specifies that each petition must contain, in the order specified: (1) the questions presented for review; (2) a list of parties; (3) a table of contents and a table of authorities; (4) citations to the decision below; (5) a jurisdictional statement; (6) the constitutional provisions, statutes, or regulations involved; (7) a statement of the case setting forth the factual and procedural background; (8) the reasons for granting the petition; and (9) an appendix with the relevant opinions below and other essential record material. Rather than exhaustively analyzing each of these sections, we instead touch on a few highlights. First, you must take care when crafting your Question(s) Presented ("QP"). As a threshold matter, you should limit your petition to one or two questions. The Court will not seriously entertain more than that, and a kitchen-sink approach makes your petition less credible. Frame the questions so that they have broad applicability and importance beyond the facts of your individual case. Flag the split of authority (or other criterion from Rule 10) that makes your case cert-worthy; do not frame the question as one of mere error correction, though your QP can hint that the court below reached the wrong result. Here is a good question presented from the petition in Madigan v. Levin:

> Whether the Seventh Circuit erred in holding, in an acknowledged departure from the rule in at least four other circuits, that state and local government employees may avoid the Federal Age Discrimination in Employment Act's comprehensive remedial regime by bringing age discrimination claims directly under the Equal Protection Clause and 42 U.S.C. § 1983.

And here is a QP that is unlikely to succeed because it smacks of mere error correction:

> Did the Eighth Circuit err in determining that the warrantless search was nonetheless permitted because of exigent circumstances arising from the fact that officers heard screams from the occupants of the apartment.

Next, the argument section — called the Reasons for Granting the Petition — also has quirks that differentiate it from routine appellate briefs. Again, given the Court's focus on the requirements of Rule 10, you should discuss the conflict or national importance of the issue immediately. Only after clearly spelling out the nature of the split should you briefly touch on the merits of why the court below erred. Finally, at the end of your argument section, you may want to briefly address what are called "vehicle" issues — why your case (as opposed to any other that the Court has entertained in the past or will see in the future) is the one the Court should take to decide this important issue.

Responsive brief strategies. The respondent may opt to waive his response to your cert petition, and respondents often do so in order to signal to the Court the view that the petition is meritless. The responsive brief at the cert stage, if filed, is called the brief in opposition. Like the petition, it is a specialized brief seeking to accomplish a specific purpose: the denial of the petition. As a result, the respondent — even more than the petitioner — must stay away from the merits of the decision below. Unlike a traditional appellee brief, where the advocate spends lots of airtime discussing why the lower court reached the correct result, a respondent at the cert stage wants to avoid drawing attention to the merits. After all, you do not want to give the Court the impression that there is fire behind the petitioner's claim of smoke. Instead, your job as respondent is to essentially tell the Court, "There's nothing to see here. Move on." In order to accomplish this, you will meticulously catalogue all of the reasons why this particular case is a bad vehicle for the Court's review.

First attack the asserted split. Did the petitioner accurately characterize it or did he rely on dicta in order to cobble together the appearance of a split? If there is a split, is it among just a few courts? If the split is shallow, you can encourage the Court to defer while the issue percolates for a few more years. Similarly, you should consider whether the question is unlikely to come up again in future litigation, debunking the petitioner's "likely to recur" argument. Are there jurisdictional, mootness, ripeness, or standing issues that would impede the Court's review? If so, point them out. Did the advocate preserve the issue that she now presents for the Court's review? The Court will not consider waived issues and generally shies away from plain error review. The respondent should also alert the Court if there is an alternative and independent basis for the ruling below; this, too, will often defeat a request for a writ of certiorari. Likewise, if the issue is one that is better resolved by an agency (like the Sentencing Commission for Guidelines interpretation issues, for example), that is another reason why the Court will decline review. Finally, complex factual or procedural postures can cause the Court to think twice before granting a petition. If the result below is inextricably tied to the facts of the case, then the Court will likely wait for another case with broader applicability. Given these many reasons most savvy respondents can convince the Court that it should take a pass; it's little wonder that so few petitions are granted each year.

4.2 Discretionary Review in State Court

In state courts most appeals to intermediate appellate courts are as of right. That is, assuming that appeal is properly and timely requested and the order is final, an intermediate court of appeal must consider it.[37] Most of the time, however, appeals to state supreme courts (or their equivalent courts of last resort) are discretionary, just as the United States Supreme Court has the power to decide which cases it will hear through the writ of certiorari process discussed above. The same rationale applies: Most state supreme courts are able to hear only a small fraction of the cases sent to them. It is critical to understand the procedures that your state supreme court uses in deciding whether to take a case and to take care in drafting the petition, for these requests are decided on the pleadings without oral argument. You must look to the court's rules to ensure that your petition is timely, that it is accompanied by any requisite fees and disclosures, and that it meets all of the court's technical requirements. Most importantly, you must emphasize the criteria that the court applies in deciding whether to take a case. Often, the highest court of a state will hear cases only if: (1) the appeal raises a question of particular importance; (2) the decision conflicts with supreme court precedent; or (3) the state's appellate courts are in conflict.[38] If you are the respondent, you also must be familiar with your state's discretionary review process. As in United States Supreme Court certiorari proceedings, respondents can waive their right to respond to the petition. But unlike the United States Supreme Court, some state courts will grant review even without a response from the respondent.[39] Counsel must account for this possibility with their clients in advance, weighing the pros and cons of responding.

Another area where discretionary review arises is in interlocutory orders. As in federal court, state courts are not required to review all nonfinal orders. But the rules often differ from those governing federal courts and vary by state as well. You must familiarize yourself with the interlocutory review rules of your court. In New York, for example, nearly all interlocutory orders are appealable as of right.[40] Other states give their courts discretion over certain interlocutory matters but not others. For example, Illinois courts have discretion whether to review many interlocutory orders, including venue-transfer orders and orders denying or granting class certification.[41] Unlike appeals of right, where a simple notice of appeal in the trial court initiates the process, petitions for review of interlocutory orders in Illinois must be filed in the appellate court, and must include the relevant facts, supported by the record, as well as the grounds for interlocutory review.[42]

REFLECTION, DISCUSSION, AND CHALLENGE QUESTIONS

Discretionary Review

- How would you prioritize considerations that state courts weigh on discretionary review? Do you think courts are more interested in resolving conflicts among courts or ensuring that lower courts are not misapplying existing precedent?
- Would you ever seek discretionary review in the absence of a split of authority or a decision contrary to existing precedent? When?
- What factors might weigh in favor or against a respondent's decision to respond to a petition for discretionary review?
- Take a look at United States Supreme Court Rule 10. How are petitions for discretionary review different from briefs? How are they similar?

Endnotes

1. Daniel Barer, *Leading the Dance: Drafting the Appellee's Brief*, CERTWORTHY (VOL. FALL 1998).
2. DANIEL J. MEADOR, APPELLATE COURTS IN THE UNITED STATES 38-39 (2d ed. 2006).
3. FED. R. APP. P. 31, 32(a)(7).
4. Richard C. Kraus, *Crafting an Influential and Effective Reply Brief*, COUNCIL OF APPELLATE LAWYERS (Summer 2012).
5. *Id.*
6. Paul J. Killion, *Having the Last Word: The Appellate Reply Brief*, CERTWORTHY (Fall 1998).
7. Richard C. Kraus, *Crafting an Influential and Effective Reply Brief*, COUNCIL OF APPELLATE LAWYERS (Summer 2012).
8. Killion, *supra* note 6.
9. *Id.*
10. *Id.*
11. MICHAEL E. TIGAR & JANE B. TIGAR, FEDERAL APPEALS JURISDICTION AND PRACTICE § 9:17 (3d ed. 2013).
12. *See, e.g.,* ILL. SUP. CT. R. 341(j); SDCL 15-26A-62; PA.R.A.P. 2113.
13. FED. R. APP. P. 29(E).
14. SUP. CT. R. 37.2. For amicus briefs in support of a petition for certiorari, the amicus brief is due 30 days after the petition is docketed. No extensions are allowed, even if the respondent requests and receives an extension.
15. *Available at* http://www.nacdl.org/.
16. *Available at* http://www.hiphopassociation.org/.
17. SUP. CT. R. 37.2(b).
18. SUP. CT. R. 33.1(a).
19. SUP. CT. R. 37.6.
20. *See* Fisher v. University of Texas at Austin, 133 S. Ct. 2411, 2433 (2013); King v. Burwell, 135 S. Ct. 2480, 2493-94 (2015); McCullen v. Coakley, 134 S. Ct. 2518, 2537-38 (2014); Obergefell v. Hodges, 135 S. Ct. 2584, 2595-96 (2015).
21. *See* Arizona State Legislature v. Arizona Independent Redistricting Commission, 135 S. Ct. 2652, 2691 (2015); Burwell v. Hobby Lobby Stores, Inc., 134 S. Ct. 2751, 2799 (2014); Graham v. Florida, 560 U.S. 48, 68-69 (2010); Obergefell v. Hodges, 135 S. Ct. 2584, 2600 (2015).
22. SUP. CT. R. 37.6.
23. 8 U.S.C. § 1252(b)(2) (2012).
24. FED. R. APP. P. 15(a)(1).
25. FED. R. APP. P. 15(a)(2). Form 3 in the Appendix of Forms to the Rules provides a template for this document.
26. FED. R. APP. P. 16(a).
27. FED. R. APP. P. 16(b).
28. FED. R. APP. P. 17.
29. 8 C.F.R. § 1003.1(b).
30. 8 C.F.R. § 1003.1(d).
31. 8 U.S.C. § 1252(b)(1) (2012).
32. APPELLATE LAWYERS ASSOCIATION, A GUIDE TO ILLINOIS CIVIL APPELLATE PROCEDURE VIII-1 (2014).
33. 735 ILCS 5/3 113; ILL. SUP. CT. R. 335.
34. MEADOR, *supra* note 2, AT 17-23.
35. *Statistics*, SUPREME COURT OF THE UNITED STATES § II (October Term 2013), http://www.supremecourt.gov/orders/journal/jnl13.pdf.
36. SUP. CT. R. 10.
37. *See, e.g.,* ILL. SUP. CT. R. 301.
38. *See, e.g.,* ILL. SUP. CT. R. 315(a).
39. *See, e.g.,* ILL. SUP. CT. R. 315(f); PA.R.A.P. 1116.
40. N.Y. C.P.L.R. § 5701.
41. ILL. SUP. CT. R. 306(a).
42. ILL. SUP. CT. R. 306(b)-(c); APPELLATE LAWYERS ASSOCIATION, A GUIDE TO ILLINOIS CIVIL APPELLATE PROCEDURE II-5 (2014).

14 Preparing for and Delivering Oral Argument

Oral argument is the capstone experience to months of intense thinking, researching, and writing. It is an important part of your case, but it cannot replace the value of your written submissions. For that reason, we have devoted the last 13 chapters of the book to the written portions of your appeal, and devote just one to oral argument. Nevertheless, you will find here all of the tools and information you need to get ready for oral argument. Section 1 outlines the fundamentals: the purposes and structure of oral argument. After this overview, Section 2 takes you through a detailed, step-by-step preparation process. Finally, we devote the last section of the chapter to tips about delivery and answering questions, both as the appellant and the appellee.

Section 1 Oral Argument Fundamentals

1.1 The Purposes, Benefits, and Challenges of Oral Argument

Every reader of this text brings different knowledge and experience to the study of oral argument. You may have only a first-year legal writing course oral argument under your belt. Or perhaps you've built on that experience by watching real-life arguments on video or in person. Your knowledge may even be deeper, having competed in moot courts, taken other appellate advocacy courses or clinics, or interned for an appellate court. Whatever your exposure to the craft, the first step in advancing your skills is to think critically about what you have already learned about oral argument. In particular, reflect on what you understand so far about: (1) the purposes of oral argument; (2) oral argument's strategic benefits and challenges; and (3) the attributes of effective and ineffective oral arguments. To stimulate your thinking, more specific reflection questions on these three topics appear below, along with an exercise.

REFLECTION, DISCUSSION, AND CHALLENGE QUESTIONS

Oral Argument

- What are the primary purposes of oral argument from the court's perspective?
- What are the primary purposes of oral argument from the advocate's perspective?
- What makes for an effective oral argument introduction?
- Categorize the kinds of questions that appellate judges ask during argument.
- What are the biggest potential mistakes an oralist might make?
- Identify three vital steps to good preparation for oral argument.
- What argument styles have you seen that you believe were effective? What argument styles have you seen that you believe were ineffective? Why?
- Compare your responses to Chief Justice Roberts's comments on oral argument at the U.S. Supreme Court (minutes 25-38): http://www.c-spanvideo.org/program/CourtChi.[1]
- Based on your Argument Assessment Memo, which arguments will be the most difficult to convert to oral form? Why?

Practice Alert #1
A Taste of Oral Argument

This exercise in the online companion asks you to read and reflect on two classic articles that offer competing views on the purposes and utility of oral argument. You will put these thoughts together with your answers to the reflection questions above. Then, either on your own or at your professor's direction together with your classmates, attend a local oral argument or watch an argument online. Using the parameters set by your professor, draft a short reflection paper recording your impressions of the argument.

1.2 The Structure of Oral Argument

As every good rhetorician knows, a persuasive oral presentation needs a beginning, middle, and end.[2] The structure of oral argument is no different, except that each segment must accommodate maximum flexibility. In this section, we define the structure of oral argument as having three components—the introduction, the body, and the conclusion—and then discuss the most important aspects of each one. Sections 2 and 3 address how to prepare for and execute these components with agility as questioning pulls you in all directions, both predictable and unanticipated.

The introduction. An effective introduction at once crystallizes the issues for decision, makes clear the advocate's position, and captures the court's attention. But the strategies for achieving these aims vary by oralist, and even by the nature of the appeal. As the next section explains, the introduction always starts by greeting the court, but what comes next is advocate-driven. Some oralists kick off with a simple statement of the issues and their positions[3] in the most appealing, direct manner possible, devoid of fanfare:

EXAMPLE **Introduction Kick-Off: Simple and Direct**

Mr. Chief Justice, and may it please the Court. The constitutionality of the Act's massive expansion of Medicaid depends on the answer to two related questions. First, is the expansion coercive, and second, does that coercion matter?
— *Paul Clement, representing the State of Florida in 2012's Affordable Care Act arguments.*[4]

EXAMPLE **Introduction Kick-Off: Simple and Direct**

Good morning, and may it please the Court. This Court's decision in *Gross* does most of the work in this case, and the plain language of the 1991 amendments to Title VII do the rest.
— *Daryl Joseffer, representing the University of Southwestern Texas Medical Center in Univ. Sw. Tex. Med. Ctr. v. Nassar.*[5]

Other advocates start with a thematic hook, framing the issues in a way that appeals to the bench's "visceral notions of doing the right thing:"[6]

EXAMPLE **Introduction Kick-Off: Thematic**

Barbara Grutter applied for admission to the University of Michigan Law School with a personal right guaranteed by the Constitution that she would not have her race counted against her. . . . The law school intentionally disregarded that right by discriminating against her on the basis of race as it does each year in the case of thousands of individuals who apply for admission.

> The law school defends its practice of race discrimination as necessary to achieve a diverse student body. . . . [That diversity] is of a narrow kind, defined exclusively by race and ethnicity.
>
> It is precisely because we are a nation teeming with different races and ethnicities . . . that it is so crucial for our Government to honor its solemn obligation to treat all members of our society equally, without preferring some individuals over others.
>
> —*Kirk Kolbo, representing Barbara Grutter in Grutter v. Bollinger.*[7]

In the next example, Paul Clement departs from his succinct opener in the Affordable Care Act arguments, using a thematic approach better suited to a case that required him to defend Arizona's immigration laws.

EXAMPLE   **Introduction Kick-Off: Thematic**

Mr. Chief Justice, and may it please the Court. The State of Arizona bears a disproportionate share of the costs of illegal immigration. In addressing those costs, Arizona borrowed the Federal standards as its own and attempted to enlist state resources in the enforcement of the uniform Federal immigration laws.

Notwithstanding that, the United States took the extraordinary step of seeking a preliminary injunction to enjoin the statute as impliedly preempted on its face before it took effect. The Ninth Circuit agreed with respect to four provisions, but only by inverting fundamental principles of federalism.

The Ninth Circuit, essentially, demanded that Arizona point to specific authorization in the Federal statute for its approach. But that gets matters backwards.

—*Paul Clement, representing the State of Arizona in Arizona v. United States.*[8]

Thematic introductions can have a high risk-reward ratio. The risk is that they invite skepticism if the court doesn't see your case through that same lens or if your framing fails to ring true. Your theme might spur a time-devouring line of questioning or negative commentary to the tune of, "that's not really what this case is about, counsel." On the other hand, the payoff can be substantial. Well-crafted thematic introductions—those with compelling ideas that unite the entire argument—can influence the court's thinking and decisionmaking in ways that a straight-up presentation of the issues might not. You and your supervisor or professor must jointly assess the right approach.

Some advocates move next to a roadmap asserting a pithy preview of their arguments, on the theory that the roadmap captures their positions just in case time runs short, and allows the court to point them in one direction or another. But especially in the hands of less experienced oralists, roadmaps have a tendency to run long with redundant or unnecessary detail. Moreover, good signposting and transitions within the argument can steer the panel from one argument to the next more efficiently. And time is precious in oral argument. All in, the best advocates protect their time by limiting introductions to about 45 seconds. The reality is that they may be interrupted far sooner.

The body. On the heels of the introduction, the body presents the advocate's arguments in capsule form, paring each one down to its essence.[9] Section 2 explains how to prepare to deliver the body of your argument, as well as how to manage intensive questioning. But for now, we offer four important points about the body's structure.

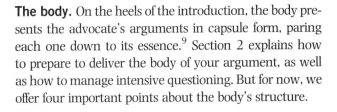

First—Each argument should be modular.[10] That is, each argument should stand on its own so that you can jump to it at an opportune time in your remarks or in answers to questions. For example, in a statutory interpretation argument, a linear structure might dictate this order: (1) plain language; (2) legislative history; and (3) policy implications of one interpretation versus another. But you mustn't depend on that order when you think about the body of your argument. The court's questioning may force you into a discussion of legislative history before you utter a word about the plain language, so your plain language argument cannot be the sole launching pad into your legislative history argument. You'll need to fashion both arguments as modular, accessible through multiple points of entry. At the same time that you are disaggregating arguments to promote agility, your structure must reflect their relationships to each other and to the result you want. Make sure you know what happens if the court agrees with any given argument but disagrees with any other. Which combinations will result in reversal? Which in affirming? Which ones are alternatives to the same result?

Second—Each argument should be point-first, that is, state your conclusion first, then give the supporting reasons. That means staking out a firm position on the argument before you launch into the "why" behind it. Even more than in the written medium, oral arguments that meander around reasons and build up to a conclusion lose focus and derail your judicial audience. Arguments presented in this upside-down manner also prompt questions that would have been unnecessary had you been more direct. Here is a point-first example:

> The trial court was correct that the police complied with the Fourth Amendment in searching the defendant's car and seizing his writing. The record shows that the police conducted a proper inventory search—both in purpose and scope. As for purpose, the officers' compliance with department inventory procedures is dispositive. . . .

Sidebar:

**Practice Alert #2
Great Oral Argument Openers**

In the online companion you will find a compilation of arresting oral argument introductions delivered by experienced United States Supreme Court advocates.

And another:

> The defendant's writing was not a "true threat" for two independent reasons. He did not intend to communicate his thoughts, and no reasonable person would have found them threatening. Intent to communicate fails because the writing itself shows it was for the defendant's eyes only, and the only steps he took were to keep the writing private, not to share it. . . .

To create the capsule form that oral argument demands, use one-step logic to articulate your supporting reasons whenever possible, rather than asking the court to stay with you through a long or multi-faceted line of reasoning. This can be done with complex arguments; it just requires you to compress your reasoning down to its purest syllogistic form. The table below compares the overly complex, meandering approach to a point-first, one-step logic approach.

Overly complex logic presented upside-down	One-step logic presented point first
A "true threat" requires the defendant to form an intent to communicate.	This court should reverse the defendant's conviction because he never formed the intent to communicate. Proving this intent is an absolute requirement for true threats.
Virginia v. Black cemented this requirement when it described true threats as where the speaker "means to communicate" a serious intent to commit violence. Several circuits confirm and define this intent requirement.	Virginia v. Black tells us that true threats must "mean to communicate" a serious intent to commit violence, but the defendant meant to communicate nothing. He simply wrote down his thoughts about a rap song on scrap paper and stashed it between the seat and console of his car.
For example, in *Doe*, the court held that the defendant had formed an intent to communicate by writing a threatening letter to his girlfriend, even though it was never delivered. The defendant showed communicative intent by addressing the letter to a recipient and sharing its content with others.	This is far cry from taking "active steps" to put speech out into the world. That's the standard that several circuits have set for the outer limits of intent. The defendant didn't write and address a letter and then talk about it with friends like the defendant in *Doe*. He didn't post and then remove a Facebook rant like the defendant in *Jeffries*. Because the defendant's only steps were to keep his writing private, the State fails the intent element. His conviction should be reversed on this ground alone.
In *Jeffries*, the defendant intended to communicate when he posted, then removed, a threatening Facebook rant.	
These cases and several others confirm that a speaker intends to communicate when he takes active steps to put his speech out into the world. Here, the defendant did not take any active steps to put his writing out into the world. He simply wrote down his thoughts about a rap song on scrap paper and stashed it between the seat and console of his car. These actions are consistent with keeping the writing private, not communicating it. Therefore, the State cannot show intent to communicate here.	
Because intent to communicate is an absolute requirement for proving a true threat, the defendant's conviction should be reversed on this ground alone.	

Third—An effective argument delivered orally should not recount all parts of a test, elements, or rules in the abstract. Your argument will be much more effective if you combine the legal rules with the actual facts of your case, rather than addressing them separately and seriatim. In other words, the articulation and application process should be simultaneous. So, for example, not: "The next element of negligence is causation. Causation fails here because . . . [facts]," but "The plaintiffs failed to prove causation as a matter of law because . . . [facts]."[11] The latter approach creates both the reality and the perception that your argument is moving faster. It also makes your presentation more forceful and explains the immediate import of any law you discuss. As with the other techniques, the result is efficiency and a lower likelihood that the court will consume argument time with questions that a streamlined presentation would head off.

Below is a chart that compares the two approaches. Try reciting each version aloud in front of a peer. The simultaneous version will probably cut about one-third off your time. Then check your peer's reaction. He is likely to tell you that he became impatient with the first version and wanted you to get to the point.

Inefficient recounting of the law, followed by application	Simultaneous articulation and application
To convict the defendant on a theory of constructive drug possession, the government must prove three elements. First, the government must show that the defendant knew about the contraband. Second, it must prove that the defendant had the ability to control the contraband. And third, it must show that the defendant had the intent to control the contraband.	This Court should reverse the defendant's conviction for constructive drug possession because the government did not prove with sufficient evidence any of the elements of the crime.
Here, the government fails for insufficient evidence on all three points. No evidence suggests the defendant was aware that the small, gray, putty-like substance in a baggie sitting on a counter 20 feet away was a cocaine precursor. Nor did she have the ability to control the substance. She had never touched it, was not near it, and had no power over it.	First, the defendant did not know about the contraband. No evidence suggests that she was aware that the small, gray, putty-like substance in a baggie sitting on a counter 20 feet away was a cocaine precursor.
Finally nothing in the record suggests that the defendant intended to control the contraband—a substance she wasn't even aware of in the first place. Therefore, the defendant's conviction should be reversed.	Second, the defendant had no ability to control the substance. She had never touched it, was not near it, and had no power over it.
	Third, nothing in the record suggests that the defendant intended to control the contraband—a substance she wasn't even aware of in the first place.

Fourth — The body of your argument must address weaknesses. Just as two-sided messaging and inoculation pay persuasive dividends for your brief, so they do in oral argument, but the strategies differ. Whether to wait for a question to deal with the weakness or to attack it head-on yourself is a tactical choice, depending on the weakness's magnitude as well as the oralist's style. Using one of our recurring examples, assume you represent a defendant convicted of constructive cocaine possession. Your theory is that she is the innocent girlfriend of a drug dealer, and that the government is pushing guilt by association. But you have a bad fact. Pre-drug bust, your client received a text message saying, "Drop off the baby at Shelby's tonight." Although your client shares custody of a toddler, "drop off the baby" is street lingo for a drug transaction, and Shelby's is a truck strop known for drug activity. As the only piece of evidence potentially connecting your client to drugs, if you don't address it head-on, it could seem like the elephant in the room, leading the court to think that you are hiding from that fact. On the other hand, perhaps the court thinks this evidence so speculative that it is not worth addressing unless asked. Whichever strategy you choose, you must have a knock-out explanation of why it doesn't matter. If the evidence shows your client and her ex-husband often use Shelby's as the drop-off location for their shared custody arrangement, and nothing suggests that drug lingo is in her lexicon, you can convincingly argue that this evidence invites pure speculation, not permissible inferences of guilt.

The conclusion. The conclusion is the shortest argument component, but how you end leaves an impression. When time expires, quickly and simply conclude by asking the court for the relief you're seeking. This brings the big picture back into focus and shows the court you respect its time. If you are in the middle of an answer to a question, you can briefly wrap it up before your conclusion. Some advocates, if not consumed with answering a question as time is waning, will finish the argument with their last best point in light of how the argument has gone — ending with a "bang," so to speak. But good advocates never strain to use the rest of their time once they have made their points and there appear to be no more questions from the court; instead they sit down. And the panel is always grateful.

REFLECTION, DISCUSSION, AND CHALLENGE QUESTIONS

The Structure of Oral Argument

- Think about the appeal you are working on. Do the issues lend themselves to a thematic introduction or a simpler beginning? Try drafting your opening sentences using both approaches. Which one is more effective and why?
- Pick the most complex argument from your brief. Try rewriting it in one-step logic form.
- What is the biggest weakness in your appeal? Strategically, would it be best to raise and attack that weakness in the argument, or wait until the court asks about it? Then draft a two-sentence explanation of why that weakness does not cut against a ruling in your favor.

Section 2 Preparing for the Argument and Anticipating Questions

Having discussed argument fundamentals and structure, we turn next to oral argument preparation and execution. The best oral arguments result from exhaustive and methodical *over*-preparation. We say over-preparation because even experienced appellate advocates spend many thousands more minutes preparing for an oral argument than the 10 to 30 minutes they will spend arguing it. As a new practitioner, you can anticipate spending 60 to 80 hours from soup-to-nuts preparing for your oral argument, and, of course, that is on top of the enormous time spent researching and writing the briefs. Though at first blush such a time commitment might seem unwarranted and inefficient, many judges report that oral argument can favorably change the outcome in 10 to 15 percent of the cases before them.[12] And one thing is certain, an advocate can lose a case during oral argument, either through sloppy concessions or by poor performance affecting the advocate's credibility, which in turn reflects poorly on the client.[13] After spending hundreds of hours reviewing the record and carefully crafting your arguments, you do not want the judges' last impression before retiring to conference to be that counsel was ill prepared or, worse, incompetent. Below is a plan that will ensure you are fully prepared.

2.1 The Briefs: Review, Refresh, and Identify

To begin your preparation, spend a few hours with the briefs. If you've prepared Chapter 12's analysis chart for your response or reply brief, it will come in handy again now. Re-read all of the briefs and make two lists. The first list (the "Points List") should contain the essential points that you may want to make during your argument and those that you expect to be raised by the other side. On your second list (the "Questions List") jot down any potential oral argument question that could be asked of you. For this list, it is important to keep an open mind so that you do not filter out potential questions by virtue of your extreme familiarity with the case. Pretend you are the judges coming to the case for the first time. What piques your curiosity? What remains unanswered by the briefs?

2.2 The Record: Review the Record and Take Notes with Purpose

Once again — like the brief analysis charts — the time that you spent digesting early in the case continues to pay dividends. You already have a template to guide you through your oral argument record review. Unlike the record review at the beginning of the case, your purpose for diving back in now is different. Your review should be thorough but efficient, targeted to the specific facts pertinent to the issues you identified for oral argument. And your review should be even more active than it was on the front end. Supplement your Points List with any specific facts from the record that you may now see in a new light with the benefit of hindsight after rereading the briefs. Draft additional questions and add them to your Questions List based on the facts in the record that might come up at oral argument. Finally, start a third, new list (the "Topics List") where you cull and organize facts from across the factual record around the topics that you now know are important. For example, in Chapter 12 we provided an example of permissible arguments in a reply brief from the *Mutombo* appeal, which dealt with an inventory search of the defendant's car. The defendant argued that the police had engaged in an unconstitutional warrantless search because they were already investigating him when they conducted the inventory search and because the police did not follow their own policies in conducting it. Together, these facts showed that the police's inventory rationale was mere pretext. If you wanted to pursue this line of argument, you would want to have at your fingertips all of the relevant testimony from the officers about their motivation and execution of that search, so one of your topics on your Topics List would look like this:

Officers' Statements About the Search and Days Leading up to It

Source	Pg	Witness	Quote
Grand Jury	2-9	Sampson	Glen Lake P.D. contacted him on 4/4/08; testifies how he went to the bank to trace the defendant's check, contacted the IRS and the local P.D.
Grand Jury	7	Sampson	Says that these actions were "[i]n furtherance of our investigation."
Suppression	12	Salles	Says he knew there was an ongoing investigation
Suppression	58-61	Wilburn	Acknowledging that a memo about the defendant had been circulated in the days leading up to the search.
Trial	33	Wilburn	"And I let my officers know just keep an eye on the car. Should they see somebody around the car, go ahead and stop and identify who may be there and jot it down for the investigators from the Glen Lake P.D. and IRS."

Notice how this chart answers one question or topic: What record evidence demonstrates that the officers' search was pretextual rather than a true inventory search? And it captures in one place all of the evidence from across the factual record on that topic. These single-topic lists allow you to synthesize and later use complex factual information during the oral argument, both in fashioning your points and in crafting answers to questions. For example, imagine you were asked this question at argument: How do you know that the police officers were targeting the defendant before they conducted the search? Because you have taken the time to analyze the facts, you can provide a truly outstanding answer, one that reflects thought and persuades through its detail and obvious mastery of the record:

> We know that the police officers were targeting the defendant because three of the four officers who worked on the case — Salles, Wilburn, and Sampson — admitted no less than eight separate times over the course of the proceedings below that they were doing so.

And then you could refer to your Topics List, which has all of this information in an easily accessible, summary form, for additional detail or record citations if the panel requires it. As you continue to prepare, you will further refine the points you want to make and so you will inevitably have to dive back into the record many times to gather the precise facts (and their location in the record).

2.3 Case Law and Other Authority: Review and Update

Your next step is to re-familiarize yourself with the relevant authority. You simply must know every case cited in the briefs and their key proposition(s). Again, it is more helpful at this point to start categorizing the cases in whatever way makes them easiest for you to remember. Here is a sample of one approach with the cases listed alphabetically, but you could also sort them by persuasive weight:

Case Name	Court/ Year	Quote
Albers	Neb. 2008	No challenge to charge of attempted terroristic threats; pointed gun at wife/daughter/husband
Boim	11th Cir. 2007	Student actually gave notebook w/ threat to other student. It left student's possess/control
Brandenberg	U.S. 1969	Speech with action only type proscribed; KKK imminent lawless act
Doe / Lafayette	7th Cir. 2004	Core First Amendment right of self expression; gov't violates if punish pure thought; can't regulate thought w/o conduct
Doe / Pulaski	8th Cir. 2002	Letter about desire to assault ex-girlfriend/school discipline; threat requires communication which happened here b/c defendant gave to friend knowing he would release
Edwards	U.S. 1963	Speech protected against censor or punish, unless shown likely to produce a clear and present danger. . . . Alternative would lead to standardization of ideas.

Case Name	Court/Year	Quote
Evans	D.C. App. 2001	Person behind in courtroom; must do more than utter a threat: must show message conveyed
Green	Penn. App. 1981	True threat because actually communicated, not attempt
Jenkins	D.C. App. 2006	Cell phone; statute requires communication in order to be a threat
Porter	5th Cir. 2004	Violent sketch case; threat must be intent and knowing communication to remove from First Amendment
Stanley	U.S. 1969	"Whole constitutional heritage rebels at . . . giving government power to control men's minds"

Not only should you review the cases cited in the briefs, you should update that research to ensure that no new cases impacting yours have come down since briefing concluded. Ensure that all of your authority is still good law for the proposition that it stood for in your brief. If new binding authority has been issued, you should file a letter with the court under Federal Rule of Appellate Procedure 28(j), alerting it to that authority *before* your argument. That rule permits advocates to flag "pertinent and significant" authorities that have "come to a party's attention after the party's brief has been filed." If you don't, you may not cite to that authority during your argument,[14] and you may draw questions from the panel as to why you did not address it.

Finally, cases are a source of potential oral argument questions, especially the sometimes-dreaded hypothetical questions. As you review the authority, take the time to consider the next logical step from the case holding: Craft a hypothetical question from that next step and see if your argument survives it. Add these to your Questions List as well. Even if you do not believe that the panel will ask you about specific cases, it is a good idea to draft some questions based on the case law so that you are prepared to answer them. At a minimum, you should be able to answer the question: What is the best case for whatever point of law you are trying to advance? Courts routinely ask that question. More broadly, questions about decided cases are also a good test of your level of preparation; if you are able to answer a question about any case in your brief, then you know (and the panel will know) that your preparation has been thorough and rigorous.

2.4 Questions and Answers: Drafting and Categorizing

Having reviewed the briefs, the record, and the relevant legal authority anew and having jotted down potential questions along the way, you now should have a formidable Questions List. Take a pass through the list and edit out the repetition, then categorize the remaining questions by topic or issue. Next take a stab at drafting answers. It's often best to have two answers to each question: the five-second answer and the one with a bit of additional explanation. Treat your five-second answer as the thesis sentence for your longer answer. You can revert to your short answer if you are running low on time, but having the longer answer — especially during your preparation — provides the reasoning that will keep you focused and hopefully avoids a lapse into robotic, unpersuasive responses. Then practice answering the questions out loud. You'll notice that your written answers are probably too complicated and too long. Simplify your answers, and then practice them aloud once again. Continually update your answers throughout your preparation based on the feedback at each moot or roundtable. By the end of your preparation you likely will have committed most of the answers to memory, but if not, start creating charts or spreadsheets to condense and summarize only the most crucial Q&As.

Building on the example of the inventory search, here is a sample Questions List that includes questions culled from each step of the prep process. Note how these questions incorporate all of the work completed thus far — they mine the record, the cases, and the briefs.

Question	5-Second Answer	Long Answer
What privacy expectation could the defendant possibly have had when he abandoned the car on campus for days? Doesn't his failure to exercise control of the vehicle (and its contents) destroy any privacy claim?	His car was not abandoned and his privacy expectation in his car remained — as the Supreme Court has said — "important and deserving of constitutional protection."	First, he didn't abandon his car. The vehicle abandonment statute defines it as a car in such disrepair that it can't be driven or a car that has been left for more than 7 days. Second, the Supreme Court in Arizona v. Gant reinforces that although an individual's privacy interest in his car is less than that in his home, it is nonetheless, "Important and deserving of constitutional protection."
Isn't it true that the P.D. didn't join the investigation until after the threat was discovered?	No; they joined it at least a week before.	No, not at all. Wilburn issued a safety alert on July 16; police went to the credit union on July 17; no less than six times during suppression hr'g Wilburn said that they were gathering information for other police units (T. at 68-72; 81-82).
Doesn't *Hoskins* tell us that his expectation of privacy was terminated because he had abandoned the car?	No, *Hoskins*'s facts are completely different; there a woman actively threw her purse away while fleeing police.	No, *Hoskins* dealt with a purse that a woman threw to ground while fleeing police, which is a different intent to abandon. The relevant statutes define abandoned car: a vehicle in a state of disrepair rendering it incapable of being driven in its condition or any vehicle that has not been moved or used for 7 consecutive days.

Question	5-Second Answer	Long Answer
Didn't Salles testify that he was merely doing an inventory. Why shouldn't we credit his testimony? (Appellee Br. 23.)	Because he did not even follow department policies in executing it.	Look at what Salles knew and did and this contradicts what he said. Salles knew it was the defendant's car before initiating the search; knew that defendant was the subject of ongoing investigation. And then Salles didn't even do a complete inventory. (R933.) This was an invalid investigatory search and under this Court's cases (*Dennison* 1978), it was invalid.
Opperman doesn't say that you cannot read personal papers during an inventory, does it?	No. But the conduct here was the type of general rummaging that the Court counseled against.	No, but given the facts underlying this search — the fact that there was an ongoing investigation — should require heightened vigilance in protecting Fourth Amendment interests.
Are you asking for a categorical rule that officers simply cannot read personal papers during an inventory search?	No.	No. The rule could be limited in many ways that don't tie the hands of officers in a legitimate inventory search. First, officers may pick up to ascertain, but then must put down. Second, no reviewing personal papers when the car owner is the subject of an ongoing investigation.

Practice Alert #3 Brainstorming Questions

The online companion contains sample briefs for you to review, then create a list of potential oral argument questions for both sides. Share your questions with your colleagues. Did you come up with the same questions? What did you learn from the questions you did not think of?

2.5 Prepared Remarks, Argument Outline, and Nonverbal Persuasion

Prepared remarks. Because you took notes when you reviewed the briefs at the beginning of the process, you should have a fairly comprehensive Points List with issues that you think are worth addressing at oral argument. But now you need to cut down your list or, as the Supreme Court Practitioner's Guide counsels, "Lay out all the clothes you think you will need [for the ocean cruise], and then return half of them back to the closet."[15] Make potency your gauge for selecting these topics or issues. Former Solicitor General Seth Waxman calls this the "kernel" approach. He defines the kernel of the case as the "one or two, or at the very most, three points that you must impress upon the court before you sit down."[16] Some advocates even omit or trim to a bare minimum any argument that, in the oralist's estimation, was well-laid out in the brief.[17]

Your next job is to translate these (often-complex) written arguments into a series of propositions that will resonate with a listening audience. Whatever you say must be tethered to your theory of the case and the themes you've developed.

Among other strategies, advocates have used the oral medium to: (1) hone and shore up themes that got lost in the written presentation;[18] (2) simplify complex arguments with conversational language, visual descriptions, and relatable examples;[19] (3) emphasize arguments with commonsense appeal;[20] (4) stress arguments that best tie into the underlying rationale behind a legal doctrine, test, or rule;[21] and (5) focus the court on real-world benefits of their position and the dangers of the opponent's.[22]

The key takeaway is this: If you simply recite the arguments from your brief, you will have accomplished nothing positive and the consequences could be much worse. It will sound like you are reading your brief and *no one* wants to listen to that. Instead, you must re-imagine those essential points with an eye towards the spoken word and group your arguments in a way that allows the judges to easily understand and visualize what you are saying.

Logistically speaking, how many lines of prepared remarks you write depends on the court in which you are arguing. If you are arguing in a "hot" court — one that asks a lot of questions — you may only need a minute or 90 seconds of prepared remarks, only a bit more than a carefully crafted introduction. If you know that your bench will be "cold," you may want to prepare more of your argument. Additionally, a lot of these decisions depend on your personal style, discussed in more detail below. Some people are more comfortable with a crafted presentation, others with a less detailed outline, and still others need only a list of topics.

Argument outline. Whatever format you choose for your structured argument, remember two things. First, you must not read. You may read a brief quotation from something that is particularly important but if you need something more fleshed out than a list or an outline, then make sure that you can easily memorize it. Second, and equally important, your chosen format must give you the flexibility to depart from your prepared presentation for questions and easily dive back in when you've finished answering. If you can't fluidly shift from "presentation" mode to "questioning" mode and back again, then the approach you've chosen simply does not work for you, and you must try something else. Try different approaches for formatting your argument on paper. Bullet points work well for some; others have tried a "tree" approach with each point (and subpoints) occupying their own branch. Columns or tables are better for others, and still others are able to follow prose in paragraphs.

Do not underestimate the amount of work this process involves. You should commit to drafting at least five to seven versions of your argument, for it will change significantly each time you practice it aloud and for others. Usually, the first stab at an argument is too complicated, filled with fussy language and, quite frankly, too many words. So in each round, continue culling the points that you want to convey. And simplify your language, because a listening audience cannot absorb the level of detail that a reading audience can.[23] Split up the compound sentences and make meaning early in each sentence. Slice out the adverbs. Replace every multisyllabic word (unless it is a legal term) with a shorter, more concrete substitute. Eliminate all double negatives — they are nearly impossible to comprehend when spoken. And eviscerate the wishy-washy lead-ins and verbal clutter such as, "I think" or "I believe" before making your points. Be deliberate in your word choice as well. Make sure what you say does not lead the court to take you down an unintended labyrinth of questioning. Work on creating "soundbites" or memorable phrases that capture thematic elements or frame the law or facts in an original way. Illustrate your points with everyday examples, plain-spoken analogies, or aphorisms. Above all, choose words that are simple, yet descriptive and visual, and that will stay with the judges long after your argument.

Nonverbal persuasion. Once you've considered what you'd like to convey verbally, think next about the nonverbal cues that should accompany your argument. This work is more vital than you might think. Studies show that nonverbal cues carry even more information to the listener than the speaker's words.[24] Professor Michael Higdon's exhaustive application of the social science on nonverbal persuasion to appellate argument emphasizes three aspects: (1) body movement, including eye contact; (2) appearance; and (3) vocal cadence, volume, and tone.[25] Together, these qualities should portray a delicate mix of deference and confidence, as we explain below. Deliberately incorporate them into your presentation, and seek feedback on them from your mooting audience.

First, good eye contact is both a crucial element of persuasion and a way to engage the judges' interest.[26] Simply put, the judges are more likely to want to hear and believe what you say if you are looking at them, especially when you answer questions. Looking down before responding conveys a lack of knowledge and confidence.[27] On the other hand, eye contact that crosses the line into staring can be unnerving, so practice striking the right balance with your eyes, aiming to look at each panelist in turn.[28] Indeed, if one judge is asking particularly hostile questions, it can be imperative for you to look at the other judges because you might prompt one of them to break into the hostile judge's attacking questions. By staring at the judge who is asking the hostile questions, you almost invite her to follow up after you have offered an answer. It is much better to look away as if your answer is directed to others on the bench.

Posture, too, sends messages about confidence. The ideal posture stems from planting your feet, standing straight, and not shifting your weight or leaning on the podium, but also staying relaxed enough to leave your hands free for natural gestures.[29] As for gestures, too many are distracting, but restrained hand movements that match your tone and verbal message—rather than seeming like random or nervous movements—can reinforce your content.[30] Conversely, fidgeting with pens, papers, or anything else detracts from persuasive value.[31] And we hardly need social science to tell us that appropriate formal dress and a clean appearance communicate an equally important nonverbal message: that you respect the court and the import of the occasion.[32] Practice in your court attire so that you are comfortable when argument time comes.

Pacing, volume, and tone. Use your moots and roundtables to experiment with vocal cadence, volume, and tone. These qualities have persuasive power apart from the content of your words. A moderate rate is the most persuasive (and intelligible), and that rate should slow as you explain difficult or important concepts.[33] Accompanied by strategic pauses used sparingly for points of emphasis, this approach to pace contributes to a perception of the oralist as a "learned counselor," intent on helping the court with its decisionmaking enterprise.[34] Many advocates, when they perceive they are gaining momentum, add a rhythmic quality to their delivery that makes the court grasp every word. As with cadence, a moderately high volume makes the speaker more persuasive.[35] At this level, the speaker conveys command and control over her argument, while a soft-spoken speaker appears timid and unconfident.[36] On matters of tone, oralists who vary their pitch are perceived more favorably than those who speak in monotone, quite possibly because varied tones create a conversational feel.[37] Finally, listen to the question that is asked and try to slow down your answer and insert a deliberate, two-beat pause before you begin to answer a question. That pause comes pretty naturally if you simply nod your head to demonstrate that you think you understand the question before you launch into an answer. This approach ensures that you have time to process the question actually asked (and not presume that it mirrors a slightly different one from earlier practice rounds). It also signals to the panel that you are listening to them.

2.6 Winnow, Study, and Memorize

In the final days before the argument, you should begin to create synthesis charts. Compiling these documents is a lot like preparing outlines for final exams in law school: It's not so much about the final product as it is about the process. Though these charts might ultimately accompany you to the podium, it is doubtful that you will ever refer to them. But the very process of identifying the categories of facts (and their location in the record) and the authorities that best support your points at oral argument allows you to internalize all of this important information. For example, here is a sample chart compiling all of the important facts from the record and their citations:

Date	Event	Record
07/02/07	Defendant receives check	McDonald Tr. 8/9/07
07/03/07	Defendant first speaks to Cotton	R00670
07/05/07	Vannick calls police b/c realizes forged check	McDonald Tr. 8/9/07
07/12/07	Vannick calls IRS	R00682
07/16/07	IRS calls back	R00693
07/17/07	Police to the bank	Williams Tr. 8/9/07
07/20/07	Preston interview	R00748
07/25/07	Press conference	R00635
08/09/07	Indictment	C00023

You may want to further winnow your Topic List into summary charts. The example from Step 2 above, which collected all of the facts relating to the officers' investigation of the defendant before the inventory search, could be winnowed down for oral argument as follows:

Fact Showing Pretext	Cite
Glen Lake police told Sampson about the forged check three days before the search; Sampson went to bank to inquire two days before search; contacted the IRS	GJ Tr. 2-9
Sampson admits that his actions were "in furtherance of our investigation"	Trial Tr. 7
Salles admitted that there was an ongoing investigation	Trial Tr. 12
Wilburn admits receiving memo about defendant three days before	Suppress. Tr. 58-61
Wilburn telling officers to surveil car three days leading up to search	Trial Tr. 1, 33

You will do similar exercises for your case authority, your oral argument questions, and your prepared remarks. Here is the case chart that you prepared in Step 3, now condensed for your final days of preparation before argument and organized by issue rather than alphabetically:

Issue	Cite
1st Amendment	Trial Tr. 237
4th Amendment	Trial Tr. 1, 33

Issue	Cite
1st Amendment	• *Stanley/Woodrum*: can't control thought • *Boim*: (1) school; (2) civil; (3) no threat/disruption; (4) gave to another • *Evans*: actual communication & required by statute • *Parr*: jury question because threat; fact question as to whether kidding • *Porter*: intentional communication required; 5th Circuit. • *Susic*: open question about the proper interpretation of Virginia v. Black

Issue	Cite
	• *Toledo*: attempt only b/c no establish fear element; actual communication • *Woodrum*: thought w/o conduct
4th Amendment	• *Opperman*: Powell concurrence says inventory "provides no general license for the police to examine all the contents of such automobiles."

By consistently condensing your outlines, you will continue to commit more to memory.

2.7 Practice Via Moots and Roundtables

All of the intense preparation thus far should culminate in roundtables and moot courts with other trusted colleagues. Even the most experienced oral advocates collaborate with others in preparation for oral argument. At a minimum, you should hold a roundtable or "pre-moot" where you sit around the table with others familiar with the case and hash out the most difficult parts of your case. Your brain trust for these roundtables should be people who will push and test you, not merely agree with you. After these roundtables you should hold a series of moot courts; include as judges those who participated in the roundtable, but also incorporate others who are new. Their perspective and level of preparedness will more closely mirror that of your actual panel. Conduct the first part of each moot as if it were the actual argument; stay in character and mind the time limits. If you can recruit someone to argue the other side, it can be incredibly valuable. Another person should take notes during each moot, recording the questions and answers, the general responses to your lines of argument during the moot, and the judges' specific feedback afterwards. Videotaping at least one moot is a great way to identify problems with your delivery. After each moot, you must tweak your presentation and answers, something that will continue all the way until the hours before your argument.

It might look silly to outsiders, but in the days before your argument, you should spend time walking around and presenting your argument in various permutations. You can stand in front of a mirror and deliver an opening statement or you can take the dog for a walk and make believe you are answering the toughest questions you expect to be asked at the oral argument.

2.8 Prepare for the Day of Argument: Research the Court and Compile the Documents

In advance of oral argument you will want to be completely familiar with the court. Consider this an extension of the research you conducted earlier on the court and its handling of appeals, discussed in Chapter 4. Attend oral arguments once or twice beforehand and observe the judges' questioning style. Review the rules governing oral argument in your court and speak to the clerk's office if you have any questions. For example, make sure you understand how the light system works. Does a yellow light mean you are five minutes from the end of the time you reserved for your opening argument, or does it mean you are now into your rebuttal time?

If you learn your panel in advance, spend some time researching the judges. Figure out whether any of those judges authored the key cases in the appeal, or if they have written at all on the topics in your case. Listen to or read the transcripts of oral arguments made before these judges so you can get a feel for their questioning style. Even if you do not find out the panel until the day of the argument, you should familiarize yourself with the judges who sit on the court.

In the day or two leading up to the argument, you will want to finalize the documents that you will bring up. Compile a full set of the briefs and appendix; those must go up to the podium with you. Make sure you have copies of the relevant statute and the top few cases. Finalize the summary charts that you may need during the argument and the final version of your remarks and/or outline. Memorize your introduction, but make the delivery sound extemporaneous. To achieve an extemporaneous effect, write out your introduction and then say it out loud. You'll probably find some words, phrases, and sentence constructions that looked fine in writing, but sound awkward orally. So choose more natural syntax and phrasing that fits your speaking style, then conform the writing to your speech. Do this over and over until the words you have written down sound conversational when spoken aloud. Having the first few seconds of your presentation down pat will counteract the inevitable jitters as you step up to the podium.

Next, decide how you would like to access your materials. Some people use a notepad, others use a binder or staple the key documents into a folder. Some bring up only a few sheets of paper or a series of notecards. A word of caution here: We have seen loose paper slide off the podium and lawyers drop the notecards, which is not only distracting, but also can completely disrupt the flow of the advocate's delivery. Finally, some people bring no notes at all to the podium, but these are only the most experienced advocates with scores of oral arguments under their belts. Most very experienced advocates take some notes with them to the podium even if they never look at them during the argument. If you are new to oral argument, just try different approaches during your moots. You will soon discover which approach works best for you.

SUMMARY

Steps to Prepare for Oral Argument

STEP 1 — Review the briefs; take notes and craft questions.
STEP 2 — Review the record; take notes and craft questions.
STEP 3 — Review the authority; take notes and craft questions.
STEP 4 — Categorize and answer your questions.
STEP 5 — Prepare your remarks or an argument outline.
STEP 6 — Winnow, study, and memorize.
STEP 7 — Practice via roundtables and moots.
STEP 8 — Prepare materials for argument day and familiarize yourself with the panel.

Section 3 Delivering the Argument and Answering Questions

After all of your preparation, the day of your oral argument has arrived. This portion of the chapter walks you through the actual presentation of argument, including answering questions and developing your personal style. Even if your oral argument is simulated, you should approach it just as if you were in court, unless your professor instructs you otherwise.

3.1 Arriving at the Courthouse

You may wonder why on the day of the argument you have so much adrenaline running through your body. It is because you have worked for weeks or months for this moment and you know that the judges who are deciding your case will be coming out to greet or perhaps confront you in a few minutes. Up to this point, you have no idea how the real decisionmakers will react to your arguments. It is that anticipation that increases the lawyers' anxiety level. But what you should remind yourself before the oral argument begins is what Rex E. Lee, the former Solicitor General of the United States, would say to his colleague on the other side of the podium before every oral argument: "Just remember, oral arguments are the most fun thing a lawyer can do with his clothes on."

If your case is the first of the day, then you can be seated at the counsel table when the judges come in. If your argument comes later in the session, then when your case is called, you should stop at the counsel table to deposit your extra items, but do not sit down. Proceed directly to the podium and take a few seconds to arrange your materials. Look up at the bench to make sure the judges are ready for you to begin. Begin every argument with some version of "May it please the Court" (in the United States Supreme Court, for example, you say "Mr. Chief Justice and may it please the Court"). Some lawyers introduce everyone at the counsel table. That is not necessary and it is a bit time-consuming and generally of no interest to the judges. You may then launch into your introduction and prepared remarks. Remember to slow down a bit and speak clearly. Aside from these general tips and our advice in Section 2, though, we don't find it all that useful to provide detailed advice on delivery. You have your own personal speaking style that reflects your personality and your strengths; you should cultivate what works best for you during your moots. Some people persuade through an active, energetic style; others persuade through quiet certainty. Any approach can be persuasive so long as it's comprehensible, fluid, and confident. If you try to shoehorn your natural presentation into a different style, it will be stilted and thus less persuasive.

Practice Alert #4
Evaluating Different Styles

The online companion contains clips of oral arguments reflecting advocates' different styles. After watching or listening to the selections, try to describe each advocate's approach and discuss what you found effective (or ineffective).

3.2 Answering Questions

Depending on the court and the issues your case presents, you will have anywhere from a few seconds to several minutes before receiving your first question. The best strategy for dealing with questions is to view them not as threats, but as opportunities. Most judges ask questions because they are legitimately confused about a point in your case and they want your guidance. If the judges care enough to ask questions about your case, that means you still have an opportunity to persuade them. So rather than viewing questions as hostile attacks or interruptions of your prepared speech, welcome them as an essential (though sometimes nerve-wracking) part of the appellate experience.

Regardless of when your first question arrives, you must stop what you are saying and *listen.* Resist the temptation to talk over the judge or to finish the point you were making. Instead, place a mark or a finger at the spot in your outline where you stopped. Then take a few seconds to collect your thoughts and to make sure that you are answering the question that was asked and no other. If you are at all confused by the question, it is fine to ask for clarification. If it is a question that calls for a "yes" or "no" answer first, be sure to provide it. Then qualify that answer if you must. Don't give a politician's evasive answer that refuses to commit to a "yes" or "no": that will only lose credibility points and invite questions that a more direct answer would have avoided. After your answer, offer your supporting reasoning, but keep it succinct. Many an advocate has surrendered the panel's attention, wasted time, and appeared unprepared by giving a rambling answer that takes the argument into the weeds. And if you can, take Carter Phillips's advice and craft your answer so that you return it "with topspin." What that means is that you not only provide the answer to the question asked but do so in a way that advances your own case. Consider the following two examples:

Question:	How is the phrase, "a shooting will occur . . . this is not a JOKE" artistic expression?
Regular Answer:	Because the only evidence at trial, unrebutted by the State, showed it was the formative stages of rap lyrics.

"Topspin" Answer: Because otherwise the Beatles, Pink Floyd, and the Dixie Chicks would be in jail. For example, in *Goodbye Earl*, the Dixie Chicks say: "We'll pack a lunch and stuff you in the trunk, Earl." The Beatles and Pink Floyd have similarly violent lyrics. Just because a song has violence in it does not strip it of its artistic value and convert it into a true threat, and the same is true of the defendant's lyrics here.

Be sure that you know what *kind* of question the judge is asking. If you can slot the question into one of the common bench query categories, you will be in a better position to answer it without giving up too much ground. Below is a chart that categorizes common types of questions from the bench:

Question Type	Example
Facts	When exactly did the police start investigating the defendant? Was it before or after they conducted the inventory search?
Law	Why should we interpret Virginia v. Black's "means to communicate" language to require a subjective intent prong? Isn't that language captured by the "reasonable speaker foresee" standard?
Standard of Review	Why should this court review the true threat determination de novo when the jury's finding of a true threat is implicit in its verdict?
Procedure	What happens if we reverse on the inventory search issue but affirm on the true threat issue? Does that mean a new suppression hearing and a new trial?
Clarification	Are you asking this court to inject a subjective test into the true threat equation, or are you satisfied with an objective test?
Implications (direct)	If this court adopted an actual communication requirement for all true threats, would that invalidate the law on attempted terrorist threats?
Seeking concession	Do you lose this case if we hold that true threats require an intent to communicate? What if we determine that true threats require actual communication?
Line drawing	Is there a difference between a "dual police motivation" that won't defeat an inventory search on the one hand, and a pretext that will render the search invalid on the other? How do we make the distinction?
Hypothetical	What if a police officer had a vendetta against a local citizen—say, someone who'd filed a lawsuit against the police department—and the officer spotted that citizen's car parked illegally on a highway for more than 24 hours. He inventoried that car because he hoped to find

Question Type	Example
	something incriminating there. The officer followed the police department's inventory procedure to the letter, and sure enough, he finds drugs. Would that qualify as pretext? Or is it "reasonable" under the 4th Amendment?
Softball	Doesn't the First Amendment protect broad swaths of speech subject only to a set of narrowly drawn exceptions?

In addition to recognizing the category into which each question falls, you should also try to detect patterns in the questioning as a whole. Doing so allows you to identify and then focus on what really matters to the panel. Do the panel's questions reflect a concern with crafting a broad rule that might have undesired results in future cases? If so, offer the panel a narrow formulation of the rule that will allow your client to win, but limit the rule's applicability in the future.

One piece of advice that seems counterintuitive is how to deal with rapid-fire questions from multiple judges. If one judge asks you a question and you begin to answer it when a different judge interrupts with another question, answer the interrupting judge's question immediately and then turn back to the first judge and resume answering hers. Though at first blush it may seem impolite to leave the first judge hanging, the judges realize that such things happen and are not offended. It's much worse to tell the second judge — who is now speaking directly to you — to "hold on and I'll get back to you in a second." In fact, never tell a judge that you will answer his question later in your remarks. Address it now, then work your way back into your argument.

Another mistake is waiting for the panel to tell you that you can move on after you answer. Just resume on your own; the court will interrupt you if it has another question. In any event, if you make a habit of returning the ball with topspin, you won't likely encounter those awkward pauses that separate the end of your answer from the beginning of your next point. When you have finished responding to the judge's question, you must seamlessly transition back into your affirmative argument and continue on until the next question. Try phrases like "And that gets me back to why [INSERT ARGUMENT] matters here . . ." or "Not only is the government's reading of the statute undermined by the legislative history, as Your Honor's question pointed out, it also would violate the Rule of Lenity because. . . ." All the while you must watch your time clock. Often the podium or the courtroom deputy's table will have a series of lights or signs indicating how much time you have remaining in your argument, and they often indicate when you are running into your rebuttal time if you are the appellant. It is critical that you protect a few minutes of time for rebuttal (more about that in a moment), so if you see your time dwindling make sure you wrap up your argument.

3.3 Troubleshooting

Every so often an argument runs into a snag. Perhaps the court asks a question to which you have no answer or refers to a case that you do not know. Other times the advocate makes a hasty concession in the heat of the argument that is damaging to the case. Sometimes a judge or judges on the panel commandeer all of your time with questions that seem off-point. Learning how to handle these complications while keeping your wits about you signals your transition to more advanced oral advocacy. With respect to the questions you cannot answer, you simply must be up front, acknowledge that you do not know, and request an opportunity to file a supplemental letter or brief to the court answering it. Similarly, if you make an unwise, hasty concession, you may write a letter to the court immediately after the argument to retract that statement.[38] If a judge tries to get you off track with her questioning, you must answer and cannot seem rude or exasperated. In a variant of "returning the ball with topspin," try responding to the question and immediately transitioning back to a more relevant point: "Your Honor is correct that excited utterance might have been a viable hearsay exception to raise below, but because it wasn't pursued, we have focused on the party-admission exception, which is dispositive here. Specifically . . ." These are just a few tips for the any number of curveballs that can be launched your way during the argument. Keep calm and weather them the best you can.

SUMMARY

Oral Argument

DO	DON'T
Over-prepare.	Read your prepared remarks.
Use one-step logic and conclusion-first sentences.	Repeat your brief.
Know the heart of your case to avoid damaging questions.	Make hasty concessions in response to tough questioning.
Use a strong voice, good cadence, and an affirmative tone.	Speak too quickly.
Use simple language geared toward your aural audience.	Use complex language not geared toward your listening audience.
Make eye contact.	Move around the podium and gesture wildly.
Treat questions as an opportunity to persuade, not an interruption.	Provide evasive or indirect answers to the judges' questions.
Answer questions with topspin.	Introduce new cases that you did not discuss in the briefs.
Make a rebuttal argument if it is allowed.	Continue to argue simply to use up your allotted time if you have finished what you have to say.

3.4 The Appellee's Argument and the Appellant's Rebuttal

All of the advice above applies equally to appellants and appellees. But if you are arguing as the appellee, there are a few additional points worth mentioning. First, it will be more difficult to stick to a set outline or presentation because your argument must necessarily be responsive. If the other side has misrepresented the law or the record, you must clear that up right out of the gate. Barring that, you have some flexibility as to where to start your argument. Listen very carefully to the appellant's points and, more importantly, to the judges' questions. Try to get a feel for where the judges are leaning and then pick up on those in your argument. For example, if a judge asks the appellant a question that favors your side or if the appellant answers a question in a way that the panel finds unsatisfying, then you could seize upon those points first:

> [Introduction . . .] Your Honor, I'd like to begin by picking up on your question relating to commercial readiness that you posed to my colleague. Although the appellant claims that the product was only days from production, the record shows — at Appendix B.34 — that due to delays in enamel manufacturing in Asia, the product would not have been ready for at least another six months. This delay is important because [transition into a prepared point] . . .

You might also begin by clarifying a point that your opponent muddled, or by focusing on a key opposing weakness or concession. In the example below, appellate specialist Maureen Mahoney uses this technique, recasting her opponent's argument and naming its flaw.

| EXAMPLE | Appellee Opener

Mr. Chief Justice and may it please the Court. The Solicitor General acknowledges that diversity may be a compelling interest, but contends that the University of Michigan Law School can achieve a diverse student body through facially neutral means.

His argument ignores the record in this case.
— *Maureen Mahoney, representing the University of Michigan in Grutter v. Bollinger.*[39]

In this example, Solicitor General Don Verrilli, Jr., responds to Paul Clement's argument in *Arizona v. United States*.

EXAMPLE **Appellee Opener**

Mr. Clement is working hard this morning to portray SB 1070 as an aid to Federal immigration enforcement. But the very first provision of the statute declares that Arizona is pursuing its own policy of attrition through enforcement and that the provisions of this law are designed to work together to drive unlawfully present aliens out of the state.

—*Don Verrilli, representing the federal government in Arizona v. United States.*[40]

These strategies build credibility by showing that you have paid attention to what the court is really concerned about, that you are using the court's time prudently, and that you are mentally agile.

Finally, remember two other points. First, as it was during briefing, you have the benefit of the lower court's decision behind you. It makes sense to emphasize that point once again at argument when appropriate. Second, as appellee you do not have rebuttal or a second chance to address the panel. Therefore, you should not leave any essential points on the table.

If you are the appellant and have reserved time for it, you will be entitled to provide the last word via a rebuttal argument. These arguments are short, typically three to five minutes. During the appellee's argument, take notes on points that you would like to discuss during rebuttal. Jot down key phrases from the judges or the advocate that you might be able to weave into your presentation. In the minute or two before the appellee sits down, narrow down the points to the top three or four and number them in the order you'd like to address them. When you return to the podium, tell the judges you have a few points to address, but do not waste time roadmapping them. Like the appellee's argument, your first order of business will be to clean up any critical loose ends because you do not want the judges retiring to conference your case with any misapprehension of the record or the law. Then you need to select your remaining two or three points based on where you have concerns or see opportunities. If you think you have one judge on your side but another is on the fence, focus your rebuttal on attempting to connect with that judge. If you are certain that one of your arguments has been rejected by the panel, make sure to emphasize your alternate basis for winning. These points should be responsive to the appellee's argument, not a continuation of your opening argument. You may receive questions from the panel during your rebuttal and, though your time is short, you should welcome them graciously and treat them as an opportunity to clear up any last-minute concerns.

**Practice Alert #5
Post-Argument Analysis**

In the online companion you will find the briefs, transcripts, and coauthors' Carter Phillips's and Jeff Green's post-argument analyses in three Supreme Court cases.

REFLECTION, DISCUSSION, AND CHALLENGE QUESTIONS

Delivering the Argument

- If you are in a jurisdiction that makes oral argument optional, should you actively pursue it? Can you envision any circumstances where oral argument would *not* enhance your case? What signal would you be sending by not requesting argument if it were available?
- How would you determine who from your team should argue the case? Would it be the person with the most familiarity with the record or the person who is most comfortable on his feet?
- How would you deal with a panel that did not appear to be familiar with your case, either the facts or the legal issues? Similarly, how would deal with a judge who is not paying attention during your argument, or even sleeping?
- Do you experience jitters when engaged in pubic speaking such as oral argument? What physiological effects occur? What strategies can you employ to ensure that the inevitable pre-argument jitters do not interfere with your performance?

Endnotes

1. *Supreme Court Chief Justice Roberts*, C-SPAN.ORG (June 19, 2009), http://www.c-spanvideo.org/program/CourtChi.
2. Aristotle, *Poetics* (S. H. Butcher trans.), *in* S. H. BUTCHER, ARISTOTLE'S THEORY OF POETRY AND FINE ART 31 (4th ed. Macmillan & Co. 1923); Linda L. Berger, *How Embedded Knowledge Structures Affect Judicial Decision Making: A Rhetorical Analysis of Metaphor, Narrative, and Imagination in Child Custody Disputes*, 18 S. CAL. INTERDISC. L.J. 259, 267 (2009).
3. Kenneth R. Berman, *Snatching Victory: Arguing to Win*, 21 LITIG. 18, 18-19 (1995).
4. Transcript of Oral Argument at 3, Nat'l Fed'n of Indep. Bus. v. Sebelius, 132 S. Ct. 2566 (2012) (No. 11-400).
5. Transcript of Oral Argument at 3, Univ. S. Tex. Med. Ctr. v. Nassar, 133 S. Ct. 2517 (2013) (No. 12-484).
6. Berman, *supra* note 3, at 19.
7. Transcript of Oral Argument at 3, Grutter v. Bollinger, 123 S. Ct. 2325 (2003) (No. 02-241).
8. Transcript of Oral Argument at 3-4, Arizona v. United States, 132 S. Ct. 2492 (2012) (No. 11-182).
9. RUGGERO J. ALDISERT, WINNING ON APPEAL 343 (2d ed. Nita 2003).
10. Rob Hochman, Lecture on Moots and Arguments at Northwestern University School of Law Supreme Court Clinic (October 2010); ALDISERT, *supra* note 9, at 344.
11. Berman, *supra* note 3, at 19 ("Reciting boilerplate is not advocacy. Being ordinary is not advocacy.").
12. Myron H. Bright & Richard S. Arnold, *Oral Argument? It May Be Crucial!*, 70 A.B.A. J. 68, 70 (1984); Myron H. Bright, *The Power of the Spoken Word: In Defense of Oral Argument*, 72 IOWA L. REV. 35, 39-41 (1986).
13. *See* Berman, *supra* note 3, at 20; BRYAN A. GARNER, THE WINNING ORAL ARGUMENT 191-92 (Thomson/West 2009).
14. *See, e.g.*, 7TH CIR. R. 34(g).
15. SUP. CT. GUIDE FOR COUNSEL 6 (October Term 2013).
16. ALDISERT, *supra* note 9, at 352 (quoting Seth P. Waxman).
17. Rob Hochman, Lecture on Moots and Arguments at Northwestern University School of Law Supreme Court Clinic (October 2010).
18. ALDISERT, *supra* note 9, at 343.

19. GARNER, *supra* note 13, at 32-35; Berman, *supra* note 3, at 22; Myron H. Bright, *The Ten Commandments of Oral Argument*, 67 A.B.A. J. 1136, 1138-39 (1981).
20. GARNER, *supra* note 13, at 35.
21. *See* ALDISERT, *supra* note 9, at 346-47.
22. *Id.* at 343-44.
23. GARNER, *supra* note 13, at 32-35.
24. Michael Higdon, *Oral Argument and Impression Management: Harnessing Nonverbal Persuasion for a Judicial Audience*, 57 U. KAN. L. REV. 631, 634-35 (2009).
25. *Id.* at 656-64 (2009).
26. *Id.* at 656.
27. *Id.* at 657.
28. *Id.* at 641-42.
29. *Id.* at 657.
30. *Id.* at 658-59.
31. *Id.*
32. *Id.* at 659-60.
33. *Id.* at 661.
34. *Id.* at 662.
35. *Id.* at 663-64.
36. *Id.*
37. *Id.* at 662-63.
38. *See* 5TH CIR. R. 28.4.
39. Transcript of Oral Argument at 28, Grutter v. Bollinger, 123 S. Ct. 2325 (2003) (No. 02-241).
40. Transcript of Oral Argument at 34, Arizona v. United States, 132 S. Ct. 2492 (2012) (No. 11-182).

Life's a Beach

First published 2012 by Elliott and Thompson Limited

27 John Street, London WC1N 2BX

www.eandtbooks.com

ISBN: 978-1-907642-39-5

9 8 7 6 5 4 3 2 1

A CIP catalogue record for this book is available from the British Library.

Printed and bound in Italy by Printer Trento

Designed by Two Associates

Life's a Beach

Gordon "Butch" Stewart and the Story of Sandals

Jo Foley

From a revolutionary concept – the all-inclusive holiday for couples – Sandals has grown to become one of Jamaica's most dynamic and successful companies.

Life's a beach: since the early 1980s,
Stewart has brought thousands
of happy couples and families to
beaches throughout the Caribbean.

Contents

MARCH IS A MAGICAL MONTH in the Bahamas, that wonderful collection of islands and cays. Seven hundred of the first and almost two and a half thousand of the latter lie scattered like the beads of a necklace, held together with a bright blue silken rope of water – the Caribbean Sea. It is a splendid time for fishermen as the waters brim bountifully with huge schools of marlin, mahi mahi, and mackerel that swirl through its deep and seduce the sportsmen who come to capture and catch. The Exuma Sound is a rich hunting ground throughout the year, but excels in the early spring, when fisherman come in their multitude to pit their wits and their strength against furiously fast and beautifully iridescent fish.

The locals spend days on the water and visitors flock to pass their weeks of holiday on the ocean. Hemingway spent several months in Bimini; lesser mortals such as Richard Nixon and Howard Hughes would rush to the clear blue waters, in some places over 6,000 feet deep, that host some of the best deep-sea fishing in the world. From Nassau to Eleuthera and all along the Exumas, the abundance is too tempting and inviting.

This is why an annual ritual takes place every March, when five men converge on a boat moored in Nassau. It is not just an ordinary deep-sea fishing boat, but a ninety footer: a Hatteras Sport Fisherman, a US built boat, custom designed for the needs and requirements of the owner. There, accompanied by the faithful captain, Neddy, a crew, a cook, a majordomo (a senior member of household staff who acts on behalf on the owner), a dog called Monty, and a box of dominoes, the fishing party sets out. (The boat is customized to include a large, non-slip, flat surface for the dominoes.) There may be a practice run the day before to get the juices running, but the two-day trip is the highlight. The group have known each other most of their lives, some since school days, and are now at the top of their respective professions. They include a couple of former government ministers, a political advisor, and a smattering of entrepreneurs. They fish, gossip, play dominoes, squabble over the scores, laugh and shout, and repeat the same jokes year after year. They are comfortable with each other, there are no secrets, no petty jealousies – any of these would remain in the past, as time and age has smoothed them like waves over craggy rocks. This is simply a group of men who have worked hard, are successful, and have lived well, men who are comfortable in their own skins. Along the way there have been

struggles as well as setbacks, but they have come out on top, they have survived – and, most of all, they have had fun. It shows on their faces, in the weather-beaten laughter lines, the grey-tinged eyebrows, the well-worn tans, but it also shows in their enjoyment of each other's company and in the shared knowledge and experiences they have accrued – this is what the Blues Brothers could be like forty years on. As their host likes to say: "There isn't a day in my life that I haven't loved."

It is the host who organizes this annual pilgrimage: a man who sweeps them all up and flies them off to the Exuma Sound to deposit them on his fishing boat; a man who at the age of seventy has all the energy, power, and bloody-mindedness of someone forty years his junior; a man who will stay up all night until he has won the final game of dominoes . . . a man unwilling (or unable) to accept defeat. He will be on one of three cellphones constantly, keeping in touch with his family and staff, and will consult with governments as easily as reel in a fish. He is a man whose zest for life is undiminished.

He is Butch Stewart, or rather the Honourable Gordon Arthur Cyril "Butch" Stewart, the man who almost single-handedly, and single-mindedly, invented the luxury all-inclusive holiday. Although christened Gordon, he has been called Butch from birth, simply because at a strapping nine and a half pounds he reminded his father of a cartoon bulldog of the same name. Stewart was someone who knew nothing about hotels and leisure until he bought a near-derelict one on the north coast of Jamaica thirty years ago. Now there are twenty-one of them strung through six islands of the Caribbean and more on the way.

There was no plan, no career structure. The company that is Sandals had an organic, almost haphazard growth. Butch would arrive at a place, look around, investigate, find the best beach and then begin to plot another pleasure palace. But in truth, for him, it is all down to the sea. He is never more at ease, at home or relaxed than when he is on the water. His friends, colleagues, and family all attest to that. "I grew up by the sea," he says, "and I love the feeling of spending a day talking, eating, and sleeping out at sea on a fishing boat." This is hardly surprising, given that Butch Stewart was born surrounded by the Caribbean in the Jamaica that is still his home and the hub of his business activities today.

"I have never wanted to leave Jamaica, even though it's been through some pretty painful periods, and there were times when it might have been easier for me to go . . . but I couldn't," he explains. "I love the Bahamas, I love the sea there and the fishing, and while it's a great second home, it is not home. To me, Jamaica is by the far the most beautiful country in the world . . ." he says, as he steams out of the mooring of his apartment in Nassau.

A scion of traders and farmers, he claims on his father's side to be sixth-generation Jamaican – "But we go back longer on my mother's side, although we have no idea where they came from – they might have been Portuguese or they could have been English, we don't know." However, while there was money in his father's family, most of it had been dissipated by the time the young Butch came along . . . and the rest was lost when his grandmother, who had a large farm in St. Ann's, died without making a will. "My old man grew up in a very wealthy household, but he had no interest in how the wealth was made, or indeed in the farm, and that upset her a lot, so much so that she refused to make a will," which resulted in the young Mr. Stewart having to make his own way in life. "My old man didn't care about that farm . . . at the time he was only interested in radio, which was all the rage in Jamaica then. But he was also a fun seeker – he loved wine, women, and song – and of course that upset his mother, even more so when he had no liking for the land."

That old man, known later in life as Daddy Stew, began life as Gordon Coxe, who was born in England to Stewart's grandfather and his English wife. The marriage was difficult from the beginning, with a husband missing the warmth and fun of the Caribbean and a wife who had never experienced it. When the family moved back to Jamaica, it did little to strengthen the bond; and, when young Gordon Coxe's mother returned to England, he stayed behind, was adopted by wealthy childless relatives and was given the surname Stewart. While he was expected to be part of an industrious tribe of traders and farmers, his childhood was also one of privilege with space, sunshine, freedom, and the sea. Little wonder he took to a sybaritic lifestyle as he grew up, despite being despatched to the Jesuits of Stonyhurst College in Lancashire, England, for his education, in an attempt to introduce some discipline and rigor into his life.

The entrepreneurial gene may have evaded one generation with Daddy Stew, but it returned with a vengeance in young Butch, who at the age of ten was selling fish he had caught to local hotels and restaurants. A few years later during weekends and school holidays, when not helping out in the farm and family business, he was offering boat trips along the Jamaican coast to tourists. It mattered little that the boat he shared with a school friend was barely seaworthy – they made a tidy sum, until it almost sank with a group of visitors on board.

There is nothing so precarious about the *Sir Jon*, the boat that now speeds over the bright blue waters surrounding the Exumas while its guests indulge in seafood chowder, the freshest sashimi straight from the ocean, and the slap of dominoes against the wooden table, as the friends wait for the sound of the next bite before rushing to the back of the boat and tightening the belts that hold their rods. Each catch is greeted with backslapping, high fives, and big smiles. Throughout the fishing party the person having the most fun is the ship's master and commander, the one with Monty the big blond Labrador at his feet and a rod in his hands, the latter frequently swapped for a cellphone that rings constantly and is never ignored: these calls, often from his son, Adam, or daughter, Jaime, are the lifeblood of Butch Stewart.

The businesses that he founded include twenty-one hotels and resorts, automobile distributors, a newspaper, a radio station, and a host of further distribution companies incorporating everything from air-conditioning units to generators, and domestic appliances to business solutions. They have, for nearly forty years, brought him wealth, power, and honors as well as tragedy and disasters along the way . . . but rarely has his enjoyment faltered or the desire to succeed waned. Despite having some 10,000 employees throughout the Caribbean, making the hotel group Jamaica's largest private-sector employer, friends in high places, partnerships with such US icons as Martha Stewart and Sesame Street, a close-knit family of seven children and ten grandchildren, more international awards for luxury resorts than possibly any other hotelier, and being the founder of one of the most recognizable brands in the world – Sandals – Butch Stewart says, hand on heart and with a huge grin, "I don't think I have ever worked a day in my life."

RIGHT *Family, friendships, and laughter are the foundations on which the empire was built.*

1. Early Days

The space, the freedom, the sun, and of course the sea all provided an ideal backdrop for a memorable childhood in Jamaica. Butch Stewart talks lovingly about how special his early years were, when he would escape to the sea at every opportunity. Being in the sea, on the sea, and by the sea is a vital component in Stewart's personality and psyche.

Growing up in Jamaica was
a free-wheeling, enjoyable start
to Butch Stewart's life.

A LUST FOR LIFE and a will to win are clearly embedded in the Hon. Gordon Arthur Cyril "Butch" Stewart's DNA. He may well, as he claims, have had a wonderful childhood with all the advantages of climate and privilege, but the money was running out. He was sent to one of the best schools in Jamaica, Campion College, on the grounds that "my grandmother would create no end of trouble if you didn't go to a Catholic school." He was much influenced by this single-minded woman, while her adopted son, his father, known to all as Daddy Stew, was mainly interested in having a good time. The young Butch left Campion College at fifteen for a school in England. This experience not only separated him from the country he was born in and loved – a feeling that is as strong as ever today – but also gave him a taste for England, the English, and English customs that he has never lost.

ABOVE *Broad horizons: Butch flew to England aged just fifteen, following an idyllic childhood in the Caribbean.*

He could easily have stayed on in the UK and become a successful businessman there, but for Stewart it was never an option. The call of the Caribbean was too strong. He returned to Jamaica with some experience of having a good time, and with firm friendships, hoping to find a job and earn some money. If he was counting on owning some land or part of the farm when his grandmother died, he was to be hugely disappointed. Angry with her son for not showing any interest in the family farm, she refused to make a will and died intestate. Even now he and his family are at pains to discount any talk that he started life with a tranche of family money behind him. The reality is that there was none.

So what was an ambitious young buck around Kingston to do? Untried and untested in any job, he cast around for something to attract his interest and harness his energy. What he lacked in experience he made up for in an abundance of charm and

a great deal of persuasion. It didn't take long for Butch and his employers to discover that the boy could sell.

Butch Stewart's first job was as a salesman with the Dutch-owned Curacao Trading Company. Not only was he successful, he also discovered he loved what he was doing: "I won a few awards and found out that I loved closing the deal," he says. It took just six years for him to become sales manager for the region and to get itchy feet. He had found his niche, but he also recognized a burgeoning market when he saw one. Domestic appliances were still new to the islands – especially air-conditioning units. In the heat and humidity of the Jamaican summers, air-conditioning was what everybody craved for their home. Stewart saw that the market was wide open and decided to specialize in these to begin with, and after some research came to the conclusion that the best ones came from a manufacturer in Edison, New Jersey – Fedders. With all the enthusiasm of youth (he was just twenty-seven) and $3,200 of savings, he decided to go it alone.

First, though, Butch had to surmount one small problem. He needed to negotiate the distribution rights from the manufacturer, who showed little interest in his initial enquiries. Fedders had not yet been exposed to the full force of the determined young man from Kingston, and Stewart's letters and requests for meetings had remained unanswered – hardly surprising, since he had no established business or reputation or even banking credentials. However, he did have firm orders for thirty units and a ramshackle office at 15 Caledonia

ABOVE *The logo of Appliance Traders Limited, founded by Butch Stewart on June 1, 1968.*

BELOW *The salesman at work . . . doing what he still does best. Butch Stewart can woo an audience, whether it is sales, press, or the public.*

Avenue in the Cross Roads area of Kingston. The orders he acquired simply by trawling the streets and knocking on doors, extolling the advantages and wonders of in-room window air-conditioning units.

The only way he saw to surmount the problem was to get to the company in person, so he flew to New Jersey to make his pitch, using every ounce of his persuasive powers – but, while the decision-makers might well have been impressed with his enthusiasm, they were reluctant to grant this young newcomer the rights for Jamaica. Luck came his way, however, when he met the company president's nephew, Bruno Giordana, who took a liking to Butch and gave him the deal he wanted – and Appliance Traders Limited (ATL) was born on June 1, 1968. To this day the two young men who struck the deal remain firm friends.

Always needing to be one step ahead of the competition – and at that time in the Caribbean there was much competition in the domestic air-conditioner market from the likes of General Electric and Westinghouse – Stewart needed a unique selling point, and he found it by promising superior service and speedy installations. He guaranteed the installation of a unit, from taking the order to the unit being in

ABOVE *From the very beginning,
Stewart was adept at using
promotional platforms such as
local newspapers when putting
his message across.*

BELOW *Dedicated to service: all ATL
engineers had two-way radios at their
disposal, ensuring a rapid response
every time.*

ON 24-HOUR CALL: Senior service technician,
Bunny Griffiths, checking in with base, from
his radio-controlled service vehicle. All Appliance Traders vehicles are equipped with two-
way radio, which allows the service team to
respond to calls at a moment's notice.

place, in just eight hours or less. Husbands would order an air-
conditioner on their way to work in the morning as a present for
their wife and it would be installed and running by the afternoon
– a fantastic concept, but much easier to deliver if the wife knew
to expect it . . .

In one famously tricky case, the wife was not at home
when Butch's boys came calling: her husband, wishing it to
be a surprise, did not tell her he'd bought an air-conditioner.
Not knowing what to do, they had to find a telephone before
calling the office for instructions, only to be told by the boss that
they must do whatever was necessary in order to get the unit
installed and working by the eight-hour guarantee. Obviously
there was nothing for it but to find some means of entering the
house – which they did. By the time the woman returned, her
air-conditioning was in perfect working order and her house was
just as she had left it.

There are many such stories about the early days of ATL
which are now part myth, part company history, but from the very
beginning service was key to the whole operation. Orders would
come in from one part of the island and employees on their way
back from another part would be told, when they called in to
report their progress, to find somewhere to stay for the night and
clean clothes, and more units would be dispatched to them so that
they would not have to waste time returning to base. They went
the extra mile and always enquired of the householder if there
was anything else they could do for them – from changing a plug
to fixing a leaking tap. Nothing was too much trouble, there was
no extra charge, and it was all part of
the service.

As soon as the company was
up and running, radio-controlled
units were issued to each van
so that there could be constant
communication between office staff
and engineers out on jobs. Engineers
had to call in every fifteen minutes
to report progress or lack of it. The
boss needed to know everything,
and there could never be any
slacking. The people who worked for

Butch had to be punctual, determined, efficient, professional and clean. Employees' uniforms had to be immaculate. Standards were to be upheld at all times: often at the end of the day Butch would inspect the vans, engines included, and they too had to be spotless. *Committed to Excellence* was the company's motto from the outset and underlines all it offers, including not just the best products, but also the best service.

Over forty years on, many of the workforce who started with Appliance Traders Limited are still there. Betty Jo Desnoes, Stewart's Executive Assistant, who has been with both ATL and Sandals almost from the start, explains his method: "He puts his stamp on the company and its organization so that people can see what he is after . . . and he never asks people to do something he wouldn't do himself. More so, he was always the first in the office and always the last to leave." Stewart's work ethic is remarked on by Checks Nicholl, who has racked up forty years of service with ATL: "Whatever time of day or night you finished your job he would be there in the office waiting for your call. And if there was work in the same area to be done, he would tell us to stay put and would send money, new units and clothes. It's no wonder we were always so busy, but everybody liked what they were doing, we didn't watch time . . . we did it for him." He continues, "But then there is nothing he would not do and he would never ask you to do stuff he wouldn't do himself . . . that is what makes me love the company, and love the man."

BELOW *"The Bluebirds," as the ATL engineers and their vehicles became known. Blue was the color of the Fedders logo and stood out as they toured the island.*

ABOVE *The famous "defaced" Mercedes Benz, this time with the addition of Stewart's two sons, Jonathan and Bobby, for extra adornment.*

Like many of his co-workers, Nicholl states that work, though fast-paced and busy, was fun. "We all had a great time. He would involve us all – we would play dominoes and cricket, we'd go fishing; we all felt as if we belonged. It was like a family. Mr. Stewart knew everything about you, whether you had a problem at home or with money, and he looked out for you. That's one of the reasons he and this company have been so successful: he cares about everyone, the staff as well as the customers."

Never one to rest on his laurels, Butch was forever thinking of new ways to develop the business. He was a natural salesman; marketing was in his blood. All the company's white Volkswagen vans had the bright blue Fedders logo on the side so that people would notice them and remember. Even Stewart's own treasured white Mercedes Benz sported the Fedders logo. "Who in their right minds would deface a Mercedes Benz? Well, he did," says Desnoes. The fleet of ATL vans became known throughout the island as "The Bluebirds" and gradually turned into mobile advertisements, sporting the logos of all the other brands the company stocked. As one person commented, they were like moving billboards throughout the island. They assured brand recogntion, as

The archetypal Caribbean: paradise islands, azure seas, and blue, blue skies – the ideal playground for a young man with big dreams.

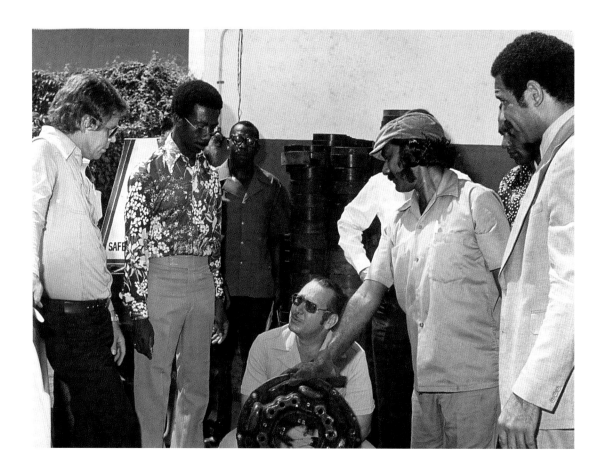

ABOVE *Having moved into automotives in 1975, Stewart (far left) takes time to meet with the Caribrake team.*

well as being an advertising tool. It should not come as a surprise that at the end of its first trading year Appliance Traders Limited exceeded its projections by 500 per cent.

On one memorable occasion, Butch got the staff to fill the vans with all the products they were selling at the time and drive through the streets of the affluent neighbourhoods of Kingston with a loudspeaker calling people from their homes to look, learn and, of course, buy. It worked, and it got the name ATL known throughout the island. Within eighteen months the company had more than fifty per cent of the domestic air-conditioning market and was moving into the commercial area. More vans and radio-controlled units were acquired, and the first ATL building was constructed at Marescaux Road.

One early setback was a fire that destroyed part of the offices. But Stewart's handling of the situation was to set the standard for how he dealt with other more serious impediments: life had to go on. According to Nicholl, Stewart called the staff together: "He just told us we had to clean up and we all got involved in the clearing and cleaning process, but he worked as hard as anybody. Luckily it was only the front of the building, but that was important as it was the showcase, so we cleaned it up, and because the storeroom was intact, we were all back at work the following day. That is what he is like, he doesn't give up and he never looks back . . . we all just got on with it."

Not looking back is one thing, but Stewart was never one for standing still either. ATL's next growth spurt was brought about by a government initiative. A limit was imposed on imports and heavy taxes were imposed on luxury goods such as air-conditioning units, so for ATL there was only one way forward: make your own. Stewart turned to manufacturing. And, in typical Butch Stewart style, he made the most of it. ATL started making not only air-conditioners, but also water pumps, electric generators, and a host of domestic appliances. Air-conditioning was never going to be enough: Butch Stewart wanted more.

The company was enjoying such expansion that it needed bigger premises, so by September 1973 it moved to its current location at Halfway Tree Road in Kingston and expanded to represent and stock even more top appliance brands. After the purchase of another company, Caribbean Brake Products Ltd (known locally as Caribrake) in 1975, Stewart diversified into automotives and motor distribution. Business was booming, and the company proceeded to grow over the next four decades. The foundation of the whole Stewart vision was here: selling air-conditioning units in and around Kingston. ATL itself has grown steadily over the years, and is now Jamaica's leading supplier of commercial and industrial equipment – it is one of the many stars of

BELOW *Business is booming: by 1973, ATL was expanding, and the firm was relocated to this office and showroom at Halfway Tree Road in Kingston.*

●MEET ERROL LEE

FACTORY MANAGER

ABOVE: *Errol Lee joined as Factory Manager and is still with the company forty-three years later.*

Jamaican commerce. Keeping customer service at its core – in true Stewart style – ATL continues to diversify and innovate, as the recent additions of car dealerships ATL Autohaus and ATL Britannia to the ATL Automotive team attest.

Errol Lee has been at ATL for forty-three years and is in charge of technical quality control. "My only regret is that Mr. Stewart has diversified and grown away from Appliance Traders. In an ideal world I would like him to spend more time there. I want other people, the new people, to see, to experience, and to understand what a difference he can make. He is an exceptional motivator. I try to instill that sense of service and loyalty in the young people who come here so that it can be passed on down the years," he says.

In 1981, with a highly successful company growing and expanding, Butch Stewart was in a strong position. However, another new government initiative struck a blow at the heart of ATL. Foreign imports were limited: only existing foreign exchange earners – companies who already brought foreign currency into Jamaica – were allowed to import foreign goods. Butch had to find a way for his business to earn some foreign currency. Fortune must have been smiling the day he was told about a hotel for sale on Montego Bay, Jamaica's most popular tourist area – the Bay Roc. Suddenly, tourism became part of Butch Stewart's vision when he bought not only the Bay Roc but also its sister property, Carlyle on the Bay, from the family that had run them for years. It was the start of a whole new love affair.

BELOW *Work and play: ATL staff gather to celebrate Stewart's birthday.*

A strong belief in and deep love of his native Caribbean shores ultimately drove Butch Stewart to develop a new kind of vacation.

2. Hotel Paradiso

Success came early to the young Mr. Stewart, who had all the drive and energy to make his first company, ATL, a force to be reckoned with in Kingston and its environs. From the very beginning, *service* was the key and the core of any business Stewart became involved with – a philosophy that eventually made him one of the most successful hoteliers of his time.

It always begins with a beach.
Wherever Butch Stewart opened,
built, or bought a resort, it was
chosen because of the beauty of the
beach that came with it.

TOURISM has long been Jamaica's largest industry, what with the island's glorious beaches, year-round sunshine, famous Blue Mountains, tropical forests, rum, great music, and easy-going attitude. However, during the 1970s, the island's image changed and Jamaica lost some of its glamour. Partly, this was brought about by travelers discovering more exciting or exotic destinations, but the various social changes taking place on the island and an increase in crime also contributed. It was not the ideal time for a hotel rookie to be entering the business. However, that is exactly what Butch Stewart did.

ABOVE *With no hotel experience and in a declining market, Stewart made his purchase of the Bay Roc in Montego Bay.*

Motivated more by getting foreign currency onto the island than any ambition to be a hotelier, Stewart bought the Bay Roc, a down-at-heel resort in Montego Bay complete with sixty-six rooms, thirty privately owned cottages that were managed and marketed by the hotel and, best of all, one of the island's largest private beaches at its edge. The only snag was that the Bay Roc was next door to the airport and its major runway.

Even Stewart's legendary optimism was dented when he realized what he had bought, and he readily admits that if he hadn't been such a proud man and committed to the purchase, he would have pulled out. Bay Roc may have once offered luxury, but now all it had to offer was broken glass, peeling paintwork, out-of-date wiring, and ancient plumbing; about the same condition of its sister property, Carlyle on the Bay, which he had also agreed to buy. "For us it was a very large investment and we really didn't know what to do. The resort was in a state of horrendous disrepair, a total nightmare," Stewart acknowledges. "We didn't own the cottages on the property and

ABOVE *Public recognition of Stewart's brave new adventure.*

RIGHT *Stewart, pictured here with his former wife, PJ, has long been a keen fisherman, making the most of the bountiful waters in the Caribbean.*

we didn't have enough rooms to make it financially viable, so we decided to convert the conference room into another twelve bedrooms just to give ourselves more rooms to sell!" Even his closest associates were dubious about the venture, as was Anthony Abrahams, the then Minister of Tourism, who thought the purchase ill advised.

With no way back and no way out, the Stewart genius for making things work was stretched to its limits, but then his limits came with knowing how to find the right help. He immediately got his workforce to start clearing up the hotel and renovating it – he had craftsmen at ATL that he could call on, as well as contacts, friends, and associates. Plumbers and electricians were dispatched from ATL alongside any spare pair of hands he could find to make the hotel habitable. But speed was of the essence: the high season was approaching and Stewart wanted, and needed, the hotel to be up and running. By the time the dated rooms and bathrooms were renovated, replumbed, rewired,

LEFT AND BELOW *The way it was – old-style colors, furnishings, and comfort at the old Bay Roc, left; and sharp, modern, chic design in Liquid Nightclub at Beaches Turks & Caicos that would look right in any twenty-first-century city, below.*

redecorated, and re-furnished, costs had dramatically escalated, but no expense was spared. Trelawny stone, Jamaica's natural indigenous pink variety, was used for a dramatic entrance and lobby, while the gardens were landscaped and replanted with tropical shrubs and trees. When completed to Stewart's satisfaction, the transformation of Bay Roc to Sandals had cost almost $2 million.

One Jamaican national recently returned from the UK was Eleanor Miller, who was called by a friend, Lex Shelton, Stewart's financial director, to meet Stewart in the ATL office one Saturday morning. As she tells it, "I was locked in for two years. He had asked me to the office to help with the final paperwork regarding the purchase of Bay Roc, and before I knew it I had a sales job." As well as having meetings with architects and interior designers for the ensuing thirty-one years, Miller has skipped between hotels, ATL, landscape design, and special projects, even at one stage taking over a furniture factory one Christmas Eve when the furniture needed for Sandals Negril wasn't finished. Not bad, she thinks, for somebody who has never had a contract, nor even a letter of employment.

"Sandals is not," she says firmly, "a job. It's a lifestyle. And you have to get with it. I have experienced all sorts of stuff I never dreamed of, so leaving the company or Mr. Stewart was never an option. I'd die of boredom." Because she was open-minded and willing to turn her hand to any number of tasks, opportunities came her way. Over the years she has found her job fascinating, at times frustrating – but always fun. Looking back at the early days of the two hotels, she says the problem with many of the people with whom Stewart and his team came into contact was that "nobody got him; they didn't understand what drove him. He entered an industry that was offering the minimum of service for the most amount of money – he revolutionized it by first concentrating on the service. You could almost see what was special about him and his vision, which is why, I suppose, we went through about five general managers for Bay Roc before it opened."

Even then, it was not without its problems, which is why the
opening night will go down in history. The hotel had all the trappings of
a new luxury resort: brand new uniforms for the staff, a band playing in
the lobby; but, even though there were forty-three dining room staff for
just twenty-seven guests, dinner took over four hours to serve – mostly
due to a chef who had a liking for the bottle and had consumed a little
too much rum!

One person who from the outset understood what Butch Stewart
was about, and understood what his business needed, was Merrick Fray.
The timing could not have been better. Fray had been running a hotel
called The Seawind that, due to the current climate in Jamaica, had closed
down and been sold, and all the staff had been let go. Fray was a man
who needed a job – and Stewart was a man who had a job. "A friend
put us together, but I sort of knew him a little before, as he had sold us
air-conditioners on occasion. During our first conversation he told me to
take the keys of the Carlyle and to start running it the way I thought it
should be done," said Fray. "But then, he knew what he wanted: he did
his research, he talked to everybody . . . more than anything he wanted
the guests to have a good time. He looked at everything and wanted to
know everything. I remember him asking me what my main weakness was
and me telling him, marketing. Did that matter? Of course not, although
I didn't know then that I was talking to the greatest marketing guru of
all time."

Fray was dispatched to the Carlyle, which was still operating and in
reasonable condition, and thirty years on he is still with the company
as Managing Director of Sandals Resorts International. He watched
from afar as Bay Roc was gradually renovated and put together, offering
help and advice whenever it was needed – which was often, as general
managers arrived and departed, and he often had to sit in until another
was found. Eventually one stayed for two years, but on his departure Fray
got the call and was made Managing Director of the two hotels, which was
the job he had originally wanted.

Both hotels were still operating under their old names and the
search was on to rebrand them. For a time Bay Roc had "Club" added to
its name. Stewart was always looking at the idea of an all-inclusive resort.
"I had always loved the idea of Club Med, I loved their energy and their
style and thought we should emulate what they were doing. However, we
kept going round in circles for about six months, not sure about anything,
and not knowing which way to go, changing our minds and then going

*The lure of the beach: Montego Bay
in the mid-1980s. Its white sand and
fringe of palm trees are essential to any
Sandals resort.*

ABOVE *"The customer is the best salesman" – this firm belief has made Sandals the success it is today. Making guests feel welcome was – and still is – paramount.*

back again, but eventually we put together a formula based on the all-inclusives of the time, but always with the idea of luxury." Stewart had suddenly remembered a small hotel in Port Antonio on Jamaica's north-east coast. "It's ironic," he says, "that the first luxury all-inclusive resort was right here in Jamaica. It had only thirty rooms and cottages, guests could have all the champagne and caviar they wanted, fresh salmon was flown in two or three times a week, and the cost was $1,000 a week, which was a lot of money in the 1950s." The resort was called Frenchman's Cove and it became his blueprint for style, luxury, and service.

So with one eye on Club Med, one eye on the forgotten Frenchman's Cove, and Stewart's focus on great service and fun, the story of Sandals began.

Nobody could think of a name, so a friend of Stewart's in Miami who had worked in tourism marketing suggested the name "Sandals" for discussion at a meeting, but nobody bit. "Nobody liked the name," said Fray, "but then nobody could come up with a better one and, after a couple of days, it sort of stuck." To begin with, it was called The Sandals Club.

Pragmatic as ever, Stewart believes that often the name is not as important as what you offer. "If what you're offering is good, people will remember and the name will then become well-known."

And all the time, Butch Stewart was planning ways to make his new resort the best, the most attractive, the most seductive, even. He had already decided on the club atmosphere and an all-inclusive approach, but he was searching for another niche. He looked at other hotels, talked to hoteliers, guests, tourist boards, and hotel associations. He also looked at figures: for the guests who traveled to Jamaica – how they traveled and where they came from. The eureka! moment came when he realized that more than eighty percent of guests from North America came in pairs, as couples. One of his mantras has always been: "When you want to be the best, specialize." So the concept of the all-inclusive, luxury, couples only, Sandals Resort Beach Club was born. Hence on the beaches there were loungers made for two, throughout the gardens love seats were dotted around, while hammocks big enough for two were strung between the trees. Every room had a kingsize bed. Detail was all.

As Eleanor Miller recognized from the beginning: "He has an eye for detail that most men, in fact most women, don't have. He sees everything, he sees what's needed, what's missing, what can be improved . . . and his eye for detail is tireless. Sometimes it could drive you crazy, but then you realized, he was always right."

Stewart was already a master on service. He had built a thriving business and overtaken all competitors because he had concentrated on the product with the added bonus of exceptional service. And, while it may have taken a little time to attain the level of service he was looking for, Stewart always had his eye on the detail, from what was provided by the kitchens (this time without a chef high on an excess of rum), to what was put into the rooms – great beds and clock

BELOW *The great unveiling, when a decision was finally made about the name.*

radios, a luxury in the late 1970s and early 1980s – and, most importantly, what the staff were like, and how they were trained. And when staff joined from other hotels they were retrained in the ever-evolving Sandals philosophy of service.

Says Stewart, "We had established a reputation for service with ATL: we would turn somersaults for people to keep them happy, and to be sure they were happy with our product and what we had done for them. And it paid off."

The taskmaster here, and key to the process, was Fray. "Staff were chosen more for their attitude and a ready smile rather than their experience, because we could always train them to be what we wanted, but if they were fun, lively and interested, with the right attitude – then they were right for Sandals," he says. To this day, each staff member has to undergo at least 120 hours of training every year.

Back then, all Stewart wanted was for the guests to have a good time. If they enjoyed themselves, if they had fun, then they would remember their holiday with warmth and, with luck, would want to return. And staff were encouraged to remember this, which helped to underline the Stewart school of optimism – turn a negative into a positive, which they managed to do with such panache when faced with

LEFT *An ingenious distraction technique – guests were encouraged to kiss their partner every time a plane flew overhead. Clever when the runway was so close!*

TOP AND ABOVE *Robert "Daddy"*
Stone, Sandals Montego Bay's first
employee . . . and still charming guests.

the problem of the airport runway next door to the resort. Stewart's idea was to make an event of every time a plane flew overhead, so staff were instructed to ask guests to wave at the plane and then kiss the person they came with. It worked. It became a game. More importantly, staff worked in a way previously unknown in hotels – they might be employed to work in the dining room, or on the beach, but if they saw a guest who needed something they did not call or wait for another staff member to come along, they took care of it themselves. This is a practice that lives on in the capable hands of Robert "Daddy" Stone, who at eighty-three years of age is still monitoring the dining room at Sandals Montego Bay. The first real employee of Sandals Montego Bay, and now Director of Services, he still watches eagle-eyed over his domain, claiming defiantly, "I'll stay till the burial ground."

Stone continues, "Mr. Stewart gave me this name, Daddy, because he knows what I am like and trusts me with all the young staff. I keep an eye on them, train them and discipline them – after all, the guests are paying us and we must always do what is right for them."

Daddy Stone spent much of his first few weeks at Sandals in one of the cottages in the grounds of Bay Roc drilling his dining-room staff. "I'd brought a few of my waiters from where I had been working so they knew what to do, but I started from the beginning with the new recruits: showing them how to set a table, how to serve and clear away. It was a very busy time with builders all over the place . . . but we knew we had to get on with it because Mr. Stewart wanted everything done quickly."

The boss may have wanted everything done quickly – and perfectly – but he knew instinctively that he also had to treat the staff well and responsibly. They were all employed year-round, a first for Jamaican hotels, which closed during the low season. Sandals staff had job security and, even more important, he paid them a better wage than any other hotelier. To this day the staff are still some of the highest paid in the hospitality industry throughout the Caribbean.

In the early days, however, it was for all of the staff, and especially for Stewart, a leap in the dark. Only the drive, energy, and enthusiasm of this soon-to-be-hotelier with a huge debt kept him going. Something had taken over, something was going on inside his mind that was to bring a whole new style of resorts and hotels to the world of travel. Back then, even Butch Stewart had no idea how this was going to grow.

LEFT *The close-knit team at Sandals was like a family.*

When the first guests arrived on November 27, 1981, they were met at the airport by the staff, given a little orientation tour on their way to the resort (spiced with a short introduction to Jamaican history), and then welcomed to their holiday home with a live band and a drink. This was the way it was going to be. Staff were advised to think not of welcoming guests into a hotel where money would change hands, but instead to think of welcoming somebody into their own homes. The question, "How would you treat a guest in your house?" was almost the basis of the training manual – greet them with a welcoming smile and offer a drink. It was to be that simple and, thirty years on, still successful.

What a difference a resort makes in bringing luxury to a tropical setting: Sandals Montego Bay today.

3.

And Then There Were Three, and Four…and More

For somebody who knew nothing about hotels or the hospitality industry, Stewart was a fast learner, and even faster at opening more resorts. As others abandoned tourism as a business, he embraced it – while Jamaica and the world stood back and shook their heads. Undaunted, he ploughed on, always providing more facilities, great service, and exceptional locations.

A tour of Sandals Montego Bay
for Jamaica's then Prime Minister,
Edward Seaga.

ONCE BAY ROC had opened, attention turned to the Carlyle, which needed a mini-revamp and had to provide the same service and meet the same standards. But, more than anything, the concept of Sandals had to be sold, and this is where Stewart's genius came into play – a peerless salesman, he set about wooing the trade. He knew he needed to get travel agents and tour operators interested in what he was offering – a little-known resort on an island that had fallen out of fashion and run out of good will.

Gordon Stewart (left), owner of Sandals Resort Beach Club, Jamaica, and president of the Jamaican Hotel and Tourist Association, shows Joe Garzilli, president of Flyfaire, Inc., some of the attractions at his resort. Sandals is designed for adult couples only and has an all-inclusive, pre-paid policy. All rooms in the 219-room property are air conditioned and have king-size beds, telephones, and balconies or patios.

ABOVE *Stewart was scrupulous in keeping the travel trade involved with his growing business. He is seen here on a visit to Joe Garzilli, President of Flyfaire.*

Stewart was a good listener and a fast learner. He did his research, spoke to tourism offices and to other hoteliers. An old friend, George Myers, was now running a resort company in Nassau, and Stewart visited him to seek advice. Myers dispatched him to New York with introductions to two of the big operators – Flyfaire and GOGO Tours. That was all Stewart needed – the rest he was sure he could do himself, just as he had all those years ago when he had persuaded Fedders to trust him, a guy with no experience, no real company, and no track record, with their Jamaican distribution rights.

The Stewart magic worked sufficiently for some of the top tourist operators to take a chance on a man with no experience selling an all-inclusive resort for romantically inclined couples – but it didn't stop there. Stewart knew that it was not just the top guys he needed on his side, he needed players throughout the States, the sales force on the ground, so he made it his business to find them, charm them, and keep in regular contact with them. He went to every travel show and sold, sold, sold. Even the most hardened wholesaler was impressed with his charm and energy. He also knew that nobody could sell anything they had not seen, so he began the great Sandals marketing experience: flying agents and operators to the properties, showing them what was on offer, telling them about the island and what it offered but, more than anything, giving them a great time. Even Merrick Fray, a hotelier to

RIGHT *Distinctive from the very beginning, Sandals' advertising and marketing materials are still some of the most recognized in the world.*

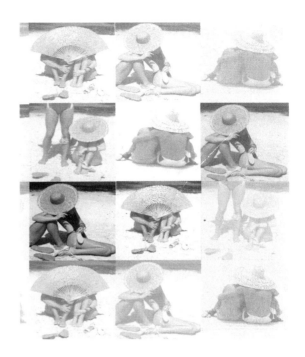

his bones, admitted that nobody had ever shown so many travel agents around any hotel. "We were told to entertain them and to make sure they had the most enjoyable experience. All the staff joined in." he says. On one occasion a senior member of staff even jumped fully clothed into a swimming pool to start a party and to help the guests ignore the rain falling around them. Of course, it worked . . . and it still works. The agents got to know the properties and what they had to offer and, more importantly, got to understand the ethos of the brand. Sandals was fun, had excellent service, and offered more than any other all-inclusive resort in the market. To this day, every year planes are chartered and travel agents are flown to Sandals resorts throughout the Caribbean.

LEFT *A smile and a friendly demeanor were essential attributes for any Sandals employee.*

What Stewart needed more than anything, however, was feedback. He wanted to know what the people who would be selling his hotels thought of them, what they did not like, and what he could do to improve them. He did the same with the staff. He would eat in each of the staff canteens, listening to what they were saying, asking their opinions, asking what the guests were saying. He played dominoes with the staff and with the taxi drivers who ferried the guests around the island. He wanted to know what was being said in the backs of cabs to see if he could improve what he was offering.

In those early days the offerings were quite simple in spite of in-room amenities such as kingsize beds, clock radios, and a hairdryer in every room. This latter item underlines Stewart's obsession with detail. As he tells it, he was on holiday in Italy, staying at a small hotel that had a hairdryer in every room – something completely new, in his experience. He almost had to dismantle it to discover where it was made, and by the time he returned home the orders were placed and his hotels became the first in the Caribbean to boast this amenity. Slowly but surely the resort began to grow in popularity, although he does admit, "The first two years were very tough."

During those two years he had started the move from all-inclusive to "Ultra All-Inclusive"

ABOVE *Sandals has employed specialists in water sports since the early 1980s – the Caribbean offers some of the best locations in the world.*

ABOVE *Stewart examines the equipment in his newly installed gym.*

BELOW *The signature Swim-up Pool Bar – one of the most popular facilities in any Sandals resort.*

– but first he needed more space, so a new block housing sixty-six new beachfront rooms was added, the first whirlpools were installed around the property (indeed, they were the first whirlpools in the Caribbean), a fitness center was introduced, and the water-sports program was upgraded.

This was just the beginning. Within four years he introduced the Sandals signature Swim-up Pool Bar, and now no Sandals swimming pool is complete without the bar that guests can swim to, and relax and make friends. Like many innovations, the Swim-up Pool Bar happened almost by accident. When the new Palms block with its sixty-six extra rooms was built at Bay Roc, it highlighted a divide between two areas of the resort, when what was needed was movement and integration. The main problem was how to move guests from the main swimming pool, which they knew, loved, and felt comfortable with, along the grounds to the new one. Butch and his architect Evan Williams were ruminating on what to do. The goal was to effect a seamless wave-like movement from one end of the property to the other. They needed an attraction, and, while throwing out ideas on what could be done, Butch wondered why there were never any bars in a pool. Hence another eureka! moment, and the Sandals signature Swim-up Pool Bar was born.

Stewart was never one to rest on his laurels. Two years earlier, with a scant two years' experience in the hotel industry, he had become President of the Jamaica Hotel and Tourist Association. That gave him a bigger platform, both to sell the island he loved, and to entice visitors to one of his hotels. Betty Jo Desnoes remembers the energy he brought to that position. He asked the government for

ABOVE *Stewart takes over as President of the Jamaica Hotel and Tourist Association in 1984, and drives the business forward.*

incentives for the hotel industry so that all hotel properties could benefit, from small inns to the big swanky hotels.

He happened upon a third property almost by accident. The late 1970s and early 1980s were a tough period for Jamaican tourism and a number of hoteliers wanted out. Many hotels at that time were bought, cheaply, by the government, who tried to run them when management contracts came to an end. Two of Stewart's executives heard that the management operators of the Royal Caribbean Hotel wanted to leave the island and they attempted to get Sandals to bid for it. Struggling a little with the two hotels he currently owned, he showed little interest. But "little interest" in the Butch Stewart vocabulary did not necessarily mean no interest, so David Roper (now Group Director of Industry Relations), and two executives headed off for Spain, won the contract, and returned home with the keys to the Royal Caribbean. Now there were three! "The government knew nothing about it, and were a little put out when

RIGHT: *Sandals Royal Caribbean in all its refurbished glory.*

Stay at ONE

Play at TWO!

Sandals All-Inclusive Club Resorts, creators of the ultimate romantic, all-inclusive vacation for couples, now offer the limitless pleasure of TWO resorts for the PRICE of ONE!

Our frequent shuttle service has joined together the two "worlds" of Sandals Montego Bay and Sandals Royal Caribbean. Guests staying at either hotel can now sample the special amenities of the other Sandals Resort at NO EXTRA COST.

So book your couples to a Sandals Resort in Montego Bay and give them

TWICE THE ROMANCE.   TWICE THE FUN.
TWICE THE SANDALS!

Sandals
All-Inclusive
Club Resorts

Sandals Montego Bay • Sandals Royal Caribbean • Sandals Negril

For further information call your favorite wholesaler, tour operator or Unique Vacations at:

ABOVE *One of the most successful promotions Sandals ever introduced: stay at one . . . and enjoy the facilities of the other resorts.*

BELOW *A menu from one of the very popular specialty restaurants that can be found throughout the Sandals empire.*

they discovered Sandals now had the management contract for the hotel," Merrick Fray explains. So more money was expended while the Royal Caribbean was welcomed into the Sandals stable with its "added value" philosophy applied every room, service, and amenity. It offered all the grandeur of an old colonial manor house as it welcomed guests, but it also had the hidden benefit of its own private Robinson Crusoe-style Caribbean island where guests could have extra privacy: another plus, another unique selling proposition. A day did not pass without Stewart coming up with yet another idea to add to the attractiveness of his hotels. Once the Royal Caribbean opened, his pitch was "Stay at one resort, play at two," allowing guests to experience what else Sandals offered and to decide whether they might like to try a different hotel on their next vacation.

David Roper became the Royal Caribbean's first general manager and brought with him all the Sandals expertise, its commitment to service, and its desire to give the customer the best holiday possible. At the same time, Sandals Resort Beach Club was renamed Sandals Montego Bay to distinguish it from Sandals Royal Caribbean, which was in the same area (Carlyle on the Bay was not yet part of the Sandals brand). By the time the third hotel was up and running, the system was beginning to operate smoothly, and staff were becoming more confident in what an all-inclusive resort was about.

"We may not have invented all-inclusive, but, because of our innovations and the high quality of the product, we perfected it," Stewart is proud of saying. One such innovation took place when the first specialty restaurant opened at Montego Bay. Until then all meals at all-inclusive hotels were buffet-style, but Butch heard a whisper that Club Med were about to open a gourmet restaurant and he beat them to it, when the Oleander restaurant opened on a verandah at Montego Bay serving traditional Jamaican fare.

While the buffet service has become more grand over the years, Sandals today also has more than 180 specialty restaurants offering twenty different types of cuisine – from Italian to Japanese, Mexican to French, and British. This latter became a passion of Stewart's when he discovered that you could buy traditional pubs that had been dismantled in the UK and transport them piece by piece across the Atlantic. To date, most Sandals resorts have a British pub, serving bangers and mash along with other traditional British fare, which have become just as popular with the American clientele.

Sandals prides itself on offering what no other resort company can – such as Sandals Cay, a private island just off Sandals Royal Caribbean in Montego Bay.

Once the difficult first couple of years were behind him, Stewart was in his element. He had found an outlet for his prodigious energy, one that appealed to his quest for all that was new and different, but which also honed his dedication to service. "Good service doesn't happen by mistake – we built one company on service, and we knew we could build another. Our job is to make sure when guests come to the hotel, we exceed their expectations."

The company's next move was to buy two old hotels on Negril's glorious seven-mile beach. Both the Sundowner and Coconut Cove were well past their prime, but Butch's idea was to knock them into one, and the ambition to have four hotels on the one island suddenly became a reality. His competitors were aghast: it was difficult enough to fill one hotel, and sure, he had managed successfully with three, but how was he going to keep four going?

The plans were drawn and work began on the the construction of Sandals Negril in February 1988. Stewart, with his usual drive and lack of patience, wanted everything finished and ready to welcome guests for the high season in the autumn and winter of that year. Negril would set the standard. By now his experience of what hotels and resorts should be was honed and he knew the additions he wanted – two specialty restaurants this time, more whirlpools around the place, and many more gazebos dotted around the gardens. The mantra was more, bigger, and better.

And even though his concentration was on this new hotel, he had also seen a property in his old home town of Ocho Rios that would make a great hotel. So, plans unfolding, mind buzzing, and company

growing, the Butch Stewart vision was unstoppable. Until it was swiftly and dramatically halted one morning in September 1988 with the arrival of Hurricane Gilbert.

In just under eight hours of fierce winds, at times gusting of speeds up to 130 miles an hour, record rainfall, and waves over twenty feet high, Butch's dream turned into a nightmare as Sandals was almost wiped off the face of the earth. "We had five broken resorts," recalls Eleanor Miller, her voice still catching as she recounts Butch's arrival at Montego Bay that day – the hurricane had affected not only Sandals Montego Bay, Sandals Royal Caribbean, and Carlyle on the Bay, but also the two newer resorts that were being developed at Negril and Ocho Rios.

"Of course, all the phone lines were down, but we still had some radio contact. He called me from the plane, but we kept losing the signal, as I tried to explain what it was like. But nothing could prepare anyone for what had happened. He cried. He stood in the wreck of Montego Bay and cried. But we all cried – all that work, all that fun, all those dreams."

BELOW *Blue skies and clear seas make the Caribbean a favorite playground for travelers from around the world. Hurricanes can strike – but Stewart would not be caught unprepared more than once.*

A unique innovation at Sandals Negril: the River Suites, which were designed to complement, not compete with, Mother Nature.

4.

Not All Plain Sailing: Stewart and the Setbacks

There are some things that are completely outside anyone's control; for instance, when nature delivers a body blow such as Hurricane Gilbert, which almost destroyed the fledgling empire. On another occasion, the Jamaican dollar nearly collapsed, while a little later the national airline, Air Jamaica, was about to go out of business. Stewart went into rescue overdrive on each occasion.

"...nothing short of a miracle."

Travel professionals respond to Sandals Resorts' incredible hurricane come-back.

After the devastation of Hurricane Gilbert, trade professionals such as Fred Kassner of GOGO Tours (left) and Joe Garzilli of Flyfaire (right) were lavish in their praise of the speed with which the resorts reopened.

IT IS NOT OFTEN that Butch Stewart is quiet and still. But those who saw him that morning amongst the debris of Sandals Montego Bay were worried. It was a Butch they had never before witnessed, and, as Miller explained, they were right to be worried: "That is when he is at his most terrifying, except this time he was deeply upset." For Betty Jo Desnoes, it was an extraordinary experience: "A speechless Mr. Stewart; he was so silent in the office, it was weird." On the plane from Kingston to Montego Bay his then wife, PJ, watched a silent Butch looking at the destruction of his island. However, nothing prepared him for what he saw on arrival at the hotel, and that is when the tears started. A whole new business that he had gone into with no experience, a business he had grown to love, but more importantly a business he had come to understand, probably better than any other Caribbean hotelier, was in bits around his feet.

As Stewart recalls, "I had some insurance, but not enough for what was needed here." But he is not one for moping and feeling sorry for himself – that is not the Stewart way. Instead, he put his mind to fixing the situation. That's what he does – if it's broken, fix it. "I have difficulty in identifying with negative stuff," he says. The extraordinary aspect of the tragedy was that all the staff turned up for work the day after, even though their own homes and lives had been badly battered and affected. Fortunately Merrick Fray had managed to evacuate the hotel before the worst of the storm hit, and bussed the guests to wherever he could find a safe place – in hotel lobbies, golf clubs, convention centers – and could oversee that they at least had food and drink.

Looking at the destruction, Stewart quickly devised a recovery plan. Sandals Montego Bay was the least damaged resort, so he decided to get that back up and running first. All the trucks and staff of ATL were

OPPOSITE AND ABOVE *A broken hotel, a broken heart . . . but both are quickly mended: the resorts were devastated by Hurricane Gilbert.*

summoned, and were told to buy every piece of wood and every nail they could find on their way from Kingston. Eleanor Miller, who lived nearby, had a generator and managed to get an ice-making machine to keep the workers' drinks cold and a baker to make sure they had bread. "Mr. Stewart did everything to make sure the staff had food. All he said to me was to take my vitamins because we were going to need all our strength to get this show back on the road. But the important thing was he did as much, if not more, than anybody else. He worked morning to night, he was determined that Montego Bay would open as quickly as he could get it together."

It was not only vital that the resorts should be renovated as quickly as possible, it was even more important to win back the confidence of the trade and keep the bookings coming. For Hurricane Gilbert had not just destroyed Stewart's dream, it had also destroyed the island's reputation. Demonstrating his firm resolve, Stewart decided halfway through the renovations to take all his sales staff to the US. And while the staff had no idea what he was going to do, they were thrilled to be asked because they could get clean clothes and a hot shower! The great marketeer went

ABOVE *Stewart was determined that nothing should get in the way of guests enjoying their time at Sandals . . . including hurricanes, which is why he issued a guarantee.*

into overdrive at a lunch for travel agents and tour operators at the Four Seasons Hotel in New York, where, armed with photographs of the devastation and the clearing-up exercise, he promised them that Sandals Montego Bay would reopen at the beginning of the new season and that it would be even bigger and better. His own staff simply sat open-mouthed at his promises – which saw the birth of another innovation, a Blue Chip Hurricane Guarantee. This vowed that if ever a resort was touched by a hurricane again, he would give a replacement vacation, including airfares, to all the guests. This generous offer was not to be used until another Sandals hotel in Antigua had been battered some years later, but it started here, as he sought to reassure agents.

And, true to his word, with renovations going on almost until the very last minute, Sandals Montego Bay reopened on October 14, 1988, a mere month and two days after Hurricane Gilbert's terrifying visit. And it reopened in style, with planeloads of agents arriving to see what had happened and what had been rebuilt, and determined to enjoy the good times that Sandals was well-known for providing for its guests.

It is not in Stewart's character, as he admits, to be stymied by problems and setbacks, so he will just knuckle down and find a way to combat them and deal with them. This is a great gift if the problem is yours – but when it is something that you feel you have no control over, there is little you can do. Stewart had to face one such ordeal when in the early 1990s the Jamaican dollar almost collapsed. Exchange-rate control had been abolished and a number of deregulation and privatization initiatives brought a new freedom to the marketplace, which in turn freed up the movement of currency on and off the island.

Many businesses and investors began to reduce spending and to hoard US dollars, preferring to speculate instead. This had disastrous consequences for the Jamaican dollar, which was almost in free-fall and devaluing by the day. In less than eighteen months the exchange rate had gone from $10 Jamaican to $1 US, to $30 Jamaican to $1 US. Nobody knew what to do. It was killing trade, investment and, of course, tourism. People were panicking, and the government was floundering . . . when to the rescue came Butch Stewart. In what has gone down in Jamaican history as the "Butch Initiative," Stewart decided single-handedly that he had to save the Jamaican dollar.

JOIN THE NATIONAL CAMPAIGN

TO SAVE OUR DOLLAR

Sell your Foreign currency each Wednesday at any branch of National Commercial Bank islandwide and so contribute to the national

SAVE THE DOLLAR FUND

Join the people's initiative NOW and help stabilise our dollar!

Today, the rate of exchange is J$23.50 to 1US$.

Each week NCB will announce the rate of purchase.

Help Stabilise our Jamaican dollar and Watch Jamaica Grow!!

NCB NATIONAL COMMERCIAL BANK JAMAICA LIMITED **TODAY**

Helping to build a strong nation

RIGHT *Butch Stewart spearheaded the massive campaign to save the Jamaican dollar . . . and it worked.*

BELOW *Locals queue up to deposit foreign exchange into Jamaican banks.*

At an outrageously bold press conference on April 21, 1992, Butch Stewart announced that he would personally deposit $1 million US every week into Jamaican banks at a rate of $25 Jamaican to $1 US – hoping secretly that others would take up the challenge and back his initiative. Says Stewart now, "I wanted to show that enough was enough and that people can make a difference, but I also wanted the people to know that the future depends on each and every one of us."

The announcement whipped up heated arguments and discussions in every town and village on the island, took up acres of newsprint, and was the

ABOVE *On the radio, Stewart (left) encourages his countrymen to help save the dollar.*

subject of every talk show and news bulletin. It was decried by many as voodoo economics, and applauded by others as inspirational. But it worked: it galvanized the populace and it created a real local hero. Within days, queues of people were lining up outside banks with everything from ten dollars to hundreds, to follow the Butch Initiative and buoy up the nation's economy and future.

And while it was of no specific advantage to Stewart and the business at the time (he was, after all, earning foreign exchange), he was fully aware of the long-term benefits it would bring to Jamaica, and of course to the businesses' operating environment. His bold, seemingly reckless gesture halted the slide and established a stable dollar rate for some considerable time.

This may well have been the first of Stewart's grand gestures to take place on a national scale, but it was not to be the last. In 1994, when Air Jamaica, the national airline, looked as if it would crash out of existence, Butch Stewart came to the rescue again. Although several consortia had attempted to save and buy the airline, all the bids failed. Stewart arrived and set up the Air Jamaica Acquisition Group, to privatize and save the airline.

Looking back on the Air Jamaica deal, Betty Jo Desnoes declares, "It was another steep learning curve for him. He didn't know anything about airlines . . . but he did know about marketing and how to sell. He made all the marketing decisions, he also knew where to position it in the marketplace. The thing about Mr. Stewart is that he puts his stamp on any organization he is involved with, because he wants people to see what he expects of them and what can be done. He did make a great success of Air Jamaica."

Many of his innovations are still remembered – for example, he prominently positioned Air Jamaica in the marketplace, devised new logos and uniforms, and brought in the best of the new planes available at that time; but he also made flying fun, in typical Stewart style, with champagne flights and an on-board chef, who produced Jamaican as well as international dishes. The crew put on fashion shows

to keep the passengers entertained and organized in-seat aerobics.

He renamed first class as "top class" and even, on some routes, introduced beachside check in, allowing passengers to check in their luggage and get their boarding cards at their hotel, so that they could enjoy every last minute of their vacation. According to Stewart, the airline should be "the island's single biggest ambassador."

An island-hopping service was introduced so that visitors could see more of the Caribbean, with a "visit two islands" deal (where, of course, they might stay at another Sandals resort – Sandals Antigua having opened by this time) as well as a "Caribbean Hopper" where they could visit as many islands as the carrier served for a special ticket price.

The Stewart philosophy was successfully at work again: show everybody a good time and they will remember and return; and always make sure you and the service you provide exceed expectations. But, despite increased loads and revenues, the airline continued to lose money and eventually Stewart walked

ABOVE *Butch Stewart at one of his legendary press conferences unveils the new livery and logo for Air Jamaica.*

BELOW *Stewart's new venture makes headlines.*

away, relinquishing his majority interest share in the carrier. Looking back on that time, Stewart says, "Air Jamaica was crazy, and although we started off on the wrong foot we did an extraordinary job in building a business. But governments have very different objectives from an organization like ours – there is too much interference based on outside objectives, which could undermine what we tried to do. In the end it was better to give it back. I never cry over spilt milk." Though soon after the event he told an interviewer: "In spite of the political hurdles, we showed the possibilities of what the airline could be. But if I were called upon again, I would still assist the airline. It is Jamaica's and there is nothing I would not do for my country."

Airline moguls: Richard Branson of
Virgin Atlantic welcomes a newcomer
to the aviation industry.

ABOVE *The Sandals clan – Adam, Jaime, Butch, and Bobby.*

Butch isn't one to take such setbacks to heart, and he instantly got back to expanding the business and driving it forward. But his redoubtable optimism, one of his great strengths, was stretched to the limit when in 1990 his treasured son, Jonathan, was killed in a car crash in Miami. Jonathan was twenty-four years old and believed by everyone to be his father's natural heir. He was Stewart's second child from his first marriage.

His older brother, Bobby Stewart, who is today the company's Technical Director, explains: "Jon was so charismatic, he was the one we all knew would take over from Dad, and he was being groomed for that. His death affected all our lives." Stewart, his wife, PJ, and their two young children had only arrived in England a few hours before they got the news of the accident and they immediately returned to the US.

"He was an incredible boy," his father states, "a natural. He was working on a couple of projects for me at the time, sourcing stuff in Miami. He was a lot better than me at that age – smarter, cleverer, nicer."

Jon's two younger siblings, half-sister Jaime McConnell and half-brother Adam Stewart, remember a golden, fun-loving young man. Adam, now the CEO of Sandals Resorts International, recalls that "I was only ten when he died and that was the biggest blow ever to happen to our

ABOVE *Butch with his son Jonathan, who tragically died in 1990.*

family. Jon was a unique human being and even though we were kids and he was in his twenties, he was always in our life, he was always with us. The sad thing is that he loved living more than anyone I've ever met, he lived life to the fullest.

"It was a huge blow for our family, but for my old man it was terrible because I think for the first time it hit him about what the family needed, and even though I've never heard him say it I think he regrets it deeply that he didn't spend more time with the family." Adam continues, "But then, how could he do it all . . . he was building a business, traveling all the time, providing for a huge workforce as well as a family . . . but it hit him hard."

Jaime, who also spent many years working for Sandals and ATL before devoting herself to motherhood, remembers that they had all been celebrating Jon's birthday in Miami before leaving on holiday: "I was only eleven but I remember it so well. My parents flew back immediately and Adam and I flew later that day. We were told he'd been in an accident but I was convinced he was going to make it. He had to – Jon was such a life force, he had a way of making everyone feel good, of making everyone laugh. A parent is not supposed to lose a child and Dad went through a lot of different stages trying to deal with it and so many emotions trying to heal."

Jaime believes that his son's untimely death brought her father back to religion. "To this day he can't go into a church without crying, sometimes he can't even pass a church. Eventually it took him back into his faith and I've noticed as he's got older he's got a lot more spiritual. He was brought up a Catholic and since I've had children he is always checking up on me that I take them to Mass on Sundays. And he now makes a conscious effort to bring us all together for holidays and weekends."

Stewart himself admits he did not know how to deal with Jonathan's death and the aftermath. "I was pretty useless for a while, couldn't see what the point was. I just holed up in a beach house and I didn't want to see anyone, or do anything. Eventually a friend came down to see me and gave me a good talking to. Pointing out that I had a lot of people depending on me and even though I had been through a parent's worst nightmare, I had responsibilities to others."

ABOVE *Butch Stewart's optimism has been an integral part of his success, and is also part of his enduring legacy.*

But grieving is often a slow process. "It takes several years to compartmentalize a tragedy like that in your life, to try and separate it and get on with stuff. I had a great friend to whom something similar had happened years before and I once asked him how long it took to get rid of the pain. When he told me that you never lose the pain, I felt better because I realized it wasn't just me who felt like this."

Even though Jonathan died over twenty years ago, his memory lives on in his father's famed fishing boat, named after him – the *Sir Jon* – and the multimedia library Stewart has donated to Campion College, where all the Stewart males went to school – the Jonathan Stewart Multimedia Library.

Jonathan's death has also affected how his siblings relate to their families: both Jaime and Adam explain that they are much more a presence in their children's lives; Adam will often break off from work to come home and see his son before bedtime. Jaime decided to become a full-time mother after her second child was born. "I was very conflicted, but knew that I was no longer a businesswoman, but a mum. I didn't know how to tell Dad so I rehearsed this great big speech for him about having to support my husband and my children. Of course when I saw him, I didn't have to say anything, he knew it, and said I just had to do what was right for my family.

"However, he did tell me not to stop working – it didn't have to be with the company, but to do something for myself. If I didn't, he said I would become very boring, and my husband would be bored. That's always in the back of my mind, so I invariably have a few projects on the go. It's at times like that that he takes off his boss hat and becomes a father again."

A refuge for a busy man: The fishing boat Sir Jon, *named in memory of Stuart's son Jonathan.*

5. Expansion

One Caribbean island was never going to be enough for Stewart's dreams of expansion, and before long both Antigua and Saint Lucia were the recipients of the maestro's "luxury-included" philosophy. At the same time, the existing properties were not allowed to rest on their laurels, and a whole tranche of added value and added excitements were introduced. Weddings became a staple offering and then, of course, as a natural progression, family resorts were added with the introduction of the Beaches brand.

The Sandals empire grows,
but the quality of the service
remains unsurpassed.

LIFE GOES ON, hotels open, tourism markets are conquered. In 1990, Sandals Ocho Rios opened, followed by Sandals Dunn's River, which boasted the largest swimming pool in Jamaica at that time. Dunn's River Falls is one of the great sights of the island and one of its top tourist attractions, a spectacular 600-foot waterfall and a natural wonder that all hoteliers advise their guests to visit. Stewart, however, decided to take things one step further, and built a replica of the falls on the property so that guests could get an introduction to this great attraction. This resulted in the enormous size of the pool and the growth

of a great water playground, setting the standard for future Sandals developments. And, of course, alongside all these new openings, a new sales slogan was born: "Stay at one, play at six".

ABOVE AND LEFT *The boy comes home: the opening of Sandals Ocho Rios was a great day for Butch Stewart, as his grandmother used to live nearby.*

...And Now Sandals Dunn's River
Ocho Rios, Jamaica

ABOVE *Sandals Dunn's River boasted the largest swimming pool of the day in Jamaica.*

With half a dozen properties, by 1991 Sandals had become the largest operator of fully all-inclusive resorts in Jamaica and the whole of the Caribbean, as well as being the home island's largest private-sector employer, which it still is to this day. It was time for Stewart to push the boat out and head towards another island and another new resort.

Sandals Antigua opened at the end of 1991. The Sandals group had bought a ninety-room property on Dickenson Bay, which was swiftly brought up to the Sandals standard with its ethos of luxury, featuring Swim-up Pool Bars, whirlpools, and a full water-sports menu. Stewart and

LEFT *Former Prime Minister Michael Manley (far left) with travel industry executives and Fred Kassner of GOGO Tours (second from left) at Sandals Dunn's River.*

ABOVE *Next port of call for Sandals was Saint Lucia, with its iconic Pitons.*

his team overcame any possible cultural difficulties by bringing Jamaican staff to train the local Antiguans, and also taking Antiguan staff to Jamaica so that they could absorb the service standards that were required. Stewart wanted to dispel any thought that this was going to be a Jamaican takeover; this Sandals was going to be an Antiguan property. As Stewart has always stated: "Even though the Caribbean is perceived as one area, each island is completely different," and this was his philosophy as he moved from island to island, and resort to resort. He wanted to underline that while the resorts offer the same level of standards and service, no two are the same, and each revels in its difference and strives to ensure and maintain that difference.

Stewart now had his eye on the island of Saint Lucia. When the new Sandals Regency was finished, it had its own nine-hole golf course within the grounds. A second Saint Lucia resort opened the following year – Sandals Halcyon Beach Resort – giving visitors to this island the opportunity to stay at one, play at two. A perfect complement to each other – the first grand and opulent, the second laid-back and luxurious.

However, the rest of the Caribbean was as yet untouched by Stewart's magic wand. So, as always, Stewart's search began with the beach: if there was a good one he noted it, if there was a great one he wanted it. For some time he had his eye on the hotels stretched along the glamorous Cable Beach in Nassau, known as the Bahamian Riviera. When a new government was voted into power in 1992, tourism became a political initiative. The Bahamas, with its multitude of islands, clear, warm, bright blue water, amazing beaches, and some of the best fishing in the hemisphere, was ripe for promotion. Butch watched and waited and

in 1991 the Sandals group purchased Le Meridien Royal Bahamian, the iconic Bahamian resort that had opened its doors as the Balmoral Club and had hosted everyone from movie stars to the Duke and Duchess of Windsor. It was a colonial-style mansion with grand marble rooms and pillars, set in beautifully landscaped tropical gardens.

No expense was spared as the Sandals team went into overdrive not just to renew the property to its original grandeur, but to improve on it. The building was renovated, new rooms added, along with massive chandeliers, antique pieces, and classical statues imported by the shipload, as well as a traditional British pub that had been dismantled and brought halfway across the world to its new home in the sun. When it was finished, Sandals Royal Bahamian Resort & Spa was unleashed on the holiday world with no fewer than six restaurants, four swimming pools, a sports complex, a European-style spa and its own private island just half a mile from the resort. And, even though the costs had escalated, the product was magnificent.

Innovations came thick and fast in the early 1990s, when all-inclusive became upgraded to "Ultra All-Inclusive" to define the Sandals difference: a number of gourmet dining options, premium accommodations and an increased number of land and water sports were included. A suite concierge service was introduced, adding cocktail parties and a *New York Times* fax special delivery and additional service and amenities to the "Ultra All-Inclusive" concept. Then came the WeddingMoon program, introduced in 1994, where guests could

ABOVE: *A special place in customers' hearts: the popularity of the Sandals wedding program brought even more romance to the resorts in the 1990s.*

combine their destination wedding and honeymoon into the trip of a lifetime. Over the years more and more couples had been looking for a different wedding experience. For some it was just the opportunity to marry in an exotic location; for others, it may have been a second or third marriage. The idea of getting married somewhere exotic was popular with those who were getting married later in life and already had all the domestic accoutrements marriage implies, while a fourth market was for couples who wished to renew their vows to mark a special anniversary. Sandals Resorts now hosts thousands of weddings a year – on the beaches, in the special wedding pavilions dotted throughout the grounds and even in a special chapel at Montego Bay that was built by a grateful guest.

In 1997, sixteen years after the first Sandals resort opened in Montego Bay, a quantum change took place in the company. Resorts that had been devoted to providing couples with their dream holidays, and that had morphed into highly successful wedding and honeymoon destinations, suddenly realized that as a result of their romantic success there was a growing market who could never frolic in a Sandals playground:

customers with children. As a natural progression, Beaches Resorts was born – the ultimate family holiday resort, a place where everyone under the sun could come and have fun. The first Beaches opened in Negril in 1997, the company's first completed new-build hotel. The Stewart attention to detail was much in evidence during the construction. If children were to be here, the resort had to be as enjoyable for them as for their parents, and, while parents had a choice of five restaurants, seven bars, and three pools, just as much effort had to be put into what would delight the kids. The kids' club offered a huge choice of activities for children of all ages, and the staff were trained to introduce different activities for the teens at certain times. Even the low-rise design of the building was child-friendly and divided into village-type clusters.

Guests loved the idea that they had somewhere safe to leave their children, so that they too could rest and relax – or that, if they so chose, there were any number of activities and outings that adults and children could enjoy together. Beaches Negril was the beginning of something big.

Only a few months later, the flagship Beaches opened in Providenciales in the Turks and Caicos Islands, and from its inception it became the blueprint for any further developments. Now fourteen years old, it is regarded as one of the premier family resorts anywhere in the world. It has not only one of the largest waterparks in the Caribbean, but also a multitude of quality inclusions, such as a wide range of land and water sports, including unlimited scuba diving. One of the most impressive inclusions is the extraordinary PADI (Professional Association of Diving Instructors) diving program. "I was determined always that scuba diving was going to be included in Sandals and Beaches

ABOVE *The launch of the Italian Village at Beaches Turks & Caicos – a $150 million expansion.*

RIGHT *Beaches was the leader in its field with the introduction of its PADI program.*

resorts, and at Beaches we dive kids from the age of eight. We are the only ones to do that," Butch says. And both he and Adam are rightly proud of the fact that they only use custom-made Newton dive boats, which are recognized as being the best in the world. For dive aficionados, Sandals and Beaches have access to more than 200 dive sites throughout the Caribbean and have more PADI dive instructors than any other company in the area – add to that water-skiing, snorkeling, hobie cat and sunfish sailing, alongside wake-boarding and banana boats. Additionally, three Beaches

The flagship Beaches resort in the Turks and Caicos Islands: four villages, one of the largest waterparks in the Caribbean, and sixteen restaurants – the highest restaurant-to-guest ratio in the world.

ABOVE *Having fun at Beaches Turks & Caicos: Michael Jordan is just one of the many celebrities who escape to the islands.*

resorts have a huge Pirate's Island waterpark with water and tube slides, water cannon and whirlpools, as well as lazy river journeys and the Caribbean's only surf simulator at Beaches Turks & Caicos. Stewart's flair for marketing has led to immensely popular collaborations with Sesame Street and Xbox, among others – children can even go bird-watching with Big Bird – and for the musical cool crowd there is a Scratch DJ Academy.

Stewart is fond of telling the story of a time when Michael Jordan and his family stayed at Beaches Turks & Caicos: "A bunch of kids decided to have a game of basketball, and the side Jordan's boys were playing for were getting trashed. Suddenly he appeared on the court – now we are talking about the most famous sportsman in the world at that time – and he gave a demonstration of the most amazing ball control ever. Word got round and people came from all over the resort to watch him. That's the sort of thing that can happen at Beaches."

While the Beaches resort at Turks and Caicos is huge, with more than 600 rooms, its size is not daunting, as the resort is styled into four village areas – Caribbean, Italian, French, and Seaside. Small wonder that in the fourteen years since the first Beaches sprung onto the scene the resorts have picked up numerous awards, including the World's Leading Family Resort, and the World's Leading All-Inclusive Family Resorts.

Perhaps most importantly, the introduction of Beaches Resorts has brought a whole new generation to Sandals. Stewart tells of being confused when, at a convention in the United States, an agent "kept talking to me about us having a multitude of little salesmen. I didn't know what she meant and thought our sales people were all short . . . and then I got it, she was talking about all these kids who had holidayed at Beaches and were talking to their friends about it." Stewart has always believed the customer is the best salesman, and here was a fine example of it. "Even Michael Jordan told me that the only reason he was at Beaches was because his kids were being harassed at school by their friends to visit, and in the end he had to bring them," he continues.

ABOVE *No adults allowed! The Trenchtown clubhouse at Beaches Negril is dedicated to teens and tweens.*

RIGHT *Butler service on the beach for one of the lucky families who vacation at Beaches.*

A thriving market also grew up to accommodate single parents, who were welcomed with special packages, programs, and cocktail parties so that they too could experience a marvelous family vacation.

Beaches catered for an entirely new vacation market, which, according to Yoni Epstein, the company's Director of Call Center Operations, is

ABOVE AND BELOW *Always improving: in the 1990s, "Ultra All-Inclusive" soon offered everything from a treatment at a Red Lane Spa (above) to a gorgeous honeymoon suite complete with private pool (below).*

the multi-generational and multi-layered family getaway – "grandparents, sisters and brothers with their kids, aunts, cousins – they want to take these big family holidays. They want to be together and yet separate, and each generation is as discerning as each other," he says. "It's not just enough that there is sufficient entertainment for the kids and a baby-sitting service – the adults need entertainment, choice, and exceptional service, too. A lot of our customers have been coming to us for years and know the product so well, they are also incredibly well-traveled and well-informed, which means they are demanding and they know what they want. The feedback we get from them is incredible, and if anything is wrong we attend to it immediately," says Epstein.

Adam Stewart explains that staff are trained to be on the alert, and if they overhear a customer complain or say they are not happy with something, then they immediately refer it to their line manager. "We are lucky, I suppose, that out of nearly a million customers a year we get very few complaints, and each we respond to instantly."

ABOVE AND BELOW *The launch of the Grand Pineapple brand (above) in 2008 made the Sandals experience available to even more people, while Royal Plantation in Ocho Rios (below) had taken opulence to a whole new level when it opened in 2004.*

As with all the Stewart companies, the Beaches resorts are constantly scrutinized, re-examined, and improved on. For instance, the newest addition to this side of the family, Beaches Sandy Bay, which lies at one end of Negril's amazing seven-mile beach, offers seven accommodation categories so that families, extended families, and groups of friends can opt for a selection that is perfect for their needs. It also includes not just a Kids Camp, but a nanny service, which allows adults to enjoy carefree evenings. The fourth resort in the Beaches family, Beaches Boscobel, has not only the usual fantastic Pirate's Island waterpark, Sesame Street, and Xbox favorites, but also a golf clinic, especially for youngsters, at the nearby Sandals Golf and Country Club. And Beaches Turks & Caicos continues to surprise and to surpass even its original offering. For instance, its renovated Pirate's Island waterpark is now ten times its original size!

Improvements and innovations were not just aimed at families, for Sandals is constant in its attention to its original clientele – couples. Couples were the heart and soul of Sandals, and its ethos is to continue to seduce and satisfy its major market. To this end, the first of the Honeymoon Villa Suites were introduced in Negril in 1998, before being rolled out to other resorts. These suites offered not just luxury and privacy, but a plunge pool and a whirlpool, as well as indoor and outdoor

ABOVE *Building for the future: construction of the Swim-up Pool Bar at Sandals Grande St. Lucian, another successful resort, which opened in 2002.*

showers and private outdoor space. To ensure guests felt relaxed and at their best at all times, spas were introduced. The Red Lane Spa concept, found throughout both Sandals and Beaches resorts, combines the finest European treatments and traditions alongside Caribbean charm. And while Sandals has a constant and loyal following, the company still wants and needs to attract the new consumer. In the early years of this century, a contemporary consumer began to emerge, a sophisticated and knowledgeable customer who was looking for a little more privacy and a little more exclusivity. So, true to form, Sandals came up with a whole new concept: a boutique resort – all-suite, all-butler service – and in the pop of a champagne cork the Royal Plantation brand was born. The first opened at Ocho Rios, complete with the only champagne and caviar bar in the Caribbean, and was the only all-inclusive resort to be granted membership of the Leading Hotels of the World. Slowly the Royal Plantation Collection added further luxuries to its offerings, from Private Villas to a private island when Fowl Cay, a fifty-two-acre island hideaway in the Exumas in the Bahamas was added. This consists of just six villas, two restaurants, and two amazingly pristine beaches as well as total privacy.

Always ahead of the game, Sandals Resorts has traditionally set the benchmark way ahead of its competitors, who are then left scrambling to catch up. From being recognized as best in the world for all-inclusive holidays, it moved several notches up when it termed its offerings "Ultra All-Inclusive" as it provided more amenities and more choice, from dining experiences to water-sport activities. But again, when you are ahead of the game there will always be some competitor on your tail – not for long, however, with Sandals, who retaliated with the "Luxury Included" vacation. This offers unprecedented services in this market, from private plunge pools and whirlpools, exclusive dining options plus amazing partnerships with the Guild of Professional English Butlers and Beringer Vineyards, all for the benefit of guests. This brought the highest level of luxury to all Sandals resorts, encompassing the ethos of the Royal Plantation brand, and eventually absorbing the resort in Ocho Rios into the "Luxury Included" brand, too.

However, there was another market whom the company felt were being denied the Sandals experience – a budget-conscious consumer. And, while the whole Sandals philosophy is devoted to value for money no matter which resort you choose, the company felt that during the tougher economic climate, a new offering could be made. Hence, Grand Pineapple Beach was born in St. John's in Antigua and Negril in Jamaica in 2008. These are all-inclusive resorts with specialty restaurants, great beaches, non-motorized water sports, and entertainment. "In creating the Grand Pineapple brand, our intention was to create an inviting atmosphere for guests to affordably enjoy the best beaches in the Caribbean," Adam Stewart explains. "It's a slice of paradise no matter your budget."

BELOW *When Bill met Butch: former President Bill Clinton visited Sandals Grande St. Lucian and had a presidential suite named in his honor.*

"Luxury Included" was always close to the Sandals psyche, and never so much as when the company, in the middle of the recession, bought, renovated and revamped the Four Seasons hotel at Great Exuma in the Bahamian out islands, and renamed it Sandals Emerald Bay. Situated on a one-mile stretch of glorious white-sand beach, the resort is a collection of beachfront villas and houses offering 245 rooms and suites. The resort features beachfront villa suites with butler service, three swimming pools, a Red Lane Spa with seventeen indoor treatment rooms and six outside gazebos, a deepwater marina with 133 slips, and an eighteen-hole Greg Norman designed golf course, all of which underlines the company's total dedication to providing luxury on vacation. This can be seen throughout its resorts with the constant updating, such as the provision of Millionnaire Suites with private pools and whirlpools and private villas.

As Adam Stewart pointed out not too long ago: "In this company we let our imaginations run wild . . . and then we cost it. We scale back here and there, where we have to, but the company spends a lot." Like his father, he recognizes that in his business the customer is king, but, even more importantly: "The customer is our biggest salesman," as one of Butch's mantras goes. It's been effective: by 2011, there were twenty-one resorts spread across six Caribbean islands.

LEFT *Sandals accommodation reached new heights with the introduction of the Millionaire Suites at Sandals Regency La Toc, Saint Lucia.*

Sandals Emerald Bay, the newest
addition to the Sandals family –
a luxury ocean-front resort at Great
Exuma, in the Bahamian out islands.

6. A Family Affair

The Sandals family is more than its natural members. For many employees, the company is as much their family as their own, and many talk fondly of a sense of belonging and of the paterfamilias who looks after them both personally and professionally. Stewart is like an old-fashioned Jamaican patriarch, reaching into the lives of his staff, encouraging them, and looking out for them. As for his own children, they, in a wider sense, see the company as a family, as they have been involved in aspects of it while growing up. All have played a part . . . and still do.

Butch and Adam Stewart
with valued members of the
Sandals team.

IT IS THE CONSTANT CARE and attention to detail, along with accolades and criticisms, that underline the success of both Sandals and Beaches, and it is also the constant involvement of the staff at all levels that helps keep the company at the top of the industry. Sandals is constantly assessing what it is doing and how it could be improved – not just for guests, but for the staff, too. The mantra of Beaches Resorts could be seen as a paradigm for the company as a whole. It really is a family affair, and those who work for Butch Stewart acknowledge it.

From those who began in the very early days to the newest recruits, all look on working for the company almost as belonging to a family. One member of staff who joined in 2011 says she has never worked anywhere where everyone seems so genuinely concerned about each other: "I've never been to an office where they hug you every morning," she says.

Betty Jo Desnoes, a stalwart of almost forty years, says it all comes down to the man at the helm. "He seems to know everything about

BELOW *A get-together: Stewart with a group of General Managers from the resorts.*

everyone, he knows who your friends are, where your family is. He keeps track of all of us." She recounts two incidents that underline the true paternalistic nature of the man and the company. "I had only been working back in Jamaica for about a year and I was going to a meeting in Miami. The minute I got to Miami I had a call to tell me my father had died in Canada. I don't know how Mr. Stewart knew, but in minutes there was a plane ticket in my hand to fly direct to Canada. Another occasion one of my sons, who was only fifteen at the time, broke his leg playing rugby. Fifteen-year-old boys are no good at doing nothing, but by the time he got home from hospital Mr. Stewart had bought him a computer and sent it round. Nobody had computers in those days . . . and it kept him amused and occupied for weeks."

Checks Nicholl has been with ATL since 1969, and admits he once thought of leaving and going it alone. "But I couldn't, it would be like leaving the family. Mr. Stewart is like a father and a brother to me, he is also my teacher and he would always look out for you. When I joined the company I had no trade, but I learned on the job. He is the most inspiring man and yet we had fun, we played dominoes and cricket. Coming to work was enjoyable. After the first week I felt like I was part of the family."

BELOW *A long-running relationship: Eleanor Miller receives recognition from Butch and Adam Stewart.*

Sandals Director Bobby Stewart with his daughters.

And like a father, Nicholl points out, Stewart knows how to chastise and bring you into line. "I once did something bad, and fiddled with my electricity meter. Of course I got it wrong and ended up with a bill for $50, which in those days I hadn't a hope of paying. That evening he came to my house and told me I had done a terrible thing, I had breached the trust of the company supplying me and I must never do it again. He then told me he would pay my bill and take it every week from my wages. Things like this make me love the company, love the man." As a reward for his long and faithful service, Nicholl was presented with a gold Rolex watch. "I never take it off," he says proudly.

Eleanor Miller, another long-serving employee who has worked for Stewart for thirty-one years, pays tribute to the man who she says is always aware of the needs of his staff. "One of his best qualities is the way he treats people – he cares about them, their lives and their families. Not that long ago he heard about a young man working in one of the resorts who had an aneurism in his brain. He wanted to know what it would cost to get him to the best hospital and the best care – it was $30,000 and he paid it without a murmur. He did the same for me when my husband needed bypass surgery, he flew him to Miami and paid for everything, and spent the day of the operation with me, making sure I was alright."

Arlene Lindo, his faithful personal assistant of eighteen years, explains, "He cares. Mr. Stewart is a very busy man but he finds time to ask you about yourself and your family. He is very hands-on and he keeps track of people, I don't know how he does it, but he does have the memory of an elephant. I once told him that he was the father that any daughter would love to have. He is so caring, so inspirational, he is somebody you would want to emulate . . . he is like my Oprah!"

Christine Taylor, Vice President of Customer Relations, simply says: "He draws you in and you become a member of a very strong family. He can be very intimidating and you have to be strong and thick-skinned to work here, because he expects perfection. But then he surrounds himself with people who expect perfection, too, and that's a recipe for success. He recognizes what sort of person you are, and if he asks you to do something and he never needs to check that you have done it, because he trusts you, then you are around for years. That's why so many of us have lasted so long . . . I love that man to death."

As his personal assistant Arlene points out, they are all one family: "I was the one who took his father to Miami when he needed medical treatment: you are trusted when you come to work for Mr. Stewart."

As for Stewart's own family, they all played their part. Even his father, Daddy Stew, when he was alive would wander into head office every day just to see what was going on and to dispense sweets and smiles to

Keeping it in the family: Butch, Jaime, and Adam on the beach at Sandals Grande Antigua.

Moving to motherhood: Jaime McConnell with husband Mark and daughters Penelope-Sky and Isla.

the girls there. The three older Stewart children are, or have been, involved with the business. Butch's eldest son, Bobby, heads up the IT side of the company; Adam is now CEO and number two in the company, while Jaime was Managing Director of the Royal Plantation Collection before her children were born, as well as Sr. Vice President of ATL for a time.

"We are a very close family," Jaime says, "but we need to be – everyone is moving at such a fast pace and there are so many stresses in life, we need contact with each other. One of Dad's great lessons in life is the importance of communication. Adam and I are very close, he is my best friend and, really, your sibling knows you best. Your parents have the first part of your life, and your husband or partner has the second, but your sibling is constant, he is there all the time. There are only twenty-four months between Adam and myself, we know each other so well and we have total trust in each other. And remember, I know his boss, too!"

Jaime continues: "And Dad is more boss than dad sometimes, because he never stops talking about the business. We're not a typical family, as there are so many units, but Dad brings us all together – wives, children, grandchildren. Dad has always been a strong and steady presence in our lives."

She explains that throughout their childhood they were always involved in the business – stuffing brochures in envelopes, going through slides in the marketing office in Miami, sitting in on meetings, working in the resorts. "We were even pulled out of school to go to WTM [the World Travel Market] in London or to ITB in Berlin [International Travel Berlin, a huge trade event]. Trade shows were part of our holidays."

Both she and Adam agree that the biggest lessons came from being able to watch their father in action and learn from him. "We learned that nothing was impossible, and it was great to be beside him at a meeting and watch the light bulb come on inside his head as he had devised another way forward," says Jaime.

"We didn't have the traditional family life," she continues, "sitting down together every evening, but we had all the same attributes of a family. Obviously, when we were growing up he was away a lot, but you can't hold it against him. He was building a company."

Adam says, "When we were growing up Dad traveled constantly and now, with a growing young family of my own, I understand the challenges. I must take about 400 flights a year, but I will come home just for bath time, and on weekends I will take some time out. Family is important. I think Dad regrets not having spent more time with us as children, especially after Jon's death, but he has learned to take time out."

Both admit that growing up as Butch Stewart's children was sometimes problematic. Adam once denied it and got beaten up and thrown in the garbage by a boy at school for lying, while Jaime, at the age of seven, heard her father being criticized on a radio phone-in, rang the station and told them off for getting facts wrong about her dad. She says, "Neither of us wanted to stand out from the crowd as Dad became more and more well-known in Jamaica, but I have to say my mum played a huge part in the people we are. At the end of the day, we are fortunate

BELOW *Butch with Cheryl and their three children.*

RIGHT *The three main loves in Butch Stewart's life are his family, Jamaica, and the sea.*

with the way we were brought up and the experiences and opportunities we were given. Dad has shown us the world, but Mum has kept our feet on the ground."

Both are very protective of their father and feel stung when he is criticized. And Adam, as his father's son, is just as proud of the company and its family atmosphere, and of how, like any family, it can nurture people and change lives. "Here in Jamaica we are very proud that we can give the staff opportunities they might never have had, with our training and our foundation. I pay huge tribute to my old man for doing this and supporting it going forward."

Though not given to boasting, Butch is proud of his children – of Adam, his chosen successor, he says: "I have never seen anybody more capable on every project. He is so decisive and he can implement anything he sets his mind to."

Adam is the fifth of Butch's eight children. Brian Jardim, the eldest, was born when Butch was in his late teens, and was adopted before moving to Guyana. Years later, father and son were reunited and for a time Brian worked for the company. Today, Brian runs his own very successful food company from Jamaica. Bobby is the eldest from Stewart's first marriage and also lives in Jamaica, along with Jaime and Adam. The three youngest children live in Miami with their mother, Cheryl.

"I'm lucky in that I get on with all my children," says Butch. "I may not be a doting father, but they all know my feelings and I try always to be there for them. I don't micro-manage but I'm lucky none of them has gone off the rails so far. They are good kids and I have tried as much as I can to make them independent – which they are."

And, although Jaime states that her father is more boss than dad on occasion, she does admit that in her teens he did his best to frighten off some of her suitors of whom he didn't approve. However, now that he is a grandfather, she has seen him take on a very different role: she will occasionally watch him with her daughter Penelope-Sky (known to all and sundry as P-Sky), "and suddenly this big, powerful, serious man turns into a clown before your eyes. It's magical to watch."

Family and business are close to Stewart's heart, and in many ways he runs the company the way he wants his family to be: "I think that's just my style, everyone has their own way and mine is to work with people I trust and like – why else would you want to spend time with them?"

And of all those people he trusts, likes and works with, many are Jamaican – products of his first great love.

The larger family: Sandals teaches caring and sharing within each local community.

7.

A Question of Loyalty

Loyalty is everything to Butch Stewart. Loyalty first to yourself, then to your family, to your community, and outwards to your country. From the early days of ATL, Stewart has expected his workforce to give back, to help out in their community, and to be aware of its needs. He even encourages members of the travel trade with whom he works to contribute to the country they are visiting by volunteering to help in local schools and hospitals, while guests often visit local communities.

Making a positive impact in Jamaica
– and across the Caribbean –
has always been part of the
Sandals philosophy.

"JAMAICA IS BY FAR THE MOST BEAUTIFUL COUNTRY IN THE WORLD," is the unbiased view of Gordon "Butch" Stewart, a son of its soil, who has spent the last thirty years selling it, promoting it, and, on occasion, saving it from disaster. And while he has traveled the world and has homes in Nassau and Miami, his real home is in Ocho Rios, just seven miles from where he was born and brought up, in St. Ann's Bay. "I had the nicest childhood and upbringing, and to this day my idea of luxury is being by the sea. I'm sixth-generation Jamaican on one side of my family and go further back on the other. I have never wanted to leave this place. There were times when it might have been a lot easier for me to go, but it's part of me and who I am," he says.

RIGHT *Three generations of Stewarts in Jamaica: Butch's great-great-grandfather, Herbert Edward Coxe, his great-grandfather, James Ernest La Cordaire Coxe, and his grandfather, James Rupert Stewart Coxe, at their farm in 1896.*

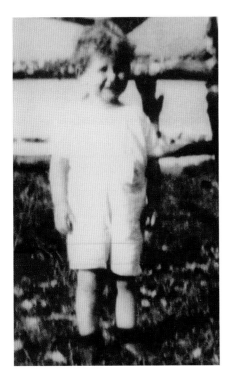

ABOVE *Gordon Leslie Stewart, Butch's father, as a child (above); his mother, Jean, and his father, Gordon Leslie (top).*

Jamaica and Butch Stewart are almost inseparable – he travels all over the world, but, a little like Mary, Queen of Scots and Calais, if you cut Butch Stewart open, you would find Jamaica carved on his heart. As he is quick to point out, all Caribbean islands have their own personality, culture, and mores, as does Jamaica – and anyone who talks about Stewart describes him as a passionate Jamaican and an archetypal Jamaican patriarch in the way he leads the business, his life, and his family.

As an ambassador for his country, Stewart is unparalleled. "I keep telling people I come from a small country, but we win awards telling us we are the best in the world – how great is that?" he says. His children have the same brand of charismatic confidence. Jaime insists: "We keep our feet in Jamaica – we want to stay close to home, which I think when we were growing up served us well. We couldn't even begin to behave ostentatiously, even if we wanted to – it would just make us feel uncomfortable."

And, while father and son recognize that the country has had some really bad times, it has always survived, and both Stewarts firmly believe it also has a great future. Adam explains, citing the crime waves that have overrun the island from time to time, "Over the years Jamaica has had a lot of bad publicity, and still gets it." The last major instance, in the summer of 2010, known as the Tivoli incident, caused much unrest when a known drug dealer refused to be extradited to the United States. He was protected in the ghettos in a small estate in West Kingston – four hours away from the tourism hub of the country, and far from the public eye – which, in the end, meant police and the army became involved. Since that time, a zero-tolerance policy has been pursued by the police and crime figures are reported to be down forty percent.

Adam Stewart explains: "The problems are mainly due to the breakdown in education and subsequently in the home, because the parents have never had opportunities, they had no teaching, no mentoring, which is why you find kids of six and seven hustling on the streets. That is why we at Sandals try to do something about it with our outreach projects to schools and further education. We can make a difference. We can give people opportunities they never dreamed of. The idea of the government waving a magic wand is nonsense. But then all governments are broke."

Some may dislike him, some may fear him, but many in Jamaica love the Sandals king. If they have not been employed by him, they have been educated by him, or have been helped in many different ways through both his public and private donations to charities, schools, and workshops. Giving back is vital to the cultural health of Sandals resorts: "We give more back to the community than any other Jamaican company, although we don't talk a lot about it. I come from the school that says if you are going to help somebody, then help them. It's not an opportunity to brag," Stewart says. The Sandals Foundation, the philanthropic arm of Sandals Resorts, is the culmination of three decades of dedication to playing a meaningful role in each of the communities in which the company operates, across the Caribbean.

Since the very early days of Sandals and ATL, the companies have always supported local causes, and each Sandals and Beaches resort is involved in an Adopt-a-School program. This means that Sandals personnel meet with school teachers and the principal to see what is needed – it could be books or computers, it might be maintenance with the buildings, teacher training, or mentoring. The resort gets to know the school, and the school then develops a relationship with the resort. Often the children from these schools are given work experience, and then full-time jobs at the hotels.

BELOW *The company mandates each resort to take part in the Adopt-a-School program.*

The resorts also work with local health authorities and clinics, whether it's helping provide medicines, providing the clinics themselves, or simply visiting sick or elderly people in the community. Each resort decides what is needed in their area and organizes what it can do.

Another outreach program is with local farmers. In 2005, the company developed a partnership with Jamaica's Rural Agricultural Development Authority whereby they provide seeds for crops – fruit, vegetables, flowers, and more – which are grown locally and the produce sold to the resorts. It's a livelihood for the farmers and a means for the resorts to get fresh, locally grown food, and is one of the most successful outreach programs throughout the island where the resorts are based.

But it's not just the staff who are asked to give back – when tour operators and travel agencies visit the resorts or have a conference or convention there, they are asked to donate half a day of their time to help the local community. Some have painted shops, some have helped build a school, while others have helped build a community center. The very latest initiative is to get the guests to do something similar. The company has recently announced a Voluntourism program – a Reading Road Trip, where guests are given the chance to give back by taking part in a volunteer literacy program. Should they wish to, the guests can attend the local school "adopted" by the resort and help children between the ages of five and seven, under supervision, with their reading, comprehension, and listening skills. Children of guests can also take part.

"The chance to give back has been a customer request for some time, so we are thrilled to be able to offer guests this program for the first time," Adam Stewart says. "It is an extraordinary thing to be able to connect with the people of a place, to know them and to make a difference

BELOW Jamaica's then Minister of Education Andrew Holness, Adam Stewart, and team officially open the Culloden Early Childhood Institute, a state-of-the-art school designed and built by the Sandals Foundation. Holness became Jamaica's ninth Prime Minister soon after this picture was taken.

in their lives. This is our first step in developing programs that allow our guests to do just that. I expect the guests who participate will leave feeling fabulous – body and soul."

Since 2003, Arlene Lindo, Stewart's personal assistant, has been running a separate project with inner-city children. She explains: "Each year we take eight busloads of kids, during their summer holidays, to one of our hotels. Mr. Stewart wanted to expose them to a totally different experience. He wanted to show them that there is another side of life, that there is more to Jamaica than the ghettos. We bring them to a hotel – and these are children who have never been anywhere near a hotel, let alone inside one. We ask them to bring a swimsuit and they spend the day at the pools, on the beach, having barbecues. It has an astonishing effect on them."

Arlene continues, "Last year, after the Tivoli affair, we brought some children from there. It was a real eye-opener. And you know these children then go back to school and write the most wonderful letters, they make thank-you cards and they say things that bring tears to your eyes. If you ask me, I love working for Mr. Stewart, I love the travel, I love the

BELOW *Giving back to the community is part of Butch Stewart's ethos and is built into the Sandals business model.*

things we do, watching him opening a hotel is magical, but the inner-city project is one of the best things about working for him."

Loyalty to the mother country is obviously part and parcel of the Stewart DNA – Stewart cares deeply about his employees and their well-being, which is why the companies that he runs pay better wages than most other hospitality companies throughout the Caribbean. He has organized illness and bereavement packages as well as educational programs for his staff, and this has not just been latterly. Even at the very beginning he took a keen interest in his employees' health and welfare, as well as introducing a lending scheme where they could invest in motorcycles rather than being dependent on local public transport. Obviously, this also ensured that they got to work on time, too.

Yoni Epstein, a relatively new employee, says, "Loyalty and trust go a long way in the Stewart family." Christine Taylor, a member of the old guard, agrees: "Mr. Stewart is loyal to a fault; he will always look out for you." And it is this two-way loyalty that establishes and cements relationships over the years.

BELOW *A letter from a teacher at the North Street Primary School in Kingston, thanking Butch Stewart and Sandals.*

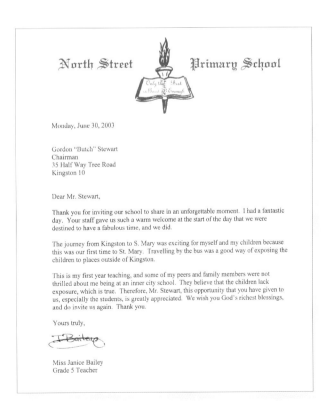

Thank You for inviting us at Beaches Boscobel

Javaun

Mr. "Butch" Stewart

Mr. Gordon "Butch" Stewart
Sandals Resorts International
36 Half Way Tree Road
Kingston 5

Dear Mr. Stewart

I am writing this letter to tell how much I appreciate going on that trip. It was a very amazing and enjoyable trip going to a hotel. The drive was'nt long for nothing. It was like (whoa) i'm in a very large hotel with a lot of tourist, and I even felt like a tourist too. even though the rain began to drizzel and I thought it was the end of the day. But it turned out to be a very enjoyable moment for me and my friends, and I just want to say a big warm thank to you. I hope you'll invite us again to Beaches Boscobel

yours truly
Renee

THESE PAGES AND OVERLEAF

*A selection of thank-you letters from
the children of inner-city schools in
Jamaica who have enjoyed day trips
to Sandals resorts.*

Mr. Butch Stewart
Air Jamaica
Beaches Boscobel
St. Mary.

Dear Sir,
This letter serves to express my
sincere gratitude to you for granting
me the privilege to be the special
guest at the Boscobel Hotel Beach
on June 13, 2003. It was truly a
rewarding experience for me, one that
I will never forget. I really enjoyed
every moment of it.
It was also an educational
experience for me. As I travelled
from Kingston to St. Mary I have
seen and enjoyed beautiful sceneries
of other parts of Jamaica. I have
also learnt the names of places.
The hotel, my destination provide
another form of enjoyment and
education. I have never enjoyed
such good hospitality before.
The staff made me feel as if I
was an oversea tourist. The layout
of the various dishes, the quantity
and the savour attracted me so
much. I stood in amazement
for quite a while before deciding

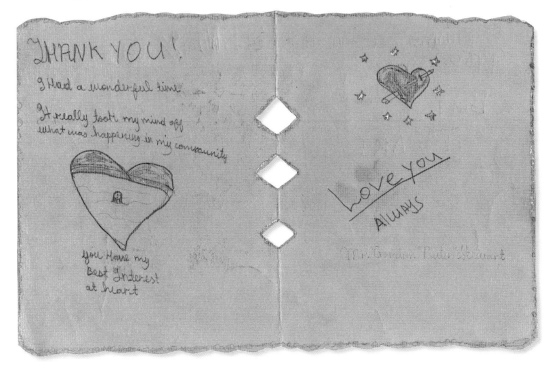

THANK YOU!

I had a wonderful time.

It really took my mind off
what was happening in my community

You have my
Best Interest
at heart

Love you
Always

Mrs Gordon Butch Stewart

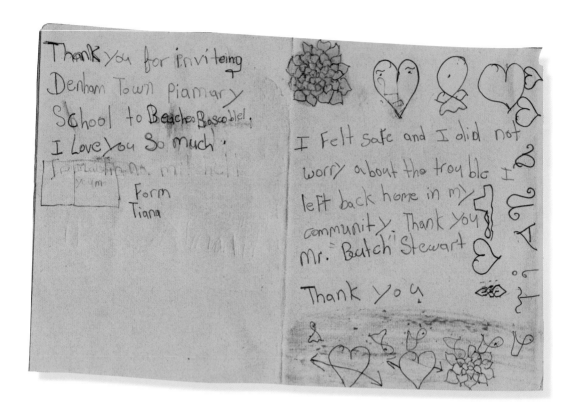

Thank you for inviteing
Denham Town piamary
School to Beaches Boscobel.
I Love you So much.

Form
Tiana

I Felt safe and I did not
worry about the trouble I
left back home in my
community. Thank you
Mr. Butch Stewart

Thank you

The Hon Gordon "Dutch" Stewart
Chairman/Sandals Group
Sandals Resort, Montego Bay
Dear Sir,
        I want to extend a big thank
you for your invitation that was extended
to me which enabled me to take part in
your tour day that was held on the 13th
of June at Beaches Bascobel in St Mary.

It was indeed a great honour for me to have
been selected to take part in such a
wonderful event because I have never been
exposed to an event of this kind before.
I would also like to say special thanks
to your wonderful Staff for their warm
hospitality, they were quite polite and willing
to serve their guest and that helped to make
our day more enjoyable.
        Over all it was a new experience for
me, a day filled with fun but also it was quite
educational.
There was a lot that I learned from it

Mr. Gordon "Butch" Stewart
Sandals Resort International
35 Half Way Tree Road,
Kingstons.

Dear Mr. Stewart, I am writing this letter to thank you for a wonderful day at the Beaches Boscobel. I enjoyed myself very much. I love the water slides most of all. The Jacuzzi was awesome. I think it was a very long journey, but it was worth it. I really appreciate what you did for us. Being there causes me to forget about the troubles I left behind. For once since May I did not think about my cousin who died during the unrest. I felt peaceful and happy. Thank you so much for helping me to relax. It was an excellent experience for us. So once again, I would like to say a big thank. I hope we can come again soon.

Yours Truly,
Shakira.

Director of Services, and Sandals' longest-serving employee, Daddy Stone proclaims he will only leave for the burial ground. Stone, who has been offered many a placement at other hotels over the last thirty years, asks, "Why would I go? Mr. Stewart is a good man to work for and he inspires me."

Errol Lee has been part of the company for many years: he joined ATL right at the very beginning and still swears undying loyalty to his boss. "He's the sort of person you want to be around, he has enormous integrity," says Lee, while confessing he had two almost insurmountable run-ins with Stewart. "I had the distinction some years ago of destroying three vehicles in one day . . . and when he suggested I should use a donkey instead, I walked out. He let me cool down then drove to my house and brought me back to work. Since then I have never had the inclination to leave."

Years before that particular incident, Lee and a friend purloined Stewart's beach house for a weekend of partying with a couple of local lovelies. "On the Sunday morning, I was making breakfast – frying fish from his freezer – when he arrived unannounced with Bobby and Jonathan. He just asked us to make breakfast for them, and he knew I would never do anything like that again!

"I work for Mr. Stewart, I don't work for ATL. He is a born leader and I have watched him and the business grow for forty years, I have grown with him both personally and financially, and the loyalty is bonding. I will always be there for him and will always be at his beck and call. One day some years ago he asked me to go to Negril with him, something needed fixing. I didn't get home for a whole month.

"I will tell anybody that you cannot find another person in this whole life who is like Butch Stewart."

As the company expanded, Butch Stewart never forgot the people and place that launched him – his beloved Jamaica. In 1993, after successfully starting companies in a variety of industries, Stewart launched the *Jamaica Observer* – the first real alternative voice to the 150-year-old *Jamaica Gleaner*. Press and publishing was another industry he knew nothing about, but Stewart remained undaunted. The *Observer* launched as a weekly and after just nineteen months it became a daily.

Stewart intended the paper to be apolitical and balanced in its presentation of the news, but also to have a strong focus on educational and developmental issues in Jamaica. It highlighted local ventures and the work of successful members of the community, and promoted hard work at school to the teenagers in its audience. "Although newspapers were totally outside his remit," Betty Jo Desnoes explains, "he was adamant the country needed another platform and that he was the person to provide it." As with the other businesses, he brought in people who knew about the newspaper industry to help set it up and run it. And while, according to Desnoes, he is very aware of what the paper is doing, "he does make the distinction between interfering and controlling. He knows that journalists must have their independence and that integrity is paramount . . . I had nightmares about him going for the *Observer* – it is high, high risk and indeed it has taken a long time to get where it is," she says.

THE JAMAICA OBSERVER

Vol 1 No 1   88 PAGES   SUNDAY, MARCH 7 1993 $10

Panasonic AIR CONDITIONING
Simply the best
ATL
appliance traders limited

The inquiring mind of Michael Manley

Michael Manley (left) and Jamaica Observer Chief Photographer, Michael Gordon.

Michael Manley, politician, journalist, trade unionist, social reformer, cricket writer, former Prime Minister, now travelling statesman for the Caribbean region and the developing world, brings his awesome intellect, sharp wit and a perspective born of hard experience earned in the socio-political arena, to the pages of the *Jamaica Observer*. Read Michael Manley's weekly THE WORLD WE LIVE IN, beginning March 21 in the *Jamaica Observer*.

Barbara Gloudon, national honoree, journalist, talk show host, communicator par excellence, outspoken commentator, Barbara Gloudon pulls no punches in FRANKLY SPEAKING, a weekly column, starting March 14 in the *Jamaica Observer*.

Dwight Nelson, orator, trade unionist, master negotiator, politician, historian and labour educator, shares his views ACROSS THE BOARD with readers, beginning March 14 and every week in Jamaica's newest sensation – the *Jamaica Observer*. Don't miss it.

WILL THE DOLLAR SURVIVE AT $22 ?

BOJ : YES
JLP : NO

Put your fears to rest. The Jamaican dollar is not about to be devalued. This is the upbeat position coming out of the Finance Ministry, though it is in sharp contrast to popular speculation that the local currency, at $22.20 to one US dollar, could snap under severe strain. "A devaluation is not imminent and there-

•Turn to DOLLAR on page 4

RODERICK RAINFORD
US$ purchases to resume

Moves to replenish STABFUND

By Desmond Allen
Editor of the Observer

The Bank of Jamaica (BOJ) is shortly to hold discussions with the commercial banks and authorised foreign exchange dealers, in preparation to resume purchases of United States dollars to re-stock the foreign exchange Stabilisation Fund (STABFUND).

No purchases have been made for the Fund by the central bank, since last November when the BOJ sold back to the commercial banks the agreed 50 per cent, or US$10 million, and used the rest to pay Jamaica's foreign exchange bills and build up the country's net international reserves.

BOJ Governor, Hon. Roderick Rainford, said the talks with the authorised dealers would seek to arrive at an agreement on when would be the most appropriate time for the central bank to resume purchases for the STABFUND.

"This would take into account the actual demand for foreign exchange by the market and the Bank's requirements for improving the net international reserves," he told the *Jamaica Observer*.

The STABFUND was established last June to help hold the Jamaican dollar, then at a rate of just over J$22 to one US dollar.

•Turn to RAINFORD

New Custos
The new custos of St Andrew, Carmen Stewart receives her seal from Governor-General Sir Howard Cooke.
Old Problem
Garments adorn the fence at Kingston Parish Church, in defiance of the Police, church authorities and MPM. (Page 61)

RIGHT A new paper is born: Butch Stewart gives Jamaica another voice with the launch of the Jamaica Observer.

On a corporate level, Butch Stewart has given back to the nation by sponsoring the West Indies Cricket Team in 2000, and has given back to his clients by introducing a loyalty program for those who return. And they do return – which is why the loyalty program has both platinum and diamond levels. One couple returned to Sandals Montego Bay ninety-eight times. For such loyalty, exceptions are made, and in this case, once the husband had died and the wife still wished to return, she was of course allowed to, becoming the only single guest at a Sandals resort.

But giving back is not totally one-sided – Jamaica itself has recognized and honored what Stewart has done and contributed to the economy, to the community, and to the perception of the island. No rich and powerful man is without enemies, and Stewart has them too, but

RIGHT *A keen cricketer in his youth, Butch still loves the game, and sponsored the West Indian team in 2000.*

even they recognize, sometimes grudgingly, that he is often a power for good. Over the years, honors have been lavished on Butch Stewart, and these go as far back as 1988, the year Stewart was made a Commander of the Order of Distinction, an award from the Jamaican Government for his exemplary contribution to industry and tourism. A few years later he received the Dr. Martin Luther King Jr. Humanitarian Award from the Jamaica-America Society. One of the island's highest accolades is the Order of Jamaica (O.J.), which was bestowed on Stewart in 1995, and brought with it the title "the Honourable." In addition to which, in 1994 Sandals was named the World's Leading All-Inclusive Company and the Top Caribbean Hotel Group, for the first time – both awards it has made its own and held on to ever since.

BELOW *Stewart pictured after receiving the Dr. Martin Luther King Jr. Humanitarian Award from the Jamaica-America Society on January 15, 1992 – the birthday of Dr. King. Betty Jo Desnoes accompanies him (left).*

A clean sweep for Sandals at the World Travel Awards 2010: Butch and Adam pose with Sandals managers.

8. Marketing Magic

Renowned throughout the travel industry is Butch Stewart's Midas touch when it comes to marketing. Nothing escapes his notice when selling his concepts and resorts. He sees things before anyone else does, he notes them, introduces them, and, with a sure touch, makes a success of them. Nothing at Sandals stands still – everything on offer can always be improved, and the customer is always king.

Sandals, a global brand in its
own right, enhances its guests'
experience by forming partnerships
with household names such as
Sesame Street, Martha Stewart,
and Xbox.

"WHEN YOU WANT TO BE THE BEST — SPECIALIZE" is a Butch Stewart mantra. At the beginning of his career, he specialized in air-conditioning units, before eventually expanding into other household appliances. Then he branched into automotives when he bought Caribbean Brake Products Ltd, and from there it was only a short skip and a jump to motor distribution. And then, out of the blue, came the giant leap into hotels and tourism. However, his methodology was the same in whichever industry he found himself. He looked, he listened, he asked, and he learned. As a young salesman for the Curacao Trading Company he came away with two great lessons: "Service is all" and "Exceed the customer's expectations."

OPPOSITE *Communication is key between staff and guests at all the resorts, which is why language experts, pictured here with manager David Roper (third from left) and Merrick Fray (fifth from left), are on call throughout.*

ABOVE *Sandals service goes the extra mile with the addition of butlers on the beach.*

These lessons were to be Stewart's lifelong guides. But, in order for these mantras to be effective, the customer had to be aware of you and what you were selling. With this in mind, when the young Butch Stewart set up on his own to import and fit air-conditioning units, his first step was to let the populace of Kingston know. Hence his desecration of his beloved white Mercedes Benz with the logo of the company he was representing and selling. And throughout those early days he kept his focus on the service the company provided. Fedders, when he launched it in Jamaica, was a relatively unknown brand, competing with some of the big boys like Westinghouse and General Electric – but ATL provided speedy installations and Stewart always went the extra mile to ensure customer satisfaction.

When it came to hotels, he was determined to offer more than any of his competitors, from the very beginning. Merrick Fray says: "I have been in hotels since I started to work and I am a hotelier through and through. I came to work for him with a lot of knowledge and experience and he listened. I also travel a lot and stay in a lot of different hotels so I knew my business, but at the beginning when he was introducing all these extra things, I thought he was mad."

ABOVE *Selling Sandals: Adam Stewart at a travel trade conference in Canada.*

Fray has a romantic way of putting it: "Mr. Stewart is a dreamer and every day he would come into my office with another idea, another little extra, another notion. I decided the best way to deal with the dreamer was for me to become the dream catcher. So I listened to these dreams and with a little team of helpers we would work out the feasibility, and then the dream catcher would let the good dreams go through, and ignore the bad dreams. It worked." Stewart himself admits that "every day I have been obsessed with improving the hotels." Eleanor Miller knew instantly what Stewart was after and what he wanted from hotels. "He just looked at it in a different way and did the opposite of everybody else. Most hoteliers at that time gave the minimum of service for the most amount of money – that was never going to be his way."

Don Cook is another of Stewart's old retainers who now works as a consultant to the hotel business, based in the Bahamas. Cook is a man who has worked in hotels all over the world; he sees Stewart as a visionary who is constantly watching and learning. "He knows instinctively what he wants and what he needs to do, but he listens. He is especially alert to guests' comments: he wants to know what they are looking for outside of what he is offering. He stores information and can listen to a hundred people and then when a new property opens it will always have another extra and different dimension. Better still, if something isn't working he will reform and revise very quickly."

BELOW *Delegates at a Sandals Ultra Convention, where they learn of new developments.*

Cook also notes that Stewart surrounds himself with people with different strengths whom he listens to. But "like a lot of smart people, he won't give you the satisfaction of letting you know it comes from you . . . but he knows and you know. He is extraordinary to watch and to work for because, although he is this huge business person, he is still dedicated to making the little things in the hotel work and be more efficient. He is a hard task master and very hands-on but he is a master at what he does."

Stewart himself admits that he knows every single room in all of the resorts – which is possibly enough to keep any general manager awake at nights. He can walk into a resort and see instantly what is not working, whether it's at a bar, at the pool, or on the beach. Says Cook, "The staff may be wary of him, but they like him and trust him. I am fascinated by the influence he has on the people who work for him and the care he takes of their lives. I just don't know how he remembers it all, and sees it all."

ABOVE *Stewart proudly displays his wares at a travel trade event.*

Stewart knew from the beginning that in order to sell what he had to offer he needed to get to know the trade – the tour operators and travel agents who would be promoting the hotels to potential customers. He needed them on his side. A salesman to his fingertips, he set about wooing them. As Merrick Fray explained: "Mr. Stewart understood that you had to show your product to those who were going to sell it. I don't think any hotels ever see the same number of travel agents and tour operators as we do." That practice continues to this day, while no trade show, no matter how small, escaped his notice. He would visit, laden with brochures and posters, his enthusiasm and charisma, and his total belief in Sandals' luxury-included product.

This latter was Stewart's first differentiation. He always wanted the resorts to be all-inclusive, but he wanted them to be more inclusive than anybody else's. He looked at what others offered and he always went one stage further. He was always

ABOVE *A panoramic view of one of the Millionaire Suites at Sandals Regency La Toc in Saint Lucia.*

searching, looking for the one thing that made the difference, and throughout the years there have been many of them. They included cold towels, chilled champagne, balloons and music to welcome guests on arrival, and luxurious bedrooms equipped with kingsize beds, clock radios, hairdryers, and fine cotton sheets. Sandals was the first all-inclusive resort to introduce suites, thus taking the luxurious holiday experience to another level. These were followed by Premium Suites and Love Nest Suites, all offering ever more luxury, including butler service provided by the Guild of Professional English Butlers. These were followed yet again by villas and Rondovals – often with private plunge pools. The resorts themselves featured expansive whirlpools and secluded gazebos dotted throughout the grounds, swim-up bars – even swim-up rooms – and beautifully landscaped gardens. As Stewart says, "People like gardens."

Another concept pioneered by Stewart is all sports being included in the price, including scuba diving. Today Sandals has the largest dive program in the Caribbean with more than 100,000 guests diving annually at the resorts, beginners as well as experienced divers, with all of the resorts offering PADI certification courses. And from the early days, fitness centers were part of the package, to be joined later by spas. All these things combined to make Sandals "Ultra All-Inclusive," while today it is known as Sandals, the "Luxury Included" vacation.

ABOVE *The magic of the deep: one of the great joys of the Caribbean is the ocean life.*

And never did Butch Stewart take his eye off the ball. Always on the lookout for ways to add to the experience he knew he could deliver, very early on he realized that he needed to sell the destination as well as Sandals resorts. The island of Jamaica had received a lot of criticism since its glamorous heyday in the 1940s and 1950s, when movie stars such as Errol Flynn and theatricals like Noël Coward brought kudos as well as tourists in their wake. When, in 1984, he became President of the Jamaican Hotel and Tourist Association, he knew that if he got all the hoteliers to work together, they would have a louder voice in the travel market. He was unstinting in his selling of the island and what it offered and, as Sandals expanded to other islands, he was just as adept and enthusiastic at selling those areas. As Butch explains, "We love to get people visiting more than one island. Culturally, each has its own national characteristics and charm, although there are still people out there who think you can canoe from one island to another – it's 1,200 miles from Nassau to Kingston."

And nobody is better placed to draw attention to these differences. To operators and agents, Stewart can sing the praises of these islands better than anyone else. He highlights the drama of Jamaica's scenery – its lush Blue Mountains, the clear turquoise sea that surrounds it, fringed

with silvery white sand dotted with a host of beautiful bays and hidden coves, all leading to some of the best reefs and diving in the world, while inland the island offers clear streams and dramatic waterfalls, swamps and wetlands host myriad bird life, and the really fortunate can find rare orchids deep in its forests. All that before you hit the towns and the villages, meet the people and hear the music.

Stewart loves Antigua for its 365 beaches, one for each day of the year, and ensures that the resorts have the best of those on offer. The coastline is also dotted with the relics of its history as an important naval outpost, and is decorated with forts and watch towers, the remains of old wars when the French and British battled it out for supremacy of the sea. The grand look-out post of Shirley Heights and Nelson's Dockyard at English Harbour are constantly high on tourists' must-see list. Saint Lucia, on the other hand, has some of the drama of Jamaica, with its volcanic black sand on one coast and its deep white sand on another, its tropical forests and lush valleys, and of course its two volcanic pyramids, the Pitons, rising dramatically from the sea. It has hidden coves and caves and the world's only drive-in volcano at La Soufrière, where the sulphurous hot springs are also used as a natural healing spot.

The Bahamas offer a quite different experience, gentle and easy, with an abundance of islands – 700 in total, and almost 2,500 cays.

Some are just simple fisherman's villages, while Nassau, the capital, is one of the most sophisticated cities in the Caribbean, with every luxury experience known to tourists and travelers. But they are all blessed with the most intense warm, blue sea fringed with silky white sand. They are a fisherman's dream, a diver's delight, and a sybarite's ideal holiday destination.

"The Caribbean has everything for the vacation of a lifetime. It offers the best tropical holiday in the world and the product itself is every hotelier's dream," Butch Stewart says. He also has the resorts to make it happen. Stewart continues, "The Caribbean people get a lot of satisfaction from pleasing others and it is up to us to ensure that that culture lives on. We built a company on service and we constantly reinvest in training. The concrete and the luxury are just the start – the rest comes from the staff. We know that the customers talk, and when they go home they tell their friends . . . that's what we always remember."

BELOW The launch of Operation Relax in 1991, in which free vacations worth $2 million were offered to active military personnel.

When exemplary service meets inspiration and chutzpah, you get Butch Stewart, the man who took his sales team to New York after Hurricane Gilbert and, armed with photographs of utter devastation, told the tour operators and travel agents assembled that the resort would be open in a couple of months' time for the new season and would be bigger and better. The man who created a Blue Chip Hurricane Guarantee if such a storm disrupted any customer's holiday. The same man who, in 2008, as fuel surcharges escalated and threatened to disturb business, agreed to pay all fuel surcharges and taxes on all holidays of fourteen nights and over. And the man who forever endeared himself to America when, after Operation Desert Storm, he launched Operation Relax, which gave $2 million in free vacations to active-duty military personnel in the US and abroad.

But, like all great entrepreneurs, Stewart also recognized that he could not do everything himself, much as he might like to, so he set about

THE DAILY GLEANER, TUESDAY, JUNE 4, 1991

STAFF Sgt. Daniel Stamaris, the U.S. Army crew chief and celebrated POW, drew the first of 500 winning names in a $1 million Sandals vacation sweepstakes for Persian Gulf vets. Lucky servicepersons will receive week-long sojourns for two at Sandals Resorts in Jamaica. Stamaris was one of three survivors in a dramatic helicopter mission during Operation Desert Shield. Sandals VP of Marketing Development Warren Cohen and Rene Stamaris (wife) assisted.

US 'Operations Desert Storm' troops get free vacations

developing partnerships that add to the style of the resorts and enhance the experience of the guests. This was particularly true when Beaches was introduced to the portfolio. Every parent knows that if a child is happy on holiday, then there is a strong chance of their parents having a good time, too.

Stewart had already introduced such innovations as Pirate's Island waterparks, every water sport imaginable . . . but what about the younger guests? Butch headed straight for Elmo, Zoe, Grover, and Cookie Monster and signed a deal with Sesame Street, which brought

RIGHT *A long-running partnership with Sesame Street brings fun and education to the younger guests.*

the characters to the resorts along with Sesame Workshops – the non-profit-making educational side of the Street. Each season more and more activities, story times, and workshops are added to the amusements – so much so that even the parents have been known to join in. Throughout the day, the characters stroll around the resorts, much to the delight of the guests.

And then, for children of all ages, another partnership was founded with Microsoft Xbox, bringing state-of-the-art Xbox 360 consoles to the resorts' Game Garages, which are regularly updated with the latest games. Hot on its heels came Scratch DJ Academy, founded by the legendary Jam Master Jay of Run-DMC, to teach kids the rudiments of scratching and mixing for their own amusement and parties.

But partnerships are not all child's play – among those devoted to adults is the relationship with Beringer Vineyards of California. This, the oldest continuously operational winery in the Napa Valley, now provides

ABOVE *The Scratch DJ Academy is one of the most popular activities with guests of all ages.*

RIGHT *Greg Norman at the launch of the golf course he designed at Sandals Emerald Bay, with Vanna White and Pat Sajak from* Wheel of Fortune.

all the house wines for Sandals and Beaches resorts, so that a consistency of taste and standard is maintained.

Once he introduced suites to the resorts, Stewart felt a little extra finesse was required and decided that butler service was in order. To provide this, he formed an exclusive partnership with the Guild of Professional English Butlers – renowned for providing butlers for every situation, from hotels to embassies, palaces to private homes – to train Sandals and Beaches butlers. "Butler service," says Stewart, "takes the suite experience to a whole new level. It is true luxury."

For another touch of luxury, Greg Norman, professional golfer and entrepreneur, designed the course at Sandals Emerald Reef Golf Club in the Bahamas, one of the most taxing as well as one of the most beautiful in the region. The stunning course opened with an equally stunning tournament, where the stars of the American reality television competition *Big Break* came out to play with the designer. The tournament not only launched the golf course but also ensured that Sandals Emerald Bay became a force to be reckoned with in Bahamian tourism. To date, many celebrities have visited Sandals Emerald Bay to play the stunning

oceanside course, including Pat Sajak and Vanna White from iconic game show *Wheel of Fortune*.

In another successful partnership, one of the most respected chefs in the United States, Walter Staib, became associated with Sandals to raise the quality and choice of cuisine to even higher standards. Conscious that Beaches was catering for a different market with different needs, Sandals Resorts International sought the best in the business to advise on global culinary trends – from changing tastes with more vegetarian options required, to the rising popularity of Japanese and Thai cuisine, plus the upsurge in food allergies. Staib, with his thirty-plus years of experience in cooking, catering, and consulting, was called in and has worked in partnership with the Sandals group ever since.

Since the WeddingMoon concept was first introduced in 1994, the company has fostered partnerships with the best in the business, such as celebrity wedding designer and planner Preston Bailey, accessories designer Beverly Clark, and luxury homeware company Waterford Wedgwood. However, it wasn't until 2009 that the Stewart flair took another great leap and formed Sandals Weddings by Martha Stewart,

*Emerald Reef Golf Club in the
Bahamas – an eighteen-hole
championship course designed by
Greg Norman and recognized as
one of the finest in the Caribbean.*

ABOVE: *Butch and Martha, both Stewarts, announcing their partnership on her US TV show.*

bringing the expert touch of the iconic style guru to all resorts. Launched by them both on Martha Stewart's own TV program, the concept offers six wedding themes designed by Martha Stewart that can be customized: colors, taste, decor, and location can all be decided by the couple. This has resulted in another upsurge in wedding business at the resorts. And at any point of the day holidaymakers might see a bride in her dream dress heading for a beautiful beach, a secluded, flower-decked gazebo, or one of the elegant gardens of the resort, where she will meet her groom and they will pledge their vows surrounded by their family and friends. Afterwards a beach party or romantic dinner for two or even a lavish meal for fifty is easily catered for in magical surroundings.

Just a few months after the wedding partnership, Martha Stewart Craft Studios at Beaches became available, where guests – children and adults alike – can learn a whole series of crafts, from stenciling to card-making. Many come and make a host of Christmas cards and gifts while on their vacation, ensuring their memories can be perfectly preserved.

From the very beginning of Sandals, image was paramount, and creating the look and the logo that would sell this very special concept took time, although the essence has remained the same. The brand is dedicated to people having a good time in the sun, on a beach. To begin with it was simply aimed at couples, so posters and brochures depicted coastlines, white sand, blue sea, and often a couple languorously enjoying the experience – under an umbrella; lying on the sand; swimming or sailing. The Sandals logo has more or less stayed the same in an informal script that occasionally varies in color or depth. Stewart knew that sea and sand were not going to be enough, so gradually the colors of the Caribbean were used to bring light and life to the images – the red of the flamboyant blooms, the lush green of palms, the fluorescent pink of bougainvillea, and the bright, bright blue of the Caribbean. "Guests come to the Caribbean

ABOVE AND BELOW *Sandals is one of the most recognizable and distinctive brands in the world.*

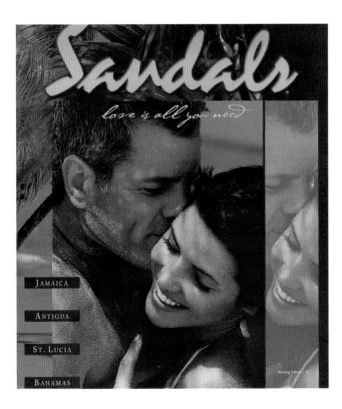

to be devoured by the tropics," he says, and these are smart yet subtle ways to highlight that experience.

The advertisements, posters and billboards showing off these brilliant shades appeared in media in the United States and Europe, on television, in travel agency windows, on the sides of buses and taxis. Some claim that over the years fortunes have been spent on advertising, although Stewart himself says: "We don't spend as much as people think, it's just very recognizable, and while you can never stop advertising and promoting, advertising has its limits. It's the returning guest who is your best tool."

And Sandals has never stopped promoting what it offers – so much so that it is now one of the most recognizable brands in the world. Research carried out by a UK-based organization, Superbrands, saw an expert council and a representative sample of consumers look at thousands of brands from all over the world. From this data, an annual Top 500 recognizable global brands is generated. Sandals was ranked 355 out of the 500. Given that the percentage of UK clients to Sandals and Beaches is but thirty percent, it is a phenomenal achievement. Stewart was thrilled with the accolade: "Achieving this status in the UK tells us that our brand strategy is working well, and to think we were chosen out of literally thousands of brands makes this achievement much sweeter."

Stewart is very proud of the Sandals brand being in the Top 500, and states that the "brand Sandals continues to do a phenomenal job at promoting our beautiful island of Jamaica, as well as showering this and other Caribbean islands with promotion, advertising, and attention, in some cases above the beyond their own resource levels."

It was particularly pleasing for Stewart, who still bemoans his initial lack of success at selling the Sandals concept to the UK holidaymaker. "I didn't have much success with the main people in England, the operators and agencies, when I first began to run around the place with my slides and screens. In those days, all-inclusive didn't have a good ring to it, they got it confused with holiday camps . . . however, it is now a lot better and growing. Which I am pleased about, because my ideal recipe for hotel guests was always to have some well-dressed Italians, some great Americans intent on enjoying themselves, mixed with the British sense of humor. These three countries together provide a great atmosphere."

BELOW *The magnificent* Lady Sandals *– a great brand ambassador.*

OPPOSITE *Tell it like it is . . . Sandals marketing constantly reminds consumers and the trade who is Number One in the all-inclusive market.*

In selling the Sandals wares, Stewart leaves no stone unturned, no opportunity missed, and indeed no wave unsailed. And it was to this end that in 1999 he unveiled one of Sandals' great selling tools – the *Lady Sandals*, a 135-foot luxury yacht from the Dutch specialist builders Feadship, built in 1985 and refitted twice, once by a leading Hollywood movie star, to whom Stewart had sold it. "I was sorry once it was sold but fortunately the company got it back a few years later. She's a great boat and works hard," Stewart explains.

Lady Sandals is of such a size that she can sail almost anywhere without requiring extra assistance from tugs and other boats as well as harbour masters and special services. Large enough to cross oceans yet slim enough to sail along rivers and canals, she looks just as much at home on lakes as she does in the Caribbean. She is the descendant of all those traveling billboards Stewart once had when he was selling air-conditioning units and plastered their names and logos across his vans as well as his own Mercedes Benz. *Lady Sandals* is a

BARS & PREMIUM BRAND

Liquors

up to 8 bars per resort

Anyone who has ever taken a cruise has experienced the shock of the bar bill at the end of the voyage—especially when they've ordered premium brand liquors and wines. But at Sandals you can order any drink, anytime you want to without worrying about the tab—drinks are always on the house. There are up to 8 bars per resort, with everything from swim-up bars and piano bars to authentic British pubs. Unlike other all-inclusive resorts, Sandals pours only the very best premium brand liquors, including El Dorado, the oldest and only rum manufacturer left in the world that uses wooden stills, and the exclusive Johnnie Walker Black. Maybe that's why our guests are always raising their glasses—because they know the next round is always on us.

premium brands include

- Bombay Sapphire
- Tanqueray
- Rémy Martin VSOP
- Dewar's
- Crown Royal
- Johnnie Walker Black
- El Dorado 15 Years
- Jack Daniels

MORE

Beringer® Wines on the House

Only Sandals includes Beringer Wines, the oldest, most respected winery in Napa Valley. With four varietals to choose from, each corked exclusively for Sandals, guests can savor the best wines at every meal and at every bar—and it's always included. Now that's the Sandals difference.

ABOVE *The mark of an expert: only awarded to those agents who undergo intensive workshop training.*

seriously upmarket selling tool. She travels the world entertaining clients, agents, and tour operators, who are invited on board to experience a taste of a "Luxury Included" vacation in their home city, and to be informed of all new developments at Sandals and Beaches resorts. She can host a glamorous cocktail party, a posh lunch party, or an elegant dinner. She's traveled the Caribbean and the Great Lakes of North America, she's crossed the Atlantic bringing news of her parent company, and she has sailed along the St. Lawrence Seaway until her sales pitch arrived in Chicago. No other travel, hotel, or resort company has anything like the *Lady Sandals*. Agents love her and never refuse an invitation . . . like Butch, she is the ultimate ambassador.

As Adam Stewart remarked: "This is how much we love our travel agents!" But Sandals does, and rewards them not just with visits onboard *Lady Sandals* during regular familiarization trips to the resorts, but also, and much more importantly, with a Certified Sandals Specialist program. This was brought about as much by the agents themselves, for a number wanted to be specialist only in selling Sandals and Beaches resorts. It came through discussions with the company's marketing agents and involved a rigorous training program. The curriculum for this includes learning everything about the different room categories, the different numbers and types of restaurants in each resort, every sporting activity, plus every new development and, naturally, learning about and absorbing the company culture. Only when they had completed such a course could an agent deem him or herself a Certified Sandals Specialist.

To highlight and promote the growth of this program and to attract more agents, Sandals Resorts created Ultra Conventions, where the company's top agents would gather for more news and information about the resorts, but very much in a celebratory atmosphere. Wooing agents has always been a priority for the great marketer, and he pays as much attention to it now as he did at the very beginning, constantly coming up with new ways to keep them up to speed and onside.

Always one step ahead: unique architecture can be found throughout Sandals resorts, such as the Beachfront Rondoval Suites at Sandals Grande St. Lucian.

9. The Bigger Picture

Long before many of his competitors woke up to conservation and preservation, Stewart was practicing them. His love for his country, its beauty, and, most of all, its beaches underlined the need to protect it. And it is this same drive that has imbued in his children and staff the sense of responsibility they owe Mother Nature – a sense of responsibility that has passed almost imperceptibly to his son Adam, who is, if possible, even more passionate about conservation.

The importance of protecting the
environment is part of ongoing
educational initiatives with
local communities.

VACATIONS ARE NOT JUST ABOUT FUN – well, not any more. For the last two decades tourists, travelers, hoteliers, airlines, and providers have become increasingly aware of the damage done to the planet by wanton waste, careless construction, and thoughtless behavior. In Rio de Janeiro in 1992, some 182 heads of state endorsed an accreditation that applied to the tourism and travel trade – the Green Globe Certification project. This is a worldwide program that sets out forty-one different criteria that tourism projects should adhere to in order to receive this certification – the criteria included everything from sustainable management through to community development and the preservation of a region's cultural heritage.

ABOVE *Staff from the Sandals Foundation receive an award for Biodiversity at World Tourism Day in Jamaica from minister the Hon. Edmund Bartlett.*

In 1998, when Sandals Negril became Green Globe certified, it was only the first all-inclusive and only the fifth resort in the world to be designated as such. Within three years, the remaining fifteen Sandals and Beaches resorts earned the award and today all twenty-one of them are certified.

Sandals has now strengthened its existing partnership with EarthCheck – an environmental management program used by travel and tourism organizations around the world, and the science behind Green Globe – by launching a new program, Sandals Earthguard, which continues to improve their commitment to sustainable tourism and reduce the company's environmental footprint. In 2010, EarthCheck undertook

a rigorous upgrade of its science and software to launch its own standard for certification. Adam Stewart says, "The partnership we now have with EarthCheck provides our group with access to a set of tools and data that is the very best there is out there . . . which in turn allows our management team to meet the more complex and demanding reporting needs of a new carbon economy and have better insight into the operational efficiencies of each resort." For years, the environmental management systems developed by Sandals have been adopted by both governments and organizations internationally, which has kept the company at the forefront of innovation.

However, the greening of Sandals had begun long before the initiatives undertaken in Negril. In fact, it literally began with the very first resorts – Bay Roc and the Carlyle – as both had lush tropical gardens that became one of their great attractions, and were the forerunners to some of the great

ABOVE AND BELOW *Working with Mother Nature in mind: Stewart testing the water and staff at Sandals Negril – the first Green Globe certified of the resorts.*

gardens of the Sandals and Beaches resorts today. Butch Stewart found the gardens to be hugely popular with his guests: "During their stay they have many different moods, many different needs, and they loved the quiet spaces and the colors given to them by the gardens.

"But then to keep the gardens looking good, they needed lots of water, and that's when we began to recycle the water. In those days the

ABOVE *Stewart with experts on site at the clearing of Negril.*

environmentalist voice was not often heard and we were recycling to keep the gardens looking more beautiful. So by doing the things that our guests liked, we stumbled onto things the environmentalists liked," Stewart explains.

But it was with the acquisition of another property in Negril at Long Bay in Jamaica that the environment took center stage. The location was stunning – a great beach backed by a lush tropical forest. Stewart explained that the previous owners had planted the forest, twenty acres of it in total, full of palms and quango trees along with a mangrove swamp, all of which gave a wild tropical air to the beach resort. Consequently, a landscape architect was employed for the first time to conserve the area, save the trees, and ensure that all the resort's buildings were below the tree-line.

Before construction began, the whole area was assessed and examined and the decision taken to leave as much of the natural setting as possible and build around it. A protection plan was drawn up: to facilitate the protection of many of the trees and plants, a nursery was built where those to be transplanted were housed temporarily. In this way almost 5,000 indigenous plants were saved and used in the resort's landscaping, while areas of swamp were left intact for turtles and crabs to nest and lay

Gardens, such as this one at Negril, are an integral part of any Sandals experience, as they showcase some of the island's most beautiful indigenous plants.

their eggs. And, when the eggs hatched, Sandals staff laid bamboo pipes on the ground, so that the young could crawl through and have a safe journey from land to sea!

The natural theme spread to the buildings, which were constructed from less concrete and more wood mixed with tiles and coral stone. Negril is one of the very few properties in the Caribbean that has rooms right on the water, an innovation that would no longer be allowed because of environmental regulations.

Care for the environment continued whenever new properties were added to the portfolio. The resort at Ocho Rios, in the garden parish of St. Ann's, where Butch was brought up and where his grandmother had a weekend house, became a project dear to his heart; he knew the area intimately having swum, fished, and played there as a child. It was known as the Garden Parish because of the lushness of the vegetation, caused by the myriad waterfalls and underground streams in the area.

During the growth of the Sandals empire, landscape was always vital to each individual hotel – along with having the best beach, fantastic reefs, which

Oceans of Life, a Sandals Foundation roadshow, educates local children on the importance of marine conservation.

Sandals Negril led the way in environmental conservation, with no buildings taller than the highest palm tree and natural vegetation preserved throughout.

ABOVE AND BELOW *Conservation
continued: recycling in the community,
above; and below, beaches are cleaned
by local volunteers.*

the company also looked after, and spectacular locations. Sandals Whitehouse, for instance, on the south coast of Jamaica, is cradled by the mountains and nestled in fifty acres of a wildlife preserve; it is both natural and splendid. Stewart often muses that he should have had all the rooms designed with double windows so that guests could have mountain as well as sea views. "Those mountains are so gorgeous, whether you are looking at them from a plane or from the ground," he says. However, the views are still glorious. Throughout the property the color and lavishness of the planting is magnificent, with flowering vines, bougainvillea of bright pink, red, and mango, jade vines with their purple flowers, bottlebrush with its green and red bulbs, night-blooming jasmine, orchids, and the powder-pink puffs of the candlestick plants, making the whole experience seem like walking through a kaleidoscope. But it is the natural beauty of the Caribbean that has been one of the great selling objectives of Butch Stewart, and he is committed to maintaining the look and the fecundity of the land and the clearness of the sea.

As Adam Stewart points out: "We are changing the way we run our hotels in order to serve Mother Nature." As a part of the company's Earthguard program, each property has a conservation and environmental

manager who monitors what needs doing, what needs implementing and what has to be changed. The beaches, of course, are an absolute priority, so constant monitoring of them and the nearby reefs and marine life is essential – Sandals Emerald Bay in the Bahamas, the company's newest resort, has even persuaded yachts mooring at the local marina to alert the resort, and Sandals will collect and dispose of their waste. In each resort, waste management is a vital daily concern, as is the recycling of everything from bread to bedspreads. In other areas, energy management is monitored with timers on whirlpool jets, spa steam rooms and external lighting in hallways and corridors, while energy-saving light bulbs are fitted throughout the properties. Adam Stewart is still aghast at the fact that when Sandals acquired Sandals Emerald Bay there was not one energy-saving bulb in the property – their first light bulb purchase order for the hotel cost $360,000! And throughout all of this, staff awareness is crucial, with workshops and seminars on conservation, recycling, and composting held regularly.

Adam Stewart explains the company's environmental perspective: "Our first environmental award was given to us for breaking down sewage and cleaning the water. There is a very sound reason for everything we do – for instance, the electricity used for air-conditioning is used to heat the pools. It annoys me in a way that so many corporations say they genuinely care, whereas I know we genuinely do. Ours even begins with our purchasing policy – we look at the chemical contents of everything we consider and everything we buy. This year we will spend $15 million on next-generation technologies such as lighting, solar and wind – now that is us planning for the future and thinking long-term. But that is how we operate; we know we have to find short-term money for such long-term planning, but that is what makes the difference between what we do, and what others do. Our customers are now very knowledgeable and very concerned about the planet so they understand and accept the boundaries we are pushing, but they also know there are rewards for this. Soon all our rooms will be fully intelligent with infrared monitoring, so that things can shut down when there is nobody in the room."

The eco-friendly programs at the resorts are also extended to the surrounding towns and communities, with many school and educational projects included through the Sandals Foundation. A recent project for schools was an essay competition on why children should be environmental ambassadors. It is extremely important, according to both Stewarts, to inculcate the importance of protecting the environment in future generations.

Protecting the environment is only one aspect of what has now become the Sandals Foundation. Social responsibility has been part of the company's culture from its inception. Sandals has always believed in giving back to the workforce, the local area and the country as a whole, from sponsoring schools to organizing health checks. Adam Stewart formalized this by creating the Sandals Foundation with its tripartite program of community, education, and environment. He heads it, aided by a board of directors who are all top Sandals executives and are as committed as he is to the Foundation, and whose knowledge and experience of both the company and the area will help it grow. As he explains, "We have always been about changing people's lives and caring for the communities in which we operate and it is my pleasure to put a formal and transparent face on the work my father began more than thirty years ago – to make the Caribbean a better place for the people who live and work here.

"We are the Caribbean," he adds. "As my father taught me long ago, we have the means and therefore the responsibility to act."

Because he believes that education is the Foundation and cornerstone for individuals as well as communities and countries to improve their lot, so it is for the Sandals foundation. Building on the already thriving Adopt-a-School policy that each resort is committed to, other community concerns are also addressed by the Foundation, including healthcare and empowerment. Sandals already sponsors several health clinics and programs aimed at all aspects of healthy living, such as senior citizen wellness and HIV/AIDS awareness, and for some years has supported the "Great Shape 1000 Smiles Project," which gives access to free dental care to communities throughout Jamaica.

The Foundation also supports programs for youth arts and sports, as well as hospitality training and agricultural partnerships with local farmers that teach lifelong skills to provide both a decent living and economic opportunities. The work organized by the Foundation to sustain and conserve the environment includes educating fishermen on environmentally sound fishing practices.

ABOVE: *A Sandals Foundation volunteer gives books to a child at one of the Readathon events.*

168

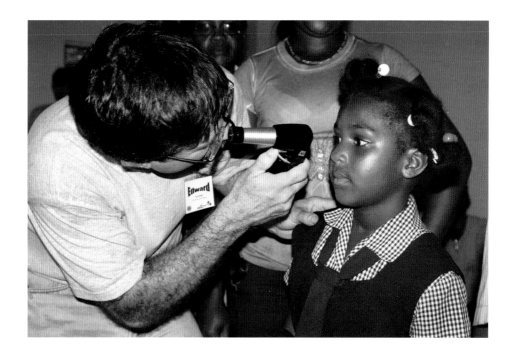

ABOVE *A volunteer optician inspects a child's eyes as part of the i-Care program.*

BELOW *A school adopted by Sandals.*

Sandals is also able to expand the partnerships developed at its resorts to benefit local communities, by involving special partners in the Foundation's work – for example, through the partnership with Sesame Workshops, characters visit local communities promoting anti-litter campaigns and teaching children about road safety awareness. Sesame Street characters also visit the sick and provide gifts for underprivileged children. Two of the most popular programs are "Story Time with Elmo," which encourages children to read, and "Exploring with Grover," which teaches local children about oceanography and how they can play a part in conserving the sea, marine life, reefs, and beaches.

Guests are encouraged to participate in the Foundation's work, either through straight donations to various projects, or through special purchases in the gift shops where a percentage of the proceeds goes to the Foundation. Better still, they can donate some of their vacation time to working alongside resort members on any number of community projects.

Over the years community projects benefiting children and young people have included providing Christmas toys and treats for thousands of children across the Caribbean, funding critical care for three

ABOVE: *Adam Stewart, with help from Santa Claus, makes one child smile.*

children undergoing heart surgery, providing scholarships across five countries with its "Care for Kids Program" and sponsoring Youth Crime Watch of Jamaica across forty schools. Environmental work undertaken by the Sandals Foundation has included funding an eight-week coral conservation show, the launch of marine sanctuaries at Boscobel and Whitehouse, helping Negril Recycling Center to purchase an extruder to help produce by-products from recycled waste, and launching a Climate Change Program at a girls' school in Antigua.

Additionally, the Foundation has supported many sports and fitness projects throughout the region, such as helping fund street cricket for twenty inner-city communities (in partnership with West Indian cricketer Courtney Walsh), launching a summer golf clinic attended by forty children – three of whom qualified for the Jamaica Junior team – and, in a high-profile partnership with the Antiguan Ministry of Sport, launched the Sandals Foundation Cricket Academy. The importance of healthy eating and nutrition is the focus of the Beaches Big Breakfast club in Turks and Caicos.

RIGHT *Students at Sandals Cricket Academy in Antigua – a graduate of the academy was recently selected to play for the West Indies team.*

Added to this, following the earthquake in Haiti in 2010, the Foundation raised $200,000 for Haiti Relief and chartered ten planes to help provide food and water purifiers to several charities on the ground.

Alongside all of these are a host of sponsorships and initiatives throughout the six islands where Sandals offers its "Luxury Included" vacations, whether it's mentoring young people, providing computers and books for schools and colleges, putting new roofs on schools, or organizing shoreline and underwater clean-ups. The company is involved in every aspect, from raising funds to providing people and ideas. As Adam Stewart explains: "This is another example of the company growing up. While we've always helped the community, now we have a mantra, an ethos in which each hotel has a mandate: to make the lives of people in our communities better."

ABOVE *Sandals staff are encouraged to help with outreach work, often in their own communities.*

The Stewarts also have another new venture in the pipeline: the Sandals Corporate University (SCU). Education is vital not just to a community and a business, but also to a country, and the company has always taken this aspect of its employment policy seriously. From the beginning, as Merrick Fray insisted, no staff were engaged unless they could read and write – skills that are recognized as the absolute basic essentials of growth for the individual and the resort. Adam Stewart is passionate about education and the part it plays in anyone's life: "We've always cared about the people who work for us and worked toward improving their lives and opportunities, and we still do." Constant training alongside educational scholarships has been very much part of the Sandals philosophy, and from the beginning help and encouragement, as well as money, were provided for those members of staff who wanted to take part in higher education up to degree level, either within the Caribbean or in the United States.

The role of the SCU is to formalize the training Sandals has always provided and take it to a new level with international partners. As Adam says, "While we've had a Sandals University for a long time, it was more of an accreditation for our internal system. I did a hospitality management degree at college, but I also did a Sandals degree, which for me was:

ABOVE *The emblem of the new
Sandals Corporate University.*

forget about your vacation and head for a Sandals resort, where I worked and studied and learned about what was going on!"

The SCU's basic principle is set out in a declaration: "To enhance team member and customer value." In order to do this, the purpose and workings of the SCU have three main strands. The first is team member development, which applies to all staff to help develop their knowledge, skills, and attitude by placing emphasis on cross-training and leadership development, regardless of their position in the company. Secondly, company innovation is taught, by which everybody is encouraged to contribute ideas and innovative suggestions to help the company and the industry to improve and grow. The third subject taught is corporate knowledge management – teaching staff to preserve and maintain the knowledge and experience within the company to secure its intellectual property for the next generations.

Grandiose as this may sound, its application is intensely practical and is based in the desire to maintain company standards, improve them, and allow them to change and grow. Staff can sign on and take the courses in various modules, and while there is a core course curriculum that all students have to take, they can all study at their own pace. The company acknowledges that while hospitality training does exist in various colleges and schools throughout the Caribbean, standards and facilities have not been consistent; this is what SCU will provide, so that eventually it will offer the courses to other hoteliers and to those who want to learn about and enter the industry. And to this end it will partner and liaise with three outside bodies: the American Hotel and Lodging Educational Institute, the Western Hospitality Institute, and the Jamaica Foundation for Lifelong Learning, which will help to upgrade facilities and standardize training and certification. The outcome will not be centered solely on improved service and staff, but also geared to improving customer value and profitability – ensuring that the hospitality industry comes of age and is taken as seriously as any other profession.

What is both extraordinary and sets the SCU apart from other corporate training schemes is that its manifesto lays out what it expects from its graduates. The SCU expects each graduate to be "A team member who can sell and contribute to revenue enhancement, who can communicate professionally at all levels and can work cohesively in a team. Someone who can display leadership regardless of position or title, and who can be conscious of cost and the bottom line as well as being aware of the environment, the community, the country and the world in which they live. They should be capable of being flexible and multi-skilled, be au fait with the latest technology, engage with and satisfy the guests while being able to think creatively and critically and come up with ideas." Phew.

And in order to facilitate this and explain to staff what the SCU will entail, there is a very simple learning aid, "The House that Butch Built," which uses six pillars of learning to encapsulate the Stewart philosophy: Team Member Engagement, Guest Retention, Environmental Responsibility, Community Involvement, Strategic Partnerships, and Profitability. Every student must study these in the "Sandalization" standard course, which is followed by a number of specific modules from line management to guest engagement through to community involvement and cost management. Alongside the core course, department-specific courses are on offer and take in everything from food and beverages to accountancy and engineering.

In addition, SCU offers two special programs: a six-week Hospitality Training Program designed for those with no previous experience to make them ready for job entry; and a two-year Management Training Program, designed to develop and managerial skills.

To help both students and teachers keep track and assess each part of the course, students are issued with a passport, which is monitored and "stamped" as each part of the learning journey is completed. And, of course, in harmony with the company's original statement about offering a "Luxury Included" all-inclusive experience, SCU offers a "change-included" experience. The university's logo sports two emblems: a torch and a shield. The former is to remind followers that it is their duty to pass on the flame of continuous learning, and the shield serves as a reminder to protect the legacy, integrity, and values of the brand for the future. As Butch says, "Our job is to ensure that when guests come to our hotels they get more than they were expecting. It begins with training, and this allows our brand to constantly lead in service, innovation, and protection of the environment."

Supporting the rich diversity of marine life is an important part of the commitment that the Sandals Foundation promises to uphold.

10.
Like Father, Like Son

With forty years of starting, building, and sustaining such successful businesses, Stewart shows little evidence of slowing down. However, he recognizes that in family businesses the act of succession has to be addressed. He acknowledges he is fortunate in having his successor to hand. Adam Stewart is more than just a chip off the old block; he's a man with a mission: to make Sandals even more of a brand leader and success story for the twenty-first century.

United we stand: father and son
working together for the future
of Sandals.

THE ARCHETYPAL JAMAICAN PATRIARCH, the Honourable Gordon "Butch" Stewart, Chairman of Sandals Resorts International, Chairman of ATL Ltd, Chairman of the *Jamaica Observer*, public figure, elder statesman, savior of the Jamaican dollar, winner of numerous awards for business and humanitarian acts, is an ace salesman and marketing genius who built up a pan-Caribbean empire starting with just $3,200. Along the way he acquired influence, enemies, and a loyal band of followers, hangers-on, and fans, alongside a close-knit family. Now aged seventy, while he is not running out of steam, or energy, or enthusiasm, but recognizing that the companies need another dimension and a renewed focus, he has appointed his son Adam Chief Executive Officer.

ABOVE *Adam Stewart at the helm, speaking at an awards ceremony.*

As old as Sandals – he, too, was born in 1981 – Adam has been working in the company since the age of eight, when he started stuffing brochures into envelopes and attending trade fairs and shows with his father. He received a hospitality management degree at Florida International University in Miami, but knew his destiny was marked out for him.

The day after he left college, Adam Stewart began working for the hotel group and, as all who were involved with Sandals and still are can vouch, for the first two years he watched, listened, and absorbed. Adam himself says: "I've grown up in this company and know it inside out, and I have a lot of fantastic people around me who love this company, sometimes more than I do. But the Chairman knows and I know that we now have to take the company to another level."

His dedication and expertise were not lost on his father. Butch Stewart went on public record some years ago when he declared that "the best decision I ever made was to make my son Adam chairman of the youth committee when he was twenty-three years old." Within a few years it became obvious that Adam was not just ready for more responsibilities, but was actually taking them.

RIGHT *Passing on the baton: a cartoon from the* Jamaica Observer.

Merrick Fray, once the dream catcher, now became the kingmaker. It was he who approached his longtime boss, friend, and associate, Stewart senior, to suggest that he should stand down as number two in the company in favor of Adam.

Butch Stewart recalls, "It was actually Merrick Fray rather than me who saw the potential and told me we were holding Adam back, and that we should give him a clear path. Merrick saw his obvious strengths. Sandals was ready for Adam and he for Sandals . . . he grows by the day. I have never seen somebody more capable of implementing on every project. He is decisive on the financial side and then is able to implement things very swiftly and successfully. He is a natural and is instinctively right on the money every time. Succession planning is the most difficult thing for any family, and much of the time it is near impossible and you see people go round and round in circles."

Meanwhile, Fray is gracious about the handover. "I thought it was time for me to step back and for him to come forward. If the company continues to grow it needs this young fellow. He is bright-eyed, no-nonsense, he listens and he takes advice. This is the kind of guy who can move things forward. I'm a Sandals man through and through and have always had the best relationship with his father, although the Chairman didn't take my idea too seriously to begin with. But he knew I was right, he knew something had to change. I liked the way it happened."

Fray understood, as Stewart did, that at the age of seventy it was prudent to plan and implement a succession strategy; and, while Butch is still vibrant and effective as Chairman, Adam has already surpassed

ABOVE *Accepting a six-star diamond award from Joe Cinque, President of the American Academy of Hospitality Sciences, for Beaches Turks & Caicos.*

expectations. While father and son work steadily and seamlessly together, talking constantly (Jaime once remarked: "Dad called Adam this morning not having spoken to him for all of ten hours and asked if he was hiding from him! They speak dozens of times a day"), the Chairman is still the Chairman. Butch insists, "I do not interfere. But then Adam doesn't do silly things. I am still very much in charge, and I'm traditionally a pretty hands-on manager. But he knows what I'm up to and I know what he's up to. I also come from the school of thought that two heads are better than one."

Adam, on the other hand, understands how his father works: "He has a lot of things to think about and there is always a lot going on in his head at any one time. But he is very much the leader of the organization. He created it and he is still the man, and he still has a lot of views – sometimes too many – on what should happen, but the best thing about working with him is that he is very respectful of me.

"We really do have a very good relationship, and I am probably one of only three people in the company who will look him in the eye and tell him he's wrong. He doesn't like it when that happens but he knows ultimately that we are telling him what he needs to know. All I want is for him, as Chairman, to make the right decision so I will always gingerly find a way to tell him."

Whatever differences there may be between them, the two men

have one guiding principle: to make Sandals resorts the best anywhere. Butch explains: "I am very lucky that there is a group of people now who know where they are going. The company is like a machine which has its own motor, its own dynamic, with people who have worked under my instruction, under my stewardship. They know where they are going and they know that I will take on board any suggestion, any comments that are constructive. But at the end of the day somebody has to make the decision. This is not a collective. Whoever is in charge has instinctively to know what is right and what is wrong for the product, and in order to do that you must have infinite knowledge of the product. We don't have a hotel that I don't know every part of, from the kitchen and dining room to all the facilities, because I have been part and parcel of its development."

And to emphasize the importance of the training that has always taken place and is now going forward in a much stronger, more formalized way, he says: "You cannot dilute the spirit of a company as it grows, because the whole thing will be at risk if you don't develop its identity, its corporate knowledge. You have to understand what works best for the guests. Some people pay up to $10,000 for their vacations and you have to deliver – I do not want a dollar of anyone's money that we haven't worked for."

BELOW *Family values: Adam goes ahead with the support of father and siblings.*

Legendary is Butch Stewart's eye for detail, an eye still as sharp and acute as ever. "Basically we all have the same wants. Everybody wants a really good bedroom and a really comfortable bed. Ours are the best because I have a bad back and I have tried every bed imaginable until I found the one that worked. We worked out our bed system long before others talked about dream bedding. Now people want bigger bathrooms and that's what we give them," he says.

Adam knows that "today you have to be better than your competition, because of the blogs and the online reviews. You need to keep up with all of those. I believe that over seventy percent of our customers go online first before booking and if you are genuinely not

BELOW *Adam receives a World Travel Award at a glitzy event in London, 2010.*

better they will swiftly find you out. We are known for our 'Luxury Included' vacations and we can keep adding to and refining that. We focus on what we're not doing or what we're not doing well enough. If we have a weakness it is that we don't pay enough attention to what everyone else is doing. We are too busy concentrating on what we are doing and going to the next heights."

And those new heights sometimes need new attitudes, new approaches. "I know that my old man is a phenomenon, but the company is no longer just about one man, and while it will always be associated with him, it is now a corporation. It is about twenty-one hotels on six different islands; it was quite different when we had only ten hotels, nine

in Jamaica and one in Antigua. Then you only had to travel once a month, but now we constantly need to visit them all because every island is different, every place has its own culture, its own labor agreements. I find myself relying on people a lot more than he did. After all, we employ more than 10,000 people throughout those islands.

"There is only so much that one man can do. He has set the standards and set the bar incredibly high; he has shown the Sandals way, which is that you can see the light at the end of the tunnel, but you'll never reach it, because we're always striving. We are at a stage in the company where we have to pay a lot of respect to the leadership within it." Adam acknowledges that his father has set the standard for luxury all-inclusive holidays, claiming, "He's a hard act to follow."

Both men are adamant that they only work with people they know, like and trust. As Butch says, you really have to like them or why else would you want to spend so much time with them? Adam employs almost the same criteria, and cites as an example a time when he was looking for a new senior member of staff and asked his own peers for a list of suggestions. "I think we are pretty unique as a family. A lot of my friends work in the company, we have known each other since we were children, so when I was given this list of names I was surprised because I didn't recognize any of them. And I suddenly thought, why would I entrust millions of dollars a year to somebody I didn't know? Well, we had somebody I knew since we were children working at one of the hotels and picked him out for the job, we trained him to the position and I trust him implicitly."

As well as learning constantly from the Chairman, Adam also pays tribute to the people who have worked over the decades with his father. "I have a lot of mentors who have all been very good to me and who I have known since I was young, all of which helps me develop and grow this company. I know that all the wisdom of Mr. Fray is available to me and it is only a phone call away."

ATL Automotive: a multi-million-dollar facility bringing high-end motoring to western Jamaica.

ABOVE *The ATL racing team show off their colors, top; while above, another generation of the Stewart line, Adam's son Aston, is looking towards the future.*

The younger Stewart has already put his own stamp on ATL and the hotel group, two of the different companies that Butch built, by adding to its portfolio. "I only ever wanted to do two other things . . . and I've done them. One was to extend our motor distribution business, which I did when I won the contract for Audi and Volkswagen in Jamaica, and the other was to set up a tour company."

Just as his father is a fan of Mercedes, Adam is devoted to Audi and to a number of prestigious British brands such as Jaguar, Land Rover, and Range Rover. To this end two new additions have been added to ATL Motors – The Home of Honda. The ATL Autohaus division celebrates the best in German engineering by adding market-leading brands Audi and Volkswagen to the ATL family. ATL Britannia, which came on stream in 2010, has the exclusive distribution rights to Land Rover as well as Range Rover and Range Rover Sport. And then, of course, there are the super-sleek and desirable Jaguar models. Stewart also provides huge support for motor racing in Jamaica and throughout the Caribbean with the Audi DMT TT, driven by super-speedster Doug "Hollywood" Gore. Gore's signature crew "Team Mobay" entered the 2011 racing season with a new name: ATL Automotive Racing.

Adam is as passionate about Jamaica as his father is, and that has spread to the other islands in which they operate. Butch Stewart was always dismissive of critics who complained that his guests never left their compound to explore where they were staying, simply stating: "I have never met anybody who pays a lot of money to stay in a jail." And as guests were encouraged to tour the islands or visit each one's places of interest, Adam Stewart has made that easier by fulfilling the second of his goals and setting up Island Routes Caribbean Adventure Tours, a tour specialist, to provide outings, tours, and excursions for guests, whether

RIGHT *With a move that paid homage to his British roots, Stewart added legendary car brands Jaguar, Land Rover, and Range Rover to the fold.*

it's a 4x4 off-road safari into Jamaica's hinterland, a horseback ride and swim through the countryside and along the coast, or ziplining through the jungle.

Whether guests want to swim with dolphins or go bird-watching in Antigua, take part in a spectacular 007 Thunderball Tour in the Exumas (where the movie was made), hike up the Pitons in Saint Lucia, or pretend to be a castaway for a day on a secluded island, it is all on offer from Island Routes Tours. "The Caribbean is all about life on the verandah, on the beach, on the sea and in the outdoors, that's why people come here," Adam says. "So I wanted to show them properly what it has to offer, what it really is. If you go to Disneyworld in Orlando you will see that they have spent billions recreating what the Lord has given us right in our backyard. It is up to us to show that to the visitors."

While their aim is the same, the Chairman and the CEO go about their business in totally different ways. Adam says of his father: "He's the kind of guy, if he receives an email over dinner, will stop and attend to it right now. I'm the kind of person who will say . . . get on with dinner and we'll deal with it later or in the morning. We're very different, he's impulsive and in the moment. If you ask him what he's doing next Wednesday he can't tell you, he'll figure that out on the Tuesday. But if you look at my iPad you'll see the next three months planned out day by day. He still has a little black book with all his numbers in and he will sit and make fifteen phone calls to tell the same thing to different people, while I will just send an email and cc them." And while Adam's iPad and BlackBerry are all in state-of-the-art cases, Butch's cellphones, little black book and the papers he is working on are all stuffed carefully into a couple of Sandals plastic carrier bags.

Says Adam, "Marketing is his real love and he is a genius at it, while I am much more involved in the day-to-day organization of the company and its operations. But what is truly amazing is that this is a big company with all its structures, checks, and balances in place that has not lost its soul, and my old man is responsible for that. And while I am a hundred percent my own man, ninety-five percent of the time, I don't think he will ever retire.

"He is seventy years old and he looks forty-five, and the amount of energy he has is absurd. He's not normal; he doesn't need more than four hours sleep at night and he is always running around. But then his work is his world, but if he gets bored for a second . . . watch out!"

And, like the rest of the family, all his friends and colleagues agree that the only time Butch Stewart really relaxes is when he is at sea, fishing or just simply being on the water. "My greatest dread," says his son and heir, "is that he will end up not as mobile as he is now and will sit on his balcony in Nassau calling us all fifty times a day."

This is a scenario that currently seems unlikely, with plans afoot to extend properties and add the first over-water suites in the Caribbean to others, while also negotiating to acquire new properties. Sandals, with the courage and drive Butch Stewart is renowned for, met the recession head-on. In an economic downturn, many hoteliers cut back, but not Sandals; the company increased its investment into the resorts, preparing for a customer he knew would return. From the very early stages the company went into overdrive rearranging and adjusting operations and, rather than downsizing its staff, it moved them to other areas and encouraged greater multi-tasking, while at the same time renegotiating more than 1,000 contracts. By the time the recession was in

full swing, the company was in a strong position to deal with it. There was no downgrading of service, no resizing of shampoo and shower gels, no penny-pinching on all the "Luxury Included" amenities. The client was never the victim.

Sandals even decided it was time to acquire another property, the old Four Seasons in Emerald Bay in the Bahamas. It is another Butch Stewart mantra that when the chips are down – as after Hurricane Gilbert, as during a recession – that is the time to promote. Little wonder that occupancy levels rarely drop below eighty-three percent and returning clients are hitting the fifty percent level.

It's the triumph of the luxury all-inclusive and the vision of one man.

BELOW *Zipping through the rainforest – one way to see the joys that a Caribbean island has to offer.*

Another first for Sandals: over-water
suites in the Caribbean are planned for
Sandals Grande St. Lucian.

An Island Routes Tours catamaran opens up the wonders of the Caribbean on land and sea.

THE AFTERNOON SUN BRINGS WITH IT A SOFTER LIGHT over the Exuma Sound, defining the gentle coastlines of the tiny islands, each held in sharp relief, while the color of the water shifts from clear aqua to deep sapphire. It flows around the boat like liquid silk, only occasionally broken by the quiver of a fishing line or the swoop of a bird. Even the dominoes become quieter. The slapping isn't quite so sharp, and the shouts, grunts, and laughter softer. Even the fish are taking a rest, as fewer appear to bite. Perhaps it is time to call it a day.

ABOVE *At home on land and sea: Stewart never strayed far from his humble beginnings and his roots in the Caribbean.*

An imperceptible gesture to Captain Neddy from the domino king means it's time to head back, to the call of Nassau and the needs of real life and business. The boat is swiftly readied and begins to ride speedily through the waves, slowing only occasionally to admire a school of dolphins who want to prance and dance in the late afternoon sun.

An hour or so later, way in the distance, the rooftops and penthouses of Nassau begin to emerge from the horizon, painted pale rose gold in the afternoon light. All too soon, *Sir Jon* noses into his mooring, rods are stacked away, decks are cleared, and the dominoes go back in their box as the friends prepare to disembark. Monty is off first, running along the boardwalk and sniffing dry land, but the party is not yet over. Within minutes the group pile into a waiting speedboat and, with Butch at the wheel, race off for the private island across from Sandals Royal Bahamian. The island closes to guests in the late afternoon, so by the time the boss and the boys draw level with the jetty the place is deserted, the beach calm and the sea empty but for the myriad fishes.

It's a rule, a way of life: all good days in the Caribbean finish in the water, and within minutes the group are swooping, diving, laughing, and joshing like a school of porpoises enjoying the warm caress of the ocean. It's what they have known all their lives, it's what has moulded their characters and firmed their friendships, and here, at the close of the day and the end of the party, it's where the Honourable Gordon "Butch" Stewart feels most at home and most relaxed.

Too soon the boat heads back to the mainland. As they clamber out a cellphone rings and is handed to Stewart, and as the others walk towards the apartment – the last one wearing a T-shirt inscribed with the words OLD GUYS RULE – Butch takes one last look at the sun slipping towards the sea. He turns away as he answers: "Hello Adam, my love."

The king is back on dry land.

BELOW *The crystal clear waters of the Exumas – a magical setting in which to share a day with friends on the open sea.*

Timeline of Sandals Resorts International

RIGHT *Sandals Grande Emerald Bay is the latest addition to the family.*

1980

November 1981: The first Sandals resort, Sandals Resort Beach Club, opens. It later becomes known as Sandals Montego Bay.

1985

1985: First signature Swim-up Pool Bar unveiled at the Bay Roc. Carlyle on the Bay in Montego Bay opens (now called Sandals Carlyle).

1986: Sandals Royal Caribbean opens – the only resort in Jamaica with its own private island.
"Stay at one, play at two" concept launched.

1988: The first specialty restaurant, the Oleander at Montego Bay, opens. Sandals Negril opens.

1989: Sandals Ocho Rios makes its debut in Butch Stewart's home town.

1990

1991: Sandals Dunn's River opens.
"Stay at one, play at six" concept introduced.
Sandals Antigua opens – the first resort outside Jamaica.

1992: Sandals Golf and Country Club, the renamed Upton Golf Course, opens in Ocho Rios.

1995

1993: Sandals introduces the "Ultra All-Inclusive" program.
Sandals St. Lucia opens.
Island hopping introduced between Antigua and Saint Lucia.

1994: Suite Concierge Service introduced.
Sandals WeddingMoons introduced.
Sandals Halcyon Beach Resort opens on Saint Lucia.
Sandals is named the World's Leading All-Inclusive and Top Caribbean Hotel Group for the first time, distinctions the chain has held ever since.
Stewart purchases and privatizes Air Jamaica.

1995: *Lady Sandals*, a 135-foot yacht, acquired as a marketing and educational tool.

1996: Sandals Royal Bahamian Resort and Spa opens in Nassau, Bahamas.

1997: Beaches Negril opens.
Beaches Turks & Caicos opens in Providenciales in the Turks and Caicos Islands.
Blue Chip Hurricane Guarantee introduced.
Poinciana Beach Resort opens in Negril.

1998: Honeymoon Villa Suites added to Sandals Negril Beach Resort and Spa.
Sandals Royal Bahamian doubles in size.
Seventy-two additional suites added to Beaches Turks & Caicos.
Spas added to Sandals Negril, Dunn's River, Antigua and St. Lucia.
Sandals Negril becomes only the fifth resort in the world to be Green Globe (the tourism industry's label for sustainable travel and operations) certified, and the first all-inclusive.
Sandals Royal Bahamian opens the Fred Kassner Convention Center.

1999: Signature Spa Collection debuts in six resorts.
Beaches Turks & Caicos opens Pirate's Island waterpark.
Sandals Ocho Rios Resort and Golf Club purchased from the Jamaican Government.
Beaches Turks & Caicos expands with the addition of the French Village.

2000

Sandals Signature Guest program launched.

The Villas on Sunset Bluff introduced at Sandals St. Lucia Golf Resort and Spa.

Negril Gardens and Plantation Inn hotels are acquired.

2000: Poinciana Beach Resort becomes Beaches Inn.

Beaches Grande Sport at Ciboney opens in Ocho Rios.

2001: Beaches Royal Plantation opens in Ocho Rios.

2002: Beaches Boscobel Resort and Golf Club opens in Ocho Rios.

Sandals Grande St. Lucian Spa and Beach Resort opens.

2004: Best Price Guarantee introduced to protect travel agents and the Preferred Sandals Specialist programme launched.

Red Lane Spa concept debuts.

Beaches Resorts introduce partnerships with Sesame Workshop and Microsoft Xbox to create Xbox Game Oasis centers.

Beaches Royal Plantation becomes Royal Plantation Ocho Rios, the flagship for the new Royal Plantation Collection. It becomes Jamaica's only Leading Small Hotel of the World.

Sandals Ocho Rios and Beaches Grande Sport merge to become Sandals Grande Ocho Rios.

Beaches Negril opens its spa.

2005

2005: Butler Service introduced at all Sandals and Beaches Resorts.

Sandals Whitehouse European Village and Spa opens on Jamaica's south coast.

2006: Adam Stewart, son of Gordon "Butch" Stewart, becomes CEO.

Sandals Destination Wedding Dress Collection with Dessy Dresses launched.

Rondoval Suites (circular cottages) added to Sandals Grande St. Lucia.

Beaches enters an exclusive partnership with Crayola to create Crayola Art Camps for children and teenagers.

2007: Sandals goes beyond all-inclusive to introduce the "Luxury Included" vacation experience.

Sandals and Beaches partner with California's legendary Beringer Vineyards for their house wines.

Mediterranean Village opens at Sandals Grande Antigua Resort and Spa.

Royal Plantation Island at Fowl Cay – a fifty-two-acre private island in the Exumas, Bahamas, opens.

Beaches Boscobel's expanded Water Park opens.

2008: Grand Pineapple Beach Resorts launched – quality all-inclusive for the budget-conscious traveler.

Eight Plantation Suites open at Negril Beach Resort and Spa.

Four Millionaire Suites are unveiled at the Sunset Bluff in Sandals Regency La Toc in Saint Lucia, and seven Sunset one-bedroom villa suites.

Beaches Resorts introduce new Teen and Tween programmes and partners with Scratch DJ Academy while Xbox 360 Game Garages are remodeled and enhanced.

Private Villas added to Royal Plantation Collection.

2009: Italian Village opens at Beaches Turks & Caicos.

Launch of the Sandals Foundation.

A renovated Pirate's Village waterpark is opened at Beaches Turks & Caicos.

Island Routes Caribbean Adventure Tours, launched by Adam Stewart, wins a Six Star Diamond Award and is named World's Leading Caribbean Attraction Company in its first year.

Sandals Weddings by Martha Stewart introduced.

Sandals Inn becomes Sandals Carlyle.

2010

2010: Sandals Grande Emerald Bay, Great Exuma, Bahamas, opens.

Beaches Inn becomes Beaches Sandy Bay.

Royal Plantation Island becomes Fowl Cay Resort.

Royal Plantation Ocho Rios becomes Sandals Royal Plantation.

After a multimillion-dollar renovation, Sandals Grande Ocho Rios becomes Sandals Grande Riviera Beach & Villa Golf Club.

Red Lane Spa introduces exclusive partnership with Dermalogica® for all skincare treatments.

The new, ground-breaking Kinect for Xbox 360 becomes a part of the Xbox 360 Game Garage experience at Beaches Resorts.

Sandals and ATL Group Companies

SANDALS RESORTS INTERNATIONAL

Jamaica

Sandals Montego Bay
Sandals Royal Caribbean Resort and Private Island
Sandals Negril Beach Resort and Spa
Sandals Whitehouse European Village and Spa
Sandals Grande Riviera Beach and Villa Golf Resort
Sandals Royal Plantation
Sandals Carlyle

Beaches Boscobel Resort and Golf Club
Beaches Negril Resort and Spa
Beaches Sandy Bay

Grand Pineapple Beach Negril

Saint Lucia

Sandals La Toc Golf Resort and Spa
Sandals Grande St. Lucian Spa and Beach Resort
Sandals Halcyon Beach

Antigua

Sandals Grande Antigua Resort and Spa
Grand Pineapple Beach Antigua

The Bahamas

Sandals Royal Bahamian Spa Resort and Offshore Island
Sandals Grande Emerald Bay
Fowl Cay Resort

Turks and Caicos Islands

Beaches Turks & Caicos Resort Villages and Spa

Cuba

Sandals Royal Hicacos Resort and Spa

THE ATL GROUP

Appliance Traders Limited
ATL Automotive – ATL Autohaus, ATL Britannia, ATL Motors

Island Routes Caribbean Adventure Tours

Jamaica Observer Limited

RIGHT *Fun at Beaches Turks & Caicos.*

Map of Sandals Group Resorts in the Caribbean

FLORIDA

THE BAHAMAS

TURKS AND CAICOS ISLANDS

CUBA

JAMAICA

ANTIGUA

CARIBBEAN SEA

SAINT LUCIA

1   THE BAHAMAS

     2 SANDALS

     1 FOWL CAY PRIVATE ISLAND

2   CUBA

     1 SANDALS

3   TURKS AND CAICOS ISLANDS

     1 BEACHES

4   JAMAICA

     7 SANDALS

     3 BEACHES

     1 GRAND PINEAPPLE RESORT

5   ANTIGUA

     1 SANDALS

     1 GRAND PINEAPPLE RESORT

6   SAINT LUCIA

     3 SANDALS

Index

Service with a smile: Butch Stewart has always gone the extra mile to create the perfect vacation.